HELLFIRE
BOYS

HELLFIRE BOYS

THE BIRTH OF THE U.S. CHEMICAL WARFARE SERVICE AND THE RACE FOR THE WORLD'S DEADLIEST WEAPONS

THEO EMERY

LITTLE, BROWN AND COMPANY

New York Boston London

Little, Brown and Company
Hachette Book Group
1290 Avenue of the Americas, New York, NY 10104
littlebrown.com

First Edition: November 2017

Little, Brown and Company is a division of Hachette Book Group, Inc. The Little, Brown name and logo are trademarks of Hachette Book Group, Inc.

The publisher is not responsible for websites (or their content) that are not owned by the publisher.

The Hachette Speakers Bureau provides a wide range of authors for speaking events. To find out more, go to hachettespeakersbureau.com or call (866) 376-6591.

ISBN 978-0-316-26410-5
LCCN 2017942376

10 9 8 7 6 5 4 3 2 1

LSC-C

Printed in the United States of America

This book is dedicated to Ann Badger Emery.

Contents

Contents

Part III
RETORT

Characters

Research Division, Bureau of Mines/Chemical Warfare Service

George A. Burrell—Chief of the Research Division. Within days of President Wilson's war declaration, Manning asked Burrell to direct chemical warfare research for the Bureau of Mines. With the consolidation of the Chemical Warfare Service in 1918, he retained his position as chief of research.

James Bryant Conant—A brilliant Harvard chemist who came to Washington in 1917. Recruited to work in the Research Division, his work on mustard hastened the mass production of the chemical warfare agent. When lewisite became a focus of offensive war research, Conant was sent to Willoughby, Ohio, to set up the secret lewisite plant there called the Mousetrap. Became president of Harvard in 1933 and later played a critical role in the Manhattan Project.

Bradley Dewey—A chemist from Burlington, Vermont, who worked on gas mask development with Warren K. Lewis. In charge of the Gas Defense Plant in Long Island City, New York.

Frank M. Dorsey—Chief of the Chemical Warfare Service's Development Division. A chemical engineer in the Lamp Development Laboratory at General Electric's Nela Park campus outside Cleveland, Dorsey was instrumental in developing charcoal for gas masks. He later played crucial roles in mustard production and construction of "the Mousetrap."

Arno C. Fieldner—An Ohio State University graduate who worked on gas masks.

Yandell Henderson—An irascible Yale physiologist accused of being an apologist for the Central powers before the war. His work on physiology and pathology paved the way for human-subject research, in which soldiers were used in testing equipment and as test subjects for the effects of chemical weapons.

George A. Hulett—A Princeton chemist and longtime consultant to the Bureau of Mines, enlisted to travel to France in April 1917 to investigate war gas research for the bureau. His observations and recommendations were pivotal to the organization of the Chemical Warfare Service in France.

Warren K. Lewis—MIT chemist who worked on gas mask research.

Winford Lee Lewis—An Illinois chemist who came to work for the Bureau of Mines in January of 1918. His Organic Research Unit No. 3 at Catholic University uncovered previous experiments that led to the development of the chemical warfare agent lewisite.

Vannoy Hartog Manning—Director of the Bureau of Mines in Washington, D.C. One of a few U.S. government officials who saw the impending need to prepare for chemical warfare. The Research Division began under his oversight and provided the nucleus for the Chemical Warfare Service.

Eli K. Marshall—A Johns Hopkins physician whose work also centered on the physiological and toxicological effects of chemical weapons.

James F. Norris—An MIT professor known as Sunny Jim with a famously ferocious intellect. Initially put in charge of both offensive and defensive chemical research problems, he later became chief of only offensive gas research. His chance encounter on the street with James Bryant Conant brought the young chemist into the orbit of the growing Research Division.

E. Emmet Reid—A chemist and early recruit of the Bureau of Mines who came from Johns Hopkins to find new chemical warfare agents.

George S. Rice—Van Manning's chief mining engineer for the Bureau of Mines. One of the earliest members of the committee that spearheaded the bureau's research efforts.

William H. Walker—An MIT chemist considered a pioneer of chemical engineering and industrial chemistry. Became the chief of Edgewood Arsenal before relinquishing control of the arsenal to Amos Fries in June of 1919.

Department of Justice/Bureau of Investigation

A. Bruce Bielaski—Chief of the Bureau of Investigation, the predecessor of the FBI. After the war, he went to work for Richmond Levering.

Charles DeWoody—The Bureau of Investigation's division superintendent in New York City who succeeded Offley.

Warren W. Grimes—Bureau of Investigation agent assigned to Jones Point, New York. Dismissed shortly after Scheele's arrival in Jones Point in April. Code name "Warren White."

Richmond M. Levering—An oilman from Indiana who worked for the Department of Justice under the auspices of the American Protective League. He retrieved Walter Scheele from Cuba in March 1918 and put the German spy to work in his factory in Jones Point, New York.

Francis X. O'Donnell—Bureau of Investigation agent assigned to Jones Point, New York. Code name "O'Dell."

William Offley—The Bureau of Investigation division superintendent in New York City.

Graham Rice—Bureau of Investigation agent assigned to Jones Point, New York. Code name "Riser."

Walter T. Scheele—A German chemist sent to the United States to conduct industrial espionage. Activated to manufacture chemicals for Germany, he was then ordered to create chemical bombs to ignite cargo on Europe-bound ships. Indicted in 1916, he fled to

Cuba and was captured in March 1918. Facing possible execution for his role in the ship-bomb plot, he agreed to work for the U.S. government and conducted research at a secret lab in Jones Point, New York, for the duration of the war. Had the code name "Nux" and gained the alias "Dr. Smith" while at Jones Point.

Bruce R. Silver—A chemist for the inventor Thomas A. Edison. Silver evaluated Scheele's expertise after his capture and worked alongside Scheele at Jones Point until shortly after the war. His tenure ended in spring of 1919, when funding for his work at Edison's lab dried up.

U.S. Army

James T. Addison—Chaplain for the First Gas Regiment. Arrived at Fort Myer in January 1918, went to France in February 1918 with Companies C and D.

Earl J. Atkisson—Commander of the Thirtieth Engineers (Gas and Flame), renamed the First Gas Regiment.

William M. Black—Chief of the Army Corps of Engineers.

Amos A. Fries—A U.S. Army engineer sent to France in July of 1917. Expecting to be appointed director of roads, he was promoted to chief of the American Expeditionary Force Gas Service. He became one of the most vocal advocates of chemical warfare in the U.S. Army; after the war, his efforts cemented the Chemical Warfare Service as an independent branch of the U.S. Army.

Harold J. Higginbottom—One of the earliest recruits to the First Gas Regiment. Trained at American University with Thomas Jabine, deployed on Christmas Day 1917 in Company B.

Thomas Jabine—A chemist from Yonkers, New York, he was among the earliest recruits to the First Gas Regiment. Trained at American University, deployed on Christmas Day 1917 in Company B. Transferred to Company C in September 1918. During the Meuse-Argonne offensive, he was gassed near Charpentry on October 3, 1918, and spent the remainder of the war recovering.

Peyton C. March—U.S. Army chief of staff in 1918. Became a vocal critic of chemical warfare and unsuccessfully tried to prevent the Chemical Warfare Service from gaining permanent footing as an independent branch of the U.S. Army in 1919.

John J. Pershing—Commander in chief of the American Expeditionary Forces.

Charles L. Potter—Appointed director of the gas service in the fall of 1917, an early attempt to organize the disparate sections of the service under a single organization. The toothless Office of the Gas Service proved ineffective, leading to Sibert's appointment and eventual consolidation of the Chemical Warfare Service.

William Luther Sibert—One of the top engineers of the Panama Canal. Sent to Europe in mid-1917 to be General John J. Pershing's right-hand man in organizing and training the American army. Dismissed and ordered back to the United States, he was put in charge of the domestic gas service and oversaw its consolidation into the Chemical Warfare Service in June of 1918. Was demoted in winter of 1920 and retired from the U.S. Army.

Others

Heinrich Albert—The German commercial attaché in New York.

Fritz Haber—One of Germany's most esteemed chemists and one of the architects of Germany's gas program in World War I. Famous before the war for having discovered how to convert nitrogen into ammonia for fertilizer—in doing so, creating the biggest boom in commercial agriculture in history—his role in Germany's gas program horrified many chemists who admired and studied under him. His award of the Nobel Prize in 1918 for fixed nitrogen was extremely controversial. A patriotic Jew, he resigned from the Kaiser Wilhelm Institute in protest of Hitler's regime and went into self-imposed exile, dying in early 1934.

Franz von Papen—The German military attaché in Washington, recalled to Germany in 1915. He was subsequently found to have been secretly fomenting sabotage and espionage against the United States, including the "cigar bomb" plot that smuggled Walter T. Scheele's chemical bombs aboard cargo ships and set dozens of fires while the vessels were at sea.

Franz von Rintelen — A captain in the German Admiralty who was central to efforts to bankroll espionage and sabotage in the United States.

Introduction

January 5, 1993

The sky over Washington sagged with rain as the construction crew arrived at the cul-de-sac in the city's Spring Valley neighborhood. Overnight, a south wind had gusted across the city, making the January morning unseasonably warm as work resumed on Fifty-Second Court NW. A workman swung up into the cab of the backhoe that hulked near one of the houses. The engine roared to life.

The excavator carved out a sewer trench toward a corner of one of the unfinished houses ringing the dead-end street. Older parts of Spring Valley were pockets of venerable Washington power, where retired generals and ambassadors lived in seclusion, separated by high hedges and rolling lawns. But in this new corner of the neighborhood, the brick homes were only a short distance apart, their front steps close to the sidewalk. The southernmost house was finished, with shrubs planted under the windows and a sapling staked with guy wires, but the house next door still needed its sewer connection. As the backhoe scooped bucket after bucket of dirt, mountains of soil grew on each side of the trench.

At around 1:40 in the afternoon, the backhoe operator cut the engine, jumped to the ground, and peered at the soil he had just excavated. A rust-covered tube about twenty inches long lay in the dirt, stubby and fat with a metal nub at the end. The bucket had punctured the metal casing. As he looked at the tube, he could hear a hiss of escaping gas. He called the fire department.

When police and firefighters arrived on the scene, they eyed the metal tube. It looked like military ordnance, the hazmat team said. A mortar maybe. Better call Fort McNair, the Washington headquarters for the U.S. Army Military District.

The ordnance-disposal detachment from Fort McNair didn't arrive until after 3:00 p.m. The unit inspected the trench and the punctured tank. They had a theory: that the shell was a long-buried relic of chemical warfare.

After sundown, a helicopter thundered in the darkness over the neighborhood. The Huey descended into a vacant lot, and a figure in a military uniform stepped down from the cabin. Lieutenant Colonel William T. Batt commanded a specialized team called a Technical Escort Unit, trained to recover chemical munitions. The trip from the unit's base at Aberdeen Proving Ground—almost seventy-five miles away—would have taken an hour and a half in the best traffic, but buried ordnance in a residential neighborhood was an emergency that called for speed. Floodlights lit Batt's path to the trench on Fifty-Second Court. Two and a half hours later, the wail of sirens announced the arrival of the rest of the team. After the entire unit had assembled beside the pit, they agreed the munitions could contain chemical warfare agents.

The subdivision became a military zone. Floodlights illuminated the area in a harsh glow. As news of the discovery spread, reporters scrambled to the scene, and television trucks clogged nearby streets. Police began round-the-clock surveillance. The army recommended that residents within three hundred yards evacuate, and three families hastily packed up and left. Away from the sealed-off street, an army spokesmen briefed reporters. The area could once have been a munitions scrap heap, he said. While the age of the mortars may have reduced their potency, he warned that they could still be dangerous. "Any time you've got a fuse in it, you're dealing with a hot potato."

No one seemed to know how the munitions had ended up there. Residents wondered what else might be buried under their feet and in their yards. The ordnance team from Aberdeen began sifting through the soil in protective suits. When they stopped at 3:30 a.m., they had found four unexploded mortar rounds and three rounds of seventy-five-millimeter artillery, all dating to World War I.

The discoveries set in motion a scramble to find other ordnance buried beneath the cul-de-sac, like old bones in a forgotten cemetery. Ultimately, 144 pieces of World War I–era munitions would be disinterred, flown to distant proving grounds, and destroyed in controlled explosions. The crisis provided daily grist for the nightly news and the morning headlines as this long-buried history spilled out into the open. In an ironic counterpoint to the discovery of chemical weapons in Washington, a United Nations inspection team across the globe was in a tense standoff with Saddam Hussein over inspections for chemical, biological, and nuclear weapons in the aftermath of the Persian Gulf War.

Soon after the excavation began, the local newspapers published an enigmatic photo from late 1918. A Washington-area woman owned the picture, which showed her father, a young officer named Sergeant Charles William Maurer, standing over a pit surrounded by carboys, bottles, and jugs of chemicals. Wearing a gas mask, he appeared to be throwing the jugs into the ground. A caption on the back of the photo had a name for the pit: "Hades, the most feared and respected place on the grounds."

Little by little, the story unfolded. During World War I, American University had turned over its campus to the army. One end of campus became a wartime training camp, but the other became the headquarters of its embryonic chemical warfare Research Division, called the American University Experiment Station (AUES). The army leased the fields and wooded dells around the campus to use as a proving ground. They lobbed mortars and dug trenches. They tested chemicals on dogs, goats, and other animals, and on men as well. Many years before the area became Spring Valley, the dell behind the campus had earned the nicknames "Death Valley" and "Arsenic Valley." The soldiers called the hilltop campus Mustard Hill.

Spring Valley has never been quite the same since that January day in 1993. After the U.S. Army Corps of Engineers closed the investigation and declared the cleanup of Fifty-Second Court complete, questions arose about another spot across Spring Valley, where houses had been built on the back side of the American University campus. A persistent city employee and other environmental officials insisted that the army had overlooked another burial site there. The corps resisted reopening the investigation, but when they did, they promptly found new chemical weapons detritus, including pits containing hundreds of munitions, some with mustard agent inside, buried in the backyard of the South Korean ambassador's residence. The new discoveries embarrassed the Army Corps of Engineers and stirred lingering suspicion about the army's commitment to cleaning up Spring Valley. The environmental remediation, estimated to eventually cost more than $300 million, was still ongoing at press time.

On a crisp November morning in 2012, I stood in a gaggle of reporters in the driveway of a stately brick two-story house across Spring Valley from Fifty-Second Court. The house sat at the bottom of the hillside behind the American University campus, abutting the South Korean ambassador's residence. At the top of the hill, just out of sight, were athletic fields and a child-care center. The frosty air pinched red the noses and cheeks of the officials from the U.S. Army Corps of Engineers in the driveway facing the reporters.

More than ninety years earlier, Sergeant Maurer had stood on the same hillside and posed beside the pit called Hades with the jars and bottles of chemicals lined up next to him. The house in front of us had been built atop that spot, and the photo helped to pinpoint the pit's location beneath the back patio of the house. A family named the Loughlins had lived there for several years before the cleanup around them forced them to move; fearful for their health and safety, they never moved back in and forced the builder to buy the house back. No one had lived there since. On that November morning, the Corps of Engineers was going to tear the house down. The cleanup of the property had proved so complicated, with so many lingering questions about what was still buried there, that the army decided that the easiest route was simply to demolish the house altogether and cart away whatever lay beneath.

After a few questions, the corps officials asked the reporters to step back down the driveway. We retreated to the street, behind a barricade of Jersey barriers. The driver in the excavator cab started the engine and raised its long hydraulic arm. Almost gently, the bucket began to pluck at the brick façade. A few bricks rained down, then the bucket raked downward, and the bricks sheered away from the side. And then the driver punched the bucket through a window and began to rip out the guts of the house.

In a sense, *Hellfire Boys* began that day. My curiosity about this history wasn't sated by the two articles I wrote for the *New York Times* about the demolition. The more I searched for information about the American University Experiment Station, the more puzzled I grew over how little was known about what had happened there. It seemed strange that this history of chemical warfare in the United States, with its mysterious laboratory tucked into the nation's capital, could be so little understood and so poorly documented. There were military histories and technical documents, to be sure, as well as articles in the Washington newspapers during the crisis on Fifty-Second Court. A handful of books have been written in the years that followed. None provides a complete picture about the day-to-day work in the labs, the men's labors over beakers of poison gas, or the men who volunteered to go to France with the First Gas Regiment.

But there were hints. I tracked down Sergeant Maurer's daughter and grandson, who showed me other photographs from the American University Experiment Station: soldiers mugging in their uniforms, perched atop casks labeled TNT; Will Maurer grinning shyly beside his sweetheart in Washington, posing at the zoo; lyric sheets from a talent show for the soldiers on Mustard Hill. Eventually, I found eight copies of the station's newspaper in the Library of Congress. The papers covered a two-month period toward the end of the war, revealing the daily lives of these men at the cutting edge of military science on the campus. Since then, I've visited or contacted dozens of libraries and archives. I've filed Freedom of Information Act (FOIA) requests with the army and the FBI. I tracked down soldiers' descendants and asked them to check their attics and closets for letters and diaries. I've combed through newspapers. I accumulated tens of thousands of documents, photographs, and reports from the National Archives and Records Administration. A chance discovery there unexpectedly led me to the hitherto unknown story of Walter Scheele's captivity and the secret laboratory where he labored over the last eight months of the war. My research took me to Flanders fields in Belgium, to see for myself where these weapons were used and how. It took me into the living rooms of descendants of the soldiers in the Chemical Warfare Service, descendants who were proud of their ancestors but not always comfortable with the work they undertook in war. The descendants wanted this story told, but some were nervous — they wanted it told fairly, dispassionately, factually. I promised to do the best that I could. I stand by that pledge.

When I began this endeavor, I saw it as a sliver of lost history, a fascinating but long-forgotten fragment of American history. I worried that the passage of a fearful century, distended and warped by anxiety over weapons of mass destruction, would make a dispassionate chronicle of this legacy impossible, fraught with latter-day perceptions about the perils of chemical weapons. I worried that the peephole of the early twenty-first century, after a century of war and tribulation, would be an imperfect lens.

And then gas warfare returned to the headlines. I would never have dreamed that chemical warfare would reappear in the news, like a phantom from beyond the grave. In 2013, the world learned of the sarin-gas attack in Damascus attributed to Bashar al-Assad's forces and saw the horrific images of civilians dying from nerve gas. Then came the reports of barrel bombs filled with chlorine — the original chemical weapon of the twentieth century unleashed in 1915 outside Ypres, Belgium. Reports of ISIS launching mustard-filled shells followed, and then another sarin attack in 2017, again blamed upon Assad's forces. Improbably, a weapon of the past became a weapon of the present, and the subject I had undertaken took on a completely unexpected relevance and urgency. As one chemical weapons expert told me, "Everything old is new again."

HELLFIRE
BOYS

Prologue

The sun beamed down on Marie Desaegher as she left her home in the west Belgian town of Boesinghe with her young sister, Emma. It was morning when the sisters set out on the road to Ypres. Marie was twenty-six and deaf, the oldest of eight children. She worked as a servant girl in Ypres, but that day she was walking the four miles south into the city for a typhoid shot. April 22, 1915, was calm and peaceful. The grass blazed brilliant green in the fields around them, and a brisk wind blew from north to south. As the two sisters walked side by side, with the cows lowing in the fields and the warm spring breeze at their backs, perhaps they even forgot they were walking across a battlefield.

If Marie had walked in the opposite direction, she would have run right into the French front lines, where soldiers crouched in trenches facing the Germans a few hundred yards away across no-man's-land. The Desaegher homestead was close to the battle lines, as were many other farmhouses and homesteads peppering the fields of western Flanders. The city of Ypres was swaddled by a five-mile radius of Allied territory that jutted into German territory—a bulge in the front lines called a salient—which insulated the city even through the First Battle of Ypres the previous fall. On the very land where fighting had raged a few months earlier, life went on. The farmers tilled their fields; the tea shops were open in Ypres. Soldiers with a few days' leave from the front could find food and companionship in the bustling town of Poperinghe. On that clear spring day as the sisters strolled parallel to the levees

of the Yperlee Canal, crossed the Ypres moat, and entered the fortified medieval city, it was as if the war had simply stopped.

In the afternoon, Marie and Emma left Ypres for home. Marie
was tired. Far off in the distance, machine guns rattled, and an
observation balloon hovered high overhead. The sun was setting.
Just before 5:30 p.m., flares exploded against the sky in the gathering dusk. The sisters were only a few minutes away from their
house when they met soldiers and villagers on the road who tried
to tell them something. Marie couldn't hear them, but her sister
froze in her tracks and refused to move. Emma was trembling,
soundless words tumbling out of her mouth, and then she bolted
toward a neighbor's house. And then the shells began to fall.

They fell all around Marie, her body turning ice cold in fear, as
if the life had drained from her and left her a corpse. She ran
toward the farmhouse. She vaulted over ditches and dikes, thorns
tearing at her, shells falling all around her, until she reached cover.

Some nervous French territorial soldiers had also taken shelter
there from the shell barrage, including an injured man. Through the
windows, she saw a horse-drawn ration wagon rumbling toward
the house. As she watched, a shell fell almost directly on the team,
the shrapnel killing the two horses instantly. After seeing that, she
fled to hide in a pigsty.

The ferocious artillery barrage went on and on, and the French
responded with their own shelling. Then the German guns fell silent.

For a few minutes, everything was stone quiet. In the observation balloon high overhead, a French soldier looking down on the
German lines saw movement. So did the French territorials peek-
ing up from their trenches, rifles leveled toward the German lines.

The distant movement wasn't the sight of German soldiers surging up from the trenches. It was something else, something they'd
never seen before. Something evanescent, something that flowed
and coiled. Wisps of bluish smoke, a haze rising from the German
trenches, turning greenish yellow as the cloud undulated toward
them on the wind. It purled, almost like water, sinking into depres-

sions in the earth as it rolled southwest across the field in a six-foot-high curtain.

A seventeen-year-old boy named Maurice Quaghebeur from Boesinghe asked a French officer billeted in his house what the cloud was. Smoke from the German guns, he told the boy. Nothing to worry about.

Up at the lines, French commanders shouted for their soldiers to take positions at the top of their trenches, believing that the cloud was a smoke screen hiding advancing infantry. But there was no sound of an advancing army as the cloud swirled toward them, drifted into their trenches, and then spilled over their heads.

From the city, a priest watching with binoculars saw soldiers begin to drop their weapons and flee wildly. Others were staggering back from the lines, blinded, gagging, tearing off their greatcoats, faces and chests turning bluish purple. Farther down the line, a British soldier crouched in trepidation as a thunder of hooves grew louder on the road. Galloping horses burst into view and raced past with two and three French soldiers per steed, in frenzied flight. Soldiers unable to escape collapsed, writhing on the ground, screaming for water.

Canadian soldiers in trenches on the fringes of the attack watched in stunned surprise as the French territorials ran toward them in their blue coats and red pants, half staggering. Some foamed at the mouth, the buttons and buckles of their uniforms suddenly green with corrosion. The Canadians tried to stop them, to rally them to turn and fight, but they continued fleeing the gas cloud. The Canadians turned and shot at them as they fled.

Boesinghe was on fire. Shells had fallen across the town, collapsing roofs and sending showers of debris over the streets. Homes were burning, the walls torn open to the sky, parents shrieking for their children, gathering a few belongings, locking their doors and windows, unsure whether to take cover or to flee. The town filled with wounded soldiers retreating south, away from the lines. The sound of bawling cows and screaming horses rent the air. An acrid smell that burned the lungs and the eyes consumed the town as the wave of gas rolled southward, surging on the breeze.

The sleeping French guns came alive, machine guns rattling, every cannon firing as fast and as often as it could be reloaded. A din like no other filled the countryside, as if the ground had peeled open and hounds of hell had bellowed forth. The cloud rolled on, growing taller and taller, like a wave gaining strength before it crashes to shore.

Then, after about fifteen minutes, the French guns began falling silent. After another fifteen minutes, everything was quiet once again. When the bullets stopped, the German troops were ordered up and out of their trenches. They stepped over the empty chlorine gas tanks they had opened up and crept forward across no-man's-land. All the rodents that burrowed under the ground had come up from out of their holes and warrens and died in the cloud. Carcasses of rabbits, moles, rats, and mice lay everywhere. The burning stench of the gas still hung in the air. At the French lines, the soldiers were gone, the trenches almost empty. Farther on, they began to find the bodies. French soldiers, then British soldiers, sprawled on the ground, marks on their faces and throats where they had clawed at themselves for breath. Some leaned against earthen fortifications, their rifles beside them, as if in sleep. Some had shot themselves. When the Germans reached the farms, they found horses dead in their stables. Chickens, cows, dead. Everything was dead.

Four miles of the Allied line had collapsed in the chlorine-gas attack. But the cautious Germans, whose protections were little more than cotton cloths soaked in a neutralizing agent, tied over their nose and mouth, did not press the advantage, perhaps too wary of their own weapons to advance. The British and Canadians rushed reserve troops back up to the lines and prevented the enemy from advancing more than a few miles past their original lines. With the gas attack finished, shelling resumed. The night lit up with shellfire and explosions, the constant rattle of bullets, and the shouts and screams of soldiers.

When Marie Desaegher finally emerged from the pigpen where she had taken refuge, she found the farm overrun with Germans. The homestead was now behind the German lines. She did not see her family again for the rest of the war.

Over the previous two and a half months, the Germans had set almost six thousand chlorine tanks into the ground in the front of their trenches. Fritz Haber, one of Germany's preeminent chemists, had come up to the front personally to inspect the preparations. They waited weeks for a day when the weather was perfect and the wind just right to open the nozzles in a carefully synchronized cloud attack, in hopes of dislodging the British and French troops and breaking the stalemate that had gripped the western front.

There had been hints that such an attack might be coming. A German deserter had told his British captors about carefully laid plans for a poison-gas-cloud attack at Ypres. No one believed him. The intelligence was dismissed in part because it seemed too outlandish to be true. But furthermore, the British could not believe that the Germans would so flagrantly violate international treaties banning asphyxiating gases, signed in 1899 and 1907.

That first successful gas attack of World War I at Ypres set the stage for an arms race in a war already steeped in horror. At first, the press and Allied governments condemned the new tactic as a descent into barbarism. Then those same governments established their own gas programs. Soon after the attack in Ypres, a new phrase entered the lexicon for the grinding conflict in Europe: "the Chemists' War." In fact, scientists had been using the phrase even before the attack at Ypres, referring to novel uses of explosives, but now the use of industrial chemicals as weapons in their own right cemented the phrase as shorthand for a new kind of technology-driven warfare, in which scientists like Haber were just as crucial as military strategists in deciding the outcome of battles. Two years later, American chemists would enter that war as well.

The attack on April 22, 1915, was not the last chlorine gas attack in Ypres. More German chlorine-cloud attacks came in the days and weeks that followed. For a young girl named Jeanne Battheu, memories of those attacks haunted her for the rest of her life. Jeanne was with her grandmother in the family's house outside Poperinghe in 1916 when her mother threw open the door. Clouds billowed in the fields, and when Jeanne's granny tried to go outside, she stumbled back, choking, "I can't breathe. We can't breathe."

The gas cloud swept past the house, and Jeanne was unharmed. Afterward, she walked into town. She was with a group of children, about ten of them, when two trucks arrived and Allied officers and soldiers jumped to the ground. They began unloading men on stretchers and lining them up alongside a ditch. The men had been gassed, their eyes bulging, their tongues hanging from their mouths. Some tore at their clothes, screaming. Jeanne and the other frightened children just stared, but the officers yelled to them, "Come on, children, come on." The officers had buckets of milk, and they told the children to fill cups and bring them to the gassed men. Jeanne walked up and down the rows of stretchers, giving sips to the soldiers. The men were dying—not peacefully, not gracefully, but miserably, drowning in the fluid filling their lungs, weeping and screaming for their mothers. A traumatized boy was so terrified by the scene of horror that he ran away from home and didn't return for three days. Slowly, the thrashing stopped. The gurgling, gasping breaths fell silent. One after another, the men died as young Jeanne tried to help them swallow sips of milk. Jeanne never forgot that sight for the rest of her life. "I have never been a child," she said many years later. "If you witnessed that, you cannot have been a child."

PART I

CATALYST

Chapter One

Holy Week

What horrors night foretells
Of the living Hells
Where thou and thy brave comrades fought for me
On the bloody tarn
Of the Meuse and Marne
I'll take a turn next month in place of thee.
But banish now the thought,
The past is wrought;
I only pray to God to make me brave,
And there in grim death smile,
Feeling the while
To-morrow we shall meet beyond the grave.

—*Robert B. MacMullin*
Company E, First Gas Regiment, AEF

The chime of glasses and the clink of cutlery filled Rauscher's banquet hall in Washington as Vannoy Hartog Manning and his wife, Emily, arrived for a late supper. On the evening of April 2, 1917, a cloud of war hung over the nation's capital. Earlier in the night, President Wilson had delivered the most momentous speech of his presidency, asking Congress to declare war upon Germany. Red, white, and blue bunting draped the city, and throngs of pro-war demonstrators roamed the rain-spattered streets, bellowing patriotic songs and jeering at protesters and pacifists in their white sashes and armbands. Here and there, fistfights broke out between opposing sides. As the night grew late, the crowds withdrew to indoor rallies, where partisans shouted the president's pleas to Congress, read from the extra editions of the newspapers rushed off the presses.

The Mannings filed into Rauscher's after the president's rousing speech, but the buffet was hardly a political affair, the stuff of neither patriotism nor politics. Rather, it was a genteel reception honoring a famous ornithologist and photographer, William Finley, who had traveled to Washington from his home in Oregon. The Mannings were among a hundred people invited for the late supper, many of them fresh from the chaos at the Capitol, President Wilson's words and the thunderous ovations from Congress still ringing in their ears.

The elegant banquet hall was a picture of Washington decorum, a gentle occasion that would be noted in the society pages of the morning papers, a bubble of civility amid the city's tumult. Members of Wilson's cabinet, society ladies, and naturalists looked admiringly at the photographs of baby birds and animals that Finley displayed. The momentous events of the day, the roar of the crowds, the president's speech, the protest and debate—all of that remained outside in the city's rainy streets.

As the guests filled the reception hall, the starchy secretary of war Newton D. Baker, still considered an upstart in the cabinet, entered with his wife, Elizabeth. Senator Miles Poindexter from Washington State, a Progressive and Republican who detested those opposing the war, came late as well. There was Senator John Beckham of Kentucky and Congressman Charles Carlin from Virginia. There was the evening's host, E. Lester Jones, the tall, lean chief of the U.S. coastal survey. There was Secretary of Commerce William Redfield, with his bristling red muttonchops. The ruddy face of Postmaster General Albert Burleson bobbed among the guests, next to his wife, Adele—both southerners, like the Mannings.

Next to the dashing men in the room, Manning cut a diminutive figure, perhaps a bit dowdy. Not even five and a half feet tall, he was slightly plump and unimposing at age fifty-five, with a boyish, padded face and a prominent chin. A fastidious dresser, he had a taste for expensive waistcoats and cutaway suits. Known as Van, he was firm and charming, and modest above all else. "I was born in a depot," he would joke about his early years in tiny Horn Lake Depot, Mississippi.

While not a top official in President Wilson's administration, Manning directed the Bureau of Mines. It was a young agency, not yet seven years old, created because of growing alarm over the thousands of deaths each year in U.S. coal mines. The bureau's mandate was to prevent accidents and improve mine safety, but also to research the poisonous gases that seeped from the rock and overwhelmed miners deep underground. Manning saw his bureau as a fulcrum of progress, an axis of science, industry, and technology. Soon, it would be at the center of the war effort as well.

Inside the elegant reception hall, the war seemed far away. Yet even here in Rauscher's, with its glowing wall sconces and linen tablecloths, the upcoming war vote loomed over the gathering. Stirring as the president's speech had been, it marked the start of what would be an acrimonious, bitter fight. In the morning, the senators and congressmen peering at Finley's wildlife photographs would begin to debate whether to declare war.

For Manning, there was little to debate. Over the winter, he had been meeting with his department heads and planning for this moment. War was coming, and the country was ill prepared.

The War College, the War Department brain trust that charted the nation's military policy in peacetime and war, had already asked for Manning's assistance, requesting that his bureau regulate explosives nationwide. Bombs and dynamite menaced the whole country—every bridge, every ship, every munitions depot, was a potential target. But explosives were not the weapons that most concerned Manning. The armies of Kaiser Wilhelm had unleashed something new and dreadful on the fields of France and Belgium, weapons concocted in Germany's industrial dye works and laboratories. Weapons that gagged and blinded and choked all those unlucky enough to stand in their path. For months, Manning had been preoccupied with the poison gases that the Germans unleashed on the battlefields, the clouds of noxious chemicals that immobilized Allied troops with fear and felled hundreds of soldiers at a time. The director contemplated a wartime role for his bureau, one that would put its scientific expertise fully at the service of the military.

For Manning, the battle had already begun.

Since an assassin's bullets struck down Austrian archduke Francis Ferdinand and his pregnant wife in June of 1914, sending Europe tumbling into war, the United States had been deeply divided over the distant conflict that had turned the Continent into a slaughter-house. The Battles of Verdun and the Somme had revealed the war's horrors: a front riddled with stinking trenches, a sodden, denuded wasteland rank with the stench of corpses rotting in the deep mud, trench lines that barely budged, and savage hand-to-hand combat. The British saw more than fifty-seven thousand casualties, with almost twenty thousand dead on the first day of the Battle of the Somme; by the battle's end there were more than four hundred thousand casualties and over one hundred thousand dead. French casualties totaled more than two hundred thousand, while the Germans suffered as many as six hundred thousand. Death arrived in new and terrifying ways. Tanks made their debut, iron alligators growling across the battlefield, mashing fences, trenches, and bodies beneath their treads. In spasms of ferocious violence, faceless soldiers in masks unleashed liquid fire into the trenches. High explosives—shells packed with incendiary material that exploded on contact—tore men's bodies to pieces. The mortar shells loaded with chemicals punctuated battles, coughing up toxic blends of phosgene, chloropicrin, and other poisons. All the rules that governed the battlefield, the codes of chivalry and honor intended to keep warfare civilized, had been abandoned.

From its earliest days, the war created sharply conflicting loyalties among Americans, some sympathizing with Germany and the other Central powers, others with the alliance of Great Britain, France, and Russia, which became the Quadruple Entente with Italy's addition in 1915. Socialists saw allies in Germany's working class and viewed the war as little more than the death throes of inbred, imperial dynasties fueled by greed of speculators and industrialists. Isolationists viewed the war as an overseas quagmire of no concern to Americans. Deep seams of pacifism and antiwar sentiment ran through the country as well, with their own bellowing champions in Congress.

It was a barbarous, grinding war, a throwback to a time before laws of warfare. Yet at the same time it was a thoroughly modern conflict, a war of science and technology. Lithe German submarines had become fearsome predators in the ocean, and a new fleet of massive dreadnoughts—swift battleships larger than any vessel at sea—brought unheard-of firepower to the British navy. An era of aviation had unfolded in the skies, with aerial warfare and bombing. Long-distance observation from the air and signaling abilities on the ground had leaped forward. While mules and horses still brought equipment to the front, so did trucks and trains. Where cavalry once charged, now tanks rumbled across the battlefield. Machine guns, though not new to the war, were mass-produced in far-greater numbers to cut apart infantry assaults, and high explosives killed more soldiers on all sides than any other weapon. Massive howitzers like the fabled Big Bertha slung shells from miles away, and later, the Germans' Paris guns bombarded France's capital city from some sixty miles away.

If there was any military weapon that epitomized this new era of lethal science, it was gas warfare. Germany was at the vanguard of industrial chemistry, its engineering and industrial dye works the envy of scientists throughout Europe and the United States. For American chemists at elite universities, it was a privilege and rite of passage to travel across the Atlantic to study with Germany's giants of the field, such as Fritz Haber at the Kaiser Wilhelm Institute for Physical Chemistry and Walther Hermann Nernst at the University of Berlin.

Gas represented a fundamental change in warfare, and the 1915 chlorine attack and others that followed shocked American scientists. Not only was gas warfare a blatant violation of international pacts signed in 1899 and again in 1907, but scientists that American chemists revered, such as Haber and Nernst, were central to the German gas warfare program. The prominent role of Haber, who had personally overseen the attack at Ypres at the front, was particularly odious for scientists because of another spectacular achievement, Haber's discovery of a process for turning nitrogen gas into a crop fertilizer. Nitrogen fixation, as it was called, was a breakthrough, one of history's greatest advances in agriculture. His enthusiastic embrace of chemical warfare earned him scorn and brought tragedy to his home. Just days after the attack at Ypres and Haber's return from Belgium, Haber's wife, Clara—an accomplished chemist herself—shot herself in the heart with his army pistol, despondent over her husband's role in this new chapter of warfare. Haber left the next morning for the eastern front and did not attend her funeral.

Chlorine was only the beginning. Once the breach had opened, France and Britain responded in kind with their own gas programs. In September of 1915, the British attempted to retaliate with chlorine in Loos, Belgium. The attack was delayed and poorly planned. When the day arrived, the winds blew toward the British lines, and their soldiers advanced through their own gas cloud. The offensive was a failure, with over 2,600 British gas casualties and more than 50,000 overall, more than twice that of their adversaries.

The Germans, always a step ahead, introduced a new war gas in December 1915: the industrial chemical phosgene. A green cross marked the shells that carried it, and when the gas burst from exploded munitions, it gave off an odor of musty hay or apples. Far deadlier than chlorine, phosgene caused uncontrollable coughing and edema of the lungs even in tiny doses. Eventually, the victims' lungs filled up with fluid, drowning the soldiers as they choked and gasped for breath. In July 1916, chloropicrin appeared in German shells. Called vomiting gas, it was rarely deadly, but it had the advantage of passing straight through the filters of the Allies' rudimentary gas masks. When the retching soldiers tore off their masks, they inhaled other deadly chemicals mixed with the chloropicrin. Terrible as these weapons were, worse was still to come.

When war finally came to America, it arrived from under the sea. On May 7, 1915, the German submarine U-20 sank the British ocean liner RMS *Lusitania* off the coast of Ireland. Of all the war's grotesque novelties, the advent of submarine warfare and the blockade that Germany announced in February of that year most inflamed American outrage. Britain's dreadnoughts had virtually eliminated German surface ships from shipping routes. Germany's response was to deploy its submarine fleet in stealthy attacks against merchant ships running the blockade. The *Lusitania,* though, was a passenger ship, and when the German submarine torpedoed the ship, more than one hundred American civilians were among the nearly twelve hundred passengers sent to their deaths, fanning fury toward Germany.

New outrages followed. Two months after the *Lusitania* sank, a former Harvard professor named Erich Muenter planted dynamite in the U.S. Capitol, shattering windows and blasting the frescoes from the ceiling, then attempted to murder the Wall Street financier J. P. Morgan Jr. Later that year, after Germany recalled its military attaché, Franz von Papen, and his naval attaché, Karl Boy-Ed, in December of 1915, Americans learned that the two of them had bankrolled a network of spies and saboteurs within the country. In July 1916, German agents set fires that detonated explosives and ammunition warehoused on Black Tom Island in

Jersey City with powerful blasts felt as far away as Maryland and Connecticut, shattering windows for miles around. A secret cabal of conspirators led by a German chemist smuggled ingenious incendiary devices onto dozens of merchant ships, delayed-action chemical bombs that set the vessels afire at sea. With each new report of sunken ships and sabotage, the anger grew.

American scientists who understood the link between Germany's scientific and industrial capacity and its success in developing new weapons began to quietly discuss the possibility that their own chemists and other scientists could be called upon if the United States entered the conflict. Soon after the attacks at Ypres and the sinking of the *Lusitania,* the astrophysicist George E. Hale wrote to William H. Welch, president of the National Academy of Sciences, about what the war meant for men of science.

However remote the possibility of war, he wrote, America needed to muster its own scientific prowess to the same ends for "development of new appliances of warfare," including chemical weapons. Hale's letter contained a prescient note of dread over the prospect of gas warfare. "I hope we should avoid the use of poisonous gases, but we must enlist the aid of our chemists in protecting our soldiers against them," he wrote. He urged Welch to keep the entire matter confidential until it became clear whether scientific mobilization was necessary.

President Wilson, a puritanical Presbyterian and pacifist at heart, maintained that armed neutrality was the best course and believed the United States should be a mediator of the warring nations. When he was renominated in 1916, Democratic delegates cheered his slogan "He Kept Us Out of War," and he rode support for neutrality back into the White House for a second term. He kept the country on a high level of alert nonetheless, adopting the slogan "America First," supporting "preparedness" campaigns, and pushing for an expanded military and navy.

Part of that preparedness for war included heeding Hale's warning. In 1916, Hale, Welch, and other scientists met with President Wilson to offer the services of scientists to the war effort. The result was the National Research Council, a think tank of leading scientists across disciplines, government agencies, and the Smithsonian Institution, to encourage government, private industry, and academia to collaborate on industry, defense, and national security issues, with Hale at its head. On August 5 of that year, President Wilson sent the names of government appointees to Hale. One of those names was Manning's.

Van Manning was an unlikely warrior. He spoke with warm, self-deprecating humor and seemed to always want to credit others for achievements. Despite his affable personality, he could appear preoccupied and dour, his mouth drawn into a thin, humorless line. In a bureau publicity photo, he looked distinctly uncomfortable, his jacket a bit too snug, his outfit a bit too formal, as he observed a lab-bench experiment of one of his chemists. He was a government man above all, a bureaucrat with an exacting nature who paid fussy attention to detail.

Yet there was more to Manning than his buttoned-up appearance revealed. Though Manning had never fought on a battlefield, he was a child of war nonetheless and had soldierly instincts. His father, also named Vannoy Hartog Manning, was a Confederate colonel. A brash Southern partisan from North Carolina, he studied law in Nashville before moving with his wife to Horn Lake Depot, Mississippi. Not long after the Civil War broke out in 1861, he helped organize an infantry regiment and marched to Vicksburg with eleven companies, leaving behind his pregnant wife. Captured at the Battle of the Wilderness, he spent the rest of the war in prison.

After the South's surrender, Manning returned to his family, his face scarred by battle wounds. His wife had moved to Holly Springs, Mississippi, with their young son, who was now four years old. The boy had been born in December of 1861, and his mother had given him his father's name without a "junior" at the end, perhaps reflecting doubt about his father's return. For more than a decade, the elder Manning practiced law and his son went to school. In 1877, Manning was elected to Congress and moved to Washington. The younger Manning studied at the University of Mississippi and worked as a schoolteacher in Holly Springs for a time before the whole family joined his father in Washington, settling in a neighborhood southeast of the Capitol.

The younger Van Manning did not become a creature of Washington right away. In 1885, the U.S. Geological Survey (USGS) hired him for a job that would lead him to the world of chemical warfare more than thirty years later. He spent two years as a topographic aide surveying land in Massachusetts before he took charge of mapping parties in Wisconsin and North Dakota and then assisted the survey of Indian Territory. Year by year, his responsibilities grew. He became section chief of surveys in Missouri and Arkansas, then was put in charge of surveys for the entire southeastern United States. Over a quarter century, Manning surveyed federal land in almost every state. Mapping was dangerous, rugged work—one slip could result in a deadly tumble or injury. Foul weather and cold brought on sickness. Wild animals prowled the territories, along with two-legged denizens potentially hostile to surveyor teams. Under his bespoke trousers, Manning had a bullet wound on his right shin.

At their core, the geological surveys were technical expeditions linked with the nation's growth, charting the nation's interior and cataloging the resources that would fuel future engines of industrial progress. Manning's mentor and predecessor at the helm of the Bureau of Mines, Joseph A. Holmes, saw science as a critical ingredient for industrial progress and believed the government should have a central role in making mineral and resource extraction safer and more efficient. His advocacy moved Congress to authorize a new technological branch of the Geological Survey.

Holmes's ultimate goal was to create a bureau dedicated solely to mines and mining. Thousands of men were dying every year in mines across the country. Holmes used his reach at the helm of the new scientific branch to deepen investigations into accidents. Private companies and trade groups like the American Mining Congress supported his efforts, and a series of disastrous explosions in December of 1907 highlighted the urgency of his work. The Technologic Branch began investigating safety lamps and mine-rescue equipment, and studied explosives and the perils of running electricity underground. Given the divergence of the scientific work from USGS surveys, as well as pressure from mining interests, Congress created the Bureau of Mines in 1910. President Taft put Holmes in charge. Holmes adopted the slogan "Safety First" for the bureau, a credo to guide its lifesaving research. He named Manning as assistant director in January 1911, and Manning remained at Holmes's side throughout the rest of his tenure.

The dangers of the work took a toll. Holmes contracted tuberculosis during an arduous survey in Alaska, and the illness forced him to step away from his duties in 1914. Manning ran the bureau in Holmes's absence—by some accounts, more efficiently than Holmes did. "Many of the things that Dr. Holmes could not find time to do, Mr. Manning has done. Many of the papers and reports which Dr. Holmes did not have time to write or edit, Mr. Manning has 'whipped into shape,'" reported one mining newsletter.

After a long decline, Holmes died in July of 1915. Manning wrote Holmes's obituary for the *Journal of Industrial and Engineering Chemistry*. "In the death of Dr. Holmes, the people of the United States lose one of their most remarkable and efficient public servants," he wrote. With a vacancy at the top of the organization, President Wilson appointed Manning to the position. Well-wishers from around the country, from state geologists to the United Mine Workers, wrote to congratulate him. The bureau held a banquet at Rauscher's to welcome Manning on November 20, 1915. More than two hundred people attended, and after the guests found their seats in the banquet room, the toastmaster asked everyone to stand for a moment of silence to remember Holmes. After everyone took their seats again, George Otis Smith, the head of the Geological Survey, remained on his feet. Manning's success, he said, was due to his work as a topographer. "He has had more hard knocks than his looks show," Smith said.

The speeches were long, and the night grew late. Finally, Interior Secretary Franklin K. Lane rose from his seat. He thanked the other speakers and spoke a few words in homage to Holmes. Then a political note crept into Lane's speech. He equated the Bureau of Mines slogan "Safety First" to President Wilson's slogan "America First." The two slogans were one and the same, Lane said—"safety for ourselves and safety for our country." The Bureau of Mines was at the nexus of both. The agency's men delved into the secrets of nature and placed them in the service of the nation, he said, "because we have passed now into an industrial world, and war seems to be the chief industry." Where war was once a clash of men with swords, those days were past. Now military might meant extracting and developing immense mineral reserves. It meant smelting ore into barbed wire, railroads, cannons, and automobiles— "everything that a great industrial nation has constitutes the army now when comes the war, and we are an army pre-eminently great in leading any onslaught, because we have mineral resources greater than those of any other country," he said.

In a world where industrial might and military might were inextricably linked, the Bureau of Mines, an agency created to save lives, was now more critical than ever, resting squarely at the axis of progress, military strength, and economic power. Lane said:

We can build a battleship out of the mines of the United States, and no other country can make that boast. And it is the plan to make the Bureau of Mines a great conservation institution, saving from waste, putting to use, and I have no doubt that the president was wise, as wise as usual, when he selected to direct the work of that bureau Mr. Manning.

As Manning rose to his feet, the guests in the hall began to sing "For He's a Jolly Good Fellow." He spoke only a few minutes, mostly in self-effacing praise of others, and he sprinkled his comments with modest adages and wry jokes. He thanked President Wilson and Secretary Lane, then the audience. "When the day is done, I will be satisfied if it is said of me: 'Living he did gain men's good opinions, and now dead leaves his work to the care of noble friends,'" he said. The room broke into applause. The speeches were done. The band struck up. The guests rose and began to dance.

By winter of 1917, Secretary Lane's bellicose words proved true, and the shadow of war grew with each passing day. Still adamant in his desire to keep America out of the war, Wilson tried to broker a peaceful solution. On January 22, 1917, he proposed a league of peace that would require the Central powers and the Allies to lay down arms and abandon the old dynastic alliances that had begun the war. It would be a global Monroe Doctrine, founded upon the notion that no nation should try to influence another. At its heart was a principle that he called "peace without victory," a puzzling concept that earned opprobrium and ridicule from critics.

For days after the speech, there was silence from Germany and Austria. Soon their views became clear. A German newspaper in Essen that served as a government mouthpiece scoffed that Wilson did not understand Europe and dismissed the plan as "beyond the bounds of practicality." Vienna expressed disappointment in the speech, dismissing Wilson's words as shiny pearls that would lose luster.

The true response came on January 31, when Wilson's secretary stepped into the president's office and laid a wire-service bulletin on the desk without a word. Wilson set down his pen. Amazement crept over his face as he read, his lips pressed together. Germany had abandoned its pledge not to attack neutral ships, including American vessels. His long face ashen and his jaw clenched, Wilson handed the paper back. "This means war. The break that we have tried so hard to prevent now seems inevitable," he said. Neutrality was no longer an option. "Peace without victory" was dead.

On February 3, Wilson returned to Capitol Hill, this time to announce that he had severed diplomatic relations with Germany and recalled the American ambassador in Berlin. In the following days, the toll of lives lost at sea rose in a grim tally. A German submarine sank the U.S. steamship *Housatonic* on its way to London. On February 6, U-boats sank fourteen ships on a single day, twelve the next day, and ten more the day after that. As Wilson went to Congress to ask for the arming of merchant ships, a new outrage inflamed the public further: the Associated Press published a secret German telegram proposing an alliance with Japan and America's adversary to the south, Mexico, if Wilson declared war.

Germany's machinations finally tipped the scale. There seemed to be no way back from the brink. With war increasingly inevitable, Secretary Lane ordered each of his bureaus to confer over how best to aid in preparedness. Manning summoned his chiefs and his top technical men to his office on February 7. Manning's chief mining engineer, George S. Rice, came from Pittsburgh. Rice was fifty, with a thatch of gray hair and piercing blue-gray eyes set back beneath a heavy brow. His specialty was mine explosions, and he had been at the bureau since its earliest days, first as senior engineer and then as chief mining engineer. He had even temporarily stepped in as director when Manning was traveling on bureau business. During Rice's frequent trips to Washington, he stayed at the Cosmos Club, one of the city's elite private dining clubs that invited only the most accomplished scholars and scientists to join.

The bureau headquarters were in the Busch Building, a brick claptrap of creaking elevators and battered wainscoting on E Street NW. About ten blocks to the west, carpenters and electricians were completing a new building for the Department of the Interior that the Bureau of Mines would move to in April. The vast stone structure would be one of the biggest office buildings in Washington.

Each bureau within the department would have its own rectangular tower, rising five levels above common floors of the building. Just a few blocks from the White House, the new building sat close to the epicenter of federal power, reflecting the department's prominence.

Manning maintained a tidy office, almost prim in its organization. He worked at a double-sized desk, polished to a gleam. When he bent over his work, pen in hand, he resembled a diminutive pianist hunched over his instrument. He protected the desktop with a wide blotter, a double inkwell centered at the top. He aligned his books in perfect rows on the shelves. A photograph of Joseph Holmes hung on one wall, his baleful eyes peering out over his walrus mustache. On another wall, Manning hung a very different print: a wilderness vista of a waterfall crashing from a rugged peak. Full of turbulence and motion, the picture showed a place that was the opposite of Washington, with its cautious order and arcane rules of conduct.

After the men settled into their seats, Manning asked each for his views on how the bureau could aid in the war effort. Rice said the bureau could almost certainly help investigate war gases, especially in finding ways to protect the soldiers with masks. After all, one of the bureau's men, an engineer named William Gibbs, had designed a breathing apparatus that allowed miners to breathe freely amid clouds of poison gas underground.

Charles L. Parsons, the bureau's chief chemist, had just returned from an expedition to Europe to study chemical processes in England, France, Italy, Norway, and Sweden. He was among the most prominent chemists in the country, and his words had clout. When it was his turn to speak, he dismissed Rice's suggestion that a gas mask was needed on the battlefield. The problem of protecting against gas had been solved with "a simple cloth mask, which dipped in certain chemicals neutralized the gases," he said.

The comment astonished Rice, and probably all the other men in the room, too. In fact, the earliest German and British masks were not far from what Parsons described, which perhaps was the reason Parsons was so convinced that more effective protection was unneeded. But those were emergency measures abandoned years ago, and all sides had long ago developed much-more-advanced gas masks. The idea that a cloth over the nose and mouth could provide a suitable defense against poison gases was preposterous, particularly coming from the bureau's chief chemist. The comment illustrated the naïveté of the Americans with respect to the gas threat, even two years after the introduction of chlorine at Ypres.

Manning, though, firmly agreed with Rice that real masks were needed and saw his bureau as the logical agency to spearhead the work. In fact, he believed it to be the only government organization with the collective scientific ability to handle the problems of war gases.

While Parson's skepticism about gas masks was wildly off the mark, some of his other observations were not. Throughout Europe, a shortage of chemists hobbled the Allies' ability to respond to Germany's weapons. Everywhere, Parsons said, anguished scientists reported that their ranks had been dangerously thinned as result of chemists being sent to the front as soldiers, their expertise and training dying in the trenches with them. Germany, by contrast, had shielded its scientists from such a fate by keeping them at home and out of combat. Realizing their mistake, generals in France, England, Italy, and Canada had all ordered their chemists back from the front. It was not a mistake that Manning intended to let the American military repeat.

The next day, he wrote to the National Research Council offering to lead war gas investigations, pointing out that the bureau could use its expertise to design gas masks for soldiers. The bureau already had testing chambers at the Pittsburgh station, and experienced scientists. The chairman of the council wrote back a few days later, saying he would bring the matter to the attention of the council's committee.

While Manning awaited further word, the bureau's work continued. There were deadly mine explosions and fires to investigate. Technical papers and reports needed review, requests from Congress demanded attention. But preparedness was never far from Manning's thoughts. At the end of March, President Wilson told his cabinet that he would seek a war declaration from Congress. The next day, the War College nudged Manning still closer to the war effort. Because explosives were mostly used in mining and related industries, the War College president, Brigadier General Joseph E. Kuhn, requested that the Bureau of Mines regulate explosives everywhere in the country. The need to control explosives was obvious to anyone who read the newspapers. Many states had no such regulations, and those that did often conflicted with other states', making for a confused patchwork of rules. Determined saboteurs could easily get their hands on dynamite. An example was right under the government's nose: the bombing of the U.S. Capitol in 1915, in which the perpetrator ordered dynamite, blasting caps, and fuses and had them delivered under an alias to a railroad freight office, where the helpful station agent had locked the dynamite in his office and held it overnight as a courtesy.

As the march toward war continued, Manning undertook an ambitious task: a nationwide census of scientists in fields that might be of use to the war effort. Like all of Manning's undertakings, the census was meticulous: twenty-five thousand letters mailed to chemists, engineers, metal-mining and coal-mining companies. The letter asked for information about the type of work and materials the scientists worked with. It asked them to name colleges they attended, military connections, citizenship status, along with marital status, number of children, and country where they were born. Manning made no secret of his desire to enlist the country's chemists and scientists into the war effort. Trade groups such as the American Institute of Mining Engineers and the American Chemical Society supported the effort. Charles Herty, the influential editor of the *Journal of Industrial and Engineering Chemistry,* was an enthusiastic booster and featured the census in the journal's pages. Completing the questionnaire, Manning said, was "a matter of patriotism."

Shipyards would have to assemble destroyers and submarines as quickly as possible, he said. Factories would have to retool to build tanks and artillery. There would be a race to counter ever-evolving weapons with more lethal ones. American expertise and skills had already produced armored battleships, submarines, machine guns, and airships. Whatever new weapons and devices were needed when war arrived, the country's technical men would find a way to make them. This was an engineers' war, Manning said. A chemists' war.

Wilson's second term had begun on March 4 with barely a whisper, a hurried recitation of the oath of office, stripped of ritual, in the President's Room of the Capitol, while antiwar senators thundered against his maritime defense bill in the chamber a few feet away. The next day, he was sworn in again in an austere, barebones public inauguration. His war address to Congress was set for Monday, April 2. Wilson spent Palm Sunday laboring over his speech, then went to church to pray. That night, opponents of U.S. intervention protested the president's reversal, and war supporters mounted patriotic demonstrations. A riot broke out at an antiwar speech in Baltimore.

On the day of the speech, protesters from throughout the country disembarked at Union Station. White antiwar sashes slung over shoulders and bands cinched around their arms, they marched under the station's flag-draped archway and past a recruiting station with a sign reading MEN WANTED FOR THE ARMY. When demonstrators tried to assemble on the Capitol steps, police herded them down to the plaza in front of jeering onlookers. War supporters turned out in huge numbers as well, trailing the pacifists' lobbying circuit through Congress. Inside the building, a heated argument between Massachusetts senator Henry Cabot Lodge and an antiwar demonstrator escalated into a fistfight. After the senator leveled the man with a punch to the jaw, a Western Union messenger beat the protester, spattering blood on the marble floor. In the hours before the speech, Secret Service and police swarmed the building, clearing out demonstrators, and mounted police guarded the entrances.

Wilson waited all day for the summons from Congress. It came just after 8:00 p.m. Thousands of people massed in the rain outside the White House, singing raucous renditions of "Dixie" and "America" that could be heard for blocks. Cavalry flanked Wilson's car as it drove slowly past the cheering crowds toward the Capitol. The car arrived at 8:30 p.m., and Edith Wilson left her husband in the President's Room to take her seat in the gallery. With only a Secret Service man and a magazine editor looking on, the president sagged against the ornate fireplace and stared into the mirror over the mantel. His face was so contorted and flushed that the alarmed editor thought Wilson might be having a stroke. Then he straightened, composed himself, and walked to the House chamber.

Onlookers jostled in the galleries, and the diplomatic corps faced the rostrum. Supreme Court justices were in the front, with Chief Justice Edward Douglass White at their center. When the president reached the dais, cheers prevented him from speaking for two minutes. The chamber finally fell silent, the lawmakers and dignitaries still. He gripped his typewritten notes in both hands and read without looking up.

"I have called the Congress into extraordinary session because there are serious, very serious, choices of policy to be made, and made immediately, which it was neither right nor constitutionally permissible that I should assume the responsibility of making," he read. The president went on, now looking up from time to time. The new German submarine policy had swept aside all restriction on the seas, he said. "Vessels of every kind, whatever their flag, their character, their cargo, their destination, their errand, have been ruthlessly sent to the bottom without warning and without thought of help or mercy for those on board." Hospital ships and relief vessels had been sunk. Men, women, and children had died on the seas. Armed neutrality, the position he had pledged, "is ineffectual enough at best.

> In such circumstances and in the face of such pretensions it is worse than ineffectual; it is likely only to produce what it was meant to prevent; it is practically certain to draw us into the war without either the rights or the effectiveness of belligerents. There is one choice we can not make, we are incapable of making: we will not choose the path of submission—

In the front row, Chief Justice White leaped to his feet, dropping his hat to the floor and startling Secret Service agents with their hands on their pistol grips. Lips pressed together as if holding back tears, White clapped his hands above his head. As if on cue, Democrats followed suit, and the entire chamber thundered with applause. The words that followed were lost in the roar of approval from the chamber.

After the speech, deflated war opponents gathered for a mass meeting at a downtown convention hall, their cause defeated, their ranks split. For Manning, the late supper for the naturalist Finley at Rauscher's may have been a welcome social occasion, a pause in a rancorous day. If it provided a respite from the war, it was a brief one.

The morning after the president's war speech, every paper in the country carried the news that Wilson had privately known when he took the rostrum: a German submarine had sunk another American ship. The steamship *Aztec* had gone down late Sunday night, with more than two dozen people feared dead. With this new atrocity, the surge of protest from pacifists and isolationists broke. At the Washington headquarters of one antiwar group, a prowar group painted over the windows with yellow paint. As war opponents scrubbed off the paint, a crowd taunted them on the sidewalk.

Inside the U.S. Senate chamber, shouting broke out when Robert

"Fighting Bob" La Follette, the radical antiwar Senate leader from Wisconsin, temporarily blocked a vote on the war resolution. When one senator insisted that the chamber adjourn to end the antiwar speeches, gallery spectators broke out into cheers. Acrimony followed one antiwar senator dining at a hotel restaurant. After the band struck up "The Star-Spangled Banner," other patrons hissed and heckled the senator when he stayed seated during the song.

The Bureau of Mines was only a few blocks down E Street NW from the offices of the National Research Council, where the military committee met at ten-thirty the morning after the president's speech. Part of the committee's business was to name the Committee on Noxious Gases and put Manning at its head. The members included army and navy ordnance officers, two men from the Army Medical Department, and two men from the council's Chemistry Committee. It was a tiny group of men chosen to steer the research, almost laughably small given the magnitude of the problems they faced.

Manning's immediate priority was a gas mask to protect the soldiers that would embark for Europe. The man in charge of raising that army was Brigadier General Kuhn, the head of the War College, who had previously asked the Bureau of Mines to regulate explosives. Now he asked Manning to meet him at the Washington Arsenal the next day, which was Wednesday, the midway point of Holy Week and two days after Wilson addressed Congress. Manning knew that creating a gas program to match that of the Germans would be a tremendous scientific challenge, and he needed a trusted lieutenant to lead the effort. Manning chose George A. Burrell. A chemical engineer, Burrell had been Manning's former chief of gas investigations and one of the top technical men in Pittsburgh. He had a soft face, with questioning eyes behind his wire spectacles. His receding hairline made him appear older than his thirty-five years. More than twenty years separated Burrell and Manning, but the two men were close, with a deep mutual respect rooted in nearly a decade of work together.

Burrell had come from humble roots, the son of a Scottish immigrant who settled in Cleveland, Ohio, to work as a mill foreman. He had studied at Ohio State University then worked as a lab aide for a company in Cleveland. The U.S. Geological Survey hired him to investigate fuels in Saint Louis, then put him in charge of the survey's fuel-testing plant in Colorado. After only a year, he came east to investigate gas and petroleum in the survey's Pittsburgh labs. When Congress created the Bureau of Mines, the new agency absorbed the survey's mine-accidents and fuel-testing divisions, and Burrell with it. He became an intellectual luminary, publishing more than fifty papers in top journals—an astonishing number for such a young man. Engineers across the country eagerly read his published studies on gas and petroleum extraction. A methane detector he patented in 1916 was a breakthrough for mining safety.

The previous October, Burrell had decided to leave the government to become a private consultant. Colleagues in Pittsburgh had toasted him at a farewell banquet and given him a gold watch to help him keep time in his new role. Now, with the country on the threshold of war, Manning summoned him back to the bureau. Not for just any job, but to head the entire war gas research operation for the U.S. government.

The road to the War College stretched alongside the Washington Arsenal and the barracks of the Engineer School, where the elite Army Corps of Engineers trained its future officers. Manning passed a parade ground lined with trees, with a baseball diamond in one corner. Wednesday of Holy Week was warm and mild. In a more peaceful time, it would have been a perfect day to stroll around the Tidal Basin, where engineers had been planting cherry trees, gifts from the Japanese government. There was no time for such luxury now. The War College was at the center of the coming mobilization, its officers shuttling back and forth to the State, War, and Navy Building for consultations over the war budget, the likelihood of a draft, and the requisitions needed to outfit a million men.

Theodore Roosevelt Hall rose from the flats of Greenleaf Point, where the Anacostia and the Potomac Rivers converged. An enormous Beaux-Arts building of red brick and marble trim, the hall spread east and west from the rounded roof of the central pavilion. The building projected military might, an imposing symbol of the country's growing power. Atop the entrance, a sculpted eagle gazed east, poised for flight.

Along with Burrell, Manning brought George Rice and William Gibbs, as well as Arno Fieldner. A bright, likable man, Fieldner had risen quickly through the bureau after the U.S. Geological Survey hired him 1907 and later put him in charge of the chemistry lab at the bureau's Pittsburgh Experiment Station. Rounding out the group was Yale University physiologist Yandell Henderson. His cardiorespiratory research had made him famous, while his pugnacious character had made him infamous. A contrarian prone to eyebrow-raising remarks, Henderson had written an inflammatory letter to the *New York Times* shortly after the *Lusitania*'s sinking in 1915. The letter scoffed at the allegations of atrocities by Austro-Hungarian troops and likened the actions of the Central powers to collegiate mischief at a school reunion. Accused of being an apologist for the Central powers, he earned a mocking editorial from the *Times* and had even been reported to the Department of Justice. He had learned to keep his opinions to himself and was now on board with the war effort.

Kuhn greeted Manning with Major Llewellyn Williamson, chief of the Medical Department of the U.S. Army and a member of Manning's Committee on Noxious Gases. Lean and commanding, Kuhn had an imperious mustache, arched eyebrows, and silver temples. The military needed to be swiftly transformed into a fighting force, and Kuhn was particularly well suited to help with the task. He had been a brilliant student at West Point and a careful observer of battlefield tactics in the Russo-Japanese War. Most recently, he'd been the American military attaché in Berlin. He visited European battlefields regularly, and his diplomatic nature had made him a favorite among German military officers. When he returned to the United States, he brought with him valuable intelligence gleaned from the Germans who had unwisely taken him into their confidence.

Manning told Kuhn of the news that the National Research Council believed the Bureau of Mines should lead gas investigations. General Kuhn embraced the idea as well. Under different circumstances, this might have been an uncomfortable discussion—the decision put the civilian Bureau of Mines in charge of a military undertaking, making the War Department a backseat passenger to a nonmilitary agency. But under the circumstances, Kuhn felt that the bureau was best positioned to work on the gas investigations and offered to help in any way he could.

Manning and his men departed, retracing their route toward downtown. As they left the arsenal once again, the Capitol dome would have been visible in the distance, where the Senate was debating the president's war resolution. When the War Department built its army, it would need more than infantry. It would call upon every profession to volunteer: blacksmiths, farriers, stenographers, wheelwrights, masons—anyone with a skill who could aid the massive mobilization that lay ahead. With Kuhn's blessing, Manning was also gathering an army. But instead of calling upon carpenters and teamsters, he would summon chemists and technicians. He was organizing an army of scientists.

That afternoon, the Senate voted to adopt the war resolution. Two days later, in the early hours of Good Friday, the House followed suit. The Senate convened briefly at noon, readying the resolution for delivery to the president. Throngs of men in boater hats pushed up onto the steps of the Capitol and clogged surrounding streets, waving flags and cheering the delegation that rushed the document up Pennsylvania Avenue. President Wilson was lunching with his wife and cousin when the delegation arrived. All three hurried to the Usher's Room off the grand entrance. Rudolph Forster, the president's clerk, waited beside a table with the document, and the first lady handed her husband a pen. President Wilson sat and scratched out his signature with its long swooping tail.

A burly navy officer named Lieutenant Commander Byron McCandless watched the strokes of the president's pen. When it was done, the officer stepped to a window, raised his arms, and wagged them in semaphore code. Across the street, another officer watched from a window in the State, War, and Navy Building. At McCandless's signal, he crossed the hallway to the wireless operators. Their fingers began to tap, sending the same coded message to every naval vessel, yard, and station: "The President has signed an act of Congress which declares that a state of war exists between the United States and Germany."

Steam whistles blasted from the Navy Yard and from factories in Georgetown. Across Washington, the crowds churning through the streets erupted in cheers. At port cities across the country, sailors boarded interned German ships and detained their marooned crews, some of whom had smashed the cylinder heads of their vessels and crippled the engines in anticipation of the long-awaited seizure. Jewels of the German merchant fleet were now U.S. property, including the *Kaiser Wilhelm II*, the emperor's favorite vessel.

Shortly after Wilson signed the declaration, the president of neutral Cuba sent a message to Congress asking permission to declare war as well. The Caribbean nation was no longer a safe haven for spies and smugglers.

For three years, scientists in the United States had watched the carnage unfold across the ocean, wondering if and when they would be pulled into the fray. In all that time, there had been virtually no preparation for the gas warfare that awaited American soldiers. Finally, the gears were turning. On the day that Congress passed the war resolution, Manning asked the secretary of the National Research Council to quickly sign off on his noxious gases steering committee, saying the men needed to convene immediately. The scientists who had dallied for so long threw their support to their colleagues in Europe. The neutrality of the U.S. government was finished, and so was the neutrality of the American scientific establishment, which had been on the sidelines of the war for so long. Hale, the chairman of the National Research Council, was also foreign secretary for the National Academy of Sciences, making him an ambassador to scientific organizations overseas. He dictated a telegram to the academy's sister organizations across Europe—in London, Paris, Rome, and Petrograd. Hale wrote,

The entrance of the United States into the war unites our men of science with yours in a common cause. The National Academy of Sciences, acting through the National Research Council which has been designated by President Wilson and the Council of National Defense to mobilize the research facilities of the country, would gladly cooperate in any scientific researches still underlying the solution of military or industrial problems.

America had joined the chemists' war.

Chapter Two

An American University

Darkness cloaked Washington, the city streets empty and still, when explosions rattled residents from their sleep in the capital's Petworth neighborhood. It was before dawn on Saturday, April 7, 1917, not even a full day since the United States had declared war. Minutes after the explosions, police detectives swarmed Georgia Avenue to find splintered electrical poles along the trolley line. Saboteurs had drilled into the poles and stuffed the holes with dynamite. The damage was minor, and the trolleys began on schedule, but as the sun rose over the capital, the violence was an unsettling reminder of the wartime peril that was at hand.

As the city prepared for a somber Easter, guards scanned the streets outside federal buildings. When residents opened the morning newspapers, they learned that German merchant sailors interned in Guam had blown up their ship to keep it from falling into American hands, killing themselves in the process. Afternoon editions reported that spotters had glimpsed German ships prowling off Nantucket Shoals and the coast of Virginia. The president's war proclamation banned German citizens within a half mile of any military or naval installation, and the attorney general ordered enemy aliens to "obey the law; keep your mouth shut." Agents had seized radio transmitters across the city.

That afternoon, George Rice flashed his credentials to the guard on his way into the Bureau of Mines offices on E Street. There he met nine other men gathered in the director's office for the first meeting of Manning's Committee on Noxious Gases. A mix of military men, scientists, academicians, and technical men from the Bureau of Mines, all of them were well known in their various fields. They needed no reminder as to why they were there. While it wasn't yet clear what the American role would be in the war, millions of U.S. soldiers could be sent. Reports from Europe laid bare that gas was an ever-growing factor on the battlefield, and it was the committee's duty to protect them. Urgent questions needed to be addressed about how the research effort would proceed, who would control it and where.

A stenographer took notes as Duncan Gatewood, the dour-looking director of the Navy Medical Department, described the work in England. Britain had fifteen thousand men working in the Army Medical School laboratory in London and analyzing German gas brought from the front. The scope of the work there was enormous: ten factories making ten thousand masks a day, with 25 million more under contract. At the same time, the British had three factories making gas of their own to use against the Germans. "It is a tremendous thing we are considering," Gatewood said.

"How extensive should the research work be? Should it be done here in Washington?" Manning chimed in with his Mississippi burr. The undertaking before them was vast—they would need millions of masks. They would need factories. They would need doctors to study the effects of war gases. They would need experienced chemists—the very best chemists in the country, and lots of them. And the research would not be simply for defensive measures. Like the British and the French, the Americans would need an offensive division to devise chemical weapons of their own. Every weapon the Germans had built—the drift gases released from tanks, the gas-filled shells launched across the lines, grenades, and flamethrowers—the Americans now needed to replicate as well.

They would need a laboratory. A place where experiments of all kinds could be carried out secretly, under guard. Manning's longtime confidant, George Burrell, had gone back to Pittsburgh briefly but was returning to Washington in a few days to take charge of the research. The men agreed that the central research laboratory ought to be in Washington, or close to it, for security and convenience. As the men debated the location of the lab, Gatewood warned that the army would probably want to be in charge of the research, and probably should be, because only the army would be able to bring back gas samples from the front to study.

"There will be no objection on our part to having the army control the work," Manning said. He suggested his bureau's laboratory, while the chief of the Bureau of Chemistry argued that his would be best. The chief of ordnance agreed with Gatewood that they should use the army's lab. The men went around and around, unable to agree on a location. When the meeting adjourned, there was still no consensus on how to proceed, but all the men recognized that a central government laboratory was crucial. It needed to be secure, it needed to be protected from spies and saboteurs, and it needed to be in Washington. The question was where.

As the committee members departed Manning's office on April 7, they could hardly be faulted if they felt daunted by the enormity of the task before them. They would be racing to catch up on a novel form of warfare they had neither seen nor experienced, which would test their scientific knowledge and their moral codes. It was also a field that was constantly changing, with new gases introduced with new types of weapons. The very week that the Americans entered the war, the British unveiled a new weapon that would reshape the battlefield for gas warfare again. The northern French city of Arras was a garrison city, a frontier outpost smashed into ruins when the Germans had seized the Artois coal-mining region almost three years before. Once famous for its tapestries, the city was a ghost of what it had been. In late 1914, shelling had reduced the sixteenth-century town hall to rubble, and the city bell tower soon after. Buildings ringing the city squares lay in piles of rock and timber. The cathedral walls still stood, the aisle columns protruding from heaps of stone, but the bombardment had smashed the vaulted roof open, leaving the nave open to whirling snowflakes. Most city residents had fled, but a few hardy souls remained, haunting the shattered homes and the cratered, vacant streets.

For months, the British had planned a major offensive at Arras to try to punch through the German lines and at the same time create a diversion from an impending French drive in the south. The immediate goal was to seize coveted high ground to the city's north, Vimy Ridge, with the more ambitious hope of breaking the back of the German army and ending the war. It would be a massive attack, carried out both belowground and above. The British First Army had prepared all winter, slowly expanding caves, mines, and underground quarries around Arras into a warren of tunnels and subterranean rail lines to allow the Allies to creep up beneath the very feet of the Germans. At the same time, they'd been busy aboveground at night, digging in the darkness, sometimes shrouded in whirling snow.

The British were introducing a new weapon for the gas attack. The soldiers digging in the nighttime were burying a mortar called a Livens projector, an old weapon being put to new use. The mechanism was simple: the projector was little more than a metal tube buried in the ground with a heavy baseplate to keep it stable. Black powder ignited inside the tube could heave an eight-inch-diameter, thirty-pound shell nearly a mile, much farther than the smaller Stokes mortars that the British had been using to deliver gas shells since the previous year. Before Arras, projectors had been used to scatter burning oil over German troops, an age-old tactic to spread panic and chaos behind enemy lines. Now the British were using the projectors to launch shells filled with gases like chloropicrin and phosgene.

The advantage of Livens projectors was both their mobility and the sheer amount of gas they could deliver. Until gas shells came into use, cloud or wave attacks like that at Ypres had been the only means of delivering gas. Cloud attacks were unpredictable, often ineffective, vulnerable to sudden changes in weather or wind, and incredibly difficult and time-consuming to carry out. Stokes mortars delivered in a more precise fashion. Now Livens projectors, which were arranged in batteries of twenty and fired simultaneously by the hundreds, sent gas farther and in much higher volume than regular mortars. Though not very accurate, they rivaled the saturation of cloud attacks and could be dropped behind enemy lines at strategic locations to maximize mayhem.

Over Holy Week, the British had used the projectors to throw the Germans into turmoil before the Easter Monday attack. The first projectors fired in a deafening cannonade in the early morning of April 4: first the tremendous blast and flash with belching smoke, then the rustle of the bombs tumbling toward their targets. With each concussion, a gas cloud burst from the shells, three thousand projectors in all, firing some fifty tons of phosgene. The dense clouds of gas that the new weapons delivered behind the lines took the Germans completely by surprise. Even if they had time to get their masks on, the chloropicrin seeped through the respirators. If the retching soldiers tore off their masks to vomit, the odor of corn or apples—the telltale smell of phosgene—reached their noses. Inhaling meant death a few hours later, drowning in the fluid that filled their lungs. The impenetrable volleys of gas threw the Germans into chaos. Overhead, the Royal Flying Corps darted in the clouds, strafing camps and bombing ammunition dumps while snapping photographs of the German positions.

The projector shelling lasted for days, keeping the Germans off guard and disorganized. On the night of Saturday, April 7, the roar of the projectors stopped. Arras fell quiet. At daybreak, Easter stole over the city, gray and rainy. Residents crept down into cellars to mark the holy day. The sound of singing seeped from basements where they huddled. Celebrants sang a Benediction hymn reflecting the bleak reality enshrouding the city: "O Saving Host, guardian of Heaven's Gate, armed foes oppress us; give us strength, bring us aid."

The lull was short-lived. When dawn broke on Easter Monday, a fifteen-mile wave of fire erupted anew from the British line, a fusillade of spitting howitzers and Livens projectors that blew apart German trenches, shredding barbed wire and coughing out clouds of gas. As the bullets whined across the heath and shells soared overhead, a flock of rooks rose from a copse of trees and wheeled in a spiral, silhouetted by the flames rising from the German positions. Behind them, to the west, Sopwith biplanes appeared, flying low over no-man's-land toward the German lines. A light drizzle turned to rain, then snow, and waves of British and Canadian soldiers rose from the underground earthworks like specters in the mist and smoke. Amid the swirling snow, the infantry advanced behind a wall of shellfire and smoke bombs—called a creeping barrage—that moved in a scorching, slow-moving curtain of fire in front of them. Tanks growled across the plain alongside the infantry, advancing yard by yard through a gale of gas and smoke and snow.

By early afternoon, Canadian troops had taken Vimy Ridge, giving the Allies the high ground. That early success, partly enabled by the projectors and the confusion they wrought, was the only clear-cut victory of the battle. The British momentum stalled, and fighting ground to another standstill, raging on for weeks with the Allies unable to advance. The potent power of the Livens projector and its far-ranging shells had not been enough to smash the German front. By mid-May, with some 150,000 dead among the British Expeditionary Force (BEF), the Battle of Arras ended, and the stalemate on the western front resumed.

The articles about Arras that appeared in the Washington papers made oblique mentions of the role of gas in the battle, but the words "Livens projectors" never appeared, with little to no technical information about the advance in gas warfare that had taken place there. Few of the scientists joining Manning's effort had any practical notion of what chemical warfare actually entailed, as they had few channels of information with their British and French counterparts, and detailed information took weeks to reach Washington on slow-moving steamships.

Manning and his cadre of scientists needed someone in Europe as soon as possible to observe, consult with allies, and report back to the nascent research organization. The day before Congress passed the war declaration, the National Research Council had begun assembling a scientific delegation to embark for Europe. One of the seven invitations to serve on the delegation went to George A. Hulett, a Princeton professor and former chief chemist at the Bureau of Mines Pittsburgh Experiment Station. Manning told Interior Secretary Franklin Lane that he wanted Hulett to represent the Bureau of Mines on the delegation to investigate gas warfare and that the bureau should subsidize his expenses. Lane agreed.

Hulett was a natural choice to be the bureau's eyes and ears overseas. Joseph Holmes, Manning's mentor at the Bureau of Mines, had recruited Hulett in 1910 as chief chemist at the Pittsburgh station. He brought new vigor to the station's work, introducing weekly seminars and guiding the younger, less experienced chemists. He had a brilliant, searching mind, and his students adored him. His skills included glassblowing, making him the only chemist at Princeton who could make his own laboratory equipment. He was also an avid golfer who scoffed at pious objections to hitting the links on the Sabbath.

The professor in charge of the scientific commission, Joseph S. Ames of Johns Hopkins, was eager to have Hulett on the delegation. He welcomed Hulett and told him of the arrangements for his passage to Europe. He would be appointed an attaché with the American embassy in London and given a diplomatic passport. Hulett would leave from New York on April 14. In the meantime, he should write to the National Research Council's top chemist,

Marston Bogert, for a list of questions about gas warfare to ask the British and French. Ames scribbled "absolute silence" at the top of his note.

After hastily getting his passport and ticket, Hulett boarded the steamship *Chicago* on April 14. He scanned the wharf for his family, but he couldn't spot them in the crowds to say goodbye before the ship cast off. As he sailed east, Hulett huddled over a typewriter and compared notes with the other delegation members on the ship, formulating questions to pose once their work began. In the afternoons, Hulett exercised with laps around and around the promenade deck. When the weather turned foul and storms tossed the ship, Hulett avoided the seasickness that befell many of his fellow passengers. The *Chicago* joined a convoy partway across, and the ships soon crossed the submarine zone in formation. The choppy weather reduced the threat from submarines, but nonetheless, many nervous passengers stayed up through the last night of the voyage. Subs had recently sunk two small ships near their destination, the Bay of Biscay in southern France. For his part, Hulett retired to his stateroom and slept soundly.

At 5:00 a.m. on April 25, the *Chicago* steamed into the mouth of the Gironde River, about sixty miles downriver from Bordeaux. The delegation arrived in Paris the following evening. Springtime had exploded in the city, with peach, cherry, and pear trees in bloom. The beauty meant little to Hulett with the horrific battle to the north. The indelible stain of the war was everywhere. Grief swaddled the city, and wounded soldiers hobbled through the streets.

The delegation went to work immediately. The morning after they arrived, the scientists motored south to a training camp near Fontainebleau, where Hulett watched gas mask training for protection against chemicals. Afterward, he saw artillery practice with gas shells, then toured a gas-manufacturing plant. He had plenty to ponder as he motored back to Paris through the dense, wild forest around Fontainebleau. He wrote home that night:

So you see my work for the Bureau of Mines studying gases to prevent the explosions in coal mines is being put to a very different use, and knowledge acquired to save life must be utilized to kill if possible whole regiments of boys for the most part. This would appall one if he didn't see that at this time the only thing that will help is to "carry on" and hope when it is over—it will be over for good.

Hulett spent his first few days studying the gases that the Germans used and promised detailed reports for Manning on how to manufacture them. "Everything is open to us and we are getting first class information," he wrote in a report back to headquarters. He also referred to a gas that the French were testing that was "distinctly better (or worse) than anything the Germans have"—probably a reference to hydrocyanic acid, which the French called *vincennite*.

He spent time studying gas masks: their stitches, the rubber pieces, the glass eyepieces, and the canisters containing charcoal and neutralizing agents through which soldiers drew their breath. He also carefully examined the differences between the British mask known as the small-box respirator and the French M2 mask. It was absolutely vital, Hulett wrote to Manning, that the Americans quickly settle on a gas mask. The U.S. military attachés and French military authorities insisted that every American soldier must have preliminary training in protection against gases before arriving on European shores. For that to be possible, the Americans needed to decide which mask to adopt, whether it was the British or the French model.

Hulett's trip had only just begun, but already he had a rudimentary grasp of the enormity of the task ahead for the Americans. Beyond the difficulty of mastering gas warfare from a purely technical viewpoint, he understood there would also be moral and ethical challenges. Like many scientists thrust into the middle of chemical warfare, he was simultaneously thrilled by the intellectual challenge and repelled by the concept of using his scientific skills for the purpose of mass killing. Seeing the maimed and scarred men in Paris, while taking in the vast apparatus of the French and British for inflicting the same grievous suffering upon Germans, he was open about his ambivalence.

"The use of these gases is a most terrible and terrifying thing, but it seems that it was absolutely necessary to fight fire with fire," he wrote to Manning.

Each morning, the front page of the *Washington Post* featured the day's war news in a special inset section, headed with the number of days since the United States entered the fray. "Twelfth Day of the War," the box read on Wednesday, April 18, with news of a submarine attack off the coast of Sandy Hook, a 7-billion-dollar war bond bill that the Senate passed, and President Wilson's push for Congress to pass a conscription bill. "Fifteenth Day of the War," for Saturday, April 21, outlined the espionage bill making its way through Congress, proposals for price controls on food, and raising new war taxes. A front-page brief reported that the British embassy had flown the Stars and Stripes for the first time to hail the U.S. entry into the war.

Burrell and Manning probably took little note of the headlines that Saturday. Burrell had sketched a tentative outline of the new gas service, and Manning had convened the gas committee to meet again to grapple with the research enterprise they had undertaken. In preparation for the next meeting of the scientists, Manning distributed a seven-page memorandum summarizing everything known so far about chemical warfare research. Two weeks into the war, the scope of the scientists' undertaking was still unknown— only that it would start small and would grow quickly. "The tremendous scale and elaborate system of the gas service abroad may never be required here; however there is enough uncertainty to necessitate our making provision in our plans for a large amount of experimental work," Burrell's memo read.

George Hulett's promised reports had yet to reach the States—transatlantic travel still took several weeks—but the War College had received other reports from abroad that Burrell planned to distribute as soon as they were compiled and reproduced. Burrell proposed that the American gas program be modeled after the British and French, both of which investigated defensive technologies and offensive capabilities in separate but coordinated efforts. Advanced laboratories had hundreds of chemists at work on gas problems, including physiologists, physicians, and engineers. Factories produced masks by the millions.

The scientists were learning some of the most elementary lessons about gas warfare that their allies had known for years. One was that even the term "gas" was often a misnomer. Most chemical weapons were liquids that required an explosion to be volatized or dispersed in misty clouds, while others were solids blown into clouds of toxic particles. The researchers needed to quickly learn how to make the chemicals already in use in Europe. When the United States entered the war, there were three basic types of chemical weapons agents. The first type was lachrymators, or tear gases, like benzyl bromide and xylyl bromide, which caused temporary blindness and made fighting impossible in the absence of masks. The second was called sternutator gases, or sneezing gases, which were mostly nonlethal but irritated the nose, throat, and eyes, causing headaches and nausea. It was the third category, though, that reaped a lethal harvest of chaos and death on the battlefield. These were asphyxiants, or suffocating gases, which included chlorine and phosgene, irritants that caused the alveoli of the lungs to slowly fill with liquid. At the same time, they also needed to investigate and develop their own gases, ones that the Germans had not yet discovered.

The scientists didn't have to start from scratch with some chemical production. In the spring, the bureau had dispatched a chemist to Midland, Michigan, to discuss gas production with the Dow Chemical Company. "They are prepared and willing to cooperate to their fullest extent," Burrell had written in his memo to the gas committee. Dow already made chlorine and bromine—both useful as war gases—as well as many other chemicals on an industrial scale. The company recommended sulfur chloride as a drift gas, had already begun experiments, and was anxious to demonstrate its findings. "This work will be transferred later to some selected and more convenient point near Washington," Burrell reported.

When Manning next reconvened the Committee on Noxious Gases—now numbering eighteen men—the Bureau of Mines had moved to the Department of the Interior Building. The men gathered around Manning's gleaming desk to discuss their next steps, particularly the problem of gas masks, which was the most immediate and urgent issue facing the bureau. The navy had already asked for fifteen thousand test models, but Burrell and Henderson said more investigation was needed before a requisition of that size was made.

Henderson told the committee that, in his opinion, mask makers always made the same mistakes. Breathing holes were too small. There was too much dead space for trapped air inside the mask, so carbon dioxide built up. Some British respirators were so hard to breathe in that soldiers tore them off and threw them aside. He argued that commercial companies couldn't be trusted to design military-grade masks; the masks would have to be designed by the government and then manufactured by private companies. He argued that researchers should take "a week or two" to go over currently available masks and remedy the defects.

A week or two was, to put it mildly, an optimistic estimate for such major research. But without Hulett's observations, the men in the room knew very little about the actual use of gas in Europe and how America's allies were researching it. The only man present with firsthand knowledge of gas was Dr. Henry Drysdale Dakin, a chemist and military surgeon who had developed an effective antiseptic to prevent infection of wounds. He had last been at the front six months earlier and explained that, though the gas situation changed rapidly, when he was there chloropicrin was the gas getting the most attention. He described the manufacturing process — British companies were paid to make gas in what were called "controlled factories" overseen by the military — and the process used to test masks: sealed chambers where test subjects could sit in a cloud of gas to determine if the mask worked properly.

There was no shortage of talent or manpower to help with these problems: because of Manning's census of chemists, private laboratories, universities, and research institutions around the country were offering to help with the gas work. The problem was still finding a secure location for the research. For Manning and his technical men, secrecy was paramount, and the threat of German spies was very real. The lead-up to war revealed Germany's espionage apparatus: labor unions, diplomatic circles, and immigrant communities were riddled with German sympathizers and collaborators. In Washington, members of the city's exclusive social clubs checked over their shoulders and eavesdropped on suspicious conversations, and the papers regularly included breathless stories about conspiracies and unsavory alliances. Over the weekend that followed the war declaration, a Department of Justice dragnet swept the country, netting hundreds of Germans suspected of being spies and jailing them without warrants or charges. Absolutely secrecy was needed for development and testing without fear of spies or leaks.

The men had discussed potential sites at the committee's first meeting without reaching a consensus. The responses to Manning's census included many offers of space and facilities; all of them should be considered, Manning said. In the meantime, they would use the laboratory in the building where they were meeting. "We will equip the office in the Bureau of Mines, and use our laboratory facilities, and Mr. Burrell will be designated as gas director, with offices and laboratories in the Bureau, without any further consideration as to expense," Manning said.

Henderson warned that the bureau laboratory would not be

adequate for long, though, and the research would soon outgrow the space. Henderson's own physiological work would require three thousand square feet of lab space alone. "My idea of the situation is, that this is a great big job, an emergency job, not like ordinary research work, where one has a year or two to get underway," Burrell said. "We are very rapidly going to outgrow the facilities of the Bureau of Mines."

The solution, it turned out, lay only a few miles up Massachusetts Avenue, at a small, struggling Methodist college called American University.

On the morning of April 26, the streets around the White House were in an uproar. French vice premier René Viviani and Marshal Joseph Joffre, France's most senior military officer and the hero of the Battle of the Marne, had arrived in Washington the previous evening and were scheduled to call on President Wilson and Secretary of State Robert Lansing that morning to seal a military pact. French and American flags draped the sides of automobiles, and crowds gathered on the sidewalks to catch a glimpse of the French delegation.

Before the pageantry got under way, Benjamin F. Leighton made his way up the steps and through the colonnades flanking the door of Washington's Riggs National Bank, less than a block down Pennsylvania Avenue from the White House. Tall and lean with untamed eyebrows, he was expected at an important meeting of the board of trustees of American University. A devout Methodist from New England, Leighton had been on the university's board for years as it struggled to establish itself and find its financial footing.

Leighton and the university trustees were meeting at a critical juncture for the school. For a quarter century, their efforts to build the endowment, construct the buildings for their campus, and attract a cosmopolitan student body had stumbled. Officially, the university had been open since 1914, but the war in Europe cast a shadow over its first few years. It boasted only a handful of graduate students, and there was no clear path to enrolling more. At the other end of Pennsylvania Avenue, Congress was debating a bill that would institute a military draft for conscripting thousands of soldiers and sailors. Young people destined for the battlefields meant fewer students, and American University couldn't spare a single one. The trustees needed to ensure that the university could survive the lean war years ahead.

Charles Glover, the president of Riggs Bank and one of Washington's wealthiest businessmen, was the university treasurer. Riggs had become a cornerstone of Washington power that would declare itself "the most important bank in the most important city in the world," and Glover's vast wealth and political leverage were enormous. When it was founded, American University saw its future in similarly grandiose terms—the most important university in the most important city in the world. But unlike the bank, American's bold aspirations had yet to become a reality.

A sense of divine providence had driven the effort to found American University a quarter century earlier. For years, prominent Methodists had urged Bishop John Fletcher Hurst to start a national university, a center of scholarship to rival Georgetown University and the Catholic University of America, the Roman Catholic universities in the city. The idea had preoccupied the bishop, who saw himself as an agent of George Washington's divine mission to establish a national university.

Bishop Hurst found the property in early 1890, after plodding across the city on horseback in search of suitable land. The church bought the land for a hundred thousand dollars and began raising money for the endowment in 1890. But despite Hurst's optimism, one obstacle after another prevented his vision from becoming a reality. Nothing, it seemed, went as planned. Fund-raising flagged. More than a thousand applications for admittance piled up. Methodists across the country, confounded by the endless delays, clamored for the school to open.

American finally opened on a warm, breezy day in late May of 1914, when President Wilson mounted a bunting-draped dais on the campus to dedicate the school. But the campus around him was a shadow of Hurst's vision, with just a single completed building, the College of History. The exterior of a second building, McKinley Hall, was finished, but the inside remained an empty shell, and the university opened with only twenty-eight graduate students. Barely a month later, an assassin in Sarajevo took the life of Archduke Ferdinand, and Europe plunged into war.

As the school's board of trustees met to decide the school's future on April 26, the crowd outside the bank broke out into noisy cheers as Joffre and the delegation arrived at the State, War, and Navy Building, then crossed the street for a brief ceremony at the White House to seal the military pact between the United States and France. The crowd swelled even larger as Joffre returned across the street to meet with Secretary of War Newton D. Baker. When the delegation left the building and drove down Pennsylvania Avenue toward the Capitol, pedestrians turned to gape, and cars stopped in the road, flags waving from windows and horns blaring.

When the trustees emerged from the meeting at the bank, they had made a fateful decision: to offer their campus to the federal government to use during the war. The two buildings and the grassy quadrangle between them, the ninety-two acres of wooded dells and meadows at the rear of the campus, would become the domain of the federal government. The grand aspirations for a world-class university, the unflagging belief in divine intervention, fell away in the face of the stark reality that the university faced. Albert Osborn, the board's treasurer and secretary, wrote a short entry in a chronicle of the university business: "On motion, the executive committee declared that the sentiment of the committee is that the buildings and grounds of the university should be tendered to the Government for such purposes as may be necessary and fit, and that the Chancellor and President of the Board communicate this offer to the President of the United States."

Bishop Hurst had envisioned the university bound up in divine purpose, moving toward a heaven-inspired destiny. The university newspaper used similarly lofty terms to describe the trustees' decision to offer the campus to the government, as dedicating the university's meager resources to a great national enterprise and accepting the "torch of war" like an Olympic relay runner.

"It is a matter of regret that the University is not thus equipped for bearing its full share of responsibility in rubbing the lamp of science in this nation's crisis, but it proposes to remedy this situation at once, to meet if possible the present demands of the war, and surely those of the future peace," the paper read. Unable to build its own laboratories or finish its facilities, the school was inviting the federal government to step in, a gesture that hopefully "wealthy and patriotic friends" would recognize and reward in the future. War might destroy the university, or it might save it.

After the board voted to offer the campus to the government, Leighton sent an official letter to President Wilson. It read like an invitation to a dinner party or a weekend in the countryside, peppered with stiff formality:

> *To His Excellency, Woodrow Wilson, President of the United States.*
>
> *Sir: In behalf of the Board of Trustees of the American University, located in the District of Columbia, I am authorized to extend to the United States Government the use of ninety-two acres of land lying within the District and composing the campus of the University, together with the use of the College of History Building containing twenty-one large and commodious rooms, and also the McKinley Auditorium, not quite completed, which could be made available as a barracks, or for such purpose as the government may desire.*

The campus may be used either for a camping ground for troops, for gardening and raising products for the Army, or for such other purpose as you may elect.

There is a bountiful supply of city water on the premises and the grounds are easily accessible by means of the Washington City trolley service.

The character of the land is such as would make it available as an aviation ground.

> *Respectfully,*
> *B. F. Leighton*
> *President, Board of Trustees, American University*

The president's secretary thanked Leighton for the offer and passed the letter to the secretary of war, who sent it on to the U.S. Army chief of engineers, Major General William Black.

During peacetime, the Corps of Engineers masterminded public works large and small, from the Panama Canal to lighthouses to coastal fortifications. At the U.S. Military Academy at West Point, the corps taught army elites the science of construction and the physics of wind and water. The corps had a special relationship with Washington itself, executing Pierre L'Enfant's plan to transform Washington into a glimmering jewel among world capitals. They graded city streets, erected grand government buildings, and completed work on the Washington Monument. Now the engineers' peacetime training was shifting to wartime endeavors. Black had planned to build cantonments for two regiments at Fort Belvoir in Virginia, the only large site available in close proximity to Washington where soldiers could train before shipping out to Europe. The offer from American University unexpectedly presented a better option within the district and the corps' jurisdiction, unconstrained by the problems of crossing the river.

On the warm, clear afternoon of May 17, two officers from the War Department drove up to American University to visit the campus. What they found was a far cry from the verdant campus bubbling with scholarly activity that its founders had envisioned. The College of History stood by itself at the corner of the campus, a lonely marble edifice facing northwest across an open expanse of fields. To its northwest, McKinley Hall sat alone at the corner of a phantom quadrangle; the buildings planned to ring its circumference had never been built. In a melancholy testimony to the school's difficulties, the building's interior was still incomplete almost ten years after it was started. The same was true of the rest of the campus—not a single cornerstone had been laid for any of the other nineteen buildings. Past the campus, Massachusetts Avenue was a rolling, dipping country lane with scrub brush hanging over the sunken roadway.

It was exactly what the army engineers were looking for. The quadrangle was a perfect parade ground for drilling. The open spaces designated for libraries and classroom buildings were ideal for barracks and mess halls and commissaries. The campus was far removed from the downtown federal offices, but trolleys made it easily accessible, running up Massachusetts Avenue to the traffic circle just outside the campus. Electric lines brought power to all corners of the campus, while water lines had been laid alongside Massachusetts Avenue. Even if they needed more space, tracts of farmland could be leased beyond the ninety-two-acre campus.

But the army engineers weren't the only contenders for using the campus. The day after the two officers scouted out the location, the phone rang on Albert Osborn's desk. The voice on the other end of the line said he was calling from the Bureau of Mines and that he, too, wanted to come out to see the campus. He was particularly interested in the unfinished McKinley Hall, and whether it could be converted for use as a laboratory. It would be for chemistry research, the man on the phone explained to Osborn. Chemistry needed for the war effort.

As perfect as the campus was for the engineers, it was equally ideal for the chemists. After Manning's meeting the day after the war declaration, the director's deputies had searched for lab locations in

Delaware, New Jersey, and other areas. Even before the trustees' offer had arrived, Manning or one of his deputies had been informed about the struggling university on the northwest heights. To Manning, the appeal wasn't the parade ground or the availability of land for barracks: it was the vacant, unfinished McKinley Hall, which anchored the campus quadrangle. The building was a blank slate, ready for whatever apparatus or equipment the scientists chose to install. Manning wrote to George Hale:

A patriotic offer of grounds and buildings by the trustees of the American University has made available for the work on noxious gases a location and opportunity for development which appear ideal. In location and in a number of other respects it will be convenient not only for investigation, but also as a center for instruction in regard to both the offensive and defensive sides of gas warfare.

Manning had found his laboratory.

Chapter Three

Diabolical Instruments

As President Wilson waited in the White House to deliver his nighttime speech to Congress, Judge William C. Van Fleet stepped out of the federal courthouse in Lower Manhattan for a brief walk around Foley Square. On April 2, 1917, a slate-gray sky hung over New York City, and there was a hint of rain in the cool midafternoon air. For more than a week, Van Fleet had presided over a trial that had transfixed New York. Six men — five Germans and one naturalized American — faced conspiracy charges for setting fire to merchant ships at sea using bombs assembled under the very noses of an unsuspecting public. Day after day, the tabloids reported the latest outrages from the courtroom: how top German diplomats had bankrolled the operation, how the bombs had been engineered in a clandestine workshop in Hoboken masquerading as a fertilizer factory, how the devices were assembled on an interned German vessel. The prisoners, all wearing black Prince Albert coats and spats, glowered at the government witnesses who took the stand to testify against them. One of the defendants, a wizened former ship's captain named Carl von Kleist, shook his head and muttered "Oh! What damn lies!" under his breath during the testimony.

When the government lawyers presented their evidence early in the trial, the counsel's table resembled a chemistry-lab bench. Tall glass jars of acids, beakers, and boxes of potassium and sodium nitrates lay jumbled on the wide tabletop. The bombs themselves—metal tubes about the size of cigars—rested on the clerk's desk and on the bar rail between the defendants and the packed gallery. The jury had watched in silence as the witness standing next to the table, a fire department chemist named Leo Lieberman, explained the reaction that set fire to dozens of ships. The bombs weren't typical explosives like the dynamite that German agents had used to blow up munitions plants and armories throughout the country. These were chemical bombs, the ingredients calibrated and separated within the chambers of lead pipes like the ones resting on the bar rail. When acid ate through the tin barrier in the middle of the device, the chemicals ignited with a furious white heat.

"Sulfuric acid," Lieberman said, holding up a liquid-filled bottle. He picked up a large jar from the table. "Coming in contact with permanganate of potash"—he held up the jar for the jury to see—"forms manganese dioxide which burns with an intense flame."

In his closing arguments, the defense attorney tried to argue that the conspiracy was political, not criminal, but the judge would have none of it, interrupting the lawyer to say that was nonsense. Still, Van Fleet knew that it was impossible to ignore the war fervor and had delivered a stern warning to the jury not to let antipathy toward Germany cloud their deliberation and judgment. After Van Fleet sent the jury to deliberate at 3:05 p.m., he went for his stroll.

He had expected to have time for at least a short walk to stretch his legs. He overestimated. The jury sent a note to the clerk after only fifteen minutes, saying they had reached a decision. It took another thirty minutes for Van Fleet to return from his walk, and after he hurried back to the bench, the jurors filed into the packed courtroom. Von Kleist, the former ship's captain, sat still as the foreman rose. The clerk asked the foreman if they had reached a verdict. They had. "We find all the defendants guilty."

The judge ordered steep bail bonds to ensure that the men couldn't leave the Tombs—the city jail—before their sentencing on Friday. But the man most responsible for the chemical devices, whose name came up again and again during the trial, wasn't among the six men in the prisoner's dock and had never been in the courtroom. Von Kleist and the five crewmen were just the footmen in the plot. The man at the heart of the sabotage, the prize who had eluded police, was a German chemist named Dr. Walter Theodore Scheele. He had engineered the bombs in his factory laboratory in Hoboken and taught the longshoremen and the boilermakers how to assemble the devices before they were smuggled into the cargo holds of ocean-bound ships. After von Kleist's arrest, agents from the Bureau of Investigation moved on the other men, plucking them up one by one. But somehow, word had reached Scheele that his cover had been blown, and as quick as one of his lab-bench conflagrations, he had vanished like a puff of smoke.

Before the war, no one would have looked twice at Walter Scheele. The chemist and his American-born wife, Marie Magdalene Scheele, lived in a rented row house in Brooklyn's Bushwick neighborhood, a few blocks from the pharmacy Scheele owned on a busy corner of Cypress Avenue. Barrel chested and balding, his face a web of scars, the chemist still had a thick German accent after almost a quarter century in the United States. He had assisted the district attorney's office for a time, helping out with investigations and testifying in murder trials involving poison and chemicals. Marie was a sharp-tongued, domineering woman, a hectoring contrast to her soft-spoken, pensive husband. Every morning, Scheele cocked an alpine hat on his head and tucked a pearl-handled revolver into his waistband for the short walk from their house to the drugstore. As he strolled the streets of Brooklyn, impeccably dressed and sharply erect, he invariably had a cigar clamped in his lips.

Scheele had come to New York in 1893 with a wave of hundreds of thousands of Germans who flooded into the United States starting in the mid-1880s. Many emigrated because of economic hardship or displacement during the unification of the German empire, but Scheele came to America for a very different reason. He was a spy, paid a yearly retainer for reconnaissance of the American chemical industry. Though Scheele worked hard to knit himself into the fabric of New York's expatriate neighborhoods, the scars on his face were a sign that he was no ordinary German: the healed wounds were marks from sabre duels that were a bloody ritual among Prussian aristocrats and military officers.

Born in Cologne, Scheele came from a prominent Rhineland family. Though Fritz Haber had become infamous as Germany's godfather of gas warfare, Scheele's bloodline also had strong ties to German chemical warfare. He claimed to be related to the great eighteenth-century Swedish chemist Carl Wilhelm Scheele, who was famous for having discovered the existence of oxygen and many other elements. Carl Scheele had also discovered chlorine gas and prussic acid—or hydrogen cyanide—both of which the German army would later adopt as war gases. Naturally, Walter Scheele studied chemistry when he attended the University of Bonn, then enlisted in the army. He reached the rank of lieutenant in an artillery regiment before he was ordered to go to the United States and report to the German military attaché. Promoted to major, the unassuming druggist became one of the top-ranking—if undercover—German staff officers in America.

An accomplice accompanied Scheele to the United States: Hugo Schweitzer, the chief chemist of the Bayer Chemical Company. Their job was to report back to the German military attaché in Washington with intelligence about chemical manufacturing, ammunition factories, and commercial food production, with details about increases in manufacturing. Schweitzer would generate the reports; Scheele would review them and bring the reports to Washington three or four times a year, where the military attaché would pay him in cash. The men were also instructed to report on promising patents; when they found them, German companies snapped them up, keeping the formulas out of the hands of American industry. They did the same with chemists themselves. When a prominent scientist emerged, German companies would hire him away, whatever the price.

The two years Scheele had planned to be in America stretched into two decades. He lived in Baltimore and then New York City, never becoming a citizen. He knit himself into Brooklyn's booming enclaves of Bavarians, Prussians, and Westphalians. Bushwick was like a little Berlin, with dozens of breweries and soaring new mansions built by the *Braumeister* who grew rich on the thirst of their expatriate countrymen. Scheele mingled with his compatriots at the German Club, sang with them at the Freemasons Lodge, and raised his glass at the pubs where German was spoken freely.

In 1913, the new German military attaché, Franz von Papen, summoned Scheele to his Manhattan office. The attaché's address was on Hanover Street, in a room above G. Amsinck & Company, a German import-export company tucked into the humming financial engine of Wall Street. War was coming, von Papen told Scheele, and he should prepare for a new kind of work. He instructed Scheele to catalog locations of ammunition and explosives factories and to study American manufacture of acid, fertilizers, and chemicals. Schweitzer would continue to investigate the commercial chemical industry, but Scheele would redirect his attention to military research and the manufacture of chemicals.

Scheele carried out his mission steadfastly. As Europe teetered on the brink of war in 1914, the doctor and Schweitzer traveled to Germany together for a briefing and to consult with government officials; they also brought back secret instructions for German embassy officials. He continued to bring reports to von Papen month after month, and the attaché handed him his pay of fifteen hundred dollars a year in twenty-dollar bills.

When the Continent finally toppled into war, another summons arrived from von Papen in early 1915: "Very esteemed doctor: I have been trying to find you since several days.... Come at once. Great haste."

When Scheele arrived at 6 Hanover Street, von Papen had new orders for him. Scheele must get free of the drugstore and begin work solely for the German government producing goods that had become difficult for Germany to acquire as a result of the Allies' naval blockade. Using his skills as a chemist, Scheele needed to devise ways to break down scarce commodities into their components, conceal them, and smuggle them safely through neutral countries and into Germany. Von Papen gave Scheele a check for ten thousand dollars to start up this new enterprise.

Scheele quickly sold the drugstore and moved with Marie from Brooklyn to Hoboken, New Jersey. They rented an apartment in a brick building six blocks from the Hudson River and the Hoboken piers, where the streets around the shipyards teemed with boilermakers streaming into the foundries, and stevedores swarmed the packet ships in the dry docks.

On von Papen's orders, Scheele looked for a factory to lease; he found one for fifty dollars a month at the intersection of Clinton and Eleventh Streets. It was an ugly two-story building with clapboard siding tucked into the industrial landscape of Hoboken. His next step was to find a manager for the business, a confidant who could be trusted. Scheele asked around in German expatriate circles, and the name he was given was Carl von Kleist, a naturalized American from a prominent German family. His wife was a former opera singer. His daughter was a morphine addict, and the family had fallen on hard times. Von Kleist himself was elderly and slow, but he was dependable enough as a watchman and superintendent for the day-to-day affairs of the factory.

Scheele began paying him fifteen dollars a week as the first employee of the New Jersey Agricultural Chemical Company, the name he chose for his firm. Rubber was one of the commodities that had become scarce in Germany, and Scheele came up with a way to break it down into a powder and ship it through neutral companies to Germany, where it could be chemically reconstituted.

He came up with a similar method of breaking down and reconstituting lubricant oil as well. The first shipment of one thousand bags labeled as fertilizer went to Copenhagen on a steamship with MADE IN U.S.A. stamped on the tags.

On April 10, 1915, the Scheeles's maid heard a knock on the apartment door. It was late on a Saturday night, a strange time for an unannounced visitor to drop by. When the maid answered, a man was standing on the stoop in the dark. *Is Walter Scheele home?* he asked. *He is out,* the maid told him. The man handed her a business card and asked that she give it to him when he returned, then disappeared into the darkness. When Scheele returned that night, the maid handed him the card. "Captain Eno Bode, Secretary, Hamburg-American Line" was printed on the card with a phone number and an address. On the back was a hand-written message from von Papen. Give the captain "any information he desires," the note read.

The next morning, Scheele headed to the address on Bode's card. The captain's house was about a mile north in Union City, on the other side of Weehawken Cove. When Scheele arrived, Bode invited him inside. They sat and talked for half an hour. Bode said von Papen had a new assignment for Scheele. A junior member of the German Admiralty named Captain Franz von Rintelen had recently arrived in the United States, Bode said, bringing stacks of cash to bankroll sabotage of Allied ships that set sail from American ports. The Admiralty had a particular form of sabotage in mind. Not exactly a bomb, nor sticks of dynamite like the anarchists used. They wanted a slow-burning incendiary device—a chemical bomb—that could be smuggled onto cargo ships. At a given hour, the device would combust, and a fire would break out, igniting anything flammable or explosive that was in the cargo hold and burning the device up in the process. Could Scheele make such a thing?

Scheele said he would have to think the matter over and told Bode to meet him at the chemical works the next morning. He put his hat back on and left, probably worrying a cigar between his teeth as he ambled back toward his house, deep in thought.

When Bode arrived at the chemical factory in the morning, Scheele told him he had devised a combination of chemicals that would function as a slow-acting incendiary device exactly as the Admiralty wanted. With funding from Bode, Scheele hired new employees and ordered new components. By April 20, they had 150 of the devices. Bode and two other men—one of whom was Captain Otto Wolpert, the pier superintendent for Atlas Lines— came to the factory for a demonstration of the devices and their assembly. Scheele had an intense dislike for one of the men who showed up for the demonstration; though he went by the name "Steinberg," his real name was Erich von Steinmetz, a captain in the German navy. He entered the United States disguised as a woman, carrying germ cultures to release in a kind of primitive bacteriological warfare. When Steinmetz brought the germs to Scheele's lab, the chemist was so infuriated that he knocked Steinmetz to the ground in a fistfight.

This time, there was no violence. One by one, Scheele let the men in after peering at them through the peephole in the door. On the way to the lab, the men walked past hogsheads of chemicals in a back room. Chickens roamed in a courtyard, and von Kleist kept a pet alligator in a tank near his office. The men crowded around Scheele as he demonstrated how the bomb worked.

The devices were roughly the same size as the cigars that Scheele smoked—a slim, seven-inch lead tube, with two compartments. One end had a larger compartment which contained a powdered mixture of one-third urotropin—the commercial name for hexamethylenetetramine—and two-thirds sodium peroxide. The smaller compartment on the other end contained about an inch of sulfuric acid. Stoppers capped each end, and a thin metal plate separated the two compartments. The acid slowly dissolved the divider until it broke through to the compartment holding the powder. When it did—two hours, four hours, four days, or eight days later, depending on the thickness of the plate—the combustion erupted from the stopped ends, igniting anything packed around the devices and melting the tube into a nugget of lead.

To demonstrate, Scheele gathered the men around. He dripped the acid from a glass tube into the urotropin-peroxide mix. A flame spat from the mixture, hot and searingly bright. "That's chemistry!" Scheele crowed. Because of the size and shape, and perhaps because they slowly smoldered for so long, the men called the bombs "cigars."

The saboteurs were satisfied. The cigars were carefully packed into wooden boxes, three to four per box, and the boxes set into satchels. Scheele packed the acid separately, in glass bottles, along with a spoon and tubes for funneling the acid into the compartments. Then the men set out with the suitcases for Scheele's old neighborhood of Bushwick. On Willoughby Street, they stopped outside a long three-story brick building called the Labor Lyceum. The men descended into a basement apartment, where they met a young building manager, Eugene Reister. Wolpert handed the satchels to Reister, and Scheele demonstrated again how the cigars worked. Wolpert took out a fat roll of bills and gave it to Reister, who was in charge of bribing the electricians and stevedores and carpenters who would assemble the cigars and plant them in the cargo holds of the ships lining the piers in Brooklyn, Manhattan, and Hoboken.

A kind of executive body, which included Scheele, met secretly in a Midtown Manhattan hotel to direct the sabotage. For weeks, German dockworkers assembled hundreds of the incendiary bombs aboard the *Friedrich der Grosse,* one of the impounded ships of the German Lloyd Line. Though the interned ships were forbidden from leaving, they were still sovereign German territory where the work could go on without fear of American authorities. Reister passed the finished devices to shipyard workers, along with bills that he peeled off from Wolpert's roll. Most of the bombs never made it on board ships, because some of the men, seeking to profit without actually carrying out the sabotage, took the money and then just threw the bombs into the water. But some of the men followed through. They smuggled the assembled bombs on board in bags of sugar, made their way to the holds, and placed them among the rest of the cargo before returning to the deck and disappearing back into the throngs on the wharf.

Scheele was never told which ships the cigars were placed in; Wolpert directed their placement. Deep in the hold, the sulfuric acid ate through the tin wall, a slow-motion chemical fuse smoldering in the darkness as the ships steamed across the open ocean. Once the acid broke through the divider separating the compartments, it reacted with the hexamethylenetetramine-sodium-peroxide mixture, an explosion that sent flames spewing from the bombs, melting the tube and setting the cargo around it ablaze.

On May 1, the crew of one of the grandest ships on the Chelsea Piers pulled in its gangplank and cast off. The great turbines shuddered to life, the whistles blasted, and the huge four-stack luxury liner set its course for Europe. The ship was the RMS *Lusitania*, sailing to its watery doom. If Scheele's devices were aboard, it's unknown whether they ignited, because on May 7, near the end of the *Lusitania*'s voyage, a German sub sank the ship, killing 1,195 passengers, including 123 Americans and inflaming American opinion against the Germans. One of the great mysteries of the *Lusitania* disaster was a second explosion that ripped through the ship. One theory for the later blast was that one of the ship's boilers exploded. Another was that a second torpedo hit the ship. Still another suggested that ammunition or ordnance detonated in the hold. The likelihood that the cigar bombs might have caused that second explosion is extremely remote but adds a layer of morbid intrigue to a horrific maritime tragedy.

During April and May alone, some thirty-five ships mysteriously caught fire at sea. Though the cigars were effective, they didn't work every time. That proved to be the undoing of the plot. The cigars aboard another ship, the SS *Kirkoswald*, never ignited, and the vessel escaped unscathed. The ship steamed to England, then passed through Gibraltar and on to Marseille, France, where it docked on June 12. After the passengers disembarked, the third officer cracked open the door of the number 2 hold, just forward of the bridge, so a gang of longshoremen could unload the cargo. The men heaved the sacks of sugar under their arms and over their shoulders. It was about 11:00 a.m. when one of the men hefted a partially opened bag on the portside of the hold. Four metal tubes dropped from the bag and clattered to the iron deck.

"La bomba! La bomba!" the Italian longshoremen screamed as they fled the hold. The *Kirkoswald's* chief officer ran belowdecks. He found the third officer gingerly holding the metal tubes in a handkerchief. The chief officer took off his hat and held it out, and the third officer carefully dropped the four pipes inside to turn over to the police.

The discovery of the chemical bombs set in motion a frenzied race to unveil who was behind the conspiracy. After the sinking of the *Lusitania,* the Bureau of Investigation had put agents on von Papen, the naval attaché Karl Boy-Ed, and Heinrich Albert, the German commercial attaché in New York. By mid-July of 1915, Bureau of Investigation agents were also investigating the New Jersey Agricultural Chemical Company and trailing both von Kleist and Scheele. Albert, who was the paymaster for the entire German spy network, made the mistake of nodding off while riding a streetcar to his office one day. When he awoke suddenly at his stop and leaped off the car, he left behind his briefcase, which the bureau agent tailing him promptly snatched. Albert realized his mistake, scrambled back on the car, and a chase ensued. The agent jumped off the car and onto another, where he told the conductor that a crazed man was pursuing him. The conductor, spotting Albert running behind the car with his arms flailing, sped through the next stop and away from Albert.

The papers in the briefcase gave bureau agents the outline for the entire German spy and sabotage network, which began to unravel as investigators traced the money trail leading from the German government. President Wilson was briefed on the whole matter, and one of his aides turned the entire dossier over to the editor of the *New York World* newspaper, which published a blockbuster article about German espionage in August.

Scheele's downfall, though, came in spring of 1916, when Scheele's factory superintendent, von Kleist, made a fatal mistake. After von Kleist took in a family friend's itinerant son who came to New York for work, the superintendent confided in the young man that Scheele owed von Kleist $235 in back pay. Scheele claimed he couldn't pay von Kleist until he received another cash infusion from a high-ranking German diplomat named Wolf von Igel. Von Kleist's young boarder claimed to know someone close to von Igel, so von Kleist wrote a complaint letter demanding his pay and gave it to the man to deliver to von Igel. Von Kleist later went to a bar to meet with an intermediary, where he spilled out the story of his owed money. When von Kleist returned to meet with the intermediary a second time, a detective walked up to the table, and von Kleist realized he had been suckered. The meeting was a sting; the young boarder had delivered von Kleist to detectives with the New York City bomb squad. Aghast, von Kleist pointed at the man he had trusted. "You Judas Iscariot!" he spat out.

The officers brought von Kleist to the Tombs, where they grilled him for twelve hours. Scheele had tried to keep von Kleist in the dark, but the superintendent turned out to know a great deal about the bomb plot and had even stolen two cigars as keepsakes, which the police found when they searched his house. He repeated the whole story to a grand jury, and in April of 1916, Scheele and eight other men in the chemical bomb plot were indicted.

Agents arrested seven of the men before they could flee, but not Scheele. Just before the indictment, von Igel tipped him off to his impending arrest and ordered him to flee to Cuba. The doctor told his wife that he would be back in six weeks or not at all, kissed her goodbye, and boarded a train to Washington. From there, he took another train to Florida. Using forged identification papers that identified him as an American newspaper correspondent named Rheinfelder, Scheele eventually boarded a Havana-bound steamship. Huffing and churning, the boat set out across the gulf, taking the most infamous chemist in America out to sea.

A few hours after the jury convicted Scheele's coconspirators in New York, President Wilson went to the rostrum in Congress to ask for the war declaration against Germany. Perhaps he was thinking about Scheele and the ship-bombing ring when he condemned Germany's "criminal intrigue...which have more than once come perilously near to disturbing the peace and dislocating the industries of the country." The morning newspapers shared the news of the president's speech and the convictions in New York; in some papers, reports of the bombers' guilty verdict ran alongside the text of the president's speech.

Toward the end of Holy Week, the trial was in the news again. On Thursday, Van Fleet was back in court in Manhattan to sentence the six ship-bomb conspirators and another German defendant convicted in a separate bombing conspiracy trial. The men showed no emotion as Van Fleet sentenced them one by one. Von Kleist received one of the steepest sentences—two years in prison and a five-thousand-dollar fine. The others, whom Van Fleet considered little more than "tools" of the ringleaders, received lesser sentences. "I am entirely satisfied with the verdict in this case," the judge told von Kleist. "You participated knowingly and intentionally in the manufacture of these instruments for a purpose which I can only characterize as diabolical."

Some of the reports of the sentencing noted that Scheele had fled and was still at large. But he was not forgotten. Even as the trial reached its conclusion, federal agents continued to investigate his whereabouts, chasing down tips and false leads. On the day before the sentencing, a man in New Mexico wrote a letter to the

Department of Justice, reporting that there was a man named Scheele in his town who he believed was the fugitive chemist. The young chief of the Bureau of Investigation, A. Bruce Bielaski, wrote back to the man with a description of Scheele. "If the man in your city answers this description, please wire me government rate collect," Bielaski wrote. A dead end. In Washington, D.C., another report of a Scheele sighting sent agents knocking on a door on N Street NW to question the man. He was definitely not the chemist. Another tip that went nowhere.

And then, a break. On April 14, a Bureau of Investigation agent went into a bank in New York City. He needed to talk to a cashier about a hundred-dollar check that had recently been remitted to the bank. Made out to Marie Magdalene Scheele, the check was from the National Bank of Cuba in Havana. It wasn't the only one. Checks from Cuban banks rolled in to Marie Scheele's bank every few weeks. At last, the German chemist had been found.

Chapter Four

Technical Men

The thunder of artillery grew closer as George Hulett's car sped east across northern France. The Princeton chemist and the rest of his scientific delegation had left Paris on May 11, driving more than one hundred miles north to Abbeville, close to where the British had their gas headquarters in France. So close to the front, civilians had fled, and in their place hundreds of thousands of British, Canadian, and Australian soldiers had amassed. Hulett watched soldiers learning to use their masks and training in fight in poisonous gas. To experience for himself what the instruction entailed, he went through the officer training course, donning a gas mask and wearing it into a gas cloud.

A few days later, the British brought Hulett and the other scientists to within six miles of the front. As they approached Arras, the city where the British had used Livens projectors, he could hear artillery rattling in the distance before they arrived in the city. Nothing he had seen of the war so far, no photo or news report, prepared him for the destruction he saw in Arras. The once glorious city had been crushed into rubble, the houses still standing too battered for habitation. Few civilians remained, and soldiers had turned the ruined city into a camp, which the Germans still periodically shelled.

Then they went south, near a British base used during the Battle of the Somme. Here, too, the destruction stunned Hulett. Ten months after the titanic battle, shell craters of all sizes pocked the landscape, trenches cleaved the fields, and barbed wire sutured the earth. Detritus of the battle lay all around—shards of hand grenades, dropped rifles, pierced helmets, and carcasses of downed airplanes. Splintered stubs of tree trunks thrust up at odd angles. Hulett walked over the fields for hours, past shattered villages, around shell holes that served as shallow graves for the dead. A member of the delegation searched for a village he knew, but the entire town had vanished, obliterated by high explosives and pounded back into the soil. Metallic husks of tanks lay where they had been stranded and abandoned. "Ever yet horrible scenes are everywhere. One cannot describe it," Hulett wrote home. "I would not have missed it for anything but it is too terrible and no one can give a real idea of the battlefield in words."

From there, it was back to Paris and then to England. Throughout his travels, Hulett absorbed an encyclopedic knowledge of war gases, their composition, and their attributes, as well as the massive enterprise required to produce them. He also gained a practical understanding of gas warfare and what it meant to use it or avoid it on the battlefield—something that most scientists in the United States would never get. With his own eyes, he saw the fearsome toll it took, as well as its limitations and strategic disadvantages.

He was also becoming acquainted with British and French officers with the greatest clout in gas warfare. Figures like Brigadier General Henry Thuillier, the director of the British gas service, deeply impressed Hulett, as did his top lieutenants, such as Major General Charles Howard Foulkes, commander of the British gas troops known as the Special Brigade, and Major Samuel J. M. Auld, a chemical adviser who, like Hulett, had been a teacher before the war.

Hulett sent back an update on May 21 that went first to George Hale at the National Research Council, then to Manning. Hulett said he planned to hurry to England to collect information about the manufacture of British gas masks for the benefit of Manning's technical men. Gathering details of the British mask was important, Hulett wrote, because "it would take a year or two to develop a satisfactory mask, and it would seem best that we select either the French or British mask, since the chemical and manufacturing details have been thoroughly worked out and would put us in a position to supply our troops in a few months."

Hulett also sent a sheaf of reports on gas warfare. One was on the organization of the gas services in France, another on offensive gas warfare. There were others on the use of charcoal for absorbing poisonous gases and on the manufacture of chemicals. Copies of all the reports should go to Manning and the Bureau of Mines, he said, to be studied and used at the laboratory set up to handle problems connected with the use of poisonous gases in warfare. He also included an urgent warning: that gas warfare was more widespread than the Americans knew, and the need for preparation far greater than what the Americans had anticipated.

"The use of poisonous and lachrymal gases, not only by the Germans but particularly by the allies, is far more extensive than we have supposed," Hulett wrote.

Hulett sent his dire missive across the Atlantic as plans for the laboratory at American University were beginning to fall into place. McKinley Hall's unfinished shell meant there was no need to rip out and replace existing features—the rough interior was ready for the lab benches and gas hoods, racks and sinks, required for chemistry research. The vacant building wasn't the sole reason that American University was ideal for the chemists. Swaths of pastures and rolling farmland swaddled the campus, land that the chemists would need as well, but not for bayonet drills or marksmanship practice. The war gas investigations would need open space where the chemists could dig test trenches, detonate incendiary bombs, ignite smoke candles, and lob shells without danger to buildings or nearby residents.

The lab could not be completed soon enough. It would be months before the laboratories at American University would be ready for the bureau's scientists, but the research was already well under way. Manning's census of engineers and chemists had set off a kind of chain reaction that activated the fraternity of chemists across the country. Offers of help poured in to the Bureau of Mines. Every colleague that he asked to commit to the war effort in turn asked the same of his colleagues and brightest students. But the flood of enthusiasm needed organization and coordination to prevent the talent from going to waste or, worse yet, being lost for good if scientists opted to go to the front instead of into military research.

In the weeks after the United States entered the war, Manning, Burrell, and the Committee on Noxious Gases organized the research into a few principal directions: one was developing war gases, and another was designing a gas mask for the millions of American soldiers who would soon be sent overseas. Without a central lab, George Burrell decided on the next-best thing: finding chemists willing to corral the volunteer scientists across the country, identify their potential contributions, and travel to their far-flung labs if necessary.

Casting about for help with developing war gases, Burrell looked to Johns Hopkins University in Baltimore, which was among the country's most prestigious research institutions. One of its chemistry professors, Joseph C. W. Frazer, had been chief of chemistry at the Bureau of Mine's Pittsburgh station. Burrell asked Frazer for names of the most promising chemists in his department. Frazer recommended E. Emmet Reid.

Reid was forty-four and an organic chemist in Frazer's lab. The son of an itinerant Baptist preacher, he had grown up in a pinprick Virginia town called Skinquarter, which boasted a post office, one store, a blacksmith, a buggy shop, and two churches. Despite a modest upbringing and only sporadic formal schooling, Reid went to Richmond College, then earned a Ph.D. from Johns Hopkins. He went on to teach at a small college in Shreveport, Louisiana, before Johns Hopkins lured him back to Baltimore. When Frazer asked Reid to help with the gas investigations, Reid didn't hesitate.

Frazer brought Reid to Washington to introduce him to Burrell, Henderson, and the other scientists at work on the gas research. Reid received his assignment: to canvass organic chemists for new chemical compounds that could be used as weapons on the battlefield. He was given no money, just a book of Bureau of Mines travel orders allowing him to roam anywhere in the country to meet with chemists. He also had a stack of postage-paid envelopes which he could use to correspond with them, and chemists could use to mail him chemical samples. Working out of the Johns Hopkins chemistry building, Reid wrote letter after letter to organic chemists across the country, asking them for chemical samples of potential war gases, in the process expanding the network of scientists that were part of this new wartime endeavor.

Reid's letter-writing campaign was haphazard, relying heavily on trial and error. And though he was corresponding with some of the country's most distinguished and experienced chemists, the chemicals they were dealing with could be dangerous if mishandled. One of Reid's letters went to Elmer Kohler at Harvard, asking him to make a batch of a chemical called chlormercaptan. A rumor later reached Reid that some of the gas had been released from the chemistry lab at Harvard and wafted into Harvard Square, causing a commotion. Another letter went to Professor William N. Dehn at the University of Washington in Seattle; Reid asked him to prepare cacodyl chloride, an extremely toxic and flammable arsenic compound. Dehn promised to make the cacodyl, along with several other chemicals. Not long after, a reeking cardboard box from Seattle arrived at the Johns Hopkins lab. When Reid opened it, he found the glass tube inside had cracked and the cacodyl had leaked out, soaking the cotton batting around it. Reid joked about the incident, but it was lucky that no harm came to him or those who handled the package on its way from

Washington. In late 1914, a chemist in Fritz Haber's lab in Germany had been experimenting with cacodyl chloride when the substance exploded. The violent detonation had blown off the man's head.

These were dangerous chemicals—in fact, the more dangerous they were, the more desirable they were as war gases—and the need to study their effects on human physiology soon became an early priority of the Research Division as well. Manning felt that research could not be delegated to scientists outside the bureau and put those efforts under the oversight of Yandell Henderson and a team of physiologists, pharmacologists, and pathologists at Yale, which had offered labs and approved the use of an athletic field for temporary laboratories. Animals would be the test subjects, "in order to avoid risking human lives in this matter."

Henderson's research quickly expanded into three sections, with a dozen scientists researching different effects of gas, from the short-term damage to tissue to the long-term health impacts. The experiments required a new pathology lab for the tests on the unlucky dogs and other animals that ended up as test subjects. Each creature that was gassed was carved open and autopsied, its tissue and organs studied under a microscope. As the tests got under way, stray dogs and cats began to vanish from the streets of cities and towns in Connecticut.

The other prong of the early research was gas masks. Burrell selected two men to spearhead the gas mask effort. One was Bradley Dewey, a Burlington, Vermont, native who had attended Harvard and the Massachusetts Institute of Technology. Dewey had been with the bureau since the first days of the war, lured away from his job as research chief of the American Sheet and Tin Plate Company in Pittsburgh. The other was Warren K. Lewis, a brilliant thirty-five-year-old chemical engineer who taught at MIT. Known as Doc, Lewis had an unruly lick of hair sprouting from his head and glasses perched atop his large nose. Famously pugnacious and dramatic in MIT's classrooms, he barked withering comments at students who failed to meet his expectations. He was also deeply religious and saw his calling as a scientist in almost evangelical terms, as a public service to better humanity. Arno C. Fieldner, the chief chemist at the Pittsburgh station, was given the task of finding the best material for the mask's filter canister.

Lewis and Dewey were among the brightest chemists in the country and believed that enterprise and ingenuity would make their assignment easy. In reality, a gas mask is a deceptively complicated piece of equipment. Designs differed, but most modern gas masks had a common feature: the wearer inhales through a filter that removes the gas and particles from the inhaled air. The main absorbent in the filter canisters is activated carbon, charcoal baked at high temperatures to expel gases trapped in its pores. Layered between cotton batting treated with soda lime, a substance that neutralizes acid, the charcoal absorbs gas as it is inhaled through the respirator. The real complexity of gas masks was in how their design needed to vary in order to protect against different chemicals. Each new war gas had different chemical characteristics, and a new gas could make existing masks obsolete, requiring weeks or months of study to determine its composition and how to reconstitute a filter for it. Chloropicrin, for example, went right through the filters of British and French masks.

The other part of the task that the men gravely underestimated was that making gas masks wasn't merely a theoretical or an academic undertaking—this was an industrial job, a manufacturing process to produce millions of perfect and identical masks. The charcoal for the filters had to be just right. So did the cotton batting that filled the canister and the soda lime that absorbed carbon dioxide. The can had to hold all three together just so. Everything needed to be assembled flawlessly, from the buckles on the straps, to the rubber hoses connecting the canister to the faceplate, to the eyepieces. Every grommet, every stitch, every flange, needed exact placement. Once the mask was designed, factories would need to quickly supply every piece to order—each one exactly matching specifications. They would then have to be shipped to a factory and assembled without flaws before they were finally provided to the soldiers. Not only did they need to work, but they needed to be comfortable and to stay in place as the soldiers fought, loaded artillery, or charged through gas.

Undaunted, Dewey and Lewis split up, with Dewey boarding a westbound train and Lewis remaining in the East, dashing between campuses and companies soliciting equipment, laboratories, and manpower. On April 28, Lewis stepped off a train in Cleveland, then went on to Nela Park, the campus of two General Electric Company subsidiaries, the National Lamp Works and the National Carbon Company. Nela Park was a logical destination for Lewis: the campus had gained a reputation as an incubator of industrial ingenuity, an engine of invention and innovation on a par with Edison's famed laboratory in Menlo Park, New Jersey. There was a man at Nela Park whom Lewis wanted to meet, a thirty-eight-year-old chemical engineer named Frank M. Dorsey who had responded to Manning's scientific census.

Dorsey had a bulldog jaw, beady, narrow eyes, and a face like a barroom tough. Outwardly, he didn't appear to have much in common with most of Manning's tweedy technical men, with their Ivy League pedigrees and burnished academic credentials. He glowered with his legs apart and his head down, with the swaggering stance of a boxer. He looked like a fighter, and he proved to be one, with a reputation as a fixer, a manufacturing genius who could quickly hammer out solutions to difficult engineering problems. Dorsey's supervisor agreed to allow Dorsey to work exclusively for the Bureau of Mines, along with four investigators turned over to Dorsey. By the end of April, an entire research laboratory at the National Carbon Company was dedicated to making charcoal for masks.

On May 1, the Army Medical Corps chief, Major Llewellyn

Williamson, asked Manning and his chemists to produce twenty-five thousand gas masks—a trial run for the millions that would be needed for the soldiers sent to the front. The draft was still months away, but soldiers had been lining up at recruitment stations to enlist. Every soldier who went to Europe would need protection from gas as surely as he needed bullets and bayonets.

Punctuating the urgency of the matter, Brigadier General Kuhn issued a supply order to his chief of staff soon after Williamson's request: Standard-issue gear for every soldier sent abroad would include two gas masks, along with their uniforms, boots, and steel helmets. Every company would have two chemical sprayers for clearing trenches of gas. Every regimental aid station would have oxygen-breathing apparatus for resuscitating the wounded. In a year, the first five hundred thousand troops expected to ship out to Europe would require one million gas masks and another one hundred thousand masks in reserve, eighty-five hundred chemical sprayers, and one thousand oxygen-breathing apparatuses. It was a colossal order to outfit an inexperienced army for what they would face in Europe.

The Bureau of Mines chemists soon realized what a difficult task they had undertaken. Lewis and Dewey's efforts had begun long before receiving Hulett's reports warning that a new mask could take a year or more to design and urging the chemists to choose either the British or the French mask in the meantime. Even though the British and the French had been working on their masks for years, Manning and Burrell naïvely believed that they could construct a mask that was superior to both the British small-box respirators and France's M2 masks in a matter of a few weeks.

Dewey and Lewis's lives became a haze of train stations and hotels and laboratories and factory floors as they raced between suppliers and labs, seeking the best materials and parts. All told, 320,000 separate pieces would have to be produced for the twenty-five thousand test masks alone. The charcoal for the filter had to come from red cedar at a coking plant in Pennsylvania. The soda lime that absorbed carbon dioxide came from the General Chemical Company in Easton, Pennsylvania. The Simmons Hardware Company in Saint Louis would make the knapsacks that held them. The Goodrich and Goodyear Rubber Companies in Akron would manufacture the face pieces. The American Can Company in New York City would make the canisters, and one of its plants in Long Island City would assemble the 320,000 parts.

For the two men, day blurred into night and back into day. At every turn, problems arose. Little in the way of directions or drawings were committed to paper; instead, verbal instructions kept the process moving. Inevitably, that led to new confusions and problems. With every complication or mishap, work had to stop while the chemists called Burrell or Fieldner or Dewey to consult over the problem before work could proceed. Mistake after mistake swallowed more time, the delays multiplying and adding up. Telegrams with test results flew back and forth between Washington and each of the satellite locations.

On June 10, a small batch of a half-dozen masks was ready for testing. On a baseball diamond across the street from the American Can Company factory in Brooklyn, Dewey, Henderson, and Burrell gathered with the new masks in hand and slipped them over their heads. The masks fit, and the men could breathe in them, but that wasn't enough of a trial. The real audition for the mask would be in the man-test chambers in the Pittsburgh Experiment Station, where the masks could be donned in a gas cloud—only then would the chemists know whether their creation actually worked.

Dewey and Henderson traveled to Pittsburgh that night. One of the men needed to be the guinea pig for the test. The newspapers had been so filled with the terrors of gas warfare that all of the men felt trepidation about testing the mask. Henderson said he would do it; he decided he had a duty to put himself at risk in service to the war effort. Perspiring and nervous, he pulled a mask over his face and entered the chamber with two large bottles of chlorine gas. The door closed behind him. He set the bottles down and uncapped them. He felt a warm sensation as the heavier-than-air chlorine gas moiled from the bottles down around his feet. The minutes ticked by.

The mask worked. Henderson, his heart racing, stayed in the chamber for a quarter of an hour, and the mask allowed him to breathe in the cloud of chlorine surrounding him. When he emerged from the man-test room, the chlorine had bleached his hair and his socks white, and when he pulled off his sweat-soaked shirt, it fell to pieces in his hands.

On July 13, the Americans shipped 19,960 gas masks to Europe for testing, promising that the other 5,000 would arrive soon. Dewey, Lewis, Gibbs, and Fieldner awaited the response. It came in an overseas telegram from General John J. Pershing, the commander in chief of the American Expeditionary Forces (AEF). The general reported that masks had been tested in French labs, and while the canister was adequate, the rubberized facepiece was "very poor." "The tissue allows chloropicrin, superpalite, and bromactone to pass through in one minute," the cablegram read. British scientists then did their own tests. Their results were even more withering, finding that the canister was also badly flawed. "Construction of entire apparatus faulty in almost every detail," another cablegram read. The masks were useless.

The Americans were crushed. The chemists had failed their first real test. But it also made them determined to improve their performance and prove their mettle in chemical warfare, even if they were the newcomers to the battlefield. Time was running out. American soldiers had already marched onto troop transports in Hoboken under cover of night and embarked for Europe in a massive convoy of twelve ships. The chemists redoubled their work, frantically retracing their steps to determine how to improve the masks.

The gas mask debacle was a learning experience in more ways than one. For Yandell Henderson, the Yale physiologist, his terrifying experience in the Pittsburgh man-test chamber in his gas mask proved to be a revelation for him. Despite his trepidation about stepping into the gas chamber, he did so because there was simply no way to determine the integrity or quality of equipment without using soldiers in the experiments. It was essential that tests on men should be run, he concluded.

As the research work expanded, the American University campus was undergoing a radical transformation. Manning had asked for $175,000 from the army and navy to pay for the necessary research facilities. The bureau's architect quickly drew up plans to convert McKinley Hall into a chemical lab. There were lab benches to install, chemical hoods where gases could be mixed, gas lines and burners, sinks and counters. The sound of hammers and saws filled the campus as construction began on barracks and mess halls for the Corps of Engineers. A YMCA building for the soldiers went up in short order, and within two weeks, there were thirteen hundred engineers stationed at the campus. A week later, that number had ballooned to twelve thousand. As the number of soldiers grew, the college trustees insisted on rules to prevent damage to the campus and the buildings, including protections for the young trees that had been planted that spring.

On the last day of May, a crowd had gathered under a gray sky at American University's tree-ringed outdoor amphitheater. For the school's third convocation, a special patriotic ceremony was planned. The Daughters of the American Revolution presented an American flag to the school chancellor, and an officer with the Sixth Engineers slowly raised the flag as the soldiers saluted. After a short musical interlude from the orchestra, the audience bowed their heads for a prayer, then joined in singing "America," before U.S. senator Hiram Johnson of California spoke.

"Now it is for you and me and all who call themselves Americans to make it plain to all our people all these things for which America stands and for which America fights," he said.

The flag raising was a patriotic gesture in wartime, but it had another symbolic meaning: the Methodist school was now government territory. On the same day as the outdoor convocation, the American University board of trustees met to approve the government's use of the campus that they had offered in April. Behind the amphitheater, hundreds of tents belonging to the Sixth Engineers Regiment radiated outward in rows.

The engineers would have only part of the campus, which would be partitioned into two jurisdictions. The eastern side would be for the Corps of Engineers, while McKinley Hall and the western end of the campus would be the domain of the chemists from the Bureau of Mines. In June, the bureau's architect carried the blueprints and schematics to Riggs Bank to present to Leighton and the rest of the university's board of trustees. The board of trustees approved the bureau's plans with minor changes, such as substituting fireproof concrete for wood floors throughout the building. When the university's board of trustees met once again, university secretary Albert Osborn down jotted the results.

"At a very important and interesting meeting of the executive committee at Riggs Bank the plans for the government occupation of McKinley Building for chemical work were approved," he wrote.

Every Tuesday, the chemists from all of the research sections gathered in Washington to update one another on progress in each of their areas and to brief army and navy officials on the work to date. By mid-July, sixty chemists were working on the investigations, many of them paid out of the Bureau of Mines budget, and forty more unpaid ones. The work on gas masks had rapidly dispersed the gas warfare work to more than twenty universities that Warren K. Lewis and other chemists traveled to, as well as the private companies that aided in the effort.

For now, the Pittsburgh Experiment Station was the center of the research, with Johns Hopkins and Henderson's lab at Yale as important secondary hubs. But when McKinley Hall was done, American University would become the central workshop for the war gas investigations. It would have another crucial function, too: ensuring the secrecy of the work. With so many scientists participating in so many locations, the need for oversight and management of the research was paramount. Security was a constant and omnipresent fear. At the top of Hulett's report from May, he scrawled "Secret," underlining the word twice. When Hale sent the reports on to the Bureau of Mines, he cautioned Manning about keeping the reports under lock and key:

> It is quite unnecessary for me to warn you regarding the extreme importance of keeping these reports on gas warfare STRICTLY CONFIDENTIAL. Every possible precaution should be taken to prevent them from falling into the hands of spies, who are undoubtedly numerous in Washington. I should like to know that you will keep them in the safe in your own office, and that you will not allow them to be seen by any one regarding whose loyalty there is even a remote possibility of suspicion.

The need for secrecy required looking no farther than corner newsstands, where the newspapers provided constant reminders of the espionage that had riddled the country before the war. The German spymaster Captain Franz von Rintelen had been caught trying to flee back to Europe. On trial in New York along with six codefendants, he had been convicted on May 20. Over the summer, an espionage bill making its way through Congress permitted censorship of newspapers, provoking the first split in the war coalition, with Republicans and some Democrats vociferously opposing censorship. Facing defeat in the House, the bill eventually passed in June stripped of the censorship provision but with harsh penalties for those convicted of conspiring against the United States.

Manning reassured Hale that he fully appreciated the sensitive nature of the reports and that everything would be kept under lock and key. Nothing was put in writing that didn't need to be, he wrote. Hale made sure Hulett's reports went to Secretary of War Newton Baker as well, with the same warnings about keeping them locked away from prying eyes. It was urgent, he noted, that the work be concentrated at the earliest possible date at American University and urged Baker to order the Secret Service to investigate all those people engaged with the work "in a case where our relations with the Allies and the safety of our Army are so clearly involved."

By July, the organization of the research was taking shape. To keep the National Research Council apprised of progress, Manning drafted a chart for Hale that folded, accordion-style, into four panels. In a box at the top, seated above the army and navy and all others, was the only name on the chart: Van H. Manning. Below his name, the chart displayed all the organization's sections and subsections, laid out in a pattern resembling piano keys. There were now seven major divisions of work: chemical investigations, physiological investigations, large-scale investigations of gas shells, gas mask design, gas mask examination, submarine gases, and gases for balloons and dirigibles.

The focus of the final category—gases for balloons and dirigibles—was far more specific than the vague description suggested. Over the summer of 1917, the British Board of Invention and Research asked the Bureau of Mines for assistance with a very specific technical problem, one which had bearing on Britain domestic security and military power. The Americans had access to a resource that the British did not, a prize locked deep in the earth beneath Texas and the American Midwest. It was a gas—not a war gas per se, but a gas that Britain hoped would give them superiority in the air. The gas was a stable, nonflammable, lighter-than-air noble gas: helium.

How exactly helium came to be part of the war gas investigations is something of a mystery; Burrell recalled that it was he who hypothesized that it might have value in the war, despite the fact that the army and navy seemed to have little interest. One of Burrell's friends, a captain in the Signal Corps, was going overseas and brought a letter from Burrell to the British about helium. The British responded like a shot, sending two officers to the United States.

The reason for Britain's interest in helium was airpower. England had long enjoyed the strategic advantage of geographic isolation from Europe, making invasion from the Continent difficult. But the advent of aviation was altering that calculus. The British feared that if Germany's airpower prevailed, England would become vulnerable to attack from the skies. Airplanes were buzzing over France, and so were lighter-than-air zeppelins, buoyed into the sky with hydrogen. The problem with hydrogen was its flammability—a single bullet that found its mark could ignite a fire and bring down a zeppelin in seconds. Out of fear of fire, the British had grounded $125 million worth of dirigibles.

Britain hoped that helium, which was noncombustible, could replace hydrogen and, if kept out of the hands of the Germans, give the British an edge in aviation. But extracting and isolating the gas was both extremely expensive and technically difficult. In the summer of 1917, a British rear admiral wrote to the National Research Council with a plea for Anglo-American cooperation on helium. "It is regarded by the British authorities as absolutely essential that every endeavor should be made to discover and produce Helium in quantities with the least possible delay, the matter being of vital importance to the future military use of lighter-than-air craft," he wrote. It was no small task—the British Admiralty hoped to buy 100 million cubic feet of helium immediately and a million cubic feet weekly after that. He ended with the caution that it is "scarcely necessary to inform you that this matter has throughout been dealt with in the strictest secrecy."

The National Research Council responded that there was a great deal of interest in helium and that the Bureau of Mines was beginning investigations under Manning. The British already had a code name for it—they called it "C gas." It was probably MIT chemist William Walker who came up with the American code name for helium. "Argon," they would call it.

On a hot day in late August, Osborn stopped by McKinley Hall. More and more tents for the engineers had sprouted in neat rows. Thousands of men in uniform drilled and paraded throughout the campus. As Osborn mounted the steps of McKinley Hall and strolled through the building with the campus superintendent, the clamor of construction met their ears. The building that had been largely empty and quiet for so many years had suddenly come alive. The two men walked past workmen finishing the floors, hammering partitions into place, and installing lab equipment for the chemists. It had taken a war, but after more than a quarter of a century, the campus was finally occupied.

Chapter Five

Amos and Goliath

In the weak half-light of early morning, the soldiers of the First Division lined up in a drenching rain along the French roadside. The perpetually overcast skies and muddy countryside were a far cry from the "sunny France" that the AEF volunteers had expected. It was July 19, 1917. The men had arrived from Hoboken in June, cheering as their transports passed through the submarine blockade to dock at Saint-Nazaire. The cantonments at the American training camp near Chaumont, about 170 miles east of Paris, weren't yet ready, and the only accommodations available were the white-walled villages and farmhouses dotting the French countryside. Divided into squads, the soldiers moved into makeshift billets in stables and barn lofts draped in cobwebs, sleeping under decaying roofs with wind and rain spitting through the rafters. Fires were forbidden except for cooking, and the soldiers grumbled as they tried to heat their meals with the twigs they scavenged from nearby woods. A bombing school was down the road; sometimes, the men could hear the boom of hand grenades detonating in the distance, as if the front lay at their doorstep.

At sunup in the villages around the American training camp, the soldiers strapped on their sidearms, buttoned up their coats, and cinched their belts tight before falling into rank along the roadside for inspection. The mutter of an engine announced their commander's arrival. His machine trundled up the road and stopped in front of his soldiers. Curious French residents cheered as Major General William Luther Sibert stepped from the vehicle and planted his boots in the mud.

Sibert was commander of the First Division and General Pershing's second-in-command. A fifty-six-year-old engineer from Alabama, he was famously contemplative and meticulous, with little tolerance for inefficiency. He was tall and powerfully built, earning him the nickname "Goliath"; but graying at his temples, with kindly eyes, round spectacles, and a moon-shaped face, he resembled a doting grandfather more than the biblical giant.

Sibert returned the regiment officers' salutes and then turned to his assembled squads of Sammies, as the French called the American soldiers. He scrutinized the soldiers from head to foot, taking in every detail, from the length of their hair to the condition of their boots. He clambered up rickety ladders to the haylofts where the soldiers were billeted, looked over their sleeping quarters, and walked through the barns, checking to make sure that their accommodations were orderly and sanitary. He ordered his aides to jot down notes for improvements, and they scribbled frantically as they tried to keep up with his pace. Striding down the ranks, he peered closely at the collars of the men's uniforms. Something was missing. Many of the soldiers lacked service pins, the two brass letters U.S. that indicated they were American. What happened to your pins? Sibert demanded. Some of the men admitted that they lost them. Others had given them away like cheap keepsakes. Sibert turned to the regimental officers and made his disapproval clear. Then as the rain continued its dreary drumbeat, he strode to the car, aides scurrying behind him, and set off down the road to the next stop, leaving his officers to dress down their soldiers.

In July of 1917, the creaking machinery of the U.S. military had begun to shed its rust, along with any doubt that involvement in the war would cost American lives. Some Americans and even members of Congress believed the nation's role in Europe would be limited to moral and logistical support and were shocked to learn that U.S. soldiers would set foot on European soil at all. The question of a draft and compulsory military duty was politically fraught and went to the very heart of the Republic. Under the existing volunteer structure of the military, state-based National Guard units fed into the relatively small Regular Army. Proponents of a draft argued that conscription into a new National Army would assimilate immigrants, level class differences, and instill military discipline in the populace. But to others—mainly Democrats in the South and West—conscription was a threat to democracy, a symptom of a coercive federal government that, unable to raise a volunteer force, must instead dragoon an army through force of law. The details of a potential draft were also deeply contentious. How many soldiers should be called up? Which ones should be exempted? How young and how old?

For Wilson and Secretary of War Baker, the fight over the draft was a distasteful one. Both men disdained the idea of compulsory military service, and Baker owed his appointment to antidraft views that he shared with the president. But the shifting tides of the war had changed their positions as a draft looked increasingly necessary, further infuriating pacifists and other war opponents who already felt betrayed by Wilson's reversal on neutrality.

Foremost in Wilson's and Baker's minds were lessons learned in Great Britain, where fervor to volunteer had sent vast numbers of potential leaders to perish in the trenches. To Wilson, raising an army demanded a methodical, organized conscription system that would avoid sending into battle American boys whose skills could be used in some critical capacity and would ensure that the country's economic and industrial foundations remained sound. An orderly approach to raising an army also served the interests of the Bureau of Mines scientists, who feared that capable technical men would be swept up in a stampede to volunteer for service. The only way to create such a system was compulsory registration that would require every eligible man to step up and make himself known to the government—a huge undertaking that had never been attempted before.

Complicating the draft's delicate politics even further, Theodore Roosevelt—one of Wilson's most ferocious critics for vacillating on whether to fight—had been agitating with his usual bombast for an all-volunteer force to go to the trenches. Huge prowar rallies thundered for a full-throttle military engagement in France, and Roosevelt's supporters advocated for the aging former president himself to be at their vanguard. When the War Department announced in May that it would send an expeditionary force to France led by General Pershing, the force did not include Roosevelt's volunteer force. Wilson complimented Roosevelt's gallantry but bluntly rejected his volunteer regiment. "The business now in hand is undramatic, practical, and of scientific definitiveness and precision," he said in his public comment.

Congress battled over the draft details for weeks, and the bill that eventually passed required all men ages twenty-one to thirty to register for selective service into the new National Army, with harsh penalties for those who shirked their duty. Registration day was set for June 5, which Wilson declared a holiday. The Council of National Defense ordered churches and fire stations to ring their bells at 7:00 a.m., when registration booths opened. Bands would play patriotic songs, fire bells would ring, and the government recommended that men of registration age should be escorted to the doors of the station by their kinfolk, neighbors, and friends.

"Registration Day should be celebrated as a consecration of the American people to service and to sacrifice. It should be a welcome to those registering. It should be a public expression by each community of willingness to surrender its sons to the country," the council director, Walter Gifford, proclaimed in his directive.

The hullabaloo wasn't for patriotism's sake alone. Recalling the draft riots during the Civil War, Baker worried about anticonscription demonstrations and even bloodshed. To Baker's great relief, the day went smoothly, with only scattered unrest and protest. With brass bands blaring and flags waving, almost 10 million men lined up at registration stations throughout the country.

The first draft drawing was on July 20, and Secretary of War Baker himself drew the first number. Standing in a packed hearing room in the Senate office building, Baker rapped on the tabletop in front of him, and the room fell silent. Dozens of reporters seated around long tables turned to look at Baker, along with members of the House and Senate Military Affairs Committees in silk summer suits and long-tailed jimswingers. On the table, a fishbowl held tiny capsules. He stood in front of a long chalkboard filled with numbers from 1 to 500.

"Gentlemen, this is a solemn and historic moment," Baker said. "We come here to determine which of ten million of our young men who have registered for national service will be selected to answer the president's call for an army of 687,000."

After Brigadier General Enoch H. Crowder explained how the drawing would work, another general broke the paper seal on the fishbowl and stirred the capsules inside with a long wooden spoon. Baker took his glasses off, and an aide tied a white blindfold over his eyes and guided him to the table. Baker stirred the jar again with the spoon, then reached in.

"I have drawn the first number," he said, and held the capsule up. A War Department clerk took it from Baker's hand, broke it open, and read the number. "The number is two hundred and fifty-eight," he said. "Two hundred and fifty-eight," the tally chief repeated, and the number went onto the chalkboard opposite the number 1. The draft had begun.

By the time of the drawing, almost 184,000 recruits had already volunteered to go to France in their state National Guard units or in the Regular Army. The troop convoys had departed Hoboken in secrecy, as had General Pershing himself—one day he was in his tiny War Department office that was barely big enough to contain him and his staff, and then one day he was gone—his desk empty, and his aides', too—only to reappear in England shortly after.

The arrival of the American soldiers was unexpected to the French. When the first convoy glided into Saint-Nazaire, France, a strange still-ness discomfited some of the American soldiers leaning over the rail-ings of the ships as crowds watched in eerie silence from the quay. By the time the second contingent arrived on June 27, the mood had changed, or at least the press accounts of it had. American flags had been hastily erected around the port, and throngs of French admirers cheered wildly as the transports brought the troops ashore.

Sibert, General Pershing's second-in-command of the American Expeditionary Forces, had no battlefield experience or training in organizing field troops. What he did have, however, was political capital, which made him a darling of Congress and helped propel him to France and, eventually, to the head of the Chemical Warfare Service.

A son of the South, Sibert was born on October 12, 1860, and grew up on his family farm in Gadsden, Alabama. He came from a long military tradition. His great-grandfather arrived in America as a regular in the British army, and his father, a Confederate infan-tryman, had been wounded at the Second Battle of Bull Run. The schoolhouse in Gadsden was a primitive, one-room school, but young Sibert excelled, particularly in math. In the lean years after the Civil War, Sibert left school to work on the family farm. His years of backbreaking farmwork provided him a personal bench-mark for the toil an able-bodied man could do in a day. Instead of returning to school, he crammed for an entire year to prepare for college applications and was accepted at the University of Alabama at age eighteen. His high marks earned him free room and board and, eventually, a spot at West Point, the U.S. Military Academy for the Corps of Engineers, where he transferred in 1880.

One of the first challenges for new cadets was a grueling, often-humiliating period in the "Beast Barracks," where first years known as plebes were segregated from the rest of the students and subjected to near-constant hazing. The Beast Barracks were a ritual that cadets whispered about with fear and awe, a trial intended to toughen the young soldiers, instill discipline, and build camaraderie. When an upperclassman burst into the tent that Sibert shared with his bunkmate, a spindly South Carolinian named David DuBose Gaillard, and asked the smaller boy's name, he replied, "David, sir." The older cadet saw Sibert standing at attention, towering over his bunkmate. "Oh yes," the older cadet gloated, "you are David and this is Goliath."

Not only was Sibert big for his age, but the farm boy could thrash bigger upperclassman in the boxing matches and fistfights that settled grudges among the cadets. Long after he graduated, the name "Goliath" stuck. More than twenty years later, David and Goliath would be thrown together again in a new backbreaking test of strength and stamina, one with far-higher stakes: construction of the Panama Canal.

Top students at West Point received appointments to the Corps of Engineers, ushering them into the ranks of the army elite. Sibert graduated seventh in his class of thirty-seven, just below Gaillard. During training at the Engineer School at Willets Point, New York, Sibert met his first wife, a Texas belle named Mary Margaret Cummings, whom he called Mamie. When they were apart, he addressed his tender letters to "My dear old darling," writing in one that "there is a charm about you that makes you surpass all other women in my eyes....I wish I could kiss you good night and tell you how dearly I love you and how hard it is to get along without you." They would have a daughter and seven sons, two of whom died in infancy. Sibert studied lock-and-dam engineering, working on the Green and Barren Rivers near Bowling Green, Kentucky, and then the Sault Sainte Marie, Michigan, locks system between Lake Superior and the lower Great Lakes. His work there earned him a command in Little Rock, Arkansas, and then an assignment in 1899 as chief engineer of the Eighth Army Corps in the Philippines, one of the fronts in the Spanish-American War. While serving on the staff of an early-rising general, Sibert adopted the habit of arriving at his office each day before dawn. When the war ended, another stint in the States followed, before President Roosevelt appointed him to the Isthmian Canal Commission, the body charged with building a canal across Panama, in March 1907.

The Panama Canal was an engineering marvel, an undertaking so vast and ambitious that it was compared to wonders like the Pyramids of Giza and the Great Wall of China. Every European explorer since Hernán Cortés had dreamed of a maritime shortcut between the Atlantic and the Pacific Oceans to avoid the arduous journey around South America. Several routes had been charted, but the French were the first to buy the rights and property from the Colombian government to build the canal. Hacking through disease-infested jungle and carving a trough through the Culebra Mountains proved too costly and complicated for the French; after twenty years, they threw up their hands and sold the canal rights to the United States. A series of short-lived appointments convinced President Roosevelt that permanent oversight was needed, leading to the seven-member Isthmian Canal Commission, which included Sibert.

The Canal Zone was an otherworldly place, an eruption of man and machinery amid primordial tropical forests teeming with perils. Tapirs thundered through the brush, and tiger cats prowled the undergrowth at night. The fer-de-lance, an irritable pit viper that could spit venom six feet, slithered underfoot. Mosquitoes carrying yellow fever, malaria, and other maladies swarmed the humid forests. The vast scale of the construction zone was staggering, with denuded hillsides sloping into a Stygian moonscape of soil and rock stitched together with rail lines. An army of steam shovels huffed clouds of smoke as they clawed through soil and substrate, and the ground trembled underfoot with the roar of dynamite blasting apart the Culebra Mountains. Showers less like rain than cataracts of water triggered flash floods and landslides that sometimes buried steam shovels and trains under hundreds of tons of soil and clay. Boneyards of abandoned French excavators and rusty train cars enveloped by jungle creepers peppered the Canal Zone, reminders of the folly that came before.

Unlike the rotating crew of civilian engineers who came and went, the new commissioners were not allowed to resign and were required to live in the Canal Zone. Sibert was one of the top engineers who together were the driving force behind the canal; the others were Colonel George W. Goethals and Lieutenant Colonel David Gaillard, his old friend from West Point. On the Atlantic side of the canal, Sibert was responsible for construction of the Gatun Locks, the system of concrete basins and watertight gates that raise southbound ships to the elevation of Gatun Lake and lower northbound ships from the lake to the Atlantic Ocean. On the Pacific side, he was also in charge of the West Breakwater in Colón, the Gatun Dam, and the channel between Gatun Lake and the Pacific. Gaillard was in charge of another stupendously difficult part of the project: the Culebra Cut, the vast trench bisecting the spine of the isthmus to link the locks on the north and south ends of the canal. Another engineer, Colonel William C. Gorgas, also had a seemingly impossible task: to rid the zone of diseases that killed laborers by the thousands.

Sibert spent six years in Panama, bringing his family to live in a house that he built for them. Acrimonious battles raged over the design of the canal. At one point, when Sibert returned to Washington for congressional hearings on the canal, a candid response to a congressman's hypothetical question about lock failure nearly resulted in his dismissal. The secretary of war was coaxed into allowing Sibert to stay. It was a wise decision. Sibert's efficiency and meticulous organization significantly cut the construction time for the Gatun Locks. The locks were expected to take two years longer than other parts of the canal; instead, Sibert completed the locks first.

After Sibert returned from Panama in 1914, the army sent him to China to work on flood mitigation. When he returned, the army put him in command of the Pacific artillery in San Francisco. Tragedy struck the family in spring of 1915 when his beloved wife, Mamie, died of malaria.

Congress was still giddy with patriotic fervor over the canal's completion and eager to reward the men who turned the dream of a canal into reality. A special act of Congress made Sibert a brigadier general, pushing him into the ranks of the general officers of the line. Trained in warfare, officers of the line resented the exalted status of the Corps of Engineers; one major general confided to Sibert that Congress might as well start promoting medical doctors as generals if it was doing the same with engineers.

When war finally came in 1917, the petrified hierarchies of the U.S. Army limited General Pershing's options for his line generals. He selected Sibert as his second-in-command, a man who knew about hydrodynamic pressure and the calculus of Pascal's law but had no battlefield experience. Sibert knew Pershing from their West Point days, although they were in different classes.

Goliath was summoned for active duty on April 26, the announcement drowned in the flood of news over the slaughter at Arras. His promotion to major general in June was similarly overshadowed by Pershing's arrival in London. Sibert was sent quietly across the Atlantic, and it was only after he had landed that the army announced his command of the First Division. In one photo that ran out on the wires, Sibert wore tweedy civilian clothes and appeared gaunt, looking more like a harried professor in his tie and vest than a general taking command of the trenches. When the ship reached Saint-Nazaire, Pershing himself had greeted the troops, standing stock-still on the wharf, intently studying the men as they walked down the gangplank. Sibert didn't know Pershing as well as the other officers who disembarked with him, but he would soon learn that Pershing's harsh scrutiny wouldn't abate, and that after the general made a judgment about someone, he rarely changed his mind.

Sibert was not the only engineer that Pershing plucked from obscurity. In the early morning of July 20, Amos A. Fries strode into the lobby of the Astor Hotel in Midtown Manhattan, uniform rumpled from a long night on the train from Washington, D.C., and set down his suitcase containing his pistol belt and riding gloves. A forty-four-year-old cattleman's son with a mustache like a Fuller brush, Fries had dark, piercing eyes that burned with a fierce intensity and a head of unruly curls that erupted on either side of a severe part down the middle of his head. He always had an indomitable confidence no matter where he found himself, and it showed in the imperial angle of his chin, in the hard glare from under his brow.

He had traveled more than two thousand miles across America, but the lavish hotel was only the midpoint of his journey, a gilded resting point before he continued on to Europe. The hotel's baroque interior, with its elegant Oriental carpets and gleaming marble columns reaching up to intricate ceiling frescoes, was hardly the kind of accommodations to which Fries was accustomed. He had gone from an austere frontier childhood to the spartan existence of the army, where he served in malarial swamps of the Philippines and then the volcanic ferment of Yellowstone Park, where he had been director of roads until just a few weeks earlier. Now he found himself in luxurious surroundings with a few days of relaxation and high-society amusement.

Before Fries retired to his room, he took care of a vital piece of business: letting his beloved wife, Bessie, know that he had arrived safely. His brisk efficiency and adherence to the army's clockwork predictability masked a sentimental streak. Every morning, he put tiny photos of all his children and his wife in his pocket and carried them with him everywhere he went, and he wrote home almost every day, addressing his letters to "My darling wifey and babies," and ending them with "With love and kisses, Amos, Daddy." Sometimes he scrawled his letters home on stationery, sometimes pecked them out on a typewriter, sometimes dictated them through the window of a telegraph office. On the night he arrived in New York, the telegram to his wife went out at 3:30 a.m. "Am stopping Hotel Astor now," he wrote. He suffered chronic indigestion, but even after his long voyage, his stomach felt fine. "Am feeling well weather warm but not so hot as June," he wrote. Finally, Fries retreated to his room to unpack his suitcase, where he had tucked some of his purchases in Washington, which included three pairs of pajamas.

Fries had learned that he would probably have the same job in France as he had in Yellowstone: grading and constructing the roads. Roads and bridge work were bedrock civil engineering, essential for victory, built upon sand and gravel, surveying and drainage. Fries knew nothing of chemicals or gas warfare; to the colonel, chemicals were potions tucked into the medicine cabinet at home, tinctures and curatives for maladies like his own unsteady stomach. For his violent indigestion, Fries took an over-the-counter purgative called calomel, a wintergreen-flavored pink tablet. A mysterious ailment also afflicted his sickly son, Stuart. Writing in his stifling hotel room, Fries suggested that their boy take the pills as well. "I think it would be wise to ask Dr. Johnson about giving Stuart two or three tenths of calomel once or twice a week. It appeared to work well, but there might be some danger in it." The compound's other name was mercurous chloride, and it was utterly toxic.

Fries was an engineer's engineer, a stern soldier with a prairie practicality, steadfast as a well-driven fence post. His upbringing could not have been more different than that of the soft-skinned chemists from Harvard and Princeton who had flocked to Manning's Research Division. Born on March 17, 1873, Fries had grown up in a remote corner of western Missouri that rubbed up against Nebraska, a lawless and violent frontier area where bands of former Civil War soldiers and bandits roamed up and down the Missouri River. When Fries's father had moved the family there from Wisconsin, they received a chilly reception. Cattlemen already grazing the prairie bitterly resented newcomers as interlopers who augured a wave of unwelcome settlers to come. Not long after the family arrived, Amos's father drew his pistol on two brothers who attacked him as he passed by with Amos and his sister in the family wagon. Word spread around Holt County about the new neighbor with the quick draw, and rumors flew that Fries packed six-shooters under his wagon seat. The family never had problems again.

Fries's childhood was one of hard work and discipline on the farm. With the nearest fence line a mile away, tending the herd meant roaming over endless prairie, hustling cattle out of the neighbor's cornfields, and driving them back to the barn. Farm life turned the boy into a stolid believer in discipline and self-sufficiency, but he also had an adventurous streak. When a teacher he admired left for the U.S. Military Academy at West Point, his student wondered about this place where young men went to become engineers and soldiers. The following spring, the Fries family left the Midwest for Oregon. Four years later, after Fries completed high school, West Point had lost neither its mystery nor its magnetism. Ignoring his mother's objections, he wrote to his congressman for assistance in applying. Wait a year, he was told; perhaps then there would be a place for him. After the year went by, he passed the qualifying exams in San Francisco and was ordered to report to West Point on June 15, 1894.

In Fries's class portrait, he wore a military cape over his uniform with an expression of smoldering poise, exuding a confidence that would stay with him throughout his life as an engineer. He had a boiling fever to prove himself; when he went to visit the

Washington Monument, he sprinted up the 897 steps to show he could beat the elevator to the top. The Spanish-American War, the "splendid little war" that made Theodore Roosevelt a household name, was under way as Fries graduated, and he was so eager to join the battle that he reported to the adjutant general's office in Washington the day after his commencement. But his zeal for war was too late. Instead of being sent overseas immediately, he was ordered to Fort Totten at Willets Point, Long Island, for instruction in laying harbor mines. By year's end, the war was over.

The year after, he was ordered back to Oregon for a stint near his hometown, Central Point, under Colonel William Langfitt, the commander in charge of the Portland district. Fries was happy to have the assignment near his home, because he was sweet on a woman there, named Bessie Wait. In early August of 1899, Langfitt granted Fries's request for leave, and he headed straight back to Central Point. For two straight weeks, Fries's spent every evening in the parlor of the Waits house in nearby Medford, where Bessie lived with her parents. On August 16, they married and, the next day, left by steamer for their honeymoon in San Francisco. At the end of Fries's leave, it was back east once again, to Willets Point. In 1901, Fries received new orders and was sent to the Philippines, America's new territory gained from the Spanish-American War.

Amos and Bessie's home was Zamboanga, a city on the western peninsula of Mindanao Island, the largest island in the archipelago. A pet monkey gnawed on the golf balls that Fries had brought with him from the United States; in the afternoons, Fries played with one of the generals, who ordered prisoners to rake the ditches of the improvised, six-hole course for lost balls. Fries astonished soldiers under his command by working alongside them in the burning equatorial heat. His standing grew when he took over the difficult job of driving wooden piles after the soldier on the job fell ill with dysentery.

Fries was not the only soldier on the island with a reputation. At the inland Lake Lanao, a Captain John J. Pershing commanded

Camp Vickers, an outpost for exploring and mapping the island's interior. Though the war was over, some of the Moro chiefs that had long defied Spanish rule also resisted the new American conquerors. Pershing's predecessor had tried and failed to pacify the Moros through brute force, causing substantial American casualties. When Pershing catapulted into the command over hundreds of higher-ranking officers, he used diplomacy and patient negotiations to slowly win the chiefs over to his side. When Fries visited the camp, he was astonished by the scene that greeted him: several Moro chiefs gathered around Pershing, listening raptly to his phonograph.

The scene made a deep impression on Fries. Long after he and Bessie departed in 1903, reassigned to Willets Point once again, he recalled his many memories of his adventures in the Philippines. Of all his recollections, his impressions of Pershing were among his sharpest. His admiration for Pershing bordered on reverence, and he marveled over the captain's daring and his skills in strategy and diplomacy. "Just as there were thousands of sailors, there was only one Columbus who had the courage, the knowledge and the leadership to 'sail on and sail on' until he discovered then an unknown continent and then (though far in the future) our glorious government and beloved home," Fries wrote of Pershing.

Fries's next assignment was back in Oregon, followed by several years as chief engineer in Los Angeles, then five years teaching at the Engineer School in Washington before he was ordered to take charge of the roads in Yellowstone Park. Founded in 1872, Yellowstone was the country's first national park, but it had been underfunded and in decline for years, overrun with poachers and memento collectors who hacked at the mineral deposits and defaced the ancient hot springs. The Department of the Interior, desperate to save the jewel of the nation's growing park system, asked for help from the army, which deployed its engineers as if it were an occupied territory. The early years were like a wilderness bivouac, with soldiers and engineers housed in tents on a high plateau near Mammoth Hot Springs. Eventually, the army built Fort Yellowstone, a permanent village of stone buildings. That made for a far-more-comfortable perch, but Yellowstone was still viewed less as a military duty than as a retirement position or an extended stay at a health spa for ailing engineers. "Fries, what's the matter with you?" one engineer asked him after he received his assignment. "I thought they only sent sick men there." Fries responded that this time the army wanted an actual living engineer in the position, rather than one with a foot in the grave.

The new assignment delighted the couple. Their newborn baby, Stuart, was a sickly child, and they felt the environment of Yellowstone would improve his health. They lived a comfortable—if simple—frontier existence at Fort Yellowstone with their young son and two daughters, amid rolling carpets of lodgepole pines and majestic valleys, burping mud pots, and thermal hot springs trimmed with rainbow-hued mineral deposits.

Fries took his responsibilities seriously. He reasserted government jurisdiction over the park's bridges and roads, whose upkeep had been ceded to private companies and hotel owners. There were almost no cars or trucks in the park when he began, and at first he navigated the park with a horse and buggy. During his watch, Fries gained a fleet of trucks, and the army assigned him an automobile—a Kissel Kar—to replace his horse and buggy. Soon tourists would arrive in cars themselves, changing the park forever, and Fries paved the way—an effort that earned him attention and accolades in Washington.

America had been at war for two months when Fries finally got his long-deferred wish to go to war. In mid-June of 1917, orders arrived to report to the engineer's examining board in New York for a promotion exam. He made the trip east, arriving with about a dozen other young officers. They took a quiz, doctors took their pulses, listened to their hearts, and tapped on their chests, and then they were ordered to report to the chairman of the exam board the following day.

When Fries arrived the next morning, he saluted the chairman and stood at attention. The colonel picked up a slip of paper from his desk, read a single sentence waiving any examination requirements, and turned his eyes back down to his desk. Fries stood there, unsure of what to do. A few seconds passed, and the colonel looked up at Fries, as if surprised to see him still there. "That is all, major," he said curtly. Fries realized he had been promoted and then dismissed. With that brief exchange, for which he had traveled more than two thousand miles, Fries was a lieutenant colonel in the National Army.

Fries had always hoped for this moment, and yet he was wracked with worry. He had three small children now, the youngest just ten months old, and Bessie was six months pregnant with their fourth. He was expected to leave for France immediately, but he convinced the army to allow him to return home first, since he had brought only a small suitcase with him for his trip east. Before he left Washington, he wired Bessie. Pack up the house, he told her. The family was leaving.

He boarded a westbound train and returned home feeling sick with anxiety and excitement. Once he was back, the family frantically stowed their belongings into crates that would follow Bessie and the children to Los Angeles, where they would live with Bessie's mother. On July 4, they finished packing, and the train left at 11:00 a.m. the next day from the park's west entrance, almost forty miles away from Fort Yellowstone. They left in the early morning, the Kissel grinding down the mountains through clouds of steam billowing from the hot springs, steadily losing elevation as the car descended to the park's west entrance. At the station, Fries helped bundle the children into their seats on the train. Both Fries and his wife were stoic and steadfast through the dry-eyed goodbye, but after the train left and Fries made the trip in reverse, a profound sense of loneliness settled over him, a deep uncertainty over his path ahead. The car trundled along the winding banks of the Madison River, gaining in altitude toward Firehole Falls. Instead of returning to Fort Yellowstone, he turned the car south, brooding as he drove toward the Paintpots and the leaping flumes of Old Faithful. He continued on, crossing the Continental Divide on his way to Yellowstone Lake. Fries saw none of it, stewing with his eyes locked on the road stretching out before him, driving with no destination in mind. "I had then that complete feeling of turning my back on all that was dear and near, perhaps forever," he recalled.

The house suddenly quiet and empty, he wrote to Bessie every day, describing the wildflowers in bloom, the level of Lake Yellowstone, the arrival of the seasonal tourists. A telegram arrived on July 13: his ship would embark from New York eight days later, on July 21. He packed a small trunk to send ahead to Washington, while his army bedroll and a larger trunk went directly to New York with the clothes he would need for France, including his enormous bearskin coat. He boarded a train east on July 15, and as he barreled across the plains, he pecked out letters on his new Corona typewriter, salting them with observations about the passing landscape, the weather and the crops, and wildlife that he spotted from the train window. He studied French and chatted with a fellow Mason he met on the train. Soldiers who filled the cars speculated about what lay ahead. "There are all sorts of ideas as to how long the war will last," he wrote to Bessie in Los Angeles. He arrived in Washington on July 18, spent the night at the Army and Navy Club, and departed for New York the next evening on the overnight train. His departure date proved more tentative than he originally thought, and July 21 arrived with no definite word on when he would leave. He spent the day instead "in high society," he wrote to Bessie, hobnobbing around Manhattan with his fellow officers in a car assigned to take him around the city.

The next day, he set out for the Chelsea Piers to see the *Orduña*, the fifteen-thousand-ton steamship that would carry him and Langfitt's regiment across the Atlantic. At 569 feet, she was not a small vessel, but alongside floating behemoths like the *Leviathan* and the *Agamemnon,* the single-funnel *Orduña* looked almost puny. As Fries walked the pier inspecting the ship, he spotted a familiar face on the quay: former president Theodore Roosevelt, whose youngest son, Quentin, would also be on the *Orduña*. Fries passed the former president several times before introducing himself and speaking with him briefly. Fries looked over the ship from stem to stern, and it looked sturdy enough. Still, his pragmatic nature led him to take precautions in case the *Orduña* encountered a submarine or some other mishap. Before he left, he went out and bought himself a full-body life preserver called an Ever-Warm Safety-Suit, which carried a hefty price tag of sixty dollars that Fries complained about bitterly to his wife. The night before he left, he spent fifty cents at target practice in a shooting gallery to make sure his marksmanship was still up to snuff. The shroud of dread and loneliness lifted, and for an army engineer accustomed to a no-frills existence, he found himself quite comfortable in New York.

> I am getting quite expert at taking it easy when I don't have to hurry, and taking it calm when I do. Guess I have grown into the feeling that this war is so vast that the only thing for me to do is to do what I can and not worry for the work one can do is so small in the total that an ounce or two of extra effort won't even be a drop in the bucket.

When he boarded the *Orduña* to set sail on July 23, Fries had a stateroom to himself—a benefit of being one of the highest-ranking officers on board—and a bathroom that he shared with another officer. His upper-level room had a wide-open view of the ocean overlooking the second deck, and as the ship carved through the waters toward Nova Scotia, Fries could see porpoises shooting through the waves alongside the ship and bobbing Portuguese man-of-wars. The ship had a ballroom and a social hall, a gymnasium with weight benches and a punching bag, and a wood-paneled smoking parlor with plush sofas lining the walls where the passengers could gather in the evening. The bracing ocean air grew colder as the ship sailed north. Thrice-daily French classes took up Fries's days, taught by a Catholic chaplain, and soon French words and phrases began to creep into his daily letters home. He joined shuffleboard games on the deck and sometimes played low-stakes poker in the evening. Fog often shrouded the ship, but occasionally the skies cleared, revealing glassine ocean and flocks of birds that darted and dove around the decks and funnel of the ship. As the ship sailed into Canadian water, the temperature dropped precipitously. Unable to tell his wife the location of the boat, he described it drily as "somewhere near the north pole, judging from how cold it is."

The ship anchored in Nova Scotia for more than a week. Fries awoke each morning at 6:00 a.m. to exercise, bathed in cool saltwater baths, walked another thirty minutes around the deck, and then went for breakfast in the dining room. The air was clear and cold, the ocean still in all directions, as the days drifted slowly past, Fries keeping time by his daily exercise and rigorous language study, boasting that he could now count, name days of the week and the months of the year in French, and order off a menu. When he wasn't studying or dining at the lavish tables in the ship's dining hall, Fries improved his skills at bridge.

Not all was relaxation and leisure on the ship. Rumors flew through the ship that a new offensive had begun against the Germans. There were other more immediate worries: the threat of German submarines. Bantering with the captain, Fries learned that the *Orduña* had made thirty-one trips across the Atlantic and had encountered a U-boat only once. In the encounter, the small ship was fired upon but escaped without damage. "Besides the ship is itself now armed," Fries wrote to his wife.

As dusk fell on August 1, fog shrouded the *Orduña* as it prepared to raise anchor. Four other ships hulked nearby in the cloud banks enfolding Halifax. The four transports and a converted cruiser would cleave through the freezing ocean air with their lights doused, the navigators charting the convoy's position in impenetrable darkness, a project that made even the steely Fries nervous. After sundown, the firemen stoked the boilers, the *Orduña*'s engines powered up, and its funnel began to belch smoke. Cloaked in darkness, the convoy slipped through the waves to France.

Chapter Six

"Fiendish Work"

The British offensive that Fries heard rumors of on the ship had begun near Ypres, not far from where the Germans had released clouds of chlorine in 1915. The decision to launch the attack had been bitterly controversial. Prime Minister David Lloyd George felt that the Flanders offensive would be "a folly and a crime," and military advisers argued that the British should wait for the Americans. But General Douglas Haig had been determined to break the German line after his failure at Arras, and intelligence from the front hinted that the Germans were on the brink of collapse. Moreover, the British wanted to seize the Belgian coast and destroy two German submarine bases. There were strategic locations within British reach that would give tactical advantage to the Allies—the high ridge of Passchendaele, the rail hub at Roulers.

In the lead-up to the battle, word quickly reached the British commanders about an unfamiliar German weapon. On the night of July 12, tens of thousands of German shells tumbled down on two British divisions near Ypres. The shells carried unknown markings on their casings: a yellow cross. When the shells landed, they made a strange sound—a plop that came from a new German fuse. Inside was a liquid compound the British soldiers hadn't experienced before. When burster charges blew open a shell and a cloud of the aerated fluid wafted over unprepared soldiers, nothing happened immediately. When shells didn't burst but cracked open, the oily liquid settled to the ground in a thick dew and slowly dispersed. Sometimes the soldiers didn't even know they'd been exposed but for a faint smell of mustard or garlic that wafted to their noses. At first, soldiers removed their masks, believing the smell to be nothing more than an odorous ruse from the Germans.

But after several hours, their eyes began to sting and redden, and soon they were half blinded, tears oozing from bulging, swollen eyelids. It caused sneezing and vomiting, and then a dry, hacking cough from an inflamed throat. On the second day, enormous blisters appeared on the most tender parts of the body—the groin, the armpits, the chest. The blisters grew until they burst, causing infections. The gas seeped through uniforms, so even those who kept their masks on were affected and had to be stripped of their clothes and washed.

Some called it yellow cross because of the marks on the shell casings. Others called it Yperite, for the place where it was used. Some named it after its odor: mustard gas.

The French border city of Armentières had been a quiet sector, a refuge for old men and children and mothers; the young men had all gone to fight. Artillery rumbled at the front just a mile away, but within the city, the tea shops were open, and at night, a restaurant or two still laid out meals for patrons.

Falling shells shattered the peace in July; high explosives pulverized houses into dust and blasted out shop fronts, pounding the church of Saint-Vaast into a heap of masonry and broken buttresses and glass, scattering organ pipes among the rubble in the nave. As fires raged, the inhabitants fled into basements, seeking refuge belowground.

Overnight on July 20, the same day that Baker drew the first draft number in Washington, thousands of yellow-cross shells began to tumble onto Armentières. Too small to pierce the paving stones, the shells burst as they clattered onto the streets and buildings, releasing their oily contents. So many fell that rivulets of liquid ran in the streets, dripped from walls and gutters, and pooled in gardens and courtyards. The fumes wafted from room to room in houses and sank down into basements where residents huddled for safety, filling the enclosed spaces with the pungent odor of mustard or garlic.

As with the British soldiers, the fumes brought only sneezing and coughing at first. After several hours, residents' throats began to burn, then their eyes. Women were affected even more than men, because it clung to their long hair. Ambulances careened through the rubble, picking up stricken residents to bring to crowded hospitals at Hazebrouck, at Aire-sur-la-Lys and Saint-Pol-sur-Ternoise. The victims felt that they were burning inside. As they died, they suffered hideous hallucinations. The hospital halls filled with the sound of delirious laughter punctuated by silence. All of the parish churches in Armentières had been destroyed in earlier shelling, and Father Camelot, dean of Saint-Vaast, was the only priest left to minister to the sick. As he tended to his afflicted congregation, the mustard gas poisoned him little by little. Soon he, too, was dead.

The gas shelling of Armentières on July 20 and again a week later caused about 6,400 casualties; 675 were civilians, 86 of whom died. News of the debut of the German war gas didn't arrive in the United States immediately. It wasn't until August that a wire report ran in newspapers across the country about the attack on Armentières and the mysterious new weapon used there. "Fiendish Work of Devils in Human Form," one headline read, the article reporting that British medical officials were scrambling to determine the nature of the new poison, which was believed to be the same gas that had felled British soldiers earlier in July.

The reports were true, but only partially so—by the time the American public learned about the gas, the British and the French had already identified it. Within a day of the first time the new gas was used, British gas defense had found unexploded yellow-cross shells and defused them. One was sent back to London and the other to the BEF's central laboratory, where they were opened and the viscous, amber liquid inside was examined.

Both the French and the British quickly identified it as dichloro-ethyl sulfide. It was not a new chemical. An impure form had been discovered more than sixty years earlier, and two other chemists described its toxic properties shortly thereafter, reporting that even its vapors "when in contact with the more delicate parts of the skin of the body cause the most serious destruction." In 1886, a German chemist named Victor Meyer developed a production process, so in spring of 1917, when the Germans began searching for a new and more effective war gas, Haber and his colleagues already had a substantial body of literature about dichloroethyl sulfide and its awful effects.

Mustard gas was different from its predecessors—the asphyxiants, lachrymators, and sternutators. Mustard was a blister agent called a vesicant. When it came in contact with skin, pustules formed hours later, often in spots where the skin was most tender. The blisters caused agonizing pain as the skin separated from the underlying tissue. Clothing didn't provide protection: the liquid soaked through cloth and leather to the skin underneath. To make matters worse, it was still toxic if inhaled, even in small quantities, and caused terrible inflammation of the throat and lungs. It caused temporary blindness if it came into contact with soldiers' eyes. It could be lethal in high concentrations, but the vast majority of cases were long-lasting injuries that took exposed soldiers off the battlefield for eight weeks or more. While it had a distinctive smell, it could be faint and was easily masked with other gases.

But mustard's greatest advantage by far was how long it took to disperse—what the chemists called persistence. Unlike other gases that quickly dispersed or were swept away by wind, mustard lingered for days, and even longer in cold weather. It clung to trench walls and trees and pooled on the ground, where unsuspecting soldiers could step in it or lie in it days after a shell burst. It coated weapons and equipment, rendering them unusable. It settled onto unprotected rations, making food inedible and water undrinkable.

It was, the French and British grudgingly concluded, the perfect war gas.

The British fired off telegrams to their five field generals with warnings about mustard and guidelines for precautions, and circulated a detailed letter a few days later with descriptions of the shells and their markings, the effects of mustard, and the cause of casualties.

With the new peril of mustard on the battlefield, the dynamics of the war changed again. Other gases depended upon the element of surprise to be effective. If soldiers were suitably prepared, a gas attack was little more than a passing threat, one danger among many. But mustard was omnipresent, requiring constant vigilance to prevent masses of soldiers from being incapacitated. It demanded entirely new equipment, clothing, and even fabrics for protection. Soldiers needed new training all the way from the front down the supply chain, to be sure that equipment could be handled safely. The interlocking processes of coordinated activities on the lines—from detection and alert and identification of gases, to individual and collective protection, to treatment and morale—all had to be changed.

Mustard had a damaging impact even in locations where it wasn't being used—its novelty and its fearful effects fired rumors that raced through the Allied troops. That it caused sterility. That it caused arms and legs to fall off. Esprit de corps, already suffering among the Allies, plummeted further.

Compounding the insidious new problem of mustard, the Germans introduced another new war gas around the same time in 1917. Diphenylchloroarsine, a kind of sneezing agent, was neither a gas nor a liquid at all—it was a cloud of odorless particles, fired with high explosives and dispersed in the blast. Though it could be toxic in high concentrations, its bigger threat was that it penetrated masks and caused sneezing, coughing, and vomiting. Sometimes it was fired by itself in shells marked with a blue cross; other times it was mixed with lethal gases, such as with phosgene in green-cross shells. When coughing, vomiting soldiers tore off their masks to breathe, they were exposed to lethal gases. Mustard so preoccupied the British that it wasn't until August 1917 that were able to identify the new substance.

General Pershing personally opposed chemical warfare as cruel and morally abhorrent, but it was a reality on the battlefield that he could not ignore. While he was learning about these harsh realities almost as quickly as his British and French allies, an ocean separated him from the War Department and the investigators in Washington. In the War Department cablegram of July 13, when he learned about the twenty thousand defective masks from the Bureau of Mines, he also learned details about the organization of the gas service in Washington for the first time.

His principal link with the efforts back in the United States was George Hulett, Manning's scientific ambassador. Hulett's scientific expedition was nearing its end. The National Research Council had sent the Princeton chemist as an emissary of chemists generally, but his singular focus on gas warfare to the exclusion of other problems provoked protest from other members of the delegation. Ames, the delegation organizer who had initially welcomed Hulett so warmly, had soured on the Princeton chemist for his constant attention to gas warfare. "Hulett has spent all his time on gas attacks, so as to help the Bureau of Mines (which pays his bills). I have protested, but in vain," he complained.

As the yellow-cross shells containing mustard tumbled onto Armentières, Hulett had been in London and beginning to get homesick—his mail had been held in France, and he hadn't heard from his family since early June. He didn't care for the bread—"hard to get and terrible when you do"—and longed for the cuisine of

France. He was even more anxious to return home when he finally got his mail in Paris and learned that his wife had been ill. "I am so anxious to see you," he wrote home plaintively. He would return to the States at once on the *Chicago,* the same ship that brought him over, bringing back the catalog of chemical warfare information that he had accumulated.

As Hulett's departure approached, he and Pershing quickly drew up plans in early August for the overseas organization, a copy of which Hulett scrawled onto Princeton University letterhead. The organizational chart that Hulett sketched out was completely different than the one Manning had drawn up in the States. Crucially, at the top of Hulett's chart was the AEF commander in chief— Pershing—and the War Department; the Bureau of Mines didn't even appear anywhere on the chart. Pershing also wrote a letter for Hulett to personally deliver to the army adjutant general with a series of recommendations. Not only should a high-ranking military officer be in charge of the domestic service, but the rapidly growing expertise of the AEF in Europe should guide the research directions, and the efforts in America should be subordinate to the overseas division, where the army was in closer proximity to the battlefield. He also recommended building a research lab in France.

Pershing sent a cablegram to the War Department on August 7, outlining his recommendations and reporting that Hulett would return shortly to the United States with the AEF's plans. Pershing made sure that Van Manning knew that his emissary was en route. "Please inform Director Manning, Bureau of Mines," Pershing added to the cablegram.

Hulett left for the United States that same day, bringing with him the plans that he and Pershing had drawn up. When Hulett stepped off the boat in New York on August 19, he carried the letter from Pershing to the army adjutant general with the same urgent recommendations for the organization of the service in France, a lab for research work, and—at the top of the list—the demand for an army officer to be put in charge of the domestic work. Not only should the military be in charge of the service, but the growing expertise of the AEF in Europe should provide the direction for the service.

Hulett didn't go immediately to Washington—first he took the train up to Princeton. He was so impatient to get home that he set out on foot from the train station to his family homestead. His wife, Dency, and their son George were away, but he checked on the garden and the chickens in their coop. Pershing had asked him to return to France as a top chemical adviser, but after Hulett came home, the homesick chemist declined the general's request, opting instead to organize a war research laboratory at Princeton and commute to Washington several days a week.

After his stopover at home, he was off to Washington to confer with the Bureau of Mines and to pass on Pershing's recommendations for organizing the gas service. Warnings about gas had barely moved military leaders in the lead-up to the war. Now, with generals in France, it had become clear how crucial chemistry had become on the battlefield, demanding offensive and defensive strategies that constantly evolved. Specially trained soldiers were needed to handle gas on the front. But the arriving officers and soldiers knew almost nothing of gas warfare, and General Pershing needed someone to take charge. Someone like Amos A. Fries.

Fries's passage across the Atlantic had been a largely uneventful trip, full of brisk exercise and French classes and hearty meals, the only discomfort the frigid cold of the North Atlantic. Nine days after leaving Halifax, the *Orduña* steamed into submarine-infested waters. As dusk approached, signal lights appeared ahead—British destroyers to escort the convoy toward Liverpool. Two days later, as the ship prepared to dock, the submarine alarm suddenly rang, and the passengers on the *Orduña* could see a commotion in the waters about a mile offshore. Two destroyers raced toward the spot, and one of them rocked suddenly in the water. With the submarine threat at hand, the *Orduña* turned and anchored offshore for safety, away from the docks. "I think most of us slept but little. It was our most uncomfortable period on shipboard," Fries recalled.

The boat docked the next morning. Fries disembarked with about twenty other engineers and boarded a train to cross Britain to the English Channel for passage to France the following day, August 13. As the train crossed the countryside, Fries marveled at the quaint villages, the rolling hills, and lush meadows. He spent the night in Folkestone on the coast. Late in the day, he boarded his transport, one of five ships in a channel convoy, and set out for France at full speed. The channel waters were placid as a fishpond in the sultry summer air. Destroyers sliced through the waters around them, and blimps hovered above. After Fries disembarked, he boarded a train to Paris. Sixteen engineers crammed into a compartment intended for eight; the men took turns standing through the night as the train rumbled across the countryside. It pulled into the Gare du Nord at 6:00 a.m. They had a meager breakfast of rolls, jam, and tea at their hotel. Fries had a top-floor room, with a view of the Eiffel Tower and the Tuileries.

At 9:30 a.m., he reported to the AEF's chief engineer, General Harry Taylor, who gave him the job he had expected, director of roads. Relieved that he knew what was expected of him, he wrote home that he was pleased with the assignment. "It will be very hard in some ways and get worse as the war develops but it is vital in any advance and I believe I can make good and help the cause here probably more than in any other capacity."

The army gave Fries an office, assigned him four clerks, provided him with equipment and supplies. He got to work, happy to be able to contribute in his area of expertise.

A few days later, a general staff officer named Alvin Barber walked into his office. Barber asked Fries if he'd rather have a different job: director of the gas service. The question took Fries aback. He stammered that he didn't know anything about gas. Barber launched into a lecture for thirty minutes or so about the importance of the British gas service, the generals who led it, and what an opportunity it would present. Fries asked Barber if he could think about it overnight. He conferred with his fellow officers in the evening and finally concluded that "I might as well be the goat as anybody else." The next day, he accepted.

Fries now had a job that he'd never heard of. "I am to be the chief of gas, O no, not hot air, but the offensive and defensive warfare with gas,—gas clouds, gas bombs, gas shells, gas masks, liquid fire, and all the rest of the hellish paraphernalia invented to date in connection with gas and liquid fire. It is a big job—Barber says one of the biggest in the whole field. I will have to organize or at least control a corps of chemists, maybe two, and several schools to teach all men how to avoid the evil effects of gas, how and when to use it, how to detect it in the air, or when being fired from bombs, ad infinitum," he wrote. The enormous British service had several thousand men, and there was a note of pride in Fries's words that he had been chosen for this task. "I get the job from having the reputation as a hustler," he wrote. "I am inclined to think myself in big luck to be here now as later I would not get half as good a chance as either one of the jobs handed me so far."

On August 18, Fries met with Pershing for the first time since his appointment. It had been a decade and a half since Fries had glimpsed Pershing in the Philippines, bent over a chessboard across from a Moro chief. The general was delighted to see him, Fries wrote home to Bessie. Despite his reservations about gas warfare, Pershing needed someone to organize and command the gas warfare work that Hulett had begun. That day, Pershing wired the War Department: "Have appointed Lieut. Col. Fries Director of Gas Service. Request organization of Gas and Flame Service regiment in United States so arranged that Lieut. Col. Fries as senior will remain in charge of Gas and Flame Service." One of the first orders of business for Fries after he took office was to order gas masks—one hundred thousand from the British and one hundred thousand from the French.

When Fries began his new job on August 22, an officer handed him a thin folder—the sum of everything the AEF knew about war gases. Fries was astonished to learn that only a few officers knew anything about gas warfare at all, and those that did had gleaned their information from the British. He had only two officers, no gas masks, no gas, no literature, and no organization. He was starting from scratch. He even invented his title, calling himself "chief" because he disliked the word "director." "It's a big job and a vital one to the army, and no one seems to have wanted to go into the thing so the dearth of information is startling," he wrote home to Bessie.

Fries began sketching the chart of the new service and drafting the order that would create it. For three days, he motored back and forth between the army's offices in a chauffeured Ford that careened through the streets, making Fries fear for the lives of pedestrians. For a month, there had been silence from Manning and Burrell in Washington. No help or information had been sent, and the reams of reports that the chemists were generating back in Washington were not making it to Europe. "Nothing is known of activities of Bureau of Mines in these matters except information received in personal letters to individuals written about the middle of July," Pershing complained in a cable to Washington on August 24. With scant help coming from Washington, Fries relied instead on his allies in Europe. In nearly every way, his new service mirrored the British organization, from the acquisition of Stokes mortars to organization of special units trained to handle and deploy gas.

When he brought a draft of his plan to Pershing, the general wanted to know why the British had special units to handle gas rather than letting artillery regiments fire gas mortars. Fries admitted he had no idea. "Well, don't you think you better beat it up to the British gas service in the field and find out about these Stokes mortars?" Pershing asked.

"General, that is exactly what I want to do," Fries told him.

"All right," Pershing said, "get going and take anybody you want with you."

Fries wrote to Bessie that he was going away on a trip for three or four days, and reassured her that he would be nowhere near the fighting and didn't expect to be away for a long time. His comforting words were far from true—in fact, he was going to the front.

On the fresh, bright morning of August 25, Fries, two other officers, and their driver left Paris in a Cadillac for Saint-Omer, the field headquarters of the British gas service about 160 miles away, on the northwest coast near Dunkirk. The few days of sun and warmth were unusual that August—for most of the month, drenching rains had been falling over France. It was a scenic drive across the countryside, and they arrived at the headquarters in late afternoon. They spent the evening in conference with their British counterparts before Fries retired to his hotel. Then, in the morning, the British took Fries and his officers up to the line.

For the first time, Fries was within artillery range of the Germans. About a mile away from the lines, they stopped and watched as high-explosive shells fell at the end of the Messines Ridge. The detonations threw huge columns of black smoke high into the air, a sight he grew accustomed to over the coming months. It also made him realize the peril facing the newly arrived American soldiers at Gondrecourt, the U.S. training grounds. There were already about twelve thousand American soldiers within thirty miles of the front, and not a single one had a mask or any training with gas.

The British volunteered everything that they knew about mustard gas and were candid about what they didn't know—it was still so new that they didn't even yet know whether blinded soldiers would regain their sight. Cordial and helpful to Fries, they seemed determined to help prevent him from repeating their mistakes of the past. They told him about their early findings that oil-impregnated fabric could block mustard gas and that uniforms soaked in linseed oil might afford protection. They showed him hand-colored photographs and drawings of mustard burns. He learned about the twenty thousand masks that Burrell's Research Division had sent over and why they were inadequate. He learned about the first airplane bombs, incendiary devices that were small but nonetheless quite deadly; aerial gas bombs were not being used. He learned about antiaircraft shells, the three-inch shells called archies that were flung by the thousands to bring down aircraft. He guessed that such defenses would only drive airplanes higher but "could not stop airplanes from bombarding cities."

The British officers made an indelible impression on Fries. They provided everything Fries asked for and attempted to answer all of his questions. "They were able, fearless, energetic and active," Fries wrote. In particular, Charles Howard Foulkes, the chief of the British gas troops promoted to brigadier general in June, made an indelible impression. Both men were engineers, and both had been thrust into their roles in charge of gas without any previous knowledge or experience. Fries's service was new and untested, an evolving improvisational organization, just as Foulkes's had been in its earliest days. "The men who came into it were not afraid of new ideas, not afraid of treading unknown paths, nor afraid of the terror of night or those of the day, of the unseen gas or the hovering airplane," he later wrote.

By the time Fries returned to Paris two days later, the sunny weather had evaporated. As his Cadillac barreled across the countryside, a powerful gale buffeted the car with whipping winds and cascades of rain.

As the front receded behind Fries, the soldiers there were not so lucky. Amid the endless rains, the British had launched yet another new offensive in Ypres in late August. The British Royal Artillery struggled to pull their guns through a soup of mud that turned shell craters into water-soaked graves. Gas was everywhere. The plop of yellow-cross fuses and spraying mustard gas forced the

British and French to keep their masks in place day and night. They slithered and waded through the mire that spread in every direction, interrupted by inverted roots of toppled trees. Hundreds of miles of wooden duckboards snaked across the front, a maze of walkways that barely kept the men above the mud. At times, impenetrable volleys of artillery and shells arched overhead. With each detonation, the mud and the water quivered like jelly, and explosions threw curtains of mud over the soldiers as they splashed in their sodden trenches. The stench of rotting bodies hung over the battlefield. After sunset each night, the flash and concussion of bursting shells lit up the night, with colored flares raking the sky with streaks of yellow, green, and red phosphorus. The rain forced the British to call off the offensive. The stalemate resumed.

The dismal conditions of the front were a world away from the bright lights of Manhattan. As the evening performance ended at the Eltinge Theater on August 22, the crowd spilled from the lobby onto the sidewalk, where the blazing marquee overhead advertised *Business Before Pleasure,* the latest smash success from director Montague Glass. It was a warm, clear Wednesday evening. As the crowd milled on the sidewalk, a sleek Rolls-Royce purred at the curb. It was a gorgeous car, all elegant lines and gleaming chrome, its lustrous body painted blue.

A group of theater-goers burst from the theater doors—two men accompanied by three young women. Richmond M. Levering was one of the five. He was tall, just under six feet, husky and solid as a boxer, with hound-dog jowls and drooping bags under his eyes. But the member of the group that drew stares was one of the three women by his side. Draped in jewels, alluring and sultry, the showgirl Billie Allen was instantly recognizable as much for her stage roles as her antics reported in the society pages of the New York tabloids. The Texas beauty was a Ziegfeld Follies dancer who had caused a minor scandal for her outlandish costumes. She was also married—very publicly so. Offstage, Billie Allen was Mrs. John A. Hoagland, the wife of a millionaire heir to a baking-powder empire.

Levering, Mrs. Hoagland, and their companions pranced through the crowd and piled inside the blue Rolls-Royce, the chauffeur slamming the doors behind them. Other theatergoers stared as the car pulled away from the curb and shot down Forty-Second Street with the glamorous Broadway star inside. But there was something else noteworthy about the flashy car: a metal sign attached to the radiator grille. Eighteen inches across, the sign read in impossible-to-ignore letters: DEPARTMENT OF JUSTICE.

Two days later, a report from the Office of Naval Intelligence landed in front of A. Bruce Bielaski, chief of the Department of Justice's Bureau of Investigation in Washington. The terse letter from Commander Edward McCauley Jr. needed little embellishment. The Office of Naval Intelligence had received a letter from New York describing the car and the flamboyant passengers. In a dry and disapproving tone, the letter made clear that the dancer and her companions had made quite a splash. "Miss Billie Allen is probably as well known as any young woman in New York," Bielaski read. "The two men and the three women entered the Rolls-Royce car bearing the inscription 'Department of Justice,' attracting a great deal of attention as they did so."

The letter went on to say that the car was registered with the secretary of state as belonging to one Mr. Richmond Levering.

Levering had been with the bureau for less than four months, and in that short time, he had already proved to be an exasperating distraction and a headache. Technically, he didn't even work for the bureau; he headed the New York branch of the American Protective League, a civilian police auxiliary of the Department of Justice. After an uneventful start for Levering, word trickled back to the department that New York businessmen were astonished that Levering had been put in charge of the organization. He wasn't exactly an exemplar of upright living, it turned out.

Bielaski already had plenty to worry about. The Bureau of Investigation was only a small agency, its meager resources stretched thin pursuing spies and labor radicals. Bielaski had just ordered his agents to begin chasing down slackers, draft dodgers who failed or refused to register. Only a few days before, saboteurs had tried to dynamite the water main in San Diego. As if that weren't enough, now he had a rogue special agent cavorting around Manhattan with a showgirl, bringing embarrassing attention to the bureau in the midst of wartime.

The escapade with the car was foolish but hardly surprising. Levering lived in a gilded world greased with the easy money of oil. A young man of thirty-six, he lived at the sumptuous St. Regis, one of New York's most luxurious hotels, and had a country estate on Long Island. He vacationed regularly in Europe and, for recreation, invited friends to sail up the coast in his yacht to fish in Newfoundland. His motorboat, the *Heather*, had won a New York–to–Bermuda race, and he owned a fleet of Rolls-Royces. Boisterous and temperamental, he drank little or perhaps not at all, cavorted with Broadway stars—particularly actresses—and invested in theatrical productions. He had always been a ladies' man. His first wife had very publicly divorced him in 1915, reverted to her maiden name, and forced him to surrender nearly all of his rights to their three children, a lopsided agreement reported breathlessly in the New York newspapers.

Levering was not a handsome man, with his large hooked nose and a pale, almost cadaverous appearance, but he had a magnetic personality that suggested supreme self-confidence in everything he did. He was a consummate dealmaker, a fast talker with a silken and reassuring nature that swept away questions about the extravagant transactions he proposed to deep-pocketed investors.

Levering had grown up in Lafayette, Indiana, the only child of Julia and Mortimer Levering, a successful banker. His parents bundled him off to a prestigious East Coast boarding school, and then he proceeded to Yale, where he rowed crew and graduated from the college's Sheffield Scientific School. His first business venture out of college was the Indian Asphalt Company. The company obtained oil leases in his home state, primarily to commercialize asphalt, but also to sell refined oil as a by-product to the Standard Oil Company. The company had a promising start, but then the finances of the company all but collapsed, revealing stock manipulation and other unsavory practices. An investigation by one of the company financiers, a New York banker, found Levering to be at fault. The banker forced him out and shuttered the troubled company, creating the first of Levering's many enemies.

One of Levering's indisputable strengths was his ability to turn failure into advantage, capitalizing off the detritus of one disastrous venture to build the next. He convinced one of his Yale classmates, William Barnum, to go into business with him in a new undertaking, the Indian Refining Company. Like its predecessor, it would lease oil properties in Kentucky, Ohio, and Indiana and sell the refined oil to Standard.

Deploying his substantial charms, Levering also courted Barnum's sister Laura. The couple married in 1905 and moved to Lexington, Kentucky. Levering asked his father-in-law to help finance the new company and then made the rounds among the wealthiest financiers in Cincinnati seeking investors. One was William Cooper Procter of Procter & Gamble, who became one of the largest shareholders; another was William Rowe, president of the First National Bank of Cincinnati; a third was Julius Fleischmann, president of the Fleischmann Yeast Company.

The company built a refinery near Indianapolis and began making money, but there was something peculiar about the finances. Levering had taken control of the company's day-to-day affairs and was shifting large amounts of money between accounts in New York and Cincinnati. He explained to shareholders that the money was for investigations of oil concessions in Russia, but an investigation showed that he was actually using the money for personal expenses to subsidize his lavish lifestyle. In 1912, the stockholders ousted him and ordered him to return some four hundred thousand dollars to the company. He never paid.

His third venture was in real estate. Before the Indian Refining Company went bad, he formed a new corporation, the Gardiner's Bay Company, to buy hundreds of acres of prime real estate on the southern tip of Long Island, a few miles west of Montauk Point, and created a community called Devon. He subdivided the land and sold the lots for large summerhouses to the same Cincinnati businessmen who invested in the Indian Refining Company. The community had its own yacht club, and Levering put himself in charge of building the houses. However, when the buyers inquired about their houses, they learned not only that none of the builders had been paid but that the houses would cost more than double the estimated twenty-five to thirty thousand dollars. Levering claimed ignorance and assigned one of his most loyal and dedicated employees to investigate, who turned over a damning report to the investors without letting Levering see it first. Levering summoned him to New York, where he was seized and involuntarily committed to a lunatic asylum. Levering, meanwhile, told the other shareholders that the records for the Gardiner's Bay Company had gone missing and that the employee was a crook who had stolen their money.

With his former investors furious, Levering all but disappeared for two years, practically abandoning his wife and three children in Kentucky. The swelling ranks of his enemies and former business partners were more than happy to be rid of him. In reality, he was still at work on other more ambitious ventures. These enterprises were overseas. Rather than enlisting the support of wealthy industrials and bankers, he would get the backing of the world's deepest pockets—the U.S. government.

During his years after the collapse of the Indian Refining Company, Levering formed a bevy of intertwined companies with stakes in overseas drilling. One of them purported to have secured rights to oil fields near Tampico, Mexico, a brawling, hardscrabble Gulf Coast boomtown about three hundred miles south of the

U.S. border. Mexico was the world's second-largest producer of oil after the United States, and millions of gallons of oil flowed through Tampico and Veracruz farther south. Levering claimed that his drilling rights would yield thousands of barrels of oil every day and more than a million each year. He also claimed to have ventures in Cuba, Colombia, and Venezuela.

Tampico was hardly a safe investment with its mixture of labor unrest, revolutionary insurrection, and volatile politics. Levering and dozens of other oilmen formed an association to secure assurances of military protection and diplomatic backing from President Wilson and the State Department, but their efforts were rebuffed. His overtures to the British ambassador for help were warmly received but also yielded no promises.

As war loomed toward the end of 1916, he made a proposal to the U.S. government to form a partnership with the Navy Fuel Board that would give the navy rights to the oil from Levering's wells, and he would set up new companies created for the sole purpose of supplying oil to the navy. All he asked was a 5 percent royalty. In March of 1917, he asked the board to ink the deal. "By the operation of the above contracts, you can see that the Navy can count on a reserve not hitherto available, and of course not obtainable by the United States itself, as none of these countries permit foreign governments to operate within their boundaries."

As part of the deal, Levering asked the navy to accept his claims regarding his foreign holdings in March of 1917, on the eve of war:

> I would be glad if you would record with the proper officials that Richmond Levering and Company has oil rights on about 60 square miles of territory in Cuba; on about 1,000,000 acres in the Republic of Columbia [sic], and are obtaining concession rights on a very large oil territory in the United States of Venezuela. We are, as you know, largely interested in about 500,000 acres of the best selected oil territory in Mexico.

The navy wasn't the only arm of the U.S. government that Levering wanted closer ties with. On March 16, 1917, an intriguing letter landed on Bruce Bielaski's desk at the Bureau of Investigation. William Offley, the Bureau of Investigation's division superintendent in New York, had had a long conversation with Levering that morning and had come away deeply impressed by the oilman and his overseas ventures. His concessions in Mexico gave him the right to build radio towers, which he would allow Bureau of Investigation radio operators to use. He was also more than willing to use the imprimatur of his company to send agents to any of the countries where he had business interests and said that he had close ties with the Cuban secret service, which would be only too happy to assist with intelligence matters. Levering was "a gentleman of standing and reputation," Offley wrote, and the bureau might have a place for Levering in an unofficial capacity: in a new organization called the American Protective League.

The American Protective League was a civilian intelligence organization, the creation of a wealthy Chicago advertising executive named Albert M. Briggs. There was little in the papers about the league; it was a quiet organization, operating in the shadows and oiled with private money. Briggs had proposed the organization to Bielaski as a way to harness the talents and zeal of hundreds of thousands of older men ineligible to serve in the army or navy but eager nonetheless to aid in the war effort.

The Bureau of Investigation was stretched thin. Prewar revelations about German espionage showed the limited abilities of existing law-enforcement organizations to root out spies, saboteurs, and seditionists. Nationwide, the Bureau of Investigation had only a few hundred agents, the Treasury Department had a similarly tiny number, as did the Office of Naval Intelligence and the Military Intelligence Division of the army. Yet men from coast to coast were eager to play a role in the war, even if they couldn't enlist. Briggs posited that if they were organized into an unpaid auxiliary corps—a patriotic civilian police force—the Department of Justice would instantly have eyes on every street corner in America, agents eager to peer into the shadows of German clubs and labor union halls. They could gather valuable intelligence about propagandists and agitators and direct badge-carrying agents to their homes. Not just anyone would be allowed to join—they would seek out well-connected men of means, with authority and resources at their disposal.

Levering seemed like a perfect candidate to head the league in New York, and his overseas businesses could extend the government's counterespionage operations far beyond U.S. borders. Agents could travel to all of these countries under the guise of working for Richmond Levering & Company, posing as engineers or oilmen. Wireless radio towers built on his territory could aid the bureau in intercepting German transmissions.

Levering was also tight with the pro-American government in Cuba. "He states that the present government in Cuba is very friendly with the United States, and that he, Levering, is in a position to secure the active aid of the secret service of the Republic, as is also our military attaché," Offley wrote. Germans considered Mexico and Cuba to be hospitable safe havens, and both countries seethed with smugglers and spies operating just outside the U.S. jurisdiction. Having a patriotic counterweight such as Levering in those places, someone who knew the terrain and could pierce the local political intrigue, would be a tremendous asset for the Americans.

Four days later, Bielaski had approved Briggs's plan for the league, on March 22, 1917, two weeks before Congress declared war. Briggs appointed Levering as head of the New York league on May 4. He undertook an ambitious organization of the New York league, proposing twelve different bureaus, each in charge of a different aspect of security against espionage. Levering offered his own company offices as the bureau headquarters, located on the twenty-ninth floor of the Equitable Building in Lower Manhattan.

The early cases he handled were not of the highest caliber. He investigated a dog club whose owner was suspected of being pro-German. He nosed around the Plaza Hotel, where the chief waiter in the café had been overheard denouncing the Allies in Europe. He dropped in on an Upper East Side art gallery because the dealer was known to be "rabidly pro-German." Still, Levering's gusto impressed his champion, Offley. "Mr. Levering is displaying some considerable enthusiasm," Offley wrote to Bielaski soon after Levering was installed in the position.

But his appointment was not greeted with the same enthusiasm in business circles. Bielaski and Offley soon learned about Levering's less-than-shining reputation. Some businessmen had been astonished by Levering's elevation to the important post and quietly told his superiors at the Justice Department that his spotty credentials threatened to tarnish the bureau and the Secret Service. And in July, stockholders of two companies had sued Levering in federal court in Virginia, accusing him of a $50 million stock swindle. After the department received yet another negative report about Levering, Bielaski passed it on to Offley with a worried note about their agent. "I enclose herewith a copy of a confidential report concerning Richmond Levering, which if it is true in any large part, indicates that we have had something put over on us," he had written. More and more, that seemed to be the case.

The dustup with the Department of Justice plate on Levering's car and flouncing around town with a notorious showgirl was now the latest headache. Even more infuriating, it wasn't the first time it had happened. His chauffeur had been arrested for speeding in Hampstead, Long Island, in the same car with the same metal sign and summoned to court to answer charges before a judge.

Levering agreed to return the plate but pleaded ignorance of wrongdoing. The letter's tone was less than contrite, even a little combative. "I desire to call your attention to the fact that all other state and city departments have the privilege of special signs, except the United States Department of Justice," he wrote. "Would it not seem fair that our people received the same courtesy as others engaged in similar volunteer war work?"

Levering had been affiliated with the league and the bureau for less than four months and had already proved to be a disaster. His reputation was so dubious that potential patrons of the league considered Levering a blight on the organization and were considering withholding their support. Briggs—the founder of the American Protective League—informed Levering that he wanted to reorganize the New York branch and asked for the resignation of Levering and his twelve deputies. Miffed, Levering stepped down. His letter to Briggs had a distinctly sour tone. "I wish to state once more that I do not approve either of your plan or methods in this reorganization," he wrote. He also managed to get into a testy squabble with a bureau agent on his way out the door. The agent, a man named Underhill, warned Bielaski that "any further connection between Mr. Richmond Levering and the department is likely to prove highly dangerous to the Department's interests."

But even before Levering had departed, he was already looking for a new angle: to use his overseas connections to leverage an ongoing relationship with the bureau. Soon he was sending letters to Bielaski about his political connections in Latin America, including in Cuba. His company had an office in Havana, and he boasted about his close ties to Cuban military officials and politicians, including the president, who he claimed was a one-third owner of his oil venture there. "Any information we wanted from Cuba, all we had to do was go to President Menocal," he wrote. Perhaps the inveterate showman, the oilman with the transatlantic connections, might prove useful after all.

On the evening of August 30, Fries took a long walk through the heart of Paris and circled the Eiffel Tower, which the French army had turned into an enormous radio antenna. In a few days, he would leave Paris for the AEF headquarters at Chaumont. He welcomed the move—he had been in Paris for several days and had tired of bouncing back and forth between government office buildings and wasting time waiting for meetings. He didn't have the staff that he needed, and he was hamstrung by the silence from the chemists in Washington, who seemed deaf to the urgency of the gas situation. Fries was at work organizing the AEF Gas Service, fortified with knowledge from his trip to the front. Earlier that day, Pershing had sent a cable labeled CONFIDENTIAL to the War Department. It was a warning about mustard. "Since July 18 the British have suffered 20,000 casualties from this gas alone. Five percent have been fatal; 14 percent have been serious, while the balance have been mild," he wrote. It was a primer on the gas, describing its properties and its symptoms—the burns and blisters, the blindness, the insidious ability to seep through clothes. "The only defense is prompt use of the gas mask, and even this only guarantees a reduction in losses," the cable read.

On the first of September, Fries set out for Chaumont. Cold had set in as his powerful Cadillac raced east across the countryside. The car sped past gleaners bringing in the harvest, and young children waved at the passing car, crying, "*Vive l'America!*" Fries's quarters in Chaumont were in a grand mansion filled with a "vast and elegant silence." There were both army offices and living quarters, but Fries rarely saw anyone else in the building except for the housekeeper and the reclusive gatekeeper's wife who admitted him every time he arrived. He was assigned an enormous high-ceilinged room with a marble fireplace, tall mirrors with gilded frames, a rolltop desk, a huge four-poster mahogany bed, and an ornate gilt-and-glass chandelier to light the room. He had to pass through five doors to reach the nearest bathroom, and he puzzled over the house's lack of bathtubs. At night, Fries would gather for an hour or so with the other resident officers for dinner before retiring to his room to write letters or study French. During one dinner, an engineer joked about how the people at home were worrying they were suffering hard times in the trenches, and Fries wrote home to Bessie that it was far from a hovel.

Two days after Fries arrived in Chaumont, Pershing approved his plan for the new gas service and sent out General Order 31. Just five sentences and an accompanying organizational chart, the order relating to the service began: "There is established a department of the American Expeditionary Forces to be known as the Gas Service." The order was broad, giving Fries latitude in building up this new service.

The day after the AEF issued the order forming the gas service, Fries received a promotion to colonel and the silver eagle pins to go with it the next day. He also became the commander of the future regiment that would be trained to use chemicals, the Thirtieth Engineers (Gas and Flame).

Fries needed men and supplies. He needed gas and factories to make it. He needed the regiment that would have the skills to use gas. He needed offensive and defensive instruction. He needed a laboratory of his own. And he needed to convince the army that gas was a vital part of the war effort. Frustrated by inertia in Washington and the shortage of staff, he cabled the War Department constantly. The War Department insisted it could spare no officers for Fries. "Well, if swearing would do any good I sure would break this silence with a roar that would shake the walls," he wrote in a letter to Bessie.

Within a few days, he had put in a massive order for offensive gas equipment: fifty thousand gas cylinders. Fifty thousand Livens drums. Twenty thousand projectors. Stokes mortars and bombs. The general staff must have been flabbergasted to receive the request for items that no one in the army knew anything about or, perhaps, had even heard of.

During his time at Chaumont, Fries went to see General William Sibert and one of his sons. Fries hoped to get Sibert's son as an aide in the new gas service. When he met the father and son for lunch, Fries noted to Bessie that the elder Sibert "looks to have aged a great deal since last January though it may be only my imagination."

It was not his imagination. Unlike Fries, who had Pershing's blessing, Sibert was having a difficult time with his commander in chief. On the same day that Fries had driven out for lunch, Pershing had inspected Sibert's First Division. It was a disaster. Sibert and his officers had only learned of Pershing's review the night before; and to make matters worse, the general announced he was going to bring the president of France with him. The location Sibert's aide hurriedly chose for the inspection was a muddy, miserable spot, and since word of the inspection had come so late, far-flung squads in billets twenty and thirty miles away had to march all night to get there in the morning. The men appeared exhausted and glum as they slithered in the mud in front of President Poincaré and the mortified Pershing. It was a ragged, amateurish display. The soldiers were still barely more than recruits, and what training they had received from the French had largely been in practical combat skills, not marching in formation.

The whole spectacle was so embarrassing for Pershing that he dressed down Sibert afterward. What was wrong? Pershing demanded. Why was progress so slow? Sibert kept a tactful silence, and Pershing angrily stalked away. As if that weren't bad enough, Sibert left later that day on a three-day trip to Montreux without informing Pershing or seeking his permission. Pershing, already irate at his second-in-command, wrote a reprimand letter for Sibert's personnel file.

Goliath was well liked among his fellow officers — he was amiable and collegial, always willing to take advice — but to Pershing he was weak and inexperienced, with little of the fortitude necessary to be a commander. He didn't even look the part of a general. To Pershing's critical eye, the men of the First Division had progressed little in their training, and he feared that they would not get the discipline that they needed from Sibert. Summer was turning into fall, and the Americans at the training fields in Gondrecourt were not ready for war. Sibert was the man charged with making them so, and he was failing. In a confidential memo to Secretary Baker, he complained that Sibert was too old, slow, and set in his ways and lacked the instincts of a soldier. "I think that I shall be compelled to replace him before his division goes into the trenches, as the responsibility is too great to take the risk of leaving him in command," Pershing wrote.

It was clear to everyone that Sibert was not among Pershing's favored and that his position was tenuous. His loyal aides, deeply sympathetic, felt he was being unfairly blamed, but who was going to risk his career to tell that to Black Jack Pershing? And so Sibert suffered in silence. Over lunch, Sibert most likely said nothing to Fries of his difficulties, but his appearance gave Fries pause.

Fries succeeded in persuading Sibert's son to come over to his fledgling organization, and within a few days, he had requested the younger Sibert for his staff. Getting officers was a universal headache; every part of the AEF was desperate for talented officers. That went double for Fries, who only had two aides. Fries soon lured over to his staff a particularly capable lieutenant named Richard Crawford, who had graduated from West Point in 1914 and was stationed with the engineers on a hillside farm near Gondrecourt. The day after Crawford started, Fries assigned him a car and sent him on a six-hundred-mile trip to find storage areas and dumps for the new gas service. He was gone for a week and found fifteen sites.

"Capt. Crawford appears to be a hustler and very desirous of doing everything in his power to make things a success, so apparently I drew a good man," Fries wrote to Bessie with satisfaction. A second officer—a lieutenant who had been stringing electrical lights for the engineers—was soon added, bringing Fries's staff to four. His fledgling organization had begun to grow, and he was waiting on four other requests, one of them Sibert's son.

Fries boasted to Bessie that he was gaining a reputation as a go-getter who was able to wrangle what he needed out of the creaking army bureaucracy. Even getting something as simple as desks for his offices was a challenge, but Fries always managed. Fellow officers were amazed that he was able to finagle supplies and staff from the army.

On September 16, Fries and his staff met in Paris for what would be the first of several conferences among the Allies about chemical warfare. The event was hosted by the French, and in addition to Fries, there were delegates from Britain, Belgium, and Italy. The conference focused largely on the medical treatment of mustard and defense against gas.

The conference invigorated the indefatigable Fries. After he returned to Chaumont, he began working on a cablegram that would go to the chief of engineers on September 25. It was a sweeping directive that, perhaps more than any previous order, illuminated the future scope of the growing overseas service. First, Fries wanted his own research lab in France. The cablegram read:

> Send at once chemical laboratory complete with equipment and personnel, including physiological and pathological sections, for extensive chemical investigations of gases and powders. Arrangements made for physiological chief from medical personnel now in Europe. The laboratory is to be auxiliary to the one in the United States and is for local emergency investigations to meet the constant changes in gases and powders used by the enemy and by ourselves.

Then he inquired about the capacity to manufacture war gases and the availability of precursor chemicals, including those for making mustard. "This material urgently needed in manufacturing a new gas for allies; also needed for our own troops. French desire about 75 tons of glycerine and 75 tons sodium cyanide each month." He went on to propose a system for manufacturing gas and packing it into shells and wrote that American troops would need the same offensive equipment as the British. "The principal material used are 4-inch Stokes mortars, 8-inch Livens projectors, and gas cylinders. Chief ordnance officer will be directed to send samples of above apparatus, including bombs," he wrote. He ended by proposing that the invaluable George Hulett be assigned to the gas service in Washington "to handle all orders and correspondence concerning gas matters and avoid duplication and possible confusion and delay."

He was, as he put it later, "selling gas warfare to the army," building a case for making it an integral part of the army's strategy. His work was also creating what would become a new and troublesome dimension in the evolution of the gas service. There were now essentially *two* services: the domestic service and his overseas service in the AEF. Fries was well aware that his constant demands probably angered his counterparts in the United States, but it didn't bother him. "Perhaps they don't appreciate it but I'm too far away to hear them swear so I won't worry," he wrote to Bessie.

As September turned to October, the weather was beautiful— too beautiful for war, Fries mused. He was ebullient in his letters home, with rosy predictions about the future of his service. "I have a man-sized job to run the game as it involves furnishing every officer and man with gas masks and respirators," he wrote home. He slept soundly at night and sometimes dreamed of Bessie and the children. Soon, a new family member began to appear in his dreams. On September 29, a cablegram arrived from home. Bessie had given birth to a seven-pound baby girl. In his letters home, he called her "Silky."

Fries was simultaneously close to the war and far from it. Occasionally, he came within a few miles of the front lines, but most of the time, danger was distant, too far even to worry about bombing runs by German planes. He was detached from the action, living in a bubble of comfort. It was a paradox that he occasionally remarked upon but that seemed to trouble him little as he motored between meals served with champagne, attended an operetta in Paris, and reveled in the mild fall weather. Still, he was aware of the travails of the soldiers on the front. Every time the Allies began a new offensive, it seemed, the weather foiled them. "They certainly have the devil's luck this season," Fries wrote.

That luck turned still worse in October. After the unrelenting rains of August, the skies had cleared, and the mud began to dry. The Third Battle of Ypres began as the British tried to take the strategic high ground of Passchendaele, just north of Ypres. The British

Royal Artillery resumed shelling, an endless cannonade of flashing concussions as the British and Australians fought their way forward. Hopes began to rise among the British generals that perhaps the time had finally arrived when the Germans' resolve would fail.

Then the rain began again. For the soldiers in the trenches, the Battle of Passchendaele would be the nadir of a war already soaked in horror. The mud turned the front into a vast, gelatinous cemetery, where bodies of men rotted where they fell, filling the air with the rank stench of decomposing corpses. Artillery turned night into day, the darkness filled with the endless roar of howitzers. Liquid metal thermite cascaded down on the trenches, an infernal rain that burned soldiers alive with a heat so intense that the ribs and walls of the trenches glowed. The quagmire underfoot swallowed artillery along with horses and men, who screamed in terror as they thrashed and struggled before they disappeared beneath the surface. A miasma of mustard and phosgene and chloropicrin and other gases poisoned the air above. That sliver of about one hundred yards created more than five hundred thousand casualties, turning the name "Passchendaele" into a shorthand for the madness of the war.

The British weren't alone in their losses. Gas also exacted a terrible setback for the Russians that would upend the war and, eventually, all of the West. In September, the demoralized Russian army had faced German general Georg Bruchmüller's troops in Riga, Latvia. Russian general Lavr Kornilov's thirteen battalions had pushed the Germans back twenty miles through sheer force of numbers, until a German counteroffensive regained the lost territory. On September 1, Bruchmüller unleashed a staggering artillery barrage. For five hours, hundreds of thousands of shells cascaded onto the Russians. About a quarter were incendiaries; the rest were gas intended to saturate the battlefield.

With the Russian army in chaos, Bruchmüller delivered the coup de grâce: the Germans' answer to the creeping barrage that the British had used at Arras. They called it the *Feuerwalze,* or "fire waltz." The *Feuerwalze* was more carefully targeted and faster moving, cleaving through the Russian line and giving the Germans an opening to thrust through the Russian defenses. The fire waltz did its work, and the German infantry crossed the Dvina River and swept the Russian positions, capturing some nine thousand soldiers and sending the rest scrambling in retreat. The Germans walked into Riga, the Russian forces shattered.

It was the last battle of the war for the Russian army. Deserting soldiers straggled home with tales of the front's horrors. As antiwar fever stoked revolutionary fervor in October, Vladimir Ilyich Lenin secretly returned to Petrograd. Within weeks, revolution swept the moderate socialist prime minister Aleksandr Kerensky from office. The Bolsheviks and left socialists seized power, and the Quadruple Entente's ally would withdraw from the war. Another member of the alliance, the Italians, suffered a calamitous defeat in October, when a massive gas attack launched at Caporetto introduced the German version of the Livens projector.

The grim tally of defeats reached Fries like a foul wind. His discomforts were limited to a restive stomach and a painful blister on his toe from a long hike across the countryside, and while soldiers shivered in the trenches, Fries bundled himself in his bearskin coat, "warm as a bug in a rug." Still, the sour news dampened his sunny outlook and dimmed his hopes for a swift return home. As he continued to build up his service, he anxiously awaited news of the gas troops he requested. Fries had a pet name for what he learned from the British: "the gas game." Like chess, checkers, or the evening games of bridge that he played with the other officers in the echoing mansion, gas demanded an exercise of wits and strategy with its own logic and rules, feints, and maneuvers to outflank an opponent. He, too, wanted to join the game.

"Things don't look quite so good for the allied cause as they did a couple of months ago, but it is always darkest just before the dawn," he wrote home. And he couldn't imagine that the night could get any darker.

PART II

FLASH POINT

Chapter Seven

"A Hotter Fire"

There's a place somewhere near Georgetown
Where the mustard blossoms grow
It was built to help the kaiser
Make a quick trip down below.
All ye chemists with your perfumes
To delight the boche's smell
Gather round and sing this anthem
It's the "kaiser's march to Hell."

—*Stunt-night lyrics from American*
University Experiment Station

The Tuesday after Labor Day was breezy and warm in Washington, a cloudless sky over the crowds assembled along Pennsylvania Avenue. President Wilson waited at the foot of the Peace Monument, jaunty and casual in white trousers, a blue blazer, and a straw boater hat, a flagpole cradled in the crook of his elbow. The president of the chamber of commerce looked starched and uncomfortable in a top hat and tails beside him, while the head of the board of trade puffed on a cigar to his left.

The September 4 parade honoring the city's first draftees was a demonstration of unity and homegrown patriotism, a celebration to drown out the naysayers and the soap-box agitators still speaking out against the war. Dissent had become the mark of traitors and slackers, and prosecutions of the war's critics had begun. The Espionage Act enacted in June made it a crime to pass information that interfered with the war or supported the country's enemies. Days before the parade, police arrested thirty Germans in South Dakota for petitioning against the war and the draft. In a Labor Day letter to American Federation of Labor president Samuel Gompers, Wilson warned that labor unions needed to be a bulwark against the "forces of antagonism." Gompers himself was suspect; Bureau of Investigation agents were tailing him, studying his movements and meetings for signs of subversive activities.

On the day of the parade, a promised pacifist demonstration never materialized, and the only arrests were a few lonely suffragists outside the White House. As the Marine Band struck up, a platoon of mounted police started down Pennsylvania Avenue. Brigadier General Joseph Kuhn, the president of the War College, led the procession, with the marshal of the First Division behind him. The president followed the Marine Band, marching with quick, measured steps, shoulders back, flag unfurled behind him in the breeze. As the parade passed, the crowds cheered for the president and the senators behind him. Then the roar fell away, and the mood grew sober. The draftees themselves came next, nine hundred dressed in civilian clothes, awkwardly trying to step in time to the martial music. The men in front carried an enormous banner that read SELECTED BY THE NATION TO ASSIST IN UPHOLDING THE WORLD'S DEMOCRACY. Some viewers wept as they watched the newly minted soldiers go by.

Then the draftees were gone and the somber mood with them. Soon the crowd was whistling and cheering for Civil War veterans in the faded uniforms of their respective sides, marching together in unity. Plodding mules pulled machine-gun caissons. Light field artillery pieces rolled by, and as infantry marched past, rifles held aloft, the sun glinted off their bayonets.

The parade along Pennsylvania Avenue was a spectacle of traditional warfare, a shiny martial display of familiar fifes and drums, cannons, and artillery caissons. The twenty-eight thousand soldiers who passed the reviewing stand outside the White House didn't carry gas masks, which would soon be one of their most vital pieces of standard-issue equipment. The day before the parade, General Pershing had issued the order forming Fries's gas service, but the War Department waited almost three weeks to publicize what had been a secret since August: that the U.S. Army would establish a chemical regiment, the Thirtieth Engineers (Gas and Flame), to answer German gas with its own.

When the War Department finally revealed its plans, the news arrived with a bang. On September 21, the lurid headline in the *Washington Herald* read "U.S. Prepared for Barbarity." America would "meet Germany at her own game of frightfulness," the article warned. "Besides poison gas and liquid fire, both of which, it was announced yesterday, would be employed by the American army, expert chemists are reported to be engaged in experiments with a new substance which will carry the campaign a step further and be the American backfire against German methods."

Newspapers across the country invoked images of sorcerous tactics conjured from a Mephistophelian cauldron. "Uncle Sam to 'Fight Devil with Fire,'" the *South Bend News-Times* proclaimed. They were brash words, hinting darkly at untested capabilities and strategies, and salted with inflated and misleading claims. "Liquid fire" would be part of the American arsenal, the articles reported, even though Fries had called flamethrowers all but obsolete. It was reported that the army had vast stockpiles of chemicals and a secret weapon at the ready—utter fabrications.

The announcement served two purposes. The first was propaganda, to send a signal rife with bluff and bluster that the United States, like its allies, intended to play the gas game, too. The second reason was that the army was laying the foundation for a sea change in warfare. For two years, the American public had read about Germany's violations of the rules of war, a flaunting of conscience and convention that laid bare the moral failings of "the Huns." Now the army needed to convince the country that it was justified in engaging in the same tactics. That wasn't all. Not only was the United States prepared to use gas, but the army suggested a desire to push chemical warfare in new directions. Aerial bombing of cities packed with civilians was one of them. "War will be carried against Germany with poison, flame and dynamite— dynamite from thousands of airplanes which will answer the Germans in their own language of 'women and children first.'" The influx of American pilots and planes would allow the Allies to shift targets from the trenches to German cities hundreds of miles behind the lines. "Berlin is the main objective. Other thriving German manufacturing towns and cities will be visited," the *Herald* promised.

The announcement that the United States would embrace gas warfare was not welcomed everywhere. "This news brings no thrill of satisfaction to the hearts of the American people," the *Free Trader-Journal* of Ottawa, Illinois, editorialized.

> We do not want to use any means of warfare so inhumane as the gas which chokes men to death in agony and the flame which shrivels their flesh beyond all healing. All forms of warfare are cruel; but in comparison with these blasting weapons, ball and shell are merciful. If lead or steel kills, it kills quickly, often without pain. If it only wounds, the hurt men have a fair chance for recovery. Gas and fire mean lingering torture.

If the scientists in Washington agreed with such doubts, they were drowned out amid the din of construction that rang across the American University campus. The rush to complete the laboratories reached a fever pitch in September. From the attic to the basement of McKinley Hall, work was under way to transform the half-finished classrooms into research spaces for the chemists.

Concrete floors had been poured in August. Workmen streamed up the curving front steps and into the high lobby under the rotunda. Carpenters hauled tables and chemical hoods up the marble steps to the labs throughout the building. Plumbers fitted pipes, installed sinks, and laid gas lines. Electricians were still unspooling wire and running it up the walls to power the building.

In a September 1 update, research chief George Burrell had written that the laboratories in McKinley Hall would be ready in eight weeks, then crossed it out and penciled in a much-shorter timeline: it would be ready in just two.

The work couldn't be finished quickly enough. Seventy-five chemists and other Bureau of Mines employees were scattered between the Pittsburgh Experiment Station, Johns Hopkins, Yale, the Interior Department building, and other labs up and down the Eastern Seaboard and beyond. Telegrams, telephones, and trains hitched the frantic investigations together. The chemists wasted precious time on travel and mailing samples to remote labs. The spring deployment to Europe was creeping closer. With Amos Fries installed as chief of the AEF Gas Service in France, cablegrams related to gas warfare flashed with increasing frequency across the Atlantic. There were battlefield updates, queries about manufacturing timelines, and requirements for officer training. Insistent requests for laboratory equipment proliferated, along with admonitions to focus investigations on mustard gas.

Every day brought new puzzles and problems. At the behest of the British, George Burrell was leading the research into cheaply produced helium for airships. After the debacle with the first gas masks, Arno Fieldner had redoubled efforts in Pittsburgh to improve their design, while the Army Medical Division had taken over the task of manufacturing them. Other divisions worked on experiments with smoke screens, explosives, and a ventilation system for scrubbing carbon dioxide from air in submarines. Another focused on large-scale manufacture of gases. In New Haven, Yandell Henderson was studying the toxicity of gas on animals in a hastily remodeled athletic clubhouse and a laboratory built beneath the bleachers of a ball field. The demand for animal test subjects was so heavy that the bureau asked mayors from Baltimore up to Bridgeport, Connecticut, to ship their stray cats and dogs to New Haven, where the division was emptying out dog pounds as quickly as animals could be scooped up.

In mid-September, while McKinley Hall was still a construction zone, the chemists began to move in. Fieldner and his gas mask division arrived first, taking first-floor rooms down the left hall-way of the L-shaped building, with more on the other side of the building next to the labs where Arthur Lamb set up his chemical defense work. James F. Norris claimed rooms for his work on offensive and defensive gas research. Eli K. Marshall moved his physiology research from Johns Hopkins up the curving lobby steps to the second floor. George Richter's pyrotechnics labs were on the top floor. A machine shop hummed in the basement.

In just a few short months, the hill became the hot center of the war gas universe, a riotous mix of construction and chemistry. Workmen brushed past chemists already at work, bent over make-shift tables and benches amid the swirling chaos of the half-finished labs. There was no time for waste or complaint, and no room for slackers. The improvisation among chaos had a lasting impression on E. Emmet Reid, the Johns Hopkins chemist. "I well remember the wild life at that time," he recalled.

But even when complete, McKinley Hall was not big enough to contain the rapidly expanding Research Division. The chemists would need outdoor stills to manufacture test batches of gases. They would need munitions pits and storage for the precursor chemicals. A firehouse in case an experiment started a blaze. Trenches and bunkers to replicate those on the front. The scientists would need man-test laboratories, chambers like the one in Pittsburgh where soldiers could test masks or expose themselves to chemicals so the effects could be studied. Kennels were needed—when Henderson transferred his operation from Yale in late September, he brought along the dogs he used as test subjects. There would be other animals, too: goats, monkeys, mice. The chemists would be designing horse masks, which meant the hill would need a stable and a blacksmith. The school had already approved construction for a concrete bomb pit, where the chemists could detonate bombs and grenades to study the clouds they released.

Besides research facilities, there was one thing the experiment station lacked: barracks. The engineers at Camp American University had their own cantonments, but the chemists boarded in private homes, and the Bureau of Mines constantly ran discreet classified ads in the newspapers seeking furnished rooms in neighborhoods nearby.

The enterprise that began in the two campus buildings inexorably spread. Over the following months, the army leased properties adjoining the campus for experimentation and training. The wealthy banker Charles Glover signed contracts with the army for one of his tracts of land, as did other area landowners like Charles Spalding and Robert Weaver, giving the bureau hundreds of rolling acres reaching all the way west toward the Dalecarlia Reservoir and north toward Maryland.

Responses to the scientific census that Manning had announced with such fanfare in April had continued to flow into the director's office through the summer and into the fall. Designed to locate scientists and chemists, it succeeded. In all, 22,500 men responded from all over the country. Some 7,500 of them were mining experts, while 15,000 were in chemical industries. Manning compiled a separate list of those with experience in foreign countries. In early October, he labeled the report *Technical Paper 179* and shipped it off to the National Research Council. "These lists are now at your service at the Bureau of Mines and should prove of great value to the country in this emergency," Manning wrote in a cover letter.

As the research in Manning's department expanded, the census continued to provide a systematic, methodical approach to identifying candidates for Manning's scientific army. Manning originally planned to have 250 scientists working on gas, but the sheer volume of new investigations was outstripping the number of men available to carry them out. In August, the War Department had approved Manning's request that 120 drafted chemists be diverted to work on gas investigations. This accommodation must have cheered Manning, because his whole enterprise relied on legions of scientists who might otherwise end up as cannon fodder in France.

Personnel problems were amplified, however, by the formation of the gas and flame regiment. The census had been designed to locate scientists and chemists who could contribute to the war gas effort, divert them from the front, and direct them instead toward technical work. Now the army was seeking chemists, too, for the gas regiment, and Amos Fries was clamoring for chemists to be sent to France for his own AEF laboratory and overseas gas service. Though Fries had been in his position since mid-August, he and Manning had never directly corresponded. Moreover, both men believed that their organizations on their respective sides of the Atlantic should guide the research, which would lead inevitably to conflict.

In the struggle to recruit the sharpest minds, Manning had a powerful tool to attract scientists that the engineers lacked: prestige. From the perspective of pure science, gas warfare represented a vanguard of technology, a new and exciting field of chemical weapons. Manning's appeal to scientists in the first weeks of the war set a chain reaction in motion, fueled by the twin engines of patriotism and intellectual curiosity that drew scientists to the chemical weapons race. Many of the chemists were "dollar-a-year" men, receiving a symbolic wage for their patriotic efforts in service to the government. Their names appeared in the *Journal of Industrial and Engineering Chemistry;* they were celebrities in their fields who had reached the pinnacle of academic success. This pantheon of intellectual luminaries, thrown together in the common cause of war and science, exerted a gravity of its own, attracting other scientists because of academic ties or informal acquaintances. Like atoms pulled by the tug of a molecule, professors convinced their students, and academicians invited their colleagues, and suddenly scientists with little inclination for picking up a gun discovered they had a place in the war effort.

The Research Division gained a crucial recruit from a chance encounter on the street. James F. Norris, a debonair MIT professor known as Sunny Jim when he attended Johns Hopkins, was walking in downtown Washington one day when he ran into a young associate professor of chemistry at Harvard. The chemist, James Bryant Conant, was just twenty-four years old, with tousled hair and piercing eyes. That fall, Conant spent his days at the Department of Agriculture's Bureau of Chemistry. Shy and retiring, Conant probably didn't socialize much with other chemists flocking to Washington from places like Harvard, Princeton, Yale, and Johns Hopkins during that summer and fall of 1917; if he had, he surely would have known all about the war gas investigations gaining steam in Washington.

Conant had grown up in Boston's Dorchester neighborhood, the child of a prosperous, middle-class family. From a young age, the power of engines and speed fascinated Conant. Transformation enthralled him—the thrill of explosions, the violent discharge of energy and heat, and currents of electricity sparking through circuits. He spent hours hitching up batteries, tinkering with motors, electric buzzers, and electromagnets.

As he grew older, chemistry captured his attention. His father built an unusual workshop for his son in a vestibule of the house. His friends had carpentry shops, but Conant had something else in mind. His father installed a gas line into the workshop, which allowed James to have a Bunsen burner, turning the space into a laboratory. He bought a blast lamp, which turned the gas flame into a blowtorch hot enough to melt glass into liquid. He experimented with glassblowing, heated red oxide of mercury to create pure oxygen, and made an apparatus for distilling water.

Conant's scientific curiosity made him a natural for Roxbury Latin School, one of Boston's storied exam schools. His grades in some subjects were middling, but he excelled in chemistry. He filled notebooks with sketches of lab apparatuses, equations, and observations far more complex than the school curriculum.

His teacher Newton Henry Black praised the advanced work in Conant's notebooks. "The experiments described in this book are quite different than the usual list offered by the boys of the school, because Conant has already done at home most of the usual experiments in elem. chemistry," Black wrote.

In the school magazine, his classmates poked fun at him for his fascination with chemistry. "This year, he has practically lived in the laboratory, concocting every kind and condition of a smell. We sincerely hope he will not blow up the laboratory at Harvard," they wrote.

Conant found his calling in the Harvard labs as an undergraduate and later as a graduate student. The outbreak of the war in 1914 polarized the campus. Many children of Boston Brahmins gravitated toward Britain and its allies, while a smaller group of German sympathizers opposed intervention. A confessed contrarian, Conant was in the latter group, contemptuous of the widespread campus support for the Allies. He called himself "a pro-German apologist," and he supported Wilson for his neutrality stance.

But the chlorine gas attack at Ypres and the sinking of the *Lusitania* in 1915 isolated pro-German chemists; many were aghast that German scientists they idolized and worked with had turned their brilliance to such ends. When unrestricted submarine warfare finally pulled the United States into the war, Conant began to worry. He didn't worry about which side was right but that the conflict would interrupt his studies. He didn't feel as though it was an option to wait until he was drafted. Many of his classmates were enlisting in the army and navy. Conant was torn. He considered joining an ambulance corps, but his former teacher at Roxbury Latin and his parents talked him out of it.

There was another route—the private sector. The war had clamped off the supply of German chemicals and equipment that American companies had long relied on. With a mix of naïveté and opportunism, Conant saw potential for wartime profit and launched an industrial chemical company with two Harvard classmates. The project ended in disaster. An explosion killed one partner and sent another to the hospital. Conant was so dismayed that he pledged to shun industrial chemistry and stick with academic work, but the problem of what to do during the war persisted. He visited chemical companies in Delaware and Washington seeking a proper wartime endeavor and wound up at the Bureau of Chemistry. There, he spent his days trying to replicate a German pharmaceutical drug that the war had made unobtainable, a task only distantly related to the war.

He lived in an apartment building on Biltmore Street NW, just east of Rock Creek. He had begun to tinker with a new idea: to enlist in the army and go overseas to train men in using and repairing gas masks. When he bumped into Norris on the street, Conant described his plans. Norris scoffed.

"You're crazy." Norris snorted. Enlisting would be a waste of Conant's time and talent, he said. "You can do more good for your country by staying here in the Bureau of Mines. We're working with gases." Chemists that Conant knew well were already working for the bureau, such as his mentor Elmer Kohler and Arthur Beckett Lamb, who headed Harvard's chemistry lab, and both were working on defensive problems around gas. Norris had been charged with organizing a research team, Organic Research Unit No. 1. He told Conant he should come to American University and lead the new research unit. Conant accepted.

Norris was almost certainly correct—Conant was not a natural fit for the army, either by disposition or experience. He had a methodical and calculating mind that carefully weighed decisions, and he expressed impatience, even disdain, at other ways of thinking. By his own admission, he was contrarian—hardly a trait suited to regimented, hierarchical army life. Still, he had been prepared to be swept into the tide of war. Had Conant gone overseas, the Chemical Warfare Service might well have gone in a very different direction.

Conant left his Bureau of Chemistry job and began work with Norris's organic unit in McKinley Hall in mid-September. There were just three men in Organic Unit No. 1 when Conant started, but it grew quickly—by mid-October he was working with seven other chemists. Conant must have found it a dismal working environment compared with what he was used to. McKinley Hall was unheated, and the windows lacked glazing to keep out drafts. Condensers for cooling hot gases and liquids dangled from shelves, suspended with bits of string. The lab lacked basic equipment, such as ring stands to secure beakers and test tubes in place over a flame, and the wind whistled in the hoods that funneled out fumes. Samples of mustard gas, chlorine, sneezing agents, and tear gases filled the lab. The chemists constantly skated on the edge of injury. Each afternoon, the scientists guzzled a quart of diluted milk to neutralize fumes they inhaled during the day.

One day, a bumbling young chemist in Conant's lab who had recently graduated from MIT leaned over an uncovered bowl and sniffed its contents. The bowl contained hydrocyanic acid. Immediately realizing what a poor idea that was, the chemist exhaled quickly to expel the gas from his lungs. That same chemist, the future Nobel laureate Robert S. Mulliken, would later be badly burned in a mustard gas experiment gone awry and spend six months recovering in a hospital.

While the lab was far from perfect, in some ways it was ideal for someone like Conant. Brilliant scientists were all around him, working feverishly on stubborn problems that would mean life or death for soldiers sent to Europe. These were not petty industrial dilemmas; they were the kinds of problems that might determine the outcome of the war. The work at McKinley Hall wasn't always efficient, but it was pure—a set of discrete problems that the men had liberty to tackle however they saw fit.

Mustard was one of those problems. Over the summer, Manning had focused on production of a handful of gases: phosgene, chloropicrin, hydrogen cyanide, and the tear gas xylyl bromide. From overseas, Fries pressured the Bureau of Mines to concentrate on mustard. "Full investigation physiological and defensive and manufacture on large scale of gas No. 475 [mustard] vital," he wrote via cablegram from Pershing's office on October 11. A week later, samples extracted from German yellow-cross shells arrived at American University, and mustard became a top priority at the experiment station. As chief of gas research, Jim Norris was in charge of learning first how to synthesize the chemical, then manufacturing enough to pack shells and mortars to launch back at the Germans. At the head of Organic Research Unit No. 1, Conant began distilling the oily liquid to study its composition.

Mustard was a vexing problem. The Germans had been using the same production method that the chemist Victor Meyer had described in 1886, known as the chlorohydrine method. Ethylene chlorohydrine treated with sodium sulfide produced thiodiglycol and sodium chloride, or salt. When thiodiglycol was treated with hydrochloric acid, a solution of dichloroethyl sulfide and water formed. Hydrolysis removed the water, leaving mustard. But removing the water was time-consuming and expensive, and this process also required chlorine, which was in limited supply because it, too, was a war gas. The process was slow and inefficient and had required the Germans to stockpile the meager output so as to have sufficient quantities to make attacks effective. There had to be a better way, and it was Conant's task to find it. He finally had the war job that he craved.

Across the campus, new facilities were rising from the hillside to meet the chemists' demands. Engineers were building a long board-walk extending northwest across the hilltop outside McKinley Hall. The wooden duckboard turned at an angle and went due west, to the top of a ravine. There, the engineers were building a bridge spanning the gulch. On the other side, a bomb pit was under construction. When the boardwalk was finished, the chemists would be able to step from McKinley Hall carrying their potions and grenades and smoke candles, walk on the level platform all the way to the bomb pit, and test their research there, safely contained inside the buried detonation chamber.

Every Thursday morning, the scientists of the organic chemistry section gathered for a meeting to compare notes, update one another on their work, and debate new avenues of research. E. Emmet Reid and his mentor, Joseph Frazer, traveled from Baltimore to Washington. Arno Fieldner, too, would have been there, discussing the latest experiments with gas masks, soda lime, and charcoal. Jim Norris was always present, along with Eli Marshall, the head of the pharmacology division, as well as Yandell Henderson, despite a cloud of suspicion over him for his incendiary writings before the war.

At the meetings, Reid acted as secretary, recording everything on notecards. When a new substance was suggested, Reid wrote down the name of the chemist proposing it; then it would be assigned to another chemist to explore further. Later meetings would include updates on the investigations, and sometimes the chemists would bring samples of the compounds to the meetings to discuss their properties. From there, they would be passed on to Marshall and Henderson's division for further exploration. The numbers of cards in Reid's file began to multiply, and Reid rated each of the substances on a toxicity scale that he invented.

The scientists didn't always have the easiest time obtaining chemicals. Since the summer, the chemists had been looking at war gases based on arsenic, rather than sulfur, so William McPherson, the chief of the Small-Scale-Manufacturing Section, pleaded with chemical companies for arsenic. At first, he begged businesses for small amounts—six pounds from one chemical company, one hundred pounds from another. By late fall, as the lethal potential of arsenic became more evident, McPherson was ordering vast quantities of arsenic trichloride. Astonished company officials warned that his requests would disrupt the market, to the detriment of commercial industries that relied on it. After he wrote to one company asking if it could manufacture eight hundred tons of arsenic trichloride, the company director wrote back to say that "it could not be furnished in the next three months without upsetting the industries of the whole country." It would have a particularly deleterious effect on companies making insecticides, so much so that a different federal agency, the Food Administration, told his company not to provide it to the Bureau of Mines.

The difficulty in obtaining chemicals was part of a still-bigger problem: producing the war gases themselves. As representatives of the War Department and the Bureau of Mines conferred with industrial chemical producers, they realized that the companies were reluctant to get in the business of manufacturing war gases. One reason was that many companies were already deep in orders for chemicals that were in heavy demand from the army, such as chlorine. Furthermore, making war gases was a dangerous and risky proposition. Unlike arms makers or shipbuilding companies that could convert factories back to peacetime purposes after the war, plants built to produce chemical warfare agents would be useless when the war ended.

A few companies, however, were willing to make chemical weapons. Dow Chemical, which was among the nation's largest chemical producers, was one of them. Herbert H. Dow had perfected a process in Midland, Michigan, for extracting chemicals from "brine wells," chemical-rich caverns deep underground that were the remnants of ancient oceans. Salt solutions pumped to the surface also contained chemicals such as magnesium, chlorine, and bromine that could be extracted through electrolysis. Midland was one of the country's richest sources of bromine, and bromine was one of the key ingredients in lachrymators, or tear gases. Midland also produced large amounts of sulfur chloride, which was a chief constituent chemical in mustard gas. Toward the end of 1917, Herbert Dow offered the plant to the Bureau of Mines, and in early 1918, the bureau would establish a Midland station which would turn the town into a hub of chemical warfare.

Another cooperative chemical maker was the Oldbury Electro-Chemical Company of Niagara Falls, New York. Carbon monoxide, one of the ingredients of phosgene, was a by-product of its furnaces. Prior to the war, phosgene was imported from Germany for industrial dyes, and when war appeared inevitable, the company had begun exploring commercial production of phosgene. Not long after Congress declared war, the company offered to assist the government in making it. An experimental lab produced batches of the chemical for the Bureau of Mines to test, and in November of 1917, Oldbury signed a contract with the government to produce twenty thousand pounds of phosgene a day.

A few other companies were also prepared to make gas, such as the American Synthetic Color Company in Stamford, Connecticut; the Frank Hemingway Company in Bound Brook, New Jersey; and Zinsser & Company in Hastings-on-Hudson, New York. But in the fall of 1917, the War Department concluded that there simply weren't enough cooperative companies. If the government wanted chemical weapons, it would have to make them itself.

The decision to manufacture war gases coincided with another effort already under way in the War Department. Since June, the Army Ordnance Department had been searching for land to build plants for filling the shells that would need to be packed with gas and sent to France by the millions. They also needed a large proving ground to test ordnance, both conventional and chemical. For that, they needed a sparsely populated area with an unobstructed, twenty-five-mile shooting range both to the north and south—fifty miles in all—to test long-range shells. They found what seemed to be the perfect spot: Kent Island, a hatchet-shaped outcropping of land jutting into the Chesapeake Bay, with open water on three sides and a short bridge to the mainland for its five hundred residents. But when army officers went to Congress for approval to buy the seventeen thousand acres, Senate hearings turned into an embarrassing spectacle, with bitter protests from Maryland lawmakers on behalf of the island's inhabitants. Secretary of War Baker himself pleaded directly with the islanders who packed the hearing room, making a patriotic appeal for sacrifice.

Baker's words fell on deaf ears. Tempers flared during the hearing, which had to be gaveled to order. An officer from the Ordnance Department, Colonel Colden L. Ruggles, set off a firestorm when he said the army would be testing gas shells on the island. In a bombastic rhetorical flourish, one senator said that if the army couldn't find another spot, "I say this country is not worth defending. Just let the Germans come and take it." Two days later, the Senate committee killed the bill.

It was a debacle, but the army had a second option. Across the Chesapeake Bay, the estuaries of the Bush and Gunpowder Rivers hugged a forlorn peninsula of marshland and thick woods known as Gunpowder Neck. Few people lived on the neck—perhaps as few as 150—and the closest settlement was the small town of Edgewood. Gunpowder Neck was a wild, solitary place. The descendant of a Civil War general owned an eight-thousand-acre game preserve which took up much of the peninsula. Deer, Mongolian pheasants, and rabbits filled the dense woods. The waterfront teemed with wild geese and flocks of redhead and canvasback ducks. The owner had a private horse-racing track and flower greenhouses. A small army of game wardens made the preserve a risky place for poachers. It was isolated and remote, far from prying eyes and civilian populations. But it was also close to a Pennsylvania Railroad line between Baltimore and Philadelphia, and the Bush River made it accessible to the Chesapeake Bay and the ocean. It would do.

A few days later, the army had a new recommendation for its proving ground and gas plants: thirty-five thousand acres of land that included Gunpowder Neck and land across the Bush River, with thirty-five hundred acres set aside for the shell-filling plant. The land would cost far more than Kent Island, and farmers and residents from Harford Country rallied to protest. This time, the army prevailed: over the objections of residents, Congress quickly approved a $7 million appropriation. On the evening of October 16, President Wilson signed an executive order to seize the land. "Barking Dogs of War Will End Gunners' Paradise," the *Sun* newspaper lamented in an editorial.

If American University was the brains of the gas research operation, Gunpowder Neck would be its muscle, sinew, and lungs. The army put Lieutenant Earl J. W. Ragsdale, the chief of the Trench Warfare Section of the Ordnance Department, in charge. In late October, work began on a rail spur, and construction started on the shell-filling station in November. As plans for the plant began to take shape, the federal director general of railroads made clear that shipping war gases to Gunpowder Neck was a dangerous proposition, requiring special trains to safeguard against accidents and sabotage. It would also be expensive to ship the chemical weapons to the shell-filling plants that would be built there, so the Ordnance Department made a decision that would shape the future of the Chemical Warfare Service for a half century to come: the army decided to build its own gas factories at Gunpowder Neck, simultaneously solving the problem of manufacturing war gases and getting those gases to the shell-filling plants.

In the fall of 1917, practically every branch of the army had some involvement with the war gas work. The Ordnance Department, the Medical Corps, the Signal Corps, the Corps of Engineers, and then, of course, the civilian Bureau of Mines. With so many offices and departments and agencies involved, it became increasingly imperative for some kind of organizational structure for all the disparate elements of gas warfare. Earlier in 1917, the

War Department had cobbled together the Gas Defense Service to take charge of making masks and organizing field training and had pressed unsuccessfully for the Bureau of Mines to turn over the research work to the military. In October, the War Department created a new Chemical Service Section, which provided a kind of umbrella organization for the loose confederation of offices and departments with an interest in chemical warfare, and placed a new director of the gas service in charge. Fries had advocated for a military officer to head the effort, and the man the army chose was an engineer named Colonel Charles L. Potter. A chemist from Maine, Potter was intended to be a kind of traffic controller, advising the work of the various agencies but with little power to control it.

When Amos Fries heard about Potter's appointment, he was not impressed: "I have been urging them to appoint someone, but I am not particularly happy over the choice of Potter because he is a dead one so far as doing anything himself is concerned," Fries grumbled. From Fries's vantage across the ocean, the various separate agencies appeared to be competing rather than cooperating, and he grew increasingly irritated with Washington. "The gas game as it was getting started under the direction of three or four departments is a fine example of running a war at a distance of 4,000 miles," he wrote in another letter.

As October came to a close, Fries had been in his position for more than two months and had still never been in direct contact with Van Manning. Each knew of the other through the reports sent overseas and cablegram traffic, but they had never personally corresponded. Fries finally wrote to Manning on November 1, apologizing for not doing so sooner. "I have been so short of personnel as to have delayed considerably writing you on subjects that I should have written you about before."

It was a courteous letter, lacking any of the criticism that Fries had confided in Bessie. Fries laid out his views of which gases were effective and why. He recommended that the bureau focus on phosgene, chloropicrin, chlorine, and mustard gas. Chlorine was still being used in conjunction with phosgene and diphosgene, he said. *Vincennite,* the French name for hydrogen cyanide, was barely of any use at all, he wrote; the British were phasing it out altogether. He ended with a plea for cooperation. "Assuring you of our appreciation of the most excellent work you are doing and our earnest desire to coordinate the work in the United States with field experience, and trust to hear from you frequently," he concluded.

Manning's reply came more than a month later. The sluggish pace of steamship mail between France and the United States likely accounted for some of the delay; still, the long gap in correspondence suggested that Manning may have been less than eager to correspond with this AEF officer who was suddenly making demands upon Manning's chemists. However, if Manning felt any resentment, he didn't indicate as such in his response.

Manning discussed the bureau's work on different chemical compounds, the research on Livens projectors, and the work on gas masks, boasting that twenty-five men were working on gas masks alone. "You will be interested to know that we have over 400 men working in the Research Division investigating war gases, and the majority of whom are chemists. Some of the very best men in the country have responded to the call for this important work," he wrote. He thanked Fries for the reports he had sent. He noted the comments from a British officer about aerial chemical bombing. He praised Fries's work in France and said it would greatly assist "the work that is being done in this country."

Manning's letter was polite, precise, and—in one respect—oddly incomplete. Despite the fact that a deadly new war gas had been unleashed in Europe—one that the AEF and its allies saw as a pressing battlefield concern and that his own scientists were actively studying—Manning barely mentioned mustard in his letter to Fries, making only a passing reference. Either he was being discreet for the censors, or perhaps he wasn't being completely forthcoming with the colonel about the work at American University.

While Fries viewed the domestic service with disdain and was displeased with the choice of Potter to lead the Office of the Gas Service, at least now there was a soldier at the head who spoke Fries's language. Fries felt that his hard work and effort were paying off, but he remained anxious about one aspect of his gas service: his gas and flame regiment. "I will certainly be glad to see them, as I want to get them underway for gas work," he wrote home.

Fries didn't have much longer to wait. In October, the War Department put out a recruitment call for the gas and flame regiment, looking for soldiers who wanted to experience a new kind of warfare, "keen, red-blooded men" who would use the new unfamiliar and frightening weapons the likes of which the modern world had never seen. The army press release called for volunteers from age eighteen to forty to enlist, including those who had not yet been drafted and men older than the draft age of thirty-one. The release listed starting pay, opportunities for commission and promotion, and the positions available within the regiment.

> The men specially needed are analytical, research, and manufacturing chemists, powdermen, men experienced in the production of gas, machinists, automobile repair men, men who can operate or repair gas or steam engines, pipefitters, electricians, designers, interpreters, carpenters, blacksmiths, plumbers, boilermakers and chauffeurs.

The effort was carefully coordinated with newspaper editors to drum up interest.

"The Hellfire Battalion," some newspapers called it, while others dubbed it "the Hellfire Regiment." "The time has gone by for any ethical discussion as to the propriety of using gas and flames against the enemy," the *Boston Transcript* wrote. "The Germans have set the pace and the practical officers of the army realize that their fire must be fought with hotter fire." At the same time, the army circulated appeals directly to gas and chemical companies, professional organizations, and industrial manufacturers, as well as to recruiting offices and district engineering officers.

In Lawrence, Massachusetts, a young factory worker named Harold J. Higginbottom spotted an article in the evening newspaper on Saturday, October 20. Higginbottom was a steadfast, easygoing sort, a chemist employed in the dye works at Pacific Mills, one of a dozen cloth factories that made Lawrence the nation's textile capital. Harold had a long face and soulful green eyes and was sweet on a girl named Irene Macreadie, the daughter of the city fire chief. When he registered for the draft in June, Harold had just celebrated his twenty-first birthday. Born in New Hampshire, he lived with his mother, Emma, and older brother, Arthur, in a boardinghouse on Cypress Street, not far from the factories along the Merrimack River. His father, James, had been an overseer at the Pacific Mills plant before he died in 1914, and eventually Higginbottom and Arthur went to work at the mill as well. Lawrence had been a cauldron of union radicalism in 1912 over low pay and insufferable working conditions in the mills. Despite the recent history of radicalism and agitation, almost ten thousand young men from the city had peacefully registered for the draft in June, along with another two thousand from surrounding towns, and only a single man was arrested for refusing to register.

The article caught Higgie's eye. The new regiment required specialists like himself who understood the alchemy of toxic substances, and the advertisement got him thinking. When he went to work at Pacific Mills on Monday, October 22, he told some of the fellows about the article and this new chemical regiment in Washington, D.C. Maybe they should enlist. Maybe this was their role in the war, this new Hellfire Regiment.

It didn't take Higginbottom long to make up his mind. During his lunch break at the mill, he strolled up to the post office and talked it over with the men at the recruiting station there. He liked what they said, and he told them that he would be back. He went back to the mill and asked if he could leave work early; he had important things to discuss at home. When he got home to Cypress Street, he told his mother and his brother, Arthur, that he was enlisting. It was probably not news that his widowed mother welcomed, but he managed to convince her it was the right thing to do. He returned to the recruiting office, where he passed his first physical examination, signed his papers, and was told to report back at the end of the week, on Friday morning. He got everything in order at the mill that night and went back one last time on Tuesday to pick up his paycheck. When he was there, the fellows at the mill surprised him with a goodbye gift of a Gillette safety razor. On Wednesday, he made plans to go bowling for what he expected to be his last frames for some time. Instead, a friend brought him over to Haverhill Street, where a group of friends from church lay in wait for him. They pounced on him when he arrived and surprised him with a nifty wristwatch with glow-in-the-dark hands, a gift that would be useful in the trenches of France.

On Friday morning, he left home at about nine o'clock for the recruiting station, where he received orders to report to Boston. On the train, he chatted with an older man who had also been recruited for the regiment. He had lunch in Boston, said goodbye to his aunt, then reported to the recruiting office. From there, he was taken to South Station and boarded a train for New York. He got to New Rochelle late that night and then caught the last boat over to Fort Slocum for training before he was sent to join the gas and flame regiment in Washington.

Pershing's order had called for six companies, but the army began modestly with only one. On paper, Fries headed the regiment, but in practice, Major Earl J. Atkisson was its leader. Atkisson had turned thirty-one in August and came from the ranks of army engineers like Fries and Sibert. Before West Point, he had studied electrical and mechanical engineering at Cornell University. Earlier in 1917, he had returned from two years as superintendent of locks in the Canal Zone and was ordered to report to Camp American University on August 30. When the War Department finally opened the lid on its plans for gas warfare, Atkisson became its face, his photograph running in papers across the country as the man at the helm of the gas regiment. Fries knew Atkisson well from when both had been posted at the U.S. Army Engineer School at Washington Barracks. He was a high achiever with a nimble mind, and an athlete to boot. Though Fries had no idea about Atkisson's appointment before it was announced, he could not have been more pleased when he heard.

The regiment's core came from the Twentieth Engineers, a forestry regiment already stationed at Camp American University. Initially, thirty-four men were hand chosen for the gas and flame regiment. While Higginbottom was still at Fort Slocum, the new recruits began to arrive at Camp American University. Thomas Jabine, a twenty-six-year-old chemist from Yonkers, New York, was among them. An amiable sort with an eye for the girls, Tom wasn't a stranger to military discipline; he had been a cadet in high school. At Columbia University, he wore starched collars and tweedy suits as he studied chemical engineering, orated in the debate society, and worshipped in the school's Christian Association. In the 1912 yearbook, his inscription read "So wise, so young, they say, do never live long."

How Jabine learned about the regiment isn't clear—perhaps from an article in the *Yonkers Statesman* or from a manager at the chemical company where he was foreman of a sulfuric acid plant. However he heard about the regiment, he wavered on enlisting but found the lure of gas warfare too powerful to resist.

When he arrived on the hill, Jabine found he was among the small number who had enlisted from outside the army rather than being picked from the Twentieth Engineers. He also discovered that the army wasn't equipped to provide much for new recruits. He had no uniform yet, and he was short on towels and soap. With fall approaching, he needed warm socks and underwear. He took it all in stride, writing a letter home to his mother for heavy underclothes, extra towels, and a brush to polish shoes, as well as the much-needed soap and socks. "I am getting along OK and guess I will be satisfied with this life for the time I am in the army. It's going to be very good for me physically I am sure," he wrote.

For the arriving recruits like Jabine, Camp American University was a booming, riotous place. With more engineers arriving every day, carpenters raced to erect new barracks, mess halls, and latrines. For $125 a month in rent, Mary Patten's properties in the cleft between Massachusetts and Nebraska Avenues became drilling and instruction grounds. A stove warmed the YMCA on the corner of Nebraska and Massachusetts Avenues where the enlisted men could write letters to their families, relax, and play cards. Just outside the campus, off-duty soldiers could get meals at two lunchrooms. An enterprising barber opened his doors, and a tailor set up shop to tuck uniforms and stitch badges into place. Braying bugles, the tramp of hundreds of boots, and the bark of drill orders filled the air. Every blade of grass on campus was gone, churned into the dirt and clay beneath, which the soldiers tramped through the hallways of the shared history building.

Jabine had been one of the first chemists to enlist for the Thirtieth, and among that early bunch, his education set him apart. The lieutenant in charge asked him to help with gas research, and he eagerly agreed. "I have been working like a horse all day and never felt better in my life. A week or two of this life would do me more good than anything I could think of. I feel like a new man already," he wrote home. At the end of October, the regiment moved into the College of History building, where soldiers slept in the hallways and in spare rooms. He didn't mind at all—it was warmer inside—but he grumbled that smoking was forbidden in the building. With the nights getting cold, he needed a warm sweater to stave off the chill. He had an idea for where to get one. "I can see where I will have to write to some of my so called girls and see which one really loves me enough to knit me a sweater," he wrote to his mother.

Jabine became fast friends with the regiment's first volunteer at

Camp American University, a Pittsburgh native named Fred Cecil Devlin. Single and twenty-five, Devlin was anything but a soldier; he had been working as a floorwalker at a department store before he joined the regiment. Arthur W. Archer was another early recruit. He was twenty-seven, slender and tall with gray eyes and blond hair. He was also single and had been working as a marine fireman on the Chelsea Piers in Manhattan when he registered for the draft. There was twenty-three-year-old Ellis Frink from Corvallis, Oregon, who was still a student at Oregon Agricultural College. Leonidas M. Shappell, a young chemist called Shap, came from Keokuk, Iowa, with his older brother, Sanborn.

Over the coming weeks, dozens more recruits arrived. On Thursday, November 8, an electric tram with about a dozen soldiers aboard trundled up Massachusetts Avenue and stopped outside the camp. Higginbottom was one of them. He was hungry and tired after twelve days of drilling and exercise, inoculations, and physical exams at Fort Slocum. A hearty meal cheered him — "a good feed," as he put it — and he got a cot to sleep on in the hall of the College of History building.

Reveille woke the new recruits the next morning at 6:00 a.m., and they got an up-close exhibition of the regiment's future that afternoon. They watched some gas experiments, a demonstration of liquid fire spewing from the nozzle of a flamethrower, and the billowing clouds of a smoke screen.

One Sunday after he arrived, Higginbottom was on police duty with Jabine, and when their work ended by noon, they went on a scenic hike with two or three other men, crossing the Potomac River into Virginia. There were still only about sixty-five men in the company then, which quickly turned into a tight-knit group of friends. Higginbottom particularly liked Jabine and Frink.

Jabine felt the same. The men in the regiment were "a dandy bunch," he wrote home. He loved camp life. The constant exercise, the camaraderie, even the location pleased him. When Jabine wasn't drilling, he was detailed to truck duty and spent his days rumbling around Washington, enjoying the sights and warm weather from the truck windows. "This is a delightful place for a camp. It is out in the country and yet not far from the city. Also, it is very high. We seem to be about even with the top of the [Washington] monument, so must be about 500 feet above the city." City life was exciting. When he went to a play with a friend, he was seated in the front row of the mezzanine. President Wilson and his wife, Edith, entered the theater and sat down in a box about fifteen feet away. "I was so excited at seeing him that I lost track of time and we nearly were late getting back to camp," Jabine wrote in an ebullient letter home to his mother.

The men became accustomed to the constant drilling, and uniforms and gear had finally begun to arrive, albeit piecemeal. Every day, the regiment's ranks swelled with new recruits, and soon there would be enough soldiers for two outfits, Companies A and B. A new name for the regiment had been spreading through camp, like flame licking through a cornfield. "They say that we are already known in the service as the 'Hellfire 30th'!" Jabine boasted.

The regiment's second company—Company B—was officially organized on November 3, and Jabine was moved to that unit, separating him from Frank Devlin but bringing him closer with Ellis Frink.

In the second week of November, he was able to move out of the crowded confines of the College of History building and into newly built barracks, which were much more comfortable and life was "much better in every way," he wrote.

The hill was becoming crowded. As the ranks of engineers grew, so did the number of chemists with the Bureau of Mines. Even with the wide-open campus and abundant land around it, the two groups were butting up against each other. The cantonments built for 1,800 engineers housed some 2,400 men, and even officers had doubled up in tiny rooms built for a single soldier. On November 20 alone, 120 men transferred in from Fort Slocum. In the College of History building that Jabine vacated, officers slept in vacant rooms, using piles of cardboard boxes as mattresses, while secretaries and stenographers worked at desks in the hallways. There was nowhere for the chemists to sleep either—all of them were traveling back and forth on Washington's streetcars each morning or sleeping in their labs.

Manning took up the space problem with the American University chancellor, asking if the university could surrender some of the rooms in the College of History building where it still maintained administrative offices. Bishop John William Hamilton wrote back granting permission for the additional space.

Chief of Engineers William Black, on the other hand, was irate over the chemists' demands and the bureau's growing footprint on the hill. Not only had the bureau positioned itself to use the campus even before receiving a formal invitation, the chemists' occupancy of rooms in the history building had never been part of the original agreement. To top it off, Manning was putting up temporary structures all around the grounds. In an attempt to rein in the chemists, Black suggested that the bureau and other government agencies needed a reminder of who was actually in charge of the campus and demanded that any changes on the hill would have to receive the engineers' approval.

Secretary of War Baker followed Black's advice, sending a reminder to all his cabinet officials about the wartime arrangements at American. But the wrangling continued. Every time it appeared settled, the bureau would make new demands for space. In the College of History building, the chemists eyed the space where the engineer officers slept. The engineers eyed the space where the bureau planned to put in a lunchroom. Finally, the bureau worked out an arrangement, divvying up the rooms in the building in a way that seemed to satisfy both sides. But even then, the bureau warned that it would probably need still more space in the future.

"I am quite confident that there will be future need for more office space than we are at present occupying, and I hope you will be able to keep this in mind, with the view to possibly accommodating us by permitting us the occupancy of such rooms as are now being used as sleeping quarters for your men," the station superintendent, Lauson Stone, wrote to the engineers.

In mid-November, a motorcade rolled into Camp American University. President Wilson stepped from one of the cars with his wife Edith to see the work of the engineers' camouflage regiments. He was bundled up against the cold in a long black coat and leather gloves, a wide-brimmed hat tipped low over his eyes. The first lady walked beside him, her polished boots gleaming as the crowd of officials made their way across the withered grass to the middle of a field. Secretary of State Robert Lansing came for the outing as well, along with Secretary of War Baker, more than a dozen generals, and a passel of colonels. With the crowd gathered in an open field, an officer asked the president to try to spot the soldier hidden nearby. Wilson scanned his surroundings. When he gave up, the officer gave a signal. A moss-covered rock a few feet away from Wilson flipped over, revealing an underground listening post with a soldier practically under the startled president's feet.

The engineers made no secret of their training at Camp American University—just the opposite: the army courted press coverage. Having the president visit the camp was a chance to publicize the engineers' ingenuity at deception. In the wide-open spaces around the campus, the camoufleurs of the Sixth Engineers practiced painting artillery to make it indistinguishable from the dun-colored ground and scrub brush. They wove reeds and leaves into netting that could be dragged over trenches or artillery. They practiced building and painting an entire dummy village that, from the vantage of aerial spies, would resemble a rural French hamlet.

The engineers sought press coverage of the Hellfire Battalion as well. Newspapers around the country carried lurid, sensational stories about how the Thirtieth Engineers gas regiment would be a ferocious response to German barbarity. "If his satanic majesty happened to drop around at the American University training camp today, he would see the 'Hellfire Battalion' at work and blush with envy," one wire article boasted.

"On the War Department records the battalion is known as the 'Gas and Flame Battalion of the Thirtieth Regiment Engineers,' " the article went on.

> Throughout the army they are known as the "Hell Fire Boys." This name is literally descriptive. A group of red-blooded Americans, most of them youths, are daily training in gas and flame fighting and learning how to make a real inferno for the Germans....Gas attacks always come in the heaviest battles, and the "hellfire boys" expect to be among those present at every big attack made by the American forces.

The Bureau of Mines, on the other hand, had little interest in publicity. Manning, Burrell, and the bureau chemists took great pains to keep their work quiet and out of the public eye. It wasn't always easy. As winter approached, more than five hundred civilians and soldiers—mostly chemists and engineers—were working in the American University laboratory and outbuildings. Detonations and explosions were daily occurrences. Tests of smoke candles and portable trench sprayers sent diaphanous clouds wafting on the breeze. Soldiers strapped on flamethrowers, the tanks of gas on their backs spewing a seething lance of flame a hundred feet from where the soldiers stood, and flares of different colors burst high over the hill.

Another factor made it difficult to keep the research under wraps: pets were disappearing all around the heights. Their owners puzzled over why they vanished and never returned. An article in the *Post* shed light on the matter. The Hellfire Boys were practicing with "liquid lightning" and "concentrated extract of vaporized brimstone calculated to reduce instantly a German field marshal to a cake of soap." As in New Haven and other Connecticut cities and towns, strays were being rounded up for use in the mysterious and deadly work on the hill.

"They would rather have the Kaiser, or the crown prince, or a

Bavarian grand duke to experiment with, for some of the fiery things they are squirting through their hose pipes are entirely too fancy to be wasted on anything less than the real Teutonic article, but in the absence of Germans, dogs and cats are providing fair substitutes, with dachshunds preferred," the article read.

Though the article painted the animal-testing issue with dark humor, the Washington Humane Society was not amused. The organization quietly fumed over the army's use of dogs for experiments, likening the hill to a torture chamber for animals, but raised no public objections, for the sake of the soldiers who needed protection from gas.

The medical investigations were fast becoming another major element of the research. The work had had a slow start in New Haven, because the physicians wanted to have more carefully controlled, methodical experimentation than the British and French. With the move to Washington, the work ballooned far beyond its modest beginnings. The 125 offensive war gases prepared on the hill all required toxicology tests, mostly with dogs and mice. Animals alone wouldn't suffice, though. In mid-October, the gas mask division set up a "man-test section," which was in charge of building gas chambers to put the masks through their paces. After Yandell Henderson tested the division's first gas mask in June, he realized that there was no way to reliably conduct gas mask tests without soldiers actually wearing them in a gas cloud to determine how well they worked. As development of the masks progressed, men would don a new model, wear it for hours on end, and then fill out a report on its comfort and fit. When new war gases came out, soldiers would wear masks into the gas chamber of the man-test house to see how well the filter worked. New chemical agents also required skin tests—putting drops of chemicals on soldiers' forearms to observe their effect on human flesh. Other developments hastened the imperatives for human testing. One was the early revelation at Yale that some animals were more resistant to gas than others, leading doctors to study treatments and medical care, including bleeding gas victims. In addition, the War Department's decision to manufacture gas in huge quantities forced Henderson's doctors to realize that workers in gas plants in the United States would soon need treatment, too, not just soldiers on the battlefield.

In addition, the potential for accidents during research experiments forced the bureau's scientists to confront the need for safety procedures, first-aid personnel, and fire alarms. After the station's opening in the fall, George Burrell had called in his division chiefs to discuss safety and first aid. They had agreed that American University needed medical personnel, particularly experts in eyes and skin. Warning signs peppered the grounds, with flags that popped up when gas was in use nearby. But now the chemists worried that they didn't have enough doctors on the grounds to take care of the men. Henderson proposed some bureaucratic sleight of hand to get more first-aid specialists on the hill. If they told the army they needed doctors for first aid, they wouldn't get them, but if they claimed the doctors were necessary for research, they would be provided, he said.

The expanding scope of the research meant that secrecy was becoming a concern. The work needed protection from snoops and busybodies, and from those with more-nefarious goals, such as spies, German sympathizers, and saboteurs. There were already safeguards in place. Burrell issued rules regarding secrecy to every member of the Research Division. Employees weren't allowed to step into laboratories that weren't their own without the permission of the section chief. Lists of each lab's employees were posted on their doors. The scientists were forbidden from speaking of their work to anyone, even bureau chemists in other research sections, to keep a firewall of secrecy between research areas. Division chiefs needed to inspect and seal important correspondence in person before it could be mailed. Papers were locked up in safes every night.

At a November 18 meeting, the bureau's brass talked about further measures. Codes were needed, Norris said, in case reports fell into the wrong hands. The men came up with a system: take the number associated with a chemical compound, multiply it by three, and add one. They'd keep the list under lock and key in Norris's office, where the chemists could consult it to refresh their memories. "The more codes we have the better off we are," he said. The men agreed that they also needed more guards around the campus to keep out interlopers.

Manning brought up the issue of security with Brigadier General Frederic V. Abbot, explaining that both McKinley Hall and the shared College of History building needed round-the-clock sentries. Abbot promised to beef up the guards. "In accordance with your suggestion I will take steps to see that an adequate guard is maintained at these buildings at all times," he said.

For Manning, it wasn't enough. He continued to fret about saboteurs and spies and, in mid-December, asked the engineers to erect a tall fence topped with barbed wire around the section of the campus where the research work was under way.

[In] view of the pernicious activity of the enemy in spying upon and attempting to destroy important government work, it seems to me desirable that a fence be erected outside of that portion of the grounds assigned to the Bureau of Mines, so as to prevent anyone from throwing fire or dynamite on to the buildings.

Sabotage wasn't the only concern. As the U.S. war plans progressed, the highest commanders in the army were discussing new ideas and tactics demanding the utmost secrecy. One of them was bombing German cities with gas. Some of the more lurid reporting on the gas and flame regiment forecasted such a tactic as a necessary response to the Germans. The *Washington Herald* had hinted at the idea of aerial bombing of German cities in its article in September, when it suggested that a secret fleet of thousands of planes was being prepared for an air offensive. Unlike other wildly exaggerated elements in those reports, this had a thread of truth.

In late November, Charles L. Potter, the director of the Office of the Gas Service, received a confidential letter from across the Atlantic. It was from Amos Fries, asking the scientists at American University to investigate several new war gases. He also told Potter that the army must prepare to use weapons or tactics outlawed by treaties, such as chemical-coated shrapnel and aerial bombing with mustard. Early in the month, the army chief of staff had asked the gas service to develop chemical-filled aerial bombs in case Germany started to use such bombs, and the army general staff approved the request with the blessing of the Ordnance Department.

It is not the idea of either this office or the General Staff, AEF, to employ such things as would be ordinarily against the laws of war, but since the enemy has shown himself utterly without conscience in other so-called laws of war, it is believed that the only policy for the Gas Service to adopt is one of preparedness to meet any attack the enemy may make.

Naturally, all such investigations must be kept strictly confidential, Fries warned. "The knowledge of them should be limited to the fewest possible people and the necessity for secrecy urged upon them."

Across the Atlantic, General Pershing had asked the chief of the Army Aeronautical School to study and report back on the possibility of dropping gas from airplanes. The commander of the army's aviation section responded that "dropping gas from airplanes is feasible if dropped in bombs," and could be much larger than incendiary bombs because the shells could be thinner and lighter.

Asked to comment, Fries wrote that "there is no doubt about the ability of planes to carry and drop gas bombs." The question was not whether the Americans could, but whether they should. The Germans had never done it, and the French and the British opposed it. Now the U.S. Army was considering it. The diplomatic sensitivity and the need for secrecy were obvious to Fries, who warned: "It is not believed necessary or advisable to go into the details of this matter further at this time."

Three days before Christmas, two prominent chemists with the National Research Council, Wilder D. Bancroft and John Johnson, wrote an urgent letter to Van Manning. Both had consulted with Fries and a top British chemist and warned Manning of the gravity of the situation relative to offensive gases. The estimates from the AEF and British gas officers were that the army would need 2,300 tons of gas each month, including 1,200 tons of mustard, 530 tons of phosgene, and 300 tons of chloropicrin. Fries recommended that half of all shells contain gas, and the AEF would likely use a million gas shells per month.

"In the opinion of those best qualified to judge, no offensive can now be successful without the use of gas; our forces, therefore, will be seriously, and needlessly, handicapped unless they are promptly supplied with an adequate provision of this essential material," the men wrote.

Two years earlier, the chairman of the National Research Council, George Hale, had warned that war might plunge the United States into gas warfare along with her allies. Now, as 1917 drew to an end, his worry had proved true. In late December, Hale wrote to the War Industries Board that chemical warfare had grown from insignificant beginnings to "an offensive weapon of the first order." Gas now filled a quarter of all shells fired on the western front and had caused twenty thousand British casualties in six weeks and poisoned morale. "There can be little doubt that gas is now becoming the determining factor in any successful offensive," he warned.

Chapter Eight

Over There

It was the strangest Christmas that Tom Jabine had ever known. Before dawn, plumes of smoke billowed over Camp American University. Winds and spitting rain made December 25, 1917, a damp, sour morning. Jabine stood in the gloom alongside the other Hellfire Boys, circled around a roaring bonfire, flames illuminating their faces. Washington was dark and still, with few astir to see the glow of the flames and the smoke coiling toward the sky. The drills were finished. It was time to go.

A month of waiting had frayed Jabine's enthusiasm for his regiment. Not long after Thanksgiving, commanding officers had stopped issuing passes to leave camp. Rumors had snaked through the ranks that their departure for France was imminent. Every time they were ordered to assemble their mess kits and rolls, Jabine wondered if it was time. Then they were ordered to unpack again, and the routine resumed. Every day, they were told they would leave as soon as transport was available to take them across, but that day never seemed to come.

As the weeks crawled by, Jabine received a promotion to corporal. When he had his picture taken with his new stripes, he didn't like how it turned out—he thought he looked too cross and tough—but he promised to send the photos to his family. When he wrote home on December 18, the word "disgusted" salted his letter. Two sergeants he liked had been demoted for not being tough enough, while officers that Jabine thought were rotten received promotions. He asked his family to write Christmas letters early, because he didn't know where he would be that day. To his surprise, he was promoted again, to sergeant.

Early on the morning of December 21, the regiment was ordered to pack again and then march out of camp. Jabine took his position at the rear of Company B, a solitary figure marching alone. It turned out to be another departure drill that sent the men down the hill, in a circle, and right back to camp. "This sudden activity may mean everything or it may mean nothing," Jabine wrote home. "But don't be surprised if you don't hear from me soon."

On Christmas Eve, the soldiers packed into the YMCA to watch vaudeville acts, and Red Cross workers handed out cigarettes and writing materials, comfort kits, and miniature stockings stuffed with candy. Secretary of War Newton Baker got up in front of the men, calling them "sons of the entire nation." Mrs. Baker sang for them, and the men roared their approval.

Dawn was still an hour away on Christmas morning when the order came to burn their mattresses and prepare to depart. Jabine joined the procession of engineers dragging straw stuffing from their barracks to the pyre. The flames leaped as they consumed the bedding the men had been sleeping on moments earlier. It was a sight to behold: hundreds of soldiers gathered in the dark around the inferno, the flames throwing a spectral glow over their ranks, a baptismal light of fire.

Everything Jabine needed for Europe had to fit in his pack. His woolen underwear, his cigarettes, his mess kit, the brushes and comfort kit from his church—all of it went into his pack. The temperature dropped, and the rain turned to snow. The men formed ranks on Massachusetts Avenue at 3:30 p.m. Daylight was slipping away. Lieutenant Colonel Atkisson took his place at the head of the column with the color guard, while Jabine fell into place behind the Third Platoon. The snow whirled in the deepening gloom as the men began to march.

With the city's pulse slowed to a holiday standstill, Washington seemed deserted. They marched down Massachusetts Avenue, past the gates of Westover, Charles Glover's mansion, and the half-finished apse of the National Cathedral atop Mount Saint Alban. The snowfall grew heavier, and soon the men marched in a blizzard. They turned south past the White House and the State, War, and Navy Building. As the men peered through the whirling flakes, they saw shapes moving on the White House lawn—the presidential flock of sheep, their white coats blending into the new-fallen snow.

The column crossed the mall and then turned east toward the train yard. At 6:00 p.m., they boarded a waiting train, which reached Jersey City at 3:30 in the morning. Just before daybreak, they boarded a ferry for the Hoboken piers where they pounded up the gangplank of the SS *President Grant,* a former German packet ship seized when the United States entered the war. Other regiments boarded as well, the 21st Engineers, the 303rd Stevedores, and an ordnance detachment. Colonel Atkisson said goodbye to his men— he was crossing later, on account of illness—and retreated back to the pier.

At 4:00 p.m., the *President Grant* set sail in a convoy with two other ships, the *Rochester* and the *Pastores,* their hulls painted with gray-and-black camouflage. The Statue of Liberty and Governor's Island fell away. The convoy turned past Staten Island, alongside Breezy Point, and out into the dark open ocean.

The Hellfire Regiment was on the fourth deck, down in the gut of the ship, with barely any room to move. Abandon-ship drills bookended each day, one first thing in the morning and another after lights-out at four-thirty in the afternoon, when the ship went dark to reduce visibility to submarines. After that, the men could remain on the decks or fumble their way into the dark interior, feebly illuminated with blue lights. Deep in the ship's thundering belly, Jabine's friend Ellis Frink, along with Arthur Archer and four other boys from the regiment, volunteered in the boiler room, their faces streaming with sweat as they shoveled coal into the furnace.

Shortly after noon on January 5, the *President Grant*'s torpedo bells clanged to life. Two soldiers on deck in the squalling wind and rain had spotted an object in the water off the port side of the ship. Everyone scrambled for their drill positions. Belowdecks, the ammunition hoists began to grind as shells and powder bags were winched up to the gunners. The ship shuddered as the engine powered up, and it began to zigzag in a submarine-evasion plan, then one of the guns opened fire with a booming concussion. The sea quieted, and the ship resumed its typical course. The soldiers had mistaken a porpoise for a submarine.

Four days later, the ship was under full steam when the bells clanged again—a periscope had been spotted to starboard. The ship shuddered as the guns boomed again and again, sending geysers of water into the air eight times as the ship fired at the object. Jabine rushed from the fourth deck for his drill station, but he was among the last to arrive at his post. By the time he had reached his station on the deck, the guns had fallen silent and the water was calm. He was too late to see anything. It was probably an unlucky fish, he mused, but afterward, word spread among the soldiers that it had been a true submarine attack, and that the ship's guns had sunk a U-boat. Both were wrong—the ship's captain recorded the object as a ship's mast floating on the waves, the detritus of another, less fortunate ship sunk at sea.

On the morning of January 10, the *President Grant* docked at Brest, France. For eight days, Companies A and B prowled the decks waiting to disembark. Finally, on January 18, they were allowed off the boat and onto trains. After two days of travel, they disembarked at Wizernes and marched to Helfaut, close to Saint-Omer, where the British trained their troops in gas warfare. Jabine was pleased to discover that winter in France was far warmer than back home, though very damp and foggy. "We are billeted still in the little village where we first stopped and I guess will be training here for some time to come so you have no cause for worrying over me for quite a while yet," Jabine wrote home. For now, Jabine was comfortable and warm—the weather was so balmy that he didn't even need a jacket at night—and he assured his mother he was as safe as if he were back in Yonkers.

The arrival of the gas and flame regiment marked a new phase for the gas service, both at home and overseas. The first American soldiers trained to use chemicals in war were just a few miles from the front. Under the tutelage of their British counterparts, Jabine and Higginbottom would learn how to bury Livens projectors, anchor Stokes mortars, and haul heavy gas tanks for drift-gas attacks. They would learn how to take wind readings before attacks, handle bombs, and dig projector emplacements both in daylight and at night.

Amos Fries had been working feverishly for months to prepare for gas warfare in France, and when Companies A and B marched into Helfaut, a crucial part of Fries's plans fell into place. The arrival of the Hellfire Regiment represented a bridge between the domestic gas service and the AEF's service under Fries. Before long, the chemists' work would burst from the laboratories, turning from technical puzzles defined by beakers and Bunsen burners into an explosive fusion of steel and flesh and gas on the battlefield.

Amos Fries's confidence in the gas service grew by the day. He kept at his work with relentless determination; he had even spent Christmas Day working in his office, except for an hour or so around lunch, when he traded stories around a fireplace with one of his majors. Three or four inches of snow blanketed the ground when he made his way to the mess to join the other officers for turkey with chestnut dressing, peas, salad, plum pudding, coffee, and champagne. A small decorated tree sat on a side table. Holly, ivy, and mistletoe draped the chandelier overhead, and the officers swapped knickknacks. They were all married, many with children, and they tried to enjoy themselves despite the distance that lay between them and their families.

Despite Fries's efforts to stay healthy in the dank, cold French winter, he took to bed with the flu, which began with a mild fever, a cold, and painful tonsils. He stayed in bed for several days, wrapped in a dressing gown that Bessie had sent him for Christmas. As he rested, he felt like Robinson Crusoe, with nothing to do but sit and think. As 1917 wound down, Fries fell into a contemplative state about the war and what lay ahead. There was a feeling among the officers that Germany was going to do something major soon, something desperate, probably by mid-1918, "before the days and nights reach an equality again," as Fries poetically put it.

New Year's Eve was a squalling, windy night, cold with a driving rain. General Pershing was throwing a party to usher in 1918. Fries felt better, but he continued to ruminate over how long the war would go on. There was talk among the officers that peace might be coming soon. Despite the hopeful talk, an end to the war seemed distant to Fries—the Germans seemed endlessly resilient despite heavy setbacks. "On the other hand the Germans are certainly sick of the war and those who know anything know they are beaten just as the South knew it was beaten in the fall of '63," he wrote home to Bessie.

His stubborn flu returned, turning into a painful sinus infection and splitting headaches that sent him to the hospital for several more days of recovery. Stuck in an officers' ward warmed with a feeble coal stove, he answered Bessie's letters from November and earlier December that were only now reaching him. In one of them, she asked about the prospects for peace. He responded:

> Frankly, I don't see anything clearly on the subject. Somebody and perhaps everybody is doing a lot of dying. Whose bluff will show threadbare first is yet to be seen. I know a great many things naturally from my position and yet I really know nothing definite. However, if peace comes before Christmas 1918, I will be most agreeably surprised.

In that first week of January, he also learned some news: General Pershing had finally acted on his long-standing reservations about William Sibert and sent the general home. "I guess he was canned. This is no place for a man nearly old enough to retire anyway," Fries wrote home.

Fries's nonchalance about Sibert's dismissal wasn't surprising. The friction between Pershing and his second-in-command was hardly a secret, particularly after the dressing-down that Sibert had received in September. On December 12, a telegram had landed on Sibert's desk at Gondrecourt saying the War Department was relieving him of his command and ordering him to return to the United States. The next day, a lengthy letter from Pershing himself arrived, marked CONFIDENTIAL. The subject of the memo: "Pessimism."

Americans visiting training areas sensed deep apprehension, leaving an impression "that the war is already well along toward defeat for our arms," Pershing wrote. Without accusing Sibert of creating a negative mood in the ranks, Pershing's rebuke was clear. An officer who isn't hopeful, inspired, and uplifted, he wrote, "should yield his position to others with more of our national courage."

Sibert fired back a blunt challenge to his commander in chief to drop the oblique accusation and make an official charge against him, which Sibert could then refute in a military court of inquiry. In the end, Sibert headed home. It was a humiliating fall for the engineer who had built and sailed through the Gatun Locks of the Panama Canal and was charged with training the largest American army ever mustered for a foreign war. Sibert didn't even land a face-saving job at the War Department; instead, his new assignment was an unglamorous post in charge of distant camps that were little more than staging areas for soldiers before they debarked for France.

Fries didn't linger much over what had happened to Sibert or reflect on the fate of his old friend; in his letter, he moved quickly to news of other officers and sartorial matters, like his torn fur coat. "About time for me to stop and do some sewing on my bear-skin coat where it has ripped under the right arm."

After he got out of the hospital, Fries threw himself back into his work with a ferocious energy. The summer before, everything the American Expeditionary Forces knew about gas warfare fit inside the manila file folder handed off to Fries. That meager beginning had ballooned into a robust organization that grew daily, and his single-minded attention to his new service had begun to pay off. Because of his agitation for staff, he now had more officers than he knew what to do with, and the experienced men he requested were arriving from the States. Other technologies were also being grouped under the banner of chemical warfare—smoke bombs, incendiaries, and phosphorus were all rapidly being subsumed into his department.

In January, the French had ordered up 240,000 gas shells from the Americans, and the two countries struck a deal under which the Americans would provide the French with three hundred tons of chlorine each month, and the French would provide the Americans with one hundred tons of phosgene monthly. The French phosgene added up to only a fraction of the amount the U.S. Gas Service calculated it would require; Fries and the AEF's chief ordnance officer had already set in motion plans for a factory in France to produce more than eighty-three tons of phosgene per day—or twenty-five hundred tons per month—as well as a shell-filling factory. Both would be near Gièvres, France, a location close to ports and a departure point for sending finished shells to the front.

By late January, his lieutenants had recommended the best chemicals for aerial gas bombs. The primary filling would be mustard or another war gas, dichloropropyl sulfide, in fifty-pound bombs. A second filling would be cyanogen bromide or cyanogen chloride in larger bombs. Phosgene or a similar substance, thiophosgene, was a third option, and bromobenzyl cyanide or bromoacetone was a fourth. One of Fries's lieutenants recommended that aerial gas bombs should not be used on a small scale, except for experimental purposes. "When available for use on a large scale, every possible bombing plane should be concentrated for the employment of these bombs on the same night so that the greatest number of rest billets, concentration camps, etc., may be taken by surprise," he wrote.

Fries described the rapid growth of the gas service as a "seven day's wonder"—an explosive expansion on a biblical scale. "We have gradually enlarged our vision until we have everything in the chemical line whether for artillery, shell, aviation bombs or anything else in that line," he wrote to Bessie.

In a sign of the growing prestige of his service, he had been promised his own limousine, an eight-cylinder Cadillac with electric lights, upholstered seats, hand-cranked windows, and an intercom to talk with the driver—"a daisy" of a car, he called it. Department heads were assigned limousines, and receiving one imparted the same prestige to Fries's service as other, more established army sections.

In letters home, Fries described the endless complications he faced. Fries's job wasn't solely to build the army's capacity for chemical warfare, get gas troops into fighting form, and send them to the front; he also had to shoehorn the new service into the army's existing structure, melding old and new seamlessly. For every problem he needed to solve, a dozen more cropped up, each of them interlocked in the slow-moving machinery of the War Department. One of the biggest challenges was determining the relationship between the gas service and the Ordnance Department, which was responsible for supplying the army with arms, ammunition, and everything else pertaining to the fighting, as well as establishing ordnance arsenals and depots. Which department would be responsible for filling shells and rebuilding stockpiles? Which department would store them, mark the tanks and projectors, and transport the new weapons up to the lines? Over the winter, Fries and the Army Ordnance Department had wrestled with that question, ultimately deciding that the Ordnance Department would make the gas shells and the gas service would fill them.

Fries faced a similar problem with respect to training. Readying recruits for gas warfare required education and drilling. For now, the American gas troops would train with the British Special Brigade, but that wasn't a long-term solution. Would artillery and gas service companies—both of which would use gas shells—train together or separately, and which department would be in charge? As he had since the beginning of his tenure, Fries followed the example of the British gas service. The British had their Porton experimental field in England and a training ground at Saint-Omer. With an ocean separating him from Washington and American University, Fries began searching for an experimental field of his own.

On Sunday, January 20, he chose a location about eight miles southeast of Chaumont, on twenty square miles of farmland outside the village of Biesles. Aligned east to west, the range was oriented in the same direction as prevailing winds on much of the front to mimic battlefield conditions. He envisioned a training field as grand as Britain's, a center of both research and teaching.

Fries had supreme confidence in the fiefdom he was building in France. He was less confident in what was happening on the other side of the Atlantic. He seemed puzzled about Colonel Charles Potter, the chief of the domestic gas service, and what exactly he did, scoffing that Potter was "more or less just a kid." From his perspective across the Atlantic, Fries believed he was in charge of the entire enterprise on both sides of the ocean, maintaining order and keeping the whole machinery running smoothly. "The arrangement now in Washington is simply a loosely jointed federation of parts of four or more other departments and except for our steering would break down in no time."

Despite Fries's skepticism, the work in Washington was not breaking down. Just the opposite, in fact: through storms and cold, the chemists carried on their research. Van Manning's January report on the offensive division's progress summarized work on almost three-dozen projects, listing success after success, each one carefully bulleted and described in cautiously positive terms or as an outright achievement. He described new smoke devices used on the battlefield to obscure troops and hide trenches, and improvements to smoke boxes that belched chemical clouds to screen ships from submarines. Experimentation with flamethrowers had produced two models that spewed liquid flame one hundred feet. The station had tested two kinds of bombs to drop from airplanes and had been making progress on an American version of the Livens projectors, using smaller drums that could be shot farther than the British version.

Production of war gases was becoming more efficient. "The situation is satisfactory in regard to the manufacture of chlorine, chloropicrin and phosgene," Manning wrote. "In fact the American Synthetic Color Company at Stamford expect to make 50,000 lbs. of chloropicrin per day from now on." While that work was in the hands of the Ordnance Department, he boasted that "the preliminary research work was done by the Bureau of Mines."

The chemists also made progress developing new gases: cyanogen chloride appeared to be a "very promising gas for use in gas shell," Manning reported, while bromobenzyl cyanide proved to be the most powerful tear gas yet discovered. Magnesium arsenide, sodium arsenide, and calcium arsenide all had good results as well.

Over the months, the chemists had developed a system for investigating new war gases. First, the offensive research chemists analyzed a new gas's physical and chemical properties, synthesizing small batches in the indoor laboratory. Samples went to the pharmacological section, where Yandell Henderson would study its properties and their effects on dogs, guinea pigs, monkeys: how lethal it was, whether it interfered with breathing, caused blisters, or had other effects. Then William McPherson, the chief of the Small-Scale Manufacturing Section, would work with his chemists on a process for synthesizing it in larger quantities, rigging up stills to make larger batches in the outdoor manufacturing shacks that dotted the grounds around the American University buildings. Fieldner's Gas Mask Research Section ran tests with masks to determine whether the gases penetrated the different models of the American, French, and British masks. The Pyrotechnic and Dispersoid Sections tested ways of delivering it to the enemy, whether in artillery shell, Stokes mortars, Livens drums, as candles, or from cylinders. Throughout all of this testing, researchers investigated the availability of the precursor chemicals that were the raw ingredients. As gases moved through the research pipeline, the chemists who had become experts in their properties moved with them, graduating to each subsequent development stage. If the gas passed all of those hurdles and still proved satisfactory, then it was approved for mass production.

Mustard topped Manning's list. Unfortunately, James Bryant Conant and Organic Research Unit No. 1 had been struggling with how to produce it. In the freezing labs of McKinley Hall, the men wrestled with a knot of problems that made the substance maddeningly difficult to make on a large scale. Toward the end of 1917, his unit had successfully prepared a batch of mustard using the slow chlorohydrine method that Victor Meyer had described and that the Germans were using. On paper, there was a better way. Mixing ethylene gas with sulfur monochloride yielded dichloroethyl sulfide and sulfur. When cooled, the sulfur then reacted with the dichloroethyl sulfide, yielding liquid mustard. But this process also produced chlorine in the solution, which made the resulting mustard impure and less effective. So much manpower and effort were expended on the king of the war gases that the experiment station gained a new nickname: Mustard Hill.

The problem consumed Conant day in and day out. The British and French had also been working on the mustard problem, so Lieutenant Colonel William H. Walker, the chief of the Chemical Service Section, cabled British counterparts for a description of their process. As Washington braced for more snow, help arrived from Britain in the form of a January 26 cablegram from the U.S.

military attaché in London. The cablegram accompanied a report from British chemist Frederick Pope, who had discovered a much-simpler process for synthesizing mustard, using a catalyst to combine ethylene and sulfur dichloride. It was a breakthrough. "The British Authorities request that more than usual precautions be observed in keeping this matter secret," the attaché warned.

Still, a viable method for synthesizing mustard was only a first step. Mass production was another problem altogether, fraught with technical obstacles. For two grueling weeks in February, Conant tried to replicate the British method for synthesizing the compound. Soon after, a second cable arrived with another break-through. The chemists discovered that lowering the temperature during the reaction prevented chlorination and helped keep the mustard pure. Even with the new information from the British, Conant still had difficulties. The British method using ethylene and sulfur monochloride worked but still yielded impure mustard when Conant's unit attempted it at American University. The resulting material was extremely unstable, breaking up into hydrochloric acid and a thick black oil. In theory the British system was better for industrial-scale production, but it was also difficult and dangerous, tending to clog pipes and machinery. To work out these problems, the Bureau of Mines set up experimental satellite labs in several locations. One was outside New York City, and another was at the Dow Chemical plant in Midland, Michigan. A third was tucked into downtown Cleveland, about two miles from Nela Park, where the industrial wizard Frank Dorsey was in charge.

Gas wasn't the only Research Division product that proved difficult to put into mass production. After the debacle with the first twenty thousand gas masks, Arno Fieldner and his mask division had worked to fix the flaws that had caused the first masks to fail so miserably, making a series of improvements on the British mask. But while the British mask worked better, it was also extremely uncomfortable and difficult to wear for more than a few minutes, and the Americans began looking closely at adopting the lighter, more comfortable French Tissot mask. Gas mask charcoal and filters had been steadily getting better. The Hero Manufacturing Company in Philadelphia had been making masks at a rate of five thousand a day, but that was nowhere near enough. The army had estimated it would need twenty thousand masks produced *every day* after January 1 but couldn't find a company that could produce that volume.

To solve the problem, the War Department had taken another unprecedented step in November 1917. Rather than contract out the manufacture of masks, the Sanitary Corps of the army decided to open its own government gas mask factory. The army had already opened a charcoal-production factory in New York at the Astoria Light and Power Company, where tons of nutshells and coconut husks were shipped to be baked into activated carbon for masks. The army quartermaster found an industrial building for rent on Jackson Avenue in nearby Long Island City.

This was an extraordinary move. The president clearly had the power to go to war, but nowhere did the Constitution say that the president had authority to go into manufacturing. War Department lawyers pored over the legal ramifications of opening a government gas mask factory. The judge advocate general of the War Department had decided the idea was legal, and Secretary of War Newton Baker issued a memo to the surgeon general ordering him to establish the factory in the Jackson Avenue building, which the government began leasing on November 24 for $112,000 a year.

On January 1, 1918, ten sewing-machine operators were hired. Eventually, the Astoria plant and the Long Island City factories would merge into a five-building campus known as the Gas Defense Plant, a million square feet and thousands of women stitching, assembling, and testing gas masks. By the war's end, 12,350 employees at the plant were turning out forty-two thousand masks per day.

By January of 1918, dozens of officers, scientists, and chemists from every corner of the Research Division now crowded into the weekly meetings at the experiment station. The research demands were outgrowing American University, and the limited space there was becoming a liability. Manning had no option: if there was no more room for research on the hill, the bureau would have to create more. Not just a room here and there—an entirely new laboratory. The spot he pinpointed as the best location was between McKinley Hall and Massachusetts Avenue, on an open area of the campus across the quad from the College of History building. He calculated it would need to be about 250 feet long, with an outbuilding for the power and heating plant. This wouldn't be just any laboratory—it would be a huge research facility intended for three hundred or more chemists, one that Manning intended to be the most advanced and well-outfitted research laboratory anywhere in existence.

The building depended on approval from the engineers at Camp American University. "Our work is growing to such proportions that it is absolutely necessary to put up more buildings to take care of it, and I trust you will grant the necessary authority for the new installation," Manning wrote to Colonel Mitchell, the commanding officer of the Twentieth Engineers.

But the engineers also coveted open space on the campus, and the colonel responded to Manning's demand with obvious irritation. There was no space remaining for recruits to train and drill, and now the bureau wanted to lay claim to one of the few areas of level ground anywhere on the hill. He suggested another spot, to the west of McKinley Hall. Manning refused.

The work would go ahead on the original spot he requested, illustrating his leverage as the founding father of the gas research work. But his persistence didn't help the bureau's already antagonistic relationship with the engineers.

It would be months before construction could even start on the new building, and the technical men struggled to do their work in the hill's cold and crowded labs. The urgency of the work and the chemists' determination required them to tolerate the unfortunate condition of the McKinley Hall labs, with all of the accompanying hazards and inconveniences.

Those very conditions, within the elastic hierarchies of the civilian Bureau of Mines, would have a consequence which would result in one of the most important research discoveries of the war. It began with a winsome recruit named Winford Lee Lewis.

Lewis was another crucial addition to the war gas work. A thirty-nine-year-old chemistry professor from Evanston, Illinois, he had first come to Washington in October of 1917 at the suggestion of Charles Parsons, the chief chemist at the Bureau of Mines and secretary of the American Chemical Society. Lewis was a native Californian, a rarity among the bureau's pedigreed scientists from Ivy League schools. His ebullient mind crackled with humor, and though he insisted that he was shy at heart, he loved dispensing advice and regaling an audience with a good yarn that reduced them to paroxysms of laughter.

Born in 1878, he had grown up in Gridley, California, a dusty village about sixty miles north of Sacramento. The Lewises were a pioneer family; both parents had come from the same town in Indiana, but his father, George, had gone west with a covered wagon train at age sixteen, joining the streams of prospectors and settlers pursuing dreams of an American El Dorado. He claimed a homestead of several hundred acres, with another 160 acres on an adjoining property, and yet another property he jointly owned with his uncle. Land rich and prosperous, he retraced his steps to Indiana several years after he left and returned to California with Lewis's mother as his bride.

The Lewis farm sat in a tawny landscape of sepia-toned hills and catkins of live oaks. When Lewis was young, the family moved to the smaller, adjoining farmhouse, which sprouted a room every time a new child was born—there were eight children in all, five by Lewis's mother, who died when he was about four, and three more from George's second wife. Lee Lewis was about five when he started school at the one-room schoolhouse in nearby West Liberty. One June, an itinerant lecturer arrived at the school. With the children watching, the woman broke an egg into a saucer of alcohol, and the children watched as the egg turned white, pickled in the alcohol before their eyes. In a second experiment, she lit a match over another dish of alcohol and set the dish aflame as the wide-eyed young Lewis watched in awe. This traveling sorceress, it turned out, was a teetotaler, a temperance advocate trying to frighten the children over the evils of alcohol. Young Lee Lewis remembered it not as an abstinence lesson but as his first chemistry experiment, a demonstration of the combustible union of fire and alcohol.

When Lewis headed off to attend a fledgling new college called Stanford, his father wanted him to study law, but Lewis was drawn instead to chemistry. Mines of all sorts riddled California, and chemists were in constant demand as assayers, to determine the mineral content and value of extracted ores. At Stanford, his chemistry skills weren't always evident. After he spilled a beaker of nitric acid onto a professor, the teacher suggested that Lewis try a different profession.

Still, Lewis stuck with it. He went to the University of Washington for graduate school, taught there for several years, then moved on to teach at Morningside College, a small Methodist school in Sioux City, Iowa. In the back of one of his classes, a dark-haired beauty named Myrtilla Mae Cook sat taking notes. He ended up marrying her in 1906.

From Sioux City, he went on to get a chemistry Ph.D. at the University of Chicago, with a minor in bacteriology. A stint followed as a chemist for the Department of Agriculture, and he began teaching at Northwestern University in 1910, serving as the city chemist for Evanston, Illinois, at the same time. He specialized in sanitation and chemistry. After a minor typhoid breakout in Evanston, he published papers about using hypochlorite—bleach—

to counter the spread of the disease. When he began contemplating how to aid in the war effort in 1917, Lewis assumed he would be most suited for work related to sanitation and food safety. Charles Parsons, a captain in the Sanitary Corps' food division, sent Lewis a job description and invited him to Washington, apologetically telling him he would have to pay his own way.

Lewis bought a train ticket to Washington in the fall of 1917, where he met with officers from both the Sanitary Corps and the Ordnance Department over several days. He decided against the former because it would almost certainly require him to go abroad; moreover, he didn't relish the idea of making nutritional surveys of army mess halls, picturing himself pursued by irate camp cooks waving meat cleavers. Instead, he reached an agreement with the Trench Warfare Section of the Ordnance Department. He would finish out his semester teaching at Northwestern and return to Washington in January to work at American University.

Lewis had wired Myrtilla on October 9 to expect him home that Friday at 2:00 p.m. Lewis's healthy sense of humor and quick wit showed even in the Western Union telegram telling her he had secured a position and a commission in the army, and a pay cut to go with it. "It seems we will have to live on prunes and beans for I am quite in beyond my means as a captain in the army," Lewis wrote. He called himself "Captain Dad," a family nickname that stuck with him for the duration of the war.

After Lewis finished teaching the semester at Northwestern, he arrived in Washington. His first job at American University was studying how metal shells corrode from the toxic liquids within. It was a crucial safety issue—new combinations of chemicals could react with the metal shells in unexpected ways, and damaged shells could leak their contents or explode. There was a fairly easy way to test the effect of the chemical agents on the metal: submerge shell shards in the liquid chemicals and observe the results. Lewis, however, took a different route. To mimic the conditions of actual shells, he instead put the liquid chemicals inside shells, heated them up, let them stand, and then reopened them to observe the effect of the chemicals on the interior.

However logical this approach, it had unpleasant side effects. On his second day, one of his assistants was gassed so badly that he was sent to the hospital. When the bureau sent Lewis replacement men, he refused to continue unless he had a safer work environment. It was well known that the chemists had little regard for the army's rigid hierarchies, and it was not the first such instance of casual rejection of military strictures. The chemists saw such displays as amusing signs of freewheeling independence. For officers, though, it showed not only insolence but disorganization and lack of discipline. Had the army been in charge of the research work at that point, Lewis might have been court-martialed for disobeying a superior officer or for insubordination. But because the bureau was a civilian-led organization, directed by scientists more concerned with problem-solving than rank, Lewis's demand got him his way.

To the east of American University, in the city's Brookland neighborhood, Catholic University of America had offered up its campus for the war effort as well. Unlike American University's hastily rigged lab, Catholic's Martin Maloney Chemistry Laboratory had been under construction long before the Bureau of Mines began looking for a laboratory, and it had opened in November of 1917. Catholic's chemistry department was an enormous granite building trimmed with limestone and marble. The entire first floor of the east wing was dedicated to a state-of-the-art inorganic chemistry lab, while an organic chemistry lab took up the west wing on the opposite site. The main analytical laboratory was big enough to accommodate almost fifty researchers, and as many as sixty more scientists could comfortably work in more labs on the second floor. Luckily for the bureau, Father J. J. Griffin, the priest who headed the lab, had attended Johns Hopkins with Sunny Jim Norris, who was the chief of the offensive section of the Research Division.

After the bureau approved moving some of the research, Norris told Lewis to requisition a truck and a driver to take him across town to Catholic, where his Organic Research Unit No. 3 would resume its work at Father Griffin's lab. Unsure of what he would need, Lewis selected an assortment of chemicals and acids that he thought would be useful, loaded the jars and vials and beakers into the truck along with a cage full of rats, and the wary driver set out across the city. It was about five miles to Brookland, but roads on Washington's outskirts were not well maintained. En route, the truck hit a rut and bounced, smashing several bottles of hydrochloric acid and ammonia. When hydrochloric acid and ammonia vapors come into contact, they create a roiling cloud of ammonium chloride. Perhaps that was what caused the nervous driver, well aware of the work on the hill, to bolt from the truck on foot. It took a few minutes for Lewis to coax him back, and they eventually continued on — most likely at a slower pace — toward Catholic University.

At the same time that Lewis left the hill, the next company of Hellfire Boys had also decamped. The recruitment call for the gas and flame regiment had brought more enthusiastic volunteers than Companies A and B could accommodate, so the engineers organized Company C in early December of 1917, then Company D a short time later, moving the new battalion across the Potomac River to Fort Myer in Virginia.

When Companies A and B marched from Washington on Christmas Day, their ranks included farriers and cooks, buglers and saddlers, but no chaplain. That changed on January 19 when James Thayer Addison walked into Colonel Atkisson's office at the regimental headquarters. Tall and slim with gray eyes, the Harvard graduate had married just before Christmas, taken his chaplaincy exam on January 4, and a few days later received his commission, with orders to report to Fort Myer. "At last, my real war job!" Addison wrote in his journal.

Affable and good-natured, the thirty-year-old chaplain knew nothing about gas warfare, or about military chaplaincy, for that matter. What he knew, he gleaned from books he read late at night after he retired to his barracks. Colonel Atkisson told Addison he was pleased to have him—the regiment needed a chaplain who could establish himself as a friend of the soldiers.

That night, an officer brought Addison up in front of the soldiers at a raucous gathering at the fort YMCA. "I am proud to belong to a regiment that's going to have such a lively future!" Addison said, and the men roared with applause. It was a warm welcome, but when he retired to his freezing barracks, he felt like a nervous schoolboy. "Oh, it's wonderful to be in uniform as an officer and soon to be in the thick of the greatest war in history!" he wrote in his diary.

Addison's ardor for camp life quickly cooled. Storms buffeted the camp, depositing ever-growing snowdrifts outside the barracks. Target practice was impossible. Motorcycles wouldn't start; trucks got stuck in the snow. Addison noted the foul weather absentmindedly, but he had other things to think about. His bride, Margaret, took up residency in one of Washington's downtown hotels. Almost daily, he taxied to see her, staying overnight in the hope of starting a family. On nights when he did sleep at the camp, he was sometimes the only person in the officers' quarters.

On one of his return trips from Washington, he picked up a moving-picture reel about gas attacks. A few days later, the regiment officers and soldiers crowded into the YMCA to watch the film of a staged gas attack at American University. *The New 30th Engineers in Action,* the newsreel was called. In the darkened room, the men watched the soldiers in their gas masks with rapt interest. There was a speech afterward, but Addison didn't stay to hear it. Instead, he hurried back to Washington to see Margaret. His time was running out. He would be leaving soon, and he might never see her again.

Chapter Nine

"A Constant Menace"

Winter barreled into Washington with bone-rattling cold. Day after day, snow fell with gloomy predictability, and drifts grew across the city. A storm on January 28 shut down trolleys, snarled traffic, and delayed freight. Another foot of snow brought the city to a standstill again two days later. Public schools ran out of coal, children stayed home, and the district ordered "heatless Mondays" to conserve fuel.

At American University, the cold seeped in through the drafty windows and between the planks of the shacks peppering the campus. The rushed renovation of McKinley Hall had created subpar working conditions for the chemists; now they had the cold to contend with, too, and drafts guttered in the fume hoods. The most detested winter duties on the hill were assignments in the unheated sheds around McKinley Hall.

Like the rest of Washington, the campus ran short on coal. Three train cars loaded with 140 tons arrived to replenish the supply. As the shipment awaited trucks to off-load the fuel, word spread through nearby neighborhoods about the arrival of the train. Hundreds of desperate residents, women and children among them, showed up with buckets and bags, pleading to buy the coal. Some began to swarm the train cars to grab what they could. Soldiers arrived with rifles to hold back the crowd with bayonets.

People in the crowd begged the soldiers to allow them to take some fuel. The pained soldiers remained stoic as the loaded trucks rumbled away to the campus. The winter seemed never to end. On February 4, another nighttime gale hammered the city, flipping planes at an airfield, cutting off train service, and freezing the Potomac River.

In February, the temperature soared, turning midwinter into spring. The frozen Potomac began to break up, releasing an ice jam that hurtled downstream, grinding up tugboats and jetties and flooding Georgetown. On the morning of February 16, Private James Smith crouched in front of an outdoor brick furnace on the north side of the campus, within sight of the barracks at Camp American University. Another private named Markle Hurtt was at his side, overseeing the experiment. Hurtt watched as Smith poured ground arsenic from a can into a galvanized pail. After he emptied the can, he reached for a second, then a third. When all three were empty, the pail contained twenty-one pounds of pulverized arsenic. Next, Smith poured in magnesium and stirred the compound with a stick.

Hurtt showed Smith how to put in the blasting fuse. It was a slow-burning fuse, which would give the men almost a minute to retreat to a safe distance down the wooden boardwalk nearby. Smith pushed the fuse into the mix of arsenic and magnesium, then slid a lid on the pail and weighted it with bricks. Smith struck a match and lit the fuse. Hurtt retreated down the boardwalk as Smith hefted the pail inside the furnace and slammed shut the cast-iron door.

The two privates were waiting for the reaction when two officers, a captain and a lieutenant, strode down the boardwalk. Private Hurtt warned them of the experiment in progress. This was at least the fifth time the experiment had been conducted. Every time the slow-smoldering fuse reached the powder mix in the bucket, it was the same result: a flash, a puff, and a cloud of granulated arsenic. It would only be a few seconds, Hurtt assured them. Best to wait. The four stood on the boardwalk, waiting for the puff of smoke.

Instead, the mixture exploded with a roar. The detonation flung off the iron cover and blasted the furnace into pieces, turning the bricks into missiles that flew in every direction, shattering windows of nearby buildings. A curtain of heat and flame roared from the furnace, searing Hurtt and Smith, and flying projectiles shredded the skin of the lieutenant and the captain. Bleeding and singed, ears ringing, the stunned men looked back at the experiment site. Nothing remained of the furnace except a circle of brick and arsenic-coated debris scattered in a wide radius.

Men came running to see what had happened. Soldiers chained a dog downwind of the blast site as a barometer for airborne toxins and sprinkled a caustic solution on the ground to neutralize the spattered arsenic. The force of the explosion had tossed a fifty-pound chunk of bricks at least thirty feet from the blast site, and more debris landed one hundred feet away. The whole area was shut down and nearby buildings evacuated, and the injured men were helped to the College of History building for first aid, and two of the men were sent to Walter Reed Hospital. While nobody died in the accident—it was never determined whether it was caused by bad luck or bad chemicals—it was a reminder of the violent power of the substances that the chemists worked with. Explosions, chemical burns, and accidental gassings were common at the station. The campus safety engineer concluded that "steps should be taken immediately to secure a much larger tract of land for experimental purposes."

It wasn't just the scientists who were vulnerable to accidents and miscalculations; the Corps of Engineers also complained about the chemists' dangerous experiments. The engineers drilled on the campus quad uncomfortably close to where the chemists occasionally fired off mortars. On March 16, Lieutenant Colonel Earl Marks was standing with a group of soldiers near the YMCA when a large piece of wood landed with a thud about ten feet away. Moments later, an iron shell casing tumbled to the ground nearby as well. As Marks watched, other fragments of debris rained down on the parade ground from hundreds of feet in the air. Marks was livid. He had heard about such carelessness, including unexploded shells landing near the engineers' cantonments, but hadn't seen it himself. He fired off an irate note to Lauson Stone, the experiment station superintendent, demanding that the chemists use greater care.

Stone wrote a contrite response a few days later. He had taken up the matter with the Research Division, and there was agreement that a new and larger proving ground was needed, farther from the activities of the engineers. "The location of such grounds, and obtaining the necessary privilege thereof will take some time, but as soon as it can be effected, this character of the work will be removed to a position where it will not be dangerous to your camp or the men therein," he wrote.

Manning, neat as a pin and fussy by nature, had already taken note of how the state of the experiment station had deteriorated. There were no paved roads around the buildings, just bare ground churned into yellowish mud or frozen into ruts. Dogs maimed in experiments limped through the campus, sometimes in a pathetic state from the injuries sustained from exposure to gas. Corpses of dogs killed in the trials rotted in buckets. The stench from the animal cages was overpowering. Gas clouds huffed from the open-air stills and sheds that the chemists erected helter-skelter around the campus. Sometimes the stench of gas wafted all the way into the city's neighborhoods, earning the campus the new nickname "Skunk Hill."

A few days after the debris rained down near the engineers, a sanitary inspector came through the experiment station. As he strolled through the campus, he jotted down what he saw: water-filled bottles, barrels, jars, and tin cans strewn on the ground—potential breeding grounds for mosquitoes when the weather warmed. He noted an enormous refuse pile of ashes, paper, scraps, and lumber. There were feces scattered around the grounds, and with the weather finally warming, flies swarmed around dog carcasses left in the sun. Flies also swarmed around empty animal crates smeared with excrement, and pools of standing water stagnated in pits and sewer trenches. "There is, apparently, no attempt to police the area and its appearance is unsightly as well as unsanitary," he wrote.

Marks forwarded the report to Brigadier General Frederic Abbot, pointing out that the unsanitary conditions of the experiment station "are not new and have existed for some time." The mess was tolerable in winter, he wrote, but as warm weather arrived, "it will prove a constant menace to the health of the men of this camp."

Abbot fired off a short note to Manning. "The within letters show that something has got to be done to improve conditions at American University." Manning's reply was prompt and courteous, indicating that he was aware of the dismal state of the experiment station and promising to do whatever was necessary to remove cause for complaint.

The sanitary and safety issues further deepened the antagonism between the Bureau of Mines and the army. Calls from within the War Department to militarize the civilian-led research arm had gained strength in the fall, and still more over the winter. In January, as organizational problems mounted, the army sacked Charles Potter as director of the Office of the Gas Service. Manning managed to stave off the military men, however, and the hill remained his fiefdom.

The Research Division also grappled with the problem of security as new enlisted men appeared every day. On March 1, there were 743 men working on chemical weapons research. By mid-May, there would be 1,125, of whom 554 were civilian chemists, 114 were commissioned officers, and 487 enlisted men. On April 3, Military Intelligence Division chief Ralph Van Deman alerted the camp's intelligence officer about a report he had received that the chemists working on the hill were not being discreet about their work and were still talking very freely "on the subject of certain poisons thought to be under consideration there."

This was not a new concern. Despite crackdowns on dissent and laws aimed at spies and domestic adversaries, a constant undercurrent of anxiety over infiltration and espionage crackled through Washington. The Military Intelligence Division carried out periodic security inspections on the hill, and coincidentally an intelligence officer had even been on the campus the day of the February 16 explosion, investigating a soldier who had written a suspicious letter. But the Research Division had a new and unexpected demand for security. A new chemist was coming to the hill. This was no graduate student who had puttered through lab experiments or graying academic moved to join the war effort. This chemist arrived in Washington under armed guard. The German spy Walter T. Scheele had been captured in Cuba, and he was coming to work for the gas service.

On Thursday, April 4, the sky over Washington was clear and cool. Two days before the anniversary of Congress's war declaration, the German army was poised at Amiens for a massive offensive, and the War Department wanted 150,000 draftees inducted in April— three times the usual monthly quota.

The Senate was debating a bill introduced by President Wilson seeking harsher penalties for German spies under the Espionage Act. State governors meeting in Washington had demanded summary execution of German agents, accusing the federal government of leniency with traitors.

In Van Manning's office in the Bureau of Mines, George Burrell awaited agents from the Bureau of Investigation. He had invited a few of his technical men to be there as well: George Richter, Wilder Bancroft, and Elmer Kohler. They were joined by a glowering twenty-seven-year-old chemist named Bruce R. Silver, who worked for the inventor Thomas Edison, and Richmond M. Levering, the Indiana oilman. If Burrell had a touch of nerves, pacing Manning's office or glancing out the window, it would have been understandable.

Just after lunchtime, two special agents with the Bureau of Investigation finally arrived at Manning's office. They hustled a third man into the office with them. Walter Scheele was easily recognizable from the long scar crossing his right cheek and more scars webbing the left side of his face. Vigilante mobs were threatening anyone suspected of disloyalty to the United States, and the agents had to usher Scheele secretly into Manning's office. Abandoned by his country and facing execution, he had offered up everything he knew about German chemical weapons in exchange for his life.

After he had fled Hoboken in 1916 steps ahead of the authorities, Scheele had assumed the identity of a journalist, using the name William Rheinfelder, to escape by boat to Cuba. He disembarked in Havana and, knowing no Spanish, made his way to the German embassy. The embassy secretary ordered him to go to a hotel, and the next day, after sleeping overnight in a train station, he went to the secretary's home, where another man arrived in a car to take Scheele away. This man, Juan de Pozas, was an agent for a German supply company, a smuggler, and a gunrunner. He brought Scheele to his house outside Havana, where he introduced him to his family and gave him an airy guest room. De Pozas politely but firmly instructed Scheele never to leave the room except for meals.

Living in seclusion in his gilded prison, Scheele felt his former life fade away, and his existence submerged into the shadowy underworld of the island. His name changed again: he became James G. Williams, American expatriate. He spent almost every waking moment in his room, sleeping in a bed draped with a mosquito netting, crossing the tiled floor to a balcony where he could stare out the window at the gardens, forbidden from even going down to the courtyard. A checkered tablecloth covered a small table where he sat and wrote home to his wife, Marie, in America, sending the letters to friends and sympathizers in the United States who delivered them to Marie. His paycheck from the German government arrived every month, but he had nothing to spend his money on, so he sent most of his pay back to his wife and some to de Pozas. When Scheele corresponded with Marie, he signed his name "Nux" or "Fritz."

Not long after he arrived, Scheele fell ill with food poisoning so severe that at one point he lapsed into a coma. He spent several months convalescing, then fell sick again, this time with a tropical fever. After Scheele was nursed back to health, de Pozas grudgingly allowed him to go outside into the garden. He became a sort of groundskeeper, tending the plants, painting murals, and overseeing maintenance around the mansion. He tried to stay abreast of current events as the United States entered the war. Not long after, Scheele's host country declared war on Germany as well. Spies or not, Germans were no longer welcome in Cuba.

In February of 1918, a police captain arrived at the gate of de Pozas's house and asked to speak with de Pozas's mysterious guest. The captain asked Scheele questions. Why did he spend all his time inside? Did he speak multiple languages? In his thick German accent, Scheele answered as best he could.

The police captain asked de Pozas to come to the station and sign a statement attesting to his guest's good character as a foreigner. The next morning, de Pozas ordered Scheele to leave. Most likely the smuggler had tired of his houseguest and his open-ended stay; he was probably panicked over the attention from police. De Pozas had worries of his own over his wartime activities for Germany, which included smuggling gold and supplying dynamite to blow up a German ship interned in Havana to keep it out of U.S. hands. Now that word was out that his guest was not an American living a leisurely expatriate life, Scheele was a liability and a danger.

Scheele packed his satchel and left on March 5, 1918. Holed up in a Havana hotel, he tried desperately to contact a fellow German for assistance and money, to no avail. Finally, he fled to Matanzas, where he tried to catch a boat for Mexico. There, the Rural Guard swooped in, bayonets lowered, and took him into custody on March 7, acting on a tip from one of the men Scheele thought was a friend. One imprisonment had ended when Scheele left de Pozas's house, and now a new one had begun. In a solitary cell deep inside the Castillo de San Salvador de la Punta, a fortresslike military prison on Havana Harbor, the chief of the Cuban army's Military Intelligence Division began to question Scheele.

The U.S. Department of Justice had no idea that Scheele was in custody, but its investigation had progressed, tracing Scheele's remittances to his wife back to Havana banks. By late February, Bureau of Investigation chief A. Bruce Bielaski was confident enough that Scheele was in Cuba to send a man to find him.

The man he chose to send to Havana was Richmond Levering. In spring of 1918, the oilman ended up at the heart of the manhunt for Scheele. After his ignominious departure from the American Protective League and the U.S. Department of Justice the previous fall, he had resumed running his companies and overseas concerns. Whenever he went abroad, he typed up reports on the political situation and sent them back to Bielaski at the Justice Department. Though he had no official title, his reports nonetheless sufficiently impressed Chief Bielaski that he considered it worthwhile to maintain ties with Levering.

In late February, Levering was about to depart for Havana on a business and pleasure trip when he received a letter from Bielaski asking him to help locate Scheele in Cuba. Bureau agents based in Key West had periodically scoured the island for Scheele, to no avail. Why Bielaski sent Levering instead of an agent is unclear, but the bureau's resources were stretched thin across the country, and Levering had well-developed political connections in Cuba through his business ventures. Bielaski wired Key West and the U.S. counsel general in Havana: Levering would proceed to Cuba to find Scheele. Once again, Levering was in the right place at the right moment, and he was thrust back into the good graces of the U.S. government.

Levering's boat arrived in Havana on March 11. That night, he learned from a high-level Cuban official that a man matching Scheele's description was being interrogated in military custody. Levering rushed to a meeting with Cuba's president, Mario García Menocal, to explain his mission, and the president pledged to help. In the morning, Levering and the U.S. military attaché in Havana, Captain Thomas F. Van Natta Jr., met with the military intelligence chief, Captain Jacinto Llaca, who had been interrogating Scheele. The situation, Llaca told them, was complicated. Several men had been arrested in the government sweep—Scheele; a second German man named Richard Guttman, who was Scheele's paymaster in Cuba; and a third man who was Cuban. All three were being held in the *castillo* where Llaca had been vigorously questioning Scheele and the other men for several days. The Americans could take Scheele back to the United States, Llaca told Levering, but on one condition: because the Cuban authorities would be presenting their case against the two other men, and Scheele had evidence in those cases, the chemist would have to return temporarily to Havana before the Americans could have him for good. Levering agreed.

Darkness had fallen over Havana when Levering's ship, a freighter called the SS *Flagler,* pulled up alongside the rock wall of the *castillo*. Levering stepped from the boat onto the pier, mounted the prison bulwarks above the quay, and peered toward the gloom of the prison. A group of men approached, members of the Cuban Rural Guard, escorting two men who wore alpine hats. One was Scheele; the other was Guttman. A Cuban army colonel signed a receipt for the two prisoners. The two sides traded salutes, then handshakes, and the Americans slipped handcuffs around the beefy wrists of the two Germans. The Americans reboarded the boat with the two prisoners, as well as Captain Llaca and a U.S.

embassy official. The boat cast off, turned its prow north, and slipped into the gulf toward Key West.

Havana fell into the distance as the *Flagler* steamed across the Straits of Florida. It was the first time in almost two years that Scheele had left Cuba. Many hours later, the *Flagler* reached the deserted pier at Key West. Agents met the boat and brought the German men to waiting automobiles. Levering and the agents took them to Fort Taylor. The cars drove into the fort's courtyard, where agents helped the handcuffed Germans from the cars. Levering and the agents brought Scheele to a room deep in the interior of the fort.

Levering warned Scheele that his crimes were so grave that only full cooperation with the Americans would save his life. Scheele was happy to oblige. During his stay at the military prison in Havana, he had been held in solitary confinement, and Llaca had been a forceful interrogator. Now in American hands and facing execution for his treachery, Scheele promised to reveal everything he knew about German weapons. He told Levering he had wanted to give himself up long ago, but de Pozas wouldn't allow him to. Since his capture, he had reflected on his situation and decided to try to right the wrongs he had committed. He also said he wanted to eke out a sliver of revenge for his abandonment by the German government after a lifetime of loyalty.

Levering was satisfied. "He has promised us that he would give us every ounce of his remaining power if we would spare his life," Levering reported. "This was not promised [but] continuance of life was based upon the importance of his revelations and absolute truthfulness in detail."

Scheele began to talk. The interrogations stretched all day and into the early morning, in a room packed with intelligence officers, Department of Justice agents, customs officials, immigration officials. Thomas Edison came to interrogate Scheele and brought his chemist, Bruce Silver, to listen and determine the veracity of his statements; Scheele held nothing back—he revealed the composition of the chemical bombs that went onto the merchant ships, who the paymasters were, who received the money. He described how the Germans used oxygen cooled and condensed into a liquid as an explosive or a propellant. He talked about how the Germans were able to shell Paris from a distance of sixty miles. How a German spy had smuggled germs into the United States in the hopes of unleashing a bacteriological plague to wipe out livestock. He described a German plan to invade Canada. He described a way to make aerial gas bombs that could be dropped from airplanes.

Astonished, Levering listened to Scheele for hours, then dashed off a wire to Washington citing how Bruce Silver confirmed Scheele's facts. Even in the dry language of the report, Levering's awe was obvious. "So far Mr. Silver states that all formulae for gas, liquid air use and other devices seem reasonable or practical from the chemical combination standpoint...some of the gases are considered to be the most devilish combination ever heard of by Mr. Silver." Copies of the interrogation reports also went to the chief of staff's office at the War Department.

Silver questioned Scheele closely, poking and prodding at his statements about chemical processes and compounds, and had the doctor demonstrate his cigar-bomb compound in front of him. He came away convinced that Scheele was telling the truth. "I would therefore, recommend that, if possible, he be given the opportunity, in a well-equipped laboratory, to demonstrate experimentally such devices and formulae as he describes. I firmly believe that his information regarding German chemical development since the outbreak of the war will be of material value to our government." Even Thomas Edison himself said that he "was much impressed" with what Scheele had to say.

Everything Scheele knew about chemistry and gas warfare would now be in the service of the Americans. Information about incendiary bombs, poison gas, liquid fire. Everything he knew, the Americans would know. The agents knew the importance of the asset they had gained. They also knew what a political powder keg they had in their hands. A German spy who had plotted to kill

Americans would be working for the U.S. government. The country was in an ugly mood toward anyone believed to be a traitor. Rage against Germans erupted in violence in Illinois, where a mob lynched a coal miner accused of being disloyal. The mob dragged him from police protection, draped him in an American flag, and hung him from a tree. In New York, police had to hold back an angry crowd in Pennsylvania Station that threatened to hang German spies and internees who were being transferred from the Tombs to prison in Georgia.

"Please keep his presence [in] this country absolute secret and code any messages you may send," one of Levering's superiors wrote to Bielaski in a telegram. Bielaski, in turn, cautioned the U.S. attorney in Newark, where Scheele would be brought before a federal grand jury, to do the same. "We are keeping the information that Scheele has given us, and the fact that he is aiding us at all, confidential," Bielaski wrote.

The message streaked through federal intelligence and law-enforcement agencies: Speak nothing of Scheele. But keeping the arrest under wraps was difficult—within a day or two, at least three newspapers carried stories about his arrest, including a detailed *New-York Tribune* account of his cooperation and grand jury testimony. The new Bureau of Investigation chief in New York City, Charles DeWoody, proved to have an alarmingly loose tongue, revealing Scheele's arrest in an interview with the *New York Times*.

Before Scheele could be brought to Washington or New York, he had to make the promised return to Havana. The group set out on March 16 on one of Thomas Edison's boats, but a storm forced it to return to Key West. Afraid that Edison's boat would be too recognizable, they switched to the SS *Flagler* and set out again the following day. This time, the weather was fair and the seas calm, and the prisoners posed for photographs on the deck, an American flag snapping in the breeze and the gulf waters stretching to the horizon.

After Captain Llaca was done with Scheele in Havana, the spy returned to the United States for good. On the morning of March 20, a Cuban naval vessel brought Scheele and Levering to Key West. The following evening, they boarded a train for Washington.

When the train pulled into Union Station, Levering and the two agents hustled Scheele from the train car to the platform. Another bureau agent greeted them. From the station, they rushed him to the Bureau of Investigation to see Chief Bielaski. Scheele spent the day there, then was escorted to his quarters: a jail cell in a police precinct.

Over the next few days, agents escorted him to American University, where the technical men from the Bureau of Mines and the Ordnance Department gathered to watch his demonstrations of chemical processes. In the evenings, the agents would return him to the jailhouse and lock him into his cell. Just before midnight on April 1, agents brought Scheele onto a northbound train to Jersey City, not far from his former chemical factory in Hoboken, then on to Newark, where Scheele testified to a federal grand jury about the ship-bomb case. From there, they went to Levering's office in Manhattan. After agents spirited Scheele up to the twentieth floor, Levering and Bureau of Investigation agents spent hours interrogating Scheele more. When the discussion ended, an agent took the men to a hotel, where they slept for a few hours and then returned to the train station. They caught a 1:18 a.m. train back to the capital for one last meeting with Washington's chemical warriors.

Burrell and the other chemists in Manning's office on April 4 recognized that Scheele was a highly trained scientist, albeit one who had been an enemy until a few days ago. As they listened to Scheele and the accounts of what he had done at the experiment station, they believed what he was telling them. His expertise and his knowledge of chemistry were sound. He had demonstrated his proficiency with experimentation. The only question, then, was how to tap this unexpected wellspring of information.

The first decision was where to put him. Keeping him at American University would have been too dangerous. There were too many opportunities for word to leak out from the chatty chemists and the many civilian employees there. Levering had a solution. Levering & Company had a subsidiary, the American Potash Corporation, which had a plant across the Hudson River from Peekskill, New York, about fifty miles north of New York City. It was a remote location, far from the press and prying eyes. Scheele could conduct experiments there while closely monitored and guarded at all times. His work would be reported back to the Ordnance Department, the Bureau of Mines, and the navy.

The Justice Department approved the plan. Back in New York on April 7, Scheele ducked into one of Levering's cars in downtown Manhattan. Warren Grimes, a bureau agent who had been at Scheele's elbow throughout his time in Washington, was behind the wheel. They went up the Hudson Valley, through Yonkers and Sleepy Hollow and Ossining. In Peekskill, Grimes turned onto Main Street and stopped outside the Eagle Hotel, a grand, four-story inn. After they lugged their bags from the trunk of the car into the lobby, Grimes registered with the clerk as Warren White. Scheele registered as Dr. Walter Smith. Then they went to the riverfront.

At the landing, one of Levering's boats waited for them. The Hudson River was wide at that point, almost a mile. The shoreline fell away as the boat puttered across the river toward Jones Point, a knob of bottomland jutting out into a bend in the Hudson. Buildings came into view: Levering's plant, the American Potash Corporation, and another subsidiary of Levering's, the Kaolin Products Company. Rail tracks hugged the riverbanks, and behind the six-acre campus, the forest rose steeply toward high, wooded hills and, farther on, Bear Mountain.

The vice president and the foreman of the plant met the boat as it pulled up to the dock. They were expecting Levering's newest employee, this Dr. Smith with the scars and the German accent, but none of the plant employees knew the true identity of the chemist delivered to the plant. The man with the policemen glued to his side, whose presence required a tall fence around the laboratory and a new system of passes and codes. The man they could never talk about, who held Germany's chemical secrets in his head.

As Walter Scheele arrived at Jones Point, Companies C and D of the gas and flame regiment were settling into new quarters in France. In late February, the chaplain, Addison, was thrilled to learn that orders had finally arrived at Fort Myer that the getaway drills in the snow would be ending. Hundreds of men celebrated that night in the gymnasium, listening to the company orchestra and watching a vaudeville spectacle that included singers, dancers, and a minstrel show that were "uniformly as poor as they could be," Addison sniffed. On the Sunday before his departure, Addison delivered a sermon, then rushed into Washington to spend his final night with Margaret. They said a wrenching goodbye in the morning, knowing he might never come back, and then Addison taxied to Fort Myer to finish packing.

At 3:30 p.m. on February 25, the five hundred men formed ranks for roll call and then marched to Rosslyn, Virginia, to board a train. Addison, in a comfortable Pullman car with other officers, had a supper of sandwiches and chocolate before the motion of the train lulled him to sleep. He awoke at 2:30 a.m., about fifteen minutes away from Jersey City. Four hours later, the regiment disembarked and boarded a ferry up the river to Hoboken. A stiff breeze blew down the river as the men crowded the decks, the rising sun blazing behind a bank of clouds and Manhattan silhouetted against the sky. After the ferry docked, the regiment stood in line as ladies from the Red Cross served them coffee and buns. The USS *Agamemnon* loomed over them, a vast four-funnel steamship, 706 feet from stem to stern, that could carry more than thirty-five hundred soldiers.

The hours wore on, the line inched forward. Finally, the Hellfire Boys boarded in groups of ten. The seized ship was the former *Kaiser Wilhelm II,* the emperor's favorite vessel, and as Addison made his way through the decks, he passed signs in German still hanging from the walls. Addison's stateroom was spacious but dark, the two portholes painted over to snuff out light during the passage. After dinner, he fell asleep in his berth, curled up in the much-too-short sofa bed.

At 6:30 p.m. the next day, tugs towed the *Agamemnon* out into the Hudson River. The night was clear and cold, moonlight spilling down across the decks and stars bright overhead. Addison remained on deck, watching Manhattan and the Battery slide slowly behind the ship. He crossed to the starboard side for a view of the Statue of Liberty, her torch bright against the night sky. Starlight illuminated the ship's path as it cruised east guarded by its flagship, the USS *Mount Vernon,* and another transport, the USS *America,* while Addison slept.

During the two-week passage, Addison's days filled with abandon-ship drills, long discussions in the stateroom, laps around the deck, and queasy days in bed as the ship pitched in the uneasy sea. On March 9, a convoy of destroyers slid up alongside the *Agamemnon.* The next morning, a Sunday, Addison strolled on deck before sunrise, the ocean placid, the sky above clear, with the morning star glimmering above a crescent moon. During his Sunday service, Addison delivered a sermon on Paul's admonitions to help the weak. He ended right on time, just before the usual 1:00 p.m. abandon-ship drill.

The drill never came. When Addison stepped onto the deck, he saw fishing boats bobbing in the waves and, in the distance, a ribbon of land. A plane circled overhead, and a dirigible kept pace with the ship. Soon he saw green hills, coastal forts, a wireless tower, and rolling forests. Buskers in dinghies scudded around the *Agamemnon,* playing music for coins tossed from the soldiers crowding the decks. In the afternoon, a rowboat bumped up alongside the *Agamemnon,* and Secretary of War Baker clambered aboard. Unbeknownst to Addison, he had been a passenger in the convoy all along, on the USS *Seattle*.

The next day, Addison and the other men disembarked to a British freighter. As the ship ferried them to shore, the rooftops and spires of Brest grew closer. The boat tied up to the pier, and at 2:15, Addison and Company C lined up in formation. They marched through the city to a busy central square, then up the hillside. No young men were to be seen, only old men, mournful women, and children. Everywhere Addison looked, the town's inhabitants wore black.

Three days of train travel brought the chaplain closer to the front. "The Ides of March," Addison jotted in his diary as the train wound through the French countryside. In the early morning of March 16, the train pulled into the station at Langres. The companies formed ranks and marched on the chalky tree-lined roads toward their destination, Humes, a village about seventeen miles southeast of the AEF general headquarters at Chaumont. Addison was assigned to a small house with a young mother and two boys; their father was at the front. His room was a good-sized one, with a window looking out on a stream and the hillsides. He had a grand supper later in the evening with other officers. Stationed in the quiet village, with its red-roofed stucco homes and picturesque church, he had a hard time believing that they were there to kill Germans.

And yet there were constant reminders of why the regiment was there. Humes was on a road and rail line, and all day long, an endless procession of muddy soldiers and guns and trucks streamed past the village toward the front, where the Germans were amassing for a new spring push toward Paris. When the fighting would begin was anyone's guess.

On March 17, the battalion was still settling into their billets in Humes when Amos Fries arrived in Tours, France, the new headquarters for the gas service. The service was still an orphan within the army, and so Pershing had put Fries's service under an army department called the Service of Supply, which was headquartered in Tours. His limousine rolled to a stop at 6:00 p.m. on his birthday after a two-day trip from general headquarters. His new office was in a former barracks about 150 miles southwest of Paris and 240 miles from his gas experimental field and general headquarters in Chaumont, hardly in close proximity to Pershing and the seat of the AEF. Fries didn't grouse to Bessie about the distance—in fact, he assured her that it would take him even farther away from the dangers of the front—but he would soon grow weary of the endless commute by train and car between far-flung corners of his jurisdiction.

The barracks building that would serve as the gas service headquarters was crude at best and needed rehabilitation work. Still, the offices hummed with activity, thronged with dozens of orderlies, officers, and as many as fifty stenographers—all of them men, Fries carefully pointed out to Bessie.

Fries managed to make his office somewhat comfortable, laying rugs on the linoleum floor. Unlike his work space, his new living quarters were luxurious, a stone house with five bedrooms filled with mahogany furniture, a parlor, a billiard room, and a live-in maid. It was an unusually modern house for France, with two toilets, gas and electricity, and fireplaces in every room. He even had a private writing room where he could peck out his letters to Bessie each night. It was only about a mile to his office, a walk that became part of his daily constitutional.

A few days before his move to Tours, Fries had been in Paris for a five-day interallied gas conference—the second since fall of 1917—to strategize and share information about chemical warfare with representatives of the Allies. He left a few days before Secretary of War Newton Baker arrived in Paris after crossing the Atlantic in the same convoy with Companies C and D of the Hellfire Regiment. While the secretary was still in the capital, German's massive cannons—the so-called Paris guns—had sent shells tumbling onto the city from sixty miles away, a distance so vast that it seemed like science fiction from a Jules Verne book. Fries gloated a bit over the fact the city was shelled while Baker was there. "Paris was bombed again last night and I guess gave the secretary a chance to say he had been under fire," Fries wrote home.

Fries expected to meet soon with Baker, but it was even more urgent that he meet with another passenger who accompanied Companies C and D: Colonel Atkisson was finally on French soil after coming across with the convoy. Sending the first two companies ahead to France without Atkisson had been "an awful bonehead piece of business on someone's part," Fries groused, and the colonel's arrival was a relief for Fries. He had great respect for Atkisson and expected him to ease the burden of day-to-day management of the gas and flame regiment. After Atkisson landed, the two men had met up briefly in Chaumont before Atkisson left for the front and Fries headed south to his new headquarters. "I certainly do need him," Fries wrote home. Back in the United States, a third Hellfire Battalion, Companies E and F, was training at Fort Myer and would soon be coming across as well.

Atkisson's arrival lightened Fries's responsibilities, but there were still myriad other tasks to attend to. In mid-March, he was consumed with plans for reorganizing his service. Like the allies before, the American service was growing. When the French and British gas services were in their fledgling stages, both countries had failed to anticipate the huge expansion ahead. Fries had no intention of repeating that mistake. During the Paris gas conference, Fries had consulted with his British and French counterparts about restructuring his service into three divisions: military, technical, and production and supply. The Military Division's task would be to care for problems related to gas offense and defense, as well as intelligence. The Technical Division, like the Research Division back in the United States, would be in charge of research at the experimental field and the laboratory. The Production and Supply Division would provide equipment.

The sheer volume of ammunition needed—whether it was artil-

lery shells, mortars, grenades, Livens drums, or gas cylinders—
was mind-boggling. Fries estimated the AEF would need roughly
17,000 gas-filled cylinders each month for cloud attacks, about
150,000 Stokes mortars filled with phosgene, thermite, white phosphorus, and other chemicals, and about 87,000 Livens drums
packed with phosgene and other chemicals.

Fries wanted an organization so efficient it ran itself, like a self-
playing pianola. But his machine was not yet complete. Fries
needed every officer he had, and yet he had to fight to prevent other
army departments from poaching his officers for their outfits. Fries
had another recruitment problem: officers assigned to the gas service had already been commissioned in their own departments, so
there was nowhere to advance in Fries's operation. As a result, officers actively tried to avoid an assignment in the gas service, seeing
it as a dead end. Fries wanted only loyal and dedicated staff, and he
judged them for their hustle or their ineptitude, as either a help or a
hindrance to his vision. He rewarded the former with praise, while
the latter rarely lasted long in his office.

As Fries pushed to reorganize the service in March, he saw the
effort as only a step toward an even more ambitious goal: an independent Gas Corps, a separate, autonomous branch of the army,
like the Ordnance Department or the Quartermaster Corps. Making the service into an independent corps would put gas warfare on
permanently solid footing, a position of power commensurate with
the growing importance of chemical warfare on the battlefield. It
would also allow Fries to vastly expand the service to thousands of
gas troops and hundreds of officers.

Fries's forceful nature and his impatient personality defined his
new service, and his endless enthusiasm for this new type of warfare propelled the enterprise forward. Had Pershing put another
man at the helm, chemical warfare might have gone in a very different direction. In February, the International Red Cross had
appealed to all the belligerents to stop using poison gases. Fries had
scoffed at the notion that the Central powers would ever agree to

such a thing. It would likely be a ruse if they did, Fries felt, and he had no interest in such a detente either, calling it "unthinkable from the point of view of the allies.

"I would be glad to see it stopped for I know the peculiar and extensive h—— that the gas game is," he wrote to Bessie at the time, using a mild expletive. "But it like some other things must go on to the end."

The Germans rejected the appeal. After the war, Fries claimed the Germans themselves later sent a Swiss intermediary to the Americans with an overture. This time, the Germans proposed that all sides stop using poison gas. Pershing asked Fries for his opinion.

Fries thought little of it. He remained adamant that gas needed to remain part of the American arsenal. He was utterly confident in his mission, impatient with skeptics, and driven in his zeal to achieve it. The Americans were preparing to produce and deploy enormous quantities of chemical weapons, and the momentum behind Fries's efforts had turned his gas service into a juggernaut, gathering speed and size as it moved forward. Had that progress slowed or ended, everything he had done would have been in vain. The Germans' increasing use of gas reinforced Fries's faith in the importance of chemical weapons. To Fries, they had become as indispensable as bullets and high-explosive shells. Tallies of American casualties at the front began to reach Fries at headquarters. Fries took note but was not overly concerned. "Bad as they are they are no worse than the mine horrors all too frequent in the U.S.," he wrote to Bessie. But it was only a taste of what was to come.

About 260 miles to the northwest, Higginbottom was training with the British in the Lens sector. Higgie and his platoon from Company B had arrived from Helfaut on March 1, after a snowy drive in the back of a truck. His billet was an old brick factory in a village called Sains-en-Gohelle just outside Lens and only a few miles from the front. The brickyard, he called it. His platoon slept on the second floor on beds made of chicken wire, while B Company of the British Special Brigade occupied the rest of the building. Their British compatriots told them the camp was within range of the German artillery, but shells rarely landed near them. The buildings were wired with explosives in case the Germans broke through. At night, artillery lit up the sky.

Companies A and B were learning the work of gas warfare at the front, training with the British Special Brigade in digging projector batteries, running detonator wires, laying smoke screens, and setting Stokes mortars. The earlier training at Camp American University—the drilling on the parade ground and the demonstrations in the fields—was little more than a faint prelude to the training they received on the front beside the British.

A few days before Higgie had arrived, the Germans had carried out their first projector attack against American troops. The nighttime barrage on February 25 took place close to the Bois de Remières, near Toul. Masked by high-explosive shells, about two hundred German gas drums rained down on the Americans, releasing phosgene and chloropicrin. Even though the clang of hammers and other sounds from the German side pointed to an impending gas attack, the Americans sustained huge numbers of casualties, largely due to poor training. About three-quarters of the casualties were the result of soldiers removing their masks too soon.

Now signs indicated a major German offensive in Higgie's sector. On his second day at the front, the British brought his squad closer to the lines. They piled into a truck and drove to the end of the road before a long hike to the forward dugout. They walked two by two, with a single British soldier as a guide. Guns fired all around, and Higgie could see shells break in the distance. The ruined landscape around him was a moonscape of shell craters and husks of barely standing buildings. He had never seen such a sight in his life. As darkness fell, star shells burst overhead in incandescent cascades.

Their dugout was an old wine cellar. The British cautioned the Americans to stay under cover during daytime. The dugout was damp and cold, but they started a fire as they curled up to sleep.

German shells boomed through the night, and a blanket hung over the dugout entrance to keep out gas. At 5:00 a.m., Higginbottom was shaken from sleep for his watch, and he pushed aside the dugout blanket to take his post. The day brightened, and mist wreathed the trench, thick and damp. A few minutes into his watch, Higginbottom began sneezing. He thought he had caught cold until he heard the men behind the gas blanket in the dugout sneezing, too. Sneezing gas, courtesy of the Germans. Not concentrated enough to merit gas masks, but enough to tickle their noses.

In the afternoon, the British engineers brought Higginbottom's squad into a warren of trenches that led right up to the line, where they helped install Livens projectors for an upcoming attack. It would be Higgie's first show, when he would launch gas shells from projector batteries that he would dig himself. The mist lingered all day. The German artillery stayed silent, their targets hidden in the fog. After the weather cleared, the German guns returned to life. Several times Higginbottom dove for cover when shells flew over. Every shell sounded as though it was going to land on him.

Everything was new, and a lesson in survival. One morning, deafening artillery fire shook Higginbottom from his sleep. The Germans had attempted a raid, coming over the top and charging British and Canadian trenches, but Allied machine guns repelled them. At daybreak, corpses of German soldiers hung all along the barbed wire separating the two sides.

That same afternoon, Higginbottom saw his first air battle. It lasted just seconds, long enough to bring down a German plane, which burst into flames as it crashed into a nearby cemetery. The soldiers scrambled to get pieces of the plane, and Higginbottom salvaged a piece to send home to his brother.

Higginbottom grew accustomed to the sound of shells streaking toward him through the air. He learned to tell the difference between the types of incoming shells, to gauge their distance, and to listen for the distinctive pop of a gas-shell fuse. He practiced how to duck for cover when the bright overhead flares known as Very lights illuminated the battlefield. As he made his way through the trench one morning, he smelled for himself the faint odor of mustard gas and learned that, when the trenches were wet, the gas lingered for days.

On March 15, he got another grim lesson. One of the British soldiers was putting a charge box down into a projector when the box stuck in the tube. When he used a wooden stick to ram it down, the charge exploded. It tore the man's arm off at the shoulder. He did not live long.

Higgie shuttled back and forth between the brickyard, the advance billets, and the dugout. At mealtime, the squad leaders meted out loaves of bread with cheese or jam. Sometimes it was hash or corned beef. One supper was just a piece of bread and a boiled onion. There was never coffee, only tea. One day, Canadian soldiers brought bread, cheese, jam, and a large chunk of bacon to share with Higginbottom and his squad. At night, the Americans laughed and joked before they went to sleep and sometimes could sleep as late as they wanted before getting up for drilling. Even at the front, there were small comforts, like a well-stocked YMCA that was open at night, the windows covered tight to smother the light from inside.

The days went by. Again and again weather delayed the projector show. Two nights in a row, Higgie slogged his way out into no-man's-land, ducking into tunnels and craters to escape shells, only to have the show called off at the last minute. One night while they waited for trucks back to the brickyard, the Germans launched another raid. Machine guns chattered all around them, and signal rockets flared across the night sky before the British and Canadian artillery opened up with a roar. Higginbottom stared up at the pyrotechnics overhead—it was a beautiful sight, he thought. A hard rain pooled in the trenches, turning into a limestone paste that clutched at Higgie's boots like glue. His mates played endless dice games in the billet.

Artillery fire shook Higginbottom from his sleep at 5:30 a.m. on March 21. Finally, the skies had cleared. If the wind was right that night, the attack would go forward. There was nothing to do until 11:00 p.m., the zero hour when the attack was to start; the projector batteries were all set, and the charges were ready. More soldiers came up from the brickyard for the attack. Higginbottom loafed around the whole day, waiting to see what would happen. In the afternoon, the wind shifted favorably for the British and the Americans. The show was on.

At 9:00 p.m., Higgie made his way up to the projector batteries. Two hours to go. As the glowing hands on his wristwatch ticked toward the start of the show, he darted through the shadows, unspooling the wires two hundred meters back to the Livens-projector batteries. He took cover, crouching behind an old building. A few minutes before 11:00 p.m., he connected the wires to the exploder. Then he waited, clenching the handle of the detonator.

Everything was quiet. All the guns were still. Nothing came over from the Germans, and in the thick darkness near the front, time seemed to stop. There was only a minute to go. In the sudden stillness, the ballooning silence seemed to fill everything. Higgie had a strange feeling, as if his own heart had stopped beating. He waited in the quiet, perfectly calm, his own internal clock at a standstill. And then he pushed the handle down as hard as he could.

A flash, and night turned to day. All around Higgie, the exploders blasted, and five thousand gas shells tumbled into the sky toward the German lines. Stones and dirt showered down on him behind the building. In the noisy aftermath of the projector show, a rainbow of multicolored flares blossomed over the German trenches, warning of gas and calling in artillery to counterattack. Higgie darted from behind the building up to the projector batteries to begin respooling the wire but quickly retreated as machine-gun fire began to hammer thick and fast around him. He was back in the trenches when the big shells started coming over from the Germans. They lasted for a while. As Higgie returned through the trenches, the sludge of lime and mud sucking at his boots, he kept his head down, a hail of machine-gun fire whining over the top of the trench. He retreated farther back through the British trenches, and the bullets followed—the German machine gunners knew exactly where the main trench was and showered an exposed section with a hail of bullets. Higgie dashed through, and he got in safe.

At twenty minutes before midnight, forty minutes after the projector show began, the British and Canadian artillery opened up with the thunder of a thousand guns going off at once. In the cyclone of noise and fire around him, Higgie sprinted back to the wine cellar and the company of the other Americans. When he reached the billet, he was finally able to slow down and ponder what had happened in that moment of pure silence just before he pushed down the plunger on the detonator. When the projectors roared and sent six hundred pounds of gas at the Germans, he felt he was in the war at last.

Chapter Ten

"Science and Horror"

The mud was six inches deep and getting deeper. The rain came down hard and fast, and German gas shells tumbled to the ground with it. Higginbottom crouched in a sloppy trench near Bully-Grenay outside Lens. No light pierced the darkness as he and his bunkmate Shap sat waiting for gas cylinders to arrive on the supply train. Other soldiers waited in the sodden dark around them, cursing the rain, cursing the Germans, cursing the war. After an hour, the train creaked up the tracks, and the men clambered out of the trench. Then, heaving and sliding in the incessant rain, they pushed the ammunition cars farther up the track. When the cars had gone as far as they could, the men unloaded the stacked gas cylinders, which weighed more than one hundred pounds each. The tanks were heavy and slick. Shap and Higgie lowered one into the trench, threaded a pole through the handles, and then hoisted the pole up onto their shoulders. With the tank slung between them, they joined the supply line of men splashing through the darkness toward the front.

At the end of March, Companies A and B of the Hellfire Battalion were supposed to peel off from the British gas companies to operate independently in the American sector. But on March 21, the same day Higgie set off his first projector show, the Germans had launched a ferocious new drive to punch through the British lines. The first phase had been to Higgie's south, an attack code-

named Operation Michael. A second phase, Operation Mars, followed at Arras. Now the third phase, Georgette, was beginning in
early April. Hundreds of thousands of British soldiers streamed
back from the Middle East, Palestine, and other far-flung fronts to
bolster the troops. As part of the surge in troops to halt the German advance, the scattered platoons of Companies A and B were
ordered to stay with the British First Army, move up, and assist
with a cloud gas attack in the Lys Valley along a five-mile line
stretching north from Lens to Bessée. Their work with the British
continued, in one of the hottest sections of the front.

As he and Shap struggled with the heavy tank, Higginbottom
fumbled for footing on the duckboard deep in the muck. His boots
skidded off the waterlogged boards or punched through rotten
ones, sinking him up to his knees in the mud. As they reached
no-man's-land, gas shells whistled overhead, and Higginbottom
and Shap squeezed into a dugout. When the barrage finally quieted, they began to move again. An old trench jutted into
no-man's-land. The water there was even deeper. The cursing from
the Americans was so loud that the Germans must have heard them
a mile away, but they didn't care. With every tentative step he took
in tandem with Shap, the cylinder swaying on the pole, Higginbottom was sure he would drop the tank into the mud. For the first
time, he wondered if he would make it out alive.

Hour after hour, the supply line snaked through the trench,
slowly bringing cylinders up to no-man's-land. With Very lights
blazing overhead, the gas companies sank their shovels into the
soil, burying the cylinders that would send clouds of gas toward
the Germans.

Toward daybreak, Higgie pulled back, returning through the
trenches for a ride to the ammunition depot. From there, he hiked
to his billet in a French family's house. He shucked off his mud-
caked clothes, laid them out to dry, then tramped through the
kitchen and up the stairs, where he collapsed on his bed. It had
been his worst twelve hours so far in the war.

He slept all day, then came downstairs for the dinner that the family made for him. Before he could go back to sleep, orders came for Higgie's platoon to slap their uniforms back on and return to the front on the supply train.

The train had just begun moving when a German shell came over and exploded close by. Gas shells followed, one after another. Higgie and his platoon leaped from the train bed and sprinted for cover across a field. In his hurry, barbed wire snagged his clothes. Bombs exploded all around him as he struggled to disentangle himself. For a few moments, he was sure he would die right there, ensnared in wire, but he tore himself free and dove into the trench.

For hours, Higgie's platoon huddled in the trench in their gas masks, peering out through the glass eyeholes as gas wafted around them. One of the men had been badly gassed when he took cover in a crater where a gas shell had just broken, and when the shelling finally eased up at 10:00 p.m., Higginbottom and the others carried him back to a dressing station. After they left him, the men got lost on their way back toward their billets behind the lines, blundering in the darkness through the blasted outskirts of Lens. About midnight, Higgie finally reached the French homestead where he was billeted. The family gave him a cup of tea before he went up to bed.

In the morning, he went to the hospital for treatment. Higginbottom, too, had gotten a dose of gas before he had gotten his mask on, but he was lucky—seven members of his platoon were in the hospital that morning. He was told to rest for the remainder of the day.

Georgette began in earnest that day. Wave after wave of shells fell in a rolling cannonade that shook the ground. The ferocious noise went on and on—some eighty thousand shells in all, most filled with mustard, showering the Lens sector. Gas was everywhere, forcing the Americans at the front to wear their masks twelve to fifteen hours a day. Ambulances careened back and forth to pick up fresh casualties. Refugees swarmed the woods and took to the roads, fleeing in straggling columns.

In the evening, Higginbottom and his platoon set out for the front once again. The rain was still falling, and an impenetrable mist swaddled the trenches as they sloshed their way forward with gas cylinders.

When they reached the end of the trench, Higgie went over the top to deliver the tank into the batteries in the wide-open wasteland beyond, following a sunken road out into no-man's-land. The phosphorescent streaks of Very lights illuminated the blasted moonscape around him. When the flares burst over his head, he froze, stock-still in the fog, until the light faded and he could keep going through the mud. On his way back toward his billet, the fog was so thick that he kept one foot on the supply-train track to avoid getting lost in the dank soup around him. He reached the depot at 4:00 a.m. When daylight finally arrived, the rising sun scarcely pierced the shroud of mist and gas that hung over the valley. Mustard shells fell everywhere. In all, the Americans suffered nearly nine hundred casualties in a single night. More than fifty men of Company A had been injured or gassed, and two men died, the company's first deaths. Company B—Higgie's outfit—had fourteen casualties, and his entire platoon was put on the sick list and told to rest. But Higgie had made it through alive.

As the battle raged across the British sector, Fries held court in the officers' mess hall in the AEF's new headquarters in Chaumont. It was April 3, and a half-dozen officers from the gas service gathered around the chief. Addison was among them, and so was Atkisson, listening closely to his genial commander, with his mop of curly black hair and healthy ego. Addison had never met Fries, but the chaplain took an immediate liking to the colonel.

As the meal went on, the conversation turned to the fighting up north. Atkisson and Fries felt that the Germans and the British were probably suffering equal numbers of casualties. One American unit had been hit badly, with hundreds of men gassed. The losses were the result of poor leadership from higher officers, Fries and Atkisson agreed.

The battle was far from over as the Germans flung themselves against the Allied defenses and drenched the front with mustard shell barrages. By the time the officers gathered over dinner, it had become clear that the German push had stalled. The greatest danger had passed, and the offensive had been contained. Paris was safe.

Yet while the lines had held, the Germans had used more gas than the Allies had ever seen, and the mustard-packed yellow-cross shells had taken their toll. Casualty numbers were rising quickly — the 88 gas casualties in the American Expeditionary Forces in February increased sixfold to 535 in March, and then to more than 600 in April. Those numbers would soon explode into the tens of thousands. The mustard shell barrages that showered Lens were a sign that gas was no longer an intermittent, occasional threat, as it had been through 1917. It had become a permanent feature of the front, as constant as the mud churned beneath the soldiers' boots and the trenches in which they fought and died.

While the Hellfire Boys waded through mud in the Lys Valley, Addison was receiving his own induction into gas warfare, albeit far behind the lines. After he returned to Humes from Chaumont, he joined the battalion for a nighttime march. Partway through the hike, the men stopped to practice putting on their gas masks in the dark. The next day he listened to a lecture about gas defense from a British officer who brought bottled gas samples and demonstrated the strombo horns and signals that warned of gas. The following day, Addison attended a long lecture on gas warfare, the various chemicals and their gruesome effects, which gave him more enthusiasm for his gas mask. "It was a long tale—a compound of science and horror, giving one a lively respect for the toxic effects of Teutonic gases," he wrote in his journal. Amid the gloom, he received a glimmer of good news from home. A letter from his wife, Margaret, had arrived with tidings he had long hoped to hear: she was pregnant.

A few days after Fries, Atkisson, and Addison dined together with the other officers, Atkisson returned to the mess hall to join the chaplain after dinner. Atkisson had spent a day driving with Fries to gas training schools and ammunition depots. The two men got along well, and they had something in common beyond chemical warfare: both were high-level Masons. In the mess hall, Atkisson spoke admiringly, almost reverently, of Fries and the gas service. Fries had been "magnificently on the job under discouraging conditions since early fall," Atkisson said. While it was only a modest regiment now, Fries was angling for a vast expansion. Soon it would have five thousand men in six battalions, Atkisson said. It would be a powerhouse.

Atkisson grew circumspect. A grim future lay ahead for the gas regiments, he told the officers. All the old rules of combat, the chivalric codes that had defined warfare, were a thing of the past. The future of warfare would be a fight to the death, *combat a l'outrance*. The regiment's goal would be simply to kill as many Germans with gas as soon and as often as possible. "Some new method to defeat them must be found—gas or the air, or a combination, or something wholly new," Atkisson mused.

After leaving Chaumont and the gas regiment, Fries had gone to the Hotel Continental in Paris just before midnight on April 6, the anniversary of the U.S. war declaration. Germany's Paris guns had shelled the city while he was there, but he assured Bessie that he was in no danger. Fries was in Paris to visit a general who was laid up in the hotel with a bump on the head, but the trip also allowed the colonel a bit of rest. Fries gave the impression of being inexhaustible, a perpetual-motion machine of energy and activity. In truth, he felt the strain of his responsibilities. He couldn't shake a stubborn cold and cough, despite his regimen of daily exercise. The dank weather at Chaumont hadn't helped, nor did his grueling travel schedule. The breakneck pace barely afforded the colonel a moment's pause. Finally, in Paris he could rest. When he got to his room, he drew a bath, took a long soak, and afterward went straight to bed.

He was in Paris only for a day or two before motoring back to his new headquarters in Tours. Since the beginning of the German drive, Fries had fretted about the raging battle, unsure of whether the attack could be repelled. Even close to the front, details were scant, and he watched with trepidation, scanning the headlines when the newspapers arrived each day at noon. He wondered just how the Germans hoped to break through. "Certainly they know the British expected them. The slaughter must be frightful," he mused. Amid the dread, a note of fatalism crept into Fries's words. "And the sun shines as brightly, the flowers bloom as prettily, and the sowing and the reaping, loving and weeping go on much the same as ever even here almost in the shadow of the terrible holocaust," he wrote home.

As the days went by and the British succeeded in stopping the German advance, Fries's doubt fell away. He was more confident than ever about the gas service as well. Just before arriving in Paris, Fries had submitted his plan for reorganizing the gas service. Soon General Pershing would review it. "It promises to go through. In fact it must," Fries wrote to Bessie.

As he wrangled with such logistics, Fries anticipated a not-so-distant future in which smoke screens, gas, and thermite attacks would be a prelude to every assault. A future in which fleets of airplanes would drop payloads of chemical and smoke bombs over enemy territory. He was convinced that gas warfare would become more of a decisive factor in the war. He hoped there would be twelve or more chemical companies producing gas for the 2 million American soldiers overseas, triple how many were working at the moment. He estimated that the United States would need to produce fifty-five hundred tons of gas per month after July 1, and that half of all shells should be filled with gas. The gas and flame regiment alone would need one thousand tons of gas per month in 1919, if the war continued.

For all of these things to come to pass, to have a chemical warfare capacity unfettered by some other army department, Fries firmly believed the gas service needed to stand on its own, as an independent department of the army that relied on no other. On May 1, Fries submitted to Pershing his most forceful argument for the creation of what he called a Gas Corps, on a par with more established sections of the military like the Corps of Engineers. Though he met regularly with the general, he made his case into a kind of dossier, with a proposal for the organization, a draft general order to create it, and a memorandum with his arguments. "Because of its vast resources, America can not only make much more gas than any of its allies, but it can make enormously more than Germany. If placed in a position to do so effectively, the Gas Service will be able to have produced, and used, enough chemicals to gas thoroughly all the Germans facing American sectors," he wrote.

The domestic gas service was reorganizing, too, and cabled Fries to send by courier his plans for the AEF's service. Fries was skeptical about the domestic service and its ability to get done what he felt was necessary. The technical men in Washington were too far from the action, and the ocean that lay between them and the army in Europe was more than just an inconvenience: it was an impediment to progress. In Fries's view, the U.S. Gas Service was like a crippled ship, "with no man at the steering wheel and a broken rudder." Nor did it help that the chemists in Washington seemed to believe that the AEF Gas Service worked for them, rather than the other way around. His harsh views of Potter softened considerably after the former gas chief wrote to Fries to lament over how bureaucracy and disorganization had hamstrung the domestic Office of the Gas Service.

With Pershing's blessing, Fries's remedy to the distance and divide had been to build the experimental field near Chaumont, as well as the laboratory that he had been pressing for since fall. The location he had found was in a former state tuberculosis hospital in Puteaux, a commune about five miles west of central Paris. Assuming no spare lab equipment was available in France, the scientists had ordered all of it from the United States: twelve hundred shipping crates containing 110 tons of chemistry paraphernalia. Much of it went astray en route, and only about eighty cases had arrived by mid-May. What happened to the rest was an enigma that sparked frantic requests for the misplaced equipment to be tracked down. Eventually, it began arriving at the laboratory around June 1. When it was up and running, the laboratory usually had about a dozen officers and between fifty and sixty enlisted noncommissioned officers and privates, all chosen for their scientific prowess. They analyzed German gas, smoke, and explosive shells sent from the front and conducted their own research into gas masks. Beginning in the spring and continuing into summer, the lab developed a protective salve, sag paste, smeared on the skin to protect it against mustard, which Fries believed would save hundreds of lives. He felt that the AEF's lab was getting things done "faster than they ever dreamed of doing them in the States. Such things can't be done there for they don't get the touch of the front so necessary to a quick understanding of the problems."

No matter how well the laboratory in Puteaux worked, there were some things Fries could never do in France. One of them was synthesizing new chemical weapons. With the exception of the phosgene plant in Gièvres, making war gases in France simply wasn't practical, due to the cost of shipping huge amounts of precursor chemicals. Back in the United States, work on producing war gases was in full swing. More than 900 people entered the American University gates each day now—about 400 civilian employees and almost 500 military men. Another 160 or so were at work at another eighteen locations under the oversight of the Bureau of Mines.

At Gunpowder Neck, a building frenzy began over the winter, plagued by the storms that paralyzed the region. Temporary barracks went up, with tar paper on the outside and composition-board walls inside. Later ones were permanent, with tile walls and showers. Pumps drew water for the filling plants from the Bush River, and potable water was piped from Winter's Run, a river four miles away. Accidents and injuries were a certainty in the plants, and so a temporary hospital went up, with plans to build three permanent base hospitals later. A twenty-thousand-kilowatt electrical plant powered the factories. The men would need distractions from the dangerous work, and so the YMCA and the Knights of Columbus both built recreation huts with libraries and movie screens. Football teams and a camp band were organized. There was a bakery and a laundry and a shower house.

On April 2, the army's General Administration Bureau had appointed William H. Walker, now a lieutenant colonel with the Army Ordnance Department, to command Gunpowder Neck Reservation, which was renamed Edgewood Arsenal in May. Edgewood turned into a boomtown of chemical weapons production. At first, the Ordnance Department had planned to erect only phosgene and chloropicrin plants at Gunpowder Neck but in time decided to make mustard there as well. Construction on the shell-filling plant, which had begun in the fall, was finished at the end of January, ready to begin packing shells full of war gases. Filling Plant 1 was an enormous facility, with four long, low buildings radiating out from a central power plant. Each one of the four filling buildings had its own gas-handling-and-mixing room, washing towers, and carefully spaced fans to keep the air moving through the building and prevent the accumulation of gas. Each building could operate independently should accidents or leaks shut down other buildings. Construction on the chloropicrin factory had begun in January, and work commenced on the phosgene factory a week later. Walker commanded dozens of engineers at the arsenal, and his jurisdiction went far beyond Gunpowder Neck: chemical-manufacturing plants in Michigan, New Jersey, Connecticut, New York, and Virginia would all be under his command as well.

Mustard took longer to manufacture. Problems with synthesizing it continued to plague Conant and Organic Research Unit No. 1, slowing the drive toward large-scale production. As the weeks slipped by, the uncertainty over making mustard frustrated the

Ordnance Department. George Burrell, the research chief, was frustrated, too. Burrell and Walker discussed the problem at one of the weekly meetings. Afterward, Burrell wrote a letter to Walker acknowledging the slow pace of progress with mustard, the most desirable offensive war gas in existence. But Burrell cautioned that it didn't make sense to lurch forward with production without knowing the best method for making it. The wrong decision could mean a waste of time and money, he wrote.

There were so many problems with the British sulfur-monochloride method that the army moved ahead with a plan to produce mustard using the chlorohydrine method, signing a contract with the Commercial Research Company on Long Island, New York, on April 13 to manufacture five tons of mustard daily. Still, work continued night and day on the monochloride method. Eventually, Conant's diligence paid off. He came up with a two-step process that maintained both the stability and toxicity of the mustard produced, with a result that was roughly 85 percent pure. Using this process, the Small-Scale Manufacturing Section produced a seven-hundred-pound batch of mustard. It soon became clear that the chlorohydrine method should be abandoned. The contract with the Long Island company was canceled, and work continued exclusively on the British method.

Finally, progress. From overseas, Fries's chemists in the AEF Gas Service sent details of a new French reactor for making mustard, and the satellite labs worked on turning Conant's small-scale production process into industrial-level production. By around May 1, the long-delayed plans for the mustard plant at Edgewood began to fall into place, and work on the plant began on May 18. It was to be a massive factory with a daily capacity of one hundred thousand pounds of mustard, consisting of four units radiating outward from a central ethylene compressor system, with each unit containing sixteen reactors. Mustard had taken so long to develop and taken so much nurturing that the Research Division chemists started calling it "the hill baby."

Conant had made his mark. On April 8, he had received a commission as first lieutenant in the Chemical Service Section. A month later, the day before work began on the plant in Edgewood, he was promoted to captain. Soon, he would have a new assignment, one so shrouded in secrecy and thought to be so vital to winning the war that its details were barely committed to writing.

This new endeavor began with Winford Lee Lewis, now at work at Catholic University. Like Conant's unit, his Organic Research Unit No. 3 had its own setbacks over the winter. Originally, the small unit of five to eight chemists had been charged with working on mustard gas. While Catholic's facilities were better than American University's in most ways, the chemical hoods that whisked toxic gases out of the lab there were inferior to those across town at the experiment station. And so the work on mustard remained at American, while Lewis moved on to other problems.

Lewis's research unit had started experimenting in March with ricin, a poisonous protein derived from castor beans. About half of the men in the unit—now numbering about a dozen—were investigating large-scale production of ricin and whether bullets could be coated with the toxin. During the week of April 8, a member of the unit inhaled ricin powder and died. Despite this gruesome outcome, it didn't hamper investigation of the poison. "Further tests of this method of administration are under way, designed to determine what promise ricin may have as a toxic dust cloud." The other half of the men worked on experiments combining TNT and chlorine to create an explosive reaction that would produce phosgene.

But the experiments that proved to have the most promise, and would eclipse all the others in urgency and create an indelible legacy of the service, came almost by accident. Father Griffin, the lab chief who had gone to Johns Hopkins with Jim Norris, recalled a 1905 dissertation by a young priest named Julius Aloysius Nieuwland. For his doctoral work, Nieuwland had studied reactions between acetylene and other compounds. During one experiment, he had combined acetylene with arsenic trichloride, using aluminum chloride as a catalyst. The contents of the flask turned black, and when he cooled it in water, a thick, gummy substance resembling tar separated out, with a noxious odor. Nieuwland sniffed it and immediately fell ill, requiring hospitalization for several days.

Griffin pulled down the dissertation and pointed out the relevant section to Lewis. Organic Research Unit No. 3's experiments began around April 13. The chemists first put one hundred grams of arsenic trichloride in a flask. Then, the chemists passed acetylene through the flask and put it in a water bath with little reaction. Then the chemists added a gram of aluminum chloride to the flask and heated it. Still nothing happened. Five more grams of aluminum chloride went in, and more acetylene was passed through the flask.

Now the chemists added more acetylene, but this time, they raised the temperature. A rapid reaction began in the flask. The liquid darkened, and a thin blue film developed on the top. The flask gave off a sickening odor that burned and irritated the eyes and noses of the chemists, who developed searing headaches that lasted for hours. They carefully distilled the substance, producing a few drops of oil that, like the undistilled liquid, had a nauseating smell and was extremely irritating to the eyes and nose. It was an auspicious result, Lewis's report noted. "The headache resulting persists several hours and the material seems to be quite toxic," he wrote.

The difficulty with the distillation process was the instability of the compound—when heated to separate it from water, it tended to explode and release arsenic trioxide. The solution to that problem came from Conant, who suggested using hydrochloric acid to remove the explosive catalyst. It worked. Lewis was able to distill and purify the mixture without danger of detonation.

About two weeks into the experiments, the scientists began testing the compounds in earnest. The work ended up producing three similar types of poisonous compounds, each one with slightly different properties. Two of them were extremely toxic blister agents and respiratory irritants, though one was far more potent than the other. The noxious fumes sickened the men and peeled the paint on the ceiling of the lab, so the chemists constructed a small-scale still on Maloney Laboratory roof, where they could produce larger batches in the open air. The compound proved to have powerful asphyxiating and lachrymal effects. The first reports on its properties appeared in mid-May with a series of skin tests. Another early report on research conducted at the University of Wisconsin in June described "very marked respiratory distress," a rash that turned into blisters, edema, and scrotal burns "quite similar to those caused by mustard." On May 24, a private named Lloyd M. Suthers arrived at the experiment station infirmary with burns on his foot—the first injury that the camp doctor attributed to the compound. The numbers grew rapidly—on June 5, the doctor saw six patients with such burns.

The research took a heavy toll on the chemists at Catholic. Organic Research Unit No. 3 suffered the greatest number of casualties of all the research units; at one point, half of the unit had suffered an injury connected to their experiments, and a third were sent away for ten days to two weeks to recover. Lewis himself was one of the casualties; after he tested the new substance on his own right hand, it swelled up painfully. Despite the injuries, reports claimed that the men's spirits remained high, in part because the lab was run so well but also because of the chemists' sense of self-sacrifice and loyalty to Lewis.

When Norris and Burrell saw Lewis's reports, they must have been thrilled by what they read. Finding new war gases was no easy task, and this new compound met all of the criteria. It appeared lethal, and it was both a vesicant and a lachrymator, causing blisters and inducing tears. It could be manufactured without great difficulty and on a large scale. The precursor chemicals were plentiful and cheap. This new poison had all the promise of mustard gas and more, since its effects were felt immediately, while mustard took time to cause its damage. Most important of all: the Germans didn't have it.

On May 1, Norris ordered Organic Research Unit No. 3 to stop all other work and focus solely on this new compound. He increased the number of chemists at Catholic to nineteen and then to almost three dozen. The experiments became a singular priority. Secrecy, as ever, was crucial. Its chemical and technical name, chlorovinyldichloroarsine, couldn't be used, so to confuse anyone who learned of the work on the hill, they adopted the same code used for mustard gas, G-34. They had another code name for it as well: "methyl," an intentionally misleading description because the word had no connection to its constituent chemicals. To the men who worked at Catholic, however, it had a different name, derived from the name of the man who concocted it. They called it lewisite.

The shroud of secrecy that covered the work at both American and Catholic Universities also extended to the outpost on Jones Point. Walter Scheele's new life as Dr. Smith had begun on April 8 in Peekskill, when he stepped through the lobby of the Eagle Hotel with his cane, accompanied by his Bureau of Investigation handler, Special Agent Warren Grimes, code-named Warren White. It was a half-mile drive to the boat landing. Levering's launch was lashed to the quay where they had left it the previous night. The men boarded, and as the boat puttered out into the current, the river yawned open both upstream and down. Iona Island jutted out into the river to the north, and the Catskills rolled away to the west. The Hudson was slow moving and placid. It had less the look of a river than of a wide lake, with rocky shores and granite cliffs rising steeply into dense forest swaddling Bear Mountain.

The far shore grew close, the launch nosed up to the landing, and the men climbed out. It was a short walk to the American Potash Corporation plant. Grimes assessed the grounds, the buildings, the proximity to the river and the rail. It was a perfect location for Scheele's work to proceed, since it would be difficult to get close to the plant unnoticed, and a secure fence would make approaching the buildings unseen impossible.

Inside the plant, Grimes and Scheele examined the facilities, took stock of the equipment, and determined what construction would be necessary. Grimes went to the office and asked for a list of the thirty or so workers on the plant payroll. He went down the list. Three Austrians worked for the company; they would have to go. He stopped at the name A. Kossovsky. A machinist and shift foreman who had brought a piano with him, Kossovsky was also a labor organizer with the radical IWW — "the Wobblies" — a union accused of pro-German leanings. Kossovsky had helped launch a strike the previous January. He had been trying to recruit employees at the American Potash Corporation to join the union. Fire him, Grimes told the company officials. Don't even let him finish his shift — tell him to clear out immediately and to take his piano from the employee bunkhouse, too.

Grimes summoned the remaining employees, asking their full name, age, birthplace, marital condition, naturalization status, and connections to radicals. He explained to them that there would be a strict pass system from that point forward. No one would get into the plant without a stamped pass and signature.

He assigned four watchmen to duty — one at the gate, three patrolling the grounds. He warned them to keep an extra close eye on the brick building where explosives would be stored. Grimes ordered fencing material for delivery the next day and put men to work digging post holes.

From the moment Scheele arrived, Jones Point became a hive of activity, but his purpose remained a closely guarded secret. Though Grimes had purged Jones Point of potential troublemakers, there were still dozens of other employees ignorant of the new purpose of the laboratory, and it was crucial that they remain in the dark. Grimes made sure that everyone in the know always used the code names and that their true names were never uttered.

The house that was being outfitted for Scheele would also have sleeping quarters for Grimes or any federal agent who was there to keep an eye on Scheele. Thomas Edison's chemist, Bruce Silver, had received permission to take a furlough from the inventor's lab and work with Scheele at the laboratory. Grimes insisted that agents observe every experiment. As soon as each day's tests finished, Scheele turned over the notes. Grimes told him nothing about the newspaper articles published after his arrest reporting that Scheele was in government custody. He also said nothing about the other figures in the bomb plot, some of whom had been in the head-lines as well. He even contemplated locking up Scheele's cabin at night, but decided that it would arouse more suspicion than it was worth.

The doctor spoke freely with Grimes. He relayed old gossip about the kaiser and his lovers in Germany. He rambled about the empire's weaponry and claimed the German military attaché in Washington had stolen an American inventor's plans for missiles propelled with liquid air. He talked about Germany's plans to invade Canada and infiltrate Mexico and how Cuba was a nest of anti-American sentiment. Grimes listened carefully and jotted it all down.

Grimes reveled in his job as wrangler of the turncoat chemist. He had been at Scheele's side almost every step of the way, and he wanted to stay there. But his time at Jones Point was coming to an end. In his report to the chief in Washington, he practically pleaded to remain on the job. "I would very much like to remain with him until the completion of the tests. It would be awkward to bring in a new man at this time," he wrote. He signed it "Warren White."

The appeal fell on deaf ears. At week's end, the bureau's new division superintendent, Charles DeWoody, ordered two other agents, Graham Rice and Francis X. O'Donnell, to Jones Point to replace Grimes. DeWoody didn't specify why he dismissed Grimes, but Grimes was from Washington, and DeWoody was assigning men from his division in New York City. Their homes were closer, and they were familiar faces in the New York office. In his orders to Agent Rice—code-named "Riser"—DeWoody described the gravity of the situation. Not only was Rice guarding against the possibility of Scheele's escape, he also had to protect the chemist. Accomplices in the ship-bombing ring were still at large, and they might want him dead. Grimes would brief Rice on the situation before returning to Washington. "All of his work must be maintained in the greatest secrecy," DeWoody wrote.

Despite DeWoody's insistence on secrecy, he had already proved himself less than reliable when he told the *New York Times* about Scheele's arrest. He demonstrated his indiscretion again when he showed up in Peekskill a few days later for an inspection of Jones Point. Grimes was stunned to discover that the superintendent had brought his wife with him, as if they were on a weekend getaway to the countryside. To Grimes's fury, the loose-lipped superintendent used Scheele's and Grimes's real names when introducing them to his wife, even though Grimes had insisted that code names must be used. When Grimes ushered DeWoody into the laboratory, he continued addressing Scheele by his real name, even though three plant employees were within earshot in an adjoining office with the connecting door open. DeWoody went on to tell Scheele facts that Grimes had carefully withheld, such as how the German spymaster Rintelen had said that Scheele would have to be "fixed"—that is, killed—and that it was common knowledge that Scheele was in the government's custody. Alarmed, Grimes interrupted to tell DeWoody that he was mistaken. Irritated, the superintendent insisted that Scheele's arrest was known all over the country. Scheele looked on as the two men argued, with the three employees still in the adjoining office.

DeWoody left after this spectacular bungle, but the damage was done. Grimes soon learned that at least two plant employees now knew that "White" wasn't his real name. Worse, Scheele turned on Grimes and angrily told him he would stop work unless conditions changed at Jones Point, insisting that he would kill himself rather than continue under the restrictive conditions of his confinement.

The furtive activities of the men did not go unnoticed outside of the plant either. A week after DeWoody came up to Peekskill, O'Donnell brought Scheele to a drugstore in town. While they were there, an Office of Naval Intelligence agent spotted them and demanded that the men accompany him to the police station, where the police chief interrogated them about why they were crossing the river each day to Jones Point. O'Donnell managed to sputter out an explanation without revealing Scheele's identity or true purpose. Placated, the police sent the men on their way.

DeWoody, however, was irate. He felt the men should never have been in the drugstore in the first place, but he grudgingly acknowledged that no harm seemed to come from it. "I do not like the incident, but O'Donnell and Dr. Scheele seem well satisfied with the whole procedure and the outcome."

There may have been another reason that DeWoody wanted men from the New York office alongside Scheele. It wasn't just the plumbers and electricians at Jones Point who concerned DeWoody; it was Richmond Levering, whose business dealings in New York were getting new scrutiny. After the oilman's departure under a cloud the previous fall, Levering's reappearance had been no small worry for the department. Amazingly, in the short period since Levering had returned to the good graces of the department by scooping up Scheele in Cuba, whispers about the oilman's transgressions had begun anew. Accusations of fraud that trailed his soured business deals gathered steam, with articles appearing in New York newspapers about angry shareholders in one of his companies. A new allegation had arisen against him: that Levering had attempted to bribe a stenographer in one of the cases against him. Then he had managed to create a diplomatic row by telling a Japanese diplomat that he was a target of Bolshevik assassins. Not only did the so-called plot prove unsubstantiated, Levering had revealed to the ambassador that he was involved with the Scheele case.

Worried anew that Levering could tarnish the bureau, Bielaski had ordered DeWoody to quietly investigate Levering. DeWoody dispatched investigators to Ohio and around the financial corridors of New York City to gather facts about Levering. The reports that came back were dismaying, peppered with words like "crook" and "totally unfit" and "unworthy of trust." "Not to be employed by the government," one former business partner said. "A man whose word should not be taken," another man said. "If ever there was a crooked crook that Levering was one," said a third. "A bad nickel," said a fourth. Though the agents had not substantiated that Levering had committed any crimes, their findings were less than flattering. DeWoody wrote to the chief:

> From one or two experiences I have had with him, noting his inclination to do rather reckless and sensational things, and his subsequent inaccurate statements in attempted explanation of same, my only thought is that if he is regularly appointed as a special agent of the department, and by any chance does commit some indiscreet act, the questionable reputation that he has borne in the past in the minds of many men is going to be raised against the judgment of the Bureau in having appointed such a man.

As the constellations of chemical warfare outposts continued to grow, it had become ever more cumbersome to keep so many agencies and individuals informed and involved. More than a half-dozen different offices and military organizations had a hand in the work, each with different responsibilities and different chains of command. The Bureau of Mines handled research; the U.S. Army Medical Department produced gas masks; the Ordnance Department manufactured explosives and shells; the Signal Corps had a role in flares, smoke screens, and smoke candles; the Corps of Engineers was responsible for the gas and flame regiment; and the American Expeditionary Forces in Europe deployed the soldiers on the battlefield, with their own separate and parallel gas service. Though more than a dozen copies of reports went to Europe alone each week, to the AEF lab and the various commanders on the ground, scientists on both sides of the Atlantic complained that vital information was not reaching them. As if that wasn't enough, the Ordnance Department, the Bureau of Mines, the navy, the Department of Justice, and Thomas Edison were all enmeshed in the work at Jones Point, which was insulated in its own bubble of secrecy.

The feeble Office of the Gas Service helped little. When the office was established in the fall and Colonel Charles Potter put at its head, it had been designed to unify and coordinate the various military and civilian departments that had a hand in gas warfare. Neither Potter nor his deputies in the Office of the Gas Service or the Chemical Service Section had provided the kind of vigorous leadership that Fries and other military chiefs hoped for; instead, it was passive, a toothless bureaucracy. After Potter was canned in the winter, a succession of directors with little military experience followed.

There was a growing recognition within the domestic gas service that the sprawl and disorganization was hindering its work — at a May meeting about procurements, Colonel Bradley Dewey admitted that gas mask production had reached a crisis point. The service couldn't keep promises made to the army. There was duplication in work. Deadlines weren't being met. Things would have to change.

A shake-up was ahead. On March 1, one of the ships returning from France had brought Major General Peyton C. March back to the United States. A tall, commanding figure, March had served as an artillery chief to Pershing. The general was a soldier's soldier, lean and sinewy, with battlefield experience. He also hated government red tape.

Recalled from France to serve as army chief of staff, he was charged with establishing order in the chaotic army structure, but while he was overseas, the general had also heard complaints about the gas service. This scattered domestic structure with no one in charge was an intolerable situation. March had someone in mind to straighten out the tangle. A soldier who had already set his boots in France and an engineer with unequaled experience in creating order from chaos.

On Saturday, May 18, an odd news item appeared in the middle of the *Washington Herald*'s Army and Navy News section. A kind of gossip column for the military, the section was a roundup of news tidbits from the ranks, anecdotes about heroes and deserters, and announcements about military rule changes. Buried in the column, a four-sentence item made a passing reference to the former head of the First Division having been in Washington. "Major General William L. Sibert, United States Army, having completed the duty for which he was ordered to this city, will return to his proper station," the item read.

Sibert's "proper station" was Charleston, South Carolina, where he had been relegated to an out-of-the-way outpost as chief of the Southeastern Division. Even before he returned from France, his sudden dismissal spurred a cascade of articles speculating about the "big Army shake-up" in France. Many hinted that the demotion resulted from some unspecified grievance that Pershing harbored toward Sibert. But after the initial flurry of reports, Sibert had been largely out of the public eye.

Sibert said nothing publicly about his fall from grace. He took up residence at the Villa Margherita, an Italian Renaissance–style hotel on Charleston's southernmost tip, across the harbor from Fort Sumter. His exile didn't dull a ferocious sense of purpose in the war. In a rare public appearance, he spoke in April to ROTC graduates at Camp Warden McLean in Chattanooga, Tennessee. His ringing words to the cadets carried a bellicose edge.

"Never will the brotherhood of man be a reality: never will the sword be forged into plowshare. Man is a fighting animal. There will always be wars. The only way to attain right is through might. Let America be prepared and mighty if she would champion the cause of right among nations," he told the graduates in what a reporter called a "grim summation of history." They were fiercely belligerent words for a man whose career was built upon civil engineering, not bloodshed.

Goliath's dismissal from the AEF just short of his retirement age had been widely seen as the sunset of his military career. But his mystery visit to Washington was likely the launch of a third act. On May 11, 1918, Sibert had quietly received a new appointment as chief of the moribund Office of the Gas Service in the National Army.

Sibert left Charleston and moved to Washington, taking a house on De Sales Street NW, near Dupont Circle. When the War Department announced Sibert's assignment, the story that went out on the wires reporting his appointment was published verbatim in many newspapers across the country. "While in France with Gen. Pershing he had every opportunity to study the uses to which gases have been put by the allied armies and the Germans and is regarded as peculiarly suited for the new post," the wire article read.

Fries was pleased when he heard the news of Sibert's reappointment toward the end of May. With Sibert at the head of the domestic service, Fries would have a commanding officer who had been in France, an engineer and a soldier who understood the war and the challenges of the gas service. The promotion gave Fries more confidence that the War Department would move ahead with consolidating the gas service, finally getting Fries the kind of results he wanted. "The gas service has been getting recognition, though there have been a few times when it felt it wouldn't become what I felt it should be."

Sibert immersed himself in the mechanics of the gas service, including the Research Division. There was little disagreement over whether the baffling, interlocking responsibilities for gas warfare needed reorganization. The question was what to do with the war gas investigations under the Bureau of Mines. Van Manning had felt that the research was his bureau's domain since the earliest days of the war, when he was one of the few voices urging action about gas. Now Manning wanted to maintain a proprietary grasp on the research and keep it out of the hands of the military. Scientists thrived on collaboration, he felt, and the creative energy fueling their achievements would suffocate under War Department command and control. Fries and Sibert, however, saw military control as an essential matter of efficiency required for clear lines of communication. Fries had been egging on the army to take over the research work since fall; the War College, too, wanted a centralized, all-military organization, calling the current mishmash of departments and agencies "thoroughly illogical." Sibert was now a powerful lobbyist for that position.

Baker asked for a conference to discuss the matter on Saturday, May 25. General March, Assistant Secretary of War Benedict Crowell, and General Sibert all attended. Marston Bogert, the assistant director of the gas service and Sibert's predecessor, was there as well. Officials who couldn't attend sent proxies, such as Assistant Secretary of the Interior Alexander T. Vogelsang representing Secretary Lane, who was traveling, and Lieutenant Colonel Raymond Bacon, Amos Fries's director of the AEF's Gas Research Laboratory in Puteaux, who had also returned from France. Van Manning also attended, taut as a trip wire and ready to deploy every rhetorical weapon he had to defend his technical men from the military.

If Baker harbored a flicker of hope that the issue could be resolved amicably, Manning promptly snuffed it out. He exuded a kind of paternal pride in this organization he had nurtured from birth, and he made it clear that he did not intend to let it go without a fight. The director launched into a lecture on the bureau's achievements, insisting that he was more responsible than anyone for the success of the chemical warfare work. Delays weren't his bureau's fault, Manning complained; slowdowns came from the development side, which the army ran. Transferring work to the military would suggest that his bureau had fallen down on the job, when he insisted he had yet to hear a single word of reproach regarding inefficiency or failure to respond to War Department requests.

When Baker asked Sibert to make the case for military control, he presented one simple reason: a more efficient organization. Manning's retort was that the research would be most efficient outside of the military. He was willing to accept consolidating the service under the army; he just felt that the research work should be exempted, because civilians preferred to work with other civilians, and not under military direction.

An embittered tone crept into Manning's arguments; his leadership challenged and his authority threatened, he hinted that his former supporters had abandoned him. He was deeply suspicious of Sibert and suspected that Bogert had coached him on questions to ask in front of Baker.

The men went around and around as Manning and Sibert argued past each other. They bickered over responsibility for improvements to the soldier's gas masks, who was to blame for delayed reports that never reached France, and whether the existing structure delayed results. By the end, nothing had been resolved. It was almost 5:00 p.m. when Baker adjourned the meeting. After almost two hours, the men were no closer to agreement than when they'd started.

After Manning and Sibert and the others had filed out of Baker's office, Assistant Secretary Vogelsang stayed behind. Baker gave the impression that he didn't agree with his generals' arguments over the need to transfer control of the war work to the army. In the now-empty office, the secretary admitted as such to Vogelsang and said that he would try to convince Sibert to maintain the status quo.

It would be a hard task, Vogelsang said. Sibert was a stubborn man.

One of the most stubborn men in the country, Baker replied.

Chapter Eleven

"He Who Gasses Last, Gasses Best"

Night fell over Chaumont as Addison joined a crowd gathering on the gas experimental field where Companies C and D were preparing a demonstration of Livens batteries and Stokes mortars. It was June 6. The weather in France had been beautiful—dry and warm, with little rain. Poppies blanketed the countryside; sometimes Addison pressed the blossoms inside letters to mail home to Margaret. As soldiers streamed onto the field in the dark, Addison saw this was no small affair; almost three companies had assembled, and Addison spotted high-ranking officers from general headquarters. When everything was ready, the men pushed the plungers on the exploders. Addison watched the projectors belch flame and smoke skyward, the shells streaking upward into the night air, detonating in the distance and sending billowing clouds of gas over the fields.

Not every member of the regiment attended the show. Some Company B platoons had departed for advance billets, but Higgie stayed behind. He had spent the afternoon fixing Livens drums at the ammunition dump up the road and hadn't been summoned for the demonstration; instead, he ate supper and retired to his bunk to read. Higgie had been struggling since he received crushing news from home. On May 29, he had stretched out on his bunk to relish a batch of letters that had arrived. The very first one he opened delivered the worst kind of shock—his mother had died on May 4.

The letter was dated three weeks before. The soldier in Higgie melted away, and the brokenhearted twenty-one-year-old threw aside the other letters, curled up in bed, and sobbed. After dinner, he went for a walk alone in the woods, unable to believe that his mother was dead all those weeks and he hadn't even known it. During the night, he drifted in and out of sleep, talking out loud and waking again and again in the darkness to wonder if it was all a dream.

The experimental field demonstration marked a year and a day since Higgie had registered for the draft in Lawrence. He didn't need fireworks to celebrate the anniversary. He'd soon be setting off his own shows. Companies A and B had received orders they'd been waiting for: they would be launching their first gas attacks independent of the British. Higginbottom's Company B would be setting off one thousand Livens projectors in the French sector of Toul. Company A would follow a few miles away and a few hours later in the American sector with nine hundred projectors.

After reveille the next morning, Higginbottom was told to get his pack ready in the afternoon. He left at about one-thirty and rode to the advance dugouts at a French camp about two and one-half miles from the front near Fey-en-Haye. The dugouts were tucked into the side of a hill, with iron roofs and wire beds and electric lights. They weren't clean, but they were roomy, with a couple of nice tables. Higginbottom and a bunch of other soldiers played cards until late that night. It was very quiet when he finally rolled into bed.

He slept late—there was no reveille this close to the front. That night, Higgie went out to the batteries to dig in projectors. There were Algerian colonial soldiers in the carrying party—he marveled at how they balanced the projector barrels on their heads. Preparations for the upcoming show lasted for days. Sometimes bullets sang over his head as he worked. The midsummer nights were short; the men had to work quickly between dusk and dawn. Even after the batteries were in place and the projectors ready, the show was postponed several times because the wind wasn't right or the weather hadn't cooperated. The men carped about the delays, blaming red tape at headquarters.

Higgie sometimes attended Addison's Sunday prayer services. Addison's training hadn't prepared him much for the reality of pastoring in a combat zone. At night, huge rats scurried through his billet; one night, a sniffling rodent scampered up on Addison's bed as he slept. One Sunday before a service, German antiaircraft guns opened up on French planes overhead. Shell bursts blossomed in the sky, and bullets rained down, one of them hitting a soldier in the back. When the firefight slowed, Addison assembled a group of fifty men down the road and passed out hymnals, and the men sang lustily on the roadside and listened to Addison's sermon. Afterward, he went up to the trenches and peered out over no-man's-land, wondering about the Germans who he knew were looking back at him in the dark. Higgie attended the following Sunday's service, listening to Addison's sermon "Christianity in Warfare." Shells began to fall in the middle of the sermon, and the singing didn't go well, but the service continued through the din. "It's interesting, holding services under these conditions," Addison mused.

On Tuesday, June 18, an officer arrived from Langres to report that conditions looked favorable for the attack that night. When the alert sounded after dinner, Addison went back to his billet to prepare. Zero hour was 10:30 p.m. The chaplain was nervous and excited; it was a big night, his first real gas show. He put on his trench coat, belt, and helmet and got his gas mask. He started off for his position at about 8:30 with two captains.

It was another beautiful evening. As dusk fell, rain clouds gave way to a clear sky. A half-moon rose, bathing the battlefield in silver light. German observation balloons floated silently above. Addison waited in a dugout, listening to a French soldier phone in the latest wind readings to the officers in charge of the show. There was little to do. It seemed strange to Addison to stand there in the quiet stillness of the evening sky, knowing that in seconds, all hell would let loose from every direction. Across the line, men's lives would be snuffed out in a curtain of fire and gas.

As zero hour approached, Higgie crouched in his trench. With the clear sky and bright moon, it was dangerous for the men to venture out into the open to wire up the projectors and pull the pins out of the shells. Finally, at 10:00 p.m., Higginbottom's platoon got word to go to the batteries. He scrambled up to the trench, trying to stay out of sight of the observation balloons as he unspooled the wire to the fuses. When he reached the projectors, the pins had been put in so tight that he couldn't get them out. Higgie was wrestling with the pins when someone yelled to get out of the way. Over the buzzer-phone wires stretching back to the command, word had come from the officers in charge: one minute to go. Heart pounding, Higginbottom scrambled up and out of the trench, getting clear as the projectors fired in a deafening roar just a few feet away. The shells launched so close to Higginbottom that he felt like they almost took him with them over to the German side.

Farther back, Addison watched in awe as almost nine hundred projectors discharged phosgene shells in thunderous waves. Some projectors didn't fire because time had been too short to prepare them all. Still, it was a spectacular display, explosions that shook the ground and turned the moonlit sky into daylight. The French artillery to the rear opened up next and continued for more than half an hour, raining shrapnel shells and high explosives over the German lines. There was little response from the Germans—nothing at all for a time and then a feeble volley of shells. Addison stayed in the entrance to the dugout for about an hour, waiting and listening and chatting, before walking back to camp. Not a single American soldier had been lost. He felt oddly calm and watched a few German shells land nearby, toward the French positions.

Back at the camp, the excited men rehashed the evening's attack, congratulating one another on a successful operation. Addison fell into bed about 12:30 a.m., around the same time as Higginbottom in his billet.

In the middle of the night, explosions jarred both men awake. Company A's show had begun about eight miles away, another 737 projectors heaving phosgene shells across the line. Addison and Higgie lay in the dark listening to the distant cannonade and the tremulous concussions that shook the ground beneath their beds. The firing resumed about thirty minutes later; this time the shelling had provoked an angry German response—continuous firing, the thunder of the ground-shaking explosions. It went on for hours. Higginbottom fell back to sleep and slept soundly until 9:00 a.m.

In the officers' quarters, Addison drifted in and out of sleep. After he awoke in the morning, he took a truck and returned to camp, where he met up with the men from Company A. The phosgene attack, it turned out, had repelled a German raid of two storm battalions. Had Company A launched its attack even a half hour later, they might have been overrun by the Germans. Every member of the gas and flame regiment survived the night.

"A few days ago the Bosche got its first taste of American gas from my regiment and I hear he didn't like it a bit," Amos Fries wrote home to Bessie. Fries had missed the solo debut of the Hellfire Boys, laid up in the hospital for almost two weeks with a mysterious ailment that the doctors chalked up to an overactive liver. The colonel was thrilled by the operation report that the projectors shot by Companies A and B—sixteen hundred in all—and artillery shelling afterward. The show caused at least forty German casualties, including ten deaths, in the 150th Landwehr Regiment and stymied the raiding party preparing to go over the top. On one night, some twenty-three tons of phosgene had been unleashed against the German regiment. "We hope to give him lots of it from now on," Fries went on.

Finding Fries fit, the medicos prescribed more exercise as the cure for his liver troubles. The hospital visit gave him a chance to rest, although he was hardly idle—he received briefings, read two novels cover to cover one day, and delivered a lecture on gas to forty doctors on another.

Fries was anxious to return to work. He was awaiting word of his proposal for a gas corps and had asked Pershing's chief of staff to sign off on a huge order: more than two thousand tons of mustard each month and more than three thousand tons of phosgene, chloropicrin, and other gases, with an expectation that this volume would double by January 1, 1919.

The chief of staff felt that the United States simply didn't have the capacity to manufacture such vast quantities, and so Fries withdrew the proposal. But the day he wrote home about the Thirtieth Engineers' attack, he received good news from Washington: the War Department had finally acted on Fries's and Sibert's recommendations for consolidating everything related to chemical warfare into a single organization, with a domestic branch and a commensurate overseas branch in Fries's corps. The name for the whole enterprise under the War Department would be the Chemical Warfare Service. "I am glad of that for it will simplify my work a whole lot," a satisfied Fries told Bessie. He was also extremely pleased with Sibert. "You were right in thinking I would be happy at seeing General Sibert at the head of the Gas Service. Things are going vastly better there now and will continue as he gets hold of the game. He is getting the work of all the Gas coordinated there along the same lines in the States that we are here," Fries wrote.

Fries was correct that the War Department was moving swiftly, but there was still a hitch. The Research Division under Manning's Bureau of Mines remained an unresolved sticking point. On June 7, what had been a behind-the-scenes fight spilled into the headlines when the *New York Times* editorialized about the issue, transforming the dispute between the scientists and the army into a national debate. The paper lamented that it would be a "tragedy" if the army took over the chemists' work. While coolly respectful to Sibert, the editorial nonetheless painted the general as a bully trying to bludgeon the country's most esteemed scientists into line:

To militarize the body of chemists whose energies, whose genius, the Government cannot do without would be to introduce red tape and generate friction between army officers who know nothing of the properties of the new instrumentality of warfare and the scientific men who are seeking and finding means to defeat the enemy at his own game.

The ultimate decision lay with President Wilson, who had emergency powers from Congress to reorganize wartime agencies. The president claimed ignorance of the matter and asked the Interior Department for more information about the wartime activities of the Bureau of Mines. Manning's allies rallied behind him, but there were louder voices on the other side, such as Assistant Secretary of War Benedict Crowell and Fries's aide Raymond Bacon, the chief of the AEF's lab who had been sent back to the States to push for Fries's consolidation plan.

On June 25, President Wilson ended the debate with an executive order placing the Research Division and the American University Experiment Station under the control of the War Department. The army would absorb all the civilian scientists. All of the existing officers would stay on. Burrell—who would be made a colonel— would remain chief of the Research Division, and each of the division chiefs would keep his position. The only person without a role in this new military organization, it seemed, was Van Manning.

The next day, President Wilson wrote to Manning that he felt confident in his decision, but that he had hesitated out of a reluctance to take the Bureau of Mines off of the work it had so effectively performed. Secretary of War Newton Baker had taken pains to praise Manning and his bureau, and the president included Baker's letter saying so. He wrote:

I want, however, to express to you my own appreciation of the fine and helpful piece of work which you have done, and to say that this sort of team work by the bureaus outside of the

direct war-making agency is one of the cheering and gratify-
ing evidences of the way our official forces are inspired by the
presence of a great national task.

Privately, Manning was surprised and hurt by the decision. He
confided in one of the officers at the National Research Council
that up until the very last minute he believed that his bureau would
remain in charge of the Research Division. He had no position or
standing in this new organization, but he knew one thing: that he
felt betrayed by scientists who had supported the army takeover
and hoped that such men would have no role in this new enterprise.

Despite Manning's bruised ego, he said nothing publicly. He
wrote a gracious response to the president, thanking him for recognizing the bureau's work. He extended no such niceties to Sibert.
Instead, he sent the general an officious letter with an unmistak-
ably curt tone stating that the transfer was only for the war's duration and that afterward the research work would revert back to his
dominion in the Bureau of Mines.

Telegrams and letters of condolence arrived for Manning from
around the country, consoling the director as if a dear family member had died. "I am sorry to hear that you have lost your chemical
section," an editor of a mining journal wrote to Manning. "I can
appreciate the keen regret you will have in parting with this work,"
another supporter wrote.

The reorganization meant that chemical warfare burst into the
public consciousness again in congressional testimony, speeches, and
articles. Americans learned not only that there were almost two
thousand chemists working on chemical weapons but that the effort
was big enough and important enough to warrant an entirely new
branch of the military dedicated solely to this novel form of warfare.
It was a front-page story in the *Washington Herald,* which declared
"1,700 Chemists Employed for Gas Service," and the wire-service
story appeared in newspapers across the country. The *New York
Times* followed up its previous editorial with another much gentler

toward Sibert, calling him "an eminent engineer with a fine Panama Canal record," saying that no more competent man could have been found. But the editorial also pointed out that Sibert had a heavy burden of responsibility. "The success of American gas warfare depends upon General Sibert; it is the man that counts in war, rarely the system, which can never be perfection."

The War Department released Newton Baker's letter about Van Manning to the press, saying "the whole subject of gas warfare has assumed a fresh pressure and intensity." After Senate testimony about the transfer, Americans read in newspapers from coast to coast that the United States had exceeded Germany's capacity for making war gases. That the introduction of chemicals to the battlefield was the most important innovation in warfare since gunpowder. And that scientists worked on these weapons in a secret laboratory in Washington that was so hush-hush that Department of War officials refused to discuss it. One article read:

> This laboratory is now perhaps the most heavily guarded stronghold of the army. It is lined with a system of electrical and mechanical alarms as intricate as those that line the vaults of the United States treasury. Only persons with the most unimpeachable references may enter it. The reason for all this secrecy is that the element of surprise is essential to the success of gas warfare. Everything depends upon suddenly attacking the enemy with a new kind of gas against which he has no protection.

A spate of public addresses, testimonials, and speeches dedicated to chemical warfare followed, with accounts published in the newspapers. Given Wilson's censorious ways and his administration's strict limitations on wartime information, the blitz of news about chemical warfare suggests a public relations campaign, aimed at both the American people and adversaries abroad. On June 21, Colonel Raymond Bacon, Fries's chemical laboratory chief, delivered a speech at a conference of mining engineers hinting darkly that a new gas more poisonous than anything that had come before would soon be used against the Germans.

"We are of the opinion that gas will win the war," he said. "It is more and more becoming something of prime importance. We are finding greater protection against gas and better gases. In time we will be able to hand the Boche a little bit more hellish gas than he has ever handed us."

Another speech noted in the Washington papers came on June 26. It was early evening as Northwestern University alumni took their seats in Cushman's Restaurant, a few blocks from the White House. The university president, Thomas F. Holgate, spoke first, then the keynote speaker, a highly regarded judge. The judge introduced the next speaker on the program. It was the chemist Winford Lee Lewis. His voice was hoarse and strained, and he apologized for the state of his vocal cords. "I have been working in poison gases for six months and my voice is all gone," Lewis croaked. "I used to be a splendid singer and a good speaker, but now I can never sing nor speak any more than the proverbial crow."

Despite his rasping voice, Lewis delivered a short but typically wry address. It was a hard time for chemistry speeches, he said. "The military lid is clamped so tight on the chemists" that he had to talk to his wife in sign language, he joked. "Our hatches are closed so tightly that most of the time I feel like a submarine ready for a dive, and I am so full of the things that I can't talk about that I simply can't talk about the things I can talk about."

But he could talk about one thing, he said: that despite Germany's head start in gas warfare, the United States would surpass her. Though he could not speak of the details, he was in a position to know, he assured the alumni. "She started this poison gas game and we are going to finish it," he rasped. "He who gasses last, gasses best."

Two days later, President Wilson signed General Order 62, entitled "Creating Chemical Warfare Service." The stroke of the president's pen on July 1 created a new branch of the army, on a par with the Corps of Engineers. "Army Takes Over All War Gas Work," the *New York Times* reported.

American soldiers had used gas for the first time only three months earlier and independently of their Allies less than three weeks earlier. Now the military would develop, manufacture, and deploy the weapons that its soldiers would wield. It demanded a new field of military study of how these new weapons should be used. Hundreds of civilian scientists and engineers abruptly became army officers. All of the research-and-development work, from California to Tennessee, was under the umbrella of the service. It was a sprawling empire stitched together beneath a single flag, and General Sibert was its standard-bearer.

One research facility, however, was absent from the reorganization plans. In Manning's May 15 report to Interior Secretary Franklin Lane on the Bureau of Mine's wartime research, he listed twenty-one different branch laboratories, from American University and Catholic University to the University of California. Jones Point was not listed. Nor did it appear in subsequent reports, and there was no description of the experiments under way there. Barely acknowledged, the secret laboratory overlooking the Hudson River was a phantom satellite in the chemical warfare universe that Major General Sibert had inherited. What Sibert learned of the secret laboratory in New York probably reached him in oral reports; the Research Division put almost nothing about it in writing.

Despite the turmoil over jurisdiction of chemical experiments and the nagging questions over Levering, the tests at Jones Point had begun. A storage building was refurbished into sleeping quarters for Scheele, so he wouldn't have to ferry from Peekskill each day. Before he left, Grimes had assisted Scheele with unpacking and storing chemicals, and he had the windows painted over to mask the activities within. He arranged for a security firm to provide twenty-four-hour guards and added a layer of surveillance from the local sheriff, too. Governor Charles Whitman gave Levering permission to use land behind the plant for open-air detonations and explosions that would be part of Scheele's experiments.

Five days after agents brought the doctor to Jones Point for the first time, an officer from the American University Experiment Station had arrived, a chemist from Arizona named Captain Paul H. M. P. Brinton. After he showed his identification and conferred with the doctor, he watched experiments and stayed only a day, returning to Washington in the morning. A few days later, he was back, and this time he stayed. During the tests, either Brinton or Edison's chemist, Bruce Silver, was at Scheele's side every day as his assistant and overseer. Brinton often authored the biweekly testing reports, which were forwarded to Bielaski, Lieutenant Commander Theodore S. Wilkinson in the Navy Bureau of Ordnance, and Lieutenant Colonel Earl J. W. Ragsdale of the Army Department of Ordnance.

Scheele began work on ten areas of experimentation. There were experiments with wing dope, the lacquers that protected airplane wings; dyes for military uniforms; designs for gas containers; shell linings impervious to corrosive chemical agents; and consultation over various war gases, including a phosgene variation. They also experimented with manufacturing mustard and other compounds for use as war gases, and when they created a particularly promising substance, they bundled up a sample and sent it to American University for further tests.

Those areas of research, however, were secondary to two main projects. The first was using liquefied oxygen as an explosive. When cooled into a liquid and detonated, oxygen proved to be a powerful explosive, perhaps even more so than TNT. Research into oxygen as an explosive had been conducted for years—including by the Bureau of Mines—but Germany had managed to iron out the technical problems and turn it into a viable explosive. From the earliest moments of his capture, Scheele had told Levering that liquid oxygen was a part of the German arsenal, used in the enormous shells that destroyed the frontier fortresses in Liège, Belgium, in the war's first days. Scheele claimed that the violence of the explosions was due to the expansion of the liquid oxygen reservoirs within the shells. Scheele also claimed that liquid oxygen accounted for the mystifying power of the so-called Paris guns that shelled the French capital from sixty miles away, a feat of firepower so stupefying that it seemed to defy physics. Scheele explained that they probably weren't conventional shells but aerial torpedoes—rockets, in other words—propelled by the rapid expansion of liquid oxygen.

The other top priority at Jones Point was Scheele's cigar-bomb compound, the mixture of hexamethylenetetramine and sodium peroxide. At first, the laboratory used the shorthand of "scheeleite" to describe the chemical combination. It didn't take long for the chemists to realize that it was imprudent to identify the substance by the name of its inventor, a traitor and a German spy, so scheeleite gained a new name: "helline."

Levering wrote frequent and enthusiastic reports about helline and its potential as a weapon. When mixed with petroleum, it burned more slowly but just as hot and with continual explosions, rather than exploding and flaring out quickly. Such a fire on a ship or in an ammunition factory "could never possibly be extinguished," Levering wrote. He proposed that they start manufacturing the substance as soon as possible. He wrote to Bielaski:

> I am quite willing and anxious to put any plant I have and quite an experienced staff of commercial manufacturers and engineers at your disposal, and would be very glad to come to some definite point where you could make some calculations as to the amount of the material which could be utilized so that a plan could be gotten up for whatever scale installation is necessary.

Bielaski wrote back praising Levering for the reports, which "should prove of great benefit to the government." But he cautioned that he wasn't in a position to respond to Levering's overture about manufacturing Scheele's compound. He suggested that Levering discuss the matter instead with the navy and other military agencies that contracted with government suppliers. Levering did just that; he soon had a deal with the War Department to produce helline and manufacture five thousand incendiary bombs for testing.

The experiments with helline initially took two forms: determining how to manufacture it on a large scale and how to weaponize it in bombs or incendiary devices, such as flares that would remain lit underwater. The manufacturing research went smoothly, and by late May, plans were under way to build a helline plant to make five hundred pounds every day. Figuring out a use for the compound started with only a few experiments. The chemists tried turning it into incendiary bombs, building a scaffolding rigged with a crane to drop three buckets filled with ninety pounds of helline through the roof of a wooden shanty below. The bottom bucket contained a glass vial of sulfuric acid that smashed on impact, igniting the helline around it, which in turn ignited the two buckets above. When the buckets were dropped, they erupted with a satisfying whoosh, creating a fifty-foot pillar of fire. But the flame was so intense and hot that it quickly flared out with little damage to the shanty. When repeated using a mixture of helline and oil, the oil ignited, too, and turned the shed into a roaring inferno.

The scientists also tested helline for use in small firebombs—incendiary "darts," Levering called them—dropped from airplanes to set crops afire behind enemy lines, or for signal flares. The Palisades Interstate Park Commission gave permission to use a nearby abandoned quarry, where explosives could be dropped from a height. A request to use other areas of the park was refused, but the commission agreed to let the chemists use condemned buildings for tests. They were not standing for long. In one experiment, three pails of helline—like the device dropped from the scaffolding—were placed inside a log cabin and ignited with a fuse. When the first bucket of helline exploded, it ignited the other two buckets, spattering flaming gobs of oil throughout the cabin. Within minutes, a raging inferno had burned the cabin to the ground.

Peekskill residents surely wondered about the mysterious activities afoot on the nub of land across the Hudson River. Just to the north of Jones Point, the U.S. Navy maintained the Iona Island Arsenal on an archipelago that jutted out into the river, so men in uniform weren't an uncommon sight in the area. Iona provided its own share of pyrotechnics; fifteen years earlier, in 1903, an explosion of defective ammunition killed six men and injured ten at the arsenal, shattering windows miles away. Still, the experiments at Jones Point were much more mysterious. Explosions threw showers of debris and fountains of flame into the air. Projectiles and rockets sizzled overhead and exploded on contact with the earth. Sometimes men gathered in boats and threw things into the river that mysteriously caught fire beneath the surface, emitting an infernal yellow and pink underwater glow. There were explosions on the river, too, underwater detonations that heaved geysers into the air. Sometimes, phosphorescence danced on the river's surface after dark, a glowing curtain that swirled and shifted in the current.

The chemists had high hopes for helline as an explosive, but comparative tests quickly found that TNT was more powerful, so Scheele's compound would have to be useful in other ways. Scheele was soon experimenting with using it as a depth charge, for signal lights, flares, and grenades. The chemists shot at it with rifles to test its stability. Though less powerful than TNT, its use for incendiary darts remained promising, and development of different variations picked up steam, eclipsing other, less promising experiments, Brinton wrote to Levering. They also began investigating it for use as a rocket propellant.

The ongoing involvement of the chemist Bruce Silver from Thomas Edison's laboratory eventually prompted Edison's assistant to write a puzzled note to Silver asking exactly what he was doing and when Edison could expect him back. Silver apologized for his absence, but said that he had been "just about as busy as possible" with his responsibilities for the chemical warfare work. The work had reached a stage that none of them would have imagined.

"The people in Washington have become so enthusiastic that the actual manufacture of the incendiary bombs is underway for rushed shipment to Europe," he wrote.

Levering, too, wrote to Edison to explain Silver's absence. "The work at Jones Point has progressed and extended beyond any possible expectations that any of us held in regard to the experiments of Dr. Scheele's various propositions," he wrote, adding that the length of time they needed Silver for was "absolutely indefinite." Levering began sending the reports to Edison as well.

Levering and the chemists at Jones Point were thrilled with the progress, but trouble was brewing. As the weeks went on, the doctor chafed more and more at his confinement. He began to agitate to spend more time with his wife under less restrictive circumstances. Marie Scheele was living alone in Hackensack, New Jersey. She occasionally traveled to Haverstraw, New York, where she stayed at a hotel about seven miles south of Jones Point and was allowed to have brief visits with her husband. But the visits were rare and always under close supervision. At the end of May, Charles DeWoody, the division superintendent, brought Marie Scheele to Peekskill for a visit. For about two hours, he allowed the doctor and his wife to sit on the outdoor veranda at the Eagle Hotel. Marie Scheele wanted to come up to Peekskill for the entire summer and asked permission as well to stay over weekends with the doctor at his quarters at Jones Point. DeWoody warned the couple that he couldn't promise that but said he would ask the bureau.

In his account of the trip to deliver Marie, DeWoody also described something that troubled him more than conjugal visits between the doctor and his wife: his agent Francis X. O'Donnell had reported that Scheele planned to go into business with Levering to manufacture his explosive compound. O'Donnell had overheard snippets of conversation between Scheele and Bruce Silver about the deal and learned that Silver met with Levering about once a week to discuss forming some kind of a holding company which would take over any patents for helline. Though the details were scant, O'Donnell had a very clear impression that Scheele would profit financially from this arrangement.

DeWoody asked the chief, Bielaski, if he knew anything about such a partnership between Levering and Scheele:

> Personally, I am surprised at it, and believe that if there were public knowledge of the fact that Dr. Scheele's offenses having been condoned for the sake of utilizing his technical knowledge, the Government had then gone further and given him the right to participate in the profits from a Government contract, it would invoke a great deal of criticism.

He added that it was not up to him to decide.

Bielaski couldn't take it up with Levering immediately, as the oilman was busy with aerial bombing tests in Montauk, Long Island. His country house was there, part of the Devon Colony that he had helped to finance and construct. Since the previous year, the U.S. Navy had maintained an air station there, where seaplanes and airships patrolled the coast all the way up to Nantucket Shoal. On Saturday, June 1, Levering accompanied the commanding officer at the Montauk station up in one of the station planes to test Mark IV aerial bombs loaded with helline. As the plane roared over Long Island Sound, there were some tense moments. One of the released bombs got jammed in the chute, and the pilot had to let go of the controls and shove the bombs out of the plane by hand. The bomb exploded prematurely about two or three hundred feet under the plane, "giving him a good kick," Levering wrote in his report to Wilkinson.

In the report, Levering discussed the mechanisms for detonating the bombs and the possibility of constructing depth charges with liquid oxygen as the explosive. He also proposed that the incendiary darts—the lightweight bombs filled with helline—could be tested on his property at Montauk, with Wilkinson's assistance. "There are about 15 miles of wasteland, some of the property belongs to me and the rest to owners whose permission I can always secure," he wrote.

The following day, Bielaski wrote to Levering to inquire about the rumored profit-sharing plan. In the earlier investigations into his background and integrity, Levering remained measured when he answered questions. But the insinuation of war profiteering was different. Levering erupted in furious indignation, writing on Department of Justice letterhead that he was "disgusted" with the accusation and insisting that there was no contract with Scheele. The accusation, he wrote, "is a very bitter pill which I deeply resent." Colonel Ragsdale, the chief of the Trench Warfare Section of the Army Ordnance Department, who was constantly kept up to date about progress at Jones Point, defended Levering, writing that his attitude "has always been most splendid and he and his staff have been placing valuable data in the hands of this Department."

Levering demanded to know who had raised the accusation of war profiteering. DeWoody doubled down, further interrogating Agent O'Donnell, who had passed on the tidbit of intelligence. The agent reiterated what he knew to Bielaski but conceded that perhaps it was just idle talk and not a fully fledged plan. Bielaski apologized to Levering, saying that he was obligated to ask about the allegation but that he couldn't reveal who had made the report.

Amid all the squabbling and snooping, helline had a setback. When scientists at American University attempted to replicate one of the Jones Point experiments, the helline exploded, an accident that almost certainly injured the men carrying out the test. Edison's chemist Bruce Silver described the incident as "discouraging" and a result that "seems to cast some doubt upon the mixture as being safe for ordinary handling and transportation."

When Colonel Ragsdale of the Ordnance Department wrote to Levering of the incident, the oilman expressed regret for the accident but placed the blame on the chemists at American University. "The first essential in handling this incendiary material is to keep organic matter away from it," he wrote. "This essential was reported when Doctor Scheele first described the formula." Hundreds of experiments had been carried out at Jones Point without any such accidents, and Levering suggested that perhaps the scientists at American University were not familiar with the work already done. It was hardly surprising that Levering would want to wave away concerns, as a thousand of the incendiary darts packed with helline were almost ready for testing on his land, and another four thousand would soon be coming.

Levering's relations with the Bureau of Investigation had resumed a more polite tenor, but in the aftermath of the caustic accusations, he began to look for some other role in the war effort. Levering didn't specify why he began to back away from the work at Jones Point; perhaps it was to disengage from the Bureau of Investigation and its probe of his business interests or to put himself at arm's length from the potential business prospects around helline. Perhaps he wanted a commission in the army and the prestige that military rank bestowed.

Whatever the reason, Levering approached the U.S. Navy seeking a commission in the American Patrol Detachment, the squadron assigned to police the Caribbean and the Gulf of Mexico against marauding German U-boats. The commander of the detachment gently rejected Levering's request, saying that his current role was of "inestimable value" and it was his patriotic duty to continue his existing work.

Undeterred, Levering turned next to the Chemical Warfare Service. He had gotten to know many military higher-ups during his involvement with Scheele, and now, as of July 1, Jones Point was part of the wide, all-encompassing umbrella of the service. Perhaps this new agency would have a place for him.

The war turned Independence Day of 1918 into an eruption of patriotic fervor. Secretary of State Lansing pronounced July 4 "an international holy day," and called the war a global campaign to destroy Prussian militarism. Washington had banned fireworks on the wartime Independence Day, allowing only sparklers, but the festivities didn't lack for enthusiasm. A ceremony raised the Stars and Stripes outside Union Station, children paraded in Petworth, and President Wilson delivered a stirring speech at George Washington's tomb at Mount Vernon, railing that "the blinded rulers of Prussia have roused forces they know little of — forces which, once roused, can never be crushed to earth again." Thousands of spectators cheered Wilson as he declared that there could be no compromise in the war, "no half-way decisions."

Afterward, he boarded a boat named the *Mayflower* to sail back to Washington for a parade down Pennsylvania Avenue. Tens of thousands of people lined the street to watch the procession of delegations from the Allies around the world. Led by the Serbians, they paraded in order of joining the war. Maria Leontievna Bochkareva, the fierce Russian warrior who organized the all-female Battalion of Death, marched with a huge sword. A woman in the blue-and-silver armor of Joan of Arc sat astride a white stallion at the head of the French contingent. A kilted Scottish Highland unit stepped to the drone of bagpipes. The procession ended at the Capitol, where spotlights bathed the dome and an elaborate, nighttime costume pageant unfolded on the steps. Children whirled in colorful robes, resembling enormous moths under the searchlights, and gowned figures representing Humanity, Justice, and finally the United States floated up and down the steps in a melodramatic allegory for the war. Several hundred volunteers ended the spectacle with the "Hallelujah Chorus" before the crowds headed home.

Sibert's office at Seventh and B Streets NW was just a block from the Pennsylvania Avenue parade route. One side of his building overlooked the National Mall, where revelers had milled on the grassy expanse all day.

When Goliath took the job in May, he had been in charge of a handful of officers whose duties constituted little more than shuttling messages between different bureaus and agencies. Now he commanded a constellation of science, engineering, and war concerns that demanded ingenuity as well as improvisation to respond to emergencies. He marshaled thousands of men — not just the seventeen

hundred chemists at American University and on campuses across
the country, but also the soldiers of the gas regiment, engineers, and
doctors. He was in charge of factories, gas masks, shell-filling plants,
experimental laboratories, and proving grounds.

In the days after the consolidation of the Chemical Warfare Service, Goliath had moved swiftly to take charge of his new organization. One of his first tasks was to smooth over the conflicts on
Mustard Hill between the chemists and the engineers at Camp
American University, which was renamed Camp Leach at the end
of May. On July 2, he had asked George Burrell, the head of the
Research Division and newly commissioned as a colonel, for a
report on all construction at the American University Experiment
Station. He wanted to know whether new buildings were permanent or temporary and what they would be used for. He also asked
for an accounting of costs for the new laboratory that was under
construction on the American University quad. That same day,
Sibert strolled the American University grounds with Brigadier
General Frederic Abbot of the Corps of Engineers, discussing the
construction debris around the new chemistry building, the chemists' car park on the parade ground, a fence line, the layout of
roads, and other sources of friction. One by one, they worked out
solutions.

Within days, Burrell had furnished a report on construction
and sent Sibert his own plan for sharing the campus in a way that
put to rest the festering antagonisms between the experiment station and the Corps of Engineers. The one unresolved issue—a coal
pile that Abbot felt was encroaching on the engineers' turf—
turned out to have nothing to do with the Research Division, and
Abbot withdrew his complaint. "I wish that all controversies could
be settled as satisfactorily and as quickly as this one," Abbot wrote.

Sibert took over the chemical warfare work right at the moment
when work on the gas-manufacturing infrastructure had begun to
bear fruit. Edgewood Arsenal had started production of chloropicrin in June. Ten days later, Edgewood's mustard plant went into

operation as well, as did the phosgene plant. By the end of June, the first shipments of American gas had gone over to Europe: 15 tons of mustard gas, 705 tons of chloropicrin, and 48 tons of phosgene loaded onto ships and sent to France. The Ordnance Department was not yet producing gas shells, so the American gas that had begun going overseas would fill French shells after it reached European shores.

Not long after Sibert took over, the AEF cabled to temporarily halt chemical shipments. The French had run out of shells, and gas sent to Europe would be useless until more could be manufactured. It was a major hiccup that increased pressure on the service to quickly make it possible for American shells to be filled and shipped.

After the initial publicity about the Chemical Warfare Service's creation died down, the press still continued to push information about gas warfare into the public domain. On July 7, the *New York Times Magazine* cover story was "Mustard Gas Warfare." The article gave Sibert almost exclusive credit for the manufacture of mustard, despite the fact that many months of research and development had preceded his rise to the top of the service. But the article also sketched out little-known aspects of gas warfare, such as the merits of persistent gases like mustard over more toxic but quickly dispersing gases such as phosgene. It carried photographs of Fritz Haber and Walther Hermann Nernst, and it predicted that the American gas program would soon eclipse the Germans'. "Those who are in a position to know what they are doing are confident that, when the full story is told, the myth that the Germans are supermen in this realm of science will be exploded," the article read.

The article reported nothing of lewisite, which was still a closely guarded secret of the Research Division. One of Van Manning's last tasks connected to the war work was to send out the monthly research summary to government agencies and officers connected to the gas investigations. As always, the July 1 report had gone out stamped CONFIDENTIAL with dozens of research reports in it, including experiments on neutralization of mustard gas, effects of mask filters against sneeze gas, and "Experiments with Tiger Slugs as Detectors of Toxic Gases."

Deep in the report, the section on pharmacological research referred to tests of lewisite's toxicity relative to other compounds. The toxic concentration of chloromethyl ethyl sulfide for mice was 20 milligrams per liter and 6.5 milligrams per liter for thionyl fluoride. Lewisite was clearly more toxic, killing mice at a concentration of just 0.6 milligram per liter. Other experiments found that lewisite had surprising qualities. One test found that lewisite passed through most rubber or rubberized protective material, which meant that rubber boots and suits didn't provide an adequate defense. Another test reached the startling conclusion that when lewisite came in contact with German gas masks, it degraded the eyepieces, making them opaque and impossible to see through, which would be a powerful strategic advantage.

For the first time, the Allies would have a lethal chemical weapon that the Germans did not have. There was a difference with lewisite, however. Every war gas, whether defensive or offensive, had been put through exhaustive testing over many months, in every conceivable fashion. But although lewisite had shown promising qualities, it had gone through testing far less rigorous than mustard, phosgene, and other chemical weapons agents had. The Research Division appears to have generated only about a half-dozen reports about lewisite by mid-July. Crucially, the technical men also appear to have done little investigation into one of the most important characteristics of a war gas—its persistence. A defining feature of mustard was its stability: the so-called king of the war gases lingered on the battlefield for days, even in rain and damp conditions, remaining dangerous long after the shells had burst. When the chemists finally got around to studying the persistence of lewisite, they found it hydrolyzed easily. In other words, water caused it to break down—hardly a desirable attribute of a war gas.

Nonetheless, Sibert decided in early July to rush lewisite into mass production along with mustard, phosgene, chloropicrin, and the other war gases. The work at Catholic and American Universities showed that lewisite could be produced at least in small quantities, but the improvised apparatus on the roof of Maloney Laboratory at Catholic University was a far cry from the industrial-sized factory needed to manufacture it by the ton. The chemists needed to design and engineer full-scale equipment, which demanded more laboratory work. Speed was crucial, and building a new factory would be time-consuming, so it would be better to find an existing building somewhere and modify it for lewisite production. There was the additional logistical problem that the precursor chemicals for lewisite, arsenic trichloride and acetylene, were not readily available commercially, and so the government would have to build plants to produce those as well.

Though lewisite was still top secret, some researchers carelessly used the name in meetings and reports, such as in a report on lewisite that had been discussed during a June meeting of the bureau's Medical Advisory Board. After Sibert took over, he ordered the chemists to stop using the name immediately. "It is directed that the word Lewisite shall not be written on paper again, neither shall it be printed. This should be communicated to the various department Chiefs, and by them to others who are familiar with the term," an aide to Sibert wrote to Burrell. From that point forward, it would only be referred to using code.

On July 12, Sibert sent new orders for Frank Dorsey—now a colonel—at Nela Park in Cleveland. His Development Division would be in charge of manufacturing lewisite. The division in Cleveland was the logical section to undertake this problem because Dorsey had already played crucial roles in production of gas mask charcoal and mustard gas. But because his existing staff was already deeply consumed in those tasks, lewisite would require an entirely new organization with its own staff. Dorsey wouldn't be alone in setting up the lewisite production: James Bryant Conant was sent to Ohio to assist. Conant received a commission as major in the new Chemical Warfare Service, and within a few days, he had his own orders to report to a town about twenty miles northeast of Cleveland called Willoughby, where he would be working for the rest of the war.

Willoughby was a small town of about twenty-six hundred people a half mile from the shore of Lake Erie, bisected by the winding Chagrin River. On July 12, Colonel Dorsey stepped from his car and surveyed a vacant building on the outskirts of the town. Dorsey was under pressure to find a factory as soon as possible to manufacture lewisite, but it needed to be secure from prying eyes. He had considered looking for properties in Cleveland or even adjacent to Nela Park but decided it was too risky. Word had leaked out about the mustard plant in Cleveland, and spies for the Germans surely knew about the building. He needed to make sure that the lewisite factory would be safe from spies, as well as Cleveland's snooping newspaper reporters.

Willoughby was far enough from Cleveland that activities there could carry on without attracting attention, but it was still convenient to Nela Park. He had asked a former tax commissioner, John D. Fackler, to find potential manufacturing sites. The attorney brought Dorsey to a rambling factory where the Ben-Hur Motor Company had made a sporty touring car with leather seats and a sixty-horsepower engine. The car made a splash when it debuted in early 1917, but only about one hundred cars rolled off the assembly line before the company went bankrupt and the factory had been abandoned ever since. The building was sixty-six thousand square feet in all, two stories high, a block and a half long by a block wide. High windows let in plenty of light. A separate office building seemed to be in decent condition as well, and the property wasn't far from train tracks where supplies could be shipped by rail. Though the factory was only a short distance from the town center, it was set off from downtown. With a fence and sentries, it would be easy to keep out trespassers and snoops. Dorsey didn't spend much time at the Ben-Hur plant. He had found what he was looking for.

PART III

RETORT

Chapter Twelve

First Gas and Flame

Three cheers for the old "Gas and Flame"
Rip 'er up for the old "Gas and Flame"
We'll smell phosgene and mustard forever
We are Vets of the old "Gas and Flame."
— *Robert B. MacMullin*
Company E, First Gas Regiment
November 11, 1924

July was the slow month for the boys of Company B. Endless drilling filled hot, dull days and somnolent afternoons. Higgie's farmhouse billet was a comfortable roost, the best in the village, and the company had the abandoned town to themselves. Nine miles from the fighting at Château-Thierry, they could hear the guns booming at the lines. Instead of setting projectors, they went for swims in the Marne. The men were bored and restless, but headquarters had ordered them to stay put. During the pause in the regiment's action, headquarters reorganized, moving Companies A and C to First Battalion, while shifting Companies B and D to Second Battalion and billeting them next to each other in Mont-Ménard and Rougeville. The battalion headquarters claimed spacious buildings nearby in Saâcy for its offices. When shells fell too close for comfort, the headquarters moved to nearby Le Ferté.

Tom Jabine led Higgie's platoon in drills, repeating the same tasks that the regiment had performed so many times. The two had become fast friends. The night after Jabine got his commission, the two men talked late into the night. "He is a swell fellow," Higgie wrote in his diary.

Company B had become a tight-knit band after many months together on the line. Jabine was well liked among the men: at an evening retreat, Higgie and the other Company B boys had given him three cheers for his promotion to second lieutenant. Jabine worried that he would miss the camaraderie of the sergeant's mess hall; fraternization between ranks was frowned on, and he worried that his friendships would fray.

Jabine also became friends with another officer, Lieutenant Joseph Hanlon, who had transferred from Company A. A chemist who had also attended Columbia University, Hanlon had introduced himself to Jabine in June. "He is one of our best—a hell of a nice fellow," Jabine wrote to his brother. Back in June, Hanlon had bunked with the chaplain Addison; they, too, had become friends.

When Jabine went to Paris on leave, he felt lonely even though the streets teemed with soldiers and sailors; he wished he had someone to see the sights with. "I never knew what it meant to be lonesome since I joined the army till I had this job wished on me!" he wrote home. After he returned to camp, Jabine drilled his men hard. He knew they hated it—it was stale and repetitive and they wanted to be at the front. But he needed to learn to lead, while the men needed something to occupy themselves. Higgie never complained. In one week, he got three letters from Irene, his sweetheart back in the States. He wrote letters, played catch, took expeditions into Le Ferté, and swam almost every day. One poker game in the billet lasted all day.

Then the shells began to fall again. On July 15, the German army crossed the Marne. A bombardment hit the next town over, and Higgie's half-empty village suddenly filled with refugees. Drilling stopped, and the men were told not to congregate outside. A shell hit the train station in Le Ferté, and some of the men went over to help dig it out. Hopes began to rise that the regiment would be pressed into action. Plans were drawn up for a projector attack at Belleau Wood, the site of a bloody battle the previous month between the Germans and U.S. Marines. But then headquarters scuttled the plan, deeming the front too fluid and the German lines too unpredictable to justify an attack.

On July 18, marching orders finally arrived. A French counter-attack had begun. Though there were no plans for gas shows, the regiment would move up to follow the retreating Germans. Higgie and his company rolled their packs to leave in the middle of the night. For several days, they marched, stopping in filthy billets that had just been abandoned. Even in retreat, the German artillery was active. Shells fell around them and lit the sky, and planes buzzed in the dark overhead.

On Sunday, July 21, Higgie gathered his platoon and marched into Château-Thierry. They were right behind the American infantry; the Germans had been driven out that same morning. Corpses sprawled everywhere. The rank stench of rotting flesh hung over the city, so putrid that men had to put on their gas masks. The air swarmed with flies, thriving in the carrion left in the battle's aftermath. Germans' helmets, bayonets, and guns lay everywhere. When Higgie had a spare moment, he ducked into a German dugout. It was an officers' bunker, with plush chairs and an open bottle of wine on the table with half-full glasses beside it. The Germans had left in a hurry.

Addison moved forward, too. As he marched through the countryside, he gaped at splintered tree trunks and towns smashed to rubble. The rank stench of rotting corpses filled his nostrils. Trekking through a forest, the men came across the curled-up corpse of an American soldier, body shrunken and charred, blackened flesh shrunk tight over the skull. Abandoned American equipment filled the woods. They came upon a half-destroyed village, the body of a long-dead German soldier splayed on the ground. Addison stared at the exposed organs, half-eaten by worms, and the back of the man's skull gnawed away. They continued through the town, past a gully filled with abandoned German gas masks and overcoats, and—unpredictably—a copy of the novel *David Copperfield*. He said a silent prayer over the grave of another American he helped bury; the soldier had been dead only about a day, shot in the mouth and chest, his skin yellowish gray. They pressed on. Outside the town of Belleau, a half-dozen decaying bodies were along the road, tattered clothes hanging from shriveled, blackened skeletons. At the edge of the village, German prisoners were digging graves for at least twenty American dead covered with a canvas tarp. Outside the canvas, the body of a young lieutenant lay exposed, his blown-off leg laid atop his lifeless body. It was the gruesome side of war that Addison hadn't yet seen, and he would never forget what it looked like.

In Tours, a hard wind battered against the windows and sent curtains of dust whirling over the rooftops. The gusts lasted all through the day on July 20, a fervent, unsettled turn to the weather, as if the sky had torn open and released a storm front galloping across the city. As the wind howled, Amos Fries spent the evening gabbing with another officer. The colonel felt cheerful. A cablegram had arrived from Washington authorizing 2,363 officers and more than 20,000 men for the gas service. "I feel I have done something that is going to contribute a great deal toward winning the war," he wrote home.

The cablegram from Washington wasn't the only reason for his high spirits. Every day, good news arrived in dispatches from the front. When he spent a night at First Corps headquarters, he heard the boom of the guns for himself, the barrage before the Americans and the French attacked along a thirty-mile front. For months, Fries had harbored a quiet pessimism about the war. When thousands of mustard shells had rained down on the Allied troops in the spring, causing huge numbers of casualties, he worried that the war would grind on in an endless collision of armies, sowing another season of death across the western front. But over the summer his outlook had been brightened by the more than eight hundred thousand Sammies that marched off transports in Brest and Boulogne to bolster the Allied armies. Many more would follow. The Americans had proved that they could fight with the best. And now a third battalion of gas troops, Companies E and F, had reached French shores as well, bringing the regiment to six companies. A seventh, Company Q, would soon join them to provide replacement soldiers when casualties thinned the ranks of the other six.

The counteroffensive had forced the Germans to retreat, but Fries knew that gains could be quickly reversed. How long the retreat would last was anyone's guess, and Fries judged that at some point—perhaps at the Aisne River—the Germans might stop, regroup, and counterattack. Many more victories would be needed to bring peace. "Confidence is increasing all the time and the people are talking everywhere of the American troops. It is fine but one hates to think of the thousands of fine fellows that will find their last resting place in sunny France before the war ends," he wrote home.

Fries would soon get new service stripes to sew onto his sleeve to mark his year of overseas duty. The gas service had been performing splendidly—twenty-five officers and men from the regiment received the French Croix de Guerre in mid-July. Positive reports arrived regularly about the gas regiment after the regiment had launched attacks on June 18 and 19 and the next month when the regiment carried out shows on the stabilized front in the Vosges region on July 8, then again between July 19 through 21.

Despite his growing optimism, Fries was troubled. Even though he was almost single-handedly responsible for the overseas work of the gas service, he had heard little from Washington hinting at a promotion. Brigadier generals commanded every service in France but his. Without a general at the helm of the Chemical Warfare

Service in France, he worried that the service would be seen as inferior, as lesser than other army departments. "Don't know what that means unless they think Gas isn't worthy of having a B.G. at the head. Maybe they are looking for a better man," he wrote home to Bessie. Still, he pretended not to care, writing breezily that if he didn't get a promotion, so be it: "c'est la guerre" — that's war.

Finally, on July 20, the War Department ordered General Pershing to name a brigadier general to serve as chief of the service, which didn't necessarily mean Fries. "They have a chance to promote me if they want to. Whether they will or not remains to be seen," he wrote home to Bessie.

While Fries fretted about his status, he didn't shirk his responsibilities. There was no end to his work, and he couldn't get new men fast enough. After his bout with grippe, Fries had tried to slow the pace of his schedule. Practically a teetotaler already, he stopped drinking completely and began resting and exercising more. He tried to stay relaxed and shorten his workdays. Sometimes he opened his collar and loosened his Sam Browne belt. Unable to sleep at night, he took afternoon catnaps and cooled down in an armchair shaded by a magnolia tree in the courtyard of his quarters.

The gas headquarters' relocation in the spring forced Fries to shuttle back and forth between Tours, Paris, and Chaumont, sometimes for meetings where he had nothing to contribute. When he wasn't in his limousine, the train rides turned into a tedious commute, the crowded cars uncomfortable in the sticky summer weather.

The tiresome 250-mile trip between Chaumont and Tours was becoming more and more frequent, as the gas experimental field had in many ways become the epicenter of Fries's work. Construction had been mostly completed by May. Though still smaller than the American University Experiment Station in Washington, it had expanded into a village of sixty-four buildings, including barracks for hundreds of enlisted men, a laboratory, and a man-test chamber, along with a mortuary, administrative offices, a warehouse, a meteorological bureau, classroom buildings, a YMCA, an infirmary, stables, and pens for goats, dogs, cats, and rats. There were three firing ranges for Livens projectors and Stokes mortars, two artillery ranges, and a cloud gas emplacement. Three areas were fenced off for persistence tests with mustard gas. Captured German machine guns, projectors, and short-range artillery called *Minenwerfer* were brought to the field for testing. Chemists cracked open and tested dud shells rushed from the front for analysis, and there were buildings for filling the Allies' own shells. With so much activity at the experimental field, Fries was there often. When the Gas Defense School opened, he spent almost a week there, hovering like a mother hen and delivering two lectures.

The experimental field resembled Mustard Hill in that it was a proving ground and a parade ground, a training campus and a school, a place to teach and to exhibit the use of chemical weapons. There was a crucial difference, though: its proximity to the front. The soldiers who made up its training corps and taught classes had hard-earned battlefield experience.

Fries was adamant that better training would reduce gas casualties substantially. Many casualties on the front resulted from poor training and inexperience; in a May 10 attack that lasted for seven hours and killed nineteen men, some of the men became hysterical with fear and knocked their comrades' masks off. Others didn't get their masks on quickly enough or removed them prematurely. In a different episode, an officer was disciplined for switching from one mask to another in the middle of an attack. "Americans yet have no real idea what gas means. Neither unfortunately, have many officers over here, but they are learning fast," Fries wrote home to Bessie.

Officers at the experimental field also solved technical problems that arose on the battlefield. When men at the front found a problem with mortar shells loaded with thermite, five hundred shells were sent to the gas field to be fixed. Equipment sent from the States could also be tested and tweaked at the field under an approximation of battlefield conditions.

In addition to training, the experimental field's staff of scientists also turned out reams of research reports. Every few days, Fries sent a passel of reports back to the States, handing them to couriers who boarded transports, carried the documents to Washington, and turned them over to Sibert in person. Some were translations of captured documents and prisoner interrogations. Many were technical reports with titles like *Cleaning of Clothes and Underwear Contaminated with Yperite*. In the July 23 packet, report number 25 from the British would be familiar to any of the scientists at Jones Point: *Hexamethylenetetramine and Sodium Peroxide Incendiary Mixture*. The British were also experimenting with Walter Scheele's ship-bomb recipe.

The experiment field was also headquarters for the Medical Division of the service. Though the physiological and pathological divisions in the United States had been studying effects of chemicals on the human body—as well as goats, dogs, mice, and other animals—they rarely got the opportunity to study and treat battlefield casualties. The number of gas cases had shot up since the Germans had begun soaking the front with mustard in the spring. Hundreds of casualties in March and April rose to almost 1,500 in May and 1,700 in the first two weeks of June. And then the numbers skyrocketed. In the second half of June, gas caused more than 6,200 casualties, and almost 6,000 more between July 1 and July 24.

With the Americans suffering so many gas casualties, the Medical Division built a mobile decontamination unit to wash mustard and other chemicals off exposed soldiers. Unveiled on July 23, the unit was designed for quick assembly near troops gassed en masse. Showers rinsed off twenty-four men every ninety seconds, and up to seven hundred men without refilling the truck. Afterward, the men received clean clothes and soldiers showing symptoms of gas poisoning were hustled off for medical treatment.

After the spring's first incidents of mass casualties, a medical gas officer was assigned to every army division. The gas officer's job was to train other officers and enlisted men in treating gas cases and supervising hospitals and dressing stations. It was also his job to sort out which exposure cases were real. Soldiers in gassed areas often claimed to be suffering from exposure when in fact they were not. In one instance, 281 men were admitted to a field hospital for treatment after a gas attack. The hospital's commanding officer, puzzled by how few men exhibited physical symptoms, asked a medical board to review the cases. The board found that fewer than a third of the men were actually exposed; the rest returned to duty. The review concluded that some men were malingerers, claiming to be gassed to escape the trenches. A greater number probably believed they had been gassed and lapsed into what the doctors called "gas mania."

Between trips to Chaumont, Fries was in the midst of an ambitious project: forming the American strategy for chemical warfare for the rest of 1918 and into 1919. With the war entering a crucial stage, Fries believed that gas ought to play a major role in the offensives to come. That meant deciding what types, sizes, and quantities of chemical weapons the American forces would need, then determining the production necessary to meet that demand and the number of men required to carry it out.

Fries envisioned gas troops that would operate very differently than the Hellfire Boys had up to that point. Rather than gas companies roving across France like a "moving circus," he believed that every American division on the front should have its own regiment, able to launch attacks anywhere, anytime. With a million Americans flooding into France, that would require a vast expansion of the gas regiment. He had received everything that he had sought from Pershing—an independent service, a laboratory and a testing ground, and latitude to make demands of the domestic service—but he would need more. And to get it, he would need evidence that the expansion of the gas troops was justified.

The problem was that the gas regiment wasn't in action as frequently as Fries believed it should be. While the Château-Thierry offensive had been a success, the Hellfire Boys had played a minimal role in the victory. Despite "splendid targets" for gas attacks, the generals felt that the fluid nature of the front and the likelihood of a German retreat would prevent gas units from being effective—in essence, the line would move more quickly than the regiment would be able to prepare for and carry out an attack. Some of the commanders on the ground reported that more gas would have yielded more German casualties and a faster advance for the infantry; their statements provided grist for Fries's schemes for an expansion of the service.

Logistical problems also complicated Fries's plans. In July, the French ran out of gas shells to supply the Americans, and the AEF ordered the domestic service to halt gas shipments to France—there was simply nowhere to put it until the problem of the shell shortage could be solved. It was only a temporary setback, however—the plants in the United States were on the brink of full production, and once the Ordnance Department could meet the demand, American gas would fill American shells, ready for shipment across the Atlantic.

During the hot days of late July, Fries went to Paris for a conference and then returned to Tours for the weekend. He had just enough time for a good night's sleep and a quiet Sunday morning before an afternoon call came ordering him to report back to the experimental field again. Fries left Tours midafternoon and drove most of the night. It wasn't until the following morning of July 29 that Fries's car turned off the Chaumont-to-Biesles road into the gas experimental field.

Fries was at the experimental field for three days. In all likelihood, the emergency summons was to meet with an assistant secretary of war named Edward R. Stettinius, who traveled to France with an entire staff of accountants to survey the army supply-and-requisition system and represent the War Department on the War

Industries Board. Fries had a vision for what his chemical corps would look like in the future. It was a vision of soldiers up and down the front with mobile gas tanks strapped to their backs. It was a vision of thermite showering down on the Germans like a molten summer rain, and fresh blankets of mustard lying like dew upon the battlefield. It was a vision of gas everywhere, omnipresent as air and earth—underfoot, overhead, and everywhere in between. For his vision to become a reality, it would have to go through Stettinius.

After he left the experiment field, he met again with Stettinius at general headquarters about a week later about the gas program. "Evidently, he was satisfied," Fries wrote.

While Fries's plans for the service gained momentum, the men of the gas and flame regiment were growing frustrated and restive over how rarely they were in action. Near the ruins of Château-Thierry, Company B was put to work with picks and shovels, not projectors and Stokes mortars. As the Americans continued to push the Germans back toward Reims, the gas regiment had been ordered to help repair the roads for the advancing American army. For a week, Company B dragged downed trees, filled shell craters, and buried the dead. Rain turned the roads into a slippery morass by day and seeped into men's tents at night. The men grumbled that their skills weren't being used and that German prisoners ought to be doing such work. Higgie carried out his duties stoically, although he got a break from the work because of a huge blister on his foot. One day, Jabine worked for twenty-four hours straight with no food and no sleep, helping to move sixteen thousand rounds of artillery ammunition up to the front.

On July 27, it was time to move again. After breakfast, Higgie set out on roads that were rivers of mud. Drenched to the bone, the men reached Épaux-Bézu about noon. Higgie and Jabine were back at work on the roads the next day and then ordered to clean up a farm for an ammunition dump. When they entered the farmhouse, something was scrawled on the wall. They deciphered the marks.

The farmhouse was a crypt—twelve Germans were buried under the floor.

Word arrived from headquarters to prepare for a Stokes mortar show with smoke and thermite. But the orders only included the First Platoon, led by Lieutenant Hanlon and another officer, Lieutenant Harry Favre. Higgie and Jabine's Second Platoon would sit out the show. Higgie had an easy day working at the ammunition depot and playing poker in the afternoon. They worked on the road for a bit and unloaded shells for that night's attack, then had a hearty supper.

Though his men were eager to get back in action, Hanlon had a bad feeling. First Platoon had had its share of casualties, and the deaths among them had turned into an eerie pattern. The first private killed in the regiment had come from the platoon, as had the first noncommissioned officer. Hanlon confessed to the chaplain, Addison, that he had a premonition that the trend would continue and that the first commissioned officer to die would come from his platoon, too.

The carrying party to lug the projectors up to the front left Épaux-Bézu at dusk, eighty men in all—twenty from Company B and sixty from Company D. They arrived at the forward ammunition depot at Villers-sur-Fère at 10:00 p.m. Division headquarters dithered for hours over whether to go ahead with the show; around midnight, they finally decided to attack in the early morning. Between the ammunition depot and the mortar position lay two miles of unfamiliar terrain infested with pockets of mustard gas, with shells falling all around. In the thick of a firefight, the carry began. With Hanlon at the rear, the long line of men stumbled through the dark, each hoisting as much as one hundred pounds of mortars and shells. Machine-gun bullets snapped over their heads, and shells whined in the distance. They crossed through marshy woods. An earsplitting crash, and clods of clay, rocks, and shell fragments rang against their steel helmets. In the darkness, a laugh, a curse, and a hoarse order to continue. The men crossed a bridge.

The path grew muddier and more slippery. Men slid and fell under the weight of their portage. They finally reached an embankment and their own infantry in dugouts.

"Are you going to relieve us?" one of the infantrymen hissed. They were not. The line crept on. More shells fell; one shell-shocked man began to crawl away into the darkness in terror. They rested in a marshy meadow. A medic ran up to the front of the line—a man was hurt, his head split open by shrapnel. He was loaded onto a stretcher and carried back toward the rear. More shells fell. Some were close, exploding toward the rear of the carrying line. The men at the front followed a line of willow trees and entered a patch of woods. Machine-gun bullets thunked into tree trunks around them. They pressed onward into the woods, where they found their hidden mortar position. Then they stopped to count their men.

There were four casualties, all from Company B. A shell had landed almost on top of the rearmost men, killing two privates and badly wounding Hanlon and a third private. Hanlon died on his way back to the dressing station. His premonition had proved true. Later that day, the smoke and thermite show went off, followed by a second several hours later led by Favre alone.

Shaken and grieving, the platoon arrived back at the billets at dawn and passed the news on to the rest of the company. Higgin-bottom noted Hanlon's death in his diary the following day in his laconic shorthand. For Jabine, who had craved the company of his new friend, the shock was deep. "He and I were becoming good friends and it was a sad blow when he was lost," Jabine wrote in a letter home.

Hanlon's funeral was at Chaumont on August 2, with members of his platoon as his pallbearers. Addison didn't know about his former roommate's death until the morning mail arrived the day after he was buried. The chaplain was still in bed in the officers' quarters when a captain stunned the other officers with the news. One officer burst into tears. They spent the rest of the day in mournful silence. "It was a painful shock to all of us," Addison recalled. By the end of August, the gas experimental field had a new name: Hanlon Field.

Each morning, streetcars trundled up Massachusetts Avenue toward American University, packed with young soldiers headed to the experiment station from their rented rooms and boardinghouses. The notoriously unreliable trolleys made for an anxious journey; if the soldiers arrived even a few minutes late, they were docked a half day's leave. In the predawn darkness, Charles William Maurer was one of the soldiers making the daily commute up to the hill and through the gates of the experiment station. Gazing out at the world through wire-rimmed glasses, Will yearned for distant places. He had wanted to go to France but ended up instead at American University.

He was twenty-three, a preacher's boy from West Texas. Short and compact, Maurer had a thatch of black hair that he combed to the side in a rakish wave. Even when he wore his uniform, his outsize ears and lopsided grin gave him a boyish look. His father was a hard-shell Baptist who had brought his wife and three boys to West Texas to preach. They settled in Marfa, a crossroads pinched between infinite sky and endless plains, where he built another Baptist church. Will and his two brothers grew up in the parsonage with a porch looking out across the rolling desert.

Like his father, Will was restless. Even before he finished his studies at Baylor University, he applied to become a medical missionary in 1915 and was rejected. He was turned down again the following year—a physical exam revealed an irregular heartbeat and a hearing problem. He tried to enlist in the army and failed the army physical, too. By 1918, he still had not graduated. Desperate to get overseas, Will saw advertisements in scientific journals seeking volunteers for the gas and flame regiment. Even though he hadn't taken many chemistry courses, he decided to take a gamble. He would go to Washington, present himself to the scientists, and try to enlist there, in the hope that the gas service might eventually land him in France. "I liked the idea of feeding the Huns their own medicine," he wrote in a letter to Baylor after the war.

After he decided on the plan, he returned to Marfa to say goodbye to his parents before leaving for Washington. He was at home when a letter from the army arrived at the parsonage. The letter ordered him to report to duty at an induction board in San Antonio at 8:30 a.m. on April 26, 1918. "From and after the day and hour just named you will be a soldier in the military service of the United States." Though the army had already rejected him once, the army physicians deemed him fit to serve. From there, he went on for training at Fort Travis in Galveston.

Many of his Baylor classmates were in his company; his former dorm roommate was in the next barracks over from his. As the unit trained for its June departure, Will imagined mighty exploits in France with his friends. Then a telegram arrived dashing Will's hopes again. Instead of sending him on to France, the telegram ordered him to report to Washington, almost exactly as he had originally planned. His chemistry classes at Baylor made him a candidate for the Research Division at American University after all, as Manning's census of scientists had intended. Will would never see the trenches of Europe. Though he was only going as far as Washington, he still boarded the train with the army unit from Fort Travis and headed east. When the train arrived at Union Station, he waved goodbye to his classmates and disembarked onto the platform by himself.

Will arrived in a city transformed. The war had turned the nation's sleepy and provincial capital into a metropolitan boomtown. Patriotic bunting hung from storefronts and window ledges, alongside HELP WANTED signs from business owners desperate for employees. Theaters filled to capacity at night, packed hotels put up guests on cots in overflowing parlors, and chefs had trouble finding enough food to serve their patrons. Every patch of dirt, including parks in sight of the Capitol, had been turned over and the soil hoed into war gardens.

Mustard Hill was going through a boom as well. New wooden buildings peppered the hill, and dozens of construction projects were under way. Construction of an explosives laboratory was finished in May, a bacteriological lab in early June, and a pyrotechnics lab a week later. A new dog kennel was built for canine test subjects and a stable for horses. Plumbers laid new water lines and hauled stone benches into the labs. On the Chemical Warfare Service's side of the campus, the buildings haphazardly dotted the hillsides all around McKinley Hall, wherever the scientists deemed it most convenient and without any clearance from their landlords at the university. Foreboding symbols and phrases decorated the shacks that cropped up all over the hill. On shack number 5, the chemists wrote LOOK AND RUN, along with a crude skull and crossbones. There were new fences, new gas lines, new electrical lines. Plans for rail lines were drawn up, so that train cars could supply the station and connect to trunk lines to Baltimore and beyond. Engineers drew up blueprints for two new explosives pits. On the back side of the campus, down the hillside from the fenced perimeter of the station, was the area that the soldiers called Death Valley and Arsenic Valley, along with a disposal pit they called Hades.

George Burrell had plans for many more projects as well. He wanted a central heating plant, a steel tower for experimental work. He wanted to expand the infirmary, the man-test laboratory, and the physiological laboratory. Work was also still under way on the huge new chemical laboratory that Manning had demanded be built across the quad from the College of History. It was, by far, the most expensive construction project on the hill, with a price tag of $250,000—an amount that would soon prove to be woefully underestimated. He also planned a new ventilation system for Catholic University's lab across town, so that work could resume there.

There was still no room on the hill for barracks, so like all the other young men, Maurer found a room to rent in a nearby neighborhood. Washington wasn't France, but it was a place to meet other young men from all over the country. Almost every college in the nation was represented on the hill, and he made fast friends with many other chemists up at American University. Though the work definitely followed army hierarchy, with higher officers mapping out the research for the lower-ranking and enlisted men, a democratic spirit suffused the work on the hill nonetheless, he wrote back to Baylor.

Will discovered that numerous Baylor classmates were in Washington, including two that he ran into one day at the Library of Congress. He met a young woman named Ruth who became his sweetheart. They went all around the city together to see the sights — to the zoo, to the Potomac River cascades at Great Falls, to downtown landmarks, where they posed together, smiling, he in his khaki uniform and she in a jaunty tam with a pom-pom on top. The Texas Club in Washington was a favorite place to mingle with fellow soldiers from home. "Washington was the gathering place for thousands [of] young war workers from every state in the U.S.A. and the social opportunities were of rare excellence," he wrote home.

Will was assigned to a shell-filling unit that worked out of a rough wooden shack that he jokingly called "my office." An upside-down horseshoe adorned the door, and DEATH VALLEY was scrawled on the planks. One of the substances he experimented with was called Paris green, a copper and arsenic compound used as both a dye pigment and an insecticide. It was also known as Scheele's green — another toxic substance discovered by Carl Wilhelm Scheele, Walter Scheele's distant relative. Members of his unit were expected to arrive early in the morning for drills, and they were rarely able to leave the station at the end of their shifts. At day's end, the men would pile into trolleys back to their rented rooms, their uniforms reeking from the chemicals they had been working with that day. The civilians who boarded farther down the line were soon sneezing and crying because of the fumes emitted from the soldiers' clothes.

The men worked long hours under risky conditions, but they were well aware that things could be worse. Every day, the Washington newspapers reported on the bloodletting in France and regularly published notices about soldiers who had been killed. Will was grateful for the relatively easy life he had, with extra pay for meals and his rented quarters. "[W]e had to suffer few of the hardships of the boys in the line," he wrote.

Nonetheless, the hill had its dangers. Periodically, gas would escape during experiments in McKinley Hall, requiring evacuation and fumigation of the building, and caged canaries in the labs would help the chemists gauge when gas had built up to dangerous levels. One morning in late June, a private stopped at a guarded gate, cradling live ordnance in his arms—a mortar shell or a Livens drum—on his way to the experimental fields beyond the fence. The two sentries asked for his pass, but the private had forgotten it. He set the bomb down and went to get his orders. Seconds later, the shell detonated, tossing both guards into the air, fracturing the leg of one and blowing off part of the other's foot. There had been two other explosions or fires in the two weeks before that. A man named George Temple was in charge of repairing all the motors across the station, including the fans in the laboratory fume hoods. Temple was constantly burned by the chemicals that collected on the fans he repaired. He was one of the lucky ones. When one of his close friends reappeared after a long absence, Temple asked where he had been. "I got a bad dose of gas," the man told Temple, "and I know I'm not going to get well." He died soon after.

While accidents were common, not all the dangers chemists like Will faced were accidental. By mid-1918, tests with human subjects— what the Research Division called man tests—were in full swing. Innumerable types of tests awaited the chemists in the man-test house, a long, low building just to the northwest of McKinley Hall. The men donned gas masks to see how long it took for an old gas to infiltrate a new filter canister or to determine if existing canisters worked for a new gas. They tested out protective gear: gloves and suits and boots. There were skin tests, where the men rolled up their sleeves and exposed their skin to drops or vapors of chemical agents.

The ever-increasing number of experiments in the man-test laboratory required the gas mask division to write a report on the various methodologies, to keep all the various types of tests straight. "The man test work has developed so rapidly and the substances tested have become so numerous that it is deemed advisable to collect under one cover all the various methods used," the report read.

Since the previous winter, the Medical Advisory Board had met regularly in the Bureau of Mines offices to confer over the findings of its pathological, physiological, and pharmacological units. Sometimes Van Manning chaired the meeting and sometimes Yandell Henderson. The doctors complained that their work wasn't valued as much as the chemists'. Before he was sidelined in June, Manning had seen to it that the doctors got the attention and resources they needed; he was always prepared to bend the rules in the interests of research.

With the organization of the Chemical Warfare Service, Sibert fused all of the domestic medical work into a new Medical Division and put the work on equal footing with that of other divisions. When the group convened in late July, the first order of business was the militarization of their work under the umbrella of the Chemical Warfare Service. The second topic was a grim one. One of the most recent additions to the division, a physician named Dr. Aldred Scott Warthin, described how he had recently taken an urgent trip to the Dow plant in Midland, Michigan, to see eight soldiers who were being treated for mustard exposure. As the doctors approached the building where the men were recovering, they recognized a telltale stench: the putrid odor of gangrene. In a basement, they found men lying on cots in crude and unsanitary conditions, with mustard burns from their necks to their ankles. A salve covered the burns; underneath the salve, infection was spreading, and gangrene with it. They had only been seen by a nurse trained in treating minor burns and blisters. No clinical tests of any kind had been done. The basement had no screen door to keep out flies, and other noisy activities were going on alongside the cots. Only seven men lay in the foul basement; one had already died, and a second soon succumbed.

The incident illustrated the problems facing the rapidly expanding service. The consolidation meant the absorption of domains that had previously fallen under other army branches—including Edgewood Arsenal—and with it, thousands of officers, enlisted men, and civilians. By July of 1918, more than ten thousand people were working at Edgewood alone. Most were civilians working on the dozens of barracks, shell-filling plants, factories, and other buildings; enlisted men made up the bulk of the remainder, with about one hundred officers. Over the fall, the number of civilians would fall sharply while the ranks of enlisted men rose. As the chemical plants at Edgewood went into production one by one, the arsenal saw its casualties go up, too. There had been just 14 casualties at Edgewood in June. In July, that rose to 63, and then 279 in August. The work in gas plants proved so dangerous that Sibert proposed that enlisted men working in them receive the same service stripes as soldiers deployed to the front lines.

In seven meetings prior to the Chemical Warfare Service consolidation, the medical unit had almost exclusively discussed tests with animals during deliberations. But in its July meeting, the Medical Service doctors discussed an expansion of man tests to gather statistics on sensitivity of human skin to mustard. Johns Hopkins physiologist Eli K. Marshall, the chief of the pharmacology division, proposed testing three thousand to five thousand men. In addition, five thousand men likely to be exposed to mustard—such as soldiers in shell-filling plants—should be tested for sensitivity before being allowed to work with the gas warfare agent, he proposed.

During morning roll call at American University, soldiers were asked to volunteer for the man tests—an unsavory aspect of army life on the hill that gave the chemists a grim sense of gallows humor. During a stunt-night talent show, the men in Maurer's unit sang a song with a refrain that went, "Oh man tests! how we did love them! / To dodge them was our only wish; / For they always came round on Friday / And gas don't mix well with fish."

The exasperated camp surgeon, Captain E. A. Brace, constantly attended to burns and blisters, lacerated arms and legs, and eyes swollen shut by gas. The injured arrived at the infirmary with skin bulging with chemical burns and blisters that were sometimes accidental but often the result of intentional experiments. He wondered about these experiments at the station, performed even without a doctor present.

In late July of 1918, the American University Experiment Station gained a new superintendent: Richmond Levering, a newly minted officer in the Chemical Warfare Service. The U.S. Navy had rejected his overture to join the American Patrol Detachment in the Caribbean, but he had found another option. Back in April, Levering had met George Burrell in Washington when they had gathered in Van Manning's office to discuss Walter Scheele's contributions to chemical warfare. In July, as Levering searched for a new role in the war effort, Burrell offered Levering a position in the Chemical Warfare Service. As Research Division chief, Burrell would have known what was taking place at Jones Point. Perhaps Levering asked Burrell directly for a job, or perhaps A. Bruce Bielaski asked Burrell on Levering's behalf. In either case, Burrell wrote to Bielaski on July 20 requesting that Levering be allowed to transfer to the service.

Bielaski wrote back with his approval of the transfer, saying that Levering would probably be more valuable with the Chemical Warfare Service in Washington than as a special agent. A former U.S. attorney separately wrote to the War Department to lobby on Levering's behalf, praising his "clear-headed judgment" and "most untiring energy."

Exactly what arrangement Levering negotiated with the Chemical Warfare Service is unclear. The operations at Jones Point continued as before, using Levering's properties and presumably relying on his financial support, but without his direct involvement. Levering moved from Manhattan to Washington, taking an apartment near Dupont Circle. Commissioned as a major, he was put in charge of the experiment station's administration, replacing Superintendent Lauson Stone.

One of Levering's jobs included a compliance review of new security rules across the Chemical Warfare Service and all of its far-flung outposts and satellite locations at universities and labs. There were still problems with leaks months after the Research Division had cracked down on loose talk among its chemists; in one incident, a contractor asked an officer about tests at American University that were supposed to be secret. New rules required all visitors to Chemical Warfare Service facilities to show a government-issued photo credential to gain entry.

The oilman wrote to campuses, laboratories, and other gas investigation sites warning of "disloyal persons or enemy Aliens" trying to infiltrate the Research Division. He demanded an accounting of all their security procedures, stressing that a confidentiality breach in one location could jeopardize information in Washington. Some of the respondents were clearly annoyed at the inquiries. "We write no reports on secret matters," Winford Lee Lewis wrote from Catholic. "I have absolute confidence in the men in my unit."

One of the locations under Levering's jurisdiction was his own stockade at Jones Point, where life for Walter Scheele had settled into a kind of repetitive rhythm. On July 4, the bureau agents had allowed him and Marie to putter across the Hudson under the stars for a rare night of freedom at the Eagle Hotel. Since then, the experiment station had returned to its former routine. Two officers from American University had arrived at Jones Point on July 10 to assist with the research; in a progress report that went to Thomas

Aerial photograph of a
French cloud gas attack in
Flanders, Belgium.
*(National Archives, photo no.
70-CW-95)*

Bureau of Mines director Vannoy
"Van" Hartog Manning. After
the war, fellow chemists praised
Manning for his foresight in preparing for the threat of chemical
warfare, but he received little public recognition for his efforts.
*(National Archives, photo no.
111-SC-56573)*

Major General William L. Sibert, director of
the U.S. Chemical Warfare Service. *(Library
of Congress, Prints & Photographs Division, photograph by Harris & Ewing, LC-DIG-hec-16794)*

Major General William L. Sibert in Gondrecourt, France, in August 1917, when he still commanded the First Division. He was later dismissed and ordered to return to the United States, where he became chief of the Chemical Warfare Service.
(National Archives, photo no. 111-SC-80078)

Brigadier General Amos A. Fries, chief of the gas service, AEF, and later chief of the U.S. Chemical Warfare Service after the dismissal of Major General William L. Sibert.
(Library of Congress, Prints & Photographs Division, photograph by Harris & Ewing, LC-DIG-hec-16690)

Fries after the war.
(National Archives, photo no. 70-CW-103)

2570

Captain Winford Lee Lewis, the chemist credited with identifying lewisite as a potential chemical weapon. *(Photo courtesy of [Philip Reiss, grandson of W. Lee Lewis)*

Sergeant Harold "Higgie" J. Higginbottom, Company B, First Gas Regiment. *(Photo courtesy of U.S. Army Chemical Corps Museum, Fort Leonard Wood, MO)*

Second Lieutenant Thomas Jabine, Companies B and C, First Gas Regiment. Wounded in mustard gas shelling in early October 1918. *(Photo by permission of the Jabine family)*

Sergeant Charles William Maurer, who was drafted and then ordered to report to American University in 1918. *(Photo courtesy of estate of Addie Ruth Maurer Olson/Olson Family Collection)*

Passport application and photo of Richmond M. Levering. *(National Archives and Records Administration, U.S. Passport Applications, 1795–1925, via Ancestry.com)*

DESCRIPTION OF APPLICANT.

Age: **27** years.   Mouth: **medium**
Stature: **5** feet, **11** inches, Eng.   Chin: **round**
Forehead: **high**   Hair: **brown**
Eyes: **blue**   Complexion: **fair**
Nose: **medium**   Face: **oval**
Distinguishing marks: **none**

AFFIDAVIT OF IDENTIFYING WITNESS.

German chemist, spy, and saboteur Walter T. Scheele, photographed aboard a vessel in the Gulf of Mexico after his arrest in Cuba. *(Investigative Case Files of the Bureau of Investigation 1908–1922, Record Group 65, National Archives Microfilm Publication M1085, Old German Files, 1909–21, case no. 8000-925, roll 279, frame 203, National Archives at College Park, MD, via Fold3.com)*

Walter Scheele, second from right, in a group photo with American and Cuban agents aboard a vessel in the Gulf of Mexico after his arrest in Cuba. *(Investigative Case Files of the Bureau of Investigation 1908–1922, Record Group 65, National Archives Microfilm Publication M1085, Old German Files, 1909–21, case number 8000-925, roll 279, frame 566, National Archives at College Park, MD, via Fold3.com)*

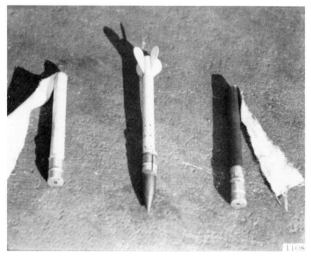

Incendiary darts developed by the Chemical Warfare Service, possibly using the chemical formula Walter Scheele developed to bomb American ships. *(National Archives, photo no. 70-CW-76)*

Kennel at the American University Experiment Station for dogs used in lab tests. Hundreds of dogs died in experiments of the Research Division; mice, cats, goats, monkeys, and other animals were also used in tests. *(National Archives, photo no. 70-CW-18)*

Future gas officers training at American University in the fall of 1917. *(Photo courtesy of the U.S. Army Chemical Corps Museum, Fort Leonard Wood, MO)*

View of the American University Experiment Station from the east, with McKinley Hall in the background. *(National Archives, photo no. 70-CW-3)*

View of McKinley Hall from the roof of the College of History building, American University. *(National Archives, photo no. 70-CW-2)*

West-facing view of the American University Experiment Station from the top of McKinley Hall. *(National Archives, photo no. 70-CW-5)*

The man-test house at the American University Experiment Station, where soldiers tested out new masks and canister designs. *(National Archives, photo no. 70-CW-6)*

Soldiers testing box respirators in the AUES man-test house. *(National Archives, photo no. 70-CW-7)*

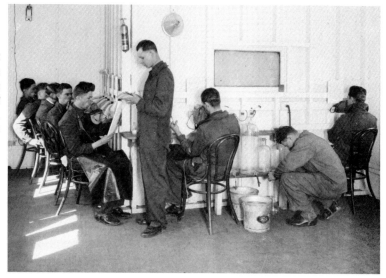

Stationary bicycle in the man-test house used to test gas mask canisters during physical exertion. *(National Archives, photo no. 70-CW-9)*

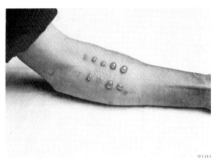 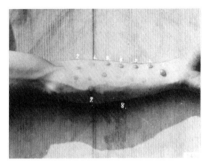

Left, example of a skin test comparing different chemical weapons agents. The photo illustrates a comparison of mustard gas and lewisite blisters. Right photo shows blisters in a test of protective salves. *(National Archives, photo nos. 70-CW-100 and 70-CW-101)*

Masked soldiers in a test trench at the American University Experiment Station. Note the Livens shells in the top-left corner of the photo. *(National Archives, photo no. 70-CW-66)*

Flamethrower demonstration at the American University Experiment Station. *(National Archives, photo no. 70-CW-56)*

Soldiers in the Research Division at the test range at the American University Experiment Station. Stokes mortars with legs, baseplates, and sandbags are in the foreground. A battery of Livens projectors, buried in the ground at an angle, is at the left-most side of the photo. *(National Archives, photo no. 70-CW-67)*

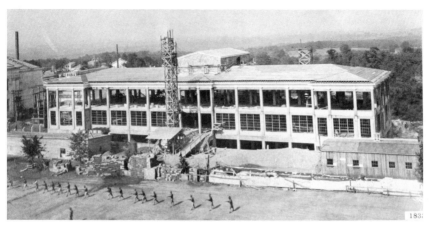

The new chemical laboratory at American University. Construction began in 1918 but stalled because of massive cost overruns. The lab was unfinished when the war ended and was turned over to American University. Today the building is known as the Mary Graydon Center. *(National Archives, photo no. 111-SC-55273)*

Members of the Research Division staff at the American University Experiment Station. Charles William Maurer is third from the right in the front row. *(Photo courtesy of estate of Addie Ruth Maurer Olson/Olson Family Collection)*

Gas warning sign at the fenced periphery of the American University Experiment Station. *(Photo courtesy of estate of Addie Ruth Maurer Olson/Olson Family Collection)*

Drum of phosgene on the grounds of the American University Experiment Station. *(Photo courtesy of estate of Addie Ruth Maurer Olson/Olson Family Collection)*

Charles William Maurer, wearing gloves to protect against mustard, posing outside the shell-filling shack he called "my office." The inscription on the back of the photo says the shack was filled with mustard and lewisite. *(Photo courtesy of estate of Addie Ruth Maurer Olson/Olson Family Collection)*

Maurer mugging inside one of the many outbuildings on the American University Experiment Station grounds. *(Photo courtesy of estate of Addie Ruth Maurer Olson/Olson Family Collection)*

Aftermath of a February 1918 explosion in which several soldiers and officers were injured at the American University Experiment Station. *(Bureau of Mines, Record Group 70, War Chemical and Gas Investigations, 1918–1919, finding aid A-1, entry 80, box 2, National Archives at College Park, MD)*

Martin Maloney Chemical Laboratory, the chemical lab at Catholic University of America, where W. Lee Lewis and his Organic Unit No. 3 tested and developed the chemical compound lewisite. *(Photo courtesy of L. Philip Reiss, grandson of W. Lee Lewis)*

Group photo of Organic Unit No. 3 outside Maloney Laboratory at Catholic University. *(Photo courtesy of L. Philip Reiss, grandson of W. Lee Lewis)*

A small-scale lewisite still set up on the roof of Maloney Laboratory, a precursor to a larger version that exploded on August 3, 1918, exposing former senator Scott and the secret industrial-scale plant dubbed "the Mousetrap" in Willoughby, Ohio. *(Photo courtesy of L. Philip Reiss, grandson of W. Lee Lewis)*

View of the Chemical Warfare Service plant at Edgewood Arsenal, 1918. At the height of wartime activity at Edgewood, more than eleven thousand soldiers and civilians worked on chemical weapons at the arsenal. *(National Archives, photo no. 111-SC-80476)*

Top photo: Panorama of Gunpowder Neck in Edgewood, Maryland, before work began on the plants. Bottom photo: Edgewood Arsenal on the same tract of land in 1918. *(National Archives, photo no. 111-SC-60480-A)*

No-man's-land in France. *(Photo courtesy of the U.S. Army Chemical Corps Museum, Fort Leonard Wood, MO)*

No-man's-land in France.
(Photo courtesy of the U.S. Army Chemical Corps Museum, Fort Leonard Wood, MO)

The AEF chemical laboratory in Puteaux, France, just outside Paris. *(Photo courtesy of the U.S. Army Chemical Corps Museum, Fort Leonard Wood, MO)*

A soldier at the gas school at Chaumont, France, loading a drum into a German projector, modeled on the Livens projector, in October 1918. *(National Archives, photo no. 111-SC-31049)*

An officer in the First Gas Regiment setting off a smoke pot near the Argonne Forest on October 8, 1918. *(National Archives, photo no. 111-SC-29510)*

The train station at La Ferté after a shell barrage, with members of Company B helping to clean up the station. *(Photo courtesy of the U.S. Army Chemical Corps Museum, Fort Leonard Wood, MO)*

Members of Company C, First Gas Regiment, attached to the Eightieth Division, load and fire phosphorus and thermite shells in Le Neufour, Meuse, France, on October 27, 1918. *(National Archives, photo no. 111-SC-31966)*

Hellfire Boys of the First Gas Regiment on the march in France. A member of Company B donated the photo to the U.S. Army Chemical Corps Museum. *(Photo courtesy of the U.S. Army Chemical Corps Museum, Fort Leonard Wood, MO)*

The gas ship USS *Elinor,* which was outfitted to carry chemical weapons to Europe. *(Photo courtesy of the U.S. Army Chemical Corps Museum, Fort Leonard Wood, MO)*

A masked soldier—probably Charles William Maurer—standing over the burial pit called Hades at the rear of the American University Experiment Station. The caption on the back of the photo calls the spot "the most feared and respected place on the grounds." The photo came to light in 1993 and helped pinpoint the location of the pit several years later. *(Photo courtesy of estate of Addie Ruth Maurer Olson/Olson Family Collection)*

Edison and officers in Washington, Bruce Silver predicted that they would be valuable assistants in future developments at Jones Point. Otherwise, little had changed at the experiment station. The same passel of experiments continued—tests with incendiary darts, wing dope, helline. The U.S. Navy disappointed the scientists after a review of their experiments found that liquid oxygen was probably incompatible for maritime use because of the difficulty of putting refrigeration plants on board navy vessels. Still, regardless of such setbacks, the humdrum nature of the agents' reports gave little hint of trouble.

But there was trouble. Walter Scheele continued to seethe at his imprisonment. He had left behind two years of confinement in Cuba only to be imprisoned again in rural New York. A tiny number of people knew that he was even alive, penned inside the stockade at Jones Point, working with the threat of execution over his head. He was allowed an occasional excursion across the river to the pharmacy in Peekskill—always escorted by a bureau agent—but after their near arrest in April, the agents took him only grudgingly. As the months went by, he festered with resentment over his predicament.

On Saturday, August 3, Charles DeWoody came up from New York to meet with the doctor and his wife. Scheele had been agitating for Marie to join him at the renovated quarters at Jones Point in some semblance of domestic normalcy, even if they were surrounded by guards and barbed wire. Agent O'Donnell—code-named O'Dell—took Levering's car, drove to Haverstraw to pick up the chemist's wife, and then brought her up to Jones Point. He fetched her husband, and all three crossed the Hudson to Peekskill. A car brought them to the Eagle Hotel, where DeWoody waited for them.

The meeting did not go well. DeWoody told the chemist and his wife that she would be allowed to move to Jones Point to be with her husband, but she could not come and go at will. She could only leave the enclosure occasionally, and then only with explicit approval from the department's agents.

Scheele exploded in anger. It wasn't enough that he'd spent months of incarceration separated from his wife. Now DeWoody was turning Marie Scheele into a prisoner as well. "Scheele for a period of a half an hour showed his teeth and his true colors," DeWoody wrote in his report. Raging at DeWoody, Scheele challenged the superintendent to prosecute him. He said he had never been arraigned, and his detention was illegal, and claimed that his deal with Levering and Offley allowed his wife to be with him permanently. He had held up his end of the bargain, he fumed, surrendering his chemical secrets to the Americans. Now that deal was broken, Scheele insisted, and he had no intention of allowing his wife to become a prisoner with him.

DeWoody countered that Scheele's treachery against America had not been forgotten and that his four months at Jones Point had not wiped away his transgressions. Moreover, the department's precautions weren't simply to isolate Scheele; the department was also protecting him from those who might want him dead, and they would have to extend that protection to Marie Scheele as well.

Scheele finally quieted. They would accept the government's terms, they said, but with their own conditions. Mrs. Scheele must be permitted to leave the enclosure upon request at least once a month—or more if the Bureau of Investigation allowed it—and DeWoody needed to establish a way for her to stay in touch with her family, in case her mother fell ill or some other misfortune befell her kin. DeWoody agreed. They also demanded that Agent O'Donnell could take the Scheeles out in the boat or in Levering's automobile from time to time, with the understanding that neither of them was allowed to talk with anyone they met en route, and Scheele insisted that he must be allowed to go to the drugstore in Peekskill to buy necessary items. DeWoody agreed, even though he suspected that the frequent drugstore trips were probably just a pretext to get away from the experiment station.

After the meeting, Agent O'Donnell brought the Scheeles back to the pier, ferried them across the river, and returned Marie Scheele to her rented room in Haverstraw. For now, Scheele had been placated.

The service had become a huge enterprise, sprawling across cities and states, one leg planted firmly in America and the other in France. On July 16, the U.S. Army surgeon general had handed William Sibert control of all the Medical Department laboratories, plants, and stations related to mask making—National Lamp Works in Cleveland, Hero Manufacturing in Philadelphia, B.F. Goodrich Company's lab in Akron, the Fulford Manufacturing Company in Providence, Rhode Island, the Plymouth Rubber Company in Canton, Massachusetts, and Pacific Gas and Electric in San Francisco—all of them flipped to Chemical Warfare Service control. In Long Island City, the Gas Defense Plant was making gas masks by the thousands to ship overseas, and a new "fighting mask" would soon be ready for the Americans to wear into combat. The helium plants in Texas were poised to begin making three million cubic feet of the gas code-named "argon" each week. Edgewood was making tons of gas each week, which would soon be shipped in American shells. A bromobenzyl-cyanide plant was under construction in Kingsport, Tennessee, as well as a sodium-cyanide plant in Saltville, Virginia. Construction was almost complete on a fourteen-thousand-acre gas warfare proving ground in Lakehurst, New Jersey, about fifty miles east of Philadelphia. It would have facilities similar to those at American University but orders of magnitude larger, with a farm to accommodate two thousand goats and kennels for more than two hundred dogs for testing, an ice plant that made two tons of ice a day, twelve barracks, a YMCA, its own post office, and a hospital and an infirmary for anyone injured, maimed, or gassed.

But the combustible heart of the service was still Mustard Hill. Burrell wanted to make sure that this fledgling science would have a place for research in perpetuity. And that place, he felt, should remain American University.

On the last day of July, Burrell proposed turning American University into a permanent seat of the Chemical Warfare Service. The plan he presented to Sibert was a simple one: the army should buy the school and the land around it. "The permanent buildings at the American University, and the equipment that has been collected at this station will furnish a fine home for such a permanent Research Division," he wrote.

The idea likely appealed to Sibert. The general didn't traffic in temporary solutions and stopgap measures; he was a man who had sunk his legacy into the Panama Canal, the most permanent solution imaginable to a problem of navigation. The idea that the army would simply have to pack up from American University after the war and abandon more than a million dollars' worth of scientific investment probably did not sit well. On August 2, Sibert passed Burrell's idea up the army chain of command, asking that the army's Real Estate Division study the feasibility of buying American University.

The very next day, that plan went up in smoke.

Chapter Thirteen

The Meuse and the Mousetrap

A brisk wind blew across the fields behind former senator Nathan Bay Scott's country house on August 3. It was a Saturday morning, and the banker sat on the porch enjoying the fresh air with his wife, Agnes, and her sister, Carrie. Chickens clucked around the veranda, and songbirds darted overhead. The temperature was already above seventy degrees at 8:00 a.m. with the sun still climbing, and the windows of the house were wide open to let in the breeze. Soon the drenching swelter of August would drive Washington's bankers and politicians out of the city and city residents to the packed municipal swimming pools. Though the war still raged toward its bloody apogee, Congress had adjourned for summer, and civil servants had departed for cooler climes.

During the week, Scott's home was the Willard Hotel, several blocks from the Continental Trust Company, where he was president. A few blocks in the other direction lay the White House and the U.S. Department of the Treasury, where his career in Washington had begun. On the weekends, Scott drove out of town to his country house and left all that behind. The road turned west alongside the barbed-wire-topped fence enclosing the hilltop campus of American University, with its ramshackle village of wooden outbuildings and storage sheds around it. Then it was down the hill to his house, where he could unload his bag and sink into a porch chair.

As Scott chatted on the porch around 8:30 a.m. with Agnes and his sister-in-law, they spotted a yellow cloud billowing from the American University property in the distance. The three watched in growing alarm as the fast-moving vapor blew toward them, undulating in the breeze. Perhaps it was smoke from a brush fire, he thought, but there was something about the mustard-colored plume that seemed sinister, dangerous even, as it curled up from the ravine behind the house and surged toward the porch. The wind brought a strange smell with it, too, a pungent, acrid odor.

Scott and the two women rose hurriedly to their feet, but their eyes and throats had already begun to burn. Half blinded, they stumbled into the house and slammed the porch door. Coughing, eyes streaming, face burning, Scott went through the house, slamming shut the open windows as the cloud enveloped the house. Barely able to see, Scott fumbled his way to the phone and dialed.

A mile away, the phone rang in the headquarters of Camp Leach. Former senator Nathan Bay Scott had been gassed.

The release of the chemical plume that engulfed the Scott house was hardly the first accident at American University. But earlier mishaps, for the most part, had been confined to the station, and the casualties were treated inside the fence at the busy infirmary at Camp Leach.

This time the gas had affected a civilian—and a famous one at that. When the call came in to Camp Leach, the officers would have instantly recognized Scott's name. When Scott left West Virginia for Washington, he had been one of the state's richest businessmen. Wealth and fund-raising prowess for Republicans earned him President McKinley's appointment as secretary of the Treasury. After that, he spent twelve years in the U.S. Senate before he retired from public service to become president of Continental Trust. He was enmeshed in the city's social life, a familiar figure at state dinners and charity galas. Since his retirement from public life, his name still appeared regularly in the Washington papers, sometimes in the society pages but even more frequently in the regular ads for Continental Trust, which urged thrifty customers to "Settle Down and Save Up."

It wasn't until 10:00 a.m. that Captain Brace, the Camp Leach surgeon, turned off Ridge Road into Scott's driveway. Two men got out of the car with him, Major C. K. Jones, the commander of the First Engineers Battalion, and G. E. McElroy, the safety engineer at Camp Leach. As they clambered from the vehicle, they lugged gas masks for the Scotts. The cloud had long since dissipated, but lifeless carcasses of chickens and farm animals lay around the house. Agnes Scott was the least affected and was already feeling better, but the gas had virtually blinded her husband and seared her sister's lungs and throat. Captain Brace attended to the former senator and his sister-in-law. Soon after, the two departed for the Willard Hotel, where Scott's personal physician was going to treat him. Agnes Scott stayed behind. One of the engineers offered her a gas mask and seemed hurt when she refused it.

"They may be just the thing to save our lives, but I cannot imagine the senator getting up 15 minutes earlier every morning to practice a gas mask drill," she said.

The phone began to ring at Camp Leach as reporters called about the incident. An explosion at the station had injured enlisted men, one reporter scribbled down. Such things should be expected because of the nature of the experiments, another was told.

In the evening, Scott roused himself from his hotel suite to speak with reporters. Face blistered, he said soberly that the incident had been a narrow escape and had given him a new appreciation for the perils that soldiers faced on the front lines.

That evening, Brigadier General Frederic V. Abbot mentioned the incident to Colonel Edward H. Schulz, the commanding officer of Camp Leach. When Schulz picked up the *Post* the next morning, the incident was a front-page story. "N. B. Scott 'Gassed,'" the headline read. "Engineers Experimenting with Elements Believed to Compose Mustard Gas, Which Escape and Descend on Surrounding Country. Chickens and Animals Killed." A muddle of fact and fiction, the article reported erroneously that the incident resulted from experiments with "mustard gas components" and claimed that the explosion nearly killed Scott. The paper reported that the "nature of the experiments could not be learned last night, as the officers in charge refused all information."

Colonel Schulz dashed to the house to speak with the Scott family. Scott was still recuperating at the Willard Hotel, but Agnes was there with other family members. She described a far-less-serious scenario than what the paper reported, telling Schulz that no one was "seriously disturbed by the gas," though they were certainly worried about a recurrence. When Schulz spoke to other nearby residents, none had any complaints.

That might have been a relief to the colonel, but it was only temporary. When the *Washington Times* came out that evening, its report of the incident was even more sensational than the *Post*'s. The incident was the paper's top news and had somehow ballooned into the accidental detonation of a bomb. In a banner atop the masthead, the paper splashed POISON GAS OVERCOMES FORMER SENATOR AND WIFE. The article reported breathlessly that the three "had a narrow escape from death yesterday when a gas bomb exploded prematurely at Camp Leach." Scott himself, who had sounded circumspect in the *Post*, sounded much angrier in his quotes to the *Times*.

"It is an outrage that a citizen cannot enjoy his home without being made to suffer like this. From what I can learn the whole thing was due to gross carelessness on the part of someone, and it has surely caused us all no end of suffering," he complained, fuming that "those in charge of operations should observe more care in protecting innocent residents."

It was a catastrophe. Not only had a prominent public figure been injured, but the secret work at American University had become a matter of public record. Scott had revealed to a jittery Washington that dangerous open-air experiments were going on within city limits. The story had the elements of a thriller: an aggrieved innocent with a tale to tell, the careless handling of deadly poisons, a mystery that defied explanation, and the whiff of a cover-up.

While the incident was a disaster for the army, there was at least one silver lining: the actual gas that escaped was not correctly identified. Even though Scott described the smell as similar to mustard, it was not mustard gas. It was lewisite.

Of course, it was no surprise that the word "lewisite" never appeared in the newspapers—Sibert had forbidden the word from even being used. But anyone familiar with physiological effects of chemical weapons agents would have known that the substance that swept over the Scott home could not have been mustard gas, as mustard required many hours to take effect. Luckily, none of the reports noted that fact, and the scientists at American were spared probing questions about the nature of the substance. Despite all the worries about leaks, loose talk among the chemists, and now the explosion, at least the secret of lewisite had remained behind the fence at American University.

By the morning of Monday, August 5, Colonel Schulz had written up a preliminary report on the accident. It was not long—just one page, with "Confidential" scrawled at the top. On Saturday morning, he wrote, three soldiers had been brewing lewisite—he described it only vaguely as "the gas"—about a fifth of a mile upwind of the Scott house. The lewisite still was inside a wooden building, manufacturing shack number 8, and was a larger-scale version of the apparatus that Winford Lee Lewis had built on the roof of the lab at Catholic University. The building was in a section of the station southwest of McKinley Hall and the College of History, tucked in a ravine dotted with structures—storage sheds, machine shops, and a laundry platform to scrub off mustard gas residue. The three soldiers had been tending the still when a pipe clogged. Pressure built, and the apparatus exploded. The blast reduced the shack to a pile of lumber and corrugated tin, scattering debris, and released the plume of lewisite. Swept by the wind, the cloud rolled southward, through the barbed-wire fence between the Scott property and American University, and over the Scott house. The camp surgeon treated the three soldiers and then sent them home to recuperate.

After such an embarrassing event, the service needed an emissary to offer an apology to the senator. That task fell to a newly appointed officer on the hill who had extensive personal experience with handling bad public relations: Richmond Levering.

Levering whipped up an apology letter to Scott. "My dear Sir," the letter began. "Permit me to express my very great regret at the accident which occurred within the enclosure at the American University Experiment Station and resulted in injury to yourself and your family." He delicately pointed out that an equipment failure caused the accident, not carelessness of the men. "I feel sure that you will realize that as our men are subjected every day to this danger in developing warfare gases for the use of the United States, it is hardly their fault that the unfortunate circumstances attendant upon their work resulted in this personal trouble to you."

It took almost a month for Burrell to complete his own report on the Scott incident. When he did, the scenario he described was far different than what Colonel Schulz had observed in his report two days after the explosion. The injury to the Scotts, he said, "was more imagined than real." Rather than a release of 120 pounds of gas, as Schulz reported, it was far less—10 pounds at most. Burrell was dismissive of the press reports, calling them "greatly exaggerated and for the most part erroneous."

The bad press could not have come at a worse moment. Only days earlier, Burrell had written to Major General Sibert with his proposal for transforming the campus into a permanent chemical warfare research station. Ironically, the plan for acquiring the campus also called for government purchase or seizure of the surrounding properties—including the Scott property—for an open-air proving ground.

All of that was thrown into jeopardy by the Scott fiasco. This incident was an unwelcome distraction that cast a harsh public glare on the research just as the machinery of chemical warfare was shifting into high gear. Gas shipments to France, which had been halted in July because of shell shortages, would soon start up again, and Sibert drew up plans for transporting gas across the ocean in specially outfitted ships. In late August, the Oldbury Electro-Chemical Company plant in Niagara Falls began filling Livens drums with phosgene for shipment overseas. Problems with manufacturing mustard were finally getting ironed out, after Fries sent a British chemist to the States with another new process, requiring an overhaul of the plants at Edgewood. Sibert asked the Department of Ordnance to furnish one hundred thousand incendiary darts and ship them to Edgewood Arsenal by September 10. The overseas division of the service ordered up hundreds of bombs to test for dropping gas from the air. The chemists were running tests on a potent new sneezing gas, diphenylaminechlorarsine, or adamsite. At last, the self-playing pianolo that Fries envisioned was making music.

Despite the inopportune timing of the Scott accident, Sibert and Burrell pressed forward with their plan to try to acquire the university and the land around it, and the army made official overtures about a possible purchase. In late August, Brigadier General Hugh S. Johnson, the army's director of purchases and supplies, wrote to American's board president, Benjamin Leighton, asking to talk with him about purchasing the school. "It is desired to have some discussion with you as to the present situation at the American University and to have your idea of what the Government would be expected to pay for the ground and the buildings if it should undertake to purchase them," Johnson wrote.

Leighton's reply arrived with a postmark from the backwoods of Maine, where he was vacationing. If the army wanted to buy the campus, it would cost $2 million for the land and the buildings. He didn't plan to return to Washington until mid-September, he wrote, but if the army was serious about moving forward, the board could convene a meeting and he would return early.

Two million dollars was too much for the army, but Sibert already had a backup plan in case Leighton asked for too much. The army would condemn the property—that is, seize it by eminent domain—reducing its value considerably, thus making it far less expensive to purchase.

There were practical reasons that Sibert wanted to acquire American University and turn it into a permanent seat of chemical warfare research, but there were also legal reasons. For the army accountants and bureaucrats, American University was a legal nightmare. When Sibert took over the Chemical Warfare Service, he investigated the arrangements in place between American University and the Bureau of Mines. He discovered that there were almost none. Manning, who had proved so adept at cutting red tape and bending bureaucratic rules for his chemists, had allowed construction everywhere on campus without any kind of written agreement or permission from their landlord. Other than the original 1917 agreement and a few ancillary documents, such as permission from the university to build bomb pits, no agreements related to construction had ever been committed to paper.

Astonishingly, that included the huge new chemistry laboratory that Manning had pressed for so urgently. The state-of-the-art lab, it turned out, was a boondoggle in several respects. As part of Sibert's push to purchase the campus, the army quartermaster investigated the half-finished project. As with most of the campus, there was no legal arrangement between the Bureau of Mines and the university over the new laboratory. Some of the university trustees had asked for a written agreement to clarify the status and ownership of the building after the war. The experiment station architect "told them to 'forget it,' that no agreement was needed; that if they wanted to get rid of it when the war was over, a few sticks of dynamite could be effectively used, or if they wanted to use it, that he had so designed it that it could be marble-faced and thus converted into a very decent building." The investigation also discovered that construction of the building had been badly bungled and its costs grossly miscalculated. Originally estimated at about $250,000, additional construction to fix the foundation and other problems would raise the price to $675,000—more than two and a half times its original price. Purchasing the property and all the buildings would allow the Chemical Warfare Service to protect the service's investments at American University, which totaled more than a million dollars, and at the same time cut through all the tangled legal problems that ensnared the experiment station.

The Scott incident had now thrown that entire plan into doubt. The accident not only put the army at odds with nearby residents and the alarmed city government, but it also inflamed the antagonism between the Research Division and the Corps of Engineers that Sibert had worked so hard to patch up. Major General William Black, the chief of the engineers, wrote a terse letter to Sibert about the incident:

> Is not your Chemical Station at the American University too close to residences and to Camp Leach for the safe handling of war gases in any such bulk as seems to be now used there? The responsibility for accidental death or injury to outsiders is very grave. I hope that you can see your way clear to such a change in procedure as will remove the existing risks.

On September 11, Sibert sat down at his desk to draft a response to the engineer's complaints. He had a difficult line to walk. Black was an extremely powerful figure, head of the army branch that had cemented Sibert's legacy in Panama. His views were not to be taken lightly. But Sibert didn't want to knuckle under to the increasing pressure on the Chemical Warfare Service to curtail its activities in Washington. There was too much at stake.

In his letter to Black, Sibert conceded that the accident was serious. Because of the blast, stockpiles of explosives at the station were reduced considerably, and new precautions had been adopted to reduce threats to residents or the engineers. But he also insisted that the work must continue at American University. "It is not practicable to transfer much of this work to any other locality without serious loss of time and efficiency as hardly appears to be justified."

Despite Burrell's and Sibert's insistence on the safety of the work, the accident would have a profound impact on Mustard Hill that would dramatically shape the future of the service. In the short term, however, the accident provided an unexpected boon in one respect: a cover story to explain to lower-level researchers at American University why the lewisite experiments were ending. Winford Lee Lewis had to tell his loyal cadres of chemists, who had endured terrible conditions and personal injury in their investigations, that the lewisite research was shutting down because the compound was too dangerous and uncontrollable to be used. The lie pained Lewis because he knew the opposite to be true — in fact, lewisite was considered wildly successful, so much so that it had become a key part of the U.S. chemical warfare strategy for the coming months. Lewis also knew that work on the large-scale manufacture of lewisite was already well under way in Willoughby, Ohio, far away from Washington and under a deep cloak of secrecy. He watched in dismay as the morale of his unit plummeted over the misinformation that their discovery had failed. "My men were depressed and the esprit de corps suffered greatly," he recalled years later.

There was something strange about Willoughby, Ohio. Nate Simpson had never heard of the town where he was headed, and no one else seemed to know anything about it either as he asked around at the YMCA in downtown Cleveland. A fresh-faced chemist with a shy smile and spectacles, Simpson had turned twenty-three a few weeks before he was inducted into the army. He was bundled off to Fort Dix in New Jersey to join the 153rd Depot Brigade, where he spent several miserable weeks slogging through bleak weather and choking down inedible food before he got new orders to pack his bag for Ohio.

The YMCA in downtown Cleveland, with its enormous illuminated sign on the roof, was a huge, bustling way station for hundreds of young men, who could exercise in gymnasium classes, take Bible classes, attend club meetings, and mingle in the packed dining room at night. Simpson was relieved to have avoided the trenches, but anxious about his mysterious destination. After a day or so, the YMCA manager told Simpson and the nine other men who had arrived at the same time to report to the General Electric Company at Nela Park. A streetcar there would take them to Willoughby.

When the ten men boarded the Willoughby trolley at Nela Park, the conductor collected their fares and told them to sit together. No one else boarded the car. The conductor didn't help the situation when he tried to make lighthearted banter with them.

"You know what? There is something mighty queer about that town, Willoughby," he told Simpson and the other men. "I've taken more than a hundred GI's out there, and never brought one back!" Not one of the men laughed.

The trolley trip ended at the Ben-Hur plant. After Simpson was ushered past the armed guards and inside the barbed-wire fence, the plant superintendent warned him that if he said anything about the plant, even the slightest word to his family back home, he would be court-martialed. There was no mailing address for the station, only a generic drop box with the inscrutable name LOCK DRAWER 426, which routed mail through Cleveland. Every letter that went in or out was read and censored. He was forbidden from leaving the plant except for meals, which he would take in town with all the other soldiers. There were no barracks; he was assigned a cot on the crowded ground floor of one of the office buildings.

Simpson was among a second wave of soldiers to arrive at Willoughby after the civilian contractors had wrapped up their work. Within days of Dorsey giving the plant the green light, a frenzy of activity had enveloped the factory. James Bryant Conant had arrived in July, with a warning from Dorsey that there were no officers' quarters at the factory, and he would have to find his own lodgings. The same day as Conant's arrival, Dorsey assigned a lieutenant colonel under his command as plant superintendent. He also assigned twenty-five soldiers to Willoughby to guard the plant day and night while it was converted into a chemical plant.

Absolutely secrecy was demanded of everyone connected to the factory, under threat of court-martial. Even uttering the word "Willoughby" was forbidden. A story circulated about the consequences of loose lips. When a Nela Park employee asked an ill-advised question about the mysterious activity at the other end of the streetcar line, he was promptly sent to Willoughby. Word of the incident spread among men in the service, and soon Willoughby Station gained a nickname. "The Mousetrap," they called it, because the men who went in never came out.

Rumors flew through the town that something big was happening down at the old Ben-Hur plant, but what it was, no one could say. The only thing that could be coaxed out of John Fackler, the attorney for the Ben-Hur Company's bankruptcy receivership, was something vague about supplies for the government. And that construction was in the offing—a lot of it, "the building of 300 houses," according to an article that ran in the *Willoughby Republican* on the same day Dorsey appeared at the Ben-Hur plant. Details in the newspaper were vague and few. The *Republican*'s editors, it turned out, knew far more about what was going on in Willoughby than the pages of the newspaper revealed. The *Republican* agreed not to report details of what was afoot down at the Ben-Hur plant in exchange for an eventual exclusive. For now, the newspaper would sit on the story.

The first job was to erect a barbed-wire fence, which went up around the perimeter of the property in short order. The plant was in rough shape—worse than Dorsey had grasped when he made his cursory tour of the property. The adjoining office building had been outfitted as a functioning headquarters for the plant, but the previous winter's cold had ruined all the plumbing, and much of the electrical wiring needed replacement. The factory building itself was in even worse condition. The rolling dirt floor dipped several feet below grade in places. No plumbing or bathrooms. No phone lines. There was no rail siding for deliveries by train.

Workmen quickly rewired the buildings and strung phone lines, graded the dirt floor, poured concrete. Draftsmen bent over improvised tables as the building took shape around them. Carpenters under Conant's supervision went to work to set up a laboratory in one corner of the factory. When Conant ordered the equipment for the plant, it was shipped in trunks, as if it were personal baggage.

Vast amounts of chemicals were needed for the Willoughby operation—Dorsey requested thirty-three tons of sulfuric acid per day, for example, a staggering quantity that required permission from the War Industries Board lest it disrupt other industrial markets. Because the orders for Willoughby piled up so quickly at Nela Park, the Development Division brought in a man to sort out the mess, a twenty-nine-year-old sergeant from Iowa named Harold French Davidson. Davidson took over the job of procuring chemicals. The best chemists in the country were hard at work in Willoughby "manufacturing something nice for the 'Huns,'" he wrote home to his mother. Of course, he never actually saw these chemists because they were sequestered inside the Mousetrap, "and if you get in there you do not get out again."

On the same Saturday that the lewisite explosion injured Senator Scott in Washington, two medical officers arrived at Willoughby to take charge of emergency care at the plant, where it was almost guaranteed that injuries would be rampant. The two officers ordered supplies and equipment and instituted physical examinations of the enlisted men and the sanitary conditions at the plant. The chief of the Medical Corps recommended that the proposed officers' quarters be made into a temporary hospital until a more permanent one could be built and equipped. Not long after, the plant had its first fatality—a civilian contractor named Anthony

Tripping from nearby Painesville, who died after a bin of castings tipped over on top of him.

Before Simpson arrived at the plant, a kind of grim, rigid martial law dictated life for the men of the Mousetrap during its first few weeks. While enlisted men like Simpson slept on the floor of the office building, officers slept in tents outside. There was no mess hall or kitchen either. At mealtimes, guards marched the men to the Willoughby Inn, where they gulped down their meals and then returned to the plant. If they met anyone from town, they were not to mention anything about what was going on behind the barbed-wire fence. Each morning, the public-address system came alive, and Major Conant's voice crackled over the speakers singing "All Up" to rouse the soldiers for the workdays that lasted from 6:00 a.m. until 10:00 p.m. or midnight, seven days a week. Confined by barbed wire, the men spent long days toiling to ensure that lewisite remained on Conant's ambitious schedule. Inside the plant, a giant war map hung on an office wall, pins denoting the positions of the armies in Europe. Other than the map and the regimented mealtime expeditions, it was as if the outside world no longer existed.

On August 10, General Sibert visited the lewisite plant to see the progress for himself. Goliath's visit proved to be a boon to the soldiers stationed there. The men who assembled to listen to their chief pledged to guard the secrets of Ben-Hur, so Sibert issued an order relaxing the strict rules at the plant, which would henceforth be governed as a regular army post, albeit with a few more restrictions. Men could receive passes to leave the plant and even visit Willoughbeach, the town to the northwest on the shores of Lake Erie. Of course, the men were still strictly forbidden from discussing the work or even acknowledging the existence of the plant. Cleveland was also off-limits, but now at least they had a modicum of freedom that they didn't have before.

Even though the purpose of the plant was shrouded in mystery, the residents of Willoughby welcomed the influx of soldiers into their midst. Each morning, town residents left fresh fruit outside the gates of the stockade and occasionally cakes and pies as well. The townspeople collected books and magazines for the men and gave them bathing suits so that they could swim in Lake Erie. Residents invited the men into their homes for dinners. The Red Cross held a dance for the soldiers on August 31, serving ice cream, cake, and punch. Music from a donated phonograph and piano brightened the evenings.

Despite the occasional chance for socializing and relaxation, the work at the plant moved ahead at a breakneck pace. Life at the Mousetrap was a monotonous blur, with Conant's voice blaring over the public-address system at the start of each day, signaling another long work shift stretching from sunup to sundown. The marches to the inn for meals punctuated the tiresome days, which ended after dark in cramped and crowded bivouacs in the half-completed buildings.

Conant's laboratory was the first part of the plant to be completed and was ready for operation on August 11. Throughout the frantic construction at the plant, Conant stayed in touch with colleagues back at American University, where the work on lewisite had gravitated from Catholic University. Conant was as tightly bound to secrecy as the soldiers under his command. In his correspondence with Elmer Kohler back on the hill, he used the code name "G-34" when he referred to lewisite. Conant reported that everything was moving smoothly in Willoughby and, in a veiled reference to Sibert's loosening of the rules at the plant, that "the stockade is more flexible than was first planned." Kohler kept Conant up to date on the work related to the work at American University and ribbed Conant for having "disgracefully abandoned" the efforts there.

The two also discussed problems resulting from the militarization of the research, when it was moved out from under the Bureau of Mines in July. It had become extremely difficult to quickly bring new scientists into the research because the army had capped the number of new soldiers who could join the effort. The service had already exceeded its quota, which meant that lower-ranking officers couldn't get promotions and new scientists couldn't be recruited to the effort unless replacing someone who was departing, creating serious personnel shortages for the scientists, Kohler wrote. Conant had hoped that a chemist he worked with at American University named Frank R. Fields could be commissioned and sent to Willoughby. But such commissions had become hard to come by under the new military rules. Moreover, Fields was injured in an explosion, perhaps even the same blast that tore apart shack number 8 and gassed former senator Scott, though Kohler wasn't specific in his letter to Conant. Even though Fields exhibited no ill effects at first, he was given a week's furlough "to get it out of his system." But he fell ill again soon after he returned to the American University lab, unable to keep down any food other than ice cream. "I doubt very much whether you can count on him doing any more G-34 work," Kohler wrote. It was a blow to Conant; now, it was impossible for Fields to come work at the Mousetrap.

The news from Kohler came just as trained chemists were most in demand in Willoughby. By mid-August, civilian contractors were finishing their work and departing the plant, replaced by chemists and engineers who would work on the manufacturing plant itself. Originally Conant had estimated that the operation would require about three hundred men. But after reexamining the plant's capacity and the demands for its output, the station superintendent calculated that the manufacturing capability would need to be doubled. Everything about the plant needed to be quickly redrawn as a result, from the layout of the factory to the ventilation system to the barracks. The plant needed more water, more electricity, more land. And above all, it needed more men to build, operate, and maintain the expanded operation; instead of three hundred men, the plant would need more than a thousand.

Inevitably, accidents occurred at the Mousetrap as well. A

chemist named John F. McGrory, a private first class who arrived at Ben-Hur on August 14, was badly burned on both hands and his head in a chemical accident. Confined to quarters for more than a month, he was unable to do work of any type, until he was eventually assigned to a clerical job, his skills as a chemist going to waste.

To protect the men, a shipment of the latest gas masks—known as the Tissot model—arrived at the plant in the third week of August. Drills became an ingrained part of the daily regimen. Masks were always in easy reach in the event of an explosion or a leak, and Klaxon horns and alarms were installed throughout the station. A fire chief made frequent inspections of protective equipment, and laundry facilities made sure that no one at the plant ever left the property wearing clothes tainted with toxins.

Experimental units for the first two steps of the five-step lewisite-production process were completed on August 30. By September 10, the men completed the apparatus for producing the raw materials for lewisite. One of the plants worked well; the other had unsuccessful early runs but was soon running smoothly as well. Within a few weeks, the apparatus for the other steps in the process had been ironed out, and full-size equipment for large-scale production was ordered. Rail sidings were placed on each side of the factory, and materials began pouring into the plant. The zero hour for full-scale production of lewisite was set. By November 15, the plant needed to be up and running.

At Jones Point, tension between Scheele and his captors had calmed and the laboratory had settled into a kind of steady, quiet rhythm. Levering was out of the picture as far as the day-to-day operations. Agent Frank X. O'Donnell filed brief daily reports, a monotonous recitation that nothing of consequence was happening at the compound. On August 15, a car went down to the Haverstraw hotel. Marie Scheele loaded her belongings and motored back to Jones

Point, where she at last took up residence with her husband in his barracks, with a federal agent sleeping in the next room.

Two days later, Walter Scheele's name surfaced in the news again. President Wilson signed an order forbidding aliens in the United States from leaving the country without special State Department permits. Quoting the State Department, articles about the order noted that several infamous Germans, Scheele among them, had escaped to Cuba in 1916 because of inadequate laws. While the articles didn't say he wasn't in custody, they left the distinct impression that he was still at large — perhaps a deliberate effort by the government to cast doubt about Scheele's whereabouts.

The calm lasted until September 16, when O'Donnell arrived for his shift. Overnight, Scheele had fallen seriously ill, and signs pointed to appendicitis. Getting medical help while keeping his identity hidden was a tricky proposition. Charles DeWoody instructed O'Donnell to find surgeons and ordered him and another agent to stay by Scheele's side. A doctor from nearby Stony Point recommended monitoring Scheele until morning; in the meantime, he suggested surgeons who could come up from Manhattan if necessary.

In the morning, the physician examined Scheele, who showed improvement. By that afternoon, though, the chemist had taken a turn for the worse. This time the doctor said Scheele needed to go immediately to Nyack Hospital, more than twenty miles away. The doctor, Scheele, his wife, and the agents all dashed to Nyack. O'Donnell frantically tried to call the surgeons in New York but couldn't reach either of them. By 9:00 p.m., Scheele's condition was considered life threatening, and there was no more time to wait. At 9:15 p.m., the chief surgeon at Nyack Hospital sliced open his abdomen and removed his appendix, with four other doctors assisting and the agents and Marie waiting anxiously outside the operating room.

The operation was a success, and by midnight Scheele was resting comfortably. He was given a private room, and no one was allowed inside without the consent of the agents guarding his door. O'Donnell got a nearby room where he could stay for as long as the doctor was hospitalized, and settled in to wait.

Celebration rippled through Paris as Amos Fries arrived in the city on August 11. A few days earlier, a long-awaited British drive on the Amiens front had proved wildly successful. The attack had surprised the Germans, throwing their troops into disarray and forcing a chaotic retreat. The Allies took tens of thousands of prisoners and seized hundreds of guns. For the first time in years, the threat to Paris had diminished. The Germans' long-range cannons briefly resumed their shelling of the city but soon fell silent. As the days went on, more good news arrived with every hour, and celebrations broke out in the sun-dappled streets.

Fries had good news of his own. For weeks, he had anxiously awaited word from Pershing or the War Department that he would reach the rank that he craved. It arrived in the form of a telegram, addressed to "Brigadier General Amos Fries." Inadvertent, perhaps, but as sure a sign as any that Washington's bureaucratic gears were turning, and he would soon have his promotion. His office erupted in celebration at the hint that their chief was moving up in the ranks. The official confirmation came a day later in another telegram recommending his promotion. It would mean more work, more travel, more long days, but it also elevated the Chemical Warfare Service another notch higher on the totem pole of the military.

Fries's wedding anniversary was only a few days away, just close enough that he joked to Bessie in a letter that the promotion would be his anniversary gift to her. It was finalized about ten days later, when another telegram reached him at Hanlon Field with notice that the promotion had gone through. He took the oath that morning and added a general's star to his uniform.

As he rode back to headquarters, Fries couldn't stop smiling to himself—his good fortune seemed too good to be true. News from the front continued to be positive. He had met with the military attaché from Switzerland, who told him that morale among the Germans had plunged. For the first time, Fries wrote to Bessie that he might be home sooner than he thought. "The Bosche is learning what it is to retreat and from many signs it appears he doesn't relish it. He is going to get it steadily from now on until the end."

As if to punctuate the regiment's rising status, the Hellfire Boys gained a new name as well: the First Gas Regiment. They were no longer an adjunct to the war machine, one regiment among hundreds. They were the first and only of their kind, with the name to prove it.

The progress reported in the newspapers and toasted in the mess halls didn't diminish Fries's ardor for chemical warfare. Just the opposite; he was more convinced than ever that chemical weapons must play a decisive role in Germany's eventual defeat. "The Bosch [*sic*] is steadily falling back, but he is far from being down and out. We have got to gas him until he wishes he had never heard the word, and we are out to do it," he wrote to Bessie.

About a week after the start of the Amiens drive, Fries presented his case to Pershing for a more muscular Chemical Warfare Service. Pershing had approved another regiment, but it wasn't enough, Fries insisted. Instead, there should be two more regiments of six companies each. That would total eighteen companies—adding 600 officers and 14,500 men, tripling the number of troops already in the First Gas Regiment. He wrote to Pershing:

> The experience so far had with our own gas companies and a careful study of the operations of the British gas troops leads to the conclusion that a continuous and extensive use of special gas troops along the entire front will be one of the most effective means of establishing the superiority which is essential to win the war without exceedingly heavy casualties.

He also recommended sharply increasing the amount of gas used. By September 1, at least 25 percent of artillery should contain gas or smoke material, he wrote, increasing to 30 percent by January 1, 1919. Eventually, gas-manufacturing facilities in the United States should prepare to supply enough chemicals to fill at least 50 percent of all shells.

To help convince Pershing, Fries sent a dossier of facts and figures to support his proposal, using evidence gleaned from the Hellfire Regiment's battlefield experience. He cited the high American gas-casualty rate—the thousands of American soldiers gassed in June and July—as evidence of how effective gas was as a weapon. He also pointed out the usefulness of mustard in rendering equipment and territory unusable because of its persistence.

But his most powerful arguments were not his; they came from American division commanders whose comments he had collected from battlefield reports. Some were specific observations, such as from the Twenty-Sixth Division commander who recommended that half of all munitions contain gas, writing that "my conversion to this instrumentality is so strong that I believe we cannot win this war unless we meet fire with fire and to the fullest extent develop this frightful agency." Fries emphasized one of the commander's statements with asterisks: "I believe it is our duty to waste not a moment in developing this gas warfare to the limit," the commander wrote.

Fries had cherry-picked comments of generals who agreed with him. But not all did. Other members of the army general staff opposed more gas troops, believing that there were already enough. "I do not see, at the present time, any necessity for an increase in the number of regiments," Lieutenant Colonel V. D. Dixon wrote to the assistant chief of staff, a West Point classmate of Fries's named Fox Conner. Another member of the general staff felt the same, and said so. Their arguments failed to sway Conner.

Fries had a dim view of Conner, believing him to be a hard worker but something of a lightweight. They were on the same side on this issue, though, and Conner pushed Fries's recommendations for the expansion up to the AEF's chief of staff for approval. The chief of staff quickly approved it, Conner sent a draft cablegram to Fries, and on September 5, the chief of staff made the request to the assistant secretary of war in Paris, with General Pershing's blessing.

Fries also began to think about more-abstract issues—public relations and image. In an effort to boost its public profile, the service had claimed some famous draftees. The baseball greats Ty Cobb and Christy Mathewson had been assigned to the chemical regiment, along with several well-known college athletes. "We are going to put them all through about 6 weeks training course before sending them into the field," Fries wrote home. In addition to prominent soldiers in its ranks, he wanted a more suitable symbol for the service. In late 1917, the chemists had adopted an insignia for the regiment: two crossed retorts, long-necked laboratory glassware shaped like teardrops used for distillation. Fries had tinkered for some time with a symbol that was "a little more warlike": two crossed gas shells superimposed over a dragon, a firebreathing embodiment of might and destruction. He convinced Pershing, and the commander in chief recommended the new insignia. The War Department snuffed out the idea with a sharply worded response that officers needed to concentrate on the war, not fiddle around with insignia changes. For now, the symbol of science and laboratory work would remain on the collars of the Hellfire Boys.

As summer turned to fall, the war's momentum had shifted. After the Germans' ferocious springtime offensive had sputtered into stalemate once again, the Allies had taken back ground with the successful counterattack at Château-Thierry. Now Pershing was laying groundwork for new attacks with the French and the British, planning a great grinding push before winter set in and the armies retrenched until spring. On September 12, an American offensive was to begin at Saint-Mihiel, in the Lorraine region near the German border. The attack was to straighten and stabilize the front line to eliminate a salient that bulged westward into Allied territory. The plan came in Army Field Order No. 9, which instructed the American I Corps and IV Corps to attack on one side of the German line and V Corps on the other, swing inward, and pinch off the salient around Saint-Mihiel. Fries anxiously awaited word of the start of the attack. When it came, he was not disappointed. "The big American push near Verdun started today and I heard a short while ago that it was going so far like a house afire," he wrote.

Addison was asleep when his bunkmates roused him a few minutes after midnight on September 12, amazed that he was slumbering as the American offensive was about to start. The sleepy chaplain roused himself and reached for his razor. In the daytime, the billet's elevation gave a spectacular view of the French countryside stretching for miles to the east and west, but as Addison began to shave, the sky outside was dark and still.

And then at 1:00 a.m., as if a switch had been flipped, the night turned to a sea of flame. Addison stood midshave, transfixed by the sight. The entire horizon, dark one moment, flared the next with the pulsing incandescence of roaring howitzers and the quick glow of smaller guns. Even from miles away, the chaplain could hear the deep and continuous percussion in the distance, the unmistakable thunder of the American artillery. The sky glowed with the heat and light of the guns, as if the countryside had been set ablaze.

Addison watched for a time. In the small hours of morning, he went up to the regiment office to join Colonel Atkisson. Together, the two waited for the 5:00 a.m. zero hour when the regimental show would begin, signaling the start of the infantry advance. All of the gas companies except for Company B had roles to play, throwing mortar barrages to create smoke screens and heave thermite onto the Germans. Projector shows, too, were planned, to lob high explosives at machine-gun nests as well as fake shows producing nothing more than a flash and a boom, to draw attention away from actual attack locations.

As Addison stood beside Atkisson at the window looking east, the colonel was distant and tense, drained of his usual warmth. The strain of battle had taken its toll; a few days earlier, he had almost collapsed with exhaustion in the mess hall. At 5:00 a.m., the regiment's work illuminated the sky anew as the projector batteries thundered. Addison watched as the searing light of thermite cascaded down in a molten wave of pyrotechnics, and thick banks of smoke billowed toward the German lines, lit with the glow from the guns below and liquid fire above.

Saint-Mihiel was neither a decisive battle nor a very hard-fought one—the Germans were preparing to abandon the salient anyway when the Americans attacked—but was an important milestone that rolled back the German line and gave the Americans their first victory without assistance from their allies. In the aftermath, the American First Army began to move once again, a lumbering pivot from Lorraine to its next target.

On the night of the Saint-Mihiel offensive, Higgie slept soundly more than one hundred miles away. He awoke at about 5:30 a.m. knowing nothing about the attack. Company B had been excluded from Saint-Mihiel, but now they were moving up to join the other battalions close to the action. He spent the day marching some twenty-five miles toward the front, stopping midday for a dinner of hot coffee and hash before continuing on toward Mézy. A thunderstorm hit midafternoon, pelting them with drenching rain and marble-sized hailstones before the sun emerged and dried them out. He ended the day back near Château-Thierry, camping under a tree, and had the next day off to go into the town on a pass to explore the elaborate German tunnels, one of which burrowed down beneath the Marne River. With the city's liberation from the Germans, residents had begun returning to pick through the rubble and ruin. Higgie got chocolate and cigars from the Red Cross and ambled through the town, peering into shopwindows.

In the days that followed, there was heavy work loading artillery shells at the train head and marching them into position under the moonlit sky. On September 15, he was ordered to move up again, and he clambered into a crowded boxcar with sixteen other men. They spread hay on the floor and fell asleep, the sky ablaze with antiaircraft fire as the train clattered toward the front. They were on the train two days before they disembarked and continued on foot. When they reached their camps at the end of each day, the men played card games late into the night. Higgie ate doughnuts for supper one night and wrote letters by candlelight. As they marched, townspeople handed champagne to the men. At night, they cheered at dogfights spiraling overhead, and watched airships roar to the earth in flames.

Jabine had an even easier time of it than Higgie. While the rest of Company B traveled toward the front, Jabine got time off and a pass for Paris. He had commanded a successful gas operation on August 28, firing phosgene, chloropicrin, and thermite at the German-occupied village of Courlandon. "Our company is 'on the move' and while waiting for moving orders I got a chance to be civilized for a couple of days," he wrote home. He got a room at the Hotel Continental across from the Tuileries. He took luxurious baths, savored meals in restaurants, and had a celebratory night on the town, taking in a show with his friend's sweetheart, a Red Cross girl from Minneapolis. "Not bad for one day with some other fellow's girl!" he wrote to his mother. He would be holing up in winter quarters soon, and there wouldn't be much fighting then, he assured his mother. There was nothing to worry about. "I explained in my last letter how comparatively safe a job this was and I want you to regard it that way," he wrote.

His respite was brief. New orders transferred him from Company B to Company C, peeling him away from Higgie and his other friends to take charge of a platoon he'd never led, into a cadre of officers he'd never fought with. Soon Jabine was in a boxcar on his way to the front. While he waited for the train to move, a lonesome weight pressed down on him. He had been with Company B since Christmas Day, when they had marched from their barracks in

Washington into the whirling snowstorm, when they were still green and the war was far away. If it meant he could have stayed with Higgie and the other boys, he would have taken a demotion to private. "I must try and get along in 'C' Co," he wrote to his mother, waiting for the train to begin its creaking passage back toward the front.

On September 15, orders went out to all companies to withdraw from Saint-Mihiel. Headquarters was already working on its next target: the Meuse-Argonne sector. With the French and the Americans in the south, the British to the west, and the Belgians to the north, the Allies planned a massive attack sweeping the length of the entire western front, a coordinated push against the Germans at every point. The American objective was to sever the Germans' main supply and communications line. If the trunk line could be choked off, the kaiser's troops up and down the front would be marooned and helpless.

Unlike in Saint-Mihiel, the push in the Argonne would be a brutal, punishing battle. The Argonne Forest was a vast natural barricade, a dense arboreal wall wrapped in miles of barbed wire, with multiple defensive trench systems and gunner nests tucked into the hills.

Addison was told he could join Company C near Ville-sur-Cousances, about eight miles southwest of Verdun. The French held the sector; but shrouded in darkness, the American First Army quietly moved artillery, soldiers, and supply trains in among their allies. Army troops and trucks swarmed the roads between the Argonne Forest and the Meuse River, and American platoons scattered in invisible billets throughout the front—in crowded dugouts the French had just vacated, in crude warrens nestled among the forests and hacked into muddy embankments, and in tents tucked among the trees. Scouts conducting reconnaissance wore French uniforms to maintain the illusion that the French held the region. Completing the subterfuge, only a thin line of French soldiers held the front.

In preparation for the attack, the engineers rushed to set mortars. The woods teemed with hungry, anxious American soldiers. Nerves were raw. No one slept. On September 25, heavy rain drenched the gas platoons tucked into their posts in the forest. Addison motored to the front with extra rations and cigarettes for the soldiers. After a slow trip back on the traffic-choked roads, he ended the day at brigade headquarters. The artillery would begin at 11:00 p.m., with zero hour for the gas platoons at 5:30 a.m. The push was on. As the uneasy night wore on, Addison headed to the ammunition depot in the woods, where regimental officers gathered in a canvas tent next to stockpiles of shells. The officers spread out maps and pored over the attack plans and division orders. An officer ducked into the tent and announced that all of his projectors were ready. Addison sat up next to a lit candle, and waited. At the front, the rain had turned the trenches into a slippery mire. Higgie's platoon slithered through the water and mud as they splashed toward their dugout, a deep hole packed with muddy, stinking soldiers like muskrats burrowed into a riverbank. He huddled in the dugout, eating crackers and jam, until the artillery began.

At 11:00 p.m., the thunder of howitzers cracked open the darkness in a deafening roar, lighting up the forest with their glow. A few minutes later, the sharp bark of seventy-five-millimeter rounds began, flinging gas shells toward the German positions. The Germans returned fire. Inside his cold, candlelit tent, Addison listened to the deafening thunder outside. As he and the other officers waited, a howitzer shell exploded nearby. The rush of air snuffed out the candle, plunging the tent into darkness.

As the deafening firestorm quaked around Higgie, the platoon ducked from the dugout to set their Stokes mortars. It was slow, slippery work—every time he scooped dirt from the trench floor, water promptly filled the hole. It took him about two hours to set his gun, then he returned to the crowded dugout and slept for an hour.

Toward daybreak, Higgie got the platoon ready. A cold, creeping fog hung in the air. The artillery began again as he struggled in the mud for the start of the show. Just before zero hour, he heard high-explosive shells arch over the top of the trenches to shred a path for the infantry through the maze of barbed wire in no-man's-land. At five-thirty, Higgie's platoon let their guns go with a roar, sending white phosphorus shells northward toward the German positions to create a smoke screen. He reloaded and fired again, then again. The concussion from the third shot pounded the gun so deep that it disappeared into the mud and water in the trench. Higgie plunged his arms into the freezing mire, thrashing under the surface to pull the heavy, slippery gun back up to be fired again. In the darkness, the red glow of Livens projectors bathed the forest in an infernal glow, the Stokes mortars and bright curtains of thermite lit up the sky like the Fourth of July, and the fog mixed with banks of smoke and clouds of phosgene in a cloak over the battlefield. The bellowing cannonade even frightened the American infantrymen waiting to charge the German positions, as if the ground had opened under their feet and the devil himself had galloped forth.

After all his shells were fired, Higgie hoisted the mortar up out of the trench, shucking the baseplate from the mud, shouldering the barrel, and clawing his way over the top. No-man's-land had disappeared into an impenetrable fog and smoke, but somewhere in the haze, the high explosives had blasted a route forward.

Sitting atop the trench, folded in a blanket of smoke and mist, Higgie lit a cigarette and waited. Soon, the second wave of infantry would emerge from the fog. Dawn was coming. The Battle of the Meuse-Argonne had begun.

Chapter Fourteen

"All to the Mustard"

Oh man tests! how we did love them!
To dodge them was our only wish;
For they always came round on Friday
And gas don't mix well with fish.
>
> —*Stunt-night song, American University*
> *Experiment Station*

From afar, the figures appeared human, but only barely. They moved slowly back and forth across the open pasture, alien creatures in rubbery shells, wide glass portholes for eyes and a ribbed tube dangling from where their mouths should have been. A hose led from the tanks strapped to their backs to the sprayers in their hands, and as they crisscrossed the field, the men in gas suits played the nozzles slowly over the bare ground in a grid, spreading an aerosol that gave off a pungent odor as it settled into the soil.

The security around the test site was tight—if the warning signs posted around the field weren't enough to keep away trespassers, the guards would be—but chances were slim that anyone could stumble across the experimental field. American University was three-quarters of a mile away, and the farmhouse of the Weaver family, who was leasing the land to the army, wasn't close. Streetcars only passed about twice per hour on the road six hundred feet away. And anyone who strayed close to the field where the men sprayed the ground would regret it soon enough.

After they sprayed the ground, the men brought dogs and mice and placed their cages on platforms at different heights above the sprayed soil. Few of the animals put an inch above the ground survived, while more of the ones at six inches lived.

When the sun was out, the men didn't last long in the suits—only about ten minutes before heat exhaustion set in. When they were done, the soldiers stripped off the suits, then the rubber boots and gloves. Masks came off next, then the sweat-soaked stockings and union suits dunked in linseed oil. Once they had stripped down, the men took hot baths with soap. Still, almost all the men working at Weaver Farm suffered injuries at some point, with chemical burns on wrists and ankles, eye inflammations, and sore throats. A half-dozen men were badly burned; one had blisters on his entire lower body. Some men's feet were burned through their rubber boots. The chemists called the field "Mustard Farm."

When the day ended on September 27, the American University chemists shucked off their gloves and gas-defense suits and hung up their masks. It had been a cool, cloudy Friday evening at the close of another week of man tests and mortar shots, and it was time to unwind. After leaving American University, hundreds of chemists crossed town for a dance at Catholic University. The school's bishop had kindly lent the administration building to the Research Division for the chemists' second social event of the season. Two officers from the American University Association, the Research Division's newly formed professional organization, had spent the afternoon decorating the building and some three hundred members of the Research Division and their dates streamed into the hall.

There was plenty to celebrate. The newspapers trumpeted the torrent of news about the successful first day of the offensive in France and the ferocious American attacks that had rolled back the German line in the Argonne. "Americans Advance 7 Miles, Take 12 Towns, 5,000 Prisoners West of Verdun" blared the *Washing-*

ton Post. The *Star* pointed out that chemical weapons may have been even more effective at the Argonne than expected. The afternoon papers arrived with still more positive news from the wires. The *Evening Star* reported that Germany's ally Bulgaria had asked for an armistice, sending a general to Paris to negotiate peace and end the fighting in Macedonia. Ottoman control of Palestine was teetering.

The festivities at Catholic University began with a reception and the soldiers lining up to shake the hand of the division chief, Colonel George Burrell, trim and commanding in his officer's cap and wire-rimmed spectacles, with his wife beside him. Next to them was Captain Winford Lee Lewis, the wizard of lewisite, and his wife, Myrtilla.

Before the music started, the colonel spoke a few words. The men faced strenuous hours of work at the station, he said, and needed rest and relaxation. Many would soon receive promotions for their work, he told them, which raised cheers from the men. A major from the publicity committee stepped up next with a pitch for membership in the American University Association and spoke for a few minutes about athletic and educational opportunities that the group planned to offer. Finally, Captain Lewis said a few words of welcome, as full of humor and dry wit as ever. Then the band struck up, the chemists took their dates by the hand, and the couples glided to the dance floor.

The daily drills, the searing heat in summer, and the freezing winter nights huddled in unheated shacks all were a dreary grind for the enlisted men of the Research Division, taking a toll on their spirits and often their skin, eyes, and lungs as well. Almost everyone working at the station had burns, blisters, or scars from their experimental work. It was grim work, this chemical weaponry, requiring a healthy sense of humor and diversions to maintain morale. But their lot wasn't all bad. While some men were disappointed not to be sent overseas, for the most part they were grateful to be spared from the battlefield. They were doing their part, even if it was in the comfortable environs of Washington, D.C., fighting "the Battle of Arsenic Valley," as they joked. While the Hellfire Boys fought their way through thickets of barbed wire and wastelands pocked with shell holes, the men of Mustard Hill sipped punch and tapped their feet to the music at Catholic University.

A strong esprit de corps developed among the soldiers in response to the difficult and sometimes-dangerous demands put on them. In the fall, the American University Association formed a committee to organize morale-raising social events, talent shows and dances. Musical clubs started up, along with intramural sports teams—the surprisingly effective football team, the Mustard Gassers, was proudly undefeated in a long stretch of games against other army squads. Evening classes could earn the men college credits, and they could practice marksmanship. The lunch counters around the station teemed with soldiers, and Washington's theaters and parks and zoo were only a streetcar ride away. With longer leave, soldiers could get on a train for Baltimore or New York or Pennsylvania. Gossip about romances spread like wildfire across the camp, and sometimes men at the station reappeared after leave with a wedding band and a marriage certificate.

As part of its campaign to boost the spirits of the men, the association published a newspaper, the *Retort*. The tabloid chronicled the station's social life, albeit with careful censorship and no clues as to the nature of the research. With the slogan "All to the Mustard" at the top, the *Retort* proclaimed itself "A Newspaper Published by the ENEMIES of GERMANY at American University Experiment Station." The paper cost five cents a copy and was packed with news articles, gossip from around the hill, engagement announcements, and features about top officers and scientists. It published long lists of promotions and dedicated a section called "Roomer Hath It" to updates on prospects for barracks that would end the detested daily commute to the station.

A wildly popular humor column called "Why Soldiers Go Wild" chronicled fictitious letters between a dimwitted stenographer named Effie Jane Smith and her friend back in Pittsburgh. The sports columns reported the latest standings in the sports leagues and the Mustard Gassers' most recent victories. There were entreaties for musicians to join a glee club and a banjo and mandolin club. The personals column was full of wry anecdotes and anonymous observations about the station.

Colonel Burrell earned a prominent place in the inaugural edition with a lengthy profile and a photo. He was also given a column to write on any subject he desired. He used it to heap praise on the chemists at the experiment station:

> You have been asked to "do your bit" on this side of the Atlantic Ocean, a part of the huge staff of men and women [in] back of the men who are in the front lines. This is a technical war, admitted by us, admitted by the enemy, and proven by the events that have transpired to date. The side with the strongest technical staff will win.

Not everything in the newspaper was lighthearted. It also asked for volunteers for the Visit the Sick Committee to comfort patients at Walter Reed with influenza or injuries too grievous for the camp infirmary. Washington had so far been spared the worst of the influenza pandemic that had jumped the Atlantic from Europe, where it was decimating cities and armies. But in September and October, deaths in the capital began to climb. On the day of the Catholic University dance, reports of new flu cases had gone up sharply. Six people died in the city in a six-day span, and 42 new cases were reported in just thirty-six hours. At Camp Leach, the very first case appeared September 24. Soon there were dozens, and the Corps of Engineers clamped a quarantine onto the entire camp on October 3 and didn't lift it for almost three weeks. A total of 110 cases developed. The majority of the men returned to duty, but five died. The virus raced like a brush fire through Camp Meade in Maryland as well, infecting fifteen hundred soldiers and requiring another emergency quarantine.

Public-health officials rushed to make sanitary masks available for soldiers and the military camps. They also prepared posters warning against coughing without covering one's mouth and sharing cups and hand towels. The precautions came too late for some. The *Retort*'s second edition, on October 19, included an obituary section, printing the names of six men and one woman from the Research Division who had recently died. Under the announcements of the seven deaths, this item appeared: "It grieves us to add to this list the names of Mrs. W. L. Sibert, wife of Major-General William L. Sibert, our Director, and Mrs. R. E. Winert, wife of Lt. R. E. Winert, of the Mechanical Section."

Though all of Sibert's six sons were in the war, the greatest threat to his family proved not to be shells, bullets, and gas but influenza. A relatively young woman at thirty-seven years old, Juliette Sibert had fallen ill and quickly succumbed on October 8. Her funeral and burial were in Pittsburgh. It would have taken a week or more for a cable to reach the Sibert boys overseas.

Major General Sibert had little time to mourn his wife's death. Projections on gas production in Niagara Falls, Bound Brook, Edgewood, Midland, and other sites came across his desk. The Ordnance Department had solved the long-standing problems that had held up production of shells. The three helium plants in Texas had proved even more successful than imagined, and bids were about to go out to build a ninety-four-mile pipeline to send the "argon" to the coast.

The service hummed along as never before, but there were still problems at American University. Work remained stalled on the new chemistry laboratory due to the accounting error that had tripled the price, and American University had begun to protest the army's treatment of their campus. The chancellor, Bishop Hamilton, complained to Assistant Secretary of War Benedict Crowell about the Research Division's activities, leaving Crowell with the distinct impression that the War Department had overstepped its bounds and was encroaching on the university. Crowell asked for an investigation of the matter. The district's board of commissioners also complained directly to Secretary of War Baker, claiming the Chemical Warfare Service's work was a danger to city residents.

Major General William M. Black, the chief of engineers, was still complaining loudly as well. The American University Experiment Station was dangerous, he wrote in a scathing memo on October 25, polluting the air, maiming dogs that hobbled around the neighborhood, and generally being a nuisance to the community:

> I would regard its continuance at this place a decided detriment to the city and one that will retard the development of the section of the city where located, and permanently depreciate the value of property. The entire establishment should be removed to a reservation where its presence will not work injury and where experiments with gases can be made freely without danger to the neighboring community.

In early morning darkness of September 26, Higgie waited in no-man's-land with his platoon. The tip of his cigarette glowed in the dense smoke and mist around him, and his mortar lay in the mud beside him. The First Army was moving up toward the German lines. With the front so fluid, Stokes mortars were the only weapons that allowed the gas regiment any mobility; projectors were impossible to move quickly enough.

After a time, the infantry emerged like ghosts from the mist behind him, and Higgie hoisted his mortar onto his shoulder to follow them forward. They waded through swamps and over brooks and across trenches in pursuit of the Germans. Higgie struggled under the weight of his gun as he slogged through the mud. The mist around him gradually brightened as daylight broke.

He was grateful for the fog and smoke—German machine gunners left behind to fire on advancing infantry were as blind as the Americans. They fumbled forward through the undergrowth and shredded barbed wire, crossing abandoned German trenches. The line had been blown to pieces in the bombardment. Equipment was everywhere, dropped in the German rush to fall back. When the mist lifted around 10:00 a.m., Higgie could see American infantry fighting on the hill ahead.

After so many months behind static entrenchments, men and machines crashed northward in a disorienting stampede. Somewhere near Higgie, Jabine's platoon of five runners plunged through the smoke and mist, sprinting through machine-gun fire and artillery rounds as they relayed movements and potential mortar positions between the infantry and Company C. Unencumbered by guns, Jabine's platoon was much more nimble than Higgie's, keeping step with the infantry. Two of Jabine's men fell wounded, but he kept on, moving northward as the infantry advanced. Blind in the thick fog, the American infantry and German machine gunners were unable to see one another, and the infantry was able to slip right past the gunners. Then the fog lifted, and the gunners took aim at Jabine. He dove into a trench, bullets snapping over his head. In the distance, he heard the growl of engines, and when he peered over the top of the trench, he saw American tanks roaring across the field toward the German gun nests. Dozens of gunners popped up and fled, and Jabine's heart leaped as he watched the terrified men shed rifles and equipment as they ran. When Jabine was able to go back for his injured men, he pulled captured Germans from a line of prisoners to carry the stretchers to the dressing station.

Higgie and his platoon hiked all day, the mortar a leaden weight on his shoulder. They stopped for only a few brief rests. The longest stop was for a meal, and the men sat puffing on scavenged German cigars. They went on. At one point a group of German soldiers stepped from the brush and surrendered without a fight.

Higgie's platoon searched them and escorted the prisoners back toward the rear. Late in the afternoon, they reached Véry, a town only about twenty miles from the Belgian border. Higgie could finally put down his mortar. Some of the fellows went out scavenging for souvenirs.

As the afternoon wore on, word arrived from farther up the line that a German counterattack was coming. Higgie was set to move again when he heard the grinding roar of engines, and twenty American tanks reared over a nearby hilltop with more infantry behind. Higgie had never seen a tank before, and he watched in awe as the machines snarled down one hill and up the next just as easy as could be. Everywhere he looked, he saw soldiers with columns of German prisoners streaming back behind the American lines.

With the front secured, it was a long hike back in the dark before Higgie could sleep. It took him five hours to retrace his steps through territory captured from the Germans and return to the ammunition dump where his day had started. He and his platoon arrived at the depot at midnight. Higgie found a truck that was returning to the barracks. The platoon rode back, and when they got to camp, they woke up the cook to get coffee and something to eat. He finally went to bed at 4:00 a.m.

Higgie slept the whole morning. When he woke up, he found thirty letters from home waiting for him. He stayed in bed reading all day, got supper, and rolled up to go to the ammunition dump again. Overhead, the battle raged on — Higgie watched two observation balloons roar down to earth engulfed in flame and an American plane get shot down in a fight with four Germans. He left in the afternoon, arrived at the dump after dark, and watched one of the platoons set off a thermite show. Ordered back to Véry, he spent the entire night on the truck, wedged in the gridlock of traffic jamming the roads leading to the front.

Higgie finally got to Véry at eight o'clock in the morning, had something to eat, and then his platoon started out for the front with mortars and bombs. He went a couple of miles up to the new battalion headquarters and then pressed on. He came to an open field that the Germans were shelling. He kept low, the shells falling quick and fast as the platoon struggled forward with the mortars. In the daylight and out in the open, he could see the mayhem wrought by the bombs, the unending detonations, the ground quaking under him, the shriek of incoming artillery. The shells were killing soldiers all around him, wounding others with flying shrapnel and gas. He kept on, still carrying the mortars closer to the front. They crouched low, trying to stay out of sight. The whistle of incoming artillery came close and fast, and a gas shell landed in the middle of Higgie's platoon. Some of the men were slow to get their masks on and got gassed. They were at the front, but the wind blew hard, too hard to launch gas shells. There was nothing for them to do, so Higgie and his men abandoned the mortars and retreated back to a first-aid station near a hill. He rested for a bit, then returned to Véry. Higgie had slept for only ten hours in five days. Exhausted to the point of collapse, Higgie and five other men crowded into a tiny room for a few hours' sleep, before they were roused for breakfast and sent back to the mortar placement they had left the previous afternoon.

All across the American sector, the Germans were retreating, abandoning their guns and surrendering by the thousands. For two days, there were no more shows, no more gas attacks. Thirty-two members of Company B were evacuated to a dressing station after they drank water contaminated with mustard gas. Dead horses lined the roadsides, and Addison joined a group of Hellfire Boys to bury the corpses of their mates where they had fallen.

Four days into the drive, all of Company B regrouped on September 30 outside Véry. Higgie could see the mountaintop ruins of Montfaucon in the distance, a prized piece of elevated territory high above the town. For the moment, the men waited. Higgie was dispatched with a message for division headquarters in Épinonville. Orders came to move that night, about a mile north. He and

Shap camped on the side of a hill, overlooking the valley outpost teeming with horses and men.

On the night of October 2, the Germans struck back. Higgie had just left the mess-hall line with a plate of food and was sitting on a hillside eating when a squadron of German bombers roared down the valley. The American encampment was full of men and horses, with a wooden road right down the middle, making for easy targets as the planes dropped their payloads. A storm of fire and explosions tore through the encampment, and bombs lit up the camp. One landed squarely on top of the kitchen that Higgie had just left, killing all the cooks and some horses. Men scattered everywhere, trying to escape the bombs, but there was nowhere to run or hide. Higgie hugged the ground, praying that no bombs would fall on him. As he looked up to the sky, a lone American plane banked and bucked overhead, chasing one of the German bombers to the ground. The air raid was the worst thing Higgie had been through so far.

A few miles to the west of Montfaucon, Jabine had crawled into a dugout near Charpentry to sleep. The battle had ripped apart the world around them as they waded through a stew of fire and rain and gas. Whole days had gone by without sleep. Over six days that were never fully light and nights that were never fully dark, the men had charged northward in pursuit of the Germans. For one night, at least, he could rest. Five other officers from Company C and a first lieutenant from the Medical Corps packed into the dugout with Jabine. Exhausted from the strain of battle, all seven men — Company C's entire officer corps — had collapsed side by side in the bunker. Confident enough in the American gains, they fell deep asleep without wearing their masks.

As they slept, bombs began to fall. Jabine was likely asleep at 2:00 a.m. when the whistle of incoming artillery split the air overhead, or perhaps the sound jolted him awake. A gas shell landed in the dugout doorway, the fuse popped, and its payload exploded into the cramped confines of the bunker, enveloping Jabine and the other officers in a choking cloud of mustard gas. As earth and rocks showered around Jabine, none of the officers got their masks on in time. Within a few days, four of the men would be dead from the gas, but Jabine would survive to see the end of the war, severely gassed but alive.

The gas troops had done a fine job, General Fries concluded with satisfaction. After daylight broke and the dense fog lifted on the first day of the drive, he had motored up to the First, Third, and Fifth Corps headquarters near Verdun. From there, he went closer to the trenches that the Germans had abandoned that morning. In 1916, the Germans and the French had both suffered more than three hundred thousand casualties in the ten-month Battle of Verdun, a grinding, eviscerating tug-of-war over the blood-soaked land where Fries now stood. What a difference a day made. What had been no-man's-land before daybreak was Allied territory by sunup, pocked with shell holes and strewn with the shattered remnants of the German defenses.

The chief could hear the crack and roar of the American artillery a few miles to the north, like a fast-moving thunderstorm rumbling into the distance. The fight was still going on—as he stood just behind the lines, he watched a burning observation balloon gutter to earth like a falling comet while the spotter parachuted to safety. The only Germans he saw were prisoners—a thousand of them, dispirited men drained of their will to fight. Fries couldn't understand it; the Germans were barely fighting back. Either they didn't have the strength to fight anymore, or they were retreating to regroup and counterattack. When they did fight, the Germans used very little gas. That made Fries suspicious. Perhaps they were running low and conserving what little they had left to spring a surprise after they retrenched and turned to face their pursuers. He would know soon enough. For now, the first day of the offensive had been a marvelous success. "We have had very few casualties today, but the Bosche may fight more tomorrow," he wrote home.

Fries returned to First Army headquarters, then general headquarters the day after that. He had a fine night's rest and spent part of a day straightening out problems at Hanlon Field. The dismal drenching rain that had fallen for days finally let up, and the weather turned cool and cloudy. He would return to the front again soon, though never close enough to be in any peril, he assured Bessie in his letters home. Every day, the papers carried more positive news—Bulgaria had had all the lead and shrapnel she could take. "Good," Fries wrote home to Bessie. "The war looks better every day but I am not setting forward my peace date yet."

The Americans were paying a heavy price in casualties, including in the First Gas Regiment. In the first two days of the drive, three enlisted men died in the fighting, and sixty-three were injured, most of them from gas. In the second week, there were seventy-two casualties, with one dead. The mustard shell that landed at the mouth of the Company C dugout where Tom Jabine had been sleeping had wiped out the company's entire officer corps. "Severe casualties have been sustained by the Regiment during the progress of the present offensive. The majority of these have been caused by enemy gas shelling. 'A' and 'C' Companies have suffered most… and 'C' Company in particular," read the weekly regimental report for October 5. "While 'C' Company officers were at their headquarters, established in a dugout in the forward area, a large calibre mustard gas shell exploded at the entrance, all became casualties, and were evacuated."

Fries had another problem. Some corps commanders were refusing to use the gas troops, fearing that deployed chemicals would wound or kill their own soldiers. And when corps commanders were assigned operations that involved gas platoons, they were sometimes resentful that their infantry units were coupled with the gas regiment. The biggest rupture came on the first day of the offensive, with Company F. Assigned to the Eightieth Division at

Béthincourt, Company F was instructed to lay a smoke screen to cover the infantry assault and fire thermite shells in a counterattack. The after-action reports indicated they did all of these things and more, including rooting out machine-gun nests, rescuing wounded infantrymen, and taking prisoners.

Infantry commanders, though, reported their performance on the battlefield very differently. Four infantry officers complained bitterly to their commander that gas platoons from Company F didn't follow instructions, failed to keep up with the infantry, or were absent altogether during the fighting. The regimental reports were so completely at odds with what the officers reported on the ground that one commanding general wondered if the official reports had been fabricated. In mid-October, the assistant chief of staff asked the commanding general of the Eightieth Division, Major General H. D. Sturgis, for his thoughts on the gas regiment. In turn, Sturgis sought comments from the infantry commanders who had gas detachments from Company F. But the men still had a war to fight. The inquiry had to wait.

On the night of the October 2 bombing raid over Montfaucon, Fries thrashed in bed, plagued with nightmares. He was hot and feverish, and sick with the flu once again, perhaps infected by one of his officers. The doctor ordered him to stay in bed. When he didn't improve, the doctor suggested recuperation on the Mediterranean coast. The doctor recommended three weeks of rest, but Fries doubted that he could be gone for so long. He had another interallied gas conference on October 25 in Paris and he was sure that the war would grind on through winter.

He left for the French Riviera on October 12 in his purring eight-cylinder car. En route to the seashore, he kept careful watch over the progress in the war. "The Bosche still retires but burns as he goes," he wrote home in a letter he posted from Combronde. "I suppose by the time I get back from this trip we can judge as to how near peace is." The day after Fries departed for the Riviera, Germany offered to negotiate a peace agreement that would end the war. Two days later President Wilson rejected the kaiser's offer. There would be no peace terms. The war would only end when Germany surrendered unconditionally. There would be no pause in the fighting, no lull in weapons production, and no halt to gas warfare. The fighting would go on.

Inside the man-test chamber at American University, Carlos Isaac Reed sat at a table reading, shirtless, as an electric fan dispersed a plume of diluted mustard gas vapor through the chamber. He tried to relax and focus on the book he had brought with him. Faces peered at him through a glass window, watching him and a second shirtless soldier in the sealed-up box. Reed had been in the man-test house many times before, but never inside the gas chamber without a shirt or a gas mask.

It was October when the thirty-one-year-old physiologist stripped down to his waist inside the man-test house. He was surrounded by stationary bicycles and gas mask stations and a poster on the wall that read ARE YOU AMERICAN ENOUGH? PROVE IT! BUY U.S. LIBERTY BONDS. He left on his khaki pants and boots, but his chest, arms, and face would be an experimental canvas for the test he was about to undergo.

Reed was a handsome specimen, with hazel eyes, a dimple in his chin, and a head of kinky hair that earned him the nickname "Curly" at Ohio State University. Reed had been at American University since July. He received his commission in September, promoted to officer status along with many of the other scientists and chemists at the station.

The title of the test that day was the Minimum Concentration of Mustard Gas Effective for Man. Hundreds of dogs and other animals had died during tests of mustard, but even so late in the war, there had never been controlled tests for toxicological effects of mustard gas on men. The purpose of the experiment was to determine the smallest amount of mustard that would incapacitate a man and knock him off the battlefield. Reed was both in charge of the experiment and its subject. It's unclear how he ended up as lab rat in his own test. Perhaps a superior officer like Eli Marshall, who headed the pharmacological division, ordered Reed to step into the chamber. Perhaps Reed volunteered out of a sense of patriotism and solidarity with other test subjects who were to follow in his steps. Perhaps he felt he had no choice.

The door closed and sealed behind Reed and the other soldier. The room was empty except for a table and chairs. The test began with the rush of air. An electric fan dispersed a weak mixture of dichloroethyl sulfide diluted with alcohol, just 0.0012 milligram per liter, a ratio of slightly less than 1 part mustard to 5 million parts air; a concentration of 0.008 milligram was deadly to animals after an eight-hour exposure. Through the chamber's glass window, Reed's audience would have been watching him closely. There was nothing to do but pace back and forth or sit at the table, reading, as mustard flooded the tiny room.

The minutes ticked by. Periodically, Reed checked the time and recorded his pulse and his breathing rate—normal so far. After three minutes, the mustard odor disappeared as the gas deadened Reed's sense of smell. Five minutes later, the other soldier said he had lost his sense of smell as well. Reed began to feel irritation in his nostrils and nasal cavities. After another twelve minutes, Reed's anxious companion asked to leave and was let out of the chamber. Reed stayed. After twenty-five minutes, his voice changed, sounding husky as if he were breathing in heavy dust. His eyelids felt heavy. He stayed another twenty minutes, then called it quits.

Once he was out of the chamber, the observation began. Hour after hour, doctors checked on Reed, recording his vitals and asking how he felt. A little more than five hours after he stepped out of the box, blindness began to set in. Light caused searing pain, and he lay in the dark with doctors hovering over him, increasingly indistinct and blurry until he could see nothing at all. Over the hours, his eyelids swelled shut and oozed liquid. Sleep was impossible, and for more than a day, he tossed in bed, nose burning and inflamed. By the end of the third day, his upper body began to itch intolerably, and his skin between his neck and waist turned bright red. An old scar from a previous chemical burn grew inflamed. Then, after seven days, the skin on his face and chest began to peel off.

The experiment was the first of its kind at American University, but it wasn't the last. In a series of experiments that followed, at least twenty-two men were exposed to mustard in the same way, most of them with lesser concentrations than Reed. At the next meeting of the Medical Advisory Board, Reed's report was one of nearly a dozen experiments that the doctors discussed. Another report presented after Reid's was titled *Individual Variation in Susceptibility to Mustard Gas V (The Susceptibility of Negroes).* The two-page report documented skin tests on eighty-four black men at American University to determine whether the skin of black soldiers was more or less sensitive to mustard than white soldiers'. The Medical Division concluded that the skin of black soldiers was more resistant to mustard than that of white soldiers. As the doctors discussed the reports, one remarked how as a practical matter, it made sense for men who were less sensitive to mustard's effects to work in jobs where exposure was expected. They went on to talk about the possibility of testing other racial groups as well, such as people from China or the Philippines.

The medical research, like the service's technical work, had expanded far beyond its modest beginnings at Yale. Thousands of soldiers had their skin burned and blistered, wore gas masks for hours on end, put on gas-defense suits, boots, and gloves to test how well they protected from chemicals, and smeared protective pastes and salves on their skin before being exposed to chemicals. As with everything in the service, the medical research was shrouded in secrecy. Anyone connected to the medical research was forbidden from publishing or presenting their research at conferences. The doctors had even written to the army's Military Intelligence Division asking for censorship of civilian medical papers related to chemical warfare. The Camp Leach surgeon, wondering why so many test subjects were arriving at his infirmary, wrote to the surgeon general asking if such experiments were authorized. The chief of the Medical Corps assured him that they were.

Now in fall of 1918, the doctors were preparing for a new kind of test. Yandell Henderson wanted large-scale man tests for the new "fighting mask" that the Gas Defense Plant in Long Island City was making. The clumsy start to the Research Division's gas mask effort was a thing of the past; the service now had an effective and well-engineered model, a variation on the French Tissot make. The improved American version was lighter and fit far better than the clumsy and uncomfortable British respirator. Production had begun in August, and soon the Gas Defense Plant would be assembling tens of thousands of them each day for U.S. troops. In the tests Henderson envisioned, soldiers wearing the masks would run for miles to replicate the exertion of masked soldiers on the battlefield. Still another improved version of the Tissot was in the works, so comfortable that soldiers could wear them indefinitely, even in their sleep. The service planned to make a million per month.

But there was a problem—there wasn't enough carbon for all the filters. The gas mask division had long ago found that the very best carbon for the canisters came from peach, plum, cherry, and olive pits, as well as from the shells of various nuts, such as walnuts, butternuts, and coconut shells. The army had a huge operation collecting shells from overseas, but getting the material to the United States was excruciatingly slow. Britain, meanwhile, had ordered fifty tons of carbon from the United States, then doubled the order to one hundred tons.

To meet the demand, the War Department needed a dependable source of shells and pits to make into carbon. Their solution was to mobilize civilians across the country to collect the materials for them. Since the war's earliest days, millions of Americans had enthusiastically supported the war effort, from buying liberty bonds to sending care packages to soldiers. They suffered through heatless Mondays to conserve coal, and meatless Tuesdays and wheatless Wednesdays to conserve food. But the nut and shell drive represented the first time the Chemical Warfare Service directly asked for help from the people of the United States.

Across the country, the army urged citizens to collect fruit pits and nutshells and deliver them to drop-off spots for the war effort. "Its meaning is that every man, woman and child can help our brave soldiers beat German poison gas. It means that fathers and mothers can help make their boys' lives safe as they go over the top in a cloud of deadly gas to meet the Hun," a publicity sheet read. Red Cross chapters would be the principal agents for collecting and delivering the shells and pits, with help from civic groups and the Boy Scouts. After barrels outside of grocery stores and fire stations and ice cream shops filled up, the day that the drive came to an end—Saturday, November 9—would be called Gas Mask Day.

The War Department printed thousands of public relations brochures and leaflets and deployed soldiers to make presentations at public meetings, movie theaters, and high schools, toting gas masks for demonstrations. Fact sheets were printed up with talking points, such as the fact that the army needed five hundred tons of shells daily, that two hundred peach pits created enough carbon for a single gas mask, and that the Gas Defense Plant had gone from thirty civilian employees in December 1917 to nearly ten thousand in September of 1918.

Over the weeks that followed the War Department appeal, articles appeared across the country, from tiny town gazettes to broadsheets in major cities. There was a ripple effect of secondary publicity, as local officials and county commissioners sent out circulars to school students and teachers, and local businesses bought ads in the papers, too. "Will you help?" the D. M. Read Company in Bridgeport, Connecticut, asked its customers. "Clean stones nicely and bring them to the store. They will be forwarded to the Chemical Warfare Service, U.S.A."

The collected shells and nuts would be shipped to New York for processing at the Gas Defense Plant. From there, the carbon would be sent to England or packed into respirator canisters and assembled into masks for American soldiers. "Let pleasure or business stop just long enough to do this important service," an army-written publicity article implored. "Gas Mask Day—what will be the results? It is a challenge. The savagery of the Hun is brought to every American door. How will it be met?"

The Mousetrap had a looming deadline, too, but its schedule was a secret too sensitive to even whisper. Under Conant's schedule, lewisite production was to start by November 15.

Earlier that fall, plans to build barracks and mess halls for five hundred men needed to be redrawn in midconstruction to accommodate the eleven hundred men that were now slated to fill the facility. In late September, hundreds more workers arrived. The supervisor at the commissary of a nearby army camp came with two trucks full of kitchen equipment, and the army began canvassing the town for additional sleeping quarters for the men, such as the local telephone company building and even the town hall.

In early October, the contractor finished the first barracks and mess hall, completed with record speed. Work soon began on a forty-eight-bed hospital. Frenzied construction filled the property as the contractor erected a storage building on the compound's north side, along with sheds, a transformer house, and a garage. The New York Central Railroad completed two rail sidings, one on either side of the plant, to at last allow materials to be brought directly to Ben-Hur by train. Vast amounts of equipment, materials, and supplies began to pour into the plant.

It was fall, and around the Ben-Hur stockade, the leaves turned shades of gold and red. For soldiers like Nate Simpson, the new barracks were surely a welcome addition, and the mess hall meant the men no longer made the hungry march down to the Willoughby Inn in front of curious townspeople and shop owners.

With the additions to the property came constant reminders of the dangers the men faced. Gas alarms sounded periodically, and leaks triggered the Klaxon horns. Sometimes they were drills, sometimes they were real, but every time, the soldiers reached for their masks. Simpson's circle of friends, the ones he called the Nifty Nine and Briggs, had become a tight-knit group since the day they all left the Cleveland YMCA together. The ten were from all over the country, each with his own distinctive regional accent, including one from Louisiana with a thick drawl. One of the ten requested duties that didn't involve making poison gas—probably out of religious conviction—and was assigned to the kitchen, where he cooked steaks to perfection.

Though the men were driven to the point of exhaustion, there were opportunities to get out of the compound. The townspeople invited soldiers for home-cooked meals; Simpson and the rest of the Nifty Nine got one of those invitations and descended on the family for dinner. Another time, when Simpson and a friend wandered through Willoughby peering into shopwindows on a Sunday, a store owner and his wife asked if they wanted an automobile tour of the area. They turned out to be Mormons trying to convert the men.

The days flowed past in a blur. On November 1, the pieces were in place. All of the station's buildings were complete. One of the two precursor chemicals was on hand in sufficient quantity to begin mass production, and the plant for the second precursor was almost finished. The lewisite factory was ready ahead of schedule.

What happened in Willoughby over the final days of October and the beginning of November 1918 was a closely kept secret of the war, one that a century later remains shrouded in mystery. It's not clear precisely when production began, but at some point, the Ben-Hur lewisite plant came to life. The building filled with the sound of purring water pumps and the compressors on the refriger-ation units. The ventilation fans roared, the agitator motors hummed as they stirred the kettles of lewisite, engine belts slapped overhead, and heating steam hissed as it vented from escape valves. After the collection kettles filled with viscous liquid, masked soldiers swad-dled in gas-defense suits slowly and carefully drained the liquid into fifty-five-gallon drums.

Reports of the exact quantity of lewisite made at Willoughby varied wildly after the war. One account claimed that the plant generated 150 tons, and Amos Fries wrote in a 1921 letter that "we were starting to make ten tons per day of lewisite" after the plant was complete. Records suggest that the factory produced much less: only a single batch of 17,300 pounds—or 8.65 tons—that filled twenty-two steel drums weighing 19,544 pounds when full, a first batch of the new gas that would be sprung upon the Germans in 1919.

Willoughby wasn't the only chemical warfare outpost that kicked into production in the waning days of October. Like water through sluice gates of a dam, a river of chemical weapons streamed out of American gas factories. In Niagara Falls, the phosgene plant at the Oldbury Electro-Chemical Company roared at full capacity, generating ten tons each day. Two units at Edgewood were making 10 tons or more of phosgene per day, with additional plants there expected to boost that output to 80 tons per day by January 1. The refurbished factories at Edgewood using the improved British for-mula produced 17 tons of mustard per day; Dow Chemical's mus-tard plants in Midland, Michigan, added 3 to 4 tons of mustard daily. The American Synthetic Color Company in Stamford, Con-necticut, was churning out 15 tons of chloropicrin each day, with Edgewood producing another 15 tons.

When all of the plants were at full capacity, the service expected to make 900 tons of mustard per month; 1,050 tons of phosgene; 1,500 tons of chloropicrin; 895 tons of chlorine and lewisite. Shell-filling plants could fill 2.4 million 77-millimeter shells per month;

450,000 7.4-inch shells; 540,000 155-millimeter shells; 750,000 gas grenades; 480,000 smoke grenades; and 30,000 Livens drums. After America's slow start, its capacity for gas warfare was greater than that of all its allies combined, and more even than Germany's.

Before the weapons could be loaded onto ships, they needed to get safely to port. Moving explosives or poison gas on the nation's rail lines demanded a carefully choreographed plan. The U.S. Railroad Administration, which President Wilson created when he nationalized the country's rail system earlier in 1918, required special gas trains outfitted according to rigorous new safety regulations. Armed guards with gas masks accompanied the freight, the tracks ahead and behind were cleared of other trains, and the trains moved slowly on carefully synchronized schedules so they could travel unimpeded.

On November 9, an officer in charge of transportation drew up a list of all of the weapons awaiting shipment overseas. There were 125,000 artillery shells packed with mustard, 125,000 chloropicrin-filled shells, 125,000 gas grenades, and 500 Livens drums, all ready for shipment.

Once the chemicals reached port, they were loaded onto ships outfitted for gas cargo per Sibert's instructions. The USS *Isabella* was finished on November 5. Work on the USS *Munwood* would be done November 10. And the USS *Elinor* would be ready to sail on November 15.

The *Elinor* had been docked in Baltimore since September 17 after a three-week passage from France. The forty-three-hundred-ton freighter was christened the *General de Castelnau* after she rolled off the dry docks in Baltimore, then was commissioned by the U.S. Navy for wartime service and renamed in March of 1918. The officer in charge, Lieutenant Commander Carl H. Anderson, had joined the crew of about ninety men in June and had been on the *Elinor* for two transatlantic voyages. Black-and-white camouflage striped her hull, curled over the bridge, and ringed the smokestack. Since the ship had docked at Baltimore, stevedores had been loading up the ship with hundreds of pounds of fish, beef, bread, and other provisions for her next voyage.

While she was docked, workmen outfitted the ship to carry chemical weapons, installing ventilation fans that sat atop the deck and exhaust ducts leading to the rear of the ship to fumigate toxic vapors from the hold in case there was a leak or a spill. On November 8, after the cargo boom and the holds had been inspected, the ship's freight began coming aboard. There were 144 gas masks for the crew, along with about 160,000 pieces of ordnance: 125,000 gas shells and 11,700 Livens drums in the holds below and 25,000 gas shells aboveboard on deck, ready for delivery to France.

Chapter Fifteen

"War to the Knife"

After a four-hour ride to the town of Romagne-sous-Montfaucon on October 27, Higgie's platoon jumped down from their truck as shells began to rain onto the village. Higgie ran for cover as artillery thundered all around them and the streets filled with sneezing gas. They finally found a dugout and squeezed inside when a shell landed outside the doorway. The blast roared in through the entrance, a shard injuring Higgie's lieutenant in the head. Higgie was all right, but they couldn't stay in the dugout, and their orders were to remain overnight in the town. He scurried through the ruined streets until the platoon found another crowded dugout with barely any room. Higgie squeezed into a corner and propped himself upright against some stairs, where he dozed until dawn.

When morning finally came, they hunted for a better shelter. They discovered a grubby dugout they cleaned up as best they could, clearing out the dirt and rubble and hauling in a small stove. The next day, they found abandoned machine guns and set them up behind the billet. When they were bored, they spent idle hours firing at German planes. Propaganda leaflets fluttered down around them, urging surrender. After lunch on October 31, Higgie and Shap went up to their position to set their Stokes mortars. It was a month into the Battle of the Meuse-Argonne, and the next phase of the offensive was starting on November 1. Company B's job was to set a smoke screen for the Eighty-Ninth Division infantry. It was a rough hike through heavy artillery fire; one of Higgie's friends was killed on the way back. When they returned to the billet, they spent the afternoon in their improvised machine-gun nest behind the dugout, spitting bullets skyward in an angry refrain.

That night, Higgie had been asleep only a few hours when someone shook him awake. Night was for fighting, a sodden cloak for an army of muddy ghosts fumbling with guns and gas masks and mortars in the mist and smoke. Around midnight, the platoon clambered up into a truck and headed toward the line, following a sunken road pocked with shell craters. The truck bounced along the torn-up road. Swaying and jolting in the back, Higgie and the other men heard artillery all around. The truck came across a crater where a shell had just landed on top of an infantry unit, killing several men. A stretcher-bearer in the truck with Higgie cracked at the sight, hysterical with fear. They sent him back behind the lines, to safety, and the truck continued on through the storm of artillery fire around them. There was no place for the men who lost their nerve as death stared them in the eye.

When Higgie reached his position, he reseated his mortar before zero hour at 5:30 a.m. Stokes mortars fired to his right, and bursting shells showered the German lines with thermite, streaks of liquid metal searing the night sky. The Germans fired back. As Higgie watched, shells fell on Company F's guns and killed an entire gun team of five men right before his eyes. At 3:30 a.m., the American artillery opened up with a bellow and a deafening chatter of machine guns. It was the heaviest barrage Higgie had ever heard. So many shells were going up that Higgie wondered if a German raiding party had come over the top at them. A dithering sergeant named Earl H. Bailey had replaced the injured lieutenant. As zero hour approached for the firing of the smoke shells, Bailey was so nervous that he scarcely knew what to do. Higgie had to yell instructions at him through the roar of the guns.

At zero hour, the show went off without a hitch. Higgie fired the guns; other men in the platoon watched the angle to make sure the mortars were shooting at the right trajectory. After the show, Higgie and his platoon took cover for a few minutes. As the firefight thundered around them, Sergeant Bailey was paralyzed with indecision, unsure of whether the men should shelter in place or move. German shells were falling behind them. Higgie knew from experience that the barrage would soon creep toward their position. *We better get moving,* Higgie yelled through the noise, and they did. Soon after they vacated the trench, bombs fell directly on it.

They sprinted away from the lines as fast as they could, toward the Romagne road. Clouds of sneezing gas filled the woods. The gas seeped through the filters and made the masks impossible to wear, so Higgie and the others left them off, praying that nothing more deadly—mustard or phosgene—was mixed in. When the platoon reached the sunken road, they lay down in some shell holes to rest.

Higgie was still trying to catch his breath when a shell whistled directly toward him through the mist and gas. Private First Class John Bleight, a stout farmer's son from Florida who had marched out of American University with Higgie, hugged the ground in the crater beside Higgie's when the shell detonated. A shell fragment whizzed into the back of Bleight's skull and killed him instantly.

Higgie and the rest of the fellows straggled back to Romagne, ate some breakfast, and then went to bed, exhausted. He slept until noon. It was a misty, overcast day. For once, no airplanes muttered overhead. The seventy-fives and the other big guns fired all through the day. Thousands of German prisoners streamed back from the Allied lines. Trucks loaded with ammunition and supplies crowded the road through Romagne, following the advancing infantry northward. Higgie wasn't prone to emotion, but as he wrote in his diary, there was a sense of disbelief, even sadness, that Bleight's life had been snuffed out beside him while he had been spared.

When daylight came, some of the fellows returned to the sunken road to find and bury Bleight. Higgie stayed behind and chopped wood by himself until rain drove him inside. The AEF printed up a leaflet to circulate among the troops announcing that Austria, Bulgaria, and Turkey had all surrendered and that Romania had declared war on Germany as well. "Now is the time to strike and strike hard," the leaflet read.

"Another day ended and another enemy country out of the war for keeps," Fries wrote home to Bessie on November 4. Austria had signed a peace deal and surrendered, leaving Germany the only member of the Central powers still fighting. Fries had returned to Tours on a beautiful, warm autumn day. Toward evening, he went for a stroll with another officer, admiring the sunset before retiring to his quarters:

> It begins to look more than ever like the war [will] end this month. If it does not I imagine it will go on until next spring though I can't see how the Bosche will be so foolish for now he can't hope for even a poor draw. And also he knows that with the coming spring the bombing of his Rhine cities will make them absolutely uninhabitable.

From the Dutch border to the Ardennes, the Allies hammered at the Germans. After four years, French, British, and Belgian infantries had finally retaken much of Flanders, as well as occupied cities in northern France. With Kaiser Wilhelm's fortunes withering by the day, the war had become a diplomatic battle as well as a military battle. Facing near-certain defeat, the Germans were attempting to exit the war with the greatest dignity, gain the best peace terms, and avoid reparations for the carnage and destruction they had wrought across Europe.

As President Wilson awaited a response to his demand of unconditional surrender, newspapers reported the spread of riots throughout Germany and shortages of raw materials. Mobs roamed through Berlin, and when the kaiser addressed the Reichstag, socialists called for the abolition of the monarchy and establishment of a democratic republic. One of the most powerful men in the German army, First Quartermaster General Erich Ludendorff, had resigned on October 27. But despite signs that the war was nearing its end, there were no guarantees. An unnamed German diplomat told the *New York Times* that his country had nothing to gain and everything to lose by surrendering. "It is war to the knife now. Germany can fight another five months, and we must take a last chance."

Pershing had unsheathed his knife for mortal combat as well, unwilling to wait for diplomatic efforts to bear fruit. The First Army had made gains in the first phase of the Argonne offensive, as the British and the French had to the north, but the advance had been slower in October. Now the new stage of the offensive that began on November 1 was turning into a rout, the kaiser's demoralized Third and Fifth Armies barely able to fight back. As in the earlier phases of the offensive, the Hellfire Boys would shoot thermite and gas, but one of their most significant roles was throwing smoke screens to obscure American infantrymen as they forded the Meuse River. "I expect to see some very hard fighting during the next week as the Bosche will drive them back if he possibly can, and he can't," Fries wrote home.

General Fries felt steady and strong, in fighting form. His convalescence on the Riviera had provided a restful interlude of sightseeing, golf, and seaside promenades. But even in his luxurious surroundings, his thoughts had never strayed from the war, and he scanned the newspapers each morning and updated his war maps. Despite his doctor's recommendation of three weeks of rest, Fries departed after two to attend a third interallied gas conference in Paris. A bit of vanity also lured him back: he got word that he was to receive the French Legion of Honor. It wasn't specific to him— the chief of every country's gas service at the conference was to receive one—but he felt honored nonetheless and duty bound to be present. He tinkered with an acceptance speech, in case he was asked to say a few words.

After a week at the Paris conference, he resumed his busy schedule, returning to Tours for meetings with officers that General Sibert had sent over from the United States. He respected Sibert, but he still had a somewhat disdainful view of the American side of the operation. "The work over there is nowhere so nearly organized as over here and there are jealousies and some bickerings over there that are entirely foreign to us over here," Fries wrote to Bessie.

With the war's end now in sight—perhaps a week away, perhaps a month, but inevitable—he had begun to fret about the future of the service. He professed not to care what happened next—"All I want is to finish this war with a fine service and the rest can go hang"—but in truth he wanted to lead the service himself, or at least be Sibert's second-in-command. The worst thing would be if it was absorbed into another branch or taken over by a newcomer.

On November 6, Fries returned to Paris in a torrential rain. As his Cadillac wound through the streets, Fries saw that the city was coming alive. The long-dark streetlamps were ablaze once again. Taxis and autos clogged the roads. Pedestrians filled the sidewalks, no longer concerned about Germany's long-range cannons. "The Bosche is quite on the run," Fries wrote, before heading out to a celebratory dinner with officers from the service.

The next day, he left for First Army headquarters, and then on to territory that the American troops had retaken. The destruction at Montfaucon stunned him, the worst mess of churned-up earth and ruins he had ever seen. In a bit of battlefield tourism, he ducked into the German crown prince's bunker to admire the elaborate concrete shelter and went to Verdun on November 9. Shells fell nearby, but he paid them no mind. "I believe the Bosche is going to give up. But we are going right on as though he were not. The Gas work is going well and a little better all the time," he wrote. "We have had to convince the army that we knew our business and had a real live means of helping to win the war. And we have succeeded."

Celebration was in the air at American University, too, as couples streamed through the experiment station gates on the night of November 5. It was a crisp autumn evening. Unlike the previous dance at Catholic University, this one was in a warehouse inside the fenced compound. Couples strolled past the sentries, admiring the fall-themed decorations of bundled cornstalks, wheat sheaves, and pumpkin pyramids. For the first time, outsiders who weren't part of the Research Division were allowed inside the gates to attend. Colonel Burrell couldn't attend, so another chemist, Dr. Arthur Lamb of Harvard, served as master of ceremonies. The orchestra played numerous encores, and Dr. Lamb danced so frequently that the men were sure he took a turn with every woman present. There was even alcohol-spiked punch—weak but wet all the same—that was gone by 10:00 p.m.

There was plenty to be cheerful about. The *Washington Times* splashed "Allies Attack on 150-Mile Front" across its front page, and the *Washington Post* carried the terms of the deal offered without negotiation to Germany, as well as the details of the armistice with Austria, breaking up the empire into five new countries and dismantling its military.

It was also a historic Election Day, with women voting for the first time in New York and control of Congress hanging in the balance. The *Washington Times* installed a massive searchlight atop a downtown building that would wigwag east to west if Democrats stayed in control of Congress and from north to south if Republicans prevailed. For good measure, the paper hired a pilot to fly over the city with the results: red lights on the plane meant Democrats won; green meant Republicans.

The night was a rare moment of openness at the experiment station, where visitors accompanying hill employees were allowed a glimpse of the gas alarms, the signs urging secrecy, the bomb pits. The station had not yet given up its secrets, but when the war was over, the chemists would reap recognition for their work, the *Retort* predicted.

Word of the chemical warfare work was already getting out into the press. Two days before the dance, one of the Washington papers published a lengthy article about the growth of the service. "In this thousands of chemists are employed making gases of various kinds and connected with it are great industrial establishments for manufacturing shells and containers and filling them with the liquids and solids which expand into gas when exploded," the paper reported. The article also included cryptic references to new, more lethal gases that the reporter wasn't at liberty to disclose. "As to our new combinations, I am not permitted to write."

On the night of the dance on November 5, one of Mustard Hill's biggest secrets was that the future of the American University Experiment Station was very much in doubt. Only the highest-ranking officers knew that the day before the dance the director of operations for the general staff, Major General Henry Jervey, had completed a sweeping review of the American University Experiment Station. He took into account the accident on August 3, the criticisms from the city board of commissioners and the Corps of Engineers. He concluded that "further use of the premises by the Chemical Warfare Service be discontinued except during such period as may be necessary to enable that Department to acquire a suitable location for carrying on its research and experimental work."

None of this was known to the men and women of the station. The hill football team, the Mustard Gassers, was still mopping up on the gridiron. Advanced chemistry classes for the soldiers were in full swing, and French classes were held every weekday night in room 22 of the College of History Building. Experiments continued, and so did whatever dry humor the men could glean from their work. "Fred is working on a new gas that is harmless in itself but deadly poison when combined with the vapor of limburger cheese. It is intended to be projected over the German lines," "Effie" wrote in "Why Soldiers Go Wild."

And then, on November 7, bedlam erupted across Washington and the whole country. Just before noon, a cablegram from the United Press in France arrived at the Western Union offices in New York City. Within minutes, a censor signed off on the cable. At noon, it was wired over to the United Press office at the Pulitzer Building. The agency then put out a news flash over the wire: "Urgent. Armistice. Allies Germany signed 11 smorning [*sic*]. Hostilities ceased two afternoon. Sedan taken by Americans."

The first edition of the afternoon *Washington Times* rolled off the press at 12:20 p.m. with the banner headline WAR IS OVER in huge type. Trying to push its competitive edge, the paper hired pilots to airdrop copies of the paper across the city. Celebrants filled Pennsylvania Avenue, with soldiers and sailors at the center. A din of sirens, horns, and signals blared from military posts through the city. Planes looped and circled overhead, and a group of post office employees propped an effigy of Kaiser Wilhelm atop a mail truck and thrashed the dummy as they drove through the streets. When night fell, Camp Leach and the other camps trained their searchlights skyward and raked the beams across the sky in celebration.

But the news was premature. A German delegation had indeed made its way to meet with the Allies that day, and a brief cessation of fighting allowed the Germans to pass through the Allied lines. The United Press apparently believed that the halt in combat signaled that an armistice had been signed. Why the government censor approved the telegram was a mystery and remained so long afterward. At 2:15 p.m., the State Department denied that an armistice had been signed, and the more circumspect *Evening Star* cautioned "Armistice NOT Signed," calling the telegram a "false report." Yet the United Press stood by its statement. Evening newspapers everywhere that carried the wire service—even those skeptical of the news—published it.

The next day, more crowds formed downtown. Parades of cars wound through the streets, sagging under the weight of flag-waving passengers hanging off the running boards. Musicians formed marching bands, and spontaneous choruses of "The Star-Spangled Banner" rang out.

The chaos must have been a noisy distraction for Secretary of War Newton Baker in his office across from the White House. He surely welcomed the tantalizing proximity of peace. Still, the war was not yet over, and he flatly rejected any de-escalation of war production until an armistice was signed. "Our policy is the same now as when the war was at its greatest height," he told reporters.

Quietly, though, he made clear in a letter that one area of war activity would be winding down. As crowds roiled through the streets, he made a decision to sharply curtail the work at the American University Experiment Station. Large-scale experiments would move to other, more remote locations, such as the new Chemical Warfare Service proving ground at Lakehurst, New Jersey. Research at American University would be confined to small-scale experiments and laboratory work. The commission "need have no apprehension as to the safety of the citizens living in the neighborhood of the American University Experiment Station," Baker wrote.

Back in April of 1917, the university trustees had eagerly asked to receive the "torch of war," so that the school might contribute to the war effort and help solidify its own fortunes. A year and a half later, that optimism had withered, and the school was at odds with the Chemical Warfare Service. The genie of science that the trustees had invited onto the hill, and the fire and smoke and poison that came with it, was no longer welcome. The short life of Mustard Hill was coming to an end.

Daylight was fading on November 8 as Higgie and his platoon started through the woods in the Argonne. Branches slapped their faces as they pushed through the undergrowth. Their packs were heavy, and it began to rain. There was no path, no road, just a compass guiding them in the dark. Whispers about an armistice had reached all the way to the front. "There was a rumor around today that peace had been declared," Higgie wrote in his journal. If there was any truth to it, he had yet to see it. Rumors of peace or no, Company B still had a show to carry out. Its next attack was some fifteen miles to the north, in an exposed spot across the Meuse River from where the Germans had withdrawn. The trucks had brought them partway, but shells were falling on the road, so the men had to get out of the open and hike undercover.

They waded across brooks and swamps and slithered down hills, cursing as they went. Some of the men kept asking the new lieutenant in charge where they were going. One man fell down twice and had trouble getting back up; the other men had to drag him to his feet. They found a road; the mud was knee deep. Arching German flares seemed to be directly overhead, and even though the men knew that the Meuse River lay between the armies, they wondered if they had somehow blundered into enemy territory. Water soaked through Higgie's boots and socks. When they finally stopped for the night, the undergrowth was so dense it was impossible to camp, so Higgie just rolled himself up in his tent as best he could and huddled on the hillside.

Higgie awoke the next morning in a pool of water. He jumped to his feet, cursing. Mud was everywhere, but at least in daylight they could see their positions and where they were going. He carried bombs up to the advance position, returned for coffee, then made another carry, sliding in the mud. More of the company joined them in carrying mortars up to the front. Higgie had begun to feel better—the hike had warmed him up, and he had found a swell place to camp that night, a spot nestled among trees felled by the Germans. Everyone was cold and wet and caked in mud, but at least Higgie had found a dry spot. When he went to bed, the air was so cold that he and another man kept warm by hugging each other all night.

When the frigid morning arrived, some of the men lit pieces of paper and tucked them into their frozen boots to thaw them out. Higgie made hot coffee and spread his blankets out to dry. Late that night, the 177th Brigade was going to ford the Meuse, and Higgie's company was to fire a smoke screen to draw fire away from the advancing infantry.

Elsewhere, the Hellfire Regiment had other shows. At 4:00 p.m., Company A shot phosgene at a machine-gun position, forcing the Germans to flee. That night, Company D fired thermite shells over German machine-gun positions about six miles north of Higgie and put up a smoke screen that allowed the Fourth Infantry to cross the Meuse. Higgie rolled himself up in blankets to sleep before the show late that night. But his show was canceled, the infantry forded the river without the smoke screen, and Higgie couldn't have been happier. He rolled himself back up in his blanket and went back to bed.

Higgie was dead asleep when a private named Charles Stemmerman shook him awake at 4:00 a.m. on November 11. Shells were falling again, and he wanted Higgie to take cover deeper in the forest. Their lieutenant and sergeant had already retreated into the woods. Higgie shrugged off the warning. If the shells got closer, he would move, he told the private. Then he rolled over and went back to sleep.

He awoke again around 8:00 a.m., several hours after Private Stemmerman had first woken him up. The early morning shell barrage had ended. In the light of morning, an impenetrable fog blanketed the forest, so dense that he couldn't see more than ten feet around him. He got up to make breakfast and prepared for the morning show, a mortar attack with thermite.

Then the lieutenant appeared through the mist with the best news Higgie had heard in a long time. All guns would stop firing at eleven o'clock. The Germans had agreed to the Armistice terms. The war had ended. Higgie thought in disbelief that maybe the lieutenant was joking. It seemed too good to be true. He rolled up his pack and retreated deeper into the woods, just to be on the safe side. They had gone through so much, had seen so many things that he would have thought impossible, that he wasn't going to take any chances now.

To the southeast, Tom Jabine's old Company C was preparing a thermite attack on a German battalion at Remoiville. Zero hour was 10:30 a.m. With fifteen minutes to go, the men saw movement across the line. The company watched warily as one hundred German soldiers stood up in plain view. As they got to their feet, they thrust their hands into their pockets—a gesture of surrender. An officer clambered up out of the German trench. The Americans watched as he crossed no-man's-land. The Armistice had been signed, the German officer said, and asked that the attack be canceled. Suspecting a trap, the Americans suspended the operation but held their positions, just in case. Minutes later, word arrived from the Eleventh Infantry. It was true: the Armistice had been signed. The war was over.

Hundreds of miles away, the sound of whistles and church bells reached Tom Jabine as he lay in his bed in the base hospital in Nantes where he had arrived a few days earlier. For days after the mustard shell detonated in the doorway of his dugout, he lay in a hospital bed in Langres, inflamed eyes swollen shut, throat and lungs burning. After a time, the bandages had come off, and he could finally see again. He still couldn't read, but even if he could, letters from home had not followed him to the field hospital. The army had not yet sent official word about his injuries, but after his letters home abruptly stopped, his family back in Yonkers must have feared the worst. In early November, the army transferred him to the base hospital in Nantes. Not a single letter had reached Tom since his injury. Jabine could walk, but his eyes still pained him, and it was difficult to write. More than three weeks after he was gassed, he had been finally able to pick up a pen and write a brief letter to his mother. "I got a slight dose of Fritz's gas which sent me to the hospital. It was in the battle of the Argonne Forest near Verdun. Well I have been in the hospital ever since and getting a little better every day."

When the pealing from the town spires reached his ears, he reached for pen and paper to write to his mother again. "The good news has come that the armistice has been signed and the fighting stopped. We all hope this means the end of the war and I guess it does. It is hard to believe it is true, but I for one am thankful it is so. When we came over I never expected to see this day so soon if I ever saw it at all," he wrote. Now, perhaps, he could rejoin his company and go home. "That seems too good to be true but I hope it won't be long."

Word reached Addison just after breakfast, when a major dashed in from corps headquarters with the news that the Germans had accepted the Armistice terms. "PEACE AT LAST!" the chaplain wrote in his diary. "The Happiest Day Mankind Ever Had!"

Amos Fries was at general headquarters in Chaumont when the news arrived. Later in the day, he drove into Paris in his Cadillac. Shells had fallen just days earlier; now the city erupted in celebration. After four years of bloodshed, euphoria spilled through the city. As Fries waited in his car, a young schoolgirl wearing a blue cape and a hood jumped up on the running board. She stuck her head in the open window and blurted to Fries with glee: *"La guerre est fini!"*—The war is over!—and then ran on. Of all the sights that day, that was the one Fries recounted in his letter home the next day. "Somehow that sight and those sweet childish words sum up more eloquently than any oration the feeling of France since yesterday at 11 am."

As the city roiled in jubilation, a splitting headache sent Fries to bed early. The festivities continued the next day; Fries celebrated with a golf game, then dinner in the evening. "Our war work is done, our reconstruction and peace work looms large ahead. When will I get home? When will we get home? is the question on the lips of hundreds of thousands."

Like the turn of the tide, the movement of the American army in the Argonne stopped and reversed, and the men of the gas regiment began retreating south. Hours earlier, the land Higgie walked on had been a shooting gallery in a firestorm. Now silence fell over the blasted countryside. For Higgie, the stillness was disquieting after months of earthshaking detonations. He still couldn't believe the end had come. The company loaded packs on a truck and started hiking to Nouart, about fourteen miles south. They arrived in the village at about five-thirty. Higgie went to bed not long after eating. He felt ill after days of unending stress and toil. But he couldn't sleep. As he lay in the dark with the quiet pressing in around him, he realized that he missed the noise of the guns.

He awoke in the morning to the same eerie stillness. After breakfast, he threw his rolled-up pack on a truck and began the twenty-mile hike back to Montfaucon. Everything seemed so different now as he retraced his steps. Everything was at a standstill. Nobody knew what to make of things. They arrived at Montfaucon after dark. The moon was bright and the air very cold with a fierce wind blowing. The men set up pup tents on the hilltop overlooking the valley. A month before, German planes had bombed the company as they camped in the same spot, scattering men and lighting up the encampment with bombs. For months, open fires had been forbidden at the front, to keep the troops invisible in the dark. Now, as Higgie sat on the moonlit hilltop, hundreds of campfires blazed in the valley below.

Across the Chemical Warfare Service, laboratories, factories, proving grounds, and shell-filling plants had all been in a nonstop sprint. The service had produced almost 11,000 tons of war gases; about 8,800 tons of which were chlorine, chloropicrin, phosgene, mustard, and lewisite. About 915 tons had been shipped to France, contained in about 868,000 Livens drums, grenades, and seventy-five-millimeter shells. The very first batch of helium had been pumped into 750 tanks that sat on the docks in New Orleans, awaiting shipment to France. The plants at Bound Brook, Niagara

Falls, Hastings-on-Hudson, and Edgewood were churning out tons of gas a day, and the lewisite plant in Willoughby had been primed and was ready for operation. The factory in Saltville, Virginia, was almost complete, too, and the new American fighting mask was in production in Astoria. Tons of fruit pits and nutshells had been collected for gas masks.

Then, as if a light switch had been flipped, the war ended. Across the service, thousands of men and women waited for word on what was to become of them. In the days that followed, technical committees convened as scheduled, their participants ordered to arrive promptly as usual and proceeding without even a mention of what had taken place; in others, officers wondered what they were expected to do now that long-sought peace had arrived.

The question hovering over Sibert and the service was whether chemical warfare would even exist after the completion of the peace deal. The heads of state would gather in Paris in the spring to deliberate over Europe's future, its borders, and how to prevent the Continent from collapsing back into war. They would also take up the question of limiting arms, chemical weapons among them. It was an open question as to whether the assembled nations would reinstate the prohibitions on gas warfare that Germany had broken in 1915.

Such questions didn't trouble the overjoyed men and women of the Research Division, who held a jubilant celebration on November 18 at a downtown Washington hall. Colonel Burrell announced a major reduction in staff in the *Retort*. While a sizable staff would remain on the hill for many months, a general demobilization would quickly reduce the division across all areas—clerical, technical, laborers, janitors, and so on. "The writer wishes those of you who are about to leave God-speed and best wishes," Burrell wrote.

In Willoughby, too, the breakneck work stopped. On November 11, Nate Simpson had been in his barracks when a friend shouted to him to look out the Mousetrap window. The window had a view of the barbed-wire stockade around the plant and the fields beyond. "There is a girl running across the field and waving her arms like crazy!" the friend yelled. The girl flailing her arms on that midautumn day meant the men of the Mousetrap would be going home.

Rules and restrictions muzzling Simpson and the rest of the men fell away. Mail censorship ended. The men could finally board the trolley to Cleveland, which had been off-limits. The YMCA set up shop in a mess hall, where they put in a movie projector, athletic equipment, and other diversions to occupy the idle men. While operations didn't stop completely, they slowed to a crawl as the men awaited word for what was to come next.

The work of the Mousetrap was already the stuff of legend among the handful of chemists who knew what had taken place behind its fence. To the public, however, the Ben-Hur plant was still a mystery, huffing bilious odors and exuding an air of secrecy. On Thanksgiving Day, the *Cleveland Plain Dealer* newspaper rolled out a front-page scoop on lewisite: "City Provides Most Deadly Gas for War."

"The most terrible weapon ever forged by man has been placed at the disposal of the United States by American chemists. And it may well be labeled 'Made in Cleveland,'" the article began. Though parochial and vague, the article set the tone for subsequent reporting on lewisite. The article claimed that it was seventy-two times more deadly than mustard, giving it an almost mystical lethality. Adding to lewisite's sorcerous aura, the plant had risen "like magic" in just six months. The men laboring within had superhuman endurance—they had "practically been prisoners within the barbed-wire fence, closely guarded, that surrounds the plant," working twenty-three-hour shifts.

Several photographs accompanied the article, including one of James Bryant Conant, looking like a solemn schoolboy with his thatch of hair and owlish spectacles. The word "lewisite" didn't actually appear in the article, nor did the name "Winford Lee Lewis"; instead, the article called the gas "methyl," the code name the scientists chose because it had no connection to lewisite's actual ingredients or characteristics.

The *Willoughby Republican,* which long ago had been promised an exclusive, had been scooped. The day after Thanksgiving, the *Republican* published its own story: "Here Is the Big Story of the Great Work of the Soldiers Who Have Been Stationed in Our Midst." In a morose companion piece, the editors explained that the paper had kept details of the plant secret in exchange for a promise of an exclusive. "We are presenting the story herewith, even with its publication in the *Plain Dealer,* but not, as we had hoped, in Willoughby first."

Harvard professor Elmer Kohler, one of the first men that Manning called upon to assist with the research, congratulated his former pupil Conant just before Christmas, writing that he had heard about the "magnificent success of the Willoughby operation" when he arrived from France a few days earlier. Everyone he had spoken with had credited Conant with being "the absolute boss on the job to which the success was largely due," Kohler wrote.

Major Conant returned to Boston for leave beginning on December 7. Colonel Dorsey extended his leave three times, giving the exhausted architect of the Mousetrap most of December to recuperate after the frenetic race in Willoughby. The army discharged Conant two days after the end of his holiday leave, on January 11. At least two job offers rolled in in quick succession — one from B.F. Goodrich, another from the University of Chicago — both of which he turned down so that he could return to his alma mater, Harvard, where he would take up teaching once again in March.

Simpson was among the men in Willoughby who cheered when an officer posted a list of the first 100 men to be discharged. Another 250 were scheduled to depart soon after, leaving several hundred to attend to the work of shutting down the plant. All of the men who remained expected to leave by the end of January.

Simpson departed on December 16. He went first to Camp Sherman and then home to Philadelphia after his discharge. Years later, he was sanguine when he wrote about his role at Willoughby. For every soldier in the trenches, ten men like him were needed on the home front. They didn't question the work they were doing, because they trusted it was in service of the soldiers at the front. "The Chemical Warfare Service ordered 'Make poison gas!' This to counter the enemy's use of chlorine, a poison gas. And so we did."

A gray pall hung over Washington as General Sibert arrived at Rauscher's hall on the evening of December 13, 1918. The weekend before, tens of thousands of government workers had gathered near the White House, singing patriotic songs. Soldiers at Walter Reed Hospital received deliveries of Christmas gifts, and every day, the army discharged another fifteen thousand men. While the crisis had ended, a sense of epochal transformation lingered. President Wilson and his wife were on their way to Paris, where crowds lining the Champs-Élysées would shower the president's car with violets, and the city council would vote to make him an honorary citizen. With General Pershing at his side, he planned to capitalize on the goodwill to advocate for his plan for a League of Nations uniting America and Europe against future wars.

While millions would cheer Wilson in the streets of Paris, the celebration at Rauscher's was a smaller fete. A virtual Who's Who of the Chemical Warfare Service, the dinner brought together commissioned officers and division chiefs from around the country to salute Sibert and the work of the chemists. The Camp Meigs band banged out the wartime rag "Too Much Mustard," and the toastmaster kept the program running smoothly.

The evening wasn't merely a tribute to Sibert and the service — it was also a public relations maneuver. With the end of censorship, reporters had been invited to the dinner to hear details of the service's work that had been kept under tight cover for so long. When Sibert rose to speak, his words revealed nothing that the officers in the banquet hall didn't already know. To the public, however, his comments were revelatory, a recitation of ingenious inventions and marvelous engineering carried out under impossible pressure.

Sibert didn't lay bare every secret during the dinner. Lewisite was never mentioned, and a casual listener would not have been able to deduce that gas was manufactured anywhere other than Edgewood. He did make oblique mentions, however, of new and more lethal weapons, and that "other endeavors in the toxic field were just coming into production." Sibert also revealed that the 1919 war strategy included using gas on a massive scale and that "had the war continued until the spring of 1919 we would have subjected the Germans to a deluge of toxic substances such as he never dreamed possible when he commenced this type of warfare."

Other speakers delved into details about the nature of the service's work. Colonel Bradley Dewey talked about the new gas masks the service had developed—no doubt glossing over the first failed prototype in 1917—which soldiers could comfortably wear whether fighting or sleeping. Colonel William Walker described Edgewood and the quantities of gas that had come out of its plants—ten tons of mustard to every ton of Germany's, he claimed. Calling Edgewood one of the most deadly institutions since time began, he startled the audience when he said the number of injuries in the plants may have matched the volume of gas casualties on the front.

The dinner wasn't the only overture to the press from the service. At least one reporter, from the *Arizona Republican* newspaper, was allowed inside Edgewood Arsenal for a tour with Colonel Walker, gaping at the vast complex erected on what had been farmland just twelve months earlier. "What I saw was a city of brick kilns, high chimneys, correlated vats in innumerable series, repeated shot towers, miles of railway, miles of elevated pipe lines, machinery of the finest type and the most perfect installation, housed in concrete and sheet iron, built apparently for permanence," he wrote. "Chiefly impressive, once one became accustomed to the thought that all this ingenious, costly mechanism was built to generate poison for the sole purpose of horribly maiming and frightfully killing, was the orderliness, the immensity, and the stability of the plant."

With the same candor as in his speech at Rauscher's, Walker spoke openly with the reporter about the gas program, including use of aerial gas bombs. The plan was to drop a ton of mustard gas at a time over fortresses like Metz or Koblenz, using a time fuse to synchronize an explosion several hundred feet over the forts, he said. Mustard being heavier than air, the gas would slowly settle. A single one-ton container could cover an acre or more, he said, "and not one living thing, not even a rat, would live through it." The targets would include fortified cities where civilians lived because the military installations within made them legitimate targets. He acknowledged that the allies of the United States, principally France and Britain, were not enthusiastic about the idea of aerial gas bombing. The British embraced the idea first, he said. Eventually, the more hesitant French followed suit. "There is not the slightest doubt in my mind that we could have wiped out any German city we pleased to single out, and probably several of them, within a few hours of giving the release signal," he said matter-of-factly.

As candid as these disclosures were, the service didn't tell the whole truth. From Sibert's comments, it would seem that the Chemical Warfare Service had sprung full-grown from the womb of the War Department in July of 1918; the crucial role Van Manning's Bureau of Mines had played was left out. Manning saw to it that his efforts were not forgotten. Not long after the Rauscher's dinner, the Bureau of Mines released its annual report outlining the Research Division's scientific investigations before it was swallowed up by the War Department. George Burrell also took pains to credit his former boss, writing a history of the division for the *Journal of Engineering and Industrial Chemistry*. "I want to pay a special tribute to Mr. Manning, the man who started the work," he wrote.

Those in the know understood Manning's contribution. Smithsonian Institution secretary Charles Walcott wrote to Manning to praise him for his work and congratulate him on his accomplishments. Walcott, who had been one of Manning's superiors at the U.S. Geological Survey, couldn't pass up the chance to take a swipe at the War Department.

"It was quite natural for the War Department to wish to take the gas work over after you had put it on its feet and the Department had made a most dismal failure on their part up to that time," he wrote. Manning reciprocated with a gracious thank-you note.

On December 4, Sibert reported to the adjutant general that the American University Experiment Station would shut down by year's end. The only work at the station would be completing unfinished research and preparing reports about the investigations. Any future experimental and research work would be handled at Edgewood, the new seat of the Chemical Warfare Service.

There was another secret of the Chemical Warfare Service that wasn't discussed. Even as the country celebrated the Armistice, the spy Walter Scheele remained at Jones Point, New York, as if he had been forgotten. Agent Frank O'Donnell, a conscientious agent who had dutifully carried out his responsibilities since the earliest days of Scheele's confinement, didn't file a single update about Jones Point between November 7 and 27. When he finally did get caught up on December 2, he submitted one report for all twenty days that read simply "During the entire period nothing of interest to the operation transpired."

Scheele presented a quandary that needed to be resolved quietly, outside of public scrutiny. As Scheele himself had angrily pointed out in August, his detention was extrajudicial. He had never been arraigned, he had never been allowed to enter a plea in response to his indictment, and he never had a bond hearing. He inhabited a legal gray area at Jones Point, living a hidden life under a pseudonym, as isolated and trapped as he had been during his exile in Cuba. His name would be back in the headlines soon enough, for reasons that none of his captors could have predicted.

With the peace, the United States and its allies would finally be forced to confront the moral and ethical questions that had been swept away the moment the Germans opened up the valves on their chlorine tanks. By the Armistice, the Americans had fired about 1,100 tons of gas at the Germans and sent over at least 111 tons in the Meuse-Argonne offensive, including between 25 and 30 tons of mustard. Artillery units used most of the gas—more than 90 percent—while the gas regiment had used the rest. The Germans had used more than 57,000 tons, France had used 28,000 tons, and Britain had used about 15,700 tons. In all, more than 124,000 tons of gas had been used in the chemists' war.

Now that the war was over, Sibert and Fries had the task before them of convincing the army, Congress, and the public to maintain a chemical arsenal. Fries appealed to General Pershing to be allowed to return to the United States as soon as possible to begin lobbying the chief of staff and Congress to make the service permanent. Pershing granted Fries's request and authorized him to bring a staff of nine officers and eight clerks. "I am going with the avowed purpose of trying to have a CWS in the regular Army," he wrote to Bessie. He began packing immediately, hoping to leave Liverpool, England, on December 7 on a fast steamer, which with luck would allow him to reach his family in Los Angeles by Christmas. He had plenty to be thankful for when he joined his fellow officers for Thanksgiving dinner on November 28, even if his roiling stomach kept him from feasting on the rum omelets and roast goose with chestnut dressing, pumpkin pie, and champagne. He also sent a missive to the men of the service, which Atkisson distributed through the ranks. "Whether the Chemical Warfare Service will be continued in peace remains to be seen. That your work will always be remembered and that it will be the guiding star for such work in any future war...is absolutely certain," he wrote.

The next day, Fries finished packing and sent his luggage ahead. He was off to Paris first, then to London. His plan to make it home for Christmas seemed less and less likely; his original ship was delayed, and the one he rescheduled on December 8 was a slower vessel. He also needed to make a stop in Washington to consult with General Sibert, which would delay him more.

Luck was on his side. The USS *Celtic* made good time and arrived in New York on December 17, earlier than expected. The ship anchored off Staten Island for the night. In the morning, hundreds of soldiers—about half of them black infantrymen from a segregated regiment—lined the rails as ships up and down the river let loose on their steam whistles. When the patrol boat arrived to greet the ship with newspapers, chocolate, cigars, and cigarettes, the police band aboard played "Home Sweet Home" and "My Old Kentucky Home," as the jubilant soldiers yelled and threw their hats into the air. After the ship glided into its berth, Fries sent a telegram to tell Bessie that he had reached New York and was headed to Washington to see Major General Sibert.

After he saw Sibert, he returned to New York City for his first stateside assignment, which was demobilizing the Gas Defense Plant in New York. It would be many weeks before the shutdown would be complete, and Fries wanted desperately to see Bessie and the children at Christmas. Eighteen months had passed since they had last seen one another, the longest time that the couple had ever been separated during their marriage. He had never met his youngest daughter, who was born after he departed for Europe, and his middle daughter, Barbara, was only ten months old when he left. The general managed to get a seat on a California-bound express train. It took five days to barrel across the country.

The locomotive pulled into Los Angeles about 5:30 p.m. on Christmas Eve. It was after nightfall, the city ablaze with lights. Fries's family waited on the platform: Bessie, their son, Stuart, and all three daughters, with Fries's father holding Barbara in his arms. In the midst of the reunion, Fries reached out to hold Barbara. Frightened, she turned her back on this unrecognizable man in a uniform and gripped her grandfather close. Fries let her be, but after they arrived at a family friend's house for Christmas Eve supper and adjourned to the living room, Fries watched his daughter carefully sizing him up as the adults talked and laughed, her eyes wide as she took in everything her parents said. After a few minutes, she tugged on Bessie's skirt and asked uncertainly, "Momma, we like that man, don't we?"

For the men of the gas and flame regiment, going home was a disconsolate waiting game, and Christmas only heightened the homesickness. They had marched out of Camp American University on December 25 a year earlier, and now they were still stuck in France, even though the war was over. Tom Jabine, wiling away the days in the officers' ward in Nantes, had given up predicting his departure. Separated from the regiment, he had hoped to be home by Christmas, too. He sometimes felt short-winded but otherwise felt fine. "I am just waiting around for a chance to go home," he wrote. While mistletoe and holly adorned most of the wards, Jabine's ward was almost bare—"Officers are too lazy to go out and get things," he carped—other than a Christmas tree decorated with improvised ornaments. For a break from the monotony, he walked into town with other officers for a Christmas Eve meal. At 6:00 a.m. on Christmas morning, soft caroling awoke Jabine. A procession of nurses wound through the hospital, singing "Silent Night," candles illuminating their faces in the darkened wards.

At least Jabine was comfortable and warm in Nantes. The same could not be said of the rest of the regiment. The Hellfire Boys had decamped from Verdun to La Ville-aux-Bois, where Thanksgiving passed and two squads from Higgie's platoon kicked up a row by stealing chickens. Every day, mail sacks bulging with packages arrived at headquarters where Higgie was detailed doing office work; he received a package containing chocolate and another with a handkerchief from Irene. In a desperate attempt at festivity, Company D decorated a Christmas tree with dangling tomato and salmon tins and draped its branches with toilet paper. It looked convincing from afar but ridiculous up close.

On Christmas Eve, some of the men in Higgie's billet got drunk and a fight broke out downstairs. One man broke his wrist, and another lost several teeth. On Christmas Day, Higgie slept until 10:00 a.m., then went into the office to fill out passes to allow the men to leave camp.

Higgie was at work on December 30 when the order came through for the regiment to start for the coast the next day. He raced back to the billets to tell the men that they were leaving. He spent the day packing and barely made an evening show at the Y before bed. "We are all ready for tomorrow and it seems too good to be true. All the fellows are happy tonight," he wrote in his journal.

When they boarded the train for Brest, sixty-three men crammed into Higgie's boxcar like livestock on their way to market. The trip took three days. Higgie thought they would march right onto a transport; instead, they hiked another six miles to a half-finished barracks. And then they waited.

It was a hellhole. For three weeks, the men bided their time in freezing, damp misery. As at the front, mud was everywhere, even inside the mess hall, a building with no roof where the men stood in ankle-deep muck in the rain while they ate. That night, Higgie's tent sank six inches into the mire. Lice infested their clothes and hair. Some days there was no firewood, and one night a powerful storm blew over many of the tents. On January 8, Higgie got to the mess hall too late, and all the food was gone. For dinner that night, he scavenged turnips from a farmer's field and ate them raw. For weeks, not a single letter arrived for him from Irene or anyone else, and he wondered if all of his friends had forgotten him. His bunk was the only place to get warm. He dried his sodden socks under his mattress tick at night. It took days for each pair to dry out. One night, he lay in the dark talking to one of the men in the squad. "We are all wondering how long we are going to be kept in this hole," he wrote in his diary.

The Hellfire Boys weren't the only regiment mired in misery; Sammies from all across the AEF were writing home to complain bitterly about the awful conditions they were in after the war. "We are still waiting after three weeks here," Addison wrote mournfully in his diary.

The day finally arrived on January 23. "Unspeakable joy at heart," Addison wrote in his diary, tempered only by fear some last-minute reassignment might keep him in France. The chaplain spent his last day trying to make sure injured members of the regiment came across with them. Higgie packed at midnight, reveille was at 2:30 a.m., and breakfast at 5:00 a.m. Just before departure time, orders arrived requiring some men to stay for several more months, sending up a howl of fury from those ordered to remain behind. Higgie wasn't one of them. The departure began at 7:00 a.m., the commanding officers demanding complete silence. Quiet as lambs, the regiment marched to the waterfront following the embarkation orders: overcoats buttoned, slickers over their packs, extra shoes cleaned and strapped to their packs. Absolutely no loud talking or singing, with the strictest march discipline.

A ferry brought them out to the USS *Celtic,* the same ship that had returned Fries to the United States a month earlier. Wounded soldiers also came aboard, but there were far fewer soldiers than on the way over. As the ship moved out of the port, Higgie crowded onto the deck to wave goodbye to France. Then he went below, strung up his hammock, and slept.

The *Celtic* set sail without Tom Jabine, who read about his regiment's departure in the newspapers. He had long since given up trying to decipher how he had become ensnared in so much red tape. Weeks earlier, a doctor had marked on his chart that he was ready to go home. Unfortunately, he still needed to go before a discharge board, which might keep him in France still longer if he was marked fit for duty. "The situation is hopeless to understand and still harder to try and explain," he said. He was beginning to feel like a prisoner. "I certainly have been fooled on this famous 'going home' proposition," he wrote in another mournful letter home.

Rather than fritter away his hours playing chess and taking walks, he set out for the Riviera with a friend for some sightseeing. They arrived on February 6 in the seaside resort town of Menton, where he strolled through villas and lush gardens filled with flowers and fruit trees, their limbs weighted down with lemons and oranges, with towering mountains rising above them and the Mediterranean to the east. They walked to the Italian border just north of the town and strolled across the bridge. "So I left France today for the first time in over a year! But alas not bound for the States just yet," he wrote home.

By the time Jabine awoke to the tropical smells of the Mediterranean coast, Higgie and the Hellfire Regiment had arrived in the United States. The *Celtic* steamed into New York Harbor before daybreak on February 2. Higgie watched the Statue of Liberty slide by in the morning light, then went below for breakfast. He returned to the deck later, when the welcome boat arrived to throw fruit and candy up to the men. Crowds waited on the pier when they disembarked, and Red Cross volunteers handed out hot coffee and rolls. The ship's arrival presented another public relations opportunity for the Chemical Warfare Service. Articles about their arrival included boastful accounts of their bravery and high casualty rates. "Very little was known in the United States of our operations," Major John Carlock told the *New York Times,* "because nothing was allowed to leak out. The nature of our work made it imperative that the greatest secrecy should be maintained and this was strictly carried out."

Higgie sent off telegrams and postcards; then the regiment took a ferry to Brooklyn and a train out to Camp Mills on Long Island.

A few days later, they moved again, this time to Camp Kendrick, at Lakehurst Proving Ground in New Jersey, the artillery testing range for the Chemical Warfare Service. Sibert and Fries came out to review the troops. For three weeks, Higgie worked in the camp office, processing discharges for men in the regiment. He was in the office one day when an order arrived with his promotion to sergeant.

The first group departed on February 12. Every day, more Hellfire Boys left the camp, and the ranks of the regiment dwindled. Higgie wondered when he would go. While he waited, he befriended the camp cooks, who served him breakfast whenever he felt like it. He took long walks in the middle of the day and played cards for hours at night. Sometimes he lay awake in the barracks, listening to his bunkmates mutter out loud in their sleep. Every night, there were fewer and fewer men in the bunks for Higgie to listen to.

Finally, Higgie's captain told him to submit his own discharge papers. When the papers came through, they were for February 22. Higgie begged the captain to let him leave a day earlier. The captain gave in, and Higgie rushed to pack. He hectored the quartermaster for his pay, gulped down dinner, and then quickly changed clothes for the trip. Higgie put on a new suit he bought, but he couldn't find his raincoat because one of the fellows had borrowed it.

He left with his pal Staples. The last train left Lakehurst at 6:30 p.m., so they had to hustle. They set out on foot. A driving rain soaked his new suit. They wouldn't have made it except a jitney appeared through the sheets of rain and gave them a ride to the station, where the friend who had nabbed the raincoat showed up just in time to return it and say goodbye. The train took them to Jersey City, where they took a ferry across the Hudson to Manhattan and on to Penn Station. It was 11:00 p.m. when they checked their bags and got their tickets for the 1:30 a.m. express train to Boston.

When they got to the platform just after midnight, a jostling crowd already awaited the train. When it pulled in, Higgie and

Staples leaped aboard and claimed seats in one of the coaches. They pulled their raincoats and mackinaws up to their chins and fell asleep. Higgie opened his eyes at daybreak and looked out the window. An overnight storm had swept over New England, and snow blanketed the landscape, as if he had been transported to another, wintery land while he slept. To Higgie, it seemed the train moved excruciatingly slowly as home grew closer, mile by mile.

At 8:00 a.m., the train finally pulled into Back Bay Station in Boston. It was February 22. Amid the crowds, Higgie spotted his aunt and a family friend waiting on the platform. He couldn't push his way out of the train fast enough to greet them. He had a suitcase with him, but he had checked his army bag through to South Station. Higgie reboarded the train for downtown Boston, so he could claim his bag. He didn't expect a soul to be there for him, so he was stunned to look out on the busy platform and see his sweetheart, Irene, searching anxiously for his face among the passengers stepping down from the car. "I had the best surprise of my life when I spotted the best little girl in the world looking for me," he wrote in his diary.

Then Higgie went north, away from the crowds, away from the patriotic bunting and the ticker tape and the brass bands in Boston, back to his little house in Lawrence. The morning *Lawrence Telegram* carried a picture of Higgie in his uniform, looking as serious as could be. The *Evening Tribune*'s headline said everything there was to say: "Higginbottom Is Home from France."

Chapter Sixteen

"Fight the Devil"

Patches of snow dappled the hillside behind American University as Charles William Maurer tramped down the slope with his gas mask. In winter of 1918, Mustard Hill had begun to empty out. Every five days, the service discharged another one hundred soldiers. As work slowed, Maurer and a friend wandered the campus, snapping pictures of the creaky sheds and huts where they had worked. Maurer clowned for the camera, holding his nose outside the man-test laboratory and crouching inside shack number 5, a skull and crossbones scrawled over the door.

A dirt road led to two shacks on the top of the hillside, just inside the barbed-wire fence encircling the station. Partway down the hill, Maurer posed at the lip of the pit called Hades. At his feet, a jumble of bottles, jars, and jugs lay on the hillside. Bending over in his gas mask, Maurer reached toward the bottles, the mask canister dangling down at his waist, as his friend snapped the shutter.

Private Maurer became Sergeant Maurer on January 1, 1919, in a flood of bottled-up promotions. His discharge came on January 20. On his way home, he stopped in Cincinnati and Saint Louis to sightsee, visited friends in San Antonio, and dropped in on his brother in the border town of Mission, Texas. Soon he was back in Marfa. As President Wilson barnstormed across Europe before the Paris peace talks, former president Teddy Roosevelt died in his sleep of a lung embolism. California banned liquor, nudging the country closer to Prohibition. Labor strikes broke out nationwide, and police rounded up Communists and anarchists. Anxiety rose over labor radicals and Bolshevik agitation. The country was moving on.

Maurer, too, had put the war behind him. Yet on the vast expanse of the West Texas plains, reminders of the Chemical Warfare Service reached him. When the Baylor newspaper, *The Lariat,* arrived in the mailbox, it included an article entitled "Dr. Gooch Tells Class of New Gas." In the article, the professor described a "wonderful gas" that American chemists developed. It was so secret that probably only three men knew its formula, and so lethal that "a minute drop of the liquid from which this gas is formed will bring almost instant death."

Soon after, a letter from Maurer's alma mater arrived, asking for an update for an alumni directory. Will mailed in a ten-page letter describing his time in Washington. He sent a folded lyric sheet from the camp stunt night, a humorous but dark ditty about the perils of the station. "Nevertheless, 'sweet were the days at the shell plant' for after all we had to suffer few of the hardships of the boys in the line," he wrote. He tucked a dollar into the envelope for the alumni directory.

Maurer also wrote about the gas that Dr. Gooch spoke of in the *Lariat* article. "He probably referred to Lewisite, named after Capt Lewis of the American U. in Washington," he wrote. "It has been called the most terrible weapon ever devised by man. American chemists proved themselves far superior to the squareheads at their own game and accomplished more and better results in two years than the Germans had in forty."

Sergeant Maurer's reminiscence of his time at American University reflected the start of a wider shift in the nation, an inflection point in how the country viewed chemical weapons. A new openness about chemical warfare had begun in fall of 1918 when the guns fell silent, and men like William Sibert unveiled the secrets of the chemists' war. But it wasn't until 1919, when soldiers like Maurer headed home, the men of the gas and flame regiment stepped off the boats in Hoboken, and the dollar-a-year men resumed their university work, that a new mythology about chemical warfare began to take root. It would be neither a single story nor a simple one. Nor would it be the entirely celebratory one that Sibert, Amos Fries, and many scientists hoped for. Like a chemical cloud bursting from compression, the story of chemical weapons proved unpredictable and difficult to control.

American University itself was emblematic of that mixed legacy. On December 30, 1918, Sibert wrote a thank-you note to Bishop Hamilton at American University for the use of the campus. The letter was intended to be a grateful handshake, a gesture of mutual admiration. Hamilton's offer of the campus in April of 1917 had been an optimistic gambit to help the army and ensure the university's continuity. But the postwar landscape yielded a more complicated reality. Debris and wooden huts reeking of poison fumes littered the once bucolic campus. Arsenic saturated the soil, and practically every blade of grass was gone. The enormous new chemistry building sat unfinished and empty. Bomb chambers, explosives pits, and test trenches riddled the campus and properties around it. Cinders and ash blanketed the campus, the trees hacked down or killed by gas. The farmer named Weaver, whose land was used for testing mustard and other chemicals, complained that his property was badly contaminated and suspected that buried mustard had killed one of his cows. Years after the war ended, area residents reported finding shell holes and dugouts used for storing explosives. And beyond the far reaches of the campus, down the hillside that the soldiers called Death Valley, chemicals and ordnance rested for generations in the pit called Hades.

Germany had been defeated, but from the moment that Amos Fries returned to Washington, he had his sights on a new adversary: the War Department. After his Christmas reunion with his family in Los Angeles, he repacked his bags and returned to the capital for what he knew would be a battle over the future of the gas service. He was Sibert's right-hand man now, the only arrangement that he would tolerate short of being the chief himself. Fries was bumped back down from brigadier general to lieutenant colonel, as he feared would happen, a postwar reduction in rank that he resented and protested fiercely.

When Fries came back to Washington on January 20, he went first to see Sibert at his office on Seventh Street. Goliath delivered what must have been disheartening, if expected, news: the War Department intended to dismantle the gas service.

Fries asked Chief of Staff Peyton C. March for a meeting. When Fries arrived at March's office a few days later, an aide went to the general to announce Fries's arrival. A moment later, the aide returned and said that the general wouldn't meet with him. When Fries asked the aide to go back and ask for just fifteen minutes, that was refused, too. The aide relayed the message that if Fries had come to plead for the Chemical Warfare Service, it was no use — March's mind was made up. The matter was closed. Still, Fries insisted that he see the chief of staff, sending the aide back a third time. This time March let him into his office. Fries launched into a diatribe about chemical warfare, but March abruptly cut him off, threw up his arms, and said, "There's not going to be any more Chemical Warfare Service."

When Fries returned to Sibert's office, he told the director what had happened. "My hands are tied, so I can do nothing," Sibert said. But he gave Fries his blessing to do whatever he could to prevent the War Department from dismantling the Chemical Warfare Service. Fries was already formulating a plan — he would appeal to Congress. He had strong relationships with two key lawmakers in particular: Congressman Julius Kahn of California and Senator George Chamberlain of Oregon, the respective heads of the House and Senate Committees on Military Affairs. Within days, both had agreed to back Fries and his position that the Chemical Warfare Service should continue in peacetime.

The chief of staff's reception shouldn't have come as a surprise to Fries. He made no secret of his views on gas warfare, and the future he envisioned could not have been further from that of March and Baker. One of Fries's most trusted officers, Lieutenant Colonel B. C. Goss, laid out Fries's postwar position on the service for Sibert. Goss called gas a "recognized weapon of warfare" and said that war without it would be like trying to fight without rifles, machine guns, or artillery. The combatants in the just-concluded war had broken their promises to shun gas, "and the same thing will happen next time," Goss wrote. The paper also anticipated what would become a defining point in the fight over chemical warfare that Fries would take up with gusto—its morality, or lack thereof: "A widespread feeling has existed in this country to the effect that gas is more barbarous and inhumane than other weapons of warfare. This is really not the case."

The War Department, however, was deep into planning for a peacetime military. That calculus did not include Fries's vision of chemical warfare. President Wilson had returned to Europe to wrangle over the terms of postwar peace, which reasserted bans on gas warfare once again. Secretary of War Baker and March backed the president's position that chemical warfare should be shunned. The rustlings of the War Department's intentions became apparent in February, when Baker stopped all gas warfare research and ordered the service's records transferred to the Corps of Engineers, effectively shutting down the Chemical Warfare Service as an independent branch of the military.

For now, the future of the Chemical Warfare Service was uncertain, with months of negotiations over the terms of the peace in Europe still ahead. One thing was clear: there was no need for mass production of chemical weapons in peacetime. The previous months had been a race against time to produce gas for the battlefield; now, after eighteen months of planning and construction, everything had stopped. The assembly lines went quiet, the factories fell silent, and tons of lethal chemicals and weapons stockpiled in warehouses and storage yards, including the lewisite that came too late.

Edgewood Arsenal, which had been a huffing, churning furnace of gas production, was eerily quiet and empty as a graveyard after months of feverish activity. At its peak, there had been more than eleven thousand people working at the arsenal producing war gases, filling shells and grenades, erecting new buildings, and keeping the existing ones running. The arsenal and its satellite factories had generated more than ten thousand tons of war gases and smoke gases. More than nine hundred men had been injured at the arsenal, most of them in the process of making mustard. William Walker had planned for the arsenal to make almost eleven thousand tons of gas every month after January 1919.

Four months later, after the Armistice, a skeleton crew of barely a thousand remained. William McPherson, whom Major General Sibert had charged with writing a history of the arsenal, wrote lonely letters back to colleagues at Ohio State University. "I have but one thing on my mind at present and that is how I can, in the shortest possible time, wind up my work and report to the University," he wrote.

Demobilization could not happen overnight—a vast number of details needed consideration, from the number of men let go, disposal of buildings, equipment, and chemicals, to continuity with any research remaining after the war. From Astoria to Willoughby, the army began to shut down the chemical warfare apparatus it had so painstakingly built, canceling leases, annulling contracts, and dismantling the factories. The buildings and plants at Kingsport, Bound Brook, and Niagara Falls were all auctioned at fire-sale prices. The Research Division began winding down its work on Mustard Hill. The Bureau of Mines, sidelined the year before, piped up to claim property that had been taken over by the army, including hammers and screwdrivers, a protractor, a vacuum cleaner, and two horses, named Happy and Hero. The War Department ordered the Army Corps of Engineers to fold up Camp Leach at American University and discharge the soldiers. By December 11, 1918, more than a thousand men had already been sent home or transferred, leaving just over two hundred men. The engineers dismantled the camp officers' club and disposed of the decorations and furniture. The camp's buildings went up for auction in June of 1919.

Disposal of surplus chemicals proved to be a complicated process. Raw chemicals with commercial value were sold to the highest bidder, but chemical agents deemed too dangerous for the marketplace needed to be either destroyed or stored. Since the latter was easier, the army's stockpiles of war gas went on the move again— not to France, but to Maryland. Since the decision in the fall to shut down the American University Experiment Station and make Edgewood the new seat for the Chemical Warfare Service, leftover chemicals, mortar shells, and Livens drums went to the arsenal.

American University had its share of gas and chemical weapons that needed to be removed. On March 1, 1919, the Research Division's ordnance officer received permission to ship thousands of bombs and shells from American University up to Edgewood. Gas shells, cylinders, jugs, and drums of various sizes containing mustard, phosgene, chloropicrin, and other chemical agents went to Edgewood by truck or train. Over the rest of the year, Sibert regularly requested more trucks to ferry armaments and weapons agents from American University to Edgewood and Fort Meade; there were at least five such requests in October of 1919 alone.

Not all of the weapons at American were shipped to Edgewood, however. Damaged or leaking gas shells posed an immediate danger. An Army Corps of Engineers memo from mid-1918 suggests those shells were "either carried out several miles to sea and sunk, or buried quite deeply in the ground," which had been the policy of the British. At American, the military took the latter approach. Time would reveal several burial pits on the American University campus. "The munitions were taken back to the limit of the University acres and there buried in a pit that was digged for them," the *American University Courier* reported in 1921. "Would that it were as deep as the cellar of Pluto and Proserpine. *Requiescat in pace.*"

Catholic University, where Winford Lee Lewis's experiments produced lewisite, was either overlooked or ignored during the demobilization. It wasn't until November 18, 1921, that a Chemical Warfare Service truck went to the university to cart away bottles of lewisite, stills for producing it, mustard, other chemicals, and equipment that had been simply stashed in a shed. Inside Maloney Hall, the fumes from the lewisite had peeled the paint off the ceilings of the labs, and the ventilation fans were broken, rendering all of the rooms unusable. The chemistry professor who insisted that the service come for their abandoned property also believed the government should pay for the repairs. Whether the army actually did so remains unclear. A letter from the chief of the Chemical Warfare Service Supply Division stated emphatically that the government had been released from all damage claims.

The process of dismantling the Mousetrap began almost immediately after the war ended but lasted more than a year. Willoughby had a unique problem. Despite the newspaper articles, lewisite's existence officially remained a secret, so getting rid of the chemicals at the Ben-Hur plant was a more delicate endeavor than at other places. When the Purchase and Storage Division advertised the sale of chemicals there, Major General Sibert reacted with alarm, chastising the division for publicizing lewisite's ingredients. The division responded that it "greatly regretted" publishing the names of the chemicals at the plant but pointed out the impossibility of selling surplus property without saying where it was located.

The lewisite that had actually been produced also posed a problem. The twenty-two steel drums had been stored in a warehouse at the Mousetrap since they had come off the production line. With no means of disposing of the material, Colonel Frank Dorsey asked Edgewood chief Colonel William Walker how to get rid of it. Walker's solution was a simple one. "The only disposition which Edgewood Arsenal can make of the material herein described is to place the same upon a lighter [a boat], take it out to sea, and throw it overboard," he wrote to Sibert. On January 30, Sibert ordered the lewisite sent to Edgewood by special train without delay. Arrangements for the rail shipment began the next day. The wheels started to turn.

Despite Sibert's warnings against delays for the special train, problems arose even before the gas train left the Mousetrap. The shipment was scheduled for Wednesday, February 5, but the New York Central Railroad didn't send enough steel-bottomed train cars that met regulatory requirements. "[The] rolling stock furnished by the New York Central was the rottenest they had in the yards around Cleveland," reported one of the officers assigned to accompany the lewisite. Two days slipped by as workmen prepared the cars for the voyage. The New York Central agent and the officer in charge argued over fares for the men accompanying the train, until they decided to let the train depart and settle the dispute farther down the line.

On Friday, February 7, the cars waited on a rail siding next to the Ben-Hur factory. Barrel after barrel from the warehouse filled the fifteen-car train. Twelve cars contained chlorine tanks, one contained miscellaneous material, and another car contained the twenty-two steel drums of lewisite. There were also containers of phosgene, mustard gas, and lewisite-impregnated carbon.

When all the drums had been loaded and accounted for, guards took their places on the train. One lieutenant was the transportation representative. There were two officers from the Mousetrap and a sergeant and six enlisted men from Edgewood. The guards had rifles and gas masks, the former to protect the cargo, the latter to protect themselves. After a final inspection, the gas train crept out of the Mousetrap at 12:20 p.m.

The train passed through the Ben-Hur stockade, clattered along the tracks a few blocks from downtown Willoughby, then crossed the Chagrin River and turned east toward Ashtabula, about thirty-seven miles away. From there, the train continued eastward along the lakeshore, stopping in Erie, Pennsylvania, to replace a broken air valve and a wheel. Nearly four hours later, dark had fallen when the gas train started up again, trundling southeast into Pennsylvania.

Hour after hour, mile after mile, the engineer kept his eyes fixed on the tracks ahead, hand steady on the throttle as the train rolled eastward. The soldiers watched for interference or obstacles, masks ready in case a cask sprang a leak, in case the train derailed, in case the cars became uncoupled, in case there was something unexpected on the tracks. Just in case. If something went wrong, if the train derailed and tumbled down one of the steep escarpments, if a car unhitched and rolled backward, if a cask shook loose and spilled a plume of toxic liquid emitting a hothouse odor of geraniums, it would be a catastrophe. And so the train had to stop again and again, to replace broken parts and ensure that its cargo reached its destination.

Just after 3:00 a.m., the locomotive huffed up to the Allegheny Plateau and into Kane, Pennsylvania. The depot at the foot of Main Street was dark, the town's residents slumbering, the brick mills and tanneries and glass factories silent. The brakes squealed, and the engine with its fourteen freight cars behind rolled to a stop at the roundhouse just outside of town.

The train idled for about a half hour in Kane. It was 3:45 a.m. when the engine began to roll slowly southward through the darkness. The train bed curved gently around the town, turning east and then southeast, as the engineer followed Wilson Run down out of the mountains toward Renovo, Pennsylvania.

Dawn broke during the 100 miles to Renovo, where the workmen replaced more air valves and six brake shoes. Another 200 miles of track lay ahead before the gas train would reach Edgewood and the sea. The train huffed on through the southern Allegheny Mountains to Marysville, Pennsylvania. Two more hours for repairs held the train there, and then the train continued on at 7:15 p.m. By then, the sun had set once again, and the cars snaked their way south. Finally, at 2:20 a.m. on Sunday, February 9, the gas train limped into Edgewood Arsenal. The train had made the 517-mile trip in thirty-eight hours, averaging 13.6 miles per hour. The men aboard must have breathed a weary sigh of relief at the sight of the smokestacks and brick filling plants. The cargo had arrived.

Precisely what happened next to the lewisite has either been lost or remains buried deep somewhere in the archives of the service. Press accounts later claimed that the barrels of lewisite were loaded onto an army vessel at Edgewood, towed out to sea, and dumped overboard. An army "historical sketch" about lewisite validates that claim: "shipment was sunk at sea after armistice to destroy gas," the brief sketch read. Some accounts claimed that a ship loaded with lewisite was already en route to France at the Armistice, an account that is almost certainly incorrect.

One possible scenario—albeit unlikely—was that the same day the train from Willoughby arrived at Edgewood, its gas cargo was sent to Baltimore, then loaded aboard the gas ship USS *Elinor*. Since the Armistice, the *Elinor* had been to France and back. When the Germans surrendered on November 11, she had still been moored in Baltimore with a cargo of chemical weapons, but Sibert ordered it to France anyway, as a hedge against a collapse of the Armistice and the peace talks that followed. The ship had set out for France on November 23 with Livens drums and artillery shells filling the holds and stacked on the deck. Toward the end of January, the *Elinor* returned still loaded with 125,000 mustard shells and 11,200 Livens phosgene drums. On January 28, she was bound fast to the number 3 pier at the Canton docks in Baltimore. Sibert asked for permission to dump the gas shells and drums into the ocean, along with another 216 tons of mustard and 102 tons of phosgene that were in leaking containers, most likely from

Edgewood. Three days later, Secretary of War Baker approved Fries's request.

Originally, the *Elinor* was going to head to sea, dump the cargo that had been to France and back, then return to Baltimore for more gas shells from another ship, the USS *Ysel Haven*. On February 1, the army director of embarkation instead ordered the *Elinor* to carry the chemical cargo of both ships out into the ocean to dump "not less than fifteen miles off the Atlantic Coast." In addition to the cargo from the ships, another 300 tons from Edgewood would also be loaded onto the *Elinor* to be thrown into the ocean as well.

On February 3, a twenty-four-soldier gas detail from Edgewood boarded the *Elinor*. That afternoon, a barge drew up alongside with drums of gas. Over the next several days, the men from Edgewood loaded drums of phosgene and other chemical weapons aboard the *Elinor*. On February 6, the USS *Ysel Haven* drew alongside so that its cargo could be transferred to the *Elinor*. Three days after that, on the same day the train from Willoughby arrived at Edgewood, more gas was loaded.

On February 10, a tugboat towed the *Elinor* from her berth. Under her own steam, the gas ship began churning south and anchored that night near the mouth of the Chesapeake. Just after 10:00 a.m. the next morning, the *Elinor* weighed anchor and continued south, turning east as she passed the Cape Henry Lighthouse in Virginia Beach. That night, when the ship was forty-two miles offshore, the gas crew began tossing seventy-five-millimeter shells overboard. Darkness fell as the men threw shell after shell into the Atlantic. The men began tossing phosgene shells overboard at 9:05 p.m. as the ship continued east. The dumping continued on February 12, pausing for meals, and into the next day. At 2:00 p.m. on Valentine's Day, the dumping was complete. Then the *Elinor* made its way toward New York City. Just before 5:00 p.m. the day after, the ship was lashed to the pier in Brooklyn. The gas detail disembarked to return to Edgewood the next day. Their work was done.

On April 20, 1919, the *New York Times* splashed a sensational story across the front of the Sunday magazine: "Our Super-Poison Gas: First Story of Compound 72 Times Deadlier than 'Mustard' Manufactured Secretly by the Thousands of Tons." Like the earlier *Plain Dealer* article, it was packed with tales of risk and ingenuity, a paean to the technical men and the chemists who toiled anonymously to make lewisite. The article told of the Ben-Hur plant, the near imprisonment of the men, and the mysterious drop box linking Willoughby to the outside world. For the first time, it described the gas train and casks of lewisite thrown into the water. There were photographs of Sibert and Frank Dorsey, the Mousetrap personnel, and a man swaddled from head to toe in a gas-defense suit. Though Dorsey was the hero of the story, it also named other scientists who played crucial roles, such as James Bryant Conant. Winford Lee Lewis—the godfather of lewisite—wasn't mentioned. Lewisite represented the pinnacle of offensive war gases—more lethal, fearsome, and faster acting than any before—and though it had been destroyed at sea, the article pointed out that the chemists were prepared to produce it again at a moment's notice.

The lengthy article was comprehensive and dramatic, calling lewisite "the most terrible instrument of manslaughter ever conceived." The article was also completely wrong in several respects, repeating the canard that lewisite was seventy-two times more lethal than mustard. Lewisite did have quicker and more aggressive vesicant properties, but the notion that a few tiny drops were lethal was completely untrue. The assertion that "thousands of tons" had been produced—"almost enough was on hand to destroy the entire people of the United States"—was untrue as well, as the only clear documentation of the quantity of lewisite produced is the twenty-two steel drums containing 8.6 tons of lewisite that was shipped east in early February of 1919.

Articles similar to the one in the *Times* soon followed. In late May, the Interior Department held an educational exposition in Washington featuring a booth with a bottle of lewisite on display, with an armed guard on duty day and night. Newspapers across the country published the newswire article about the expo, repeating many of the same outlandish claims about lewisite that were in the *Times* article.

The most egregious exaggeration in the *Times* article and articles like it related to its effectiveness. If lewisite sounded too good to be true, it was. The most closely guarded secret about lewisite turned out to be that it was not a particularly good war gas. While it was powerful and highly toxic, the handful of chemists acquainted with its properties knew that lewisite hydrolyzed in water—in other words, moisture caused it to break down and lose its toxicity. Mustard had no such problem. Its value was its stability in water or in damp conditions. In theory, lewisite would be effective in winter or in dry conditions—in the desert, perhaps—but it would be less than ideal for rainy environs such as Belgium and France.

Of course, the experts who knew the truth weren't in a hurry to correct the record. The actual efficacy of lewisite remained a deep secret. In March, Sibert warned Dorsey, "There are several subjects, as you know, that we are not publishing in any of our reports, and that we are surrounding with as much secrecy as possible." As late as 1927, Fries acknowledged in a letter to Lewis that it wasn't clear how effective lewisite actually was.

The articles about lewisite appeared as Congress was deciding the future of the Chemical Warfare Service. In early August of 1919, the War Department sent over the legislation that would reorganize the army, known as the General Staff Bill. As expected, it reflected the view that the Chemical Warfare Service should be abolished as a free-standing branch of the military and that the work of the gas service should belong to the Corps of Engineers.

Whatever chemical warfare work remained would not have the same sprawling wartime scope—it focused on defense, with only enough offensive research to allow a counterattack against a chemical-armed adversary.

The Senate Subcommittee on Military Affairs called General March to testify in early August. March was a trim and vigorous soldier, his uniform dripping with medals and citations, the opposite of the bookish, sclerotic-looking Newton Baker with his starched collars and fussy hair. When asked about the future of the service, March didn't mince words. "The War Department believes that the Chemical Warfare Service ought to be abolished in warfare," he said. As he pressed his case to the committee, he warned of the dangers that chemical warfare posed to civilians, such as a child drinking from a poisoned well or a gas cloud that sweeps over noncombatants.

"That is horrible, General, but suppose in order to protect that child and these non-combatants from that sort of warfare, it becomes necessary for us to fight the devil with fire," one committee member interjected. "Then what?"

"Then we have got to do it," March admitted.

"The Philistines are still after us," Fries complained afterward. Chemical warfare had become political warfare. From Fries's earliest days as chief of the AEF Gas Service, he had had a keen appreciation of the political dimensions of this work and the need to "sell" gas to the army. With the future of the service now in question, he needed to sell it to the American public, too. Doing so required two lines of attack. One was public relations. The other was tilting Congress toward Fries's goals and using legislation to further his ends. With his typical zeal, Fries zeroed in on Senator Chamberlain, his powerful ally.

In a late-August hearing over the bill, Sibert and Fries pulled chairs up to the committee witness table. With the sympathetic Senator Chamberlain and other members listening, Fries said American ingenuity had given U.S. troops an edge in gas warfare that should not be surrendered. Fries also addressed what he called "the question of humanity" of gas warfare; that is, whether it was a more- or less-cruel kind of weapon than others that were commonly used. It was a question woven into the weft of gas warfare since its earliest inception, and now it was becoming a focus of congressional inquiry as well.

As with most of Fries's beliefs, he had an unequivocal answer to that question: "It is the most humane," he told the committee. As the afternoon wore on, Fries's words became darker. He described an apocalyptic vision of ever-more-savage warfare. When Chamberlain asked if a time was coming when nations would agree not to use gas, Fries responded: "If we could make war so terrible that there would not be any chance for it to last more than five or ten minutes, then they would stop all wars." In other words, the only way to end war is to make it too barbaric to tolerate, he argued, despite the fact that he posited in the very same testimony that it was the most humane kind of weapon. It was a glaring contradiction, almost absurd in its convoluted logic, and yet it went unchallenged by the committee.

Away from the hearing rooms, Fries worked methodically to channel experts' voices into opposing the War Department. "Enclosed herewith are some ideas that I think need the attention of all technical societies, journals and individuals in the United States," Fries wrote to the president of a Los Angeles engineering society. "If you agree with me, get busy and spread the gospel."

Not every aspect of the wartime work could be publicized or even publicly discussed at all. As debate over the Chemical Warfare Service gained steam, Walter T. Scheele remained quietly bound by his obligations to the government and the threat of punishment over him. By 1919, the government's investment in Scheele and Levering was no longer certain, and the sheen of promise on the German spy had begun to fade. Over the winter, Bielaski had written to the Military Intelligence Division about the explosive-propelled German torpedoes that Scheele had described, asking if they thought his insights had any value. The chief of the inventions division concluded that Scheele's information "does not offer anything new or of value to the Department." This must have been astonishing news to the officers and scientists at Jones Point, given their confidence in his professed knowledge of Germany's weapons. The exchange so many months into Scheele's captivity suggests that perhaps Scheele never knew as much about German weapons — chemical or otherwise — as he claimed.

By summer of 1919, Scheele had been at Jones Point for more than a year. Though the war was over, he remained beholden to the government and to Levering under whatever murky arrangement the oilman and the Justice Department had agreed upon. Support from Thomas Edison's navy-funded laboratory had dried up, and the salary for the chemist Bruce Silver with it. "At last, the Government has brought out its little guillotine! The axe has fallen and if you will look in the basket, you will see your head," Edison's assistant wrote to Silver.

Even though Scheele was out of the public eye, his name unexpectedly surfaced again in the news. During a conference of the National Cotton Manufacturer's Association, a Department of Justice official named Francis P. Garvan delivered a stem-winding speech leveling a new accusation against Scheele. Garvan, whose job as alien property custodian allowed him to seize German assets, talked about the "master spy" Hugo Schweitzer, the Bayer Chemical Company chemist who had been Scheele's partner in espionage before Scheele was pressed into service making his cigar bombs. And then Garvan dropped a bomb of his own: that Scheele was the inventor of mustard gas. "This is the mustard gas which laid low your brothers on the plains of France."

Newspapers across the country published the electrifying claim. It was a sensational allegation, and it was also dead wrong. The chemical compound had been discovered in 1886 in Germany, not in 1913 in New Jersey. Despite Garvan's claim that the formula was discovered in the suitcase that Scheele had left with family friends when he fled to Cuba, an inventory of the suitcase's contents turns up no mention of mustard or its composition.

Nonetheless, the statement spread quickly. Bruce Silver grilled Scheele until he was satisfied that the claim was false. Nevertheless, in June, Garvan repeated the claim to a congressional committee, and eventually published a book making the accusation again. At least one chemist tried to refute Garvan's claim with a letter to the *Times,* to no avail. Perhaps the claim was a preemptive effort from the Justice Department to smear Scheele so indelibly that it would drown out any complaints he might make about his wartime internment.

Scheele's imprisonment came to an end on June 4, 1919, when the phone rang at Jones Point. Agent Victor J. Valjavec, who had taken over as Scheele's minder, answered the phone. It was the Bureau of Investigation's assistant division superintendent, calling from Manhattan. Valjavec listened. Then he hung up the receiver, went to find Scheele, and told him to get ready to leave. Scheele had a bail hearing that afternoon in federal court in Manhattan.

Valjavec brought Scheele down to the pier. Together, they boarded Levering's launch and sped across the Hudson to Peekskill. From there, they went by car to Manhattan. Ever since he had gone on the lam in 1916, Scheele had been a hunted man, always running, always in the shadows. He was about to get his first taste of independence in four years. The car made its way through the city streets to the Park Row Building in Lower Manhattan, near City Hall Park and across the street from the federal courthouse where Scheele would be expected later in the day. Before going to the courthouse, though, Agent Valjavec brought Scheele to the Bureau of Investigation office.

Most likely the reason for bringing Scheele to the bureau office, and not to the courthouse, was to keep him off the streets and out of the public eye. Two days earlier, anarchist bombs targeting judges and prosecutors had exploded in eight cities around the country, including one that ripped through the Manhattan home of a judge on East Sixty-First Street and another targeting the Washington, D.C., home of Attorney General A. Mitchell Palmer. The whole country erupted in fear and fury, with banner headlines screaming from the top of every newspaper in the country. The last thing the bureau agents needed was for the infamous ship-bomb plotter to be recognized on the streets of Manhattan.

The court postponed the bail hearing until late afternoon. The hours dragged by until finally Judge John Knox called the case at 4:00 p.m. By that late in the day, the courtroom was probably empty, the other cases dispatched. The judge set Scheele's bail at ten thousand dollars. Scheele paid it himself, most likely with cash from Marie, who had received a sizable inheritance from her foster father. Then he walked out of the courtroom a few minutes later. Reporters remained in the dark about the sudden reappearance of the long-absent chemist; newspaper briefs two days later misidentified the date of his hearing. With that, the chemist with the face webbed with scars slipped from the headlines once again. But the chemist did not vanish completely. As part of the conditions of his release, he informed the court that he would have a job: he would be going to work for Levering.

He continued to work for Levering until at least December of 1919, when an agent reported that Scheele—whom he misidentified as Carl von Scheele—"now is in the employ of Richmond Levering & Company who have provided von Scheele with a laboratory in which to conduct his experiments, which they are financing."

Scheele had good reason to keep a low profile, but his former handler, Richmond Levering, had no such need. Since the war ended, Levering had not been idle, jumping immediately back into business. Using his formidable powers of persuasion, he coaxed several wartime colleagues to join him as peacetime partners. George A. Burrell, the former chief of the Research Division, was one. Though he insisted on being addressed as "Colonel" for the rest of his life, Burrell made a swift exit from the military in mid-January of 1919 to go into the oil business with Levering. Within days, he applied for a passport to travel to Tampico, Mexico, and Cuba on behalf of Levering & Company. His goal was to build three oil-refining plants in Tampico that would have a combined capacity of 5.4 million barrels. Levering himself wrote a letter to the State Department on Burrell's behalf, urging a speedy approval of the passport.

Levering's former boss at the Bureau of Investigation, Chief A. Bruce Bielaski, also joined forces with Levering. The chief, who had been both Levering's supervisor and bulwark against accusations of wrongdoing, left the Bureau of Investigation in January of 1919 to become vice president of Levering & Company. If Bielaski's Justice Department colleagues harbored any ill will over his going into business with Levering, they didn't show it—in late February, his former staff bought him a car as a goodbye gift.

At the same time that he launched his new business enterprise, Levering also stayed involved with the Chemical Warfare Service. Early in 1919, war veterans revived the American Legion, which had been a prointervention "preparedness" association before the war but disbanded when the United States entered. The legion would become one of the war's most important veterans' organizations, serving as both a social organization and a lobbying voice in support of the military. In July, Chemical Warfare Service veterans formed their own post within the legion with Levering as the president and Burrell as vice president. Sibert accepted a charter membership.

When Levering offered himself up as president of the Chemical Warfare Post of the American Legion, it's possible he did so out of patriotism and a heartfelt desire to defend chemical warfare. But as always with Levering, there may have been another reason. Keeping the Chemical Warfare Service separate from the engineers and other military branches could have insulated Levering's business enterprises from the upper tiers of the War Department. The very arrangement he had so vociferously denied in 1918—that he had a business deal with Scheele—had proved true in 1919. He had also hired the chief chemist of the Chemical Warfare Service and the top lawman in the federal government. As with many other aspects of Levering's business undertakings, these actions may have been entirely legal. But certainly there was a whiff of insider dealings and self-promotion. Of banking on public trust. Of using patriotism for personal gain. Keeping the service independent might have been good for the service, but it was probably good for Levering, too.

On August 30, the American Legion flexed its muscles over chemical warfare. With congressional hearings about the army reorganization bill just days away, Levering's Chemical Warfare Post urged Congress to maintain the service as an independent branch of the military as Fries and Sibert wanted. With a goal of a million members, the American Legion was a voice that was impossible for Congress to ignore.

With so many business undertakings, Levering would resign from the American Legion in the fall because of his other obligations. In addition to his plans for Tampico, he was building a new business headquarters a few blocks from Wall Street. The federal government was investigating him yet again, this time for his relationship with Bielaski, and the old lawsuit from the Metropolitan Petroleum Corporation shareholders still staggered on. But before he stepped down, he had another obligation to the Chemical Warfare Service, this one in Philadelphia.

When the music swelled from the stage in the ballroom of the Bellevue-Stratford Hotel in Philadelphia, so many chemists crushed through the doors that there was nowhere left to sit. The blue-and-gold banner of the American Chemical Society hung from the balcony of the hotel, announcing that the association's annual meeting had begun on September 2, 1919. Billed as both the "victory meeting" and the "peace meeting," it was a riotous event. The chemists' war had transformed a fusty scientific field into a cutting-edge frontier of military science. This event was their moment in the sun. The organizers planned an 800-seat banquet, but almost 1,700 chemists attended. Hundreds more showed up without bothering to register. Bewildered officers calculated the actual attendance as more than 2,000, with Philadelphia chemists among the most shameless gate-crashers—only 150 registered, but two to three times that number actually attended. For the first time in the society's history, the organizers set up a pressroom for their own in-house publication and a second room for reporters. A row of typists hammered away at abstracts and resolutions and transcripts. A coat-check room was turned into a kind of post office, the cubbies assigned to reporters and filled with updates from the meeting. The publicity committee gloated that news from the meeting was appearing in newspapers across the country.

Chemical warfare was front and center. The 13,500-member American Chemical Society had been an aggressive advocate of chemical warfare from its inception. Now with the future of the service in doubt, the society was pushing even harder. In the September issue of the *Journal of Industrial and Engineering Chemistry,* the lead editorial was entitled "Beware the Ide[a]s of March!" In other words, the army chief of staff was a devious Brutus to the Chemical Warfare Service, ready to plunge his knife into the backs of the patriots congregating in Philadelphia. Charles Herty, the journal's editor, warned that the War Department's plan to abolish the service "bodes ill for the future safety of this country and possibly for the peace of the world." In the months preceding the meeting, the journal had published article after article about gas warfare, the wonders of Edgewood, the achievements of the First Gas Regiment, and technical aspects of the work. The organization also sided with Fries on the question of the service's continued existence, passing a unanimous resolution urging President Wilson and

Congress to maintain the Chemical Warfare Service as an independent branch of the military and to develop and maintain a chemical arsenal. The letter went to Baker just two days after Germany finally signed the Treaty of Versailles, which prohibited Germany from importing or producing chemical weapons and required disclosure of all explosive and chemical production to the Allies.

The September meeting was a show of muscle for the chemists, but it was also a reunion for service veterans. Amos Fries made the trip from Edgewood; Levering came down from New York, along with his new business partner George Burrell.

The general membership meeting got under way in earnest on the morning of September 3 in the hotel ballroom. When the music began, the crowd flooded into the ballroom. Scarcely a seat remained, and the chemists streamed up the sweeping staircases to pack the galleries above. A hearty rendition of "The Star-Spangled Banner" filled the ballroom, and then the hall quieted. The president of the society, William H. Nichols, spoke first. It was a long speech, and quite boring. It was the next speaker on the program who would grab the headlines in the morning papers.

To veterans of the service watching that day, the figure in the stiff collar ascending to the podium was a familiar ideological adversary. Secretary of War Newton D. Baker had received the society's resolution in support of the Chemical Warfare Service and replied with a cordial response and nary a word of criticism. Now he was here to address the chemists in person. He earned polite applause as he took to the stage. He was there not because he had anything to contribute to their field, Baker said, joking that there was "scarcely anyone who would be less competent" than he to discuss even the most elemental aspects of chemistry. No, he said, he was there to thank them. The War Department owed a debt of gratitude to the nation's chemists, "to which I want to give the most formal public expression."

Of the seventeen thousand chemists in the United States, a third of them worked directly for the government during the war, he went on. Another third worked in industries crucial to the war effort, and the final third were engaged in other types of war-related work. "I do not believe it will be discovered that any profession contributed a larger percent of its members directly to the military service, or the results of the activities of any profession were more essential to our national success than that of the chemists," he said. He praised the foresight of the society in mobilizing members when the War Department lagged in its preparation. He praised the Chemical Warfare Service for both its offensive and defensive activities, as well as the First Gas Regiment. "The chemists did their share. They did it superbly," he said.

If there was any acrimony toward Baker from the crowd, it wasn't exhibited in the official proceedings of the meeting, which noted only that Baker received "earnest and serious attention." The chemists puffed on cigars at an evening social hour at the Scottish rite temple down the street, featuring opera singers, moving pictures, and a play. The entertainment made up for the "undue solemnity" from being a booze-free event.

The next evening, about 125 of the chemists from the Research Division gathered for a private reunion. George Burrell presided over the dinner. Amos Fries was the guest of honor. Van Manning was there, too, as well as William Walker. Richmond Levering was the host. Major General Sibert couldn't attend because of General Pershing's return from Europe, but he sent a telegram with his salutations.

When Manning rose to speak, he looked out on a room of familiar faces, men who had labored over test tubes and beakers, whose hands had reddened and blistered from the chemicals they handled. The war had transformed chemistry into a groundbreaking new realm of military technology and jumped-started a sluggish industry long inferior to Germany's. Diminutive in stature, Manning had become a giant in scientific circles, praised for his foresight and his dogged efforts. But the recognition was not universal, and his contributions were largely overlooked by the public and even disparaged by the military.

All that was behind him now. Manning told the veterans of the service that he hoped that the lessons of the war and the spirit of cooperation it required would have practical value in their postwar lives. The Bureau of Mines had returned to peacetime pursuits, he told the men. He would need their help with those problems, too.

The War Department was getting the message. The day after the American Chemical Society meeting, Chief of Staff March returned to the House Military Affairs Committee hearing room to take up the issue of army reorganization and gas warfare. He praised the work of the service but reiterated his position that gas warfare was inhumane and ought to be abolished. In a dry aside, he said he was "well aware of the fact that the chemical-warfare-service people themselves are very much on the other side of the question," a tacit nod to the lobbying from the American Chemical Society, the American Legion, and his own officers, Sibert and Fries.

Out of the spotlight, Fries was a publicity dervish, pressing the benefits of chemical warfare publicly and privately. The seemingly boundless energy he used to build up the service remained in an unflagging defense of the service as he envisioned it. How he found enough hours in the day for his campaign is a mystery. He authored article after article about the humaneness of chemical warfare, about its strategic advantages, about its deterrence possibilities for preventing all-out gas warfare. No letter to the service went unanswered—every inquiry or criticism earned a personal response from the service, sometimes from Fries himself. Newspaper articles that Fries deemed to contain errors, misinformation, or falsehoods—however great or small—earned stern but always polite letters from Fries.

All of the publicity had the ancillary effect of fanning public interest in chemical weapons. The War Department sponsored speeches and public presentations about gas warfare. Letters flooded into the Chemical Warfare Service offices from chemical companies wanting to snap up the stockpiles of chemicals. Others were from enterprising businesspeople with a poor understanding of chemistry, seeking gas for all varieties of uses, from protection of bank vaults to exterminating rodents. One man sought mustard gas to make into a skin cream.

Around the country, political radicalism, socialism, and labor activism were on the rise, which Fries saw as another opportunity to argue for the Chemical Warfare Service's continuation. Police departments clamored for access to chemical weapons to put down domestic unrest. One of his many screeds he sent to the War Department included one called "Mob Control," in which he wrote that "handling of mobs" was another reason to preserve the service.

Fries confided in letters to his allies that he was increasingly certain he had secured the political support he needed. Still, he continued to deploy his lieutenants in the publicity fight. Many of the men who surrounded him in France had returned to private life but continued to finance the public relations effort against the army staff. Fries admiringly called these men "true gold," unrelenting chemical warriors giving up time and money toward their cause. Even General William Black, the chief of the Corps of Engineers who had been an adversary of the service at American University, sided with Fries, a switch that astonished even Fries.

In fall of 1919, there was a crucial shift in the debate over chemical warfare. It was a subtle change, but it would have ramifications on the political wrangling over its future, its moral dimensions, and the stance of the United States toward international treaties. Throughout 1919, both sides of the chemical warfare debate agreed that gas caused an extremely high number of casualties. But in the waning days of August, the surgeon general completed a study of American casualties resulting from chemical attacks. The data showed that while gas caused 27.3 percent of American casualties, only 1.87 percent of gas casualties resulted in death. In other words, gas caused huge number of injuries but a relatively small number of fatalities. The statistics were incomplete for a simple reason: it only counted soldiers treated at U.S. field hospitals and dressing stations. Soldiers killed on the battlefield or treated by the Allies in their first-aid stations weren't included. Nonetheless, the findings gave proponents of chemical warfare a new and powerful rhetorical weapon: gas was more humane because it disabled but rarely killed.

Despite its flaws, the data appeared to confirm Fries's argument that gas was less deadly than bullets or bombs. When the study was published, even Fries had trouble believing that it was possible that gas had killed so few soldiers. But he eagerly seized on the statistics, recognizing a political opportunity. "It would seem that in the face of these figures the cry of inhumanity against gas must soon cease through a realization of the criers of the absolute absurdity of their position," he wrote to a friend in the chief of staff's office.

When Sibert was called to testify again to Congress in October, the hearing had barely gotten under way when Goliath asked that statistics about gas casualties be entered into the record. He returned to the issue of casualties later in the hearing. "You can put more men out of business—take them out of the ranks for a month or two—with gas than with anything else," Sibert said.

The army couldn't ignore its own statistics. In November, General March released a statement highlighting the efficiency of chemical weapons in causing injuries and its inefficiency in killing. "In other words, based on the statistics, the claim is advanced that a man gassed has twelve times as many chances to recover as the man put out of action by other causes," he said.

The *New York Times* editorialized on March's words the next day, reinforcing the argument that chemicals were a more humane form of weapon. The *Times* even noted that March and Sibert now agreed on this issue. The editorial went further, sympathetically reporting Sibert's argument that "a nation without toxic gas, and without means of administering it, and without protection from it, will be almost at the mercy of its adversary."

The War Department gave in. Just before Congress adjourned, the chairman of the House Military Affairs Committee announced that an accord had been struck with the War Department that would preserve the Chemical Warfare Service as an independent branch of the army. It took months for the army reorganization legislation to pass through Congress, but in May of 1920, the House and Senate eventually reached agreement on the legislation. Fries had won.

As weather in Maryland cooled and summer turned to autumn of 1919, Fries and his family settled into their new lives at Edgewood. Two and a half years earlier, Fries had been little more than a custodian in Yellowstone Park, a ruler of dirt roads, maintaining order in a bubbling, volcanic laboratory of the nation's untamed hinterlands. Back then, he rode by horseback among the mud pots burping clouds of sulfur and chloride, the boiling geysers spewing potassium and magnesium, pools of arsenic simmering in limestone cauldrons. Now he sat on the throne of a new military frontier, the king of a chemical empire. Edgewood was a fortified city of brickwork furnaces and factories. Through his force of will and unbending confidence, he had fought for chemical warfare to continue, and the tide had turned in his direction. The critics and the naysayers of gas warfare, the feeble pacifists and sympathizers with the nation's enemies abroad, all of them had been beaten back.

There on Gunpowder Neck, surrounded by furnaces and factories, Fries made his new home. Bessie put the house in Los Angeles up for sale, packed up the household, and brought the children east to Maryland. She shopped for milk, bread, and coffee at the officers' mess, scoured the house with Old Dutch Cleanser, and scrubbed the children with Ivory soap. When she tucked the children in each night, their beds were less than a thousand yards away from seventeen hundred tons of phosgene, chloropicrin, mustard, and chlorine.

Fries brought the same officious, no-nonsense sensibility to Edgewood that he did to the gas service in France. Innumerable practical considerations needed attention, such as razing fire-prone buildings scattered across the arsenal, safely storing the roughly two hundred thousand mustard shells on the premises, and dealing with leaking shells. The fens of Gunpowder Neck, which once teemed with ducks and wildlife, had become toxic pools from the chemical agents dumped into the water, including phosgene and chloropicrin. Fries halted the practice of disposing of chemicals in the swamps.

He also drew up a long memo on future operations at the arsenal, including maintenance, training, and administration. The letter contained broad outlines of his vision for what he believed to be necessary for a thriving and prepared service. Barracks for twenty-five hundred officers and enlisted men, along with living quarters to accommodate families, since he felt that married men made the best officers. A complete research-and-development laboratory to replace the one at American University. A gas mask factory that could produce twenty-five hundred masks per day to supply a peacetime army. A small-scale manufacturing section to produce limited quantities of new chemical weapons, should the research yield promising compounds. In other words, he wanted to replicate the service's wartime capacity on a smaller scale, a fiefdom in miniature of the chemical empire that the war had created.

As the future of the Chemical Warfare Service brightened, one of the shipments of cylinders and shells from American University arrived at Edgewood. The tanks had been poorly marked, and some of the valves had blown out, releasing their contents. Fries and another officer went to inspect the damaged shipment. For more than a year in France, Fries had held forth on gas warfare, lecturing on its superiority as a weapon and on strategies for its use. He strode confidently across the experimental field at Chaumont and among the shells piled at the Puteaux lab for analysis. He had crawled without fear under the fiery tongue of a flamethrower and instructed seamstresses in how to repair defective gas masks. Fries knew gas warfare as well as anyone in the U.S. Army, and still he didn't wear a mask when he went to look at the damaged tanks.

Fries smelled nothing as he entered the storage area. Still, he held his breath to avoid inhaling any gas fumes, just in case gas had gotten loose. That paltry precaution did him little good. Soon after, his eyes began to water, and a few hours later, a deep exhaustion came over him. Chills racked his body. The chemical warrior, who survived the war without harm from the substances that he now defended so adamantly, had been gassed. Shivering and limp with paralyzing fatigue, he crept to the officers' quarters, where he crawled under the covers to recover. "I had the greatest feeling of depression, accompanied by a chill," Fries wrote in a letter to Atkisson. "I reached my quarters just in time to go to bed."

"The Devil's Perfume"

On a scorching September afternoon in 2015, I finished my research at the archives of the U.S. Army Chemical Corps Museum at Fort Leonard Wood in Missouri. I had time to kill, so I wandered through the museum. The rooms were cool and quiet as I looked over the World War I exhibits, peering at small-box respirators, Livens projectors, and Stokes mortars behind the glass. I walked through an ersatz trench, complete with toilet paper stamped with the image of Kaiser Wilhelm. I examined Harold Higginbottom's uniform in a glass case, with the regiment's crossed retorts pinned to the collar, a bright yellow "1" for the First Gas Regiment stitched on the shoulder and his service chevrons sewn onto the sleeve.

I had started this project three years earlier, when I stood in Spring Valley and watched the demolition of the house built on top of Hades. Since then, I had become familiar with projectors and mortars and cylinders that made up the chemical arsenal of World War I. In my mind, they were barely weapons—they had become harmless antiques or quaint artifacts, like arrowheads dug up from the soil. But as I wandered through the rooms of the U.S. Army Chemical Corps Museum, and the years on the exhibit placards rose, the items behind the glass became less and less familiar. The name of the organization changed, too; in a 1946 reorganization, it became the Chemical Corps. Finally, in a room displaying weapons from the 1960s, I stood in front of a display case. On the other side of the glass was a model of an M51 Little John rocket. The rocket had a range of eleven miles, and its payload held fifty-two round bomblets containing the nerve gas sarin. In flight, the payload would open, flinging out the bomblets. As they tumbled, the spinning armed the fuses. On impact, a burster charge in the middle of the orb would explode and spray 1.3 pounds of sarin gas into the air. The next room held a mock-up of an MC-1, a 750-pound bomb built to contain 75 gallons of sarin, made to be dropped from airplanes.

Since World War I, the United States has never used lethal chemical weapons in combat, although during the Vietnam War, it used the flesh-burning incendiary napalm as well as tear gas to dislodge Vietcong and North Vietnamese soldiers from tunnels. (Arguably, the defoliant Agent Orange was a kind of chemical weapon as well.) But these weapons on display in the U.S. Army Chemical Corps Museum, the rockets and bombs to deliver sarin and the deadly nerve gas VX, were clearly intended to kill as many people as possible, in as efficient a manner as possible, in the shortest time possible. The insistence of early proponents that chemical warfare was more humane because it incapacitated rather than killed—an argument central to the successful efforts in 1919 to maintain an independent service—was a compelling one at the time, even if flawed and possibly a cynical ploy. These weapons put the lie to that argument, exposing it for what it was: a politically expedient line of reasoning that ultimately left the door open for weapons that could in no way be mistaken for anything humane.

Of course, the U.S. military's inroads into chemical warfare did not wither away with the end of World War I. Just the opposite— the unrelenting efforts of Amos Fries and his allies in and out of government ensured a robust future for the service, one that would stretch for another half century.

The 1919 fight to maintain the Chemical Warfare Service was only the first skirmish in what would become a six-year battle over chemical warfare. Fries savored the victory, but he did not rest on his laurels. He continued to advocate aggressively for the service, writing articles that he mailed to members of Congress, fellow veterans, and newspapers editors, extolling the humanity of gas warfare and its superiority as an airborne weapon to be dropped over enemy lines. Around spring of 1921, he began using the term "dew of death" for lewisite, describing how, when sprayed from airplanes, it would settle to the ground in a lethal cloud, killing everything it touched. The service also began publishing its own in-house publication, a magazine called simply *Chemical Warfare,* in which Fries could publish his own articles and then send them out to his supporters and associates.

Fries's aggressive advocacy had begun get attention, and not all of it positive. "The magazine 'Chemical Warfare' is as terrifying as General Fries himself," the *New York Times* editorialized. Fries's rhetoric appeared to have had the opposite affect that he intended, stirring public opposition to gas warfare.

Fritz Haber also helped jump-start the scientific debate over the morality of gas warfare. In November 1919, the Nobel Prize committee belatedly awarded him the 1918 prize for chemistry for his discovery of fixed nitrogen. An international outcry ensued, and many scientists boycotted the award ceremony. As debate over Haber raged into 1920, a chemist wrote to an American University Experiment Station veteran, Arthur B. Lamb, for his opinion. Lamb responded that if Haber was not the originator of the gas program, then "he isn't in a very different boat from many of us here." But if Haber did start and advocate for gas warfare, "realizing its terrible potentialities, he deserves the contempt and execration of humanity! And he will get it. But that doesn't affect his deserts as a scientist." Haber's mixed legacy remained imprinted upon American University. At the fixed-nitrogen laboratory that the government maintained at American University after the war, the equipment included a "Haber synthetic ammonia catalyst testing plant."

In late 1921, public opposition to chemical warfare surged during the Conference on the Limitation of Armament, an arms-control summit held in Washington with representatives from

Great Britain, France, Italy, Japan, and the United States. The conference convened on November 12, 1921, three years and one day after the Armistice. The conference was expected to be short and adjourn by Christmas. Instead, the conference negotiations proved more difficult than expected, lasting more than twice that long.

As the talks over chemical weapons and other armaments dragged on, a reporter went to speak to soldiers still recuperating at Walter Reed Army Hospital about gas warfare. Though not unanimous, many of the injured men felt chemical warfare should be banned. One Rhode Island man called it "the Devil's perfume." Another who had lost a leg and an arm in addition to being gassed told the reporter that gas "was born out of a thirst for torture. These guys all went through it," he went on, sweeping his remaining arm to point at all the other wounded soldiers, some of whom applauded. "They'll say 'cut out the gas.'"

The men who fought in the trenches weren't the only voices raised against chemical warfare. During the disarmament conference, General John J. Pershing, the hero of the Great War, became a vocal opponent of chemical warfare. Though Pershing had supported the establishment of the Chemical Warfare Service and had put Fries into his position, in the war's aftermath he made clear his personal opposition to gas, views that he had kept silent about during the war. During the disarmament conference, he chaired a subcommittee on land armaments, which forcefully denounced chemical weapons. His words rang with an undisguised moralism all the more striking for the fact that they came from a military man, not a pastor or a pacifist. "Chemical warfare should be abolished among nations, as abhorrent to civilization. It is a cruel, unfair and improper use of science. It is fraught with the gravest danger to non-combatants and demoralizes the better instincts of humanity," he wrote of the subcommittee's findings in November 1921.

The conference finished its work in February, drafting multiple treaties over naval power and submarine and gas warfare. The U.S.

Senate ratified the gas and submarine treaty in March 1922, banning wartime use of "asphyxiating, poisonous and other gases, and all analogous liquids, materials and devices." The treaty wasn't binding, though, without ratification by all participating countries. France subsequently balked, preventing the treaty from going into effect, but it did put the United States on record as opposing chemical warfare.

Major General Sibert was absent from the proceedings. In late February of 1920, Goliath had been relieved from duty as chief of the Chemical Warfare Service and ordered to assume command of Camp Gordon in Georgia. The War Department scuttlebutt was that the demotion was punishment for Sibert's opposition to Baker and March's plans to reduce the status of the Chemical Warfare Service, a view that Charles Herty, editor of the *Journal of Industrial and Engineering Chemistry,* expounded upon in the journal. The demotion was an unmistakable rebuke, akin to Sibert's dismissal from France two years before. This time, though, there was no new surprise position—Goliath had been put out to pasture. Rather than bow to this indignation, he retired. He moved to a farm in Bowling Green, Kentucky, where he raised hounds and spent his leisure time fishing and hunting foxes. He remarried, wedding a Scottish woman named Evelyn Clyne Bairnsfather as his third wife in 1922. He returned to work for several years in his native Alabama to oversee construction of the port in Mobile but eventually returned to Kentucky. He died at the farm in 1935.

Fries faced no such exile. He replaced Sibert as head of the service, even though he had worked as fiercely to oppose the War Department's plans in 1919, with now-major Earl J. Atkisson appointed as commanding officer at Edgewood. How exactly Fries avoided the ax and Sibert did not is something of a mystery—one possible reason is that Fries had support from line officers and from Pershing, who replaced Peyton March in 1921 as army chief of staff, despite their opposite views on chemical warfare.

The year 1925 proved to be a turning point for chemical weapons internationally. Wilson was dead, but his League of Nations lived on. That year, the league held its first major arms-limitation talks, the International Conference for the Control of the Traffic in Arms and Ammunition in Geneva. There were forty-three countries at the talks when they opened. The United States proposed a sweeping ban that prohibited not only chemical warfare but also export of chemical weapons agents. Other participating countries protested, pointing out that many common chemicals, such as chlorine and phosgene, had dual uses, for both industrial purposes and warfare. A compromise banned chemical warfare but not development, manufacture, or possession of chemical weapons. It also permitted their use against nonsignatory nations and retaliation against any nation that launched an attack with chemical weapons.

The resulting treaty was the 1925 Geneva Protocol for the Prohibition of the Use of Asphyxiating, Poisonous or Other Gases, and Bacteriological Methods of Warfare. After the delegates returned to the United States, many of the organizations that fought in 1919 to preserve the Chemical Warfare Service geared up again, this time to convince the U.S. Senate to reject the gas warfare treaty. It took a year for the Senate Foreign Relations Committee to take action on the treaty and send it on for a vote by the full Senate. Debate still would not start for months, giving opponents plenty of opportunity to organize. The American Legion distributed some twenty-five thousand pamphlets entitled *The Truth about the Geneva Gas Protocol—America Should Reject Stand—Preparedness Essential to Our National Security*. A lobbying organization called the National Association for Chemical Defense was also cobbled together in November of 1926 to work against the Geneva Protocol. The organization's treasurer, John Thomas Taylor, was director of the American Legion's legislative committee and a close friend of Amos Fries; Fries was also Washington's district commander of the American Legion. Many other members of the organization were Chemical Warfare Service veterans, such as Wilder Bancroft, Marston Bogert, and Sunny Jim Norris. The American Chemical Society also remained a vocal opponent of gas disarmament and the Geneva Protocol.

Shortly after the Geneva talks, Lewis was recalled to Edgewood for two weeks of active duty. During the disarmament fight, he had spoken out against banning chemical weapons, along with many of his wartime colleagues and fellow members of the American Chemical Society. Lewis and Fries appeared together in September of 1925 at the City Club of New York. Fries spoke of how preparation for chemical warfare was the only way to avoid war. "When we let the enemy know that we are able to pour on him ten tons of chemicals for every one he can pour on us, we won't have war," Fries told the audience. Following Fries, Lewis went on to talk about the humanity of gas warfare, an argument he regularly made in speeches, using the surgeon general's statistics about low fatality rates of gas cases. The back-to-back speeches embodied the contradictions in the arguments of chemical warfare supporters—that gas could be simultaneously the most humane weapon and so awful and barbaric that it could deter future wars.

The lobbying paid off, and the Senate never voted on the treaty. Even General John Pershing, America's champion of the war, was unable to convince the Senate to approve the treaty, pleading with the chairman of the Senate Foreign Relations Committee, "I cannot think it possible that our country should fail to ratify the protocol which includes this or a similar provision." The United States was the protocol's sole holdout. The rejection so enraged Congressman Hamilton Fish Jr. of New York—an opponent of chemical warfare—that he stormed to the House floor to personally excoriate Taylor, the American Legion representative. "I charge him with carrying on a tremendous propaganda financed by the chemical industries to defeat the poison gas treaty in the Senate," Fish ranted. "I charge him with having bamboozled members of the other body which has to pass on the treaty....I charge him with misrepresenting the views of the rank and file of the veterans and misleading our colleagues in the other body into believing they will incur the wrath of the Legionnaires if they vote for the gas treaty."

The 1920s were lean years for the service. Fries worked to keep the service in the public eye with tours of Edgewood, public demonstrations of gases, and regular speeches about chemical warfare. For a time, he claimed that gas was not just humane but that it was healthy, insisting that sitting in a chlorine-filled gas chamber was a kind of spa-treatment cure for colds and pneumonia, despite doctors' assessment that this was nonsense. Some of the top scientists at American University and satellite campuses of the Research Division—George Burrell, William Walker, Warren K. Lewis, Yandell Henderson, and others—remained active advisers to the Chemical Warfare Service.

Van Manning never truly gained credit for setting in motion the research that would turn into the Chemical Warfare Service. In fact, he had to fight for the recognition that he felt the Bureau of Mines deserved after the navy took credit for many of the bureau's discoveries. Manning had stepped down in 1920 to become director of research for the American Petroleum Institute and a consultant to the Cuban government. When President Hoover wrote to thank Manning for his service, the president lamented: "I do not feel that the country can afford to lose you." Years after the war ended, Manning remained embittered about how little credit the Bureau of Mines received for its efforts. When he died in 1932, the legacy ascribed to him was that he had made helium cheap and plentiful. His role in chemical warfare was scarcely mentioned. A brief burial notice in the *Washington Post* noted: "During the World War, he established the chemical laboratories at American University."

After Winford Lee Lewis returned to teaching, he became a vocal champion of chemical warfare, a foot soldier in the fight against disarmament. Forever hitched to the substance that bore his name, Lewis spoke frequently and enthusiastically about his wartime service. Both fame and infamy accompanied that association. "I have been accused of inventing a gas so poisonous that one drop on the tongue of a dog would destroy a whole city," Lewis said in a speech he delivered in 1922 to the City Club Forum in Rochester, New York. "Forsworn to silence by the War Department, I have been cussed and discussed by my colleagues and cajoled and flattered and upbraided generally."

The War Department had initially refused to allow Lewis to publish articles about lewisite, but after a British journal printed a step-by-step process for producing lewisite, Lewis published his own article in 1923. He retired from teaching in 1924 to work for a trade group, the American Meat Institute, where he worked until ill health forced him to retire in 1941. Some of that ill health was certainly the result of his war work — he almost completely lost his voice late in life because of the toxic fumes he had inhaled. In January of 1943, Myrtilla found Captain Dad unconscious on the snowy driveway beneath a second-floor porch. He had apparently tumbled from the porch after he slipped or suffered a heart attack. He died in the hospital a day later, on January 20, 1943.

The consummate deal maker Richmond M. Levering had no second act to his brief tenure with the Chemical Warfare Service. In late January of 1920, when the influenza pandemic surged in a lethal wave across the country and the world, New York City reported 2,855 new flu cases on a single day and 386 pneumonia cases, an alarming outbreak for the city's public health officials. Levering, who was living in an apartment on East Fifty-Sixth Street, was one of those cases. Despite his temperance and his relative youth — he was only thirty-nine years old — he died of pneumonia within a few days, on Wednesday, January 28, 1920.

Had Levering lived longer, he might have left a more precise account of his wartime activities and his arrangement with Walter Scheele. Even the Department of Justice couldn't complete the puzzle of Levering. In an investigation of Levering and Bielaski's relationship in late 1919, the lengthy report concluded that "there is not much material in the files to denote Levering's activities."

Scheele continued to work for Levering until December 1919. On December 9, Scheele applied for four patents. All four were variations of a familiar "incendiary mixture": two parts sodium peroxide and one part hexamethylenetetramine that produced a "mixture or composition of matter well adapted for use as material in warfare when filled into aero bombs or incendiary shells." It was, in other words, the combination of chemicals that he had used to try to set cargo ships afire.

Scheele would have one more moment in the sun. On September 16, 1920, a bomb exploded on Wall Street, an act of terrorism that has never been solved. Bureau of Investigation Chief William J. Flynn, the man who replaced A. Bruce Bielaski, asked Scheele to analyze the composition of the explosives. His report identified blasting gelatin as the explosive. Reporters were perplexed by the report authored by the former ship bomber. The *New York Times* attempted to prove that the government witness was the same Walter Scheele who had tried to blow up merchant ships. The secrecy around his case extended even to federal agencies he worked for. Just before the Wall Street bombing, a rear admiral in the U.S. Navy trying to sort out the unpaid Nyack Hospital bills from Scheele's hospitalization wrote to Thomas Edison's assistant asking who Scheele was. Edison's assistant provided a synopsis of how Scheele came to work at Jones Point. "Dr. Scheele was a German spy," the assistant wrote. "Scheele was a fine Chemist."

Five years after his indictment, Scheele's criminal case came to an end. On February 25, 1921, the chemist stood before Judge Julius M. Mayer in U.S. District Court and pleaded guilty to the 1916 charges. Then the judge sentenced Scheele to one day in the custody of the U.S. marshal. The light sentence resulted from the prosecutor's statement that Scheele had turned informant after his arrest and had aided the War and Navy Departments. The prosecutor provided scant details, saying that he did not know the specifics of Scheele's services. Few people did.

Eventually, Scheele opened a new chemical laboratory in Hackensack, New Jersey. He bought advertisements in the city directory that read simply "Dr. Walter T. Scheele, Research Laboratories." He and Marie moved into a nearby home. Perhaps Scheele strolled the 1.5 miles from the house to the laboratory, as he had in Bushwick years earlier, hat cocked on his head and chomping on a cigar, just an elderly man with a scarred face and an accent, ambling to work.

In 1921, the U.S. Patent Office approved Scheele's applications for his incendiary mixtures, as well as two other patents. The following year, he died of pneumonia at age sixty-two, two weeks after he applied for U.S. citizenship. His four-sentence obituary in the *Washington Post* stated that he had been imprisoned in Atlanta for the war's duration.

Fries remained a staunch defender of chemical weapons long after public opinion had turned against them. He left his position as chief of the Chemical Warfare Service in 1929. Rather than accept a reduced rank, he retired from the army. But there was no quiet retirement for Fries. Over the next several years, Fries became increasingly vociferous in his support of gas, lashing out at those he saw as enemies of gas warfare and condemning critics as Bolshevik lapdogs. His conservatism found other outlets as well—he became a virulent critic of labor unions, particularly those in Washington, D.C., schools. He championed legislation that forbid even the mention of communism in public schools. In his view, anyone who opposed chemical warfare was a subversive or a Communist seeking to undermine America. The Ku Klux Klan invited him to apply for membership. As World War II began, he predicted that chemical weapons would be a part of that savage war as well.

Fries was only partially correct. Chemical weapons were never launched on the battlefield in World War II. No nation wanted to be first, which would have permitted adversaries to respond in kind under the Geneva Protocol. President Franklin Roosevelt was also a fierce opponent of chemical warfare, calling it "inhuman and contrary to what modern civilization should stand for." While the Nazis technically abided by the Geneva Protocol, they wielded gas in another horrifying fashion: killing untold numbers of Jews in the gas chambers of Auschwitz, using hydrogen cyanide, or Zyklon B. It was also known as prussic acid, one of the discoveries of Carl Wilhelm Scheele, the chemist that Walter Scheele claimed as his relative. In an unspeakable irony, Fritz Haber had a role in that horror as well; the lab of the Jewish chemist had helped develop Zyklon B. The Nazis also had scientists at work on new, still more powerful compounds, as permitted under the Geneva Protocol. After World War II ended, the extent of the Nazi gas program became clear with the discovery that Germany had developed the nerve gases sarin and tabun. Historians have speculated on why the Germans never used chemicals on the battlefield. One hypothesis is that Adolf Hitler may have had an aversion to chemical warfare, having been gassed himself near Ypres in 1918, as he described in *Mein Kampf*. After the war, the secret U.S. Nazi relocation program, Operation Paperclip, brought German chemists to work on the American chemical warfare program.

Though chemical weapons were not used on the battlefield in World War II, the U.S. chemical weapons program in World War I was in many ways a dry run for another weapon program. James Bryant Conant, the shy chemist sent to Willoughby, had gone on to a professorship at Harvard. He became the university's president in 1933. As World War II loomed, President Roosevelt named him as chemical adviser to the National Resources Defense Council; he became chairman the next year. Named to the Military Policy Committee the year after, he became a prime architect of the Manhattan Project, and he personally participated in making the decision of where to drop the atom bomb on Japan.

Fries never abandoned his views that gas warfare was a more humane type of warfare because it only debilitated enemies and rarely killed them. Politics and dogmatic ideology laced his arguments. Enemies of America—pacifism and communism—lurked behind the efforts to ban gas warfare. He also maintained a sincere, if disturbing, belief that America needed to be prepared for an apocalyptic warfare in which gas steeped the battlefield. In his unpublished memoir, he wrote,

It will be used in grenades, field guns, by heavy artillery and by tanks and ships. Airplanes will drop it in bombs, or sprinkle it in large drops like a tropical rain storms [sic] or yet spread it as a fog coming over the land from the sea, but with a speed no wind ever knew. It will search out woods, deep trenches, cellars, and rocky canyons with the thoroughness of giant ants of Africa that devour everything in their path.

He also argued that gas would create what he called "continuous warfare." Rather than the sporadic conflict of episodic battles, chemical warfare would be constant, with diaphanous gas weapons everywhere all the time, like air itself. "Gas makes battles as continuous as heart beats and protection as necessary as breath itself....Gas makes the battle continuous and adds new force to the old adage, 'Eternal vigilance is the price of success.'" After he died in 1963, the words chiseled into his headstone at Arlington National Cemetery read CHIEF OF CHEMICAL WARFARE SERVICE.

Fries's dark vision never came to pass. In 1974, almost fifty years after the Geneva Conventions, the U.S. Senate finally adopted the treaty, and President Gerald Ford signed the ban in January 1975. The reason for the belated ratification was that momentum was gathering internationally for stronger disarmament measures that would do away with chemical weapons altogether. The Geneva Protocol still had the same provisions for developing chemical weapons and using them against violators of the ban and nonsignatories. Diplomatic efforts to ban biological and chemical weapons had diverged, but when the United States ratified a 1975 treaty against germ warfare, it included a provision affirming the goal of a complete ban on chemical weapons. Chemical weapons had been used several times over the years — in Ethiopia in the 1930s and in

Yemen in the early 1960s—but it was Saddam Hussein's use of chemical weapons against Iran and Iraqi Kurds in the late 1980s that opened a window for a stronger international agreement. The result was the Chemical Weapons Convention; more sweeping and aggressive than the earlier treaty, it banned the use, development, and production of chemical weapons and had a verification system to snuff even early efforts to create such weapons. The United States signed in 1996, and the convention went into effect in 1997.

Finally, the world would be free of chemical weapons. At least, that seemed to be the case until 2013, when Syrian president Bashar al-Assad's forces were accused of attacking a Damascus suburb with sarin-filled mortars, then chlorine-filled barrel bombs. ISIS, or the Islamic State, followed suit with mustard shells in August of 2015. In a gruesome first, the estranged half brother of North Korean leader Kim Jong Un died in a Malaysian airport in February of 2017 after hired assailants smeared the nerve agent VX on his face in an apparent assassination. Then on April 4, 2017, Assad again faced accusations of using sarin, this time in an attack in the northern Syrian province of Idlib. Images of dead children filled television screens, prompting American air strikes against Syrian targets. In 1919, Chief of Staff Peyton C. March had invoked the image of "innocent little children who had nothing to do with this game at all" to argue for the abolition of gas warfare. President Trump used similar language of outrage, decrying how "even beautiful babies were cruelly murdered in this very barbaric attack." Though Syria had joined the Chemical Weapon Convention after the 2013 attack, international law had again proved toothless, just as in 1915.

Today, chemical weapons are seen as anachronistic throwbacks, almost medieval in their clumsy simplicity and brutal deployment. Their patina of atavism has turned gas masks into a visual shorthand for latter-day apocalypse. Arguably, that's because chemical weapons today seem like both a throwback to an early form of warfare as well as forward looking to a nightmarish tomorrow when chemicals saturate land, sea, and air—a vision not that distant from Amos Fries's predictions of chemical weapons as the ultimate weapon of the future. If there was a doomsday ring to his predictions, it's because he saw chemical weapons as doomsday weapons. Fries was full of contradictions. Despite his insistence in the "humanity" of gas warfare, he also predicted a battlefield so toxic, so drenched in blistering, suffocating poisons, that it needed to be avoided at all costs.

The legacy of the U.S. Chemical Warfare Service in World War I proved to be conflicted and ambiguous. Chemical weapons unquestionably made an already horrific war worse and may have hastened the end, but gave neither side the game-changing edge that could end the war. And while some in the military argued that chemical weapons—like nuclear weapons later—would prevent future wars, few today would argue the human race is well served or the world has ever been a more peaceful place because of chemical weapons.

Yet far from being a mere footnote, the American experience with chemical warfare in world war had much more than a passing influence on the country; rather, it left indelible impressions on the military and on American society.

One of the changes wrought by World War I was a reconfiguration of the relationship between the military, scientists, and academia. The Chemical Warfare Service could not have come into being without the energetic contributions of scientists in the public and the private sectors. The rapid expansion of the service, in turn, gave an enormous boost to the burgeoning field of industrial chemistry. "The new profession got its trial by fire in World War I.... The war put [the] American chemical industry firmly on its feet," Warren K. Lewis wrote after the war.

Skeptics in later generations would criticize such cozy relationships as corrosive to science and the integrity of scientists. President Dwight Eisenhower coined the phrase "military-industrial complex" in 1961, but this wedding of public and private in wartime endeavors began in World War I. Never before had the military worked so closely with private industry in a cooperative enterprise, so closely that factories were militarized, soldiers worked side by side with civilians, and government and business became almost indistinguishable, as they did at Nela Park, the Dow plants in Midland, Michigan, and other chemical production centers. James Bryant Conant, who would become the president of Harvard only a few short years after the war, noted the change.

"To those of us who remember the situation in 1914 when the European conflagration broke out, the United States' entry into World War I marked a turning point in the relation of scientists to the Federal Government and, what is more important, to the national economy," Conant wrote in notes for an autobiography.

Chemical weapons also had a profound impact upon military strategy in the twentieth century. Though nuclear weapons far eclipsed chemical agents in power and lethality, the world's experience with chemical warfare in World War I is the DNA at the heart of the nuclear arms race. In a sense, the seeds of the Cold War were planted in Flanders fields. In the aftermath of World War I, proponents of chemical warfare, such as Amos Fries, firmly believed that chemical weapons could and would be used on a mass scale and that civilian population centers behind enemy lines were legitimate targets. That premise sprouted in the war's aftermath into a strategic framework that undergirded the notion of deterrence. Even the most vociferous critics of chemical arms within the War Department agreed that some stockpile, however small, must be maintained in case another country broke the arms conventions again, as Germany did in 1915. There was also agreement that an embryonic program needed to stay in place, with contingencies for swiftly expanding back into a full-scale chemical weapons program on a wartime footing, in the event of a new outbreak of gas warfare.

Under the rubric of deterrence, complete disarmament is never truly an option. Banning a weapon, no matter how repugnant or how widespread a consensus against it, was out of the question for the simple reason that no player on the world stage can be trusted to abide by international conventions. The risk of violation demanded "eternal vigilance"—Fries's words—to ensure that the United States would not be attacked with chemical arms in the future. The genie cannot be forced back into its bottle; a weapon, once discovered or used, can never be abandoned. In the decades to come, the United States would develop chemical weapons such as those on display at Fort Leonard Wood, including those appropriated from Germany after World War II and newer ones such as the nerve agent VX, one of the most lethal chemical weapons in existence. With the dawn of the nuclear age and the dropping of atomic bombs on Hiroshima and Nagasaki, the same strategy of deterrence undergirded the Cold War, requiring more-powerful weapons with greater reach, and in greater quantities.

In this context, lewisite's legacy is both fascinating and infuriating. The postwar reporting on the "super-poison gas" that the Mousetrap produced did not square with the reality, in terms of its potency or persistence. Despite my best efforts, I was unable to locate primary documentation that answered how, or if, lewisite would have been used had the war continued. Conclusive documentation about how much was made, and what became of it after the war, also eluded me. Similarly, I was stymied in my efforts to find clear documentation of the extent to which aerial gas bombardment was part of the 1919 war strategy, postwar statements to the press notwithstanding. In one of the AEF's postwar histories of the service, I discovered a telling hint to the War Department's reluctance to disclose such information. In a draft of a document I found, entitled *History of Chemical Warfare Service, AEF,* the section referring to development of aerial gas bombs and approval from the general staff was crossed out and marked for deletion.

So were the pronouncements about drenching German armies and cities with lewisite real, or were they bluster and propaganda, an empty threat that the United States could not — or would not — deliver had it been capable of doing so? My uneasy conclusion, based on the documentary evidence I have seen, is that the War Department was prepared for massive gas use in 1919 but was probably not prepared to deliver aerial gas bombs — whether lewisite or other weapons — on a large scale (though development of incendiary bombs was quite advanced by that time). Unquestionably the United States was poised to become a chemical warfare powerhouse, but if the reports about lewisite seem far-fetched, they were. Exaggerated and inflated, the stories about America's monstrous new weapon were stitched into a new era of deterrence. Fries himself acknowledged this in a startlingly candid letter to a newspaper editor in 1923. In his letter, he debunked some of the myths about lewisite, writing that it was "unfortunate that such extravagant statements are made concerning chemical warfare materials":

> The real reason for many of the extravagant statements which continue to appear in the Press from time to time is that during the war it was considered wise by both sides to use this propaganda to bolster up the inventions, and to raise the morale of one's own side while depressing or casting a damper on the other. Gas being so new and powerful, particularly against unprotected peoples, it appealed to the imagination of both sides.

There was another legacy of the Chemical Warfare Service — a very concrete one. The work at American University and the lightning-fast stand-up of the Willoughby plant was in many ways a dry run for the Manhattan Project. Some of the very scientists who participated in the Chemical Warfare Service — James Bryant Conant, Warren K. Lewis, and Robert A. Millikan among them — also worked on the atom bomb. The organization of the Manhattan Project followed a similar organizational structure as lewisite's development in World War I, with scientists ignorant of the work of their colleagues within the same project, keeping each segment of the work segregated through secrecy.

When I began this project, I expected to find plentiful personal accounts of the soldiers stationed at American University. After all, these were bright young men educated at top universities who must have written letters home, kept diaries, and recorded their thoughts for posterity. I was mistaken—it proved difficult to find first-person accounts from American University. My theory was that the soldiers at the station maintained their wartime silence about their work long after the work ended. Perhaps they did so out of a sense of patriotic duty. Perhaps it was because of the prevailing public sentiment that turned against gas warfare. Or perhaps it was simply because the war was over, and it was time to move on.

One group that enthusiastically documented its wartime endeavors, however, was the veterans of the First Gas Regiment, who maintained a vibrant veterans' organization called the First Gas Regimental Association. They held regular reunions for many decades, all the way into the 1980s. At the U.S. Army Chemical Corps Museum, I looked through dozens of issues of the gas regiment association newsletter. Called *Gas Attack,* it was full of rich anecdotes, funny stories, poetry, and a deeply melancholic obituary section that got longer with each edition, as members of the group slowly passed away. Doubts, criticisms, questions about chemical warfare, were not to be found in the pages of *Gas Attack,* which was still published quarterly into the 1990s. This was a veterans' organization, and these original chemical warriors took great pride in what they had done.

Tom Jabine rarely spoke of his service and, according to his son, developed a strong aversion to war. After he returned from France, he married and had children and worked for the Central Hudson Gas and Electric Company. He died in Poughkeepsie, New York, on February 1, 1938. His gassing at Charpentry in October 1918 caused health problems that plagued him for the rest of his life and that his son believed contributed to his early death at the age of forty-six.

Harold Higginbottom—"Higgie"—became a consistent reunion attendee and, eventually, the association president. After the war,

Higgie had left Lawrence to take a job as a textile chemist in Duluth, Minnesota, and returned six months later to get married and take Irene away with him to Minnesota. On December 25, 1920, three years to the day after he marched off to war in a snowstorm, he and Irene married in her parents' house, underneath an evergreen arch. Irene wore a white silk gown trimmed with pearls and carried a bouquet of lilies of the valley. She also carried a white handkerchief—perhaps the very one she mailed to Higgie in France to signal her devotion to him. The pastor from Lawrence Street Congregational Church wed them. The wedding announcement that ran in all three Lawrence newspapers the following Monday noted his overseas duty: "he served overseas as a sergeant in Company B, First Gas Regiment, and for a period of fifteen months saw very active service in the front line trenches."

In the reunion photographs, Higgie is reliably present, his long, mournful face immediately recognizable, Irene at his side. After her death he attended alone. In 1986, he told a fellow regimental association member, "Jack, the parts are plain worn out." He died just a few days later, on September 11, 1986, in Towson, Maryland, just outside Baltimore. About two weeks after Higgie's death, his son brought his father's footlocker to the association trustee. In it, neatly folded, was Higgie's uniform, along with his .45, leggings, overcoat, and, of course, his gas mask.

Acknowledgments

When I read the diary of Harold J. Higginbottom at the U.S. Army Chemical Corps Museum, I found a letter with it from the outgoing Gas Regimental Association president, Robert B. MacMullin. "Great source material in case some future historian or novelist takes a notion to write about the war," MacMullin wrote to Higgie. I don't know if I am that historian or there is another yet to come, but I am certain of this: *Hellfire Boys* is not the work of one person. Over the course of working on this book, I have had more consultations, discussions, and exchanges online, in person, and over the phone than I can count, so many in fact that it seems ridiculous to consider myself the sole author of this book. Thanking every individual who has assisted me along the way will inevitably omit some helpful soul, so let me apologize in advance to anyone unintentionally excluded from this recitation of thanksgiving.

The many descendants of scientists, soldiers, and officers of the Chemical Warfare Service I've talked to and corresponded with have been legion. Without them, this endeavor would have been impossible. I'm particularly indebted to the Olson family, the descendants of Charles William Maurer. Addie Ruth Maurer Olson, who sadly passed away in early 2016, graciously invited me into her home twice and allowed me to look at her father's papers and letters, which provided me with a glimpse of life at the American University Experiment Station. Erik Olson, her son and Sergeant Maurer's grandson, generously provided me with the photos of the American University Experiment Station and extended permission to use those photos in this book, for which I am extremely grateful. L. Philip Reiss, Winford Lee Lewis's grandson, welcomed me to visit him at his home in Sonora, California, over two days, to conduct an extensive interview and review Lewis's papers, photographs, letters, and memoir, all of which provided invaluable insight into an important character at the heart of this book. Not satisfied with discussing the subject of my book alone, Phil—or "Mr. Science Dude"—also gave me a crash course on the history of the gold rush, introduced me to the breathtaking beauty of the Sierra Nevada, and showed me such an enthusiastic welcome that I still grin to this day when I think back on my visit with him.

I was thrilled to have met Thomas Jabine Jr., the son of Thomas Jabine, who invited me to lunch and shared with me his recollections of his father. Descendants of William L. Sibert showed great interest in my book as well, including George and Kathy Sibert, who met with me for coffee and answered my questions, and Anne Sibert Buiter, who allowed me to read her grandfather's letters and sat for a photo portrait in her living room.

I'm grateful as well to three descendants of Vannoy H. Manning: Kim Zvik put me in contact with her relatives, Pam Manning Fein and Petrie M. Wilson, both of whom provided me with documents about Van Manning. Rosalind Williams, the granddaughter of Warren K. Lewis, invited me to her office at MIT to look through a box of documents about her grandfather. Her reminiscences of him and his comments about the ethical dimensions of his work in both world wars—a fraught subject not easily broached—helped me grasp the moral quandaries these scientists faced in wartime. I'm deeply grateful to her for her guidance and patience. I had a wonderful visit with Theodore Conant, the son of James Bryant Conant, sitting on the porch of his lovely home in Hanover, New Hampshire.

The most exciting historical discovery of my research came from Louise Cass, the granddaughter of James Thayer Addison, who investigated his papers at my request and discovered his complete war diaries. It was humbling to be entrusted with those diaries, and such an astonishing act of faith for her to send them to me, that I am moved even by the thought of it. Louise's cousin, Margot McCain, similarly provided invaluable documents, for which I'm deeply appreciative. I had wonderful exchanges with Holly Lake and Kathy Atkisson, descendants of Colonel Earl Atkisson, as well as with Connie Ann MacMullin Aust, the grand-daughter of Robert MacMullin. While his reminiscences from his time with Company E did not find their way into this book, I'm pleased to include his haunting poems, which are so evocative of the trials at the front. I'm grateful as well for the interest of Jennifer Lawrence, granddaughter of A. Bruce Bielaski, and for my conversations with Betty Higginbottom, the daughter-in-law of Harold and Irene Higginbottom.

Parts of this story have been told in various ways. The outstanding book *War of Nerves* by the late Jonathan B. Tucker brushed up against this early history. Other scholars have more recently dove into the World War I legacy, such as Joel A. Vilensky's *Dew of Death* and Thomas I. Faith's *Behind the Gas Mask,* both excellent, meticulously researched works that provided invaluable guidance for me. My interview with Vilensky was among the first I did as I set out to report on Spring Valley for the *Times* in 2012, and his research pointed me toward document sources that would have been easy to overlook. My discussions with Faith came toward the very end, when he guided me toward General Pershing's papers and other overlooked caches of valuable documentation and generously shared documents that I had trouble locating.

So many archivists and librarians have patiently guided me to files along the way that I can scarcely find space for them. Here are the ones I can recount: Dominiek Dendooven at the In Flanders Fields Museum in Ieper (Ypres), which I visited in April of 2015; Gertjan Remmerie, formerly of Talbot House in Poperinge, Belgium, who generously provided the transcript of Jeanne Batteu's interview; Susan McElrath, the archivist at American University Library; Becky

Jordan, reference specialist at Iowa State University Special Collections; Carol Mowrey at the Mystic Museum in Mystic, Connecticut; the Abraham Lincoln Public Library; the Deer Island Historical Society; Scott Sanders at Antioch College; Louise Sandberg at the Lawrence (Massachusetts) Public Library; Amita Kiley, collections manager and research coordinator at the Lawrence History Center; the Lake County Historical Society in Willoughby, Ohio; the Willoughby Historical Society; Ann and Pat Lewis at the Willoughby Public Library; Richard Bly and Scott Morgan at the Kane Depot Preservation Society; Patrick Raftery, librarian at the Westchester County Historical Society; the Peekskill Public Library; Marianne Leese, senior historian of the Historical Society of Rockland County (New York); Lindy Smith, research services archivist at Ohio State University; Andrea Mohr, Special Collections and University Archives, Oregon State University; the Washingtonia Room at the Martin Luther King Library in Washington, D.C.; the staff at the Kiplinger Research Library of the Historical Society of Washington, D.C.; the U.S. Army Heritage and Education Center in Carlisle, Pennsylvania; the archives of the Smithsonian Institution; Daniel Barbiero at the National Academy of Sciences Archives; and Mike Hanson at the Pentagon Library. I'm also grateful for the assistance and guidance of archivists and librarians at Catholic University, MIT, Harvard University, Princeton University, Yale University, Johns Hopkins, and Columbia. Maria Asp, archivist at the Royal Swedish Academy of Sciences, directed my genealogical questions about Carl Wilhelm Scheele to historian Anders Lennartsson.

Jeffery Smart, command historian at Edgewood, fielded many an off-base question, and Kathy Chiolfi similarly provided me guidance when I reached research dead ends. While I've not quite gained senior status as a regular at the National Archives, I did receive a great deal of help from the diligent research assistants there, who guided me through the struggles of navigating century-old records. The U.S. Army Corps of Engineers has been extremely helpful, both with providing archival documents and allowing me access to contemporary events. For a time, I embedded with the corps during the cleanup in Spring Valley, allowing me some behind-the-scenes observations that helped my understanding of technical aspects of the cleanup. I particularly want to thank Brenda Barber, Andrea Takash, J. R. Martin, and Dan Noble, who answered my endless litany of questions for years on end. Numerous activists and neighborhood residents of Spring Valley have helped me to understand this history as well: Kent Slowinski, Ginny Durrin, and others. Thank you to Tom and Kath Loughlin, who shared their painful story of living in the house that I saw razed in 2012. Simon Hankinson gave me a firsthand glimpse of the interior of Theodore Roosevelt Hall and a vantage point of the city as it might have appeared in April of 1917. Amy Smithson provided invaluable background during my reporting, as did Michael Neiberg at the U.S. Army War College. Seth Carus of the National Defense University and John Ellis van Courtland Moon, professor emeritus of history at Fitchburg State College, both provided insight and feedback regarding my conclusions. Hampton Sides and Anne Goodwin Sides gave me sage advice and guided me to speak with Gregg Bemis about the sinking of the *Lusitania*.

This book would have never reached the stage it did without the assistance of Kip Lindberg, director of the U.S. Army Chemical Corps Museum at Fort Leonard Wood, Missouri, who welcomed me for two days of research and guided me to the journal of Harold Higginbottom, who of course ended up as a major figure in this book. Christy Lindberg, the archivist at Fort Leonard Wood, assisted me with my FOIA request for records. Historian Simon Jones was my intrepid battlefield guide and also gave invaluable feedback for my prologue, not to mention the occasional historical lifeline when I ran up against vexing questions about the Great War and chemical warfare.

This book would not exist but for the sorcery woven in the classrooms and workshops of Goucher College's creative nonfiction MFA program, the literary womb from which this entire enterprise sprang. Tom French, Suzannah Lessard, Jacob Levenson, and Dick Todd helped me to mold and shape the earliest iterations of this book, and Laura Wexler was my research oracle. The program's director emeritus, Patsy Sims, and its current director, Leslie Rubinkowski, have been encouraging throughout. That goes, too, for all my amazing classmates, who have cheered me on throughout the process, ever since my first workshop in summer of 2012 when I told Jim, Laura, Andrea, and Julie about Spring Valley. If it weren't for Jesse Holland, who beamed at me from across the table at the Root 100 dinner in 2012, I might still be laboring in some parallel universe of daily deadlines. Fellow alums in the D.C. area and beyond—Jim Dahlman, Erica Johnson, Tom Kapsedelis, Carol Marsh, Pam Kelley, and others—read sections along the way. Wil Hylton and Pamela Haag provided much-needed advice at a crucial juncture (i.e., deadline time). There have been innumerable editors and reporters at the *New York Times* who have helped and encouraged me over the years—two in particular are Ian Urbina and Hillary Stout. I'm indebted to the Alicia Patterson Foundation and its director, Margaret Engel. The foundation's 2015 fellowship allowed me to explore topics related to the book and dig deep in my research. NARA historian and author Mitch Yockelson swooped in like an angel of history for a final, fine-tooth fact check—an astonishing act of generosity for which I am humbly in his debt.

I'm extremely grateful to Little, Brown, and in particular my former editor, John Parsley, who was a supporter of *Hellfire Boys* even before I stepped off the train in Manhattan in the fall of 2014. John's calming voice and editorial advice, along with the insightful questions of his colleague Will Boggess and guidance from his assistant Gabriella Mongelli, steadied the helm throughout the writing of the book and improved the book immeasurably. A huge thank-you to my indefatigable copyeditor, Susan Bradanini Betz, whose untiring patience and diligence saved me from many an embarrassing error, and to Peggy Freudenthal, who kept the editorial trains running on time. My new editor, Phil Marino, stepped into the role with gusto and style, and became an enthusiastic partner in no time.

My intrepid agent, Howard Yoon, hauled me to the conclusion that the better book was the bigger story. My readers suffered through the earliest draft of the book and gave me advice and thoughtful criticism that helped me spin some of the straw into gold: Lewis "Goat" Robinson, Sasha Abramsky, Jonathan Green, and Beverly Gage. Sam Williamson, in his lawyerly way, prodded me toward writing a book long before I ever thought it possible— thanks, Spud.

My family has been a stupendous source of support and encouragement—my father, Stan, and my sisters, Alice and Margaret. The keystone to it all, the person who has held the whole thing together, is my dazzling wife, Audie. She nudged me toward new endeavors, to color outside the margins of journalism that I had grown too comfortable with, and allowed me to experiment with writing in ways I had dreamed of but never dared to try.

Last, my mother, Ann Badger Emery, died in spring of 2013, before this undertaking had germinated into a full-fledged book. She was a pacifist in spirit with a gentle soul who hated violence in any form. Her generosity, love of family and music and art, and unwavering faith in humanity was a beacon of clarity for me when she was alive. She remains so today, even in moments when the world has appeared most dark. This book is dedicated to her. I hope that it would have made her proud.

Notes on Sources

"If you can't find it, you don't have it." That statement became my mantra while working on *Hellfire Boys* because of the mountain of documents—a digital mountain, for the most part—that I collected over the course of my research.

As a rule, I relied on primary documents whenever possible. Finding supporting documentation for the three strands of this story—the work of the Research Division, the stories of the Hellfire Boys sent to France, and the saga of Walter T. Scheele—each presented its own challenges. With respect to the Research Division, the National Archives has a vast number of records related to the Bureau of Mines and the Chemical Warfare Service, and yet some documents crucial to a full understanding of this history have proved difficult to find or don't exist, such as definitive documentation of the quantities of lewisite created and how it was disposed of. Moreover, the bifurcated history of the CWS—spread under a multitude of departments and agencies in its first year, then reorganized as the CWS—means that records are spread among numerous record groups in the archives. Some records may never be found. One archivist I spoke to described a specific research errand as "looking for a needle in a stack of needles." It was an apt description.

Compounding that problem, Fort Leonard Wood has a large repository of World War I–era documents related to the CWS that have never been accessioned to the National Archives; some have never even been processed. In 2015, I filed a Freedom of Information

Act request for records related to lewisite and other aspects of the book. In summer of 2017, that FOIA was still being processed and the request was incomplete.

The U.S. Army Corps of Engineers responded quickly to FOIAs related to Spring Valley and the American University Experiment Station. Specifying locations of those records in the endnotes was difficult. The documents, which largely originated from the National Archives, arrived in large batches using an organizational system specific to the Army Corps of Engineers. In the endnotes, those records are denoted as U.S. Army Corps of Engineers (USACE). Seeking out specific documents was not as difficult as it might seem: the corps compiled a finding aid of supporting documents for a history of Spring Valley from 1994, entitled *A Brief History of the American University Experiment Station and U.S. Navy Bomb Disposal School,* which can be found in the bibliography. That list allowed me to request specific historical records.

While I attempted to use multiple document sources for verification when possible, oftentimes that was not an option. That was particularly the case with Walter T. Scheele. The Old German Files at the National Archives in College Park are by far the most comprehensive chronicle of Scheele's story during the war, but they also are the only such repository of information that I'm aware of, and I had to rely heavily on those records as a result. Many of the postwar books about German espionage (such as Emerson Hough's *The Web,* Frank Strother's *Fighting Germany's Spies,* and especially Rintelen's *The Dark Invader*) are entertaining, colorful, and rich in detail, but not to be relied upon. While the Old German Files can be viewed on microfilm at the National Archives at College Park, for the most part I used the digital document service Fold3.com to access, search, and view these documents.

The AEF records from overseas are the most comprehensive and best organized of the documents I relied on. The most complete repository of records about the First Gas Regiment is at the U.S. Army Chemical Corps Museum in Fort Leonard Wood, which has an astonishingly comprehensive library of battle reports, division histories, and other official records of the regiment. The museum also has a number of personal histories in the form of diaries, letters, photographs, and scrapbooks, as well as the always entertaining *Gas Attack*. It was there, seated at a folding table in the office of the museum director, Kip Lindberg, that the story of the Hellfire Regiment came to life for me.

While rich material for the book came from private sources, such as the priceless war diary of James Thayer Addison, I suspect that far more archival treasures remain buried in family archives, file boxes, and forgotten corners of attics. I only hope that if such documents exist they are discovered, preserved, and shared before they are lost forever.

Notes

Abbreviations
AEF—American Expeditionary Forces
BOI—Bureau of Investigation
BOM—Bureau of Mines
CCM—U.S. Army Chemical Corps Museum
CWS—Chemical Warfare Service
NAB—National Archives Building, Washington, D.C.
NACP—National Archives at College Park, MD
NARA—National Archives and Records Administration
OCE—Office of the Chief of Engineers
OGF—Old German Files
RG—record group
USACE—U.S. Army Corps of Engineers
WDG—War Department General and Special Staffs

Introduction: January 5, 1993

xv The sky over Washington: NOAA historical weather data; *Washington Post,* Jan. 5, 1993.

xv At around 1:40: USACE, *After Action Report for the Service Response Force Conducting Operation Safe Removal 5 Jan.–3 Feb. 1993* (Edgewood Research, Development & Engineering Center, Mar. 1994).

xvi He called the fire department: Ibid., 12.

xvi The area could: Martin Weil and Santiago O'Donnell, "WWI Munitions Unearthed at D.C. Construction Site," *Washington Post,* Jan. 6, 1993.

xvii Ultimately, 144 pieces: USACE, *After Action Report for the Service Response Force Conducting Operation Safe Removal, 5 Jan.–3 Feb. 1993* (Edgewood Research, Development & Engineering Center, Oct. 1994).

xvii In an ironic counterpoint: "U.N. Inspection Team Cools Heels in Bahrain: Crew Was Headed for Iraqi Toxic Arms Dump," *Washington Post,* Jan. 13, 1993, A17.

Prologue

3 Ypres: The book generally uses spellings from the war era, when west Flanders was more French influenced than it is today. Flemish nationalism has replaced almost all French names with Dutch, turning "Ypres" into "Ieper."

3 Marie was twenty-six: Dominiek Dendooven, archivist at the In Flanders Fields Museum in Ypres (Ieper), Belgium, compiled eyewitness accounts of Apr. 22, 1915, in a document entitled "Overview: 22 April 1915—Eyewitness Accounts of the First Gas Attack." This included the accounts of Marie Desaegher, Maurice Quaghebeur, and others, from scanned diaries, letters, and other supporting documentation.

4 Just before 5:30 p.m.: Major Charles E. Heller, *Chemical Warfare in World War I: The American Experience, 1917–1918,* Leavenworth Papers, no. 10 (Fort Leavenworth, KS: Combat Studies Institute, U.S. Army Command and General Staff College, 1984).

5 From the city: Owen S. Watkins, "Personal Glimpses," *Literary Digest,* Sept. 4, 1915, 483.

5 Others were staggering: Jonathan B. Tucker, *War of Nerves: Chemical Warfare from World War I to al-Qaeda* (New York: Pantheon Books, 2006), 15.

5 The Canadians turned: Max Arthur, *Forgotten Voices of the Great War: A History of World War I in the Words of the Men and Women Who Were There* (Guilford, CT: Lyons Press, 2004), 79–80. This account from Private W. Underwood of the First Canadian Division is quoted in Dendooven's "Overview: 22 April 1915."

6 neutralizing agent: Sodium thiosulfate. Ludwig Fritz Haber, *The Poisonous Cloud: Chemical Warfare in the First World War* (Oxford: Clarendon Press, 1986), 32.

7 There had been hints: Amos A. Fries and Clarence J. West, *Chemical Warfare* (New York: McGraw-Hill, 1921), 11.

7 "the Chemists' War": "A Chemists' War," *Evening World,* May 6, 1915, 18.

7 In fact, scientists had been: "Government Expert on Explosives Tells of Important Part Played by Chemistry in War," *Evening Star,* Nov. 29, 1914, 6.

8 "I have never": Videotaped interview with Jeanne Battheu and transcript courtesy of Talbot House, Poperinge, Belgium. Ms. Battheu's recollections came close to the end of her life, and in the videotape, she recalled the year as 1916 and was not specific as to the dates of her memories. Military historian Simon Jones confirmed that records from Poperinge indicate that there was a 1916 chlorine gas attack.

Chapter One: Holy Week

11 "What horrors night foretells": Excerpt from "Prelude to Battle," Robert B. MacMullin, First Gas Regiment Collection, CCM, Fort Leonard Wood, MO.

11 Red, white, and blue bunting: "Pacifists Meeting Proves Big Fizzle," *Washington Times,* Apr. 3, 1917, 4.

12 Rather, it was a genteel reception: "Give Dinner for William F. Finleys," *Washington Times,* Apr. 3, 1917, 7.

12 The elegant banquet hall: "Political Affairs Crowd Society," *Washington Herald,* Apr. 3, 1917, 6.

14 For months: *War Expenditures: Hearings before Subcommittee No. 3 (Foreign Expenditures) of the Select Committee on Expenditures in the War Department,* vol. 3, 66th Congress, 3406 (1920).

14 Tanks made their debut: "Tank Was Juggernaut to Helpless Germans," *New York Times,* Oct. 13, 1916, 3.

15 From its earliest days: "Voice Protest Against War," *Northwest Worker,* Feb. 7, 1917, 1.

15 Isolationists viewed the war: Senate Majority Leader Robert La Follette of Wisconsin was most prominent.

16 The prominent role: Sharon Bertsch McGrayne, *Prometheans in the Lab: Chemistry and the Making of the Modern World* (New York: McGraw-Hill, 2001), 66.

16 Just days after the attack: Diana Preston, *A Higher Form of Killing: Six Weeks in World War I That Forever Changed the Nature of Warfare* (New York: Bloomsbury Press, 2015), 113.

16 The offensive was: Peter Hart, *The Great War: A Combat History of the First World War* (New York: Oxford University Press, 2013), 154.

17 Britain's dreadnoughts had: Cyril Falls, *The Great War: 1914–1918* (New York: Capricorn Books, 1959), 153.

17 Two months after the *Lusitania:* The suspect, Frank Holt, was arrested the next day, after he later shot banker J. P. Morgan Jr. Holt was believed to be an alias for Erich Muenter, a Harvard professor who had disappeared after killing his wife in 1905.

17 In July 1916: "Munition Explosions Cause Loss of $20,000,000," *New York Times,* July 31, 1916, 1.

18 However remote the possibility: Letter from George E. Hale to William Welch, July 3, 1915, NAS-NRC Central File, 1914–1918, Executive Committee: Projects, Helium Production, 1917, National Academy of Sciences Archives.

18 He kept the country: David M. Kennedy, *Over Here: The First World War and American Society* (New York: Oxford University Press, 1980), 33.

19 The result was: Rexmond C. Cochrane, *The National Academy of Sciences: The First Hundred Years, 1863–1963* (Washington, DC: National Academy of Sciences, 1978), 212.

19 On August 5: Ibid., 213.

21 Given the divergence: "Bureau of Mines Formed," *New York Times,* July 3, 1910, 6.

21 "Many of the things": "Van H. Manning," *The Black Diamond* 55, no. 6 (1915): 110.

21 Manning wrote Holmes's obituary: Van H. Manning, "Joseph A. Holmes," *Journal of Industrial and Engineering Chemistry* 7, no. 8 (Aug. 1915): 712.

22 "We can build": "Dinner to Director Van H. Manning of the Bureau of Mines," *Metallurgical and Chemical Engineering* 8, no. 16 (Dec. 15, 1915): 979.

23 As Manning rose: Transcript of Manning banquet, Nov. 20, 1915, courtesy of Petrie M. Wilson.

23 "peace without victory": "Text of President's Address to the Senate," *New York Times,* Jan. 23, 1917, 1.

23 A German newspaper: "Germans Criticize Wilson's Proposal," *New York Times,* Jan. 26, 1917, 1.

24 "This means war": Joseph Patrick Tumulty, *Woodrow Wilson as I Know Him* (Garden City, NY: Doubleday, Page and Company, 1921), 256.

24 A German submarine: "Relations with German Are Broken Off; American Ship *Housatonic* Sunk, Crew Safe," *New York Times,* Feb. 4, 1917, 1.

24 On February 6: "14 More Ships Sunk by Germany in a Day," *New York Times,* Feb. 7, 1917, 1; "U-Boats Sink Ten More Ships," *New York Times,* Feb. 9, 1917, 1.

24 As Wilson went: "President Asks Broad Powers to Meet U-Boat Warfare," *New York Times,* Feb. 27, 1917, 1.

24 a new outrage: "Germany Seeks an Alliance Against Us," *New York Times,* Mar. 1, 1917, 1.

24 Manning summoned his chiefs: Van H. Manning, "War Gas Investigations," advance chapter of *War Work of the Bureau of Mines,* Bulletin 178-A, BOM, Department of the Interior (Washington, DC: U.S. Government Printing Office, 1919).

24 The bureau headquarters: Historic American Buildings Survey, Busch Building, 710 E Street, Northwest, Washington, District of Columbia, DC (Washington, DC: Library of Congress Prints and Photographs Division, documentation compiled after 1933).

25 Manning maintained a tidy office: Photo of Van H. Manning at desk, Nov. 1918, RG 111, Signal Corps, photo 56573, box 456, NACP. Though the photo is dated Nov. 1918, which would have been after the Department of the Interior moved from its E Street location, I presume that details from the photo, such as furnishings and orderliness, would have applied equally to the earlier office.

25 "a simple cloth mask": George S. Rice, Chief Mining Engineer, Department of the Interior, BOM, Washington, DC, Memorandum by GS Rice regarding Early History of Mask and Gas Investigations for the Army, Jan. 9, 1918, War Gas Investigations, Reports and Other Records, Records of the BOM, RG 70, finding aid A-1, entry 46, box 110, NACP.

26 While Parson's skepticism: Charles L. Parsons, "The American Chemist in Warfare," *Science* 48, no. 1242 (1918): 377.

26 The next day: Manning, "War Gas Investigations," 2.

27 At the end of March: "Cabinet Weighs War Plans," *New York Times,* Mar. 24, 1917, 1.

27 Because explosives were: Letter from Van H. Manning to the National Research Council, Apr. 6, 1917, Administration, Executive Committee, Committee on Noxious Gases, National Academy of Sciences Archives.

27 a nationwide census: "War List of Experts," *Washington Post,* Mar. 31, 1917, 4.

28 Wilson's second term: "President Takes the Oath," *New York Times,* Mar. 5, 1917, 1.

28 The next day: Until the ratification of the Twentieth Amendment in 1933, Inauguration Day was Mar. 4, an arbitrary date that the Continental Congress chose for the nation's first inauguration in 1789. The Twentieth Amendment fixed the inauguration as Jan. 20 in perpetuity.

28 His war address: "50,000 See Inauguration," *New York Times,* Mar. 6, 1917, 1.

28 On the day: "War Congress Is Besieged by Pacifists," *Washington Times,* Apr. 2, 1917, 1.

28 When demonstrators tried: "Pacifists in Riots; Lodge is Assaulted," *Washington Post,* Apr. 3, 1917, 3.

29 Wilson waited all day: Arthur Walworth, *American Prophet,* rev. ed., vol. 2 of *Woodrow Wilson* (Cambridge, MA: Boston Riverside Press, 1965), 97.

29 "I have called the Congress": "President Calls for War Declaration," *New York Times,* Apr. 3, 1917, 1.

30 At the Washington headquarters: "Pacifists Enraged over Yellow Paint," *Washington Times*, Apr. 3, 1917, 2.

31 After the band: "Hiss Senator Who Sat as Hotel Band Played the National Anthem," *Washington Post*, Apr. 4, 1917, 2.

31 The Bureau of Mines: Robert A. Millikan, *The Autobiography of Robert A. Millikan* (New York: Prentice-Hall, 1950), 140.

31 Part of the committee's business: Meeting of the NRC Military Committee, Apr. 3, 1917, NAS-NRC Central File, 1914–1918, Executive Committee: Projects, Helium Production, 1917, National Academy of Sciences Archives.

32 Burrell had come: James Terry White, *The National Cyclopaedia of American Biography*, vol. 46 (New York: James T. White and Co., 1963), 228.

32 The U.S. Geological Survey: Mary C. Rabbitt, *The United States Geological Survey: 1879–1989*, U.S. Geological Survey, U.S. Department of the Interior (Washington, DC: U.S. Government Printing Office, 1989). The document is available at http://pubs.usgs.gov/circ/c1050/second.htm.

32 The previous October: "Movements of the Geologists," *Oil Trade Journal*, Dec. 1916, 98.

33 Rounding out: John B. West, *Yandell Henderson 1873–1944*, vol. 74 of *Biographical Memoirs of the National Academy of Sciences* (Washington, DC: National Academies Press, 1998), 145. The memoir can be found online at http://www.nasonline.org/publications/biographical-memoirs/memoir-pdfs/henderson-yandell.pdf.

33 Accused of being: Memorandum from file, In re: Prof. Yandell Henderson, Mar. 11, 1918, Investigative Case Files of the BOI, 1908–1922, NARA M1085, OGF, 1909–21, case no. 8000-75606, roll 443, NACP.

33 Lean and commanding: "Gen. J. E. Kuhn Dies; Army Engineer, 71," *New York Times*, Nov. 13, 1935.

34 It would call: "Chance to Aid Your Country in the Quartermaster Corps," *Evening Star*, Apr. 21, 1917, 9.

35 "The President has signed": "President Proclaims War; Warns Enemy Aliens Here; 91 German Ships Seized and Spies Put Under Arrest," *New York Times*, Apr. 7, 1917, 1.

35 At port cities: "German Ships All Damaged," *Washington Times*, Apr. 6, 1917, 1.

35 Shortly after Wilson signed: "Cuba to Be US Ally," *Washington Times*, Apr. 7, 1917, 3.

35 On the day: Van H. Manning letter to Charles Walcott, Apr. 6, 1917, NAS-NRC Central File, 1914–1918, Executive Committee: Projects, Helium Production, 1917. National Academy of Sciences Archives.

36 "The entrance of the United States": Letter from George E. Hale to overseas academies, Apr. 6, 1917, NAS-NRC Central File, 1914–1918, Executive Committee: Projects, Helium Production, 1917. National Academy of Sciences Archives.

Chapter Two: An American University

37 Minutes after the explosions: "Two Trolley Poles Wrecked," *Evening Star*, Apr. 7, 1917, 2.

37 When residents opened: "Germans Blow Up Ship," *Washington Post*, Apr. 8, 1917, 6.

37 The president's war proclamation: "President Wilson's War Proclamation," *Washington Times,* Apr. 6, 1917, 1.

37 the attorney general ordered: "Germans Warned to Keep Mouths Shut," *Washington Times,* Apr. 6, 1917, 1.

38 While it wasn't yet clear: "Gas in Warfare: Considered from the Medical Standpoint," Apr. 6, 1917, Frank P. Underhill Papers, numbered folders, 80–106, group no. 514, box 6, Yale University Library Manuscript Collections, New Haven, CT.

39 The men agreed: Minutes of Apr. 7, 1917, meeting of the Committee on Noxious Gases, BOM, War Gas Investigations and Other Records, BOM, finding aid A-1, entry 46, box 110, NACP.

39 The northern French city: "Town Hall, Belfry and Squares of Arras," The Remembrance Trails of the Great War, Comité Régional de Tourisme Nord-Pas de Calais, accessed Apr. 7, 2017, http://www.remembrancetrails-northernfrance .com/visit-the-sites/post-war-reconstruction/town-hall-belfry-and -squares-of-arras.html.

40 Buildings ringing the city: Richard Harding Davis, "Arras an Unburied City," *New York Times Magazine,* Dec. 12, 1915.

41 three thousand projectors: Brooks E. Kleber and Dale Birdsell, *The Chemical Warfare Service: Chemicals in Combat* (Washington, DC: Center of Military History, 1990), 13.

41 The dense clouds: Haber, *Poisonous Cloud,* 182.

41 Even if they had time: Kleber and Birdsell, *Chemical Warfare Service,* 13.

41 Celebrants sang a Benediction hymn: Frank Fox, *The Battles of the Ridges: Arras–Messines, Mar.–June, 1917* (London: C. Arthur Pearson, 1918), 28.

42 By early afternoon: Kleber and Birdsell, *Chemical Warfare Service.*

43 Manning told Interior Secretary Franklin Lane: Letter from Van Manning to Franklin Lane, Apr. 9, 1917. NAS-NRC, Executive Committee: Projects, Helium Production, National Academy of Sciences Archives.

43 He had a brilliant: E. C. Sullivan, *George Augustus Hulett, 1867–1955,* vol. 34 of *Biographical Memoirs of the National Academy of Sciences* (Washington, DC: National Academy of Sciences, 1960). Available online at http://www.nasonline .org/publications/biographical-memoirs/memoir-pdfs/hulett-george.pdf.

43 His skills included: Charles P. Smyth, draft of biographical sketch of George A. Hulett, George A. Hulett Papers, 1909–1962, call no. C0460, box 2, folder 3, Manuscript Division, Department of Rare Books and Special Collections, Princeton University Library.

43 He was also: "George Augustus Hulett," compiled by E.C.S., box 2, folder 3, Hulett Papers, Princeton University Library.

43 The professor in charge: Letter from J. S. Ames to George Hulett, Apr. 6, 1917, box 2, folder 3, Hulett Papers, Princeton University Library.

44 Hulett boarded the steamship *Chicago:* One postwar profile of Hulett describes his passage as being aboard the steamship *Rochambeau,* but other records strongly suggest that he sailed on the *Chicago.*

44 He scanned the wharf: Letter from George Hulett to family, May 4, 1917, box 2, folder 10, Hulett Papers, Princeton University Library.

44 For his part: Ibid., Apr. 19, 1917, Hulett Papers, Princeton University Library.

44 The beauty meant little: Ibid., May 1, 1917, Hulett Papers, Princeton University Library.

45 "Everything is open": Fries and West, *Chemical Warfare*, 15.

46 "The use of these gases": Letter from George Hulett to Manning, May 5, 1917, Hulett Papers, Princeton University Library.

46 "The tremendous scale": Report of Noxious Gas Investigations, prepared for meeting of Subcommittee of National Research Council, Apr. 21, 1917, NAS-NRC Central File, 1914–1918, Executive Committee: Projects, Helium Production, 1917, National Academy of Sciences.

48 The only man: "Henry Drysdale Dakin, 1880–1952," *Journal of Biological Chemistry* 198 (1952): 491–94.

49 The men had discussed: Minutes of Apr. 21, 1917, meeting of the Committee on Noxious Gases, 14, Central Correspondence, 1918–1941, War Department, CWS, RG 175, finding aid PI-8, entry 1, box 166, NACP.

50 to seal a military pact: "Wilson Seals French Pact," *Washington Times,* Apr. 26, 1917, 1.

50 French and American flags: "With Gen. Joffre, M. Viviani Calls on President," *Evening Star,* Apr. 26, 1917, 1.

50 Before the pageantry: E-mail from American University archivist Susan McElrath.

51 The idea had: Letter from George Washington to Virginia Governor Robert Brooke, March 16, 1795. University Archives and Special Collections, American University Library.

51 Bishop Hurst found: Rev. Albert T. Osborn, "The Genesis of the American University," *Methodist Magazine* 2, no. 1 (July–Aug. 1899): 153.

51 But despite Hurst's optimism: Untitled brief, *American University Courier* (Dec. 1900); "Open the Doors for Work, *American University Courier* (Dec. 1901); "Why Not Open for Work?," *American University Courier* (Apr. 1904); "The University of the White Deer Grotto," *American University Courier* 15, no. 4 (Mar. 1909): 3.

52 American finally opened: "President Wilson Opens the American University," *American University Courier* 21, no. 1 (June 1914): 1–7, University Archives and Special Collections, American University Library.

52 "On motion": Albert Osborn, "Chronology of Events 1907–1940," Apr. 26, 1917, University Archives and Special Collections, American University Library.

53 The university newspaper: "The American University in the Service of the Nation," *American University Courier* 23, no. 3 (Apr. 1917): 3.

53 Leighton sent an official letter: "Judge Leighton's Letter to President Wilson and the Reply," *American University Courier* 13, no. 3 (Apr. 1917): 1; Memorandum from Major General Henry Jervey to Assistant Secretary of War, Subject: Purchase of American University Property, Washington, DC, Nov. 4, 1918, 1, Spring Valley–Baltimore District, Records for Project C03DC091801 (Spring Valley—Military Munitions Response Program), USACE.

54 On the warm: Osborn, "Chronology of Events 1907–1940," May 17, 1917.

55 The day after: Ibid., May 18, 1917.

55 After Manning's meeting: Yandell Henderson, *History of Research at Yale University,* Nov. 20, 1918, USACE.

56 "A patriotic offer": Letter from Van H. Manning to George S. Hale, May 26, 1917, NAS-NRC, Executive Committee: Projects, Helium Production, National Academy of Sciences Archives.

Chapter Three: Diabolical Instruments

57 "Oh! What damn lies!": "Court Says Spies Pleas Shield Others," *New-York Tribune,* Mar. 23, 1917, 5.

57 When the government: "Bomb Chemicals Shown in Court," *New York Sun,* Mar. 27, 1917, 11.

58 "Sulfuric acid": "250 Bombs to Fire Ships of Allies Made on German Liner Here in Twelve Days," *Evening World,* Mar. 27, 1917, 2.

58 In his closing arguments: "German Plotters Soon Found Guilty," *New York Sun,* Apr. 3, 1917, 9.

59 Before the war: Scheele statement, Mar. 23, 1918, 4, NARA M1085, BOI, OGF, 1909–21, case no. 8000-925, roll 279, NACP.

59 Barrel chested and balding: BOI report on surveillance of Walter and Marie Scheele, July 17–19, 1915, 2, NARA M1085, BOI, OGF, 1909–21, case no. 8000-925, roll 279, NACP.

59 Every morning: BOI report from Agent L. M. Cantrell, Apr. 18, 1916, and BOI report from Agent Ralph H. Daughton, Apr. 27, 1916, Investigative Case Files of the BOI, 1908–1922, NARA M1085, OGF, 1909–21, case no. 8000-925, roll 279, NACP.

59 Scheele had come: Scheele statement, Mar. 23, 1918, 1, NARA M1085, BOI, OGF, 1909–21, case no. 8000-925, roll 279, NACP.

60 the scars on his face: "When Student Swords Ring in Germany," *New York Times,* July 23, 1933.

60 Born in Cologne: Letter from Richmond Levering to A. Bruce Bielaski, Naval Station, Key West, Fla., March 15, 1918, NARA M1085, BOI, OGF, 1909–21, case no. 8000-925, roll 279, NACP.

60 Naturally, Walter Scheele studied: Scheele statement, Mar. 23, 1918.

60 He reached the rank: Richmond M. Levering to A. Bruce Bielaski, *First Section Report of Dr. Walter T. Scheele,* Mar. 25, 1918, 2, Investigative Case Files of the BOI, 1908–1922, NARA M1085, OGF, 1909–21, case no. 8000-925, roll 279, NACP.

60 Their job was: Walter T. Scheele interview, Mar. 23, 1918, BOI, 1908–1922, NARA M1085, OGF, 1909–21, case no. 8000-925, roll 279, NACP.

60 The men were also instructed: French Strother, *Fighting Germany's Spies* (Garden City, NY: Doubleday, Page and Co., 1918), 262. Strother's somewhat breathless account of Scheele and his tasks in the United States is not reflected in the primary documents from the case files of the BOI.

61 In 1913: Scheele statement, Mar. 23, 1918, 2, BOI, 1908–1922, NARA M1085, OGF, 1909–21, case no. 8000-925, roll 279, NACP.

61 He instructed Scheele: Scheele statement, 3, BOI, 1908–1922, NARA M1085, OGF, 1909–21, case no. 8000-925, roll 279, NACP.

61 As Europe teetered: Levering to Bielaski, *First Section Report of Dr. Walter T. Scheele,* 2.

61 When the Continent: Scheele statement, Mar. 23, 1918, 41.

62 Scheele quickly sold: Ibid., 5.

62 On von Papen's orders: Ibid., 18.

62 Scheele began paying: *Second Section Report of Walter T. Scheele,* Schedule B, 5, Investigative Case Files of the BOI, 1908 1922, NARA M1085, OGF, 1909–21, case no. 8000-925, roll 279, NACP.

63 On April 10, 1915: Scheele statement, Mar. 23, 1918, 15.

63 Bode said von Papen: Ibid., 14–16. There are conflicting accounts about how the order to make the incendiary bombs reached Scheele. Von Rintelen claimed decades later in his unreliable memoir, *Dark Invader,* that he directly instructed Scheele to make the bomb under very different circumstances. Scheele's account appears more credible.

64 Scheele hired new employees: Levering to A. Bruce Bielaski, Mar. 28, 1918, and "Information Given by Dr. Scheele concerning List of Names and Incidents Submitted by Mr. Offley," 4, NARA M1085, BOI, OGF, 1909–21, case no. 8000-925, roll 279, NACP.

64 von Kleist kept: Agent report on Scheele, "Capt. Kleist," New York, July 17–23, 1915, NARA M1085, BOI, OGF, 1909–21, case no. 8000-925, roll 279, NACP.

65 To demonstrate, Scheele gathered: Statement of Ernst Becker, Apr. 13, 1916, 9, Investigative Case Files of the BOI, 1908–1922, NARA M1085, BOI, OGF, 1909–21, case no. 8000-925, roll 279, NACP.

65 The cigars were carefully packed: Scheele statement, Mar. 23, 1918, 24, NARA M1085, BOI, OGF, 1909–21, case no. 8000-925, roll 279, NACP.

65 A kind of executive body: Ibid., 25.

65 Most of the bombs: Levering to Bielaski, *First Section Report of Dr. Walter T. Scheele,* 4.

66 On May 1: "Tells of a Plot to Bomb *Lusitania,*" *New York Times,* Jan. 24, 1918, 20.

66 If Scheele's devices were aboard: It is not clear from primary documents that I viewed, including BOI reports, whether the cigars were placed aboard the *Lusitania.* There is a high likelihood that they were; multiple coconspirators confirmed that the bomb making was concurrent with the departure of the *Lusitania,* and prosecutors alleged their placement on the ship during the trial of von Papen in early 1918.

66 The cigars aboard: Scheele statement, Mar. 23, 1918, 25.

67 It was about 11:00: "Fire Bombs Put on Allies' Ships by a Ring Here," *New York Times,* July 11, 1915, 1.

67 By mid-July: In re: Dr. Walter T. Scheele, Captain Kleist, July 15, 1915, BOI Report, OGF, 1909–21, NACP.

67 The papers in the briefcase: Howard Blum, *Dark Invasion:1915: Germany's Secret War and the Hunt for the First Terrorist Cell in America* (New York: Harper Collins, 2014), 346.

68 von Kleist wrote: Copy of letter from Charles von Kleist to von Igel, March 31, 1916, NARA M1085, BOI, OGF, 1909–21, case no. 8000-925, roll 279, NACP.

68 "You Judas Iscariot!": Notes from meeting with Charles von Kleist, Monday, Oct. 30, 1916, NARA M1085, BOI, OGF, 1909–21, case no. 8000-925, roll 279, NACP.

69 Using forged identification papers: Letter from Offley to E. S. Chasten, Apr. 25, 1918, Investigative Case Files of the BOI, 1908–1922, NARA M1085, BOI, OGF, 1909–21, case no. 8000-925, roll 279, NACP.

69 Scheele eventually boarded: BOI report from Agent Leverett F. Englesby, Apr. 20, 1916, NARA M1085, BOI, OGF, 1909–21, case no. 8000-925, roll 279, NACP.

69 A few hours: "Six Germans Convicted," *Baltimore Sun,* Apr 3, 1917, 2.

69 "I am entirely satisfied": "7 German Plotters Are Sent to Prison," *New York Times,* Apr. 7, 1917, 3.

69 Some of the reports: "Find Germans Guilty," *Sumter (SC) Watchman and Southron,* Apr. 7, 1917, 3.

70 "If the man": A. Bruce Bielaski, Letter to P. H. Sisney, *Esquire,* Apr. 16, 1917.

70 On April 14: Agent L. C. Munson, report for Apr. 14, 1917, In re: *US vs. Walter T. Scheele et al.,* European neutrality matter, NARA M1085, BOI, OGF, 1909–21, case no. 8000-925, roll 279, NACP.

70 It wasn't the only one: Agent Thomas P. Merriless, report for July 21, 1917, In re: Marie Scheele, Neutrality Matter, NARA M1085, BOI, OGF, 1909–21, case no. 8000-925, roll 279, NACP.

Chapter Four: Technical Men

71 The thunder of artillery: Letter from George Hulett to Dr. Hugh S. Taylor, Munitions Inventions Department, University College, London, May 16, 1917, George A. Hulett Papers, 1909–1962, box 2, folder 7, Princeton University Library.

72 "Ever yet horrible scenes": Letter from George Hulett to family, May 15, 1917, Hulett Papers, Princeton University Library.

73 "it would take": Letter from George A. Hulett to George E. Hale, May 21, 1917, BOM, "Miscellaneous Reports," RG 70, finding aid A-1, entry 46, box 111, folder 3, NACP.

74 In the weeks: Letter from Manning to Hale, May 7, 1917.

74 Despite a modest: Transcripts of Reid's tapes, Oct. 25, 1971, box 3, Ebenezer Emmet Reid Papers, MS 104, Special Collections, Johns Hopkins University.

75 Not long after: E. Emmet Reid, "Reminiscences of World War I," *Armed Forces Chemical Journal* 9 (July–Aug., 1955): 37.

76 In late 1914: Letter from Assistant Secretary of War Walter M. Gilbert to Van H. Manning about explosion in Haber's lab, May 30, 1917, NAS-NRC, Executive Committee: Projects, Helium Production, National Academy of Sciences Archives.

76 "in order to avoid": Letter from Manning to Hale, May 26, 1917.

76 unlucky dogs and other animals: Letter from Yandell Henderson to Major H. C. Bradley, Nov. 20, 1918, in Henderson, *History of Research at Yale University;* "Gas Stray Dogs in Experiments with New War Discovery," *Bridgeport Evening Farmer,* Sept. 26, 1917, 12.

78 On April 28: General Electric, National Lamp Works, *The National in the World War, Apr. 6, 1917–Nov. 11, 1918* (Cleveland: General Electric, 1920), 170.

78 By the end of April: Ibid., 172.

79 Brigadier General Kuhn issued: Memorandum to Chief of Staff, Subject: Gas Masks and Helmets, May 16, 1917, Technical Document Files, 1917–1920, CWS, RG 175, finding aid PI-8, entry 8, box 6, NACP.

79 Even though the British: After the Germans used chlorine at Ypres, Britain's secretary of state for war, Lord Kitchener, appealed to women of Britain and France to quickly make rudimentary masks. Rushed to the front by the millions, they were little more than cotton wads soaked in a neutralizing solution. Within a few

weeks, black veil respirators followed—a long swath of black fabric tied around the head, with a cotton pad for the mouth and nose soaked in sodium carbonate, water, and glycerin to keep it moist. Next was the hypo helmet, a flannel sack dipped in sodium thiosulfate, soda, and glycerin, with a celluloid rectangular window to see out of. In July 1915, British intelligence learned that the Germans planned to unleash phosgene later that year and began preparing a new mask. The result was the P helmet, similar to the hypo but dipped in a substance that reacted and neutralized phosgene, then the PH helmet, using another substance discovered by the Russians that was even more effective at neutralizing phosgene. The large-box, or tarbox, respirator followed, the first British mask to have a canister with chemical neutralizers inside, containing charcoal, soda lime, and potassium permanganate. Finally, in Apr. 1916, the British began issuing the small-box respirator, which was considered the most effective European mask but was uncomfortable to wear for long periods of time. The first French effort, called the M2, was also rudimentary, a snoutlike bag stuffed with layers of muslin soaked in neutralizing chemicals. The next French mask, the Tissot, made of rubber, had a canister and an intake valve that stuck straight up from the nose like a snorkel. The Russians had their own mask, considered the least effective of all.

79 Manning and Burrell: Draft of letter from Van H. Manning to George Hale, May 26, 1917. NAS-NRC, Executive Committee: Projects, Helium Production, National Academy of Sciences Archives.

79 All told, 320,000 separate pieces: "C. E. Mask," Technical Document Files, 1917–1920, Major McPherson's Personnel File—Masks, CWS, RG 175, finding aid PI-8, entry 8, box 10, NACP.

79 The charcoal for the filter: George A. Burrell, "Contributions from the Chemical Warfare Service, USA," *Journal of Industrial and Engineering Chemistry* 2, no. 2 (Feb. 1919): 93.

80 Henderson said he would: Henderson, *History of Research at Yale University,* 2.

81 The mask worked: Daniel Patrick Jones, "The Role of Chemists in Research on War Gases in the United States during World War I" (PhD thesis, University of Wisconsin, 1969), 96.

81 On July 13: *War Expenditures,* 3413.

81 Dewey, Lewis, Gibbs, and Fieldner: Manning, "War Gas Investigations," 11.

81 It came in an overseas telegram: Cablegram no. 103-S from John J. Pershing to Adjutant General, Aug. 17, 1917, *War Expenditures,* 3420.

81 masks had been tested: Burrell, "Contributions," 96.

81 "Construction of entire apparatus": *War Expenditures,* 3421.

81 The masks were: Letter from George Burrell to Llewellyn Williamson with report on first twenty-five thousand masks, July 25, 1917, Technical Document Files, 1917–1920, CWS, RG 175, finding aid PI-8, entry 8, box 16, NACP.

81 American soldiers had already: Society of the First Division, *History of the First Division During the World War, 1917–1919* (Philadelphia: John C. Winston, 1922), 6.

82 It was essential: Letter from Henderson to Major H. C. Bradley.

82 within two weeks: Osborn, "Chronology of Events," June 21, 1917.

82 As the number: "How Our Grounds and Buildings Are Protected," extract from General Order 10, *American University Courier* 24, no. 1 (Oct. 1917): 6.

82 "Now it is": "Must Follow Flag, Says Hiram Johnson," *Washington Herald,* June 1, 1917, 4.

83 On the same day: Osborn, "Chronology of Events," May 31, 1917.

83 Behind the amphitheater: "Army Engineer's Camp to Be Established Here," *Evening Star,* May 22, 1917, 1.

83 radiated outward: Osborn, "Chronology of Events," May 31, 1917.

83 "At a very important": Ibid., June 25, 1917.

83 By mid-July: Van H. Manning, *Report on Work Done on Noxious Gases,* July 23, 1917, NAS-NRC, Executive Committee: Projects, Helium Production. National Academy of Sciences Archives.

84 It would have: Letter from Manning to Hale, May 26, 1917.

84 "It is quite unnecessary": Letter from George E. Hale to Van H. Manning, June 12, 1917, NAS-NRC, Executive Committee: Projects, Helium Production, National Academy of Sciences Archives.

84 Over the summer: "House Defeats Censorship Law 184 to 144," *New York Times,* June 1, 1917, 1.

84 Manning reassured Hale: Letter from Manning to Hale, June 15, 1917, NAS-NRC, Executive Committee: Projects, Helium Production, National Academy of Sciences Archives.

85 It was urgent: Letter from George E. Hale to Secretary of War Newton Baker, June 12, 1917, NAS-NRC, Executive Committee: Projects, Helium Production, National Academy of Sciences Archives.

85 In a box: Letter from Manning to Hale, June 29, 1917, NAS-NRC, Executive Committee: Projects, Helium Production, National Academy of Sciences Archives.

85 Burrell recalled: Memorandum from George Burrell to Director, CWS, Re: Helium Investigation, Dec. 28, 1918, Office of Chief, Central Correspondence, 1918–1942, War Department, CWS, RG 175, finding aid PI-8, entry 1, box 347, NACP.

86 "It is regarded": Letter from Vice Admiral R. H. Peirse to George Hale, NAS-NRC, Executive Committee: Projects, Helium Production, National Academy of Sciences Archives.

86 The British already: Ibid., 2

86 It was probably: Van H. Manning, "Petroleum Investigations and Production of Helium," from *War Work of the Bureau of Mines* (Washington, DC: Government Printing Office, 1919), 81.

87 As Osborn mounted: Osborn, "Chronology of Events," Aug. 20, 1917.

Chapter Five: Amos and Goliath

88 In the weak half-light: Society of the First Division, *History of the First Division,* 17.

89 Sibert returned: "Sibert Inspects Camp in France," *New York Times,* July 20, 1917, 9.

90 For Wilson: David M. Kennedy, *Over Here* (New York: Oxford University Press, 1980), 146.

91 Huge pro-war rallies: "12,000 Cheer for Hard-Hitting War," *New York Times,* Mar. 23, 1917, 1.

91 When the War Department: "Regulars under Pershing Will Go to France; Will Not Send Roosevelt," *New York Times,* May 19, 1917, 1.

91   "Registration Day should be celebrated": "Prepare for Registration," *New York Times,* May 23, 1917, 2.

92   The first draft drawing: "Draft Lottery Selects 1,374,000 Men for Examination to Provide 687,000 of First Increment Troops," *Washington Post,* July 21, 1917, 1.

92   "Gentlemen, this is a solemn": "Work on National Draft Continues to Early Hours of Morning," *Washington Herald,* July 21, 1917, 1.

92   By the time: "1,971 More Recruits Obtained for Army," *New York Times,* July 29, 1917, 6.

93   The troop convoys: "First American Troops Reach France, Setting Record for Quick Movement," *New York Times,* June 28, 1917, 1.

93   The arrival of the American: Society of the First Division, *History of the First Division* (Philadelphia: Winston, 1922), 7.

93   American flags had been: "First American Troops Reach France," *New York Times,* June 28, 1917, 1.

94   Not only was Sibert big: Edward B. Clark, *William L. Sibert: The Army Engineer* (Philadelphia: Dorrance, 1930), 26.

94   "there is a charm": Letter from William Sibert to Mamie Sibert, Oct. 17, 1898, Anne Sibert Buiter Collection.

94   They would have a daughter: Clark, *William L. Sibert,* 48.

95   When the war ended: Ibid., 95

96   At one point: Ibid., 120.

96   Sibert's efficiency: Ibid., 128.

97   A special act: "Promote Canal Builders," *New York Times,* Mar. 3, 1915, 5.

97   Trained in warfare: Clark, *William L Sibert,*157.

97   When war finally came: John J. Pershing, "My Experiences in the World War," *New York Times,* Jan. 17, 1931, 19.

97   Goliath was summoned: *Ogden Standard,* Apr. 26, 1917, 1

97   When the ship: Frank E. Vandiver, *Black Jack: The Life and Times of John J. Pershing,* vol. 2 (College Station: Texas A & M University Press, 1977), 723.

98   Before Fries retired: Letter from Amos Fries to Bessie Fries, Apr. 26, 1918, Amos A. Fries Papers, 1896–1953, Ax234, box 1, folder 11, Special Collections and University Archives, University of Oregon Libraries, Eugene, Oregon.

99   On the night: Night telegram from Amos Fries to Bessie Fries, July 20, 1917, Amos A. Fries Papers, 1896–1953.

99   The compound's other name: Larry E. Davis, "Unregulated Potions Still Cause Mercury Poisoning," *Western Journal of Medicine* 173, no. 1 (July 2000), http://www.ncbi.nlm.nih.gov/pmc/articles/PMC1070962.

101   "splendid little war": Though the phrase "splendid little war" is often credited to Teddy Roosevelt, the term actually came from then–U.S. ambassador to Great Britain John Hay in a letter to Roosevelt.

102   "Just as there were thousands": Unpublished Fries memoir, Amos A. Fries Papers, 1896–1953, box 3, folder 1, Special Collections & University Archives, University of Oregon Libraries, Eugene, Oregon.

105   "I had then": Ibid.

105   he wrote to Bessie every day: Letter from Amos Fries to Bessie Fries, July 13, 1917, Amos A. Fries Papers, 1896–1953.

105   He packed a small trunk: Ibid., July 14, 1917.

105 "There are all sorts": Ibid., July 21, 1917.

106 "I am getting quite expert": Ibid.

106 The ship had: Björn Larsson, *Maritime Timetable Images,* http://www.timeta
bleimages.com/maritime/images/rmspb1.htm.

107 "somewhere near the north pole" Letter from Amos Fries to Bessie Fries, July 25,
1917, Amos A. Fries Papers, 1896–1953.

107 "Besides the ship": Ibid., Aug. 1, 1917.

Chapter Six: "Fiendish Work"

108 The British offensive: Hart, *Great War,* 352.

108 fuse: The technical term for the explosive insert that detonates ordnance is a
"fuze," a term still in use today in the military.

109 The French border city: "Ruined Armentières Is a City of the Dead," *New York
Times,* Sept. 18, 1917, 2.

109 Overnight on July 20: Haber, *Poisonous Cloud,* 193.

110 After several hours: "New Shells Poison Town," *New York Times,* Sept. 8, 1917.

110 The gas shelling: Haber, *Poisonous Cloud,* 249.

110 "Fiendish Work": "Fiendish Work of Devils in Human Form," *Bourbon News,*
Aug. 17, 1917, 6.

110 The reports were true: Haber, *Poisonous Cloud,* 111.

110 Within a day: Charles H. Foulkes, *"Gas!" The Story of the Special Brigade*
(Edinburgh: William Blackwood and Sons, 1934), 265.

111 "when in contact": Augustin M. Prentiss, *Chemicals in War* (New York:
McGraw-Hill, 1937), 181.

112 The British fired: Foulkes, *"Gas!,"* 267.

112 The interlocking processes: Haber, *Poisonous Cloud,* 195.

113 Mustard so preoccupied: Ibid., 191.

113 "Hulett has spent": Letter from J. S. Ames to Charles Hale, May 17, 1917, NAS-
NRC, Executive Committee: Projects, Helium Production, National Academy of
Sciences Archives.

113 "hard to get": Letter from George Hulett to Dency Hulett, July 31, 1917, George
A. Hulett Papers, 1909–1962, call no. C0460, box 2, folder 10, "Personal
Letters," Princeton University Library.

114 The organizational chart: "American Expeditionary Forces—Chemical Organization," Hulett Papers, call no. C0460, box 2, folder 2, "War Work."

114 Pershing also wrote: John J. Pershing letter to Adjutant General, Aug. 4, 1917,
Hulett Papers, "War Work," Princeton University Library.

114 Pershing sent a cablegram: "Cablegram Sent from General Headquarters American Expeditionary Forces to the Adjutant General of the Army, Washington,
DC," Aug. 7, 1917, *War Expenditures,* 3420.

114 he carried the letter from Pershing: Letter from John J. Pershing to Adjutant General, Aug. 4, 1917, Hulett Papers, "War Work," Princeton University Library.

115 Hulett didn't go: Letter from George A. Hulett to Dency Hulett, Aug. 23, 1917,
Hulett Papers, Princeton University Library.

116 "I think most": Fries memoir, "An Engineer Goes to War," 4–5.

116 "It will be": Letter from Amos Fries to Bessie Fries, Aug. 15, 1917, Amos A. Fries
Papers, 1896–1953.

117 "I might as well": Fries memoir, "An Engineer Goes to War," 6.

117 "I am to be": Letter from Amos Fries to Bessie Fries, Aug. 17, 1917, Amos A. Fries Papers, 1896–1953.

117 "Have appointed Lieut. Col. Fries": Fries and West, *Chemical Warfare,* 77.

118 When Fries began: Fries memoir, 7, Amos A. Fries Papers, 1896–1953.

118 He even invented: Letter from Amos Fries to Bessie Fries, Aug. 22, 1917, Amos A. Fries Papers, 1896–1953.

118 "Nothing is known": *War Expenditures,* 3421.

118 "Well, don't you think": Fries memoir, "An Engineer Goes to War," 8, Amos A. Fries Papers, 1896–1953.

119 On the fresh, bright morning: West and Fries, *Chemical Warfare,* 75.

120 "could not stop": Fries memoir, 11.

120 "They were able": Ibid., 10.

122 Levering, Mrs. Hoagland: Letter from Commander McCauley, Office of Naval Intelligence, to A. Bruce Bielaski, Aug. 24, 1917, NARA M1085, Investigative Reports of the BOI, 1908–1922, OGF, 1909–21, case 12490, roll 335, NACP.

122 Technically, he didn't: Letter from A. Bruce Bielaski to Richmond Levering, May 23, 1917. NARA M1085, Investigative Reports of the BOI, OGF, 1909–21, case 2910, roll 302, NACP.

122 After an uneventful start: Letter from E. S. Underhill to William Offley, Sept. 27, 1917, NARA M1085, Investigative Reports of the BOI, OGF, 1909–21, case 12490, roll 335, NACP.

123 Only a few days: "San Diego City Main Blowout," *Ogden Standard,* Aug. 18, 1917, 1.

123 A young man: Letter from Richmond Levering to British ambassador Sir Cecil Spring Rice, June 23, 1915, NARA M1085, Investigative Reports of the BOI, OGF, 1909–21, case 12490, roll 335, NACP.

123 His first wife: "Divorce for Mrs. Levering," *New York Times,* Feb. 24, 1915, 18.

124 An investigation: Report on Richmond Levering from William Offley to A. Bruce Bielaski, 4, Sept. 13, 1917, NARA M1085, Investigative Reports of the BOI, OGF, 1909–21, case 12490, roll 335, NACP.

124 He explained: Report from Agent W. B. Matthews for Apr. 25, 1918, In re: Richmond Levering (Confidential), NARA M1085, Investigative Reports of the BOI, OGF, 1909–21, case 12490, roll 335, NACP.

125 Levering summoned him: Letter from William Offley to A Bruce Bielaski, Sept. 13, 1917; Report on Richmond Levering, 7, Investigative Reports of the BOI, OGF, 1909–21, case 12490, roll 335, NACP.

125 One of them: Affidavit of Mr. Arthur J. Ronhagan, in case of Prentiss vs. Metropolitan Petroleum Corp and Island Oil and Transport Co., Aug. 4, 1917, NARA M1085, Investigative Reports of the BOI, 1908–1922, OGF, 1909–21, case 12490, roll 335, NACP.

126 "By the operation": Letter from Richmond Levering to Omar D. Conger, Navy Department, Washington, DC, Mar. 19, 1918, NARA M1085, Investigative Reports of the BOI, OGF, 1909–21, case 12490, roll 335, NACP.

127 On March 16, 1917: Letter from William Offley to A. Bruce Bielaski, Mar. 16, 1917, Investigative Reports of the BOI, 1908–1922, OGF, 1909–21, case 97452, roll 473, NACP.

128 "He states that": Ibid.

128 Levering offered his own company: Letter to Mssrs. Jose Marimon y Juliach, Sept. 26, 1916, NARA M1085, Investigative Reports of the BOI, 1908–1922, OGF, 1909–21, case 12490, roll 335, NACP.

129 "Mr. Levering is displaying": Letter from William Offley to A. Bruce Bielaski, May 21, 1917, Investigative Reports of the BOI, 1908–1922, OGF, 1909–21, case 2910, roll 302, NACP.

129 And in July: Bill of Complaint, Franklin D. L. Prentiss v. Metropolitan Petroleum Co. & Island Oil and Transport Corp., U.S. District Court for the Eastern District of Virginia, NARA M1085, Investigative Reports of the BOI, 1908–1922, OGF, 1909–21, case 12490, roll 335, NACP.

129 "I enclose herewith": Letter from A. Bruce Bielaski to William Offley, June 20, 1917. NARA M1085, Investigative Reports of the BOI, 1908–1922, OGF, 1909–21, case 97452, roll 473, NACP.

129 His chauffeur had been: Letter from Charles Offley to A. Bruce Bielaski, Aug. 23, 1917, NARA M1085, Investigative Reports of the BOI, 1908–1922, OGF, 1909–21, case 12490, roll 335, NACP.

129 "I desire to call": Letter from Richmond Levering to William Offley, Aug. 28, 1917. NARA M1085, Investigative Reports of the BOI, OGF, 1909–21, case 12490, roll 335, NACP.

130 His letter to Briggs: Letter from Richmond Levering to A Briggs, Aug. 29, 1917, NARA M1085, Investigative Case Files of the BOI, 1908–1922, OGF, 1909–21, case number 12490, roll 335; NACP.

130 "any further connection": Letter from E. S. Underhill to A. Bruce Bielaski, Sept. 14, 1917, BOI, OGF, 1909–21, case number 12490, roll 335, NACP.

130 "Any information we wanted": Letter from Richmond Levering to A. Bruce Bielaski, Oct. 19, 1917. BOI, OGF, 1909–21, case number 12490, roll 335; NACP.

130 He didn't have: Letter from Amos Fries to Bessie Fries, Aug. 31, 1917, Amos A. Fries Papers, 1896–1953.

131 "Since July 18": War Expenditures, 3422.

131 The car sped: Letter from Amos Fries letter to Bessie Fries, Sept. 1, 1917, Amos A. Fries Papers, 1896–1953.

131 "vast and elegant": Ibid., Sept. 25, 1917.

131 He was assigned: Ibid., Sept. 8, 1917.

131 Fries wrote home: Ibid., Sept. 1, 1917.

132 "There is established": General Order 31, Sept. 3, 1917; Fries and West, Chemical Warfare, 76.

132 "Well, if swearing": Ibid., Sept. 9, 1917.

132 "looks to have": Ibid., Sept. 6, 1917.

132 Unlike Fries: Donald Smythe, Pershing: General of the Armies (Bloomington: Indiana University Press, 1986), 46.

133 The whole spectacle: Vandiver, Black Jack, 796.

133 Pershing, already irate: Papers of General John J. Pershing, 1916–24, 1931–39, index and case files relating to Reclassification & Reassignment of Officers— Regular Army Officers: Major Generals, Brigadier Generals, RG 200, finding aid NM-10, entry 22, box 8, NACP.

133 In a confidential memo: "Comment on General Officers," *Baker Letters: Confidential Correspondence Between Secretary of War Baker and General Pershing, 1917–20*, John J. Pershing Papers, 1882–1971, General Correspondence, 1904–48, box 20, Manuscript Division, Library of Congress, Washington, DC.

134 "Capt. Crawford": Letter from Amos Fries to Bessie Fries, Sept. 11, 1917, Amos A. Fries Papers, 1896–1953.

134 A second officer: Fries memoir, 14.

135 "Send at once": Cablegram no. 181-S from John Pershing to Adjutant General, Sept. 25, 1917, *War Expenditures*, 3423–24.

135 "This material": Ibid.

136 "Perhaps they don't": Letter from Amos Fries to Bessie Fries, Sept. 21, 1917, Amos A. Fries Papers, 1896–1953.

136 As September turned: Ibid., Oct. 2, 1917.

136 "I have a man-sized job": Ibid., Sept. 29, 1917.

136 On September 29: Cablegram from Amos Fries to Bessie Fries, Sept. 29, 1917, Amos A. Fries Papers, 1896–1953.

136 It was a paradox: Letter from Amos Fries to Bessie Fries, Sept. 25, 1917, Amos A. Fries Papers, 1896–1953.

136 "They certainly have": Ibid., Sept. 21, 1917.

137 Then the rain: Hart, *Great War*, 365.

137 On September 1: Ibid., 301.

138 The fire waltz did: Ibid.

138 It was the last battle: Falls, *Great War*, 185.

138 As antiwar fever: Haber, *Poisonous Cloud*, 186.

138 His discomforts were: Letter from Amos Fries to Bessie Fries, Oct. 7, 1917, Amos A. Fries Papers, 1896–1953.

138 "Things don't look": Ibid., Nov. 11, 1917.

Chapter Seven: "A Hotter Fire"

141 "There's a place somewhere": Olson Family Collection.

141 The September 4 parade: "Soap Box Sedition to Feel Heavy Hand," *New York Times*, Aug. 16, 1917, 7.

142 Days before the parade: "30 Germans Are Arrested in South Dakota for Opposing the War and the Draft Law, *New York Times*, Aug. 28, 1917.

142 In a Labor Day letter: "President Tells Labor of Country's War Aims," *Washington Herald*, Sept. 3, 1917.

142 Gompers himself was suspect: Unsigned report, In re: Dr. W. T. Scheele et al. (Samuel Gompers), July 16, 1915, Investigative Case Files of the BOI, 1908–1922, NARA M1085, OGF, 1909–21, case no. 8000-925, roll 279, NACP.

142 As the Marine Band: "President Wilson Leads District's New National Army," *Washington Herald*, Sept. 5, 1917.

143 On September 21: "U.S. Prepared for Barbarity," *Washington Herald*, Sept. 21, 1917.

143 Newspapers across the country: "Uncle Sam to 'Fight Devil with Fire,'" *South Bend News-Times*, Sept. 20, 1917.

144 The announcement served: "Gas and Flame," *Ottawa (IL) Free Trader-Journal*, Sept. 27, 1917, 4.

144 From the attic: National Park Service, Department of the Interior, *American University, Ohio Hall of Government (McKinley-Ohio Hall of Government)*, Historic American Buildings Survey, HABS DC-458.

145 At the behest: George A. Burrell, "Organization of Work," Sept. 1, 1917. War gas investigations, semi-monthly project reports pertaining to gas warfare, Aug. to Sept. 1917, BOM, Record Group 70, finding aid A-1, entry 47, box 115, NACP.

145 In New Haven, Yandell Henderson: Leo P. Brophy, Wyndham D. Miles, and Rexmond C. Cochrane, *The Chemical Warfare Service: From Laboratory to Field* (Washington, DC: Center of Military History,1959), 8.

146 The improvisation among chaos: Reid, "Reminiscences of World War I."

147 "These lists are now": Letter from Van Manning to George Hale, Oct. 2, 1917, NAS-NRC, Executive Committee: Committee on Noxious Gases, National Academy of Sciences Archives.

150 In the school magazine: Roxbury Latin School, *Tripod* (June, 1910), call no. UAI 15.898, box 1, Papers of James Bryant Conant, 1862–1987, Harvard University Archives.

150 When unrestricted submarine warfare: James B. Conant, *My Several Lives* (New York: Harper and Row, 1970), 48.

151 He visited chemical companies: Ibid., 26.

151 He lived in an apartment: *District of Columbia Directory* (Washington, DC: R. L. Polk and Co., 1918).

151 He had begun: Conant didn't specify what this unit was. Perhaps it was the Thirtieth Engineers (Gas and Flame), but he could have been angling to work in the planned gas laboratory in France.

151 He told Conant: James F. Pringle, "Mr. President—I," Profiles, *New Yorker,* Sept. 12, 1936, 24.

152 There were just three men: James B. Conant, *Progress Report of the Organic Division,* Oct. 15, 1917, War Gas Investigations, Semi-monthly Project Reports, BOM, RG 70, finding aid A-1, entry 47, box 116, NACP.

152 Conant must have found: "American University, the Chemical Warfare Service's First Training Ground and Research Center," USACE.

152 The chemists constantly skated: "Lewis Tells of Perils of Gas Research Work," *Evanston (IL) News-Index,* Oct. 27, 1919.

152 One day, a bumbling young chemist: Robert S. Mulliken, *Life of a Scientist* (New York: Springer-Verlag, 1968), 23.

153 "Full investigation": War Expenditures, 3424.

153 A week later: Report on G-34, Dec. 1, 1917, call no. UAI 15.898, box 141, Papers of James Bryant Conant, 1862–1987, Harvard University Archives.

153 Mustard was a vexing problem: W. D. Bancroft, *Bancroft's History of the Chemical Warfare Service in the United States* (Washington, DC: Research Division, CWS, American University Experiment Station, 1919), 14 (70).

154 despite a cloud of suspicion: Letter from Frank P. Underhill to BOI, 1908–1922, Nov. 6, 1917, Frank P. Underhill Papers, Correspondence File B-Z, group no. 514, box 11, Yale University Library Manuscript Collections.

154 Reid rated each: E. Emmet Reid, *Compounds Tested for Toxicity,* Report of Division of Chemical Research—Offense, Feb. 1, 1918, War Gas Investigation,

Semi-monthly Reports, Dec. 1917–Feb. 1918, BOM, RG 70, finding aid A-1, entry 47, box 117, NACP.

155 After he wrote: Letter from director of Edward Hill's Son & Co. to William McPherson, Nov. 14, 1917, Technical Document Files, 1917–1920, "Cotton Seed Hulls, Fillings etc," CWS, RG 175, finding aid PI-8, entry 7, box 6, NACP.

155 The difficulty in obtaining: Bancroft, *History of the Chemical Warfare Service,* 229.

156 Toward the end of 1917: General Electric, *Story of the Development Division,* 209.

156 Another cooperative chemical maker: Lieutenant Colonel William McPherson, "An Historical Sketch of the Development of Edgewood Arsenal," *An Historical Sketch of Edgewood Arsenal,* DTIC Technical Report AD 498494 (Washington, DC: Army CWS, Mar. 1919), 9.

156 An experimental lab: Bancroft, *History of the Chemical Warfare Service,* 241; McPherson, "Historical Sketch," 17.

156 They found what seemed: "War Comes Home to Kent Island," *Washington, DC, Evening Star,* Sept. 16, 1917, 16.

157 Secretary of War Baker: "Bitter Clashes Mark Kent Island Hearing," *Baltimore Sun,* Sept. 16, 1917, 1.

157 Tempers flared during the hearing: Ibid., 2.

157 Two days later: "Kent Island Plan Killed," *Baltimore Sun,* Sept. 18, 1917, 1.

157 Across the Chesapeake Bay: "Neck Losing Its Glory," *Baltimore Sun,* Dec. 11, 1917, 8.

158 On the evening: "Takes Over 35,000 Acres," *(Baltimore) Sun,* Oct 17, 1917, 1.

158 In late October: McPherson, "Historical Sketch," 14.

158 Earlier in 1917: Memorandum from P. D. Lochridge to Chief of Staff, Sept. 26, 1917, Correspondence of War College Division and Related General Staff Offices, 1903–19, WDG, RG 165, microfilm publication M1024, reel 306, NACP.

159 Fries had advocated: Cablegram to General Pershing, Nov. 8, 1917, Correspondence of War College Division and Related General Staff Offices, 1903–19, WDG, RG 165, microfilm publication M1024, reel 306, NACP.

159 "I have been urging them": Letter from Amos Fries to Bessie Fries, Nov. 11, 1917, Amos A. Fries Papers, 1896–1953.

159 "The gas game": Ibid., Nov. 15, 1917.

159 Fries finally wrote to Manning: Letter from Amos Fries to Van Manning, Nov. 1, 1917, Technical Document Files, 1917–1920, Correspondence, RG 175, finding aid PI-8, entry 8, box 5, NACP.

160 Manning's reply came: Letter from Van H. Manning to Amos A. Fries, Dec. 10, 1917, Technical Document Files, 1917–1920, Correspondence, RG 175, finding aid PI-8, entry 8, box 5, NACP.

161 "I will certainly be glad": Ibid., Dec. 11, 1917.

161 "The men specially needed": "Need Gas and Flame Men," *New York Times,* Oct. 17, 1917, 18.

161 "The time has gone by": James Thayer Addison, *The Story of the First Gas Regiment* (Boston: Houghton Miflin, 1919), 7.

162 In Lawrence, Massachusetts: Author phone interview with Betty Higginbottom, daughter-in-law of Harold Higginbottom, Nov. 13, 2015.

162 the daughter: "Wedding Bells; Higginbottom-Macreadie," *Lawrence Evening Tribune,* Dec. 27, 1920, 13.

162 When he registered: Harold Higginbottom draft registration card, Ancestry .com.

162 Arthur went to work: Arthur Higginbottom draft registration card, Ancestry.com.

162 Lawrence had been a cauldron: Philip S. Foner, *History of the Labor Movement in the United States,* vol. 4, *The Industrial Workers of the World, 1905–1917* (New York: International Publishers, 1965), 307.

162 almost ten thousand young men: "Nearly 12,000 Young Men Registered for Draft Here," *Lawrence Telegram,* June 6, 1917, 2.

162 During his lunch break: Harold Higginbottom diary entry, Tues., Oct. 23, 1917, CCM.

163 On Wednesday: Ibid., Oct. 24, 1917.

163 On Friday morning: Ibid., Oct. 26, 1917.

163 Atkisson had turned thirty-one: *Gas Attack,* spring 1984, CCM.

164 Though Fries had no idea: Fries memoir, Amos A. Fries Papers, 1896–1953.

164 In the 1912 yearbook: Columbia University, *The Columbian* (yearbook), 1912, 363.

164 How Jabine learned: Bureau of Labor Statistics, *The Industrial Directory of New Jersey* (Trenton, NJ: Bureau of Labor Statistics, Department of Labor, 1918).

164 where he was foreman: Thomas Jabine draft registration card, Ancestry.com.

164 He took it all: Letter from Thomas Jabine to mother, undated letter no. 1, American University WWI file, University Archives and Special Collections, American University Library.

165 A stove warmed: "Activities at Camp American University," *American University Courier* 24, no. 1 (Oct. 1917).

165 "I have been working": Letter from Jabine to mother, Oct. 27, 1917.

165 Jabine became fast friends: Addison, *Story of the First Gas Regiment,* 4.

166 Single and twenty-five: Devlin draft registration card, Ancestry.com.

166 Leonidas M. Shappell: "Father and Three Sons Are Fighting in Uncle Sam's Army—Formerly Lived Here," *Keokuk (IA) Daily Gate City,* Nov. 2, 1917, 7.

166 On Thursday, November 8: Higginbottom diary entry, Nov. 7, 1917. In Higginbottom's diary, the dates and days of the week do not always correspond to the calendar. In this case, it appears that the entry should have been labeled Nov. 8.

166 Reveille woke the new recruits: Ibid.

166 One Sunday: Ibid., Nov. 7, 1917.

166 Jabine felt the same: Jabine diary entry, Nov. 2, 1917.

167 In the second week: Ibid., Nov. 15, 1917.

168 Manning took up: Manning, "War Gas Investigations," 7.

168 Bishop John William Hamilton: Letter from American University chancellor to Van Manning, Oct. 13, 1917, Purchase of American University Property, USACE.

168 To top it off: Memorandum from Chief of Engineers Major General William Black to Adjutant General, regarding use of American University grounds, Oct. 13, 1917, USACE.

169 With the crowd: "Camouflage at Meade," *Washington Post,* Nov. 21, 1917.

169 "If his satanic majesty": "U.S. Red Blooded Challenge Satan with 'Hellfirers,'" *Washington Times,* Nov. 15, 1917, 8.

170 As winter approached: Van H. Manning, *Research Work of the Bureau of Mines on Gases Used in Warfare for the Year 1917,* Frank P. Underhill Papers, "Poison Gas Experiments," group no. 514, box 4, Yale University Library Manuscript Collections.

170 Another factor made it difficult: "Dogs and Cats Do War Service at American University Camp; Prove Gas and Flame Tests There," *Washington Post,* Nov. 4, 1917, 2.

171 Though the article: "Society Protests 'Gassing' of Dogs: Experiments by the Army No Longer Necessary," *Washington Post,* Dec. 1, 1918, 24.

171 The 125 offensive war gases: *Report of the Toxicology Division of the Physiological Section,* Oct. 24, 1917, Frank P. Underhill Papers, "Poison Gas Experiments," group no. 514, box 4, Yale University Library Manuscript Collections.

171 In mid-October: Henderson, *History of Research at Yale University,* 3.

172 Burrell issued rules: Order from George Burrell to Research Division employees, no date, American University WWI file, University Archives and Special Collections, American University Library.

173 Manning brought up the issue: 4-SV Letter Regarding Posting of Sentries at Buildings at American University—Nov. 3, 1917, located in Army Corps Documents, subfolder "AUES Admin Info–Purchase of Land."

173 Abbot promised to beef up: Letter from Frederic V. Abbot to Van H. Manning, Nov. 3, 1918, USACE.

173 He continued to fret: Letter from Van H. Manning to Brigadier General Frederic V. Abbot regarding fence around experiment station, Dec. 13, 1917, "Correspondence Regarding Repairing Road on American University Campus—1917," USACE.

174 Early in the month: *History of Chemical Warfare Service, AEF,* 17, History of the CWS 1918, First Gas Regiment Collection, Carlisle Attic Collection, box 96, folder H-12, CCM.

174 "It is not the idea": Letter from Amos Fries to Director of Gas Service, U.S. Army, Confidential Investigations, Nov. 29, 1917, General Fries' Files, 1918–1920, O–S, Edgewood Arsenal, 1917–43. RG 175, CWS, finding aid PI-8, entry 7, box 19, NACP.

174 The commander of the army's aviation: Memorandum from Major Carol Spatz to Adjutant General, AEF, Nov. 25, 1917, Technical Document Files, 1917–1920, CWS, RG 175, finding aid PI-8, entry 8, box 7, NACP.

174 Asked to comment: Memorandum from Amos Fries to Adjutant General, AEF, Dec. 14, 1917, Technical Document Files, 1917–1920, CWS, RG 175, finding aid PI-8, entry 8, box 7, NACP.

175 Three days before Christmas: Letter from Wilder D. Bancroft and John Johnson to Van H. Manning, Dec. 22, 1917, War Gas Investigation Reports, RG 70, BOM, finding aid A-1, entry 46, box 110, NACP.

175 In late December: Letter from George E. Hale and G. N. Lewis to Daniel Williard, chairman of the National Industries Board, Dec. 22, 1917. NAS-NRC, Executive Board, Committee on Gases Used in Warfare, 1918, National Academy of Sciences Archives.

Chapter Eight: Over There

176 It was the strangest Christmas: Letter from Jabine to mother, Jan. 1918.

176 When he wrote home: Ibid., Dec. 18, 1917.

177 "This sudden activity": Ibid., Dec. 21, 1917.

177 On Christmas Eve: "Santa Claus in Camp," *Washington Post,* Dec. 25, 1917, 5; "Christmas Greeting Carried to Soldier, Sailor, Marine," *Evening Star,* Dec. 25, 1917, 7. The *Washington Post* and the *Evening Star* have slightly different accounts of Baker's speech. In the *Star* article, he said "sons of the entire nation," but in the *Post* he was reported as saying "children of the entire nation."

177 Dawn was still: Presumably the burning of mattress ticking was to kill bedbugs or lice, which carry typhus.

178 As the men peered through: "President Wilson's Sheep," *Gas Attack,* May 1979, 2.

178 At 4:00 p.m.: *President Grant* logbook, Jan. 5, 1918, Logbooks of US Ships and Stations, 1916–1940, USS *President Grant,* Aug. 2, 1917–Dec. 31, 1918, RG 24, entry 118-G-P, A1, box 1, NAB, Washington, DC.

179 Four days later: Ibid., Jan. 9, 1918.

179 On the morning of January 10: Addison, *Story of the First Gas Regiment,* 15.

179 "We are billeted": Letter from Jabine to mother, Feb. 3, 1918.

180 The arrival of the gas and flame regiment: *History of the First Gas Regiment,* part 2, section 1, "Training, Companies A and B," First Gas Regiment Collection, CCM.

180 He kept at his work: Letter from Amos Fries to Bessie Fries, Dec. 26, 1918, Amos A. Fries Papers, 1896–1953.

181 There was a feeling: Ibid., Dec. 31, 1917.

181 "Frankly, I don't see": Ibid., Jan. 8, 1918.

182 The next day: Confidential letter from John Pershing to William Sibert, Re: Pessimism, Dec. 13, 1917, Papers of General John J. Pershing.

182 his new assignment: "Relieve General Sibert!," *Tacoma Times,* Jan. 2, 1918, 5.

182 in charge of distant camps: "Pershing's Split with Sibert Caused Recall," *New-York Tribune,* Jan. 3, 1918, 5.

183 "About time": Letter from Amos Fries to Bessie Fries, Jan. 3, 1918, Amos A. Fries Papers, 1896–1953.

183 he now had: Ibid., Jan. 10, 1918.

183 Fries and the AEF's chief ordnance officer: Memorandum from Augustin M. Prentiss to Chief of Gas Service, Dec. 10, 1917, War Department Records, CWS, General Amos Fries Papers 1918–1920, A–C, CWS, RG 175, finding aid PI-8, entry 7, box 15, NACP.

183 Both would be near Gièvres: Memorandum from Chief Ordnance Officer, AEF, and Chief of Gas Service, AEF, to Chief of Staff, AEF, Dec. 12, 1917, War Department Records, General Amos Fries Papers 1918–1920, A–C, CWS, RG 175, finding aid PI-8, entry 7, box 15, NACP.

184 "When available for use": Memorandum from B. C. Goss to Amos Fries, Chemical Fillings for Aeroplane Bombs, Jan. 28, 1918, Technical Document Files, 1917–1920, Flame Bombs—Gas Masks, CWS, RG 175, finding aid PI-8, entry 8, box 7, NACP.

184 Fries described the rapid growth: Letter from Amos Fries to Bessie Fries, Jan. 15, 1918, Amos A. Fries Papers, 1896–1953.

184 One of the biggest challenges: Major Jason A. Moss, *Officer's Manual,* 6th ed. (Menasha, WA: George Banta, 1917), 79.

185 "The arrangement now in Washington": Letter from Amos Fries to Bessie Fries. Dec. 29, 1917.

186 "The situation is satisfactory": Van H. Manning, *Research Work of the Bureau of Mines on Gases Used in Warfare for the Month of Jan. 1918,* Chemical Research (Offense Problems), 3, "War Gas Investigations, Special World War I Work," BOM, RG 70, finding aid A-1, entry 45, box 2, NACP.

186 Over the months: Burrell, "Contributions," 99.

187 Mustard topped Manning's list: Van H. Manning, *Research Work of the Bureau of Mines on Gases Used in Warfare for the Month of Jan. 1918.*

187 In the freezing labs: Captain William B. Loach, "Mustard Gas Production in the United States," *Chemical Warfare* 1, no. 10, Oct. 23, 1919, 8–14.

188 "The British Authorities": Memorandum from Office of the Military Attaché, American Embassy, London, to Chief of Gas Service, War Department, Washington, on Manufacture of B.B. Dichlorethyl Sulphide, Jan. 26, 1918, Technical Document File, 1917–1920, Correspondence, CWS, RG 175, finding aid PI-8, entry 8, box 5, NACP.

188 For two grueling weeks: James B. Conant, *Progress Report, Organic Section,* Feb. 18, 1918, Technical Document Files, 1917–1920, CWS, RG 175, finding aid PI-8, entry 8, NACP.

188 The British method: James B. Conant, Organic Section Report 8, *Progress Report on Preparation of G-34 from Sulfur Dichloride,* 1, call no. UAI 15.898, box 142, Papers of James Bryant Conant, 1862–1987, Harvard University Archives.

188 extremely unstable: Bancroft, *History of the Chemical Warfare Service,* 71; Conant, *Progress Report on Preparation of G-34 from Sulfur Dichloride,* 2.

188 A third was tucked: First set up on Mar. 12, 1918. General Electric, *Story of the Development Division,* 176.

189 The judge advocate general: Memorandum from Newton Baker to surgeon general, Establishment of a Government Operated Plant for Gas Mask Manufacture, Nov. 20, 1917, Technical Document Files, 1917–1920, CWS, RG 175, PI-8, entry 8, box 6, NACP.

189 the Jackson Avenue building: Memorandum of Lease, Nov. 15, 1917, Technical Document Files, 1917–1920, CWS, RG 175, PI-8, entry 8, box 6, NACP.

189 On January 1, 1918: Bradley Dewey, "Contributions from the Chemical Warfare Service, USA," *Journal of Industrial and Engineering Chemistry* 11, no. 3 (Mar. 1919): 189–90.

190 The spot he pinpointed: Memorandum from Major General Henry Jervey, Director of Operations, General Staff, to Assistant Secretary of War, Nov. 4, 1918, USACE.

190 "Our work is growing": Letter from Van H. Manning to Frederic V. Abbot, Jan. 19, 1918, USACE.

191 Born in 1878: Winford Lee Lewis, "An Autobiography of an Ordinary Man" (unpublished manuscript), 46, L. Philip Reiss Collection.

191 The Lewis farm: Ibid., 68.

191 there were eight children: Ibid., 69.

192 Lee Lewis was about five: Winford Lee Lewis, "Why I Became a Chemist, and If So, to What Extent," *Chemical Bulletin* 11, no. 4 (Apr. 1924): 100.

192 In the back of one: Winford Lee Lewis personal data, L. Philip Reiss Collection.

192 A stint followed: J. A. Hynes, "W. Lee Lewis, the New Chairman," *Chemical Bulletin* 7, no. 6 (June 1920): 166.

193 Charles Parsons, a captain: Letter from Frank Genhart to W. Lee Lewis, Oct. 1, 1917, L. Philip Reiss Collection.

193 He decided against the former: Telegram from W. Lee Lewis to Myrtilla Lewis, Oct. 8, 1917, L. Philip Reiss Collection.

193 moreover, he didn't relish: Winford Lee Lewis, "Certain Organic Compounds of Arsenic" (speech delivered to Rochester chapter of the American Chemical Society, Nov. 21, 1921), 3, L. Philip Reiss Collection.

193 Lewis had wired Myrtilla: Telegram from Winford Lee Lewis to Myrtilla Lewis, Oct. 9, 1917, L. Philip Reiss Collection.

194 When the bureau sent Lewis: Lewis, "Certain Organic Compounds of Arsenic."

194 To the east: *Catholic University Bulletin*, Dec. 1919, 271.

194 Unlike American University's: Ibid., Nov. 1917.

194 Luckily for the bureau: William L. Sibert, "Summary of Achievements 1917–1918" (partial document), L. Philip Reiss Collection.

194 After the bureau approved: Lewis, "Certain Organic Compounds of Arsenic."

195 "At last, my real war job!": James Thayer Addison diary entry, Jan. 19, 1918, Louise Cass Collection.

196 That night, an officer: Ibid., Jan. 20, 1918.

196 Addison's ardor for camp life: Ibid., Jan. 26, 1918.

196 On one of his return trips: Ibid., Feb. 15, 1918.

196 A few days later: Ibid., Feb. 18, 1918.

Chapter Nine: "A Constant Menace"

197 Day after day: "Snow! Snow! Beautiful Snow!," *Washington Times,* Jan. 30, 1918, 1.

197 A storm on January 28: "Snowstorm Equals 1910 Record; More, and Cold Wave, Predicted," *Washington Post,* Jan. 31, 1918, 2.

197 Public schools ran out: "Obeys 'Heatless' Day,'" *Washington Post,* Jan. 22, 1918, 1.

197 The rushed renovation: Jones, "Role of the Chemists in Research on War Gases," 118.

197 Three train cars: "Coal Seekers Kept at Bay by Soldiers," *Washington Herald,* Jan. 31, 1918, 1.

198 On February 4: "Coldest February Day Here in Years," *Evening Star,* Feb. 5, 1918, 1.

198 The frozen Potomac: "Potomac in Greatest Flood Since 1889," *Washington Times,* Feb. 14, 1918, 1.

198 The two privates: Jason F. Adams, *Report of Explosion at American University,* Accidental Explosion at American University—Feb. 16, 1918, 3–5, USACE.

199 The campus safety engineer: G. E. McElroy, safety engineer, *Report of Chemical Explosion at American University Experiment Station of the Bureau of Mines, Feb. 16, 1918,* Records Relating to War Chemical and Gas Investigations, 1918–1919, BOM, RG 70, finding aid A1, entry 80, box 2, NACP.

200 He fired off: Letter from E. H. Marks to Lauson Stone, Mar. 17, 1918, Correspondence Relating to Military Affairs, 1918–1923, Camps, Posts, and Stations, OCE, RG 77, finding aid NM-78, entry 104, box 98, NACP.

200 "The location of such grounds": Letter from Lauson Stone to E. H. Marks, Mar. 21, 1918, OCE, RG 77, finding aid NM-78, entry 104, box 98, NACP.

200 Sometimes the stench: Letter from Burton Logue to his sister Marion Logue, Sept. 24, 1971, American University WWI File, University Archives and Special Collections, American University Library.

200 A few days: Memorandum from Sanitary Inspector to Camp Surgeon, Subject: Conditions in area surrounding Experiment Station, Mar. 20, 1918, OCE, RG 77, finding aid NM-78, entry 104, box 98, NACP.

201 Marks forwarded the report: Memorandum from E. H. Marks to General Frederic V. Abbot, Subject: Sanitary condition at Bureau of Mines Experiment Station, Mar. 20, 1918.

201 Abbot fired off: Memorandum from General Frederic V. Abbot to Van Manning, Mar. 20, 1918.

201 Manning's reply was prompt: Letter from Van Manning to Abbot, Mar. 21, 1918.

201 On March 1: *Historical Report to the Secretary of the Interior on the Origin and Development of the Research Work of the Bureau of Mines on Gases Used in Warfare, Feb. 1, 1917, to Mar. 1, 1918*, 5, BOM, RG 70, NACP.

201 By mid-May: *Report to the Secretary of the Interior on the Research Work of the Bureau of Mines on War Gas Investigations, July 1, 1917 to May 15, 1918*, 1.

201 On April 3: Confidential memorandum from Colonel Van Deman, Chief, Military Intelligence, to camp intelligence officer, Camp American University, Apr. 3, 1918, USACE.

202 In Van Manning's office: Report from Agent S. D. Bradley, Apr. 4, 1918, Richmond Levering report to Bruce Bielaski, Investigative Case Files of the BOI, 1908–1922, NARA M1085, OGF, 1909–21, case no. 8000-925, roll 279, NACP.

203 Abandoned by his country: BOI report, Apr. 6, 1918, Investigative Case Files of the BOI, 1908–1922, NARA M1085, OGF, 1909–21, case no. 8000-925, roll 279, NACP.

203 After he had fled: Summary of Walter T. von Scheele, "Associates," Apr. 3, 1917, Investigative Case Files of the BOI, 1908–1922, NARA M1085, OGF, 1909–21, case no. 8000-925, roll 279, NACP.

203 Living in seclusion: Scheele statement to Cuban Police Captain Llaca, Schedule A, Richmond Levering report to Bruce Bielaski, Investigative Case Files of the BOI, 1908–1922, NARA M1085, OGF, 1909–21, case no. 8000-925, roll 279, NACP.

204 De Pozas had worries: Military Intelligence synopsis, Walter Theodore (von) Scheele, June 1, 1918, 6, and Richmond Levering, BOI Report, no date, Investigative Case Files of the BOI, 1908–1922, NARA M1085, OGF, 1909–21, case no. 8000-925, roll 279, NACP.

205 In a solitary cell: Summary of Scheele Case, Mar. 4, 1921, Investigative Case Files of the BOI, 1908–1922, NARA M1085, OGF, 1909–21, case no. 8000-925, roll 279, NACP.

205 In late February: Richmond Levering to A. Bruce Bielaski, Mar. 15, 1918, *First Section Report of Dr. Walter T. Scheele*, 1, Investigative Case Files of the BOI, 1908–1922, NARA M1085, OGF, 1909–21, case no. 8000-925, roll 279, NACP.

206 Several men had been arrested: Scheele statement to Cuban Police Captain Llaca, Schedule A. Levering's reports back to the BOI are not definitive as to the identity

of the third man, referring to him as "the man who had kept Scheele in hiding and who was a Cuban citizen."

206 All three were being held: Report from Richmond M. Levering to BOI chief A. Bruce Bielaski on arrest of Walter T. Scheele, *Dr. Scheele's Proposition for Immunity,* Mar. 15, 1918, Key West, Fla., Investigative Case Files of the BOI, 1908–1922, NARA M1085, OGF, 1909–21, case no. 8000-925, roll 279, NACP.

206 Darkness had fallen: Strother, *Fighting Germany's Spies,* 261. This account, while colorful, is a bit suspect. It's impossible to know whether this account describes the first or second trip from Havana to Key West, although presumably it is the first, as it specifies that Scheele was on the SS *Flagler.* (On his second trip to Key West, he was on a Cuban naval vessel.)

207 Agents met the boat: Report from Agent Arthur E. Gregory, Mar. 13, 1918, Re: Dr. William Scheele, et al.—Espionage—German Agents, Investigative Case Files of the BOI, 1908–1922, NARA M1085, OGF, 1909–21, case no. 8000-925, roll 279, NACP.

207 Levering warned Scheele: Levering, "Dr. Scheele's Proposition for Immunity."

207 Scheele began to talk: Agent E. P. Martin report on Scheele interrogation, Mar. 14, 1918, Investigative Case Files of the BOI, 1908–1922, NARA M1085, OGF, 1909–21, case no. 8000-925, roll 279, NACP.

207 Thomas Edison came: Report by Agent Arthur C. Gregory, Investigative Case Files of the BOI, 1908–1922, NARA M1085, OGF, 1909–21, case no. 8000-925, roll 279, NACP.

208 "So far Mr. Silver": Richmond M. Levering, Report to BOI chief A. Bruce Bielaski on arrest of Walter T. Scheele, "Second Section of the Report by Levering," Mar. 16, 1918, Key West, Fla., Investigative Case Files of the BOI, 1908–1922, NARA M1085, OGF, 1909–21, case no. 8000-925, roll 279, NACP.

208 Copies of the interrogation reports: Richmond M. Levering report to A. Bruce Bielaski, Mar. 21, 1918; letter from Bruce Silver to Richmond M. Levering, Correspondence of War College Division and related general staff Offices, 1903–19, WDG, RG 165, microfilm publication M1024, reel 355, NACP.

208 Silver questioned Scheele: Letter from Bruce Silver to Richmond Levering, Mar. 21, 1918, Investigative Case Files of the BOI, 1908–1922, NARA M1085, OGF, 1909–21, case no. 8000-925, roll 279, NACP.

208 "I would therefore": Ibid., Mar. 16, 1918, Investigative Case Files of the BOI, 1908–1922, NARA M1085, OGF, 1909–21, case no. 8000-925, roll 279, NACP.

208 Even Thomas Edison: Levering, "Dr. Scheele's Proposition for Immunity."

209 Rage against Germans: "Draped in US Flag, Victim Is Marched to Destruction," *Washington Times,* Apr. 5, 1918, 1.

209 In New York: "Crowd Threatens to Hang Germans," *Washington Herald,* Apr. 6, 1918, 1.

209 "Please keep his presence": Telegram from William M. Offley to Bruce Bielaski, Key West, Fla., Mar. 15, 1918, Investigative Case Files of the BOI, 1908–1922, NARA M1085, OGF, 1909–21, case no. 8000-925, roll 279, NACP.

209 "We are keeping the information": Letter from Bruce Bielaski to Charles F. Lynch, U.S. attorney for New Jersey, Mar. 25, 1918, Investigative Case Files of the BOI, 1908–1922, NARA M1085, OGF, 1909–21, case no. 8000-925, roll 279, NACP.

209 The message streaked: "Long-Sought Data on Spies Given by German Plotter," *New-York Tribune,* Mar. 27, 1918, 16.

209 The new Bureau of Investigation: "New Hunter of Spies in New York District," *New York Times,* Mar. 31, 1918, sec. 4, 8.

209 The group set out: Agent Arthur E. Gregory report for Mar. 17, 1918, Investigative Case Files of the BOI, 1908–1922, NARA M1085, OGF, 1909–21, case no. 8000-925, roll 279, NACP.

209 This time, the weather: Photos of Jacinto Llama, Walter Scheele, Ricardo Guttman, and group, Investigative Case Files of the BOI, 1908–1922, NARA M1085, OGF, 1909–21, case no. 8000-925, roll 279, NACP.

210 On the morning: Report from Agent C. B. Treadway, Mar. 20, 1918, Investigative Case Files of the BOI, 1908–1922, NARA M1085, OGF, 1909–21, case no. 8000-925, roll 279, NACP.

210 The following evening: Telegram from Agent C. B. Treadway to A. Bruce Bielaski, Mar. 21, 1918, Investigative Case Files of the BOI, 1908–1922, NARA M1085, OGF, 1909–21, case no. 8000-925, roll 279, NACP.

210 When the train: Report of BOI Agent S. D. Bradley, Re: Dr. Walter T. Scheele (German Matter), Mar. 23, 1918, Investigative Case Files of the BOI, 1908–1922, NARA M1085, OGF, 1909–21, case no. 8000-925, roll 279, NACP.

210 Scheele spent the day: Report by Agent J. E. Elliott in Washington, DC, Re: Dr. William Scheele, et al.: Espionage—German Agents, Apr. 4, 1918, Investigative Case Files of the BOI, 1908–1922, NARA M1085, OGF, 1909–21, case no. 8000-925, roll 279, NACP.

211 Warren Grimes, a bureau agent: Letter from Warren W. Grimes to A. Bruce Bielaski, Apr. 8, 1918, Investigative Case Files of the BOI, 1908–1922, NARA M1085, OGF, 1909–21, case no. 8000-925, roll 279, NACP.

211 The vice president: Agent Warren Grimes report for Apr. 7, 1918, written Apr. 20, 1918, *Dr. Walter Scheele: German Matter,* Investigative Case Files of the BOI, 1908–1922, NARA M1085, OGF, 1909–21, case no. 8000-925, roll 279, NACP.

212 Hundreds of men: Addison diary entry, Feb. 24, 1918.

212 They said a wrenching goodbye: Ibid., Feb. 25, 1918.

212 The USS *Agamemnon:* USS *Agamemnon,* NavSource Photo History: Photographic History of the U.S. Navy, http://www.navsource.org/archives/12/173004.htm.

213 At 6:30 p.m.: Addison diary entry, Feb. 26, 1918.

213 Starlight illuminated the ship's path: Ibid., Feb. 28, 1918.

215 Fries didn't grouse: Letter from Amos Fries to Bessie Fries, Mar. 18, 1918, Amos A. Fries Papers, 1896–1953.

215 Still, the offices hummed: Ibid., Apr. 16, 1918.

215 all of them men: Ibid., Apr. 9, 1918.

215 Fries managed to make: Ibid., Mar. 22, 1918.

215 A few days before: Ibid., Mar. 24, 1918.

216 "an awful bonehead": Ibid., Feb. 10, 1918.

216 He had great respect: Ibid., Mar. 12, 1918,

216 During the Paris gas conference: Ibid., Mar. 5, 1918.

216 about restructuring his service: *History of Chemical Warfare Service, AEF,* 24.

217 Fries estimated the AEF: Memorandum from Chief of Gas Service to Lieutenant D. W. Salisbury, Re: Automatic Monthly Supplies for 1918, Mar. 15, 1918, War

Department Records, General Amos A. Fries Papers 1918–1920, A–C, CWS, RG 175, finding aid PI-8, entry 7, box 15, NACP.

217 Fries wanted an organization: Letter from Amos Fries to Bessie Fries, Mar. 20, 1918, Amos A. Fries Papers, 1896–1953.

217 As a result: *History of the Chemical Warfare Service, AEF,* 29.

217 As Fries pushed: Ibid., 28.

217 Making the service: Letter from Amos Fries to Bessie Fries, Apr. 7, 1918, Amos A. Fries Papers, 1896–1953.

218 "I would be glad": Ibid., Feb. 11, 1918.

218 The Germans rejected: "Germans Don't Intend to Give Up Poison Gas," *New York Times,* Feb. 28, 1918, 3.

218 He remained adamant: Fries memoir; Fries and West, *Chemical Warfare,* 399.

218 "Bad as they are": Letter from Amos Fries to Bessie Fries, Mar. 12, 1918, Amos A. Fries Papers, 1896–1953.

218 About 260 miles: Higginbottom diary entry, Mar. 1, 1918.

219 About three quarters of the casualties: *Report on Projector Attack on American Troops,* Feb. 28, 1918, AEF General Headquarters, G-3 Reports, Secret Correspondence, Records of the AEF (World War I), RG 120, finding aid NM-91, entry 268, box 3141, NACP.

220 At 5:00 a.m.: Higginbottom diary entry, Mar. 4, 1918.

220 In the afternoon: Ibid., Mar. 5, 1918.

220 That same afternoon: Ibid., Mar. 6, 1918.

221 On March 15: Ibid., Mar. 15, 1918.

221 Two nights in a row: Ibid., Mar. 19, 1918.

221 One night while they waited: Ibid., Mar. 16, 1918.

223 In the cyclone of noise: Ibid., Mar. 21, 1918.

Chapter Ten: "Science and Horror"

224 The mud was six inches: Higginbottom diary entry, Apr. 6, 1918.

225 As part of the surge: Addison, *Story of the First Gas Regiment,* 26.

226 For hours: Higginbottom diary entry, Apr. 7, 1918.

226 In the morning: Ibid., Apr. 8, 1918.

226 Georgette began: Addison, *Story of the First Gas Regiment,* 27.

227 More than fifty: Ibid.

227 But Higgie: Higginbottom diary entry, Apr. 9, 1918.

228 Casualty numbers: *Gas Casualties in AEF, Compiled from Gas Officers' Reports,* no date, General Fries' Files, 1918–1920, A–C Edgewood Arsenal, 1917–1943. CWS, RG 175, finding aid PI-8, entry 7, box 15, NACP.

228 Addison was receiving: Addison diary entry, Apr. 4, 1918.

228 "It was a long tale": Ibid., Apr. 6, 1918.

229 "Some new method": Ibid., Apr. 8, 1918.

229 After leaving Chaumont: Letter from Amos Fries to Bessie Fries, Apr. 7, 1918, Amos A. Fries Papers, 1896–1953.

229 he assured Bessie: Ibid., May 7, 1918.

229 a general who was: The general appears to have been Chief of Engineers William Black, but it's unclear from Fries's letter about the visit.

230 "Certainly they know": Letter from Amos Fries to Bessie Fries, Mar. 25, 1918, Amos A. Fries Papers, 1896–1953.

230 "It promises": Ibid., Apr. 7, 1918.

231 "Because of its vast": *History of the Chemical Warfare Service, AEF,* folder H-12, First Gas Regiment files 1984–87, box 96, Carlisle Attic Collection, CCM.

231 cabled Fries: Letter from Amos Fries to Bessie Fries, May 1, 1918, Amos A. Fries Papers, 1896–1953.

231 "with no man": Ibid., May 9, 1918.

231 With Pershing's blessing: Letter from Commander in Chief to Adjutant General, U.S. Army, Re: Chemical or Gas Service, Aug. 4, 1917, George A. Hulett Papers, call no. C0460, Manuscripts Division, Department of Rare Books and Special Collections, Princeton University Library.

232 What happened to the rest: Memorandum from Assistant Director Gas Service Laboratory to Acting Chief of Technical Division, Gas Service, Re: Shipment of Chemical Supplies from the United States, May 15, 1918, War Department, General Fries' Files, 1918–1920, O–S, CWS, RG 175, finding aid PI-8, entry 7, box 19, NACP.

232 Eventually, it began arriving: *History of the Chemical Warfare Service, AEF,* Technical Division, part 2, Paris Laboratory, 1.

232 When it was up: Ibid., 4.

232 Beginning in the spring: Letter from Amos Fries to Bessie Fries, May 9, 1918, Amos A. Fries Papers, 1896–1953.

232 He felt that: Ibid., Apr. 12, 1918.

232 More than 900 people: *Analysis of President Staff,* Personnel Report, May 4, 1918, War Gas Investigation, Reports and Other Records, BOM, RG 70, finding aid A-1, entry 46, box 110, NACP.

232 Temporary barracks went up: McPherson, "Historical Sketch," 54.

232 Pumps drew water: Ibid., 62.

233 A twenty-thousand-kilowatt electrical plant: "Central Power Station, Bush River," General Fries' Files, 1918–20, O–S, War Department, CWS, RG 175, finding aid PI-8, entry 7, box 19, NACP.

233 On April 2: Bancroft, *History of the Chemical Warfare Service,* 3 (227).

233 Edgewood turned into a boomtown: Benedict Crowell and Robert Forrest Wilson, *Armies of Industry II: Our Nation's Manufacture of Munitions for a World in Arms* (New Haven, CT: Yale University Press, 1921), 492.

233 Walker commanded dozens of engineers: Letter from Brigadier General C. B. Wheeler to Colonel William Walker, Apr. 2, 1918, Establishment of Gunpowder Reservation, Technical Document Files, 1917–1920, Major McPherson's Personnel File—Masks, CWS, RG 175, finding aid PI-8, entry 8, box 10, NACP.

234 Afterward, Burrell wrote: Letter from George A. Burrell to Lieutenant Colonel William Walker, Mar. 2, 1918, Technical Document File, 1917–1920, CWS, RG 175, finding aid PI-8, entry 8, box 3, NACP.

234 There were so many problems: Bancroft, *History of the Chemical Warfare Service,* 22 (245), Spring Valley.

234 By around May 1: Ibid., 25 (248).

234 Mustard had taken so long: Letter from Elmer Kohler to James Bryant Conant, Aug. 9, 1918, call no. UAI 15.898, folder "War Work at Willoughby Near

Cleveland—1918," box 142, Papers of James Bryant Conant, 1862–1987, Harvard University Archives.

235 Conant had made his mark: U.S. Army commission, Apr. 13, 1918, folder "War Work at Willoughby Near Cleveland—1918," box 142, Papers of James Bryant Conant, Harvard University Archives.

235 A month later: Western Union telegram, folder "War Work at Willoughby Near Cleveland—1918," box 142, Papers of James Bryant Conant, Harvard University Archives.

235 This new endeavor began: *Report to the Secretary of the Interior on the Research Work of the Bureau of Mines on War Gas Investigations, July 1, 1917 to May 15, 1918,* 19 (59), War Gas Investigations Reports and Other Records, BOM, RG 70, finding aid A-1, entry 46, box 110, NACP.

235 "Further tests of this method": Report for the week ending Apr. 13, 1918, of work at the Catholic University Annex, Offensive Chemical Research Division, War Gas Investigations, BOM, American University Experiment Station—Washington, DC, Apr. 15, 1918, L. Philip Reiss Collection.

235 Father Griffin: *Report to the Secretary of the Interior on the Research Work of the Bureau of Mines on War Gas Investigations, July 1, 1917 to May 15, 1918,* 19 (59).

236 The difficulty: Report for the week ending Apr. 13, 1918 of work at the Catholic University Annex, Offensive Chemical Research Division, War Gas Investigations, BOM, American University Experiment Station—Washington, DC, Apr. 15, 1918, 173, L. Philip Reiss Collection.

236 Lewis was able: Joel A. Vilensky, *The Dew of Death* (Bloomington: Indiana University Press, 2005), 23.

237 The first reports: Wilder Bancroft, Index to Reports, Aug. 1, 1918, BOM, Semi-Monthly Reports, finding aid A1, entry 48, box 113, NACP.

237 Another early report: *Preliminary Report on Lewisite,* June 25, 1918, Medical Advisory Board Minutes and Reports, Frank P. Underhill Papers, numbered folder 80–106, group no. 514, box 6, Yale University Library Manuscript Collections.

237 On May 24: "Surgeon's Morning Report for May 24, 1918," May 25, 1918, "Records Relating to War Chemical and Gas Investigations, 1918–1919," BOM records, finding aid A1, Entry 80, box 1, NACP.

237 The numbers grew: Ibid., June 6, 1918.

237 Lewis himself was one: "Lewis Tells of Perils of Gas Research Work."

237 Despite the injuries: *Report to the Secretary of the Interior on the Research Work of the Bureau of Mines on War Gas Investigations, July 1, 1917 to May 15, 1918,* 24 (64), L. Philip Reiss Collection.

238 On May 1: Ibid., 21 (61).

238 Walter Scheele's new life: Warren Grimes report for Apr. 15, 1918, *Dr. Walter Scheele: German Matter.*

239 Grimes went to the office: Employee list, Kaolin Products Corp., Jones Point, NY, Investigative Case Files of the BOI, 1908–1922, NARA M1085, OGF, 1909–21, case no. 8000-925, roll 279, NACP.

239 Fire him: Grimes report for Apr. 8, 1918, written Apr. 22, 1918, *Dr. Walter Scheele: German Matter.*

240 Grimes insisted that agents: Grimes report for Apr. 12, 1918, written Apr. 22, 1918.

240 The doctor spoke freely: Warren W. Grimes, Memorandum for the Files, Apr. 23, 1918, Investigative Case Files of the BOI, 1908–1922, NARA M1085, OGF, 1909–21, case no. 8000-925, roll 279, NACP.

240 Grimes reveled in his job: Letter from Grimes to Bielaski, Apr. 8, 1918, 3, Investigative Case Files of the BOI, 1908–1922, NARA M1085, OGF, 1909–21, case no. 8000-925, roll 279, NACP.

240 At week's end: Letter to Special Agent Rice from Div. Supt. Charles DeWoody, Apr. 13, 1918, Investigative Case Files of the BOI, 1908–1922, NARA M1085, OGF, 1909–21, case no. 8000-925, roll 279, NACP.

242 DeWoody, however, was irate: Letter from Charles DeWoody to A. Bruce Bielaski, May 2, 1918, Investigative Case Files of the BOI, 1908–1922, NARA M1085, OGF, 1909–21, case no. 8000-925, roll 279, NACP.

242 Accusations of fraud: "Oil Shareholders to Quiz Promoter," *New York Times,* Apr. 14, 1918, 20.

242 about angry shareholders: Letter from William Offley to A. Bruce Bielaski, Apr. 16, 1918, Investigative Case Files of the BOI, 1908–1922, NARA M1085, OGF, 1909–21, case no. 8000-16110, roll 473, NACP.

242 A new allegation: Memorandum from A. Bruce Bielaski to Mr. Offley, Apr. 6, 1918, Investigative Case Files of the BOI, 1908–1922, NARA M1085, OGF, 1909–21, case no. 8000-12490, roll 335, NACP.

242 Then he had managed: Personal and confidential letter from DeWoody to A. Bruce Bielaski, Apr. 18, 1918, Investigative Case Files of the BOI, 1908–1922, NARA M1085, OGF, 1909–21, case no. 8000-16110, roll 473, NACP.

243 Worried anew that Levering could: Letter from A. Bruce Bielaski to Charles DeWoody, Apr. 8, 1918, Personal and confidential letter from DeWoody to A. Bruce Bielaski, Apr. 18, 1918, Investigative Case Files of the BOI, 1908–1922, NARA M1085, OGF, 1909–21, case no. 8000-16110, roll 473, NACP.

243 DeWoody dispatched investigators: Report from Agent W. B. Matthews, In re: Richmond Levering (Confidential), Apr. 26, 1918, Investigative Case Files of the BOI, 1908–1922, NARA M1085, OGF, 1909–21, case no. 8000-97452, roll 473, NACP.

243 "If ever there was": BOI report from Agent Leonard M. Stern, In re: Richmond Levering—Investigation, May 20, 1918, Investigative Case Files of the BOI, 1908–1922, NARA M1085, OGF, 1909–21, case no. 8000-97452, roll 473, NACP.

243 "A bad nickel": Report from Agent W. B. Matthews, In re: Richmond Levering (Confidential), Apr. 22, 1918, 3, Investigative Case Files of the BOI, 1908–1922, NARA M1085, OGF, 1909–21, case no. 8000-97452, roll 473, NACP.

243 "From one or two experiences": Letter from Division Superintendent Charles DeWoody to A. Bruce Bielaski, May 8, 1918, 2, Investigative Case Files of the BOI, 1908–1922, NARA M1085, OGF, 1909–21, case no. 8000-97452, roll 473, NACP.

244 Though more than a dozen: Van H. Manning, *Historical Report to the Secretary of the Interior on the Origin and Development of the Research Work of the Bureau of Mines on Gases Used in Warfare,* Feb. 1, 1917, to Mar. 1, 1918, RG 70, NACP.

244 There was a growing recognition: Minutes of procurement meeting, May 30, 1918, "Cotton Seed Hulls, Fillings etc," Technical Document Files, 1917–1920, CWS, RG 175, finding aid PL-8, entry 7, box 6, NACP.

244 Recalled from France: "March to Make Changes," *New York Times,* Mar. 2, 1918, 2.

245 This scattered domestic structure: *Army Reorganization: Hearings before the Committee on Military Affairs,* U.S. House of Representatives, 66th Congress, 1st session, on HR 7925, A Bill to Establish a Department of Aeronautics and for Other Purposes, 58 (Sept. 5, 1919) (statement of Chief of Staff Peyton March).

245 On Saturday, May 18: Army and Navy News, *Washington Herald,* May 18, 1918, 4.

245 Even before he returned: "Many Generals Affected by Big Army Shake-Up," *Washington Times,* Jan. 2, 1918, 1.

245 He took up residence: Charleston, South Carolina, city directory, 1918, 466.

245 "Never will the brotherhood": " 'Might' Only Salvation of Nation, Declares Gen. Sibert," *Chattanooga News,* Apr. 19, 1918, 16.

246 On May 11, 1918: Memorandum from Peyton C. March to Adjutant General, May 11, 1918, Correspondence of War College Division and Related General Staff Offices, 1903–19, WDG, RG 165, microfilm publication M1024, reel 306, NACP.

246 Sibert left Charleston: "Death Toll Grows from Influenza," *Evening Star,* Oct. 9, 1918, 18.

246 When the War Department: "Gen. Sibert in New Post," *Washington Post,* May 20, 1918, 6.

246 Fries was pleased: Letter from Amos Fries to Bessie Fries, May 25, 1918, Amos A. Fries Papers, 1896–1953.

246 "The gas service": Ibid., May 20, 1918.

247 Fries had been egging on: D. W. Ketcham, Memorandum for Chief of Staff, Subject: Chemical Service, National Army, Feb. 9, 1918, Correspondence of War College Division and Related General Staff Offices, 1903–19, WDG, RG 165, microfilm publication M1024, reel 306, NACP.

247 Baker asked for a conference: Letter from Secretary of War Newton Baker to Interior Secretary Franklin Lane, May 21, 1918, War Gas Investigations Reports and Other Records, BOM, RG 70, finding aid A-1, entry 46, box 110, NACP.

248 One of the most stubborn: Van H. Manning, Memorandum Regarding Conference Held in the Office of the Secretary of War, from 3:00 p.m. to 4:45 p.m., May 25, 1918, War Gas Investigations Reports and Other Records, BOM, RG 70, finding aid A-1, entry 46, box 110, NACP.

Chapter Eleven: "He Who Gasses Last, Gasses Best"

249 Night fell over Chaumont: Addison diary entry, June 6, 1918.

249 The very first one: Emma Higginbottom died on May 4, 1918, https://www.findagrave.com/cgi-bin/fg.cgi?page=gr&GRid=166998399&ref=acom.

250 The letter was dated: Higginbottom diary entry, May 29, 1918.

250 He left at about one-thirty: Report on CWS operations at the front, June 19, 1918, 4, AEF General Headquarters, G-3 Reports, Secret Correspondence, Records of the AEF (World War I), RG 120, finding aid NM-91, entry 268, box 3173, NACP.

250 The dugouts were tucked: Higginbottom diary entry, June 7, 1918.

250 He slept late: Ibid., June 9, 1918.

251 Addison's training hadn't prepared him: Addison diary entry, June 12, 1918.

251 When the firefight slowed: Ibid., June 9, 1918.

251 Higgie attended: Addison diary entry, June 16, 1918; Higginbottom diary entry, June 16, 1918.

251 Addison waited in a dugout: Addison diary entry, June 18, 1918.

252 As zero hour approached: Higginbottom diary entry, June 18, 1918.

252 Farther back, Addison watched: Addison diary entry, June 18, 1918.

253 Company A's show: Report on CWS operations at the front. Operation by 30th Engineers, June 22, 1918, Special Report, First Gas Regiment Operations, 18 June–11 Nov. 1918, First Gas Regiment Collection, CCM.

253 Addison and Higgie lay: Higginbottom diary entry, June 19, 1918.

253 "A few days ago": Letter from Amos Fries to Bessie Fries, June 21, 1918, Amos A. Fries Papers, 1896–1953.

253 The show caused at least: Report on CWS operations at the front.

253 On one night: Special report on operations of 30th Engineers, June 18, 1918, CCM.

253 Finding Fries fit: Calomel, which Fries took for his digestion, was eventually found to cause liver damage as well as other permanent injury.

254 He was awaiting word: Memorandum from Chief of Gas Service Fries to Chief of Staff, AEF, Gas Program, Appendix A, text of proposed telegram, AEF General Headquarters, G-3 Reports, Secret Correspondence, Records of the AEF (World War I), RG 120, entry 268, finding aid NM-91, box 3141, NACP.

254 But the day he wrote: Letter from Amos Fries to Bessie Fries, June 21, 1918, Amos A. Fries Papers, 1896–1953.

254 He was also extremely pleased: Ibid., June 23, 1918.

255 "To militarize the body": "The War Gas Controversy," *New York Times,* June 7, 1918, 12.

255 On June 25: Woodrow Wilson, Executive Order, June 25, 1918, War Gas Investigations, Reports and Other Records, BOM, RG 70, finding aid A-1, entry 46, box 110, NACP.

255 Secretary of War Newton Baker: Newton Baker, letter to Woodrow Wilson, June 25, 1918, War Gas Investigations, Reports and Other Records, BOM, RG 70, finding aid A-1, entry 46, box 110, NACP.

255 "I want, however, to express": Woodrow Wilson, letter to Van Manning, June 26, 1918, War Gas Investigations, Reports and Other Records, BOM, RG 70, finding aid A-1, entry 46, box 110, NACP.

256 Privately, Manning was surprised: Letter from John Johnston to George Hale, June 29, 1918, NAS-NRC, Central File, 1914–1918, National Academy of Sciences Archives.

256 Despite Manning's bruised ego: Letter from Van Manning to President Woodrow Wilson, June 29, 1918, War Gas Investigations, Reports and Other Records, BOM, RG 70, finding aid A-1, entry 46, box 110, NACP.

256 He extended no such niceties: Letter from Van Manning to William Sibert, June 29, 1918, War Gas Investigations, Reports and Other Records, BOM, RG 70, finding aid A-1, entry 46, box 110, NACP.

256 Telegrams and letters of condolence: Letter from to W. R. Ingalls to Van H. Manning, July 1, 1918, War Gas Investigations, Reports and Other Records, BOM, RG 70, finding aid A-1, entry 46, box 110, NACP.

256 "I can appreciate": Letter from F. S. Peabody to Van H. Manning, July 1, 1918, War Gas Investigations, Reports and Other Records, BOM, RG 70, finding aid A-1, entry 46, box 110, NACP.

256 It was a front-page story: "1,700 Chemists Employed for Gas Service," Washington Herald, June 29, 1918, 1.

257 "an eminent engineer": "Sibert and the Chemists," New York Times, June 30, 1918, 22.

257 The War Department released: "Defenders of the Country," Yorkville (SC) Enquirer, June 18, 1918, 1.

257 That the introduction of chemicals: "How Trained Scientists Are Meeting Modern Destructive Agencies—Gas Warfare and Aviation Hold First Place," Maui News, June 28, 1918, 2.

257 "This laboratory is now": "American Gas Organization," Topeka State Journal, July 18, 1918, 4.

258 "We are of the opinion": "Mining Engineers Plan War Work," Bisbee (AZ) Daily Review, Mining Section, July 07, 1918, 2.

258 Another speech noted: 607 Fourteenth Street NW (Washington Herald ad, Feb. 12, 1918, 14).

258 The university president: The Town Crier, Washington Herald, June 24, 1918, 10.

258 the keynote speaker: "Judge Hitt to Address Alumni," Washington Post, June 24, 1918, 5.

258 "The military lid": Text of W. Lee Lewis speech, courtesy of L. Philip Reiss.

258 Two days later: "Chemical Warfare Service: Its History and Personnel," Chemical Engineer, 16, no. 10 (Sept. 1918): 380.

258 The stroke of the president's pen: "Army Takes Over All War Gas Work," New York Times, June 29, 1918, 7.

259 Before he left: Grimes report for Apr. 9, 1918, Dr. Walter Scheele: German Matter.

259 He arranged: Agent Francis X. O'Donnell report for May 24, 1918, Protection at Jones Point, NY, Investigative Case Files of the BOI, 1908–1922, NARA M1085, OGF, 1909–21, case no. 8000-925, roll 279, NACP.

259 Governor Charles Whitman: Letter from Richmond Levering to Bruce Bielaski, Apr. 12, 1918, Investigative Case Files of the BOI, 1908–1922, NARA M1085, OGF, 1909–21, case no. 8000-925, roll 279, NACP.

260 Five days after: Grimes report for Apr. 12, 1918.

260 Scheele began work: Francis X. O'Donnell report for Apr. 30, 1918.

260 They also experimented: Report from Bruce Silver to Richmond Levering, Report of Progress in the Jones Point Experimental Laboratory for the Period May 28–31, 1918, May 31, 1918, Investigative Case Files of the BOI, 1908–1922, NARA M1085, OGF, 1909–21, case no. 8000-925, roll 279, NACP.

260 and when they created: Report from Bruce Silver to Richmond Levering, Report of Progress in the Jones Point Experimental Laboratory for the Period June 4–14, 1918, Investigative Case Files of the BOI, 1908–1922, NARA M1085, OGF, 1909–21, case no. 8000-925, roll 279, NACP.

260 From the earliest moments: Hart, Great War, 35.

260 Scheele claimed that the violence: Richmond Levering report to A. Bruce Bielaski, *Uses of Liquid Air,* Second Section report of Dr. Walter T. Scheele, Investigative Case Files of the BOI, 1908–1922, NARA M1085, OGF, 1909–21, case no. 8000-925, roll 279, NACP.

261 Scheele also claimed: Ibid., 3.

261 The other top priority: Report from Captain Paul H. M. P. Brinton to Richmond Levering, *Report of Progress in Experimental Laboratory at American Potash Corporation Plant, Jones Point, NY,* Apr. 25, 1918, Investigative Case Files of the BOI, 1908–1922, NARA M1085, OGF, 1909–21, case no. 8000-925, roll 279, NACP.

261 It didn't take long: Report from Silver to Levering, *Report of Progress in the Jones Experimental Laboratory for the Period May 28–31, 1918.*

261 Such a fire: Letter from Richmond Levering to Lieutenant Commander Theodore Wilkinson, Apr. 30, 1918, Investigative Case Files of the BOI, 1908–1922, RG 65, NARA M1085, OGF, case no. 8000-925, roll 279, NACP.

261 Bielaski wrote back: Letter from Bruce Bielaski to Richmond Levering, May 5, 1918, Investigative Case Files of the BOI, 1908–1922, RG 65, NARA M1085, OGF, 1909–21, case no. 8000-925, roll 279, NACP.

262 The manufacturing research: Report from Silver to Levering, *Report of Progress in the Jones Point Experimental Laboratory for the Period May 28–31, 1918,* 2.

262 The chemists tried turning it: Report from Captain Paul H. M. P. Brinton to Richmond Levering, *Report of Results Obtained in the Experimental Laboratory at American Potash Corporation's Plant, at Jones Point, NY,* April 23, 1918, Investigative Case Files of the BOI, 1908–1922, RG 65, NARA M1085, OGF, case no. 8000–925, roll 279, NACP.

262 The scientists also tested helline: Report from Brinton to Levering, *Report of Progress in Experimental Laboratory at American Potash Corporation Plant, Jones Point, NY.*

262 In one experiment: Memorandum from H. H. Armstrong to Lieutenant Commander Wilkinson, Demonstrating Tests, May 22, 1918, Investigative Case Files of the BOI, 1908–1922, NARA M1085, OGF, 1909–21, case no. 8000-925, roll 279, NACP.

263 Iona provided its own share: "Six Men Killed in Arsenal Explosion," *New York Times,* Nov. 5, 1903, 1.

263 The chemists had high hopes: Report from Captain Paul H. M. P. Brinton to Richmond Levering, *Report of Progress,* May 7, 1918, Investigative Case Files of the BOI, 1908–1922, NARA M1085, OGF, 1909–21, case no. 8000-925, roll 279, NACP.

263 so Scheele's compound: Letter from Richmond Levering to Lieutenant Commander Wilkinson, May 13, 1918, Investigative Case Files of the BOI, 1908–1922, NARA M1085, OGF, 1909–21, case no. 8000-925, roll 279, NACP.

263 Though less powerful: Report from Captain Paul H. M. P. Brinton to Richmond Levering, *Report of Progress,* May 24–28, 1918, Investigative Case Files of the BOI, 1908–1922, NARA M1085, OGF, 1909–21, case no. 8000-925, roll 279, NACP.

263 The ongoing involvement: Letter from Edison assistant W. H. Meadowcraft to Bruce Silver, June 10, 1918, Naval Consulting Board and Related Wartime Research Papers, Correspondence, Feb. 1918, Edison Papers, reel 280, frames 432–33.

263 Silver apologized for his absence: Ibid., frame 438.

264 Levering, too, wrote to Edison: Ibid., frames 441–42.

264 Levering began sending the reports: Letter from Richmond Levering to Thomas A. Edison, July 16, 1918, Edison Papers, frame 831.

264 Marie Scheele was living alone: Francis X. O'Donnell report for June 5, 1918.

264 At the end of May: Letter from Charles A. DeWoody to A. Bruce Bielaski, May 31, 1918, Investigative Case Files of the BOI, 1908–1922, NARA M1085, OGF, 1909–21, case no. 8000-925, roll 279, NACP.

264 Though the details were scant: Letter from Charles DeWoody to A. Bruce Bielaski, June 6, 1918, BOI report from Agent Leonard M. Stern, In re: Richmond Levering—Investigation, May 20, 1918, Investigative Case Files of the BOI, 1908–1922, NARA M1085, OGF, 1909–21, case no. 8000-97452, roll 473, NACP.

265 DeWoody asked the chief: Letter from DeWoody to A. Bruce Bielaski, May 31, 1918, Investigative Case Files of the BOI, 1908–1922, NARA M1085, OGF, 1909–21, case no. 8000-925, roll 279, NACP.

265 Since the previous year: "Montauk Quick Facts," Montauk Library, http://www.montauklibrary.org/other_pages&key=QUICK-FACTS.

265 On Saturday, June 1: Report from Richmond Levering to Lieutenant Commander Wilkinson, June 3, 1918, Investigative Case Files of the BOI, 1908–1922, NARA M1085, OGF, 1909–21, case no. 8000-925, roll 279, NACP.

265 He also proposed: Ibid., 2.

266 The following day: Letter from Richmond Levering to William Offley, Apr. 30, 1918, Investigative Case Files of the BOI, 1908–1922, NARA M1085, OGF, 1909–21, case no. 8000-97452, roll 473, NACP.

266 Levering erupted in furious indignation: Letter from Richmond Levering to A. Bruce Bielaski, "Attention of WMO," June 4, 1918, Investigative Case Files of the BOI, 1908–1922, NARA M1085, OGF, 1909–21, case no. 8000-97452, roll 473, NACP.

266 Colonel Ragsdale, the chief: Letter from Lieutenant Colonel Ragsdale to A. Bruce Bielaski, June 6, 1918, Investigative Case Files of the BOI, 1908–1922, NARA M1085, OGF, 1909–21, case no. 8000-97452, roll 473, NACP.

266 DeWoody doubled down: Letter from Charles DeWoody to A. Bruce Bielaski, June 6, 1918, Investigative Case Files of the BOI, 1908–1922, NARA M1085, OGF, 1909–21, case no. 8000-97452, roll 473, NACP.

266 Edison's chemist Bruce Silver: Report from Silver to Levering, *Report of Progress in the Jones Point Experimental Laboratory for the period June 1–4, 1918*.

266 "This essential was reported": Letter from Richmond Levering to Lieutenant Colonel E. J. W. Ragsdale, Incendiary Material, June 3, 1918, Investigative Case Files of the BOI, 1908–1922, NARA M1085, OGF, 1909–21, case no. 8000-925, roll 279, NACP.

267 Whatever the reason: Anne Cipriano Venzon, *The United States in the First World War* (New York: Routledge, 2003), 752.

267 The commander of the detachment: Letter from E. A. Anderson to Richmond Levering, July 3, 1918, Investigative Case Files of the BOI, 1908–1922, NARA M1085, OGF, 1909–21, case no. 8000-97452, roll 473, NACP.

267 A ceremony raised: "Flags Raised Breezingly at Union Station," *Washington Herald*, July 5, 1918, 2.

268 children paraded in Petworth: "Children Up Betimes to Start Full Day," *Evening Star,* July 4, 1918, 2.

268 President Wilson delivered: "President Wilson's Speech at Tomb of Washington," *Washington Herald,* July 5, 1918, 1.

268 Afterward, he boarded: "The Greatest of Fourths," *Washington Post,* July 5, 1918, 2.

268 Sibert's office: G. Wm. Baist, *Baist's Map of the Vicinity of Washington D.C.* (Philadelphia: G. Wm. Baist, 1918), http://www.loc.gov/resource/g3850.la002292.

269 One of his first tasks: Memorandum from Adjutant General of the Army to All Departments, Designation of Name for Camp, Order of the Secretary of War, May 28, 1918, OCE, RG 77, finding aid NM-78, entry 104, box 98, NACP.

269 On July 2: Memorandum from Major General William Sibert to Colonel George Burrell, Building Program American University, July 2, 1918, USACE.

269 That same day: Memorandum from Frederic V. Abbot to Chief of Engineers and General Sibert, July 2, 1918, OCE, RG 77, finding aid NM-78, entry 104, box 98, NACP.

269 Within days, Burrell had furnished: Memorandum from George A. Burrell to William L. Sibert, Building Program of American University, July 5, 1918, USACE.

269 sent Sibert his own plan: Memorandum from George A. Burrell to William L. Sibert, Agreement with Brigadier General F. V. Abbot, July 6, 1918, USACE.

269 The one unresolved issue: Letter from Frederic V. Abbot to William L. Sibert, July 2, 1918, OCE, RG 77, finding aid NM-78, entry 104, box 98, NACP.

269 Edgewood Arsenal had started production: McPherson, "Historical Sketch," 17.

269 Ten days later: Ibid., 46.

270 By the end of June: Memorandum from William L. Sibert to Chief of Staff, Feb. 5, 1919, Central Correspondence, 1918–40, CWS, RG 175, finding aid PI-8, entry 1, box 459, NACP.

270 The Ordnance Department: *Journal of Industrial and Chemical Engineering* 2, no. 4 (Apr. 19, 1919): 381.

270 Not long after Sibert: Memorandum from William Sibert to Chief of Staff, Feb. 5, 1919.

270 On July 7: "Mustard Gas Warfare," *New York Times Magazine Section,* July 7, 1918, 1.

271 Deep in the report: Wilder Bancroft, "Summary of July 1 Report," Pharmacological Research, War Gas Investigations, July 1, 1918, 6, BOM, RG 70, finding aid A-1, entry 47, box 119, NACP.

271 One test found: A. C. Walker, Report 13, *Report on Penetration of Fabric by Mustard 1 (Lewisite),* June 28, 1918, USACE .

271 When the chemists: L. T. Satler and Clarence J. West, *Arsenic Derivatives, Miscellaneous Organic Analysis,* Apr., 1919, USACE.

272 The work at Catholic: General Electric, *National in the World War,* 214.

272 Though lewisite was still: *Preliminary Report on Lewisite,* University of Wisconsin Medical School, Bureau of Mines Laboratory, Frank P. Underhill Papers, numbered folder 80–106, group no. 514, box 6, Yale University Library Manuscript Collections.

272 "It is directed": Memorandum from Office of Director, CWS, to George A. Burrell, *Conference Report of July 3,* July 12, 1918, Central Correspondence, 1918–1942, CWS, RG 175, finding aid PI-8, entry 1, box 166, NACP.

272 Dorsey wouldn't be alone: James Bryant Conant commission, July 13, 1918, call no. UAI 15.898, box 142, Papers of James Bryant Conant, 1862–1987, Harvard University Archives.

273 had his own orders: Memorandum from Frank Dorsey to James Bryant Conant on lack of quarters for officers in Willoughby, box 141, Papers of James Bryant Conant.

273 The attorney brought Dorsey: "Auto Show Breaks Record for Sales," *New York Times,* Jan. 13, 1917, 15.

273 but only about one hundred: *The Hub,* May 1917, 30.

273 the factory had been abandoned: Willoughby Historical Society.

Chapter Twelve: First Gas and Flame

277 During the pause: Memorandum from Colonel Earl Atkisson to Commander-in-Chief, attn Asst Chief of Staff, Location of Units of 30th Engineers, AEF General Headquarters, G-3 Reports, Secret Correspondence, Records of the AEF (World War I), RG 120, finding aid NM-91, entry 269, box 3141, NACP.

278 The night after Jabine: Higginbottom diary entry, July 5, 1918.

278 Jabine also became friends: Letter from Thomas Jabine to Louis Jabine, July 15, 1918.

278 "He is one of our best": Ibid., July 9, 1918.

278 "I never knew": Letter from Jabine to mother, July 9, 1918.

278 But he needed to learn: Ibid., July 11, 1918.

278 A bombardment hit: Higginbottom diary entry, July 15, 1918.

278 A shell hit: Ibid., July 16, 1918.

279 Plans were drawn up: Addison, *Story of the First Gas Regiment,* 57.

279 Addison moved forward: Addison diary entry, July 21, 1918.

280 The colonel felt cheerful: Letter from Amos Fries to Bessie Fries, July 20,1918, Amos A. Fries Papers, 1896–1953.

281 And now a third battalion: *History of the First Gas Regiment,* part 1, section 3.

281 The counteroffensive had forced: Letter from Amos Fries to Bessie Fries, Aug. 6, 1918, Amos A. Fries Papers, 1896–1953.

281 "Confidence is increasing": Ibid., July 10, 1918.

281 The gas service had been: Record of Operations at the Front, 4, G-3 Reports, General Correspondence, Records of the AEF (World War I), RG 120, finding aid NM-91, entry 268, box 3173, NACP.

281 Despite his growing optimism: Letter from Amos Fries to Bessie Fries, July 11, 1918, Amos A. Fries Papers, 1896–1953.

282 "They have a chance": Ibid., July 20, 1918.

282 While Fries fretted: Ibid., Aug. 14, 1918, Amos A. Fries Papers, 1896–1953.

282 Practically a teetotaler: Ibid., July 11, 1918, Amos A. Fries Papers, 1896–1953.

282 Though still smaller: *History of the Chemical Warfare Service, AEF,* Technical Division, part 3, Hanlon Field, appendix 1, 3.

283 There were three firing ranges: Ibid., 4.

283 When the Gas Defense School: Letter from Amos Fries to Bessie Fries, July 15, 1918, Amos A. Fries Papers, 1896–1953.

283 Many casualties: *Projector Attack, 26th Division, May 10, 1918,* operational reports, 7–32, Thirtieth Engineers/First Gas Regiment, First Gas Regiment Collection, CGM

283 In a different episode: Memorandum from Fries, May 25, 1918, AEF, General Headquarters, General Correspondence, Records of the AEF (World War I), RG 120, finding aid NM-91, entry 268, box 3141, NACP.

283 "Americans yet have": Letter from Amos Fries to Bessie Fries, May 9, 1918, Amos A. Fries Papers, 1896–1953.

283 When men at the front: Memorandum from Fries, May 25, 1918, Records of the AEF (World War I), RG 120, AEF, General Headquarters, General Correspondence, finding aid NM-91, entry 268, box 3141, NACP.

284 Hundreds of casualties: *Gas Casualties in AEF, Compiled from Gas Officer's Reports,* War Department, CWS, Edgewood Arsenal, 1917–1943, General Fries' Files, 1918–1920, A–C, CWS, RG 175, finding aid PI-8, entry 7, box 15.

284 And then the numbers skyrocketed: Memorandum to accompany letter of Aug. 18 to the C-in-C, relative additional gas regiments for the AEF, Aug. 18, 1918, General Headquarters, G-3 Reports, General Correspondence, folders 948–65, Records of the AEF (World War I), RG 120, finding aid NM-91, entry 268, box 3141, NACP.

284 Unveiled on July 23: *History of the Chemical Warfare Service, AEF,* Medical Director, 6.

285 After the spring's first incidents: Ibid., 4.

285 In one instance: Ibid., 17.

286 In July, the French ran out: Memorandum from Captain H. Sharkey to Major Wagnor, Cancelling Arrangements for Guards, July 27, 1918, Central Correspondence, 1918–1940, CWS, RG 175, finding aid PI-8, entry 1, box 543, NACP.

286 Fries was at the experimental field: "Stettenius in France," *New York Times,* July 24, 1918, 13.

287 After he left: Letter from Amos Fries to Bessie Fries, Aug. 11, 1918, Amos A. Fries Papers, 1896–1953.

287 One day, Jabine worked: Letter from Jabine to mother, July 24, 1918.

287 After breakfast, Higgie set out: Higginbottom diary entry, July 29, 1918.

288 Higgie had an easy day: Ibid., July 30, 1918.

289 There were four casualties: Addison diary entry, 62–66.

289 Later that day: *History of the First Gas Regiment,* part 3, section 3, "Report of Operations by (30th Engineers) First Gas Regiment on Château-Thierry Front," June 30 to Sept. 12, 1918.

289 Hanlon's funeral was at Chaumont: Funeral of Second Lieutenant Joseph T. Hanlon, Special Order 229, Aug. 1, 1918, World War I Organization Records, CWS, First Chemical Regiment, Orders, Records of the AEF (World War I), RG 120, finding aid NM-91, entry 248, box 85, NACP.

289 Addison didn't know: Addison diary entry, Aug. 3, 1918.

290 By the end of August: Order of the Chief of Gas Service, Aug. 30, 1918, World War I Organization Records, CWS, 1st Chemical Regiment, Orders and Memos, Records of the AEF (World War I), RG 120, finding aid NM-91, entry 1249, box 81, NACP.

290 The notoriously unreliable trolleys: "Heard and Seen," letter to the editor, *Washington Times,* July 14, 1918, 22.

291 "I liked the idea": Letter from Charles William Maurer to Miss Burr Powell, Baylor University, Mar. 2, 1919, Olson Family Collection.

291 "From and after the day": Charles William Maurer induction letter, Olson Family Collection.

291 Though the army: Letter from Maurer to Powell, Mar. 2, 1919.

291 Many of his Baylor classmates: Ibid.

291 Patriotic bunting hung from storefronts: Harrison Rhodes, "War-Time Washington," *Harper's Magazine,* Mar. 1918

291 Every patch of dirt: Justin R. Cook, "Summer Vacation War Work," *St. Nicholas,* July 1918, 789.

292 Construction of an explosives laboratory: *Weekly Construction Progress Report,* BOM, RG 70, NACP.

292 On shack number 5: Memorandum from H. C. Hutchins to Major Burt, Bureau of Mines Experiment Station and Camp Leach, Washington, DC, July 12, 1918, USACE, Spring Valley–Baltimore District, Project C03DC0918.

292 George Burrell had plans: Memorandum from George A. Burrell to William L. Sibert, July 5, Building Program of American University, 1918, USACE.

292 There was still no room: Biographical sketch of Maurer, Olson Family Collection.

293 Though the work: Letter from Maurer to Powell, Mar. 2, 1919.

293 "Washington was the gathering place": Ibid.

293 One of the substances: "Dangers in the Manufacture of Paris Green and Scheele's Green," *Monthly Review of the U.S. Bureau of Labor Statistics* 5, no. 2. (Aug. 1917): 79.

293 Members of his unit: "Camp AU Scene of World War Training Trenches, Drill Field," *(AU) Eagle,* Jan. 15, 1965, 6.

294 Will was grateful: Letter from Maurer to Powell, Mar. 2, 1919.

294 One morning in late June: "Loses Foot by Bomb: Surgeons Operate on One of Two Soldiers Hurt at University Camp," *Washington Post,* July 1, 1918, 12.

294 A man named George Temple: *(AU) Eagle,* Jan. 15, 1965.

295 The ever-increasing number: *Chemical Control of Man Tests,* Aug. 15, 1918, USACE, Spring Valley–Baltimore District, Project C03DC0918.

295 With the organization: Minutes of the 8th meeting of the Medical Advisory Board, July 23, 1918, Frank P. Underhill Papers, numbered folders 80–106, group no. 514, box no. 6, Yale University Library Manuscript Collections.

295 One of the most recent: Dr. Warthin was an internationally renowned pathologist whose early groundbreaking research into cancer provided the foundation for future study of hereditary cancer.

295 As the doctors approached: Minutes of the 8th meeting of the Medical Advisory Board, July 23, 1918, Frank P. Underhill Papers, numbered folders 80–106, group no. 514, box no. 6, Yale University Library Manuscript Collections.

296 Over the fall: Bancroft, *History of the Chemical Warfare Service,* 229.

296 The work in gas plants: Memorandum from Gen. William Sibert to Chief of Staff Peyton March, Aug. 2, 1918, War Department, General Correspondence, Office of Chief, 1918–1940, CWS, RG 175, finding aid PI-8, entry 1, box 459, NACP.

296 Johns Hopkins physiologist: Minutes of the Medical Advisory Board, July 23, 1918, appendix 2b, Frank P. Underhill Papers, numbered folders 80–106, group no. 514, box no. 6, Yale University Library Manuscript Collections.

297 The exasperated camp surgeon: Memorandum from surgeon, Experiment Station, American University, DC to Surgeon General, Sept. 28, 1918, USACE.

297 In either case: Letter from George Burrell to A. Bruce Bielaski, Mr. Richmond Levering, July 20, 1918, Investigative Case Files of the BOI, 1908–1922, NARA M1085, OGF, 1909–21, case no. 8000-97452, roll 473, NACP.

297 A former U.S. attorney: Letter from H. Snowden Marshall to Benedict Crowell, July 26, 1918, Investigative Case Files of the BOI, 1908–1922, NARA M1085, OGF, 1909–21, case no. 8000-97452, roll 473, NACP.

298 Levering moved from Manhattan: U.S. city directory, Washington, District of Columbia, 1919, 918.

298 There were still problems: Memorandum from L. G. Wesson to Major E. E. Free, Oct. 29, 1918, CWS Correspondence, 1918–1940, CWS, RG 175, finding aid PI-8, entry 1, box 448, NACP.

298 New rules required all visitors: Circular letter to the chief of all divisions under the jurisdiction of the Director of CWS, Sept. 26, 1918, Gas Defense Production Division: subject file 1917–19, CWS, RG 175, finding aid NM-38, entry 4-K, NACP.

298 "disloyal persons": Letter from Executive Officer, Research Division, to Catholic University, DC, Sept. 24, 1918, Gas Defense Production Division: subject file 1917–19, CWS, RG 175, finding aid NM-38, entry 4-K, NACP.

298 "We write no reports": Memorandum from W. L. Lewis to Safety Engineer, Cath. Univ. Annex, Am. Univ. Exp. Sta., Washington, DC, Oct. 16, 1918, Technical Document Files, 1917–1920, Reports, CWS, RG 175, finding aid PI-8, entry 8, box 4, NACP.

298 On July 4: Progress report from Bruce Silver to Richmond Levering for July 4–14, 1918, 1, Investigative Case Files of the BOI, 1908–1922, NARA M1085, OGF, 1909–21, case no. 8000-925, roll 279, NACP.

300 "Scheele for a period": Letter from Charles DeWoody to A. Bruce Bielaski, Aug. 6, 1918, Investigative Case Files of the BOI, 1908–1922, NARA M1085, OGF, 1909–21, case no. 8000-925, roll 279, NACP.

300 After the meeting: Frank O'Donnell report for Aug. 3, 1918, written Aug. 15, 1918, *Protection at Jones Point, NY.*

301 On July 16: Memorandum from Surgeon General to Major General William Sibert, Transfer of Plants and Station, Gas Defense Service, July 16, 1918, Records of the CWS, RG 175, Technical Document Files, 1917–1920, finding aid PI-8, entry 8, box 6, NACP.

301 In Long Island City: Memorandum from H. N. Davis to Lieutenant Colonel R. A. Millikan, The Need for Discovering and Conserving Supplies of Argon Bearing Gas, July 31, 1918, AG&Depts, Interior, BOM, 1916–1918, NAS-NRC Central File, 1914–1918, Executive Committee: Projects, Helium Production, 1917, National Academy of Sciences Archives.

301 Edgewood was making: McPherson, "Historical Sketch," 65.

302 On the last day: Memorandum from George A. Burrell to General William L. Sibert, Permanent Organization for Research Division, Chemical Warfare, July 31, 1918, USACE.

302 On August 2: Memorandum from William Sibert to the chief of staff, Aug. 2, 1918, USACE.

Chapter Thirteen: The Meuse and the Mousetrap

303 Soon the drenching swelter: "Many Driven by Heat to the Bathing Pools," *Evening Star,* Aug. 7, 1918, 2.

303 Though the war: "Congress Summer Vacation Started," *Washington Post,* July 16, 1918, 4.

303 As Scott chatted: "N. B. Scott 'Gassed,'" *Washington Post,* Aug. 4, 1918, 1.

304 This time the gas: "The New Senator," *Wheeling (WV) Daily Intelligencer,* Jan. 31, 1899, 7.

304 Wealth and fund-raising prowess: "Nathan Bay Scott," *The National Cyclopaedia of American Biography* (New York: James T. White and Co., 1926), 59.

305 which urged thrifty customers: Continental Trust display ad, *Washington Times,* July 24, 1918, 8.

305 The cloud had: "Family Is Gassed in D.C. Home When Tear Gas Bomb Breaks," *Washington Times,* Aug. 4, 1918, 1.

305 That evening: Confidential memorandum from Colonel Edward Schulz to General Frederic Abbot, Aug. 5, 1918, USACE.

305 When Schulz picked up: "N.B. Scott 'Gassed.'"

306 Colonel Schulz dashed: Confidential memorandum from Colonel Edward Schulz to General Frederic Abbot, Aug. 5, 1918, USACE.

306 "It is an outrage": "Family Is Gassed in D.C. Home When Tear Gas Bomb Breaks."

307 By the morning: Confidential memorandum from Colonel Edward Schulz to General Frederic Abbot, Aug. 5, 1918, USACE.

308 Levering whipped up an apology: Letter from Richmond Levering to Nathan Bay Scott, Aug. 5, 1918, USACE.

308 It took almost: Letter from George Burrell to William Sibert, Sept. 5, 1918, Correspondence Relating to Military Affairs, 1918–1923, Camps, Posts, and Stations, OCE, RG 77, finding aid NM-78, entry 104, box 98, NACP.

309 Gas shipments to France: Memorandum from Director, CWS, to Chief, Embarkation Services, Directions for Gas Shell Handling on Shipboard, Aug. 5, 1918, Chemical Warfare Correspondence, Central Correspondence, 1918–1940, CWS, RG 175, finding aid PI-8, entry 1, box 477, NACP.

309 In late August, the Oldbury: McPherson, "Historical Sketch," 60.

309 Problems with manufacturing mustard: Memorandum to Chief, CWS, Data from History of Edgewood Arsenal re: Mustard Production, Mar. 22, 1934, Office of the Chief, Central Correspondence, 1918–1942, War Department, CWS, RG 175, finding aid PI-8, entry 1, box 488, NACP.

309 Sibert asked: Memorandum from Chief, CWS, to Chief of Ordnance, Incendiary Darts," Aug. 22, 1918, Office of the Chief, Central Correspondence, 1918–1942, War Department, CWS, RG 175, finding aid PI-8, entry 1, box 528, NACP.

309 The overseas division: Memorandum from Chief, CWS, AEF, to Captain J. E. Zanetti, Liaison Service, Report Z-389, Aug. 21, 1918, Technical Document Files, 1917–1920, CWS, RG 175, finding aid PI-8, entry 8, box 7, NACP.

309 In late August, Brigadier General: Memorandum from Brigadier General Hugh S. Johnson to Benjamin F. Leighton, Aug. 22, 1918, USACE.

309 Leighton's reply arrived: Letter from Benjamin F. Leighton to Hugh S. Johnson, Sept. 3, 1918, USACE.

310 The experiment station architect: Memorandum from William L. Sibert, Director, CWS, to Director of Operations, American University, 2, USACE.

311 The investigation also discovered: Memorandum from Major Paul V. Hyland to Captain Marlow, Additional Funds, American University Experiment Station, Washington, DC, Aug. 23, 1918, USACE.

311 Major General William Black: Letter from Major General William Black to Major General William Sibert, August 13, 1918.

311 In his letter to Black: Letter from Major General William Sibert to Major General William Black, Chief of Engineers, Sept. 11, 1918, USACE.

312 "My men were depressed": W. Lee Lewis, "Certain Organic Compounds of Arsenic," speech delivered to the American Chemical Society sectional meeting in Rochester, NY, Nov. 21, 1921, L. Philip Reiss Collection.

313 The YMCA in downtown Cleveland: Elroy McKendree Avery, *A History of Cleveland and Its Environs: The Heart of New Connecticut,* vol. 1 (Chicago: Lewis Publishing, 1918), 645–48.

313 "You know what?": Nate Simpson Papers, Lake County Historical Society, Willoughby, OH.

313 There was no mailing address: General Electric, *National in the World War,* 217.

313 James Bryant Conant had arrived: Memorandum from Frank Dorsey to James Bryant Conant, no date, call no. UAI 15.898, box 141, Papers of James Bryant Conant, 1862–1987, Harvard University Archives.

314 "The Mousetrap": "Gas Intended to Wipe Out Hun Armies Dumped into the Sea," *Cleveland Plain Dealer Sunday Magazine,* June 15, 1919.

315 Dorsey requested: Memorandum from General William Sibert to Mr. Charles H. McDowell, Chemical Division, War Industries Board, War Department, Availability of Raw Materials, Aug. 21, 1918, Chemical Warfare Correspondence, 1918–1940, CWS, RG 175, finding aid PI-8, entry 1, box 459, NACP.

315 "manufacturing something nice": Harold French Davidson Letters, file 1-2 0001-2, Parks Library Special Collections, University of Iowa.

315 the plant had: "Man Killed in Accident at Ben Hur Plant," *Willoughby Republican,* Aug. 16, 1918, 1.

316 While enlisted men: General Electric, *National in the World War,* 215.

316 Each morning: Ibid., 218.

316 On August 10: Ibid., 217.

317 Each morning: Ibid., 218.

318 The service had: Letter from E. P. Kohler to James Bryant Conant, Aug. 19, 1918, call no. UAI 15.898, folder "War Work at Willoughby Near Cleveland"—1918, box 142, Papers of James Bryant Conant, 1862–1987, Harvard University Archives.

318 Originally Conant had estimated: General Electric, *National in the World War,* 222.

318 And above all: Ibid., 221.

319 chemist named: Letter from Lieutenant Colonel W. G. Wilcox to Captain Lee G. Cover, Promotion, Dec. 21, 1918, Office of the Chief, Central Correspondence, 1918–1940, War Department, CWS, RG 175, finding aid PI-8, entry 1, box 571, NACP.

319 Experimental units: Ibid., 220.

319 On August 15: Francis X. O'Donnell report for Aug. 15, 1918.

320 President Wilson signed an order: "Special Permits for Aliens Leaving U.S. after Sept.15," *Evening Star,* Aug. 17, 1918, 8.

320 The calm lasted: Francis X. O'Donnell report for Sept. 16, 1918.

321 O'Donnell got: Francis X. O'Donnell report for Sept. 17, 1918.

321 The Germans' long-range cannons: "Paris Region Again under Bombardment," *Evening Star,* Aug. 9, 1918, 1.

321 As the days went on: "Boche Route in Picardy," *Washington Herald,* Aug. 11, 1918, 1.

321 The official confirmation: Letter from Amos Fries to Bessie Fries, Aug. 11, 1918, Amos A. Fries Papers, 1896–1953.

321 As he rode: Ibid., Aug. 26, 1918.

322 "The Bosche is learning": Ibid., Aug. 13, 1918.

322 They were the first: John C. Feeley, Special Order 246, Aug. 18, 1918.

322 "The Bosch is steadily": Partial letter from Amos Fries to Bessie Fries, no date, Amos A. Fries Papers, 1896–1953.

322 Instead, there should be two: Letter from Amos Fries to General John Pershing, "Additional Gas Regiments," Aug. 18, 1918, Records of the AEF (World War I), RG 120, finding aid NM-91, entry 268, box 3141, NACP.

322 He also recommended: Memorandum from Amos Fries to Chief of Staff, Aug. 22, 1918.

323 "my conversion": Memorandum from Amos Fries to Commander in Chief, Aug. 18, 1918, Records of the AEF (World War I), RG 120, finding aid NM-91, entry 268, box 3141, NACP.

323 "I do not see": Memorandum from V. D. Dixon to Assistant Chief of Staff, Additional Gas Regiments, Aug. 26, 1918, Records of the AEF (World War I), RG 120, finding aid NM-91, entry 268, box 3141, NACP.

323 Another member: Memorandum to Assistant Chief of Staff, Additional Gas Troops, Aug. 28, 1918, RG 120, Records of the AEF (World War I), finding aid NM-91, entry 268, box 3141, NACP.

323 Fries had a dim view: Amos Fries letter to Bessie Fries, July 7, 1918, Amos A. Fries Papers, 1896–1953.

323 Conner pushed Fries's recommendations: Memorandum from Chief of Staff, Additional Gas Troops, Sept. 6, 1918, RG 120, Records of the AEF (World War I), finding aid NM-91, entry 268, box 3141, NACP.

324 chief of staff quickly: Memorandum from Assistant Chief of Staff, G-3, to Chief, CWS, AEF, Gas Program, Sept. 7, 1918, G-3 Reports, General Correspondence, Records of the AEF (World War I), RG 120, finding aid NM-91, entry 268, box 3141, NACP.

324 Conner sent a draft: Suggested cablegram, Sept.7, 1918, G-3 Reports, General Correspondence, RG 120, Records of the AEF (World War I), finding aid NM-91, entry 268, box 3141, NACP.

324 on September 5: Letter from Chief of Staff to E. R. Stettinius, Sept. 5, 1918, General Headquarters, G-3 Reports, General Correspondence, RG 120, Records of the AEF (World War I), finding aid NM-91, entry 268, box 3141, NACP.

324 "We are going": Letter from Amos Fries to Bessie Fries, Sept. 4, 1918, Amos A. Fries Papers, 1896–1953.

324 an insignia: "Chemical Warfare Service," American Society of Military Insignia Collectors, Oct.–Dec. 1917, 31. First Gas Regiment Collection, CCM.

324 the commander in chief recommended: Cablegram from General Pershing to Adjutant General, Sept.16, 1918, First Gas Regiment Collection, CCM.

324 The War Department snuffed: Memorandum from Brigadier General Henry Jervey, Sept. 23, 1918, First Gas Regiment Collection, CCM.

325 "The big American push": Amos Fries letter to Bessie Fries, Sept. 12, 1918, Amos A. Fries Papers, 1896–1953.

325 All of the gas companies: *History of the First Gas Regiment,* part 1, section 4, "Report of Operations by (30th Engineers) First Gas Regiment during Saint Mihiel Operation of First Army."

326 Saint-Mihiel was neither: Falls, *Great War,* 381.

326 On the night: Higginbottom diary entry, Sept.12, 1918.

327 On September 15: Ibid., Sept.15, 1918.

327 They were on the train: Ibid., Sept. 19, 1918.

327 He had commanded: *History of the First Gas Regiment,* part 3, section 3, "Report of Operations by (30th Engineers) First Gas Regiment on Château-Thierry Front."

327 "Our company is": Letter from Jabine to mother, Sept. 14, 1918.

327 He got a room: Ibid.

328 If the trunk line: "Our Drive Nearing Vital Supply Line," *New York Times,* Oct. 6, 1918, 7.

329 As the deafening firestorm: Higginbottom diary entry, Sept. 25, 1918.

330 At five-thirty: *Report of 21st Operation by First Gas Regiment,* Sept. 27, 1918, Operational Reports, 30 Eng/1 Gas, 7–32, First Gas Regiment Collection, CCM.

330 Sitting atop the trench: Higginbottom diary entry, Sept. 26, 1918.

Chapter Fourteen: "All to the Mustard"

331 A hose led: Paul W. Carleton, *Report on Field Experiments on Persistency of War Gases,* Defense Chemical Research Section, Research Division, CWS, American University Experiment Station, Mar. 1919, USACE.

331 The security around the test site: Paul W. Carleton, *Outline of Proposed Large Scale Field Experiments on Persistency of G-34,* Defense Chemical Research Section, Research Division, CWS, American University Experiment Station, June 25, 1918, USACE.

331 American University was three quarters: Paul W. Carleton, *Report of Field Experiments on Persistency of G-34,* Defense Chemical Research Section, Research Division, CWS, American University Experiment Station, Sept. 27, 1918, USACE.

332 When the sun was out: G. W. Wilson, *Report on Lewis Gloves to Be Used as Protection against G-34,* Sept. 18, 1918; *Tests of Lewis Suits for Protection in Spraying G-34,* Sept. 18, 1918; *Use of Protective Clothing While Spraying G-34 on Soil,* Sept. 18, 1918, USACE.

332 Still, almost all the men: G. W. Wilson, *Report of Casualties Caused on Weaver Farm by G-34,* Sept. 19, 1918, USACE.

332 Some men's feet: *Use of Protective Clothing While Spraying G-34 on Soil.*

332 After leaving American University: "Activities Galore Assured for Fall and Winter Season," *Retort,* Oct. 6, 1918, 1.

332 some three hundred members: According to the Catholic University archives, the building referred to was most likely the administration building for the affiliated Catholic Sisters College. It was later renamed Brady Hall. It has since been demolished.

332 The newspapers trumpeted: "Americans Advance 7 Miles, Take 12 Towns, 5,000 Prisoners West of Verdun," *Washington Post,* Sept. 27, 1918, 1.

333 The *Star* pointed out: "Americans Fight All Night," *Evening Star,* Sept. 27, 1918, 1.

333 The *Evening Star* reported: "Bulgaria Asks Armistice and Peace," *Evening Star,* Sept. 27, 1918, 1

333 The festivities at Catholic University: "Activities Galore Assured for Fall and Winter Season."

333 Almost everyone working: John Bassett veteran questionnaire, CWS, World War I Veterans Survey, U.S. Army and Heritage Education Center, U.S. Army War College Library, Carlisle, PA.

334 They were doing their part: Letter from Burton Logue, Sept. 24, 1971, University Archives and Special Collections, American University Library.

334 In the fall: "Activities Galore Assured for Fall and Winter Season."

335 It also asked for volunteers: "Influenza Report," *Record of Events,* Camp Leach, Washington, DC, June, 1918, USACE.

336 The virus raced: "Influenza Brings Death to Three More," *Evening Star,* Sept. 27, 1918, 1.

336 Public-health officials rushed: "6,139 New Grip Cases in Army," *Washington Herald,* Sept. 27, 1918, 1.

336 Under the announcements: Obituary, *Retort,* Oct. 19, 1918, 4.

336 A relatively young woman: "General Sibert's Wife Dead," *Washington Post,* Oct. 9, 1918, 14.

336 Major General Sibert had little time: Memorandum from Captain Sidney Cadwell to General William Sibert, Projected Production of Gases, Sept. 30, 1918, Office of the Chief, Central Correspondence, 1918–1942, War Department, CWS, RG 175, finding aid PI-8, entry 1, box 448, NACP.

336 The Ordnance Department had solved: Memorandum from H. N. Davis, to Lieutenant Colonel R. A. Millikan, Monthly Report, Oct. 2, 1918, A&G Depts, Interior, BOM, 1916–1918, NAS-NRC, National Academies Archives.

336 The chancellor, Bishop Hamilton: Memorandum from D. H. Allen to Mr. C. William Hare, Special Assistant to Mr. Crowell, Oct. 16, 1918, USACE.

337 The district's board of commissioners: Letter from Board of Commissioners to Secretary of War Baker, Oct. 25, 1918, USACE.

337 Major General William M. Black: William M. Black, Memorandum on the Use of the American University Grounds by the United States, Oct. 25, 1918, USACE.

338 Somewhere near Higgie: Letter from Jabine to mother, letter no. 64. This letter is out of chronological order in the compilation of his letters. Dated Sept. 2, it clearly refers to events that happened after the start of the Argonne offensive on Sept. 26. Higginbottom also refers to tanks coming over the hills that day, so it's my belief they were witnessing the advance of the same tank division.

339 Higgie was set to move: Higginbottom diary entry, Sept. 26, 1918.

339 Higgie slept the whole morning: Ibid., Sept. 27, 1918.

339 Higgie finally got to Véry: Ibid., Sept. 29, 1918.

341 As they slept: *Progress Report Week Ending Oct. 5, 1918*, AEF, Headquarters First Gas Regiment, folder "Weekly Progress Reports," HQ 1st Gas Regiment, 21 Sept.–16 Nov. 1918, CCM; Addison diary entry, 155

342 Within a few days: Addison, *Story of the First Gas Regiment*, 156.

342 That made Fries suspicious: Letter from Amos Fries to Bessie Fries, Sept. 28, 1918, Amos A. Fries Papers, 1896–1953.

342 "We have had very few": Ibid., Sept. 26, 1918.

343 He would return: Ibid., Sept. 28, 1918.

343 "Severe casualties have been sustained": Earl J. Atkisson, *Progress Report for Week Ending Oct. 5th, 1918*, Weekly Progress Reports, 21 Sept. to 16 Nov. 1918, HQ First Gas Regiment. History of First Gas Regiment, Carlisle Attic Collection, CCM.

344 The after-action reports: *Report of 21st Operation by First Gas Regiment*, Oct. 3, 1918, AEF General Headquarters, G-3 Reports, RG 120, finding aid NM-91, entry 268, box 3141, NACP.

344 including rooting out: Supplemental Report (Extracts from Platoon Officers Reports), *Operations of First Gas Regiment on III Corps Front from 26th Sept. 1918*, AEF General Headquarters, G-3 Reports, RG 120, finding aid NM-91, entry 268, box 3141, NACP.

344 Infantry commanders, though: Major General S. D. Sturges, *Investigation Report*, Dec. 26, 1918, AEF General Headquarters, G-3 Reports, RG 120, finding aid NM-91, entry 268, box 3141, NACP.

344 On the night: Letter from Amos Fries to Bessie Fries, Oct. 3, 1918, Amos A. Fries Papers, 1896–1953.

344 "The Bosche still retires": Ibid., Oct. 12, 1918.

344 The day after Fries departed: "No Peace, Says Wilson, Until Kaiserism Ends," *New York Times*, Oct. 15, 1918, 1.

345 It was October: Carlos I. Reed, *The Minimum Concentration of Mustard Gas Effective for Man (Preliminary Report)*, Oct. 26, 1918 (presented at the 11th meeting of the Medical Advisory Board, CWS, Nov. 4, 1918, Frank P. Underhill Papers, group no. 514, box 6, Yale University Library Manuscript Collections.

345 Reed was a handsome specimen: *Makio*, 1915 Ohio State University yearbook, (Columbus: Sears and Simpson Co., 1915), 149.

345 The title of the test: Reed, *Minimum Concentration of Mustard Gas Effective for Man*.

347 In a series of experiments: Ibid., 5.

347 At the next meeting: Eli K. Marshall, H. W. Smith, and J. W. Williams, *Individual Variation in Susceptibility to Mustard Gas V (Susceptibility of Negroes)*, Oct. 31, 1918 (presented at the 11th meeting of the Medical Advisory Board, CWS, Nov. 4, 1918), Frank P. Underhill Papers, group no. 514, box 6, Yale University Library Manuscript Collections. References to the study may also be found here: http://history.amedd.army.mil/booksdocs/wwi/VolXIV/VolX-IVhtml/CH12.htm.

347 The doctors had even written: Minutes of the 7th Meeting of the Medical Advisory Board, June 25, 1918, 2, Frank P. Underhill Papers, group no. 514, box 6, Yale University Library Manuscript Collections.

348 The Camp Leach surgeon: Memorandum from surgeon, American University, to Surgeon General, Sept. 28, 1918; Colonel William J. Lyster, Chief, Medical Corps, Oct. 10 1918, USACE.

348 Yandell Henderson wanted: Prentiss, *Chemicals in War,* 542.

348 Britain, meanwhile, had ordered: Letter from British War Mission to Brigadier General U.S. Johnson, Sept. 7, 1918; Memorandum from Major H. W. Dudley to Major Woodruff, Subject: Correcting My Memorandum on Further Supplies of Charcoal for England, Sept. 25, 1918, Technical Document Files, 1917–1920, CWS, RG 175, finding aid PI-8, entry 8, box 3, NACP.

349 Across the country: "Sends Car Loads of Peach Stones," *Cleveland Plain Dealer,* Nov. 7, 1918, Technical Document Files, 1917–1920, CWS, RG 175, finding aid PI-8, entry 8, box 3, NACP.

349 "Its meaning is that every man": Memorandum from Lieutenant H. M. Jackson to Captain L. B. Dane, Campaign to Collect Fruit Pits and Nut Shells, Nov. 5, 1918, Gas Defense Production Division, subject file 1917–1919, CWS, RG 175, finding aid NM-38, entry 4-K, NACP.

349 The War Department printed: Ibid., Oct. 14, 1918.

349 Fact sheets were printed: *Facts and Figures concerning Gas Defense Division for Use in Publicity in Connection with Fruit Pit and Nut Shell Campaign,* no date, Gas Defense Production Division, subject file 1917–1919, CWS, RG 175, finding aid NM-38, entry 4-K, NACP.

349 Over the weeks: "Save the Fruit Pits," *Denison Review,* Sept. 11, 1918, 13.

349 "Will you help?": *Bridgeport (CT) Times and Evening Farmer,* Sept. 6, 1918, 6.

350 "Let pleasure or business stop": Ibid.

350 In late September: "Two Hundred Civilians Arrive in Willoughby," *Willoughby Republican,* Sept. 20, 1918, 1.

351 The building filled: L. Philip Reiss, Lewis's grandson, wrote to me in an e-mail that these could have been the sounds from the lewisite plant, based on his understanding of the apparatus and how it worked.

352 One account claimed: Letter from Amos A. Fries to Bruce Bliven, Managing Editor, *Globe and Commercial Advertiser,* May 13, 1921, Office of the Chief, Central Correspondence, 1918–1942, War Department, CWS, RG 175, finding aid PI-8, entry 1, box 463, NACP.

352 Records suggest: Memorandum from Frank Dorsey to William Walker, Disposal of Toxic Chemicals, Jan. 22, 1919, Office of the Chief, Central Correspondence, 1918–1942, War Department, CWS, RG 175, finding aid PI-8, entry 1, box 571, NACP.

352 that filled twenty-two steel drums: Memorandum from William Sibert to Frank Dorsey, Jan. 30, 1919, Central Correspondence, 1918–1940, CWS, RG 175, finding aid PI-8, entry 1, box 542, NACP.

352 Like water through sluice gates: Memorandum from Sidney Cadwell to William Sibert, Projected Production of Gases, Sept. 30, 1918, Office of the Chief, Central Correspondence, 1918–1942, CWS, RG 175, finding aid PI-8, entry 1, box 448, NACP.

352 When all of the plants: Letter from Newton Baker to R. H. Graves, *New York Times,* Oct. 1920, Central Correspondence, 1918–1940, CWS, RG 175, finding aid PI-8, entry 1, box 463, NACP.

353 On November 9: Memorandum from H. M. Schwietert to Lieutenant Colonel Noonan, Nov. 9, 1918, Central Correspondence, 1918–1940, CWS, RG 175, finding aid PI-8, entry 1, box 477, NACP.

353 Once the chemicals reached port: Memorandum from Lieutenant Colonel R. C. Morse Jr. to Captain H. R. Sharkey, Oct. 22, 1918, Central Correspondence, 1918–1940, CWS, RG 175, finding aid PI-8, entry 1, box 318, NACP.

353 The *Elinor*: Memorandum from Captain Howard R. Sharkey to Captain Cadwell, Nov. 7, 1918, Central Correspondence, 1918–1940, CWS, RG 175, finding aid PI-8, entry 1, box 318, NACP.

353 docked in Baltimore: USS *Elinor* deck logs for Sept. 17, 1918, Logbooks of U.S. Ships and Stations, 1916–1940, Mar. 20, 1918–Apr. 26, 1919, USS *Elinor,* Records of the Bureau of Naval Personnel, RG 24, entry 118-G-E, box 1, NAB.

353 The forty-three-hundred-ton freighter: USS *Elinor* deck logs for Sept. 19 to Nov. 4, 1918, Logbooks of U.S. Ships and Stations, 1916–1940.

354 On November 8: USS *Elinor* deck logs for Nov. 9, 1918, Logbooks of U.S. Ships and Stations, 1916–1940.

Chapter Fifteen: "War to the Knife"

355 After a four-hour ride: Higginbottom diary entry, Oct. 31, 1918.

356 A stretcher-bearer in the truck: Ibid., Nov. 1, 1918.

357 Higgie wasn't prone to emotion: Ibid.

358 The AEF printed: AEF circular, Nov. 1, 1918, Corporal John C. McMann file, First Gas Regiment Collection, CCM.

358 "Another day ended": Letter from Amos Fries to Bessie Fries, November 4, 1918, Amos A. Fries Papers, 1896–1953.

358 From the Dutch border: "Allies Sweeping Flanders," *New York Times,* Oct. 17, 1918, 1.

358 As President Wilson awaited: "Confer on Reply in Berlin," *New York Times,* Oct. 26, 1918, 1.

359 One of the most powerful: "Ludendorff Steps Down," *New York Times,* Oct. 28, 1918, 1.

359 An unnamed German diplomat: "Says Germany Can Fight Five Months," *New York Times*, Oct. 26, 1918, 1.

359 "I expect to see": Letter from Amos Fries to Bessie Fries, Nov. 5, 1918, Amos A. Fries Papers, 1896–1953.

359 Despite his doctor's recommendation: Ibid., Oct. 28, 1918.

360 "The work over there": Ibid., Nov. 2, 1918.

360 With the war's end: Ibid., Nov. 5, 1918.

360 On November 6: Ibid., Nov. 6, 1918.

360 The next day: Ibid., Nov. 9, 1918.

361 Celebration was in the air: "Big Attendance Is Expected at Our Third Dance Monday," *Retort,* Nov. 16, 1918, 1.

361 The *Washington Times* installed: "Watch the Sky for *Times* Election Results," *Washington Times,* Nov. 5, 1918, 1.

362 Two days before the dance: "America Answers the Hun's Gas Arguments," *Sunday Star Magazine,* Nov. 3, 1918, 2.

362 Only the highest-ranking officers: Memorandum from Henry Jervey to Assistant Secretary of War, Purchase of American University Property, Washington, DC, Nov. 4, 1918, USACE.

362 The hill football team: "Venez. Apprendez parlez Francais," *Retort,* Nov. 2, 1918, 4.

363 The first edition: "Airplanes Drop Peace Extras," *Washington Times,* Nov. 7, 1918, 1.

363 Celebrants filled Pennsylvania Avenue: "Nation Joy-Mad at Peace Report: Wild Revel in Washington Lasts Till Midnight," *Washington Post,* Nov 8, 1918, 1.

363 A din of sirens: "Armistice Signed? Yes! No! We Had a Good Time Anyhow and So Did New York," *Washington Herald,* Nov. 8, 1918, 4.

363 At 2:15 p.m.: "Armistice NOT Signed," *Evening Star,* Nov. 7, 1918, 1.

363 Yet the United Press: "United Press Men Sent False Cable," *New York Times,* Nov. 8, 1918, 1.

364 Still, the war: "Our War Activities Not Yet Curtailed," *New York Times,* Nov. 9, 1918, 8.

364 The commission: Memorandum from Newton Baker to the board of commissioners for the District of Columbia, Nov. 8, 1918, USACE.

364 Daylight was fading: Higginbottom diary entry, Nov. 6, 1918.

365 Water soaked through: Ibid., Nov. 8, 1918.

366 At 4:00 p.m.: *Report of 30th Operation by First Gas Regiment,* Nov. 14, 1918, Operational Reports 7–32 (not inclusive), Thirtieth Engineers/First Gas Regiment, First Gas Regiment Collection, CCM.

366 That night, Company D: *Report of Thirty-First Operation by First Gas Regiment,* Nov. 13, 1918.

367 With fifteen minutes to go: *Report on the 32nd Operation by First Gas Regiment,* Nov. 14, 1918.

367 The army had not yet: Letter from Adjutant General to Jabine family, Dec. 16, 1918, American University WWI file, University Archives and Special Collection: American University Library.

367 More than three weeks after: Letter from Jabine to mother, Oct. 27, 1918.

368 "The good news": Ibid., Nov. 11, 1918.

368 Word reached Addison: Addison diary entry, Nov. 11, 1918.

368 As Fries waited: Letter from Amos Fries to Bessie Fries, Nov. 12, 1918, Amos A. Fries Papers, 1896–1953.

368 As the city roiled: Ibid.

369 The company loaded: Higginbottom identified the village as "Nonort" in his diary, but Addison wrote in *The Story of the First Gas Regiment* that it was Nouart.

369 Higgie went to bed: Higginbottom diary entry, Nov. 11, 1918.

369 They arrived at Montfaucon: Ibid., Nov. 12, 1918.

369 The service had produced: Memorandum from Amos A. Fries, Subject: Gases Produced by the CWS, Aug. 13, 1919, General Fries' Files, 1918–1920, C–E, CWS, RG 175, finding aid PI-8, entry 7, box 16, NACP.

370 In the days that followed: Minutes of the Army Commodity Committee on Gases and Containers, Nov. 12, 1918, Chief's Office, Central Correspondence, 1918–1940, War Department, CWS, RG 175, finding aid PI-8, entry 1, box 7, NACP.

370 in others, officers wondered: Memorandum to Colonel Bogert, Re: Hand Tools and Hardware Meeting, Nov. 13, 1918, Office of the Chief, Central Correspondence, 1918–1940, War Department, CWS, RG 175, finding aid PI-8, entry 1, box 7, NACP.

370 Such questions didn't trouble: "Big Crowd Turns Out for Third Party Dance," *Retort*, Nov. 23, 1918, 1.

370 "The writer wishes": George A. Burrell, "Reduction of Staff of Research Division," *Retort*, Nov. 30, 1918, 1.

370 On November 11: Nate Simpson reminiscence, Nate Simpson Papers.

371 While operations didn't stop: General Electric, *National in the World War,* 223.

371 On Thanksgiving Day: "City Provides Most Deadly Gas for War," *Cleveland Plain Dealer,* Nov. 28, 1918, 1.

372 The *Willoughby Republican:* "The Story of the Soldiers in Willoughby" and "Here Is the Big Story of the Great Work of the Soldiers Who Have Been Stationed in Our Midst," *Willoughby Republican,* Nov. 29, 1918, 1.

372 "magnificent success": Letter from Elmer Kohler to James B. Conant, Dec. 18, 1918, call no. UAI 15.898, box 142, Papers of James Bryant Conant, 1862–1987, Harvard University Archives.

372 Major Conant returned: Memorandum from Colonel Frank Dorsey to Major James B. Conant, Dec. 4, 1918; Extension of Leave of Absence, Dec. 12, 1918; Special Order 84, Dec. 12, 1918; Special Order 94, Dec. 23, 1918, box 142, Papers of James Bryant Conant, Harvard University Archives.

372 The army discharged Conant: Untitled and undated chronology of war record and discharge, box 1, Papers of James Bryant Conant.

372 At least two job offers: Harvard appointment letter, Mar. 10, 1919, box 1, Papers of James Bryant Conant.

372 Simpson was among the men: "Three Hundred and Fifty Willoughby Soldiers to Leave," *Willoughby Republican,* Nov. 6, 1918, 1.

372 Simpson departed: Nathan A. Simpson veteran's compensation application, Pennsylvania, WWI Veterans Service and Compensation Files, 1917–1919, 1934–1948, Pennsylvania Historical and Museum Commission, Ancestry.com.

372 Years later: Nate Simpson reminiscence, Nate Simpson Papers.

373 The weekend before: "Thunder Voice of City Peals in Liberty Sing," *Washington Herald,* Dec. 8, 1918, 1.

373 President Wilson and his wife: "Two Million Cheer Wilson," *New York Times,* Dec. 15, 1918, 1.

373 With General Pershing: "Text of President's Two Speeches in Paris," *New York Times,* Dec. 15, 1918, 1.

373 The Camp Meigs band: "American Ready to Smother Huns with Gas," *Washington Post,* Dec. 14, 1918, 5.

374 Sibert also revealed: "Prepared to Deluge Germans with Gas," *New York Times,* Nov. 14, 1918, 13.

374 Calling Edgewood: "Yankees Ready to Deluge Foe with Gas Flood," *Harrisburg Telegraph,* Dec. 14, 1918, 12.

375 "There is not the slightest": "Big Poison Gas Plant for US at Full Blast When Huns Decided to Stop War," *Arizona Republican,* Dec. 22, 1918, 6.

375 Not long after: "Tells of Mobilizing Scientists for War," *New York Times,* Dec. 18, 1918, 4.

375 George Burrell also took pains: "Contributions from the Chemical Warfare Service, USA," *Journal of Engineering and Industrial Chemistry,* Feb. 1919.

376 "It was quite natural": Letter from Charles D. Walcott to Van H. Manning, Dec. 26, 1918, National Academy of Sciences Archives.

376 On December 4: Memorandum from William Sibert to Adjutant General, U.S. Army, Dec. 4, 1918, USACE.

376 "During the entire period": Francis X. O'Donnell report for Nov. 7 to Nov. 27, 1918, *Protection of Jones Point, NY.*

377 By the Armistice: Prentiss, *Chemicals in War,* 656.

377 sent over at least: Memorandum to intelligence section, Reactionary Attitude toward Gas Warfare Only Overcome by CWS Accomplishments, Technical Document Files, 1917–1920, Reports (Laboratory Summary—National Electrolytics), CWS, RG 175, finding aid PI-8, entry 8, box 14, NACP.

377 The Germans had used: Prentiss, *Chemicals in War,* 656.

377 "I am going": Letter from Amos Fries to Bessie Fries, Nov. 26, 1918, Amos A. Fries Papers, 1896–1953.

377 He had plenty: Menu, Thanksgiving Dinner 1918, Nov. 28, 1918, Chemical War Service, Chinon, France, Amos A. Fries Papers, 1896–1953.

377 He also sent a missive: Earl J. Atkisson, General Order 5, Nov. 28, 1918, First Gas Regiment Collection, CCM.

378 The next day: Letter from Amos Fries to Bessie Fries, Nov. 29, 1918, Amos A. Fries Papers, 1896–1953.

378 The USS *Celtic:* "Three More Ships Bring 4,500 More Troops," *New York Times,* Dec. 18, 1918, 3.

378 In the morning: "Negro Troops Hail New York with Joy," *New York Times,* Dec. 18, 1918, 3.

378 After the ship glided: Western Union telegram, Dec. 17, 1918, Amos A. Fries Papers, 1896–1953.

378 The locomotive pulled into: Fries memoir.

379 Tom Jabine, wiling away: Letter from Jabine to mother, Dec. 25, 1918.

379 The Hellfire Boys had decamped: Higginbottom diary entry, Nov. 30, 1918.

380 In a desperate attempt: Addison diary entry, Dec. 25, 1918.

380 On Christmas Eve: Higginbottom diary entry, Dec. 24, 1918.

380 That night, Higgie's tent: Ibid., Jan. 13, 1918.

381 "We are all": Ibid., Jan. 10, 1918.

381 The Hellfire Boys: Telegram from Secretary of State Polk to John J. Pershing, Feb. 3, 1919, John J. Pershing Papers, 1882–1971, General Correspondence, 1904–48, box 19. Library of Congress.

381 The day finally arrived: Movement orders no. 7, Re: Embarkation of First Gas Regiment for U.S., Jan. 14, 1919, CWS, First Gas Regiment, AEF records, RG 120, finding aid NM-91, entry 1248, box 86, NACP.

381 As the ship moved out: Higginbottom diary entry, Jan. 24, 1918.

382 "The situation is hopeless": Letter from Jabine to mother, Jan. 10, 1918.

382 "I certainly have been fooled": Ibid., Feb. 4, 1918.

382 "So I left France": Ibid., Feb. 7, 1919.

382 The *Celtic* steamed: "*Celtic* Arrives with Gas Troops," *New York Times,* Feb. 3, 1919, 8.

382 Higgie sent off: Higginbottom diary entry, Feb. 2, 1919.

384 "I had the best surprise": Ibid., Feb. 22, 1918.

384 The morning *Lawrence Telegram:* "Higginbottom Returns Home," *Lawrence Telegram,* Feb. 25, 1919, 12.

384 The *Evening Tribune's* headline: "Higginbottom Is Home from France," *Lawrence Evening Tribune,* Feb. 25, 1919, 1.

Chapter Sixteen: "Fight the Devil"

385 In winter of 1918: "Demobilization of Chemical Service Now Under Way," *Retort,* Dec. 7, 1918.

385 As work slowed: Maurer photo, Olson Family Collection.

385 Private Maurer became Sergeant Maurer: U.S. Army promotion certificate, Olson Family Collection.

385 His discharge came: Charles William Maurer discharge paper, Olson Family Collection.

385 California banned liquor: "California Joins in Vote to Ratify Dry Amendment," *New York Times,* Jan. 14, 1919, 1.

386 When the Baylor newspaper: "Dr. Gooch Tells of New Gas," *Lariat* 20, no. 19 (Feb. 20, 1919): 3.

386 Will mailed: Letter from Maurer to Powell, Mar. 2, 1919, Olson Family Collection.

387 On December 30: Letter from William Sibert to Bishop J. W. Hamilton, Dec. 31, 1918, reprinted in *American University Courier,* World War I History Collection, University Archives and Special Collections, American University Library.

387 But the postwar landscape: Letter from Bishop John W. Hamilton to Van H. Manning, Apr. 21, 1919, World War I History Collection, University Archives and Special Collections, American University Library.

387 Bomb chambers: "Preservation of Grounds of the American University in re: The Necessary Treatment to Restore the Grounds to Their Original Condition Prior to Their Being Taken Over by the Government," Nov. 30, 1918, USACE.

387 The farmer named Weaver: Memorandum from H. S. Kimberly to Chief, CWS, Aug. 5, 1920, Central Correspondence Files, 1918–1942, RG 175, finding aid PI-8, entry 1, box 558, NACP.

387 Years after the war ended: "Delayed Opening an Advantage in American University Park," *Washington Post,* Nov. 14, 1939, 15.

387 After his Christmas reunion: Letter from Amos Fries to unnamed senator, July 24, 1919, War Department, CWS, General Amos A. Fries Papers, 1918–1920, RG 175, finding aid PI-8, entry 7, box 15, NACP.

388 When Fries arrived: *Army Appropriation Bill: Hearings before the Subcommittee of the Committee on Military Affairs,* 66th Congress, 1st session on HR 5227 (1920).

388 "There's not going to be": Whether Fries met with March was not completely clear. In testimony to Congress, Fries said he did not meet with March that day, but in his later unpublished memoir, he claimed that March did eventually allow him in but cut short the discussion.

388 When Fries returned: Fries memoir.

389 One of Fries's most trusted: Memorandum from B. C. Goss to William Sibert, Re: Future Gas Warfare, Jan. 16, 1919, War Department, CWS, General Amos A. Fries Papers, 1918–1920.

389 The rustlings: Memorandum from Major General Henry Jervey to Chief of Engineers, Re: Chemical Warfare, Feb. 21, 1919, General Fries' File, 1917–1943, A–C, CWS, RG 175, finding aid PI-8, entry 7, box 15, NACP.

390 At its peak: McPherson, "Historical Sketch," 53.

390 Four months later: Report of Edgewood Arsenal for week of Mar. 16 to Mar. 22, inclusive, Mar. 24, 1919, Central Correspondence, 1918–1940, War Department, War Department, CWS, RG 175, finding aid PI-8, entry 1, box 166, NACP.

390 William McPherson: Letter from William McPherson to Professor W. E. Henderson, Dec. 17, 1918, Technical Document Files, 1917–1920, Major McPherson's Personnel File—Masks, RG 175, finding aid PI-8, entry 8, box 10, NACP.

390 The Bureau of Mines: Memorandum from Newton Baker to Secretary of the Interior, Mar. 22, 1920, Central Correspondence, 1918–1940, War Department, CWS, RG 175, finding aid PI-8, entry 1, box 345, NACP.

391 The War Department ordered: Memorandum from Adjutant General's Office, Dec. 23, 1918, OCE, RG 77, finding aid NM-78, entry 104, box 98, NACP.

391 By December 11, 1918: Memorandum, Organizations at Camp Leach, This Date, Dec. 11, 1918.

391 The engineers dismantled: Memorandum, Received from the Officer's Club, Camp Leach, DC, Dec. 27, 1918.

391 The camp's buildings: Circular accounting date of bid opening for buildings and government-owned property at Camp Leach, June 18, 1919, USACE, Spring Valley–Baltimore District, administrative record, Property C03DC0918.

391 American University had its share: "Toxic Gases Received at Edgewood from the American University Experiment Station," Apr. 14, 1919, War Department, Central Correspondence, 1918–1940, CWS, RG 175, finding aid PI-8, entry 1, box 460, NACP.

391 On March 1, 1919: Memo from William L. Sibert to George F. Moulton, Mar. 1, 1919, USACE.

391 Gas shells, cylinders, jugs: "Toxic Gases Received at Edgewood from the American University Experiment Station."

391 An Army Corps of Engineers: Memorandum from Wm. Black, Chief of Engineers, to Ordnance Office Supply Division, Storage of Gas Shells, June 3, 1918, Central Correspondence, 1918–1940, War Department, CWS, RG 175, finding aid PI-8, entry 1, box 477, NACP.

391 Time would reveal: "A Burning Village," *American University Courier* 27, no. 2 (Jan. 1921): 4–5.

392 It wasn't until November: Memorandum from chemistry professor H. P. Ward to Chief, CWS, regarding (a) Removal of Toxic Materials (b) Clearance to CWS, Jan. 13, 1922, Central Correspondence, 1918–1940, CWS, RG 175, finding aid PI-8, entry 1, box 3, NACP.

392 Inside Maloney Hall: Memorandum from Captain E. P. H. Gempel to Major W. C. Baker, CWS, regarding (a) Repairs Damages to Buildings and Equipment (b)

Removal of Toxic Materials, Nov. 23, 1921, Central Correspondence, 1918–1940, CWS, RG 175, finding aid PI-8, entry 1, box 3, NACP.

392 A letter from the chief: Letter from Major W. C. Baker to Professor Hardee Chambliss, Catholic University of America, Nov. 28, 1921, Central Correspondence, 1918–1940, CWS, RG 175, finding aid PI-8, entry 1, box 2, NACP.

392 The process of dismantling: A letter from A. M. Heritage to Colonel Frank Dorsey, Nov. 19, 1919, indicates that there were seventy-two thousand pounds of aluminum and two thousand tons of arsenic still stored at the Ben-Hur plant a year after the war ended. Office of Chief, Central Correspondence, 1918–1942, War Department, CWS, RG 175, finding aid PI-8, entry 1, box 347, NACP.

392 When the Purchase and Storage Division: Copy of memorandum from Major William Wilson, Chief, Raw Materials and Scrap Section, to Office of Director of Storage, Aug. 19, 1919, Office of the Chief, Central Correspondence, 1918–1940, CWS, RG 175, finding aid PI-8, entry 1, box 461, NACP.

392 With no means: Memorandum from Frank Dorsey to William Walker, Disposal of Toxic Material, Jan. 22, 1919, Chemical Warfare Correspondence, 1918–1942, CWS, RG 175, finding aid PI-8, entry 1, box 571, NACP.

392 Walker's solution: Memorandum from William Walker to William Sibert, Jan. 27, 1919, Chemical Warfare Correspondence, 1918–1942, CWS, RG 175, finding aid PI-8, entry 1, box 571, NACP.

393 On January 30: Memorandum from William Sibert to Frank Dorsey, Special Train Movement, Jan. 30, 1919, Chemical Warfare Correspondence, 1918–1942, CWS, RG 175, finding aid PI-8, entry 1, box 543, NACP.

393 Arrangements for the rail shipment: Copy of memorandum from Chief, Inland Traffic Service, to Director, CWS, Property Movement, Gases, Poisonous, from Various Points to Edgewood Arsenal, Edgewood, MD, Jan. 31, 1919, Office of the Chief, Central Correspondence, 1918–1940, War Department, CWS, RG 175, finding aid PI-8, entry 1, box 543, NACP.

393 Despite Sibert's warnings: Letter from Lieutenant H. M. Scheitert, Transportation Section, CWS, to Major Neil Bailey, Special Train Movement from Willoughby, Ohio, Feb. 10, 1919, Office of the Chief, Central Correspondence, 1918–1940, CWS, RG 175, finding aid PI-8, entry 1, box 543, NACP.

393 Two days slipped by: Letter from Chief, Inland Traffic Service, to Director, CWS, Property Movements, Gases, Poisons, from Various Points, Transportation of Guards, Feb. 13, 1919, Office of the Chief, Central Correspondence, 1918–1940, CWS, RG 175, finding aid PI-8, entry 1, box 543, NACP.

393 until they decided: Letter from William Sibert to Major N. E. Bailey, Inland Traffic, Transportation of Guards on Toxic Gas Train, Feb. 12, 1919, Office of the Chief, Central Correspondence, 1918–1940, CWS, RG 175, finding aid PI-8, entry 1, box 543, NACP.

393 On Friday, February 7: Letter from Captain C. H. Hawley to First Lieutenant H. M. Schwietert, Shipment of Toxic Gases, Feb. 3, 1919, Office of the Chief, Central Correspondence, 1918–1940, CWS, RG 175, finding aid PI-8, entry 1, box 543, NACP.

393 There were also containers: Memorandum from Major General William Sibert to Colonel Dorsey, Re: Special Train Movement, Jan. 30, 1919, Office of the Chief, Central Correspondence, 1918–1942, War Department, CWS, RG 175, finding aid PI-8, entry 1, box 543, NACP.

393 When all the drums: Memorandum from Lieutenant H. M. Schweitert to Major General Sibert, Re: Special Train Movement of Toxic Gases, Feb. 10, 1919, Office of the Chief, Central Correspondence, 1918–1942, CWS, RG 175, finding aid PI-8, entry 1, box 543, NACP.

393 The train passed: 1918 Ohio Railway Map, listed on the website of the Northern Ohio Association of Railway Societies. Available at www.trainweb.org/noars/railroads.htm.

394 From there, the train continued: Memorandum from Schweitert to Sibert, Re: Special Train Movement of Toxic Gases.

394 Just after 3:00 a.m.: Author interview with Richard Bly, Kane Historic Preservation Society.

394 The train idled: Memorandum from Lieutenant H. M. Schweitert to Major General Sibert, Re: Special Train Movement of Toxic Gases.

395 The train had made: Ibid.

395 Precisely what happened next: Many years later, Amos Fries contradicted that account when he responded to an insistent letter-writing critic that "no lewisite was ever thrown into any sea." Exactly what happened to the lewisite, how it was disposed of and where, officially remains a mystery.

395 albeit unlikely: A U.S. Army researcher believes this is unlikely because of the quick turnaround that would have been required for the lewisite to be sent from Edgewood to Baltimore the same day. It would require orders from high in the army command and coordination of multiple army offices.

395 On January 28: Memorandum to Director, Operations Division, General Staff, Jan. 27, 1919, Central Correspondence, 1918–1940, War Department, CWS, RG 175, finding aid PI-8, entry 1, box 477, NACP.

395 Sibert asked for permission: Ibid.

396 Three days later: Memorandum from Adjutant General to Sibert, Jan. 30, 1919, CWS Correspondence, 1918–1940, CWS, RG 175, finding aid PI-8, entry 1, box 477, NACP.

396 Originally, the *Elinor*: Memorandum from Captain John E. Craig to Superintendent of Water Transportation, Re: *Elinor* and *Ysel Haven*—Disposal of Mustard Gas and Phosgene Cargo, Feb. 1, 1919, Office of the Chief, Central Correspondence, 1918–1942, War Department, CWS, RG 175, finding aid PI-8, entry 1, box 477, NACP.

396 On February 10: Deck logs of the USS *Elinor,* Mar. 20, 1918–Apr. 26, 1919, Records of the Bureau of Naval Personnel, RG 24, entry 118-G-E, National Archives Building, Washington, DC.

397 On April 20, 1919: "Our Super-Poison Gas," *New York Times Magazine,* Apr. 20, 1919, 1.

398 In late May: "Most Deadly Gas Was US Invention," *Washington Times,* May 25, 1919, 12.

398 In March, Sibert warned Dorsey: Memorandum from William Sibert to Frank Dorsey, Mar. 11 1919, Office of the Chief, Central Correspondence, 1918–1942, CWS, RG 175, finding aid PI-8, entry 1, box 166, NACP.

398 As late as 1927: Letter from Amos Fries to W. Lee Lewis, Feb. 2, 1927, War Department, Office of the Chief, Central Correspondence, 1918–1942, CWS, RG 175, finding aid PI-8, entry 1, box 466, NACP.

399 "The War Department believes": *Reorganization of the Army: Hearings before the Subcommittee of the Committee on Military Affairs*, 66th Congress, 2nd session 93 (Aug. 8, 1919) (statement of Peyton March, Chief of Staff, U.S. Army), 93.

399 "The Philistines are": Letter from Amos Fries to Bradley Dewey, Aug. 18, 1919, General Fries' Files, 1918–1920, C–E, box 16, CWS, RG 175, finding aid PI-8, entry 7, box 16, NACP.

400 "It is the most humane": *Reorganization of the Army: Hearings before the Subcommittee of the Committee on Military Affairs*, 66th Congress, 1st session, 365 (Aug. 26, 1919) (statement of Major General William L. Sibert, Director, CWS).

400 Away from the hearing rooms: Letter from Amos Fries to Mr. H. Z. Osborne Jr., Aug. 7, 1919, General Amos A. Fries Papers, 1918–1920, CWS, RG 175, finding aid PI-8, entry 7, box 19, NACP.

400 Over the winter: Letter from A. Bruce Bielaski to Colonel John M. Donne, General Staff, Dec. 21, 1918, Investigative Case Files of the BOI, 1908–1922, NARA M1085, OGF, 1909–21, case no. 8000-925, roll 279, NACP.

401 The chief of the inventions division: Letter from Colonel John M. Donne, General Staff, to A. Bruce Bielaski, Jan. 18, 1919, Investigative Case Files of the BOI, 1908–1922, NARA M1085, OGF, 1909–21, case no. 8000-925, roll 279, NACP.

401 Support from Thomas Edison's: Letter from W. H. Meadowcraft to Bruce R. Silver, Feb. 28, 1919, Special Collection Series, Naval Consulting Board and Related Wartime Research Papers, Correspondence, Feb. 1919, Edison Papers, reel 281, frame 39.

401 Even though Scheele: "Master German Spy," *Chattanooga News,* Apr. 26, 1919, 3.

402 Bruce Silver grilled Scheele: Agent V. J. Valjavec, *Protection at Jones Point, NY,* report for May 11, 1919, Investigative Case Files of the BOI, 1908–1922, NARA M1085, OGF, 1909–21, case 8000-925, roll 279, NACP.

402 Nevertheless, in June: "Bernstorff Used Dyes as War Club," *New York Times,* June 16, 1919, 4.

402 At least one chemist: "Deadly War Compound More Than Thirty Years Old," *New York Times,* June 18, 1919, 16.

403 The judge set Scheele's bail: "Wall Street Explosion Laid to Gelatin," *New York Times,* Oct. 16, 1920, 16.

403 Then he walked out: Agent V. J. Valjavec, *Protection at Jones Point, NY,* report for June 4, 1919.

403 Reporters remained: Two BOI documents, the backdated report from Agent Valjavec and a later partial report in bureau records, date his bail hearing as June 4. The newspaper accounts that appeared June 6 report that he appeared the day before, on June 5.

403 As part of the conditions: Report from BOI agent E. P. Martin, *In Re. Dr. Walter v. [sic] Scheele—Violation Espionage,* May 12, 1919, Investigative Case Files of the BOI, 1908–1922, NARA M1085, OGF, 1909–21, case no. 8000-925, roll 279, NACP.

403 "now is in the employ": Letter from unnamed agent in charge to Mr. J. M. Nye, Chief Special Agent, Department of State, Dec. 5, 1919, Investigative Case Files of the BOI, 1908–1922, NARA M1085, OGF, 1909–21, case no. 8000-925, roll 279, NACP.

404 His goal was: "Form New Oil Company," *New York Sun,* Apr. 1, 1919, 13.

404 Levering himself wrote: Letter from Richmond M. Levering to State Department on behalf of George A. Burrell, Jan. 20, 1919, U.S. Passport Application, 1795–1925, Ancestry.com.

404 If Bielaski's Justice Department colleagues: "Gift Car for Mr. Bielaski," *Evening Star,* Feb. 26, 1919, 2.

404 In July, Chemical Warfare Service: "Gas Veterans Organize," *Evening World,* July 23, 1919, 5.

405 On August 30: "Helping Soldiers Keep Insurance," *New York Times,* Sept. 1, 1919, 7; "Chemical Warfare Post of the American Legion Protests the Abolition of the Chemical Warfare Service," *Chemical Age* 1, no. 4 (Sept. 10, 1919): 170.

405 With so many: Legion Drive Will Be Extended Week," *New York Sun,* Sept. 20, 1919, 18.

405 When the music swelled: *Journal of Industrial and Engineering Chemistry* 11, no. 10 (Oct. 1, 1919): 915.

406 Billed as both: "Peace Meeting of the American Chemical Society," *Catalyst* 4, no. 8 (Oct. 1919).

406 For the first time: "National Publicity for Philadelphia Meeting," *Catalyst,* Oct. 1919.

406 Now with the future: Letter from Charles L. Parsons to Newton Baker, June 25, 1919, General Fries' Files, 1918–1920, O–S, CWS, RG 175, finding aid PI-8, entry 7, box 19, NACP.

408 If there was any: "Annual Meeting American Chemical Society," *Journal of Industrial and Engineering Chemistry* 11, no. 10 (Oct. 1, 1919), 911.

409 The day after: *Hearings before the Committee on Military Affairs,* House of Representatives, Washington, DC, Government Printing Office, 1919, 59.

410 The War Department: Letter from Bradley Dewey to W. Nephew King, Apr. 10, 1919, Office of the Chief, Central Correspondence, 1918–1942, War Department, CWS, RG 175, finding aid PI-8, entry 1, box 388, NACP.

410 Around the country: Amos A. Fries, Mob Control, General Fries' Files, A–C, CWS, RG 175, finding aid PI-8, entry 7, box 15, NACP.

410 Even General William Black: Letter from Amos A. Fries to Lieutenant Colonel Earl J. Atkisson, Sept. 25, 1919, General Fries' Files, A–C, CWS, RG 175, finding aid PI-8, entry 7, box 15, NACP.

410 But in the waning days: *Casualties from Gas in the AEF (Official Figures Compiled by Surgeon General's Office),* General Fries Files, 1918–1920, O–S, CWS, RG 175, finding aid PI-8, entry 7, box 19, NACP.

411 But he eagerly seized: Letter from Amos Fries to Colonel George S. Watson, Sept. 3, 1919, General Fries' Files, 1918–1920, S–Z, CWS, RG 175, finding aid PI-8, entry 7, box 20, NACP.

411 In November, General March: "Finds Gas Humane in War," *New York Times,* Nov. 26, 1919, 6.

412 Two and a half: J. J. Rowe, R. O. Fournier, and G. W. Morey, "Chemical Analysis of Thermal Waters in Yellowstone National Park, Wyoming, 1960–65," *Geological Survey Bulletin* 1303 (Washington, DC: U.S. Government Printing Office, 1973).

412 Bessie put the house: Telegram from transportation officer to Amos Fries, July 16, 1919, General Fries' Files, 1918–1920, S–Z, CWS, RG 175, finding aid PI-8, entry 7, box 20, NACP.

412 brought the children: Amos A. Fries, *Personnel Report and Statement of Preferences for All Officers,* Jan. 15, 1920, General Fries' Files, 1918–1920, O–S, RG 175, War Department, CWS, Fries' Files, finding aid PI-8, entry 7, box 19, NACP.

412 She shopped for milk: Receipt for officers' mess, Oct. 27, 1919, receipt for Edgewood Bargain House, Nov.1, 1919, General Fries Files, 1918–1920, O–S, RG 175, War Department, CWS, Fries' Files, finding aid PI-8, entry 7, box 19, NACP.

412 When she tucked the children in: *Reorganization of the Army,* 504.

413 The fens of Gunpowder Neck: Memorandum from Amos Fries to Executive Officer, Edgewood Arsenal, July 21,1919. General Fries Files, 1918–1920, O–S, RG 175, War Department, CWS, Fries' Files, finding aid PI-8, entry 7, box 19, NACP.

413 He also drew up: Memorandum from Commanding Officer, Edgewood Arsenal, to Director, CWS, Re: Project for Future Operation of Edgewood Arsenal, July 8, 1919, War Department, CWS, General Fries' Files, 1918–1920, RG 175, PI-8, entry 7, box 19, NACP.

414 Fries smelled nothing: Letter from Amos Fries to Lieutenant Colonel Earl J. Atkisson, Sept. 25, 1919, General Fries' Files, A–C, RG 175, finding aid PI-8, entry 7, box 15, NACP.

Epilogue: "The Devil's Perfume"

417 Around spring of 1921: "World Mastery Lies in Dew of Death," *New York Herald Magazine and Books,* May 8, 1921, 79.

417 Fries's aggressive advocacy: "Gas Warfare," *New York Times,* May 13, 1921, 14.

417 Fritz Haber also helped: "Nobel Prizes to Germans," *New York Times,* Nov. 15, 1919, 11.

417 An international outcry: McGrayne, *Prometheans in the Lab,* 73.

417 As debate over Haber: Letter from Arthur B. Lamb to Ellwood Hendrick, Feb. 13, 1920, HUG 4508.7, Special Personal Files for 1918–19, General A–L, box 5, Arthur B. Lamb Papers, Harvard University Archives.

417 At the fixed-nitrogen laboratory: Signal Corps photo 111-SC-67774, NACP.

418 As the talks over chemical: "Do Away with Gas, Is Plea of Maimed Boys out at Walter Reed," *Washington Times,* Dec. 14, 1921, 1.

418 During the disarmament conference: Committee on Limitations of Land Armaments report, Nov. 30, 1921, John J. Pershing Papers, 1882–1971, General Correspondence, 1904–48, box 81.

419 In late February of 1920: "Sibert to Leave Chemical Warfare Service," *New York Times,* Feb. 29, 1920, 10.

419 ordered to assume command: "Sibert's Transfer Stirs Army Men," *New York Times,* Mar. 1, 1920, 15.

419 The War Department scuttlebutt: "Sibert Transfer Punishment, Says Herty," *Chemical Engineer,* 28, no. 3 (Mar. 1920): 78.

419 The demotion was an unmistakable rebuke: "General Sibert Resigns," *New York Times,* Apr. 7, 1920, 10.

419 He moved to a farm: "Kentucky Calls to the Fox Hunter," *New York Times,* Nov. 2, 1924,

419 He remarried: Clark, *William L. Sibert,* 175–87.

419 How exactly Fries: "Pershing on Duty as Chief of Staff," *New York Times,* July 2, 1921, 4.

420 That year, the league held: "Arms Sale Parley Opens in Geneva," *New York Times,* May 5, 1925, 23.

420 After the delegates returned: Frederic J. Brown, *Chemical Warfare: A Study in Restraints* (Princeton, NJ: Princeton University Press, 1968), 104

420 Many other members: "Will Fight Abolition of Poison Gas," *New York Times,* Nov. 15, 1926, 2.

421 Shortly after the Geneva talks: "Signing of Accords Ends Arms Parley," *New York Times,* June 18, 1925, 4.

421 Lewis was recalled: War Department order, June 16, 1925, courtesy of L. Philip Reiss.

421 Fries spoke of how preparation: "Gas Upheld as Humane in War," Sept. 25, 1925, publication unknown, L. Philip Reiss Collection.

421 Even General John Pershing: Letter from John J. Pershing to Senator W. W. Borah, Dec. 10, 1926, John J. Pershing Papers, 1882–1971, General Correspondence, 1904–48, box 81.

421 The rejection so enraged: "Hits Legion on Poison Gas," *New York Times,* Jan. 22, 1927, 7.

422 For a time, he claimed: "Gen. Fries Defends Chlorine Treatment," *New York Times,* Jan. 6, 1925, 14.

422 Years after the war: Letter from Van H. Manning to George A. Burrell, Nov. 24, 1923, Correspondence 1917–23, A–Cha, HUG 4508.5, box 5, Arthur B. Lamb Papers. 1. Letter from unnamed agent in charge to Mr. J. M. Nye, Chief Special Agent, Department of State, Dec. 5, 1919, Investigative Case Files of the BOI, 1908–1922.

422 When he died: "Dr. Van H. Manning to Be Buried Today," *Washington Post,* July 15, 1932, 5.

423 In late January of 1920: "2,855 New Cases of Influenza; 30 Deaths Reported," *New York Times,* Jan. 26, 1920, 2.

423 Despite his temperance: "Richmond Levering Dies of Pneumonia," *New York Times,* Jan. 30, 1920, 15.

423 Even the Department of Justice: *Alien Property Custodian Investigation Report into Richmond Levering and A. Bruce Bielaski,* Investigative Case Files of the BOI, 1908–1922, NARA M1085, OGF, 1909–21, case no. 8000-12490, roll 335, NACP.

424 On December 9: U.S. Patent Office, patent no. 1,382,804, US1382804-0.

424 On September 16, 1920: Beverly Gage, *The Day Wall Street Exploded: A Story of America in Its First Age of Terror* (New York: Oxford University Press, 2009), 30.

424 His report identified: Ibid., 199.

424 The *New York Times:* "Wall Street Explosion Laid to Gelatin," *New York Times,* Oct. 16, 1920, 16.

424 Just before the Wall Street bombing: Letter from Rear Admiral W. Strother Smith to W. H. Meadowcraft, July 25, 1920, Edison Papers, reel 281, frame 164.

424 Edison's assistant provided: Letter from W. H. Meadowcraft to Rear Admiral W. Strother Smith, July 28, 1920, Edison Papers, reel 281, frame 166.

424 Five years after his indictment: "Dr. Scheele Let Off with One-Day Term," *New York Times,* Feb. 26, 1920, 7.

425 He bought advertisements: City directory, Hackensack, NJ, 1921–22, 24.

425 The following year: "Dr. Walter T. Scheele Dead," *Washington Post,* Mar. 6, 1922, 3.

425 As World War II began: "Gen. Fries Says Planes Will Decide War: Holds Neither Side Can Hope to Win Unless It Dominates in Air," *Washington Post,* Sept. 5, 1939, 1.

425 President Franklin Roosevelt: "President Assails War Gases in Veto," *New York Times,* Aug. 5, 1937, 8.

425 While the Nazis: Brown, *Chemical Warfare,* 230.

426 In an unspeakable: McGrayne, *Prometheans in the Lab,* 77.

426 After the war: Annie Jacobsen, *Operation Paperclip* (New York: Little, Brown, 2014).

427 "It will be used": Fries memoir.

427 In 1974, almost fifty years: Tucker, *War of Nerves,* 235.

428 President Trump used: "Transcript and Video: Trump Speaks about Strikes in Syria," *New York Times,* Apr. 6, 2017.

429 "The new profession": Warren K. Lewis, "Chemical Engineering: A New Science, date unknown, Warren K. Lewis Papers (MC 578), box 3, Institute Archives and Special Collections, MIT Libraries, Cambridge, MA.

430 James Bryant Conant: James B. Conant, Memorandum I: Teaching and Research in the 1920s (outline and notes for Conant's 1970 memoir *My Several Lives*), call no. UAI 15.898, box 11, Papers of James Bryant Conant, 1862–1987, Harvard University Archives.

431 In a draft of a document: *History of Chemical Warfare Service, AEF,* 17.

432 Fries himself acknowledged this: Amos A. Fries, letter to the editor, *San Francisco Journal,* Mar. 29, 1923, Chemical Warfare Correspondence, 1918–1940, RG 197, finding aid PI-8, entry 1, box 469, NACP.

433 He died in Poughkeepsie: "Tom Jabine," *Gas Attack,* May 1938, 2.

433 His gassing at Charpentry: Thomas Jabine Jr., "Learning to Fly for the Navy."

433 Harold Higginbottom—"Higgie": Phone interview with Betty Higginbottom.

Selected Bibliography

Archives

American University Library, University Archives and Special Collections
American University Early History Files.
Jabine, Thomas. Letters.
Osborn, Albert. "Chronology of Events, 1907–1940."
WWI History Collection.

Antioch College, Olive Kettering Library, Antiochiana
Adams, Clyde S. Papers.

Catholic University of America, American Catholic History Research Center and University Archives
Assorted articles about lewisite and Martin Maloney Chemistry Laboratory.
Catholic University Bulletin, 23, no. 8 (Nov. 1917); 25, nos. 1–2 (Feb. 1919); 25, no. 9 (Dec. 1919).

Columbia University, Rare Book and Manuscript Library
Zanetti, Joaquin Enrique. Papers, 1917–52. Call no. MS 1405.

Harvard University Archives
Conant, James Bryant. Papers, 1862–1987. Call no. UAI 15.898.
Lamb, Arthur B. Papers. Call no. HUG 4508.5.

Historical Society of Washington, D.C.
American University photos. General Photograph Collection. Whetzel Aerial Photograph Collection.
Baist Map Collection. Washington, DC.
Photo collection of Spring Valley, Rauscher's banquet hall, Cosmos Club, and book *In Memoriam, Benjamin Farnsworth Leighton.*

In Flanders Fields Museum, Ieper (Ypres), Belgium

Dendooven, Dominiek, archivist and compiler. "Overview: 22 April 1915—Eyewitness Accounts of the First Gas Attack."

Johns Hopkins Medical Institutions, Alan Chesney Medical Archives

Marshall, Eli K., Jr. Papers, 1899–1966.

Johns Hopkins University, Special Collections, Milton S. Eisenhower Library

Reid, E. Emmet. Reid (Ebenezer Emmett) 1889–1974 Papers. Call no. MS 104.

Lake County Historical Society

Simpson, Nate. "Nineteen-Eighteen in Willoughby, Ohio." Assorted photos and articles related to the Mousetrap.

Library of Congress

Pershing, John J. Papers, General Correspondence, 1904–48.

MIT

Keyes, Frederick. Papers, 1917–80. Call no. MC-318.
Lewis, Warren K. Papers. Call no. MC-578.
Richter, George A. Papers, 1919–58. Call no. MC-401.

National Academy of Sciences Archives

National Academy of Sciences—National Research Council Central File, 1914–1918, Executive Board records.

> Agencies and Departments, Dept. of the Interior, Bureau of Mines, 1916–1918.
> Committee on Gases Used in Warfare, 1918.
> Committee on Noxious Gases, 1917.
> Projects, Helium Production, 1917.

National Archives and Records Administration, Washington, D.C.

Record group 24, Records of the Bureau of Naval Personnel, Logbooks of US Ships and Stations, 1916–1940, US Navy Logbooks.

> Muster Rolls of Ships and Shore Establishments, Jan. 1898–June 30, 1939. Vol. 2240. PI 123, entry 134.
> USS *Agamemnon*, Jan. 1, 1918–Aug. 27, 1918. Entry 118-G.
> USS *Elinor*, Mar. 20, 1918–Apr. 26, 1919. Entry 118-G-E.
> USS *President Grant*, Apr. 2, 1917–Dec. 31, 1918. Entry 118-G-P.
> USS *Western Front*, May 11, 1918–Aug. 18, 1919. Entry 118-G-W.

Record group 41, Bureau of Marine Inspection and Navigation, Official Number Files, 1867–1958. USS *Elinor*. Box 1323.

Record group 45, Navy Subject File.
   Logistics File, 1916–20. Entry 522, box 53.

National Archives and Records Administration II, College Park, MD
Record group 18, Air Service.
Record group 70, Bureau of Mines.
Record group 77, Records of the Office of the Chief of Engineers.
Record group 92, Office of Quartermaster General.
Record group 120, Records of the AEF.
Record group 165, War Department General Staff.
Record group 175, Chemical Warfare Service.
Record group 200, Papers of General John J. Pershing.
Signal Corps, 111-SC.

Ohio State University Archives
Burrell, George A. Records.
McPherson, William. Papers. Record group 3/g/1.
Reed, Carlos Isaac. Records.

Princeton University Archives
Hulett, George A. Papers, 1909–1962. Call no. C0460.

Smithsonian Institution Archives
Records of the Audubon Naturalist Society of the Mid-Atlantic States, 1893–1980.

Talbot House, Poperinge, Belgium
Batteu, Jeanne. Video and transcript of oral history.

University of Iowa, Parks Library Special Collections
Davidson, Harold French. Papers. Call no. MS-605.

University of Oregon Library, Special Collections and University Archives
Fries, Amos A. Papers, 1896–1953. Collection no. Ax 234.

U.S. Army Chemical Corps Museum, Fort Leonard Wood, MO
Carlisle Attic Collection.
First Gas Regiment Collection.
Individual soldier files.

U.S. Army Corps of Engineers
Records and historical documents for project C03DC091801 (Spring Valley—
   Military Munitions Response Program).

U.S. Army Heritage and Education Center at Carlisle Barracks, Carlisle, PA
World War I Veterans Survey, Chemical Warfare Service.

Washingtoniana Room, Washington, D.C., Public Library
"Artificial Collection," Collection 60.

Yale University

Henderson, Yandell. Collected Papers. 1873–1944. Call no. Sl21 38.

Underhill, Frank Pell. Papers. Call no. MS 514.

Yale University Military and Wartime Activities Photographs. Call no. RU 750.

Microfilm

Edison, Thomas A. Papers. Part 5, 1911–19, Notebook Series, reel 231, NBK-55, reel 237, NBK-61; Edison General File Series, reel 268, DOC-90, reel 270, DOC-92; Letterbook Series, reel 277, LBK-20. University Publications of America.

Investigative Case Files of the Bureau of Investigation, 1908–1922. Record group 65. National Archives Microfilm Publication M1085. Old German Files, 1909–21. National Archives at College Park, MD.

> Levering, Richmond M. Case nos. 8000-184, 8000-12490, 8000-16110, 8000-16950, 97452.
>
> Scheele, Walter T. Case no. 8000-925.

Willoughby Republican, Willoughby-Eastlake Public Library, Willoughby, OH.

Personal Papers, Books, Unpublished Manuscripts, and Private Collections

Addison, James Thayer. War diary. Louise Cass Collection. Additional Addison records courtesy of Margot McCain.

Bielaski, A. Bruce. Documents. Courtesy of Jennifer Lawrence.

Jabine, Thomas. Photos and documents. Courtesy of Thomas Jabine Jr.

Lewis, Winford Lee. Papers. L. Philip Reiss Collection.

MacMullin, Robert Burns. *Odyssey of a Chemical Engineer: The Autobiography of Robert Burns MacMullin.* Smithtown, NY: Exposition Press, 1983. Courtesy of Constance Aust.

Manning, Van H. Articles, letters, transcripts. Courtesy of Petrie M. Wilson and Pamela Manning Fein.

Maurer, William Charles. Papers, letters, and photos. Addie Ruth Maurer Olson/Olson Family Collection.

Sibert, William L. Letters, photos, and records. Anne Sibert Buiter Collection.

Smith, Harold Clinton. Papers and photos. Courtesy of Dorothy Smith Coleman.

Articles and Periodical Collections

The following list does not include newspaper articles or individual articles cited in the endnotes.

Black Diamond 55, nos. 1–26 (July 3–Dec. 25, 1915). Chicago: Black Diamond Co., 1915.

Brophy, Leo P. "Origins of the Chemical Corps." *Military Affairs* 20, no. 4 (1956): 217–26.

Catalyst: Official Bulletin of the Philadelphia and Delaware Sections of the American Chemical Society 4, nos. 1–8 (Jan.–Oct. 1919).

"The European War," *New York Times Current History* 11 (Apr. –June 1917).

Faith, Thomas. "It Would Be Very Well If We Could Avoid It: General Pershing and Chemical Warfare." *Historian* 78, no. 3 (fall 2016): 469–85.

Fitzgerald, Gerard D. "Chemical Warfare and Medical Response during World War I." *American Journal of Public Health* 98, no. 4 (Apr. 2008): 611–25.

Forum 62 (July–Dec. 1919).

Fuel Oil Journal/Oil Trade Journal 7, nos. 1–12 (Jan.–Dec. 1916).

Gordon, Martin K., Barry R. Sude, and Ruth Ann Overbeck. "Chemical Testing in the Great War: The American University Experiment Station." *Washington History* 6, no. 1 (1994): 28–45.

Jaffe, Harry. "Ground Zero." *Washingtonian,* Dec. 2000. https://www.washingtonian.com/2000/12/01/ground-zero/.

———. "The Toxic Pit Next Door." *Washingtonian,* Mar. 2013. https://www.washingtonian.com/2013/02/28/the-toxic-waste-pit-next-door/.

Journal of Industrial and Engineering Chemistry 9, nos. 1–12 (Jan. 1.–Dec. 1, 1917); 10, nos. 1–12 (Jan. 1.–Dec. 1, 1919); 11, nos. 1–12 (Jan.–Dec. 1919).

May, Leopold. "The Early Days of Chemistry at Catholic University." *Bulletin of Historical Chemistry* 28, no. 1 (2003): 18–25.

McLamb, Margaret E. "From Death Valley to Spring Valley: A Case Study in Contamination in Washington, DC." *Sustainable Development Law and Policy* 3, no. 1 (fall/winter 2003): 3–9.

Mining and Engineering World 45 (July 1–Dec. 30, 1916).

Mining Congress Journal 2, nos. 1–12 (Jan.–Dec. 1916).

Stockbridge, Frank Parker. "War Inventions That Came Too Late." *Harper's Monthly Magazine,* Nov. 1919.

Verrell, Benefsheh D. "Spring Valley, Washington, DC: Changing Land Use and Demographics from 1900–2000." *Geographical Bulletin* 49 (2008): 103–19.

Books and Monographs

Addison, James Thayer. *The Story of the First Gas Regiment.* Boston: Houghton Mifflin, 1919.

———. *War, Peace and the Christian Mind.* Greenwich, CT: Seabury Press, 1953.

Albright, Richard. *Death of the Chesapeake: A History of the Military's Role in Polluting the Bay.* Beverly, MA: Scrivener Publishing, 2013.

Arthur, Max. *Forgotten Voices of the Great War: A History of World War I in the Words of the Men and Women Who Were There.* Guilford, CT: Lyons Press, 2002.

Auld, Major Samuel James Manson. *Gas and Flame in Modern Warfare.* New York: George H. Doran, 1918.

Baker, Newton B. *Why We Went to War.* New York: Harper and Brothers, for the Council on Foreign Relations, 1936.

Berg, A. Scott. *Wilson.* New York: G. P. Putnam's Sons, 2013.

Blum, Howard. *Dark Invasion: 1915: Germany's Secret War and the Hunt for the First Terrorist Cell in America.* New York: Harper Collins, 2014.

Brophy, Leo P., and George J. B. Fisher. *The Chemical Warfare Service: Organizing for War.* Washington, DC: Center of Military History, 1989.

Brophy, Leo P., Wyndham D. Miles, and Rexmond C. Cochrane. *The Chemical Warfare Service: From Laboratory to Field.* Washington, DC: Center of Military History, 1959.

Brown, Frederic J. *Chemical Warfare: A Study in Restraints.* Princeton, NJ: Princeton University Press, 1968.

Christianson, Scott. *The Last Gasp: The Rise and Fall of the American Gas Chamber.* Berkeley, CA: University of California Press, 2010.

Clark, Edward B. *William L. Sibert: The Army Engineer.* Philadelphia: Dorrance and Co., 1930.

Cochrane, Rexmond C. *The National Academy of Sciences: The First Hundred Years, 1863–1963.* Washington, DC: National Academy of Sciences, 1978.

Coleman, Kim. *A History of Chemical Warfare.* New York: Palgrave Macmillan, 2005.

Conant, James B. *My Several Lives: Memoirs of a Social Inventor.* New York: Harper and Row, 1970.

Crowell, Benedict, and Robert Forrest Wilson. *The Armies of Industry II: Our Nation's Manufacture of Munitions for a World in Arms, 1917–1918.* New Haven, CT: Yale University Press, 1921.

Dickey, Robert W. *Goliath of Panama: The Life of Soldier and Canal Builder William Luther Sibert.* Morley, MO: Acclaim Press, 2015.

Faith, Thomas I. *Behind the Gas Mask: The U.S. Chemical Warfare Service in War and Peace.* Chicago: University of Illinois Press, 2014.

Falls, Cyril. *The Great War: 1914–1918.* New York: Capricorn Books, 1959.

Ferrell, Robert H. *Woodrow Wilson and World War I: 1917–1921.* New York: Harper and Row, 1985.

Foulkes, Charles H. *"Gas!" The Story of the Special Brigade.* Edinburgh: William Blackwood and Sons, 1934. Facsimile. Uckfield, East Sussex: Naval and Military Press, 2009.

Fox, Frank. *The Battle of the Ridges: Arras–Messines, March–June, 1917.* London: C. Arthur Pearson, 1918.

Freemantle, Michael. *Gas! Gas! Quick Boys! How Chemistry Changed the First World War.* Gloucestershire, England: Spellmount, 2013.

Fries, Amos Alfred, and Clarence J. West. *Chemical Warfare*. New York: McGraw-Hill, 1921.

Gage, Beverly. *The Day Wall Street Exploded: A Story of America in Its First Age of Terror*. New York: Oxford University Press, 2009.

General Electric, National Lamp Works. *National in the World War, April 6, 1917–November 11, 1918*. Cleveland: General Electric, 1920.

Haber, Ludwig Fritz. *The Poisonous Cloud: Chemical Warfare in the First World War*. Oxford: Clarendon Press, 1986.

Hart, Peter. *The Great War: A Combat History of the First World War*. New York: Oxford University Press, 2013.

Hershberg, James. *James B. Conant: Harvard to Hiroshima and the Making of the Nuclear Age*. New York: Alfred A. Knopf, 1993.

Jacobsen, Annie. *Operation Paperclip: The Secret Intelligence Program That Brought Nazi Scientists to America*. New York: Back Bay Books, 2014.

Jankowski, Paul. *Verdun: The Longest Battle of the Great War*. New York: Oxford, 2013.

Jones, Daniel Patrick. "The Role of Chemists in Research on War Gases in the United States During World War I." PhD thesis, University of Wisconsin, 1969.

Jones, Simon. *World War I Gas Warfare Tactics and Equipment*. Long Island City, NY: Osprey Publishing, 1994.

Junger, Ernst. *Storm of Steel*. New York: Penguin Classics, 2016.

Kennedy, David M. *Over Here: The First World War and American Society*. New York: Oxford University Press, 1980.

Kleber, Brooks E., and Dale Birdsell. *The Chemical Warfare Service: Chemicals in Combat*. Washington, DC: Center of Military History, 1990.

MacMullan, Margaret. *Paris 1919: Six Months That Changed the World*. New York: Random House, 2003.

———. *The War That Ended Peace: The Road to 1914*. New York: Random House, 2013.

Marchand, C. Rowland. *The American Peace Movement and Social Reform, 1898–1918*. Princeton: Princeton University Press, 1972.

Mayor, Adrienne. *Greek Fire, Poison Arrows and Scorpion Bombs: Biological and Chemical Warfare in the Ancient World*. Woodstock, New York: Overlook Duckworth, 2003.

MacMullin, Robert Burns. *With E of the First Gas*. Brooklyn, NY: Holton Printing, 1919.

McCullough, David. *The Path Between the Seas: The Creation of the Panama Canal 1870–1914*. New York: Simon and Schuster, 1977.

McGrayne, Sharon Bertsch. *Prometheans in the Lab: Chemistry and the Making of the Modern World*. New York: McGraw-Hill, 2001.

Millikan, Robert A. *The Autobiography of Robert A. Millikan.* New York: Prentice Hall, 1950.

Millman, Chad. *The Detonators: The Secret Plot to Destroy America and an Epic Hunt for Justice.* New York: Little Brown, 2006.

Mills, J. Saxon. *The Panama Canal: A History and Description of the Enterprise.* New York: Thomas Nelson and Sons, 1913.

Mulliken, Robert S. *Life of a Scientist.* New York: Springer-Verlag, 1968.

Osborn, Albert. *John Fletcher Hurst: A Biography.* New York: Eaton and Mains, 1905.

Palmer, Frederick. *Newton D. Baker: America at War.* Vols. 1 and 2. New York: Dodd, Mead and Co., 1931.

———. *John J. Pershing: General of the Armies.* Harrisburg, PA: Military Service Publishing, 1948.

Pershing, John J. *My Experiences in the World War.* Vols. 1 and 2. New York: Harper and Row, 1931. Reprint. Blue Ridge Summit, PA: Tab Books, 1989.

Pollard, Captain Hugh B. C. *The Story of Ypres.* New York: Robert M. McBride and Co., 1917.

Powell, Edward Alexander. *The Army behind the Army.* New York: Charles Scribner's Sons, 1919.

Powell, Fred Wilbur. *The Bureau of Mines: Its History, Activities and Organization.* New York: D. Appleton and Co., 1922.

Prentiss, Augustin M. *Chemicals in War.* New York: McGraw-Hill, 1937.

Preston, Diana. *Lusitania: An Epic Tragedy.* New York: Walker and Co., 2002.

———. *A Higher Form of Killing: Six Weeks in World War I That Forever Changed the Nature of Warfare.* New York: Bloomsbury Press, 2015.

Reed, Germaine M. *Crusading for Chemistry: The Professional Career of Charles Herty Holmes.* Athens: University of Georgia Press, 1995.

Rintelen von Kleist, Franz. *The Dark Invader.* New York: Macmillan, 1933.

Romano, James A., Jr., Brian Luckey, and Harry Salem. *Chemical Warfare Agents: Chemistry, Pharmacology, Toxicology, and Therapeutics.* 2nd ed. Boca Raton, FL: CRC Press, 2008.

Smythe, Donald. *Pershing: General of the Armies.* Bloomington: Indiana University Press, 1986.

Society of the First Division. *History of the First Division During the World War, 1917–1919.* Philadelphia: John C. Winston, 1922.

Spaulding, Thomas M. *The Cosmos Club on Lafayette Square.* Manasha, WI: George Banta Publishing, 1949.

Stevenson, David. *With Our Backs to the Wall: Victory and Defeat in 1918.* London: Penguin, 2011.

Stockbridge, Frank Parker. *Yankee Ingenuity in the War.* New York: Harper and Brothers, 1920.

Strother, French. *Fighting Germany's Spies*. Garden City, NY: Doubleday, Page and Co., 1918.

Terraine, John. *To Win a War: 1918, The Year of Victory*. Garden City, NY: Doubleday, 1981.

Theoharis, Athan G. *The FBI: A Comprehensive Reference Guide*. Phoenix, AZ: Oryx Press, 1999.

Tuchman, Barbara W. *The Guns of August*. New York: Presidio Press, 2004.

Tucker, Johnathan B. *War of Nerves: Chemical Warfare from World War I to al-Qaeda*. New York: Pantheon Books, 2006.

Tumulty, Joseph Patrick. *Woodrow Wilson As I Know Him*. Garden City, NY: Doubleday, Page and Co., 1921.

Tunney, Thomas J., and Paul Merrick Hollister. *Throttled! The Detection of the German and Anarchist Bomb Plotters*. Boston: Small, Maynard and Co., 1919.

Underhill, Frank Pell. *The Lethal War Gases: Physiology and Experimental Treatment*. New Haven: Yale University Press, 1920.

Vandiver, Frank E. *Black Jack: The Life and Times of John J. Pershing*. Vol. 2. College Station: Texas A&M University Press, 1977.

Venzon, Anne Cipriano. *The United States in the First World War*. New York: Routledge, 2003.

Vilensky, Joel A. *Dew of Death: The Story of Lewisite, America's World War I Weapon of Mass Destruction*. Bloomington: Indiana University Press, 2005.

Warthin, Aldred Scott, and Carl Vernon Weller. *The Medical Aspects of Mustard Gas Poisoning*. St. Louis: C. V. Mosby, 1919.

Watkins, Owen Spencer. *With French in France and Flanders*. London: Charles H. Kelly, 1915.

Wilkinson, Christina L. *Willoughby*. Charleston, SC: Arcadia, 2012.

Wilson, Edith Bolling. *My Memoir*. New York: Bobs-Merrill, 1939.

Yerkes, Robert M. *The New World of Science*. New York: Century, 1920.

Yokelson, Mitchell. *Forty-Seven Days: How Pershing's Warriors Came of Age to Defeat the German Army in World War I*. New York: NAL Caliber, 2016.

Zieger, Robert H. *America's Great War*. Lanham, MD: Rowman and Littlefield, 2000.

Government Documents

The following list does not include individual documents cited in endnotes that are included in larger archival collections.

Bancroft, W. D. *Bancroft's History of the Chemical Warfare Service in the United States*. Washington, DC: Research Division, Chemical Warfare Service, American University Experiment Station, 1919.

Cochrane, Rexmond C. *The 26th Division East of the Meuse, Sept. 1918*. U.S. Army Chemical Corps Historical Studies, Gas Warfare in World War I. U.S.

Army Chemical Corps Historical Office. Washington, DC: Office of the Chief Chemical Officer, 1960.

Fries, Amos A. *Gas in Attack and Gas in Defense.* 1919.

Gordon, Martin K., Barry R. Sude, Ruth Ann Overbeck, and Charles Hendricks. *A Brief History of the American University Experiment Station and U.S. Navy Bomb Disposal School.* American University Office of History, U.S. Army Corps of Engineers, 1994.

Grandine, Katharine, William R. Henry Jr., and Irene Jackson Henry. *Aberdeen Proving Ground (Edgewood Arsenal), Written Historical and Descriptive Data.* Historic American Engineering Record, no. MD-47. Washington, DC: U.S. Department of the Interior, 1985.

Heller, Major Charles E. *Chemical Warfare in World War I: The American Experience, 1917–1918.* Leavenworth Papers, no. 10. Fort Leavenworth, KS: Combat Studies Institute, U.S. Army Command and General Staff College, 1984.

Hendricks, Charles. *Combat and Construction: U.S. Army Engineers in World War I.* U.S. Army Corps of Engineers, Office of History. Fort Belvoir, VA, 1993.

Manning, Van H. "Petroleum Investigations and Production of Helium." Advance chapter from *War Work of the Bureau of Mines,* Bulletin 178-A. Bureau of Mines, U.S. Department of the Interior. Washington, DC: U.S. Government Printing Office, 1919.

———. "War Gas Investigations." Advance chapter from *War Work of the Bureau of Mines,* Bulletin 178. Bureau of Mines, U.S. Department of the Interior. Washington, DC: U.S. Government Printing Office, 1919.

Navy Directory, Officers of the United States Navy. Washington, DC: U.S. Government Printing Office, 1919.

Sidell, Frederick R., Ernest T. Takafuji, and David R. Franz, editors. *Medical Aspects of Chemical and Biological Warfare.* Washington, DC: Office of the Surgeon General, 1997.

U.S Army. *Potential Military Chemical/Biological Agents and Compounds.* U.S. Army Field Manual 3-11.9. 2005.

U.S. Army Corps of Engineers. *The U.S. Army Corps of Engineers: A History.* Washington, DC: U.S. Government Printing Office, 2008.

U.S. Army Department of Ordnance. *History of Pyrotechnics in World War.* Washington, DC: U.S. Government Printing Office, 1920.

U.S. Bureau of Mines. *Seventh Annual Report by the Director of the Bureau of Mines to the Secretary of the Interior for the Fiscal Year Ended June 30, 1917.* Washington, DC: U.S. Government Printing Office, 1917.

———. *Eighth Annual Report by the Director of the Bureau of Mines to the Secretary of the Interior for the Fiscal Year Ended June 30, 1918.* Washington, DC: U.S. Government Printing Office, 1918.

U.S. Chemical Warfare Service. *Report of the Chemical Warfare Service.* Washington, DC: U.S. Government Printing Office, 1918.

U.S. Department of the Interior. *Annual Report of the Secretary of the Interior for the Fiscal Year Ended June 30, 1915.* Washington, DC: U.S. Government Printing Office, 1915.

———. *Annual Report of the Secretary of the Interior for the Fiscal Year Ended June 30, 1920.* Washington, DC: U.S. Government Printing Office, 1920.

U.S. House of Representatives. *Army Reorganization: Hearings before the Committee on Military Affairs.* 66th Congress, 1st session, on HR 8287, HR 8068, HR 7925, HR 8870. Part 1. Washington, DC: U.S. Government Printing Office, 1919.

———. *War Expenditures: Hearings before Subcommittee 3 (Foreign Expenditures) of the Select Committee on Expenditures in the War Department, House of Representatives.* 66th Congress, 2nd session, on War Expenditures. Vol 3. Washington, DC: U.S. Government Printing Office, 1920.

U.S. Senate. *Army Appropriation Bill: Hearings before the Subcommittee of the Committee on Military Affairs, United States Senate.* 66th Congress, 1st session, on HR 5227. Washington, DC: U.S. Government Printing Office, 1919.

———. *Reorganization of the Army: Hearings before the Subcommittee of the Committee on Military Affairs, United States Senate.* 66th Congress, 1st session, on S. 2691, S. 2693, S. 2715. Washington, DC: U.S. Government Printing Office, 1919.

Index

About the Author

THEO EMERY is a journalist who has written for the *New York Times*, the Associated Press, the *Washington Post*, the *Boston Globe*, *The Tennessean*, and other publications. A native of South Burlington, Vermont, he graduated from Stanford University in 1994 and earned an MFA in creative nonfiction from Goucher College in 2014. He was a 2015 Alicia Patterson Foundation Fellow. He lives outside Washington, D.C.